THE WORLD RELIGIONS READER

— ●◆● —

The World Religions Reader includes material relating to six of the world's most influential faiths: Judaism; Christianity; Islam; Hinduism; Buddhism and Sikhism. Each is considered in a global context, and the selection of readings strikes a balance between providing an account of their historical development and exploring their beliefs and practices in the context of the latter half of the twentieth century. A study of three themes – sacred place; women in religion; making moral decisions – provides further perspectives on the same traditions.

The World Religions Reader includes examples from the foundational and classical texts of each religion, readings that signpost significant developments within the faiths and more recent statements from those within the traditions. Religion's resurgence as a political force in many parts of the world, during the latter half of the twentieth century, is also addressed in a number of readings.

Readings are grouped under each religion and arranged in chronological order under headings and sub-headings appropriate to the concerns of that religion. Revised and expanded for this new edition, *The World Religions Reader* now has new introductions to each tradition covered, as well as new readings on Hinduism and a completely new selection of readings on Buddhism. The comprehensive and diverse range of material gathered together here makes *The World Religions Reader* a superb resource for any student of religion.

GWILYM BECKERLEGGE is a member of the Department of Religious Studies at the Open University.

WORLD RELIGIONS READER

— •◆• —

Second edition

Edited by
Gwilym Beckerlegge

London and New York

in association with

The Open University

First published 1998
by Routledge
11 New Fetter Lane, London EC4P 4EE

Simultaneously published in the USA and Canada
by Routledge
29 West 35th Street, New York, NY 10001

Reprinted 2000

This edition first published 2001

Reprinted 2002

Routledge is an imprint of the Taylor & Francis Group

Typeset in Baskerville by
Florence Production Ltd, Stoodleigh, Devon
Printed and bound in Great Britain by
TJ International Ltd, Padstow, Cornwall

British Library Cataloguing in Publication Data
A catalogue record for this book is available from the British Library

Library of Congress Cataloging in Publication Data
A catalog record for this book has been requested

ISBN 0–415–24748–9 (hbk)
ISBN 0–415–24749–7 (pbk)

CONTENTS

— ◆◆◆ —

From the Rabbinic Tradition

Different Voices from the Past

The Holocaust and Post-Holocaust Theology

Judaism and Israel

Torah and Covenant: Recent and Contemporary Voices

PART TWO: CHRISTIANITY

The Church Fathers

The Churches: Their Life and Faith

Women's Voices and Feminist Theology

Christianity and Social Justice

PART THREE: ISLAM

From the Qur'an

Islam in the Late Twentieth Century

PART FOUR: HINDUISM

Village Hinduism

Hindu Patterns of Liberation

The Modern Period

PART FIVE: BUDDHISM

Buddhist Practices

Recent and Contemporary Buddhist Concerns

PART SIX: SIKHISM

Guru Nanak and Guru Gobind Singh

The Sikh Tradition

Khalistan and Sikh Identity

INTRODUCTION TO THE
SECOND EDITION

——— ◆◆◆ ———

This Reader examines six of the world's most influential religious traditions, namely, Buddhism, Christianity, Hinduism, Judaism, Islam and Sikhism, considered in their global setting. The Reader endeavours to strike a balance between providing an account of their historical development and exploring their beliefs and practices in the context of the latter half of the twentieth century. A closer study of the thematic topics of sacred place, women in religion, and making moral decisions provides another perspective on these same faiths. The balance and arrangement of this book reflects these concerns. Though this Reader is designed to support students following the Open University course, *World Religions*, the prominence of the six chosen religions in the contemporary world and the centrality of the course's chosen themes to the study of religion means that this compilation should be of interest to a wider readership.

The present volume incorporates some materials included in a Reader compiled for an earlier Open University course on world religions, Whitfield Foy (ed.) *Man's Religious Quest: A Reader* (Croom Helm/The Open University, 1978). This new Reader, however, covers a more limited range of religious traditions than its predecessor and thus is able to offer a wider range of readings relating to its six chosen traditions. This volume includes examples from the foundational and classical sources of each religion, readings that signpost significant developments within the faiths, and more recent statements from those within these traditions. A more limited selection from critical studies by scholars is also included. When deciding upon what new materials to include, I have sought in particular readings that indicate something of the preoccupations of the six religions in the latter part of the twentieth century, as well as reflecting the themes that Open University students will study. The resurgence of religion as a political force in many parts of the world during the latter half of the twentieth century has been much discussed of late and a number of readings address this phenomenon.

Readings are grouped under each religion and arranged in chronological order under headings and sub-headings appropriate to the concerns of that religion.

Abridgements and editorial comment are clearly shown. The second edition of this Reader contains brief introductions to the six religions covered, which explain the basis for the selection of readings. The section on Buddhism has been substantially revised and translations of certain Hindu texts have been replaced with more recent versions.

Many people have had a hand in producing this Reader, not least the authors of the course units used in *World Religions* who were largely responsible for the materials that have been retained from the earlier Reader edited by Whitfield Foy. I am grateful to my course team colleagues, and in particular to David Herbert and Susan Mumm for suggesting new readings, which were included in the first edition, and to Helen Waterhouse who substantially revised the selection of extracts on Buddhism for the second edition. The revision of the section on Buddhism was carried out with advice from Peter Harvey, Cathy Cantwell and Kate Crosby. I am also indebted to Mary Baffoni for her considerable assistance in preparing the original manuscript of this Reader.

Gwilym Beckerlegge
The Open University
May, 2000

PREFACE

———— •◆• ————

This Reader examines six of the world's most influential religious traditions, namely, Buddhism, Christianity, Hinduism, Judaism, Islam and Sikhism, considered in their wider global setting. The Reader endeavours to strike a balance between providing an account of their historical development and exploring their beliefs and practices in the context of the latter half of the twentieth century. A closer study of the thematic topics of sacred place, women in religion, and making moral decisions provides another perspective on these same faiths. The balance and arrangement of this book reflects these concerns. Though this reader is designed to support students following the Open University course, World Religions, the prominence of the six chosen religions in the contemporary world and the centrality of the chosen themes to the study of religion mean that this compilation should be of interest to a wider readership.

The present volume incorporates some materials included in a Reader compiled for an earlier Open University course on world religions, Whitfield Foy (ed.) *Man's Religious Quest: A Reader* (Croom Helm/The Open University, 1978). This new Reader covers a more limited range of religious traditions than its predecessor and thus is able to offer a wider range of readings relating to its six chosen traditions. This volume includes examples from the foundational and classical sources of each religion, readings that signpost significant developments within the faiths, and more recent statements from those within these traditions. A more limited selection from critical studies by scholars is also included. When deciding upon what new materials to include, I have sought in particular readings that indicate something of the preoccupations of the six religions in the latter part of the twentieth century, as well as reflecting the themes that Open University students will study. The resurgence of religion as a political force in many parts of the world during the last quarter of the twentieth century has been much discussed of late, and a number of readings address this phenomenon.

Readings are grouped under each religion and arranged in chronological order under headings and sub-headings appropriate to the concerns of that religion. Abridgements and editorial comment are clearly shown.

Many people have had a hand in producing this volume, not least the authors of the course units used in World Religions who were largely responsible for the materials that have been retained from the earlier reader edited by Whitfield Foy. I am also grateful to my course team colleagues, and in particular to David Herbert and Susan Mumm for suggesting new readings. I am also indebted to Mary Baffoni for her considerable assistance in preparing the typescript of this book.

Gwilym Beckerlegge
The Open University
March 1997

ACKNOWLEDGEMENTS

———— ◆ ◆ ◆ ————

The publishers would like to thank the following for permission to reprint their material:

Advaita Ashrama for *The Complete Works of Swami Vivekananda*, vol. 1, © 1989, pp. 3f, 364f.

Beacon Press: from *Four Centuries of Jewish Women's Spirituality* by Ellen M. Umansky and Dianne Ashton © 1992 Ellen M. Umansky and Dianne Ashton. Reprinted by permission of Beacon Press, Boston.

Beshara Press for Muhyi al-Din Ibn Arabi, *The Wisdom of the Prophets*, © 1975, pp. 27–9.

The Buddhist Society for 'Selected Sayings' from the *Perfection of Wisdom*, translated by Edward Conzi, London: The Buddhist Society, 1968. Reprinted by permission of the publisher.

Cambridge University Press for *An Introduction to Buddhist Ethics* by P. Harvey. Published by Cambridge University Press, 2000; extracts from *The Book of Common Prayer*, the rights for which are vested in the Crown, are reproduced by permission of the Crown's Patentee, Cambridge University Press.

Cassell for Desmond Tutu and J. Webster, *Crying in the Wilderness*, © Mowbray 1986, pp. 11–13; Muhammad Ali (ed.), *The Living Thoughts of the Prophet Muhammad*, © Cassell 1947, pp. 62, 68, 71, 75, 83–5, 89, 92, 110, 114–15, 117, 123, 125–6, 135–7.

The Church of England: Extracts from *One in Hope* (Church House Publishing/Incorporated Catholic Truth Society, 1989) © The Central Board of Finance of the Church of England, reproduced by permission; Extract from *Christians Believing* (SPCK, 1976) © The Central Board of Finance of the Church of England, reproduced by permission.

Columbia University Press for extracts from *Scripture of the Lotus Blossom of the Fine Dharma* translated by L. Hurvitz. Published by Columbia University Press, 1976; *Sources of Indian Tradition*, vol. 2, William Theodore de Bary (ed.) © 1988 reprinted with permission of the publisher; *Selected Writings of Nichiren* by Philip Yampolsky (ed.). © 1990 Columbia University Press. Reprinted with permission of the publisher.

Curzon Press for *The Sutta-Nipāta* by H. Saddhatissa, 1985 and *Kappa's Question*. Reprinted by permission of the publisher.

Darton, Longman and Todd Ltd for: 'The Chosen People', taken from *A Jewish Theology*, by Louis Jacobs © 1973 Darton, Longman and Todd Ltd, used by permission of the publishers; 'A Declaration of the Second Vatican Council (1964)', taken from the English translation of *Constitution of the Church, Lumen Gentium, of the Second Vatican Council*, © 1965 Darton, Longman and Todd Ltd, used by permission of the publishers.

David Higham Associates Ltd for 'Before I was Born', 'Lament on the Devastation of the Land of Israel', and 'All Glory to His Name' in David Goldstein (trans.), *The Jewish Poets of Spain*, © 1965 Penguin, pp. 39–40, 97, 158.

The Dharam Parchar Committee (S.G.P.C) Amritsar for Dharam Parchar Committee (Shiromani Gurdawara Parbandhak Committee), © 1950, chs 1, 2, 3, 10; Dharam Parchar Committee (Shiromani Gurdawara Parbandhak Committee), © 1995, pp. 7f, 21–5.

Dover Press, for F. Max Muller (ed.), *The Sacred Books of the East*, vol. 25, © Clarendon Press, Oxford 1886, reprinted by Dover Press, New York 1969, pp. 327–45.

Luis O. Gomez for *Land of Bliss*. Published by University of Hawaii Press, 1996. Reproduced by permission of the author.

Harcourt Brace & Company Ltd: Reprinted from *Religion*, vol. 26, no 2, April 1996, J.G. Lochtefeld, 'New Wine Old Skins', pp. 101–7, © 1996, by permission of the publisher Academic Press Limited London.

HarperCollins Publishers Ltd for A.J. Arberry, *The Koran Interpreted*, © Allen and Unwin 1964, Surahs 2, 17, 23, 24, 36, 52, 57, 59, 90–114; M. Lings, *A Sufi Saint of the Twentieth Century*, 2nd edn, © Allen and Unwin 1971, pp. 109–14, 117; S Radhakrishnan, *The Hindu View of Life*, © Allen and Unwin 1927, pp. 79–82; S. Radhakrishnan, *The Bhadavadgita*, F. Edgerton, trans., © Harper & Row 1944, pp. 2–8, 9–16, 38–41, 55–61, 83–91.

Hartford Seminary for A.J. Arberry (trans.) 'Uyub al-Nafs' (attributed to al-Ghazali) in *The Muslim World Quarterly 30* (1940) pp. 140–3.

Henry Holt and Company, Inc.: From *This People Israel* by Leo Baeck © 1964 The Union of American Hebrew Congregations. Reprinted by permission of Henry Holt & Co., Inc.

The Johns Hopkins University Press for Richard L. Rubenstein, 'Muslims, Jews and the Western World – A Jewish View' from Richard L. Rubenstein, *After Auschwitz: History, Theology and Contemporary Judaism*, 2nd edn, pp. 281–2, 286–8, 290–2, © 1990 The Johns Hopkins University Press.

The Jewish Publication Society for *Tanakh – A New Translation of the Holy Scriptures According to the Traditional Hebrew Text*, © 1985.

K. Kabbani for 'Veiled Threats', in *Letter to Christendom*, London, Virago, © 1989, pp. 22–38.

Libreria Editrice Vaticana for *Evangelium Vitae*, Dublin, Veritas, © Libreria Editrice Vaticana, 00120 Citta del Vaticano, pp. 103–4, 112–13.

Macmillan Press Ltd for extracts from *Religion in Contemporary Japan*. Copyright © Ian Reader 1991. Reprinted by permission of Macmillan Press Ltd.

Hew McLeod for his kind permission to reprint 'From the Dasam Granth of Guru Gobind Singh', 'The Jap', 'In Praise of the Eternal One', 'We are Not Hindus', in W.H. McLeod (ed. and trans.), *Textual Sources for the Study of Sikhism*, © Manchester University Press, 1984.

National Council of the Churches of Christ in the USA, for scripture quotations from the *Revised Standard Version of the Bible*, copyright 1946, 1952, 1971 by the Division of Christian Education of the National Council of the Churches of Christ in the USA. Used by permission.

Navajivan Trust for M.K. Ghandhi, *An Autobiography, or the Story of My Experiments with Truth*, © 1982, pp. 14–16; M.K. Ghandhi, *Hindu Dharma*, © 1950, p. 13, 3, pp. 158–60, 220–8, 6–9.

Orbis for Jean Zaru, 'The Intifada, Nonviolence and the Bible' in U. King (ed.), *Feminist Theology and the Third World*, © SPCK/Orbis, 1994, pp. 230–5, also in Naim S. Ateek *et al.*, *Faith and the Intefada: Palestinian Christian Voices*, © Orbis 1992; 'Summary Statement of Feminist Mariology', in U. King, *Feminist Theology from the Third World*, © SPCK/Orbis 1994, p. 273; Sister Mary John Mananzan, 'Conclusion' from 'Theological Perspectives of a Religious Woman Today: Four Trends of the Emerging Spirituality', in Marc H. Ellis and Otto Maduro (eds), *The Future of Liberation Theology: Essays in Honor of Gustavo Gutierrez*, © 1989 Orbis Books, Maryknoll, New York, and in U. King (ed.), *Feminist Theology from the Third World*, © SPCK/Orbis 1994, p. 34.

The Orion Publishing Group Ltd for L. Dumont, *Homo Hierarchicus*, (trans. Mark Sainsbury) © 1972 Weidenfeld and Nicholson, pp. 123–9.

Oxford University Press for: H. Danby, *The Mishnah*, © 1933, pp. 287–8; Henry Bettenson, (ed.), *Documents of the Christian Church*, 2nd edn, © 1963, pp. 63–4, p. 25f; R.E. Hume (trans.), *The Thirteen Principal Upanishads*, © 1931, pp. 362–6; F. Max Muller, *Sacred Books of the East*, vol. 1, © 1879, pp. 12–13, 92–109, 120–24, 181–3, 203–4; F. Max Muller, *Sacred Books of the East*, vol. 11, © 1881, pp. 6–11, 36–9, 90–1, 189–91; F. Max Muller, *Sacred Books of the East*, vol. 13, ©1881, pp. 80–1, 84–5, 90–1, 94–6, 134–5, 144–8, 211, 230; F. Max Muller, *Sacred Books of the East*, vol. 21, ©1884, pp. 224ff, 292, 317, 386ff, 413–18; F. Max Muller, *Sacred Books of the East*, vol. 35, ©1886, pp. 40–5, p. 50, 120, 65, pp. 101–2; F. Max Muller, *Sacred Books of the East*, vol. 49, ©1884, p. 1, 2, 8ff, 91, 97f, 133, pp. 147–9; H. McLeod, 'Sikism', in A.L. Basham (ed.), *A Cultural History of India*, © 1975, pp. 294–302. Reprinted by permission of Oxford University Press.

The Pali Text Society for extracts from *The Word of the Doctrine* by K.R. Norman, 1997; *Milinda's Questions*, vol. I, translated by I.B. Horner, 1990; 'Kālāma Sutta', in *Gradual Sayings*, vol. I, translated by F.L. Woodward, 1989; *The Collection of Middle Length Sayings*, vol. II, translated by I.B. Horner, 1989; 'The Anguttara Nikaya' in *Gradual Sayings*, vol. I, 1932; *The Book of Discipline*, vol. I, translated by I.B. Horner, 1970. Copyright © The Pali Text Society; F.L. Woodward, *Gradual Sayings*, vol. 1 © 1932, pp. 117–19, 128–9; Mrs Rhys Davids, *Kindred Sayings*, vol. 1, © 1917, p. 98; Mrs Rhys Davids, *Kindred Sayings*, vol. 5, © 1930, p. 343; Mrs Rhys Davids, *Kindred Sayings*, vol. 4, © 1927, pp. 34–7; I.B. Horner, *Middle Length Sayings*, vol. 1, © 1954, pp. 204–7, 217–19; I.B. Horner, *Middle Length Sayings*, vol. 2, © 1957, pp. 98–101. Reprinted by permission of The Pali Text Society.

Penguin Books Ltd for *The Laws of Manu* translated by Wendy Doniger O'Flaherty with Brian K. Smith (Penguin Classics, 1981). Copyright © Wendy Doniger O'Flaherty and Brian K. Smith, 1991. Reprinted by permission of the publisher.

Pennsylvania State Press for 'The True Lion's Roar of Queen Śrīmālā' from *A Treasury of Mahāyāna Sūtras* by Garma C.C. Chang. Published by Pennsylvania State University Press, 1983. Reproduced by permission of the publisher.

Ramakrishna-Vivekananda Center: *The Gospel of Sri Ramakrishna*, as translated into English by Swami Nikhilananda and published by the Ramakrishna-Vivekananda Center of New York, © 1942 Swami Nikhilananda.

Random House, Inc. / Alfred A. Knopf, Inc., for pp. 115-7, from *Days of Awe* by S.Y. Agnon. © 1948, 1965, renewed 1975 by Schocken Books Inc. Reprinted by permission of Schocken books, distributed by Pantheon Books, a division of Random House, Inc.

A. Rippin for A. Rippin and J. Knappert (eds. and trans.), *Textual Sources for the Study of Islam*, © Manchester University Press 1986, pp. 108-110.

Routledge for Whitfield Foy (ed.), *The Religious Quest*, Croom Helm, © 1978, 1982, pp. 267-86; for A.S. Ahmed and H. Donnan, *Islam, Globalization and Postmodernity*, © 1994, pp. 93-8.

The Royal Anthropological Institute of Great Britain and Ireland for H.N.C. Stevenson, 'Status evaluation in the Hindu caste system', in *Proceedings of the Royal Anthropological Institute of Great Britain and Ireland*, vol. 84, 1954, pp. 63-4; U. Sharma, 'Theodicy and the Doctrine of Karma', in *Man*, vol. 8, no. 3, 1973, pp. 347-64.

Sangha Bung Wai Forest Monastery for Bodhinyāna. *A Collection of Dhama Talks* by the Venerable Ajan Chah. Copyright © 1980 by the Sangha Bung Wai Forest Monastery.

SCM Press Ltd for Gustavo Gutierrez, *A Theology of Liberation*, © 1974, 1988, pp. 300-2.

Simon & Schuster: From David Novak, 'The structure of Halakhah'. Excerpted with permission of Macmillan Library Reference USA, a Simon & Schuster Macmillan Company, from *The Encyclopedia of Religion*, Mircea Eliade (ed. in chief), vol. 6, pp. 164-73 © 1987 by Macmillan Publishing Company; Shlomo Deshen, 'Domestic Observances: Jewish Practices.' Reprinted with permission of Macmillan Library Reference USA, a Simon & Schuster Macmillan Company, from *The Encyclopedia of Religion*, Mircea Eliade (ed. in chief), vol. 4, pp. 400-2 © 1987 by Macmillan Publishing Company.

The Society for Promoting Christian Knowledge for The St Hilda Community, *Women Included: A Book of Services and Prayers*, © 1991 SPCK, p. 48; and U. King (ed.), *Feminist Theology from the Third World*, © 1994 SPCK/Orbis, pp. 230-5, p. 273, 349. Reprinted by permission of SPCK.

Sri Aurobindo Ashram Trust for Sri Aurobindo, *Birth Centenary Library*, vol. 17, © 1972-5, pp. 9-11; Sri Aurobindo, *Birth Centenary Library*, vol. 24, © 1972-5, pp. 594-6; The Mother [of the Sri Aurobindo Ashram], *Auroville: Cradle of a New World*, © 1972, pp. 1-6.

Suffolk Educational and Training Services Ltd for Cynthia Capey, *Finding our Way and Sharing our Stories: Women of the Nineties Reflect on their Traditions*, © 1995 Suffolk College Publishing, pp. 110-12.

UBS Publishers' Distributors Ltd, for Khushwant Singh, *My Bleeding Punjab*, © 1992, pp. 161-4.

Union of American Hebrew Congregations Press for Leo Baeck, 'Kol Nidre Prayer', Z.Kolitz, 'Yossel Rakover's Appeal to God', and J. Bemporad, 'The Concept of Man after Auschwitz', in A.H. Friedlander (ed.), *Out of the Whirlwind*, © 1968, pp. 131-2, 396-7, 484-7.

Union of Liberal and Progressive Synagogues for Z.H. Kallisher, 'The Redemption of Israel' in A. Hertzberg (ed.), *Judaism*, © Prentice Hall 1961, pp. 221-2; a new revised version has been since printed in *Siddur Lev Chadash*, Union of Liberal & Progressive Synagogues, 1995, pp. 520–1.

University of Chicago Press for extracts from *The Edicts of Asoka* by Nikam and McKeon. Published by University of Chicago Press, 1959; R.B. Ekvall, *Religious Observances in Tibet*, © 1964, p. 31; M.E. Marty and R.S. Appleby (eds), *Fundamentalism Observed*, © 1991, pp. 617–19.

Verso: the extract from *Islams and Modernities* by Aziz Al-Azmeh is reprinted by kind permission of the publishers, Verso.

Vikas Publishing House Pvt Ltd, for U. Sharma, *Contributions to Indian Sociology*, © 1973, pp. 1–21.

Wadsworth for extracts from *Experience of Buddhism Sources and Interpretations*, 1st Edition by J.S. Strong, copyright © 1995. Reprinted with permission of Wadsworth, a division of Thomson Learning. Fax 800 730 2215.

Wisdom Publications for extracts copyright © Maurice Walsh 1987, 1995. Reprinted from *The Long Discourses of the Buddha: A Translation of the Digha Nikaya* with permission of Wisdom Publications, 199 Elm Street, Somerville MA 02144 USA, www.wisdompubs.org.

World Council of Churches (WCC) Publications for K. Sivaraman, 'The Meaning Moksha in Contemporary Hindu Thought and Life', in S.J. Samartha, ed., *Living Faiths and Ultimate Goals*, © 1974, pp. 2–11.

Every effort has been made to contact the copyright holder for each extract. The publishers would be happy to hear from any copyright holder we have not been able to trace.

PART ONE

— ◆ ◆ —

JUDAISM

INTRODUCTION

— ● ◆ ● —

The history of Judaism has been punctuated by events that have fragmented and scattered the Jewish community and others that have drawn the community back together. Behind the workings of human history, Jewish prophets and teachers have seen a divine plan in which they believe Jews have a vital part to play. This understanding is encapsulated in *torah* ('instruction'), contained in the Jewish Bible, and Covenant, the belief that God established a relationship with the Jews, which brings with it special responsibilities.

Jewish tradition looks back to the figure of Abraham and a migration from Mesopotamia to Canaan as marking the beginning of a collective sense of religious identity. Guided by God, Abraham is depicted as working within the framework of a covenant relationship with God. Subsequent catastrophes and setbacks were interpreted by the prophets as the penalties inflicted by a just God for backsliding. Memories of slavery in Egypt, and the later collapse of the twin kingdoms of Israel and Judaea, followed by the fall of Jerusalem and exile in Babylon, heightened prophetic insistence upon the need for adherence to the demands of *torah*. It was believed that only this would hasten the coming of the Messiah, God's anointed one, who would gather the Jews back to their homeland and inaugurate a golden age.

In the period of exile after the fall of Jerusalem, a new style of Judaism began to develop that no longer centred on the temple in Jerusalem and its sacrificial cult. The reading and interpretation of *torah* in new circumstances, far removed from Judaea, saw the growth of the institution of the synagogue and the role of the rabbi, religious teacher. The experience of exile led many to focus their hearts and minds on returning to Jerusalem and rebuilding the temple but also to a growing recognition that their God was the lord of all human history. The return of Jews from Babylon saw the rebuilding of the temple in Jerusalem, but this was to prove to be no more than a prelude to a far longer exile. When the Romans destroyed Jerusalem and its temple in 70CE, Jews scattered widely into a diaspora that has continued to the present day. They drew upon their experience yet again of maintaining and adapting their faith as minority and often-persecuted communities. In so doing, they built up vibrant and highly distinctive centres of Jewish culture.

Persecution in Europe, culminating in the Holocaust, increased the spread of the diaspora as the United States became a haven for many Jews, whilst other Jews campaigned and fought to return to Palestine and create the modern state of Israel. Responses to Enlightenment thinking, the experience of persecution and the founding of Israel shaped different positions within Judaism now commonly recognised as Ultra-orthodox, Orthodox, Reform and Liberal Judaism. In fact, all these experiences have tested long-held Jewish theological assumptions and have complicated debates between Jews about what now constitutes Jewish identity.

The readings begin with selections from the Jewish Bible and rabbinic tradition, chosen to illustrate some of the central principles of Jewish belief and practice. *Different Voices from the Past* gives a flavour of Jewish perspectives within Europe and the different ways in which Jewish thinkers responded to the European Enlightenment. The remaining sections include Jewish responses to the Holocaust and the creation of the modern State of Israel, and recent reflections on the covenant relationship.

PASSAGES FROM THE
JEWISH BIBLE

— ◆◆◆ —

1.1 TORAH: THE FIVE BOOKS OF MOSES

1.1.1 God's covenant with the Jews

God spoke to Moses and said to him, 'I am the LORD. I appeared to Abraham, Isaac, and Jacob as El Shaddai, but I did not make myself known to them by My name יהוה.[1] I also established My covenant with them, to give them the land of Canaan, the land in which they lived as sojourners. I have now heard the moaning of the Israelites because the Egyptians are holding them in bondage, and I have remembered My covenant. Say, therefore, to the Israelite people: I am the LORD. I will free you from the labors of the Egyptians and deliver you from their bondage. I will redeem you with an outstretched arm and through extraordinary chastisements. And I will take you to be My people, and I will be your God. And you shall know that I, the LORD, am your God who freed you from the labors of the Egyptians. I will bring you into the land which I swore to give to Abraham, Isaac, and Jacob, and I will give it to you for a possession, I the LORD.'

(Exodus 6:2–8)

1.1.2 God's encounter with Moses on the mountain

On the third new moon after the Israelites had gone forth from the land of Egypt, on that very day, they entered the wilderness of Sinai. Having journeyed from Rephidim, they entered the wilderness of Sinai and encamped in the wilderness.

Israel encamped there in front of the mountain, and Moses went up to God. The LORD called to him from the mountain, saying, 'Thus shall you say to the house of Jacob and declare to the children of Israel: "You have seen what I did to the Egyptians, how I bore you on eagles' wings and brought you to Me. Now then, if you will obey Me faithfully and keep My covenant, you shall be My treasured possession among all the peoples. Indeed, all the earth is Mine, but you shall be to Me a kingdom of priests and a holy nation." These are the words that you shall speak to the children of Israel.'

Moses came and summoned the elders of the people and put before them all that the LORD had commanded him. All the people answered as one, saying, 'All that the LORD has spoken we will do!' And Moses brought back the people's words to the LORD. And the LORD said to Moses, 'I will come to you in a thick cloud, in order that the people may hear when I speak with you and so trust you ever after.' Then Moses reported the people's words to the LORD, and the LORD said to Moses, 'Go to the people and warn them to stay pure today and tomorrow. Let them wash their clothes. Let them be ready for the third day; for on the third day the LORD will come down, in the sight of all the people, on Mount Sinai. You shall set bounds for the people round about, saying, "Beware of going up the mountain or touching the border of it. Whoever touches the mountain shall be put to death: no hand shall touch him, but he shall be either stoned or shot; beast or man, he shall not live." When the ram's horn sounds a long blast,[2] they may go up on the mountain.'

Moses came down from the mountain to the people and warned the people to stay pure, and they washed their clothes. And he said to the people, 'Be ready for the third day: do not go near a woman.'

On the third day, as morning dawned, there was thunder, and lightning, and a dense cloud upon the mountain, and a very loud blast of the horn; and all the people who were in the camp trembled. Moses led the people out of the camp toward God, and they took their places at the foot of the mountain.

Now Mount Sinai was all in smoke, for the LORD had come down upon it in fire; the smoke rose like the smoke of a kiln, and the whole mountain trembled violently. The blare of the horn grew louder and louder. As Moses spoke, God answered him in thunder. The LORD came down upon Mount Sinai, on the top of the mountain, and the LORD called Moses to the top of the mountain and Moses went up. The LORD said to Moses, 'Go down, warn the people not to break through to the LORD to gaze, lest many of them perish. The priests also, who come near the LORD, must stay pure, lest the LORD break out against them.' But Moses said to the LORD, 'The people cannot come up to Mount Sinai, for You warned us saying, "Set bounds about the mountain and sanctify it."' So the LORD said to him, 'Go down, and come back together with Aaron; but let not the priests or the people break through to come up to the LORD, lest He break out against them.' And Moses went down to the people and spoke to them.

(Exodus 19)

1.1.3 The Ten Commandments

God spoke all these words, saying:

I the LORD am your God who brought you out of the land of Egypt, the house of bondage: You shall have no other gods besides Me.

You shall not make for yourself a sculptured image, or any likeness of what is in the heavens above, or on the earth below, or in the waters under the earth. You shall not bow down to them or serve them. For I the LORD your God am an impassioned God, visiting the guilt of the parents upon the children, upon the third and upon the fourth generations of those who reject Me, but showing kindness to the thousandth generation of those who love Me and keep My commandments.

You shall not swear falsely by the name of the LORD your God; for the LORD will not clear one who swears falsely by His name.

Remember the sabbath day and keep it holy. Six days you shall labor and do all your work, but the seventh day is a sabbath of the LORD your God: you shall not do any work – you, your son or daughter, your male or female slave, or your cattle, or the stranger who is within your settlements. For in six days the LORD made heaven and earth and sea, and all that is in them, and He rested on the seventh day; therefore the LORD blessed the sabbath day and hallowed it.

Honor your father and your mother, that you may long endure on the land that the LORD your God is assigning to you.

You shall not murder.

You shall not commit adultery.

You shall not steal.

You shall not bear false witness against your neighbor.

You shall not covet your neighbor's house: you shall not covet your neighbor's wife, or his male or female slave, or his ox or his ass, or anything that is your neighbor's.

All the people witnessed the thunder and lightning, the blare of the horn and the mountain smoking; and when the people saw it, they fell back and stood at a distance. 'You speak to us,' they said to Moses, 'and we will obey; but let not God speak to us, lest we die.' Moses answered the people, 'Be not afraid; for God has come only in order to test you, and in order that the fear of Him may be ever with you, so that you do not go astray.' So the people remained at a distance, while Moses approached the thick cloud where God was.

(Exodus 20:1–18)

1.1.4 God's law: its extension

The LORD spoke to Moses, saying: Speak to the whole Israelite community and say to them:

You shall be holy, for I, the LORD your God, am holy.

You shall each revere his mother and his father, and keep My sabbaths: I the LORD am your God.

Do not turn to idols or make molten gods for yourselves: I the LORD am your God.

When you sacrifice an offering of well-being to the LORD, sacrifice it so that it may be accepted on your behalf. It shall be eaten on the day you sacrifice it, or on the day following; but what is left by the third day must be consumed in fire. If it should be eaten on the third day, it is an offensive thing, it will not be acceptable. And he who eats of it shall bear his guilt, for he has profaned what is sacred to the LORD; that person shall be cut off from his kin.

When you reap the harvest of your land, you shall not reap all the way to the edges of your field, or gather the gleanings of your harvest. You shall not pick your vineyard bare, or gather the fallen fruit of your vineyard; you shall leave them for the poor and the stranger: I the LORD am your God.

You shall not steal; you shall not deal deceitfully or falsely with one another. You shall not swear falsely by My name, profaning the name of your God: I am the LORD.

You shall not defraud your fellow. You shall not commit robbery. The wages of a laborer shall not remain with you until morning.

You shall not insult the deaf, or place a stumbling block before the blind. You shall fear your God: I am the LORD.

You shall not render an unfair decision: do not favor the poor or show deference to the rich; judge your kinsman fairly. Do not deal basely with[3] your countrymen. Do not profit by[4] the blood of your fellow: I am the LORD.

You shall not hate your kinsfolk in your heart. Reprove your kinsman but incur no guilt because of him. You shall not take vengeance or bear a grudge against your countrymen. Love your fellow as yourself: I am the LORD.

You shall observe My laws.

You shall not let your cattle mate with a different kind; you shall not sow your field with two kinds of seed; you shall not put on cloth from a mixture of two kinds of material.

If a man has carnal relations with a woman who is a slave and has been designated for another man, but has not been redeemed or given her freedom, there shall be an indemnity; they shall not, however, be put to death, since she has not been freed. But he must bring to the entrance of the Tent of Meeting, as his guilt offering to the LORD, a ram of guilt offering. With the ram of guilt offering the priest shall make expiation for him before the LORD for the sin that he committed; and the sin that he committed will be forgiven him.

When you enter the land and plant any tree for food, you shall regard its fruit as forbidden. Three years it shall be forbidden for you, not to be eaten. In the fourth year all its fruit shall be set aside for jubilation before the LORD; and only in the fifth year may you use its fruit – that its yield to you may be increased: I the LORD am your God.

You shall not eat anything with its blood. You shall not practice divination or soothsaying. You shall not round off the side-growth on your head, or destroy the side-growth of your beard. You shall not make gashes in your flesh for the dead, or incise any marks on yourselves: I am the LORD.

Do not degrade your daughter and make her a harlot, lest the land fall into harlotry and the land be filled with depravity. You shall keep My sabbaths and venerate My sanctuary: I am the LORD.

Do not turn to ghosts and do not inquire of familiar spirits, to be defiled by them: I the LORD am your God.

You shall rise before the aged and show deference to the old; you shall fear your God: I am the LORD.

When a stranger resides with you in your land, you shall not wrong him. The stranger who resides with you shall be to you as one of your citizens; you shall love him as yourself, for you were strangers in the land of Egypt: I the LORD am your God.

You shall not falsify measures of length, weight, or capacity. You shall have an honest balance, honest weights, an honest *ephah*, and an honest *hin*.

I the LORD am your God who freed you from the land of Egypt. You shall faithfully observe all My laws and all My rules: I am the LORD.

(Leviticus 19)

1.1.5 Hear, O Israel

And this is the Instruction – the laws and the rules – that the LORD your God has commanded [me] to impart to you, to be observed in the land that you are about to cross into and occupy, so that you, your children, and your children's children may revere the LORD your God and follow, as long as you live, all His laws and commandments that I enjoin upon you, to the end that you may long endure. Obey, O Israel, willingly and faithfully, that it may go well with you and that you may increase greatly [in] a land flowing with milk and honey as the LORD, the God of your fathers, spoke to you.

Hear, O Israel! The LORD is our God, the LORD alone. You shall love the LORD your God with all your heart and with all your soul and with all your might. Take to heart these instructions with which I charge you this day. Impress them upon your children. Recite them when you stay at home and when you are away, when you lie down and when you get up. Bind them as a sign on your hand and let them serve as a symbol on your forehead; inscribe them on the doorposts of your house and on your gates.

(Deuteronomy 6:1–9)

---

1 The divine name is traditionally not pronounced; instead, Adonai, '(the) Lord', is regularly substituted for it.
2 'Sounds a long blast': meaning of Hebrew uncertain.
3 'Deal basely with': others 'go about as a talebearer among'; meaning of Hebrew uncertain.
4 'Profit by': literally 'stand upon'; precise meaning of Hebrew uncertain.

Source: The Jewish Publication Society, *Tanakh – A New Translation of the Holy Scriptures according to the Traditional Hebrew Text* (Philadelphia: The Jewish Publication Society, 1985).

1.2 THE PROPHETS

1.2.1 Prophetic words of judgement

The prophecies of Isaiah son of Amoz, who prophesied concerning Judah and Jerusalem in the reigns of Uzziah, Jotham, Ahaz, and Hezekiah, kings of Judah.

Hear, O heavens, and give ear, O earth,
For the LORD has spoken:
'I reared children and brought them up –
And they have rebelled against Me!
An ox knows its owner,
An ass its master's crib:
Israel does not know,
My people takes no thought.'

Ah, sinful nation!
People laden with iniquity!
Brood of evildoers!
Depraved children!
They have forsaken the LORD,
Spurned the Holy One of Israel,
Turned their backs [on Him].

Why do you seek further beatings,
That you continue to offend?
Every head is ailing,
And every heart is sick.
From head to foot
No spot is sound:
All bruises, and welts,
And festering sores –
Not pressed out, not bound up,
Not softened with oil.
Your land is a waste,
Your cities burnt down;
Before your eyes, the yield of your soil
Is consumed by strangers –
A wasteland as overthrown by strangers!
Fair Zion is left
Like a booth in a vineyard,
Like a hut in a cucumber field,
Like a city beleaguered.
Had not the LORD of Hosts
Left us some survivors,

We should be like Sodom,
Another Gomorrah.

Hear the word of the LORD,
You chieftains of Sodom;
Give ear to our God's instruction,
You folk of Gomorrah!
'What need have I of all your sacrifices?'
Says the LORD.
'I am sated with burnt offerings of rams,
And suet of fatlings,
And blood of bulls;
And I have no delight
In lambs and he-goats.
That you come to appear before Me –
Who asked that of you?
Trample My courts
                      no more;
Bringing oblations is futile,
Incense is offensive to Me.
New moon and sabbath,
Proclaiming of solemnities,
Assemblies with iniquity,
I cannot abide.
Your new moons and fixed seasons
Fill Me with loathing;
They are become a burden to Me,
I cannot endure them.
And when you lift up your hands,
I will turn My eyes away from you;
Though you pray at length,
I will not listen.
Your hands are stained with crime –
Wash yourselves clean;
Put your evil doings
Away from My sight.
Cease to do evil;
Learn to do good.
Devote yourselves to justice;
Aid the wronged.[1]
Uphold the rights of the orphan;
Defend the cause of the widow.

Come, let us reach an understanding,[2]
                               – says the LORD.
Be your sins like crimson,
They can turn snow-white;

Be they red as dyed wool,
They can become like fleece.'
If, then, you agree and give heed,
You will eat the good things of the earth;
But if you refuse and disobey,
You will be devoured [by] the sword. –
For it was the LORD who spoke.

(Isaiah 1:1–20)

1.2.2 Prophetic words of promise

Comfort, oh comfort My people,
Says your God.
Speak tenderly to Jerusalem,
And declare to her
That her term of service is over,
That her iniquity is expiated;
For she has received at the hand of the LORD
Double for all her sins.

A voice rings out:
'Clear in the desert
A road for the LORD!
Level in the wilderness
A highway for our God!
Let every valley be raised,
Every hill and mount made low.
Let the rugged ground become level
And the ridges become a plain.
The Presence of the LORD shall appear,
And all flesh, as one, shall behold –
For the LORD Himself has spoken.'

A voice rings out: 'Proclaim!'
Another asks, 'What shall I proclaim?'
'All flesh is grass,
All its goodness like flowers of the field:
Grass withers, flowers fade
When the breath of the LORD blows on them.
Indeed, man is but grass:
Grass withers, flowers fade –
But the word of our God is always fulfilled!'

Ascend a lofty mountain,
O herald of joy to Zion;
Raise your voice with power,
O herald of joy to Jerusalem –
Raise it, have no fear;

Announce to the cities of Judah:
Behold your God!
Behold, the Lord GOD comes in might,
And His arm wins triumph for Him;
See, His reward is with Him,
His recompense before Him.
Like a shepherd He pastures His flock:
He gathers the lambs in His arms
And carries them in His bosom;
Gently He drives the mother sheep.

(Isaiah 40:1–11)

1.2.3 The Jewish people: God's servant

This is My servant, whom I uphold,
My chosen one, in whom I delight.
I have put My spirit upon him,
He shall teach the true way to the nations.
He shall not cry out or shout aloud,
Or make his voice heard in the streets.
He shall not break even a bruised reed,
Or snuff out even a dim wick.
He shall bring forth the true way.
He shall not grow dim or be bruised
Till he has established the true way on earth;
And the coastlands shall await his teaching.

Thus said God the LORD,
Who created the heavens and stretched them out,
Who spread out the earth and what it brings forth,
Who gave breath to the people upon it
And life to those who walk thereon:
I the LORD, in My grace, have summoned you,
And I have grasped you by the hand.
I created you, and appointed you
A covenant people,[3] a light of nations[4] –
Opening eyes deprived of light,
Rescuing prisoners from confinement,
From the dungeon those who sit in darkness.
I am the LORD, that is My name;
I will not yield My glory to another,
Nor My renown to idols.
See, the things once predicted have come,
And now I foretell new things,
Announce to you ere they sprout up.

(Isaiah 42:1–9)

1.2.4 The treachery of God's servant

When Ephraim spoke piety,
He was exalted in Israel;
But he incurred guilt through Baal,
And so he died.
And now they go on sinning;
They have made them molten images,
Idols, by their skill, from their silver,
Wholly the work of craftsmen.
Yet for these they appoint men to sacrifice;[5]
They are wont to kiss calves!
Assuredly,
They shall be like morning clouds,
Like dew so early gone;
Like chaff whirled away from the threshing floor,
And like smoke from a lattice.
Only I the LORD have been your God
Ever since the land of Egypt;
You have never known a [true] God but Me,
You have never had a helper other than Me.
I looked after you in the desert,
In a thirsty land.
When they grazed, they were sated;
When they were sated, they grew haughty;
And so they forgot Me.
So I am become like a lion to them,
Like a leopard I lurk on the way;
Like a bear robbed of her young I attack them
And rip open the casing of their hearts;
I will devour them there like a lion,
The beasts of the field shall mangle them.

You are undone, O Israel!
You had no help but Me.[6]
Where now is your king?
Let him save you!
Where are the chieftains in all your towns
Whom you demanded:
'Give me a king and officers'?
I give you kings in my ire,
And take them away in My wrath.

Ephraim's guilt is bound up,
His sin is stored away.[7]
Pangs of childbirth assail him,
And the babe is not wise –

For this is no time to survive
At the birthstool of babes.

From Sheol itself I will save them,
Redeem them from very Death.
Where, O Death, are your plagues?
Your pestilence where, O Sheol?
Revenge shall be far from My thoughts.
For though he flourish among reeds,
A blast, a wind of the LORD,
Shall come blowing up from the wilderness;
His fountain shall be parched,
His spring dried up.
That [wind] shall plunder treasures,
Every lovely object.

(Hosea 13)

1.2.5 God's promise of forgiveness

Samaria must bear her guilt,
For she has defied her God.
They shall fall by the sword,
Their infants shall be dashed to death,
And their women with child ripped open.

Return, O Israel, to the LORD your God,
For you have fallen because of your sin.
Take words with you
And return to the LORD.
Say to Him:
'Forgive all guilt
And accept what is good;
Instead of bulls we will pay
[The offering of] our lips.[8]
Assyria shall not save us,
No more will we ride on steeds;[9]
Nor ever again will we call
Our handiwork our god,
Since in You alone orphans find pity!'
I will heal their affliction,
Generously will I take them back in love;
For My anger has turned away from them.
I will be to Israel like dew;
He shall blossom like the lily,
He shall strike root like a Lebanon tree.
His boughs shall spread out far,

His beauty shall be like the olive tree's,
His fragrance like that of Lebanon.
They who sit in his shade shall be revived:
They shall bring to life new grain,
They shall blossom like the vine;
His scent shall be like the wine of Lebanon.
Ephraim [shall say]:
'What more have I to do with idols?
When I respond and look to Him,
I become like a verdant cypress.'
Your fruit is provided by Me.[10]

He who is wise will consider these words,
He who is prudent will take note of them.
For the paths of the LORD are smooth;
The righteous can walk on them,
While sinners stumble on them.

(Hosea 14)

1.2.6 God's choice of the Jews carries justice with it

Hear this word, O people of Israel,
That the LORD has spoken concerning you,
Concerning the whole family that I brought up from the land of Egypt:
You alone have I singled out
Of all the families of the earth –
That is why I will call you to account
For all your iniquities.

Can two walk together
Without having met?
Does a lion roar in the forest
When he has no prey?
Does a great beast let out a cry from its den
Without having made a capture?
Does a bird drop on the ground – in a trap –
With no snare there?
Does a trap spring up from the ground
Unless it has caught something?
When a ram's horn is sounded in a town,
Do the people not take alarm?
Can misfortune come to a town
If the LORD has not caused it?
Indeed, my Lord GOD does nothing
Without having revealed His purpose

To His servants the prophets.
A lion has roared,
Who can but fear?
My Lord GOD has spoken,
Who can but prophesy?

(Amos 3:1–8)

1.2.7 God will establish his rule

In the days to come,
The Mount of the LORD's House shall stand
Firm above the mountains;
And it shall tower above the hills.
The peoples shall gaze on it with joy,
And the many nations shall go and shall say:
'Come,
Let us go up to the Mount of the LORD,
To the House of the God of Jacob;
That He may instruct us in His ways,
And that we may walk in His paths.'
For instruction shall come forth[11] from Zion,
The word of the LORD from Jerusalem.
Thus He will judge among the many peoples,
And arbitrate for the multitude of nations,
However distant;
And they shall beat their swords into plowshares
And their spears into pruning hooks.
Nation shall not take up
Sword against nation;
They shall never again know war;
But every man shall sit
Under his grapevine or fig tree
With no one to disturb him.
For it was the LORD of Hosts who spoke.
Though all the peoples walk
Each in the names of its gods,
We will walk
In the name of the LORD our God
Forever and ever.

In that day

        – declares the LORD –

I will assemble the lame [sheep]
And will gather the outcast
And those I have treated harshly;

And I will turn the lame into a remnant
And the expelled[12] into a populous nation.
And the LORD will reign over them on Mount Zion
Now and for evermore.

And you, O Migdal-eder,[13]
Outpost of Fair Zion,
It shall come to you:[14]
The former monarchy shall return –
The kingship of Fair Jerusalem.

(Micah 4:1–8)

---

1 'Aid the wronged': meaning of Hebrew uncertain.
2 'Let us reach an understanding': meaning of Hebrew uncertain.
3 'Covenant people': literally 'covenants of a people'; meaning of Hebrew uncertain.
4 'Opening eyes deprived of light': an idiom meaning 'freeing the imprisoned'.
5 'Yet . . . sacrifice': meaning of Hebrew uncertain.
6 'You are undone . . . help but Me': meaning of Hebrew uncertain.
7 I.e. for future retribution.
8 'Forgive all guilt . . . our lips': meaning of Hebrew uncertain.
9 I.e. we will no longer depend on an alliance with Egypt.
10 'Your fruit . . . by Me': meaning of Hebrew uncertain.
11 I.e. oracles will be obtainable.
12 Meaning of Hebrew uncertain.
13 Apparently near Bethlehem.
14 'Outpost . . . come to you': meaning of Hebrew uncertain.

Source: The Jewish Publication Society, *Tanakh – A New Translation of the Holy Scriptures according to the Traditional Hebrew Text* (Philadelphia: The Jewish Publication Society, 1985).

1.3 THE WRITINGS

1.3.1 God's majesty and humanity's great vocation

For the leader; on the *gittith*.[1] A psalm of David.

O LORD, our Lord,
    How majestic is Your name throughout the earth,
    You who have covered the heavens with Your splendor![2]
From the mouths of infants and sucklings
    You have founded strength on account of Your foes,
    to put an end to enemy and avenger.
When I behold Your heavens, the work of Your fingers,
    the moon and stars that You set in place,
    what is man that You have been mindful of him,
    mortal man that You have taken note of him,

that You have made him little less than divine,
and adorned him with glory and majesty;
You have made him master over Your handiwork,
laying the world at his feet,
sheep and oxen, all of them,
and wild beasts, too;
the birds of the heavens, the fish of the sea,
whatever travels the paths of the seas.
O LORD, our Lord, how majestic is Your name throughout the earth!

(Psalm 8)

1.3.2 God demands righteousness of his people

A psalm of David.

LORD, who may sojourn in Your tent,
who may dwell on Your holy mountain?
He who lives without blame,
who does what is right,
and in his heart acknowledges the truth;
whose tongue is not given to evil;[3]
who has never done harm to his fellow,
or borne reproach for [his acts toward] his neighbor;
for whom a contemptible man is abhorrent,
but who honors those who fear the LORD;
who stands by his oath even to his hurt;
who has never lent money at interest,
or accepted a bribe against the innocent.
The man who acts thus shall never be shaken.

(Psalm 15)

1.3.3 God's providential care

A psalm of David.

The LORD is my shepherd;
I lack nothing.
He makes me lie down in green pastures;
He leads me to water in places of repose;[4]
He renews my life;
He guides me in right paths
as befits His name.
Though I walk through a valley of deepest darkness,
I fear no harm, for You are with me;
Your rod and Your staff – they comfort me.

You spread a table for me in full view of my enemies;
   You anoint my head with oil;
    my drink is abundant.
Only goodness and steadfast love shall pursue me
   all the days of my life,
    and I shall dwell in the house of the LORD
    for many long years.

(Psalm 23)

1.3.4 Psalm of thanksgiving to God

Of David.

Bless the LORD, O my soul,
   all my being, His holy name.
Bless the LORD, O my soul
   and do not forget all His bounties.
He forgives all your sins,
   heals all your diseases.
He redeems your life from the Pit,
   surrounds you with steadfast love and mercy.
He satisfies you with good things in the prime of life,[5]
   so that your youth is renewed like the eagle's.

The LORD executes righteous acts
   and judgments for all who are wronged.
He made known His ways to Moses,
   His deeds to the children of Israel.
The LORD is compassionate and gracious,
   slow to anger, abounding in steadfast love.
He will not contend forever,
   or nurse His anger for all time.
He has not dealt with us according to our sins,
   nor has He requited us according to our iniquities.
For as the heavens are high above the earth,
   so great is His steadfast love toward those who fear Him.
As east is far from west,
   so far has He removed our sins from us.
As a father has compassion for his children,
   so the LORD has compassion for those who fear Him.
For He knows how we are formed;
   He is mindful that we are dust.

Man, his days are like those of grass;
   he blooms like a flower of the field;

a wind passes by and it is no more,
   its own place no longer knows it.
But the LORD's steadfast love is for all eternity
   toward those who fear Him,
   and His beneficence is for the children's children
   of those who keep His covenant
   and remember to observe His precepts.
The LORD has established His throne in heaven,
   and His sovereign rule is over all.

Bless the LORD, O His angels,
   mighty creatures who do His bidding,
   ever obedient to His bidding;
   bless the LORD, all His hosts,
   His servants who do His will;
   bless the LORD, all His works,
   through the length and breadth of His realm;
   bless the LORD, O my soul.

(Psalm 103)

1.3.5 Psalm of praise to God

Hallelujah.
Praise God in His sanctuary;
   praise Him in the sky, His stronghold.
Praise Him for His mighty acts;
   praise Him for His exceeding greatness.
Praise Him with blasts of the horn;
   praise Him with harp and lyre.
Praise Him with timbrel and dance;
   praise Him with lute and pipe.
Praise Him with resounding cymbals;
   praise Him with loud-clashing cymbals.
Let all that breathes praise the LORD.
   Hallelujah.

(Psalm 150)

1.3.6 True wisdom

There is a mine for silver,
And a place where gold is refined.
Iron is taken out of the earth,
And copper smelted from rock.
He sets bounds for darkness;

To every limit man probes,
To rocks in deepest darkness.
They open up a shaft far from where men live,
[In places] forgotten by wayfarers,
Destitute of men, far removed.[6]
Earth, out of which food grows,
Is changed below as if into fire.
Its rocks are a source of sapphires;
It contains gold dust too.
No bird of prey knows the path to it;
The falcon's eye has not gazed upon it.
The proud beasts have not reached it;
The lion has not crossed it.
Man sets his hand against the flinty rock
And overturns mountains by the roots.
He carves out channels through rock;
His eyes behold every precious thing.
He dams up the sources of the streams
So that hidden things may be brought to light.
But where can wisdom be found;
Where is the source of understanding?
No man can set a value on it;
It cannot be found in the land of the living.
The deep says, 'It is not in me';
The sea says, 'I do not have it.'
It cannot be bartered for gold;
Silver cannot be paid out as its price.
The finest gold of Ophir cannot be weighed against it,
Nor precious onyx, nor sapphire.
Gold or glass cannot match its value,
Nor vessels of fine gold be exchanged for it.
Coral and crystal cannot be mentioned with it;
A pouch of wisdom is better than rubies.
Topaz from Nubia cannot match its value;
Pure gold cannot be weighed against it.

But whence does wisdom come?
Where is the source of understanding?
It is hidden from the eyes of all living,
Concealed from the fowl of heaven.
Abaddon and Death say,
'We have only a report of it.'
God understands the way to it;
He knows its source;
For He sees to the ends of the earth,
Observes all that is beneath the heavens.
When He fixed the weight of the winds,

Set the measure of the waters;
When He made a rule for the rain
And a course for the thunderstorms,
Then He saw it and gauged it;
He measured it and probed it.
He said to man,
'See! Fear of the Lord is wisdom;
To shun evil is understanding.'

(Job 28)

---

1 'For the leader; on the *gittith*': meaning of the Hebrew uncertain.
2 'You ... splendor!': meaning of Hebrew uncertain; or 'You whose splendor is celebrated all over the heavens!'
3 'Whose tongue is not given to evil': meaning of Hebrew uncertain; or 'who has no slander upon his tongue'.
4 'Water in places of repose': others 'still waters'.
5 'The prime of life': meaning of Hebrew uncertain.
6 'They open up ... far removed': meaning of Hebrew uncertain.

Source: The Jewish Publication Society, *Tanakh – A New Translation of the Holy Scriptures according to the Traditional Hebrew Text* (Philadelphia: The Jewish Publication Society, 1985).

—— ● ◆ ● ——

FROM THE RABBINIC TRADITION

— ● ◆ ● —

1.4 THE SANHEDRIN FROM THE *MISHNAH*

This passage deals with the trying of capital cases before the Sanhedrin, the supreme Jewish court until the Fall of Jerusalem in 70 CE. It is taken from the *Mishnah*, the rabbinic legal code compiled in the second century CE.

How did they admonish the witnesses in capital cases? They brought them in and admonished them, [saying,] 'Perchance ye will say what is but supposition or hearsay or at secondhand, or [ye may say in yourselves], We heard it from a man that was trustworthy. Or perchance ye do not know that we shall prove you by examination and inquiry? Know ye, moreover, that capital cases are not as non-capital cases: in non-capital cases a man may pay money and so make atonement, but in capital cases the witness is answerable for the blood of him [that is wrongly condemned] and the blood of his posterity [that should have been born to him] to the end of the world. For so have we found it with Cain that slew his brother, for it is written, *The Bloods of thy brother cry*. [Genesis 4:10] It says not "The blood of thy brother", but *The Bloods of thy brother* – his blood and the blood of his posterity. (Another saying is: *Bloods of thy brother* – because his blood was cast over the trees and stones.) Therefore but a single man was created in the world, to teach that if any man has caused a single soul to perish Scripture imputes it to him as though he had caused a whole world to perish; and if any man saves alive a single soul Scripture imputes it to him as though he had saved alive a whole world. Again [but a single man was created] for the sake of peace among mankind, that none should say to his fellow, "My father was greater than thy father"; also that the heretics should not say, "There are many ruling powers in heaven." Again [but a single man was created] to proclaim the greatness of the Holy One, blessed is he; for man stamps many coins with the one seal and they are all like one another; but the King of kings, the Holy One, blessed is he, has stamped every man with the seal of the first man, yet not one of them is like his fellow. Therefore everyone must say, For my sake was the world created. And if perchance ye would say, why should we be at these pains – was it not once written, *He being a witness, whether he hath seen or known [if he do not utter it, then shall he bear his iniquity]?* [Leviticus 5:1] And if perchance ye would say, why should we be guilty of the blood of this man? – was it not once written, *when the wicked perish there is rejoicing?*' [Proverbs 11:10]

Source: H. Danby, The *Mishnah* (OUP, 1933), pp. 387–8.

1.5 LAWS OF PRAYER FROM THE *SHULKHAN ARUKH*

The *Shulkhan Arukh*, literally, 'the prepared table', was written by Joseph Caro and first printed in Venice in 1565. It has become accepted as the authoritative code of Jewish law.

One who prays must be conscious of the meaning of the words he utters, as it is written, 'You will strengthen their heart; You will incline Your ear' [Ps. 10:17]. Many prayer books with explanations in other languages have been published, and every man can learn the meaning of the words he utters in prayer. If one is not conscious of the meaning of the words, he must at least, while he prays, reflect upon matters which influence the heart and which direct the heart to our Father in heaven. Should an alien thought come to him in the midst of prayer, he must be still and wait until it is no more.

One should place his feet close together, as though they were one, to be likened to the angels, as it is written, 'Their legs were a straight leg' [Ezek. 1:7], that is to say: their feet appeared to be one foot. One should lower his head slightly, and close his eyes so that he will not look at anything. If one prays from a prayer book, he should not take his eyes off it. One should place his hands over his heart, his right hand over his left, and pray whole-heartedly, in reverence and awe and submission, like a poor beggar standing at a door.

One should utter the words consciously and carefully. Every person should pray according to his own tradition, whether it be Ashkenazic or Sephardic or other; they share a sacred basis. But one should not mix the words of two traditions, for the words of each tradition are counted and numbered according to major principles and one should neither increase nor decrease their number.

One must be careful to pray in a whisper, so that he alone will hear his words, but one standing near him should not be able to hear his voice, as it is written of Hannah, 'Hannah was speaking in her heart; only her lips moved, and her voice was not heard' [I Sam. 1:13].

One should not lean against any object for even the slightest support. One who is even slightly ill may pray while seated or even whilst lying down, provided that he is able to direct his thoughts cogently. If it is impossible for one to pray with the words of his mouth, he should at least contemplate with his heart . . .

When one who is outside of the Land rises to pray, he must face in the direction of the Land of Israel, as it is written, '. . . and they pray to You toward their land . . .' [I Kings 8:48], and in his heart he should be directed toward Jerusalem and the Temple site and the Holy of Holies as well. Therefore those who dwell to the West of the Land of Israel must face the East (but not precisely East, for there are idolaters who pray in the direction of sunrise and their intention is to worship the sun), those who dwell to the East should face West and those who dwell to the South should face North (and those who dwell to the Northwest of the Land of Israel should face Southeast, etc.).

One who prays in the Land of Israel should face Jerusalem, as it is written, '. . . they pray to the Lord toward the city which You have chosen . . .' [I Kings 8:44], and his thoughts should be focused toward the Temple and the Holy of Holies as well. One who prays in Jerusalem should face the Temple site, as it is written '. . . when they come and pray toward this House . . .' [II Chron. 6:32], and his thoughts should be focused toward the Holy of Holies as well.

Thus the entire people of Israel in their prayer will be facing one place, namely, Jerusalem and the Holy of Holies, the Heavenly Gate through which all prayer ascends . . .

If one is praying in a place where he cannot discern directions, so that he is unable to know if he is facing in the proper direction, he should direct his heart to his Father in heaven, as it is written, '. . . and they pray to the Lord . . .' [I Kings 8:44] . . .

Source: Text in A. Hertzberg (ed.) *Judaism* (Prentice-Hall, 1961), pp. 231–3.

1.6 LAWS CONCERNING THE SEVEN DAYS OF MOURNING

J. GOLDIN

1 One is obliged to observe the rite of mourning on the death of the following seven next of kin: one's father, mother, son, daughter, brother and sister, whether from the father's side or mother's side, a wife, and a husband.

2 For the death of a child that did not live thirty days one need not observe the rite of mourning.

3 A minor, less than thirteen years old, is not obligated to observe the rite of mourning.

4 The period of mourning begins as soon as the dead is buried and the grave is filled up with earth.

5 During the seven days of mourning cohabitation is forbidden. It is also forbidden to wear leather footwear.

6 During the first three days of mourning, the mourner is not allowed to do any work, even if he is poor and is supported by charity. From the fourth day on, if he lacks food, he may do work privately in his home. But the sages said: 'May poverty overtake his neighbours, who forced him to do work', for it is their duty to provide for the poor, especially during the period of mourning . . .

12 During the seven days of mourning, the mourner is not permitted to study the Torah, but he may study the books and laws concerning mourning; as, for instance: The Book of Job; the Treatise Semahot; the mournful parts of Jeremiah, and the laws relating to mourners . . .

14 During the first three days of mourning, the mourner should neither greet any one, nor should other people greet him. If others, unaware that he is in mourning, do greet him, he is not allowed to respond to their greetings; he should inform them that he is a mourner. After the third day and until the seventh, he must not greet others, but he may respond to the greetings of people who, not knowing of his condition, do greet him.

15 During the seven days of mourning, laughter and any kind of rejoicing is forbidden.

16 During the seven days of mourning, the mourner is not permitted to sit on a chair or bench; he should sit on a low bench or stool. It is not obligatory for him to sit; he may either walk about or stand. When people come to offer him condolence, he must sit down . . .

19 During the seven days of mourning, a mourner is forbidden to leave his house. If death occurred in his family, or if it occurred elsewhere and there are not enough people to attend to the bier and the burial, he is permitted to leave the house even on the first day. If he has to attend to a matter of great importance, as where his absence would involve a great loss, he is permitted to go out, but he should put dirt in his shoes.

20 No mourning should be observed for the death of him who had committed suicide . . .

26 A candle or a lamp should be kept burning for the departed soul during the seven days of mourning, especially when the prayers are offered.

Source: J. Goldin, *Hamadrikh, The Rabbi's Guide* (New York: Hebrew Publishing Company, 1956), pp. 142ff. (Nos 1–6, 14–16, 19–20, 26.)

1.7 READINGS FROM THE *AUTHORISED DAILY PRAYER BOOK*

The *siddur* (literally, 'the order') is the term used by Ashzenazi Jews to refer to the book containing daily prayers. Simeon Singer (1848–1906), an English rabbi and headmaster, was responsible for translating and editing the *siddur* as the *Authorised Daily Prayer Book*.

1.7.1 Ethics of the Fathers

A chapter such as the following is read on each Sabbath from the Sabbath after Passover until the Sabbath before New Year. On each of the last three Sabbaths before New Year two chapters are read.

All Israel have a portion in the world to come, as it is said (Isaiah 1x, 21). And thy people shall be all righteous; they shall inherit the land for ever, the branch of my planting, the work of my hands, that I may be glorified.

Chapter I

(1) Moses received the Torah[1] on Sinai, and handed it down to Joshua; Joshua to the elders; the elders to the prophets; and the prophets handed it down to the men of the Great Synagogue. They said three things: Be deliberate in judgement; raise up many disciples, and make a fence round the Torah. (2) Simon the Just was one of the last survivors of the Great Synagogue. He used to say, Upon three things the world is based: upon the Torah, upon the Temple service, and upon the practice of charity. (3) Antigonos of Socho received the tradition from Simon the Just. He used to say, Be not like servants who minister to their master upon the condition of receiving a reward; but be like servants who minister to their master without the condition of receiving a reward; and let the fear of Heaven be upon you. (4) Jose, the son of Joezer, of Zeredah, and Jose, the son of Jochanan, of Jerusalem, received the tradition from the preceding. Jose, the son of Joczer, of Zeredah, said, Let thy house be a meeting house for the wise; sit amidst the dust of their feet, and drink their words with thirst. (5) Jose, the son of Jochanan, of Jerusalem, said, Let thy house be open wide; let the poor be the members of thy household, and engage not in much gossip with women. This applies even to one's own wife; how much more then to the wife of one's neighbour. Hence the sages say, Whoso engages in much gossip with women brings evil upon himself, neglects the study of the Torah, and will in the end inherit Gehinnom. (6) Joshua, the son of Perachyah, and Nittai, the Arbelite, received the tradition from the preceding. Joshua, the son of Perachyah, said, Provide thyself a teacher, and get thee a companion, and judge all men in the scale of merit. (7) Nittai, the Arbelite, said, Keep thee far from a bad neighbour, associate not with the wicked, and abandon not the belief in retribution. (8) Judah, the son of Tabbai, and Simeon, the son of Shatach, received the tradition from the preceding. Judah, the son of Tabbai, said, (In the judge's office) act not the counsel's part; when the parties to a suit are standing before thee, let them both be regarded by thee as guilty, but when they are departed from thy presence, regard them both as innocent, the verdict having been acquiesced in by them. (9) Simeon, the son of Shatach, said, Be very searching in the examination of witnesses, and be heedful of thy words, lest through them they learn to falsify. (10) Shemayah and Abtalyon received the tradition from the preceding. Shemayah said, Love work, hate lordship, and seek no intimacy with the ruling power. (11) Abtalyon said, Ye sages, be heedful of your words, lest ye incur the penalty of exile and be exiled to a place of evil waters, and the disciples who come after you drink thereof and die, and the Heavenly Name be profaned. (12) Hillel and Shammai received the tradition from the preceding. Hillel said, Be of the disciples of Aaron, loving peace and pursuing peace, loving thy fellow-creatures, and drawing them near to the Torah. (13) He used to say, A name made great is a name destroyed; he who does not increase his knowledge

decreases it; and he who does not study deserves to die; and he who makes a worldly use of the crown of the Torah shall waste away. (14) He used to say, If I am not for myself, who will be for me? And being for my own self, what am I? And if not now, when? (15) Shammai said, Fix a period for thy study of the Torah; say little and do much; and receive all men with a cheerful countenance. (16) Rabban Gamaliel said, Provide thyself a teacher, and be quit of doubt, and accustom not thyself to give tithes by a conjectural estimate. (17) Simeon, his son, said, All my days I have grown up amongst the wise, and I have found nought of better service than silence; not learning but doing is the chief thing; and whoso is profuse of words causes sin. (18) Rabban Simeon, the son of Gamaliel, said, By three things is the world preserved: by truth, by judgement, and by peace, as it is said, Judge ye the truth and the judgement of peace in your gates (Zech. viii, 16).

Rabbi Chananya, the son of Akashya, said, The Holy One, blessed be he, was pleased to make Israel worthy; wherefore he gave them a copious Torah and many commandments, as it is said, It pleased the Lord, for his righteousness' sake, to magnify the Torah and make it honourable (Isaiah xiii, 21).

---

1 The word Torah is left untranslated. It is variously used for the Pentateuch, the Scriptures, the Oral Law, as well as for the whole body of religious truth, study and practice.

Source: S. Singer (ed.) *Authorised Daily Prayer Book* (Singer's Prayer Book Publication Committee, 1963), pp. 251–4.

1.7.2 Morning Service: From the Mishnah

These are things which have no fixed measure (by enactment of the Law): the corners of the field, the first fruits, the offerings brought on appearing before the Lord at the three festivals, the practice of charity and the study of the Law – These are the things, the fruits of which a man enjoys in this world, while the stock remains for him for the world to come: viz., honouring father and mother, the practice of charity, timely attendance at the house of study morning and evening, hospitality to wayfarers, visiting the sick, dowering the bride, attending the dead to the grave, devotion in prayer, and making peace between man and his fellow, but the study of the Torah leadeth to them all.

Source: S. Singer (ed.) op. cit., p. 6.

1.7.3 Morning Service: Three Prayers

(i) O my God, the soul which thou gavest me is pure; thou didst create it, thou didst form it, thou didst breathe it into me; thou preservest it within me; and thou wilt take it from me, but wilt restore it unto me hereafter. So long as the soul is within me, I will give thanks unto thee, O Lord my God and God of my fathers, Sovereign of all works, Lord of all souls! Blessed are thou, O Lord, who restorest souls unto the dead.

(ii) And may it be thy will, O Lord our God and God of our fathers, to make us familiar with thy Law, and to make us adhere to thy commandments. O lead us not into sin, or transgression, iniquity, temptation, or shame; let not the evil inclination have sway over us; keep us far from a bad man and a bad companion: make us cling to the good inclination and to good works; subdue our inclination so that it may submit itself unto thee; and let us obtain this day, and every day, grace, favour, and mercy in thine eyes, and in the eyes of all who behold us; and bestow loving kindnesses upon us. Blessed art thou, O Lord, who bestowest loving-kindnesses upon thy people Israel.

(iii) Sovereign of all worlds! Not because of our righteous acts do we lay our supplications before thee, but because of thine abundant mercies. What are we? What is our life? What is our piety? What is our righteousness? What our helpfulness? What our strength? What our might? What shall we say before thee, O Lord our God and God of our fathers? Are not all the mighty men as nought before thee, the men of renown as though they had not been, the wise as if without knowledge, and the men of understanding as if without discernment? For most of their works are void, and the days of their lives are vanity before thee, and the pre-eminence of man over the beast is nought, for all is vanity.

Nevertheless we are thy people, the children of thy covenant, the children of Abraham, thy friend, to whom thou didst swear on Mount Moriah; the seed of Isaac, his only son, who was bound upon the altar; the congregation of Jacob, thy first born son, whose name thou didst call Israel and Jeshurun by reason of the love wherewith thou didst love him, and the joy wherewith thou didst rejoice in him.

It is, therefore, our duty to thank, praise and glorify thee, to bless, to sanctify and to offer praise and thanksgiving unto thy name. Happy are we! how goodly is our portion, and how pleasant is our lot, and how beautiful our heritage! Happy are we who, early and late, morning and evening, twice every day, declare: Hear, O Israel, the Lord our God, the Lord is One. Blessed be His name, whose glorious kingdom is for ever and ever.

Source: S. Singer (ed.) op. cit., pp. 6, 8, 9.

1.8 PRAYER FROM *SERVICE OF THE HEART*

Let us now praise the Lord of all, the Maker of heaven and earth; for he chose us to make known his unity, and called us to proclaim him King. We bow in reverence and thanksgiving before the King of Kings, the Holy One, praised be he. He spread out the heavens and established the earth; he is our God, there is none else. In truth, he alone is our King, as it is written: 'Know then this day and take it to heart: the Lord is God in the heavens above and on the earth below; and there is none else.' Trusting in You, O Lord our God, we hope soon to behold the glory of Your might, when false gods shall cease to take Your place in the hearts of men, and the world will be perfected under Your unchallenged rule; when all mankind will call upon Your name and, forsaking evil, turn to You alone. Let all who dwell on earth understand that unto You every knee must bend, and every tongue swear loyalty. Before You, O Lord our God, let them humble themselves, and to Your glorious name let them give honour. Let all accept the yoke of Your kingdom, so that You may rule over them soon and for ever. For the kingdom is Yours, and to all eternity You will reign in glory, as it is written: 'The Lord shall reign for ever and ever.' And it has been said: 'The Lord shall be King over all the earth; on that day the Lord shall be One and his name One.'

Source: *Service of the Heart* (Union of Liberal and Progressive Synagogues, 1967), pp. 364–6.

1.9 KOL NIDRE PRAYER
LEO BAECK

Leo Baeck (1873–1956) was a German rabbi and leader of German Jewry who felt it his duty to remain in Germany during the Second World War. Having survived incarceration in a concentration camp, Baeck came to London after the war and served as the chair of the World Union for Progressive Judaism. Kol Nidre (literally, 'all vows') are the opening words of recitation of the annulment of thoughtless and hasty vows that is made on the eve of the Day of Atonement. This prayer was prohibited by the Nazis but was still read in many synagogues in the early days of 1935.

In this hour all Israel stands before God, the judge and the forgiver.
In his presence let us all examine our ways, our deeds, and what we have failed to do.
Where we transgressed, let us openly confess: 'We have sinned!' and, determined to return to God, let us pray: 'Forgive us.'
We stand before our God.
With the same fervor with which we confess our sins, the sins of the individual and the sins of the community, do we, in indignation and abhorrence, express our contempt for the lies concerning us and the defamation of our religion and its testimonies.
We have trust in our faith and in our future.
Who made known to the world the mystery of the Eternal, the One God?
Who imparted to the world the comprehension of purity of conduct and purity of family life?
Who taught the world respect for man, created in the image of God?
Who spoke of the commandment of righteousness, of social justice?
In all this we see manifest the spirit of the prophets, the divine revelation to the Jewish people. It grew out of our Judaism and is still growing. By these facts we repel the insults flung at us.
We stand before our God. On Him we rely. From Him issues the truth and the glory of our history, our fortitude amidst all change of fortune, our endurance in distress.
Our history is a history of nobility of soul, of human dignity. It is history we have

recourse to when attack and grievous wrong are directed against us, when affliction and calamity befall us.

God has led our fathers from generation to generation. He will guide us and our children through these days.

We stand before our God, strengthened by His commandment that we fulfil. We bow to Him and stand erect before men. We worship Him and remain firm in all vicissitudes. Humbly we trust in Him and our path lies clear before us; we see our future.

All Israel stands before her God in this hour. In our prayers, in our hope, in our confession, we are one with all Jews on earth. We look upon each other and know who we are; we look up to our God and know what shall abide.

'Behold, He that keepeth Israel doth neither slumber nor sleep' (Psalm 121:4).

'May He who maketh peace in His heights bring peace upon us and upon all Israel' (Prayer book).

Source: A. H. Friedlander (ed.) *Out of the Whirlwind* (New York: Union of American Hebrew Congregations, 1968), pp. 131–2.

—— ●◆● ——

DIFFERENT VOICES FROM THE PAST

———— •◆• ————

1.10 HASIDIC: SAYINGS OF THE BRATZLAVER

Naham of Bratzlav (1772–1811) was a Ukrainian Hasidic leader who drew
many followers. His teachings were characterized by a stress upon faith
and prayer.

1 Every man should devote much time to meditation between his Creator and
himself. He should judge himself and determine whether his actions are correct,
and whether they are appropriate before the Lord Who has granted him life,
and Who is gracious to him every moment. If he finds that he has acted properly, he should fear no one – no officials, no robbers, no beasts – and nothing
in the universe except the Lord. When he learns this, he will have attained, first:
perfection in the study of the Torah and in meekness; and second, perfect worship
wherein all material considerations are forgotten: worship which asks for no
personal benefits, and which prompts one to forget his very existence.

2 He who meditates in solitude before God receives divine inspiration.

3 He who is pure of heart will find new thoughts and new phrases every time he
meditates in solitude.

4 A man's longing and intense desire to cast away any evil within himself and to
attain goodness recreates his soul in pure goodness. It should be expressed in
words in order to give it actual and true expression.

5 Meditation before God brings forth the holy spark that is found in every Jew;
it lights up his heart, and thereby deprives him of all desire for evil.

6 The chief object of meditation is truthful confession of a man's every act, and
the cultivation of a sense of contrition for his sins.

7 Meditation and prayer before God is particularly efficacious in grassy fields and
amid the trees, since a man's soul is thereby strengthened, as if every blade of
grass and every plant united with him in prayer.

8   In meditation a man may discuss his tribulations with God; he may excuse himself for his misdeeds and implore the Lord to grant him his desire to approach nearer to God. A man's offenses separate him from his Maker.

9   It is impossible to be a good Jew without devoting each day a portion of the time to commune with the Lord in solitude, and to have a conversation from the heart with Him.

10   Even though a man may feel he cannot concentrate adequately upon the theme of his meditation, he should nevertheless continue to express his thoughts in words. Words are like water which falls continually upon a rock until it breaks it through. In similar fashion they will break through a man's flinty heart.

11   A man should say every day in his meditation: 'I shall commence today to cleave unto Thee, O Lord.' No man can remain in the same position without change, and hence in the achievement of goodness we must frequently alter our place. Whether he falls back or moves forward, he will at least have commenced afresh.

12   In true meditation a man cries to the Lord like a child to his father who is about to take his departure. There is no sadness in this weeping – only longing and yearning.

Source: C. Newman (ed.) *The Hasidic Anthology* (New York: Schocken Books, 1963), pp. 175–6.

1.11 JEWISH POETS OF SPAIN

1.11.1 All glory to his name

Joseph Ibn Abithur (born in the mid tenth century CE) spent much of his time in the Middle East. His verse has been used in Jewish prayer books.

> To him who delights in music and rhyme,
> I proclaim:
> 'All glory to his name.'
>
> I consider. His work is good.
> I sing to him who has numbered the world,
> And created man from an earthen clod,
> And has put a soul in his inmost core,
> Pure,
> Like a king in his tower.
>
> He exists in all. From his hand comes all.
> Nothing approximates him to the full.
> Compared with him, all is null.
> What shall I say? The world entire
> Is poor.
> His knowledge is far from man's power.

His might and the mystery of his skies are far.
Around his throne are his servants of fire.
His awe extends through the hosts of the air.
He has built his home on the waters above.
He moved
His lips. The heavens were clothed.

There are wonderful things in all his work.
Creation bears witness for his glory's sake.
To the prophets he revealed all that was dark.
The soul that appears to him to be dear
He will steer
In the pathway of those that fear.

1.11.2 Before I was born

Solomon Ibn Gabirol (born in 1021/22 CE) was both a philosopher and a poet who composed a number of liturgical poems.

Before I was born your love enveloped me.
You turned nothing into substance, and created me.
Who etched out my frame? Who poured
Me into a vessel and moulded me?
Who breathed a spirit into me? Who opened
The womb of Sheol and extracted me?
Who has guided me from youth-time until now?
Taught me knowledge, and cared wondrously for me?
Truly, I am nothing but clay within your hand.
It is you, not I, who have really fashioned me.
I confess my sin to you, and do not say
That a serpent intrigued, and tempted me.
How can I conceal from you my faults, since
Before I was born your love enveloped me?

1.11.3 Lament on the Devastation of the Land of Israel

Abraham ben Meir Ibn Ezra (born c. 1092 CE) travelled widely through Europe, including a visit to England. His poetry is characterized by wit and satire.

Weep, my brothers, weep and mourn
Over Zion with great moan,
Like the lament of Hadadrimmon,
Or of Josiah, son of Amon.

Weep for the tender and delicate ones
Who barefoot now tread upon thorns,
Drawing water for barbarians,
Felling trees at their commands.

Weep for the man who is oppressed,
In bondage inexperienced.
They say to him: 'Carry! Make haste!'
And he, among burdens, finds no rest.

Weep for the fathers when they see
Their sons, none more praiseworthy,
Whose price gold cannot buy,
At the hands of Cushites condemned to die.

Weep for the blind who wander on,
Defiled, through the land of Zion,
With the blood of pregnant women,
The blood of the aged and young children.

Weep for the pious, whom the unclean goad,
Force them to eat forbidden food,
To make them forget their bond with God,
And the land, where their joys reside.

Weep for the women pure and chaste,
Whose fidelity has never ceased,
Subject to Hamitic lust,
Conceiving, with terror in their breast.

Weep for the daughters, noble
And upright as sculptured marble,
Forced to be slaves to the ignoble,
Who are themselves a servile rabble.

Weep, Weep and mourn
The synagogues forlorn,
That wild beasts have torn down,
And desert birds have made their own.

Weep for those in the enemies' grip,
Gathered together for a day without hope,
For those poor souls who have drained the cup,
Who are suffering now murder and rape.

Weep, weep for our living.
Do not weep for our dying;

For, as long as we have being,
To be like the dead is our desiring.

Therefore, my friend, do not recall
Consolation for my soul,
For those torn in pieces, all
In Zion, with no burial.

Source: *The Jewish Poets of Spain, 900–12 C.E.*, trans. David Goldstein (Penguin Books, 1965), pp. 39–40, 97 and 158.

1.12 MAIMONIDES

Maimonides, or Rabbi Moses ben Maimon (1135–1204), was born in Cordoba but settled in Fez. The most important Jewish scholar and philosopher of the Middle Ages, he was responsible for numerous compilations of, and commentaries on, Jewish law.

1.12.1 On Charity

If the poor asks of you and you have nothing in your hand to give him, soothe him with words. It is forbidden to rebuke a poor man or to raise one's voice against him in a shout, for his heart is shattered and crushed and it is written, 'A broken and contrite heart, O God, You will not despise' [Ps. 51:19]. And it is written, 'I dwell in the high and holy place and also with him who is of a contrite and humble spirit, to revive the spirit of the humble and to revive the heart of the contrite' [Isa. 57:15]. Alas for anyone who has humiliated a poor man, alas for him. He should rather be like a father both with compassion and with words, as it is written, 'I was a father to the poor' [Job 29:16] . . .

There are eight degrees in the giving of charity, each one higher than that which follows it:

1   The highest degree, exceeded by none, is giving a gift or a loan or taking one as a partner or finding him employment by which he can be self-supporting . . .
2   Giving charity to the poor without knowing to whom one gives, the recipient not knowing the donor's identity, for this is a good deed of intrinsic value, done for its own sake. An example of this is the Hall of Secret Donations which was maintained in the Temple. The righteous would donate in secret and the poor would be supported from it in secret. Approximating this is giving to a charity fund. One should not give to a charity fund unless he knows the collector is trustworthy and wise and conducts himself properly, like Rabbi Hananiah ben Tradyon.
3   Giving to one whose identity one knows, although the recipient does not know the donor's identity. An example of this would be the action of those great sages

who would walk about in secret and cast coins at the doors of the poor. It is fitting to imitate such a custom and it is a high degree indeed, if the charity collectors [through whom one can give impersonally] do not conduct themselves improperly.

4   Giving without knowing to whom one gives, although the recipient knows the donor's identity. An example of this would be the action of those great sages who would wrap up coins in a bundle and throw it over their shoulder. The poor would then come to take it without suffering any embarrassment.
5   Giving before being asked.
6   Giving only after being asked.
7   Giving inadequately, though graciously.
8   Giving grudgingly.

The great sages would give a coin for the poor before each prayer service and then pray, as it is written, 'I shall behold Your face in righteousness' [Ps. 17:5]. Giving food to one's older sons and daughters (though one is not obligated to do so) in order to teach the males Torah and to direct the females on the proper path, and giving food to one's father and mother is considered to be charity. And it is a great degree of charity, for relatives should have precedence . . .

One should always press himself and suffer rather than be dependent upon others; he should not cast himself upon the community as a responsibility. Thus the sages commanded: 'Rather make your Sabbath like a week day than be dependent upon others' [*Pesahim* 112a]. Even if a man was learned and respected and then became poor he should occupy himself with a trade, even a lowly trade, rather than be dependent upon others. It is better to strip the hide of dead animals than to say 'I am a great sage, I am a Priest; support me.' Among the great sages there were wood choppers, those who watered gardens and those who worked with iron and charcoal. They did not ask the community for money and they did not take it when it was offered to them.

Source: A. Hertzberg (ed.) *Judaism* (Prentice-Hall, 1961), pp. 106–8.

1.12.2 On Free Will

Every man is given free will. If he wishes to turn to the good way and to be righteous, he has the power to do so. Or if he wishes to turn to the evil way and to be wicked, he has that power, too. Thus it is written in the Torah: 'Behold, the man is become as one of us, to know good and evil' (Gen. 3:22). That is to say, this species, man, has become unique in the world, there being no species like him in the respect that, of himself and from the exercise of his own knowledge and reason, he knows good and evil. He can do whatever he wishes, and there is no one to hinder him from doing good or evil. This being so – 'lest he put forth his hand' (ibid.).

Do not believe what the fools among the nations of the world and most of the blockheads among the children of Israel say: to wit, that the Holy One, blessed be he, decrees whether a man will be righteous or wicked at the moment of his creation. It is not so. But every man may become righteous like Moses our master, or wicked like Jeroboam, wise or foolish, compassionate or cruel, miserly or generous, and so with all the other qualities. There is no one to coerce a man, and no one to determine his actions, and no one to draw him into either one of the two ways: he himself of his own free will turns to whatever way he wills. That is what Jeremiah meant when he said, 'Out of the mouth of the Most High proceedeth not evil and good' (Lam. 3:38). That is to say, the Creator does not determine that a man will be good or that he will be evil. Since this is so, the sinner is responsible for any injury he does to himself. Therefore, it is fit for him to cry and to bewail his sins and what he has done to his soul and the evil he has brought upon it. This is expressed in the next verse: 'Wherefore doth a living man complain?' (Lam. 3:39). Jeremiah continues, saying as it were, 'Since we have free will and committed all these evils knowingly, it is fit that we turn in Teshuvah and forsake our wickedness, since we have the power to do so.' This is expressed in the next verse: 'Let us search and try our ways, and return to the Lord.'

And this is an important principle, the pillar of the Torah and of the commandment, as it is said, 'See, I have set before thee this day life and good' (Deut. 30:15), and 'Behold, I set before you this day a blessing and a curse' (Deut. 11:26). That is to say, you have the power, and whatever a man wishes to do he can do, whether it be good or bad. And because he has this power, it is said, 'Oh that they had such a heart as this always . . .' (Deut. 5:26), implying that the Creator does not coerce the sons of man, nor decree that they are to do either good or evil, but all they do is in their own discretion.

If God had decreed whether a man were to be righteous or wicked, or if there were some force inherent in his nature that irresistibly drew him to a particular course, or a special science, or a particular view, or a special action, as the stupid astrologers pretend, how could He have commanded us through the prophets, 'Do thus and do not thus, better your ways and do not follow your wicked impulses' – if from the moment of a man's creation his destiny had already been decreed, or if his nature irresistibly drew him to that from which he could not free himself? What place would there be for all of the Torah, and by what right or justice would the wicked be punished or the righteous rewarded? 'Shall not the Judge of all the earth do justly?' (Gen. 18:25).

Source: S. Y. Agnon (ed.) *Days of Awe* (Schocken Books, 1948), p. 116.

1.12.3 To Obadiah the Proselyte

'While we are the descendants of Abraham, Isaac and Jacob, you derive from Him, through whose word the world was created'

Thus says Moses the son of Rabbi Maimon, one of the exiles from Jerusalem, who lived in Spain:

I received the question of the master Obadiah, the wise and learned proselyte, may the Lord reward him for his work, may a perfect recompense be bestowed upon him by the Lord of Israel, under whose wings he has sought cover.

You ask me if you, too, are allowed to say in the blessings and prayers you offer alone or in the congregation: '*Our* God' and 'God of *our* Fathers', 'Thou who hast sanctified *us* through Thy Commandments', 'Thou who hast separated *us*', 'Thou who has chosen *us*', 'Thou who hast inherited *us*', 'Thou who has brought *us* out of the land of Egypt', 'Thou who hast worked miracles to *our* fathers', and more of this kind.

Yes, you may say all this in the prescribed order and not change it in the least. In the same way as every Jew by birth says his blessing and prayer, you, too, shall bless and pray alike, whether you are alone or pray in the congregation. The reason for this is, that Abraham, our father, taught the people, opened their minds, and revealed to them the true faith and the unity of God; he rejected the idols and abolished their adoration; he brought many children under the wings of the Divine Presence; he gave them counsel and advice, and ordered his sons and the members of his household after him to keep the ways of the Lord forever, as it is written, 'For I have known him to the end that he may command his children and his household after him, that they may keep the way of the Lord, to do righteousness and justice.' Ever since then whoever adopts Judaism and confesses the unity of the Divine Name, as it is prescribed in the Torah, is counted among the disciples of Abraham, our father, peace be with him. These men are Abraham's household, and he it is who converted them to righteousness.

In the same way as he converted his contemporaries through his words and teaching, he converts future generations through the testament he left to his children and household after him. Thus Abraham, our father, peace be with him, is the father of his pious posterity who keep his ways, and the father of his disciples and of all proselytes who adopt Judaism.

Therefore you shall pray, 'Our God' and 'God of our fathers', because Abraham, peace be with him, is *your* father. And you shall pray, 'Thou who hast taken for his own our fathers', for the land has been given to Abraham, as it is said, 'Arise, walk through the land in the length of it and in the breadth of it; for I will give it unto thee'. As to the words, 'Thou who hast brought us out of the land of Egypt' or 'Thou who hast done miracles to our fathers' – these you may change, if you will, and say, 'Thou who hast brought Israel out of the land of Egypt' and 'Thou who has done miracles to Israel'. If however, you do not change them, it is no transgression, because since you have come under the wings of the Divine Presence and confessed the Lord, no difference exists between you and us, and all miracles done to us have been done as it were to us and to you. Thus it is said in the book of Isaiah, 'Neither let the son of the stranger, that hath joined himself to the Lord, speak, saying, "The Lord hath utterly separated me from His people."' There is no difference whatever between you and us. You shall certainly say the blessing, 'Who hast chosen us', 'Who hast given us', 'Who hast taken us for Thine own' and 'Who hast separated us': for the Creator, may He be extolled, has indeed chosen you and separated you from the nations and given you the Torah. For the Torah has been given to us *and* to the proselytes, as it is said, 'One ordinance shall be both for you of the congregation, and also for the stranger that sojourneth with you, an ordinance for ever in your generations; as you are, so shall the stranger be before the Lord.' Know that our fathers, when they came out of Egypt, were mostly idolators; they had mingled with the pagans in Egypt and imitated their way of life, until the Holy One, may He be blessed, sent Moses, our teacher, the master of all prophets, who separated us from the nations and brought us under the wings of the Divine Presence, us and all proselytes, and gave to all of us one law.

Do not consider your origin as inferior. While we are the descendants of Abraham, Isaac and Jacob, you derive from Him through whose word the world was created. As is said by Isaiah: 'One shall say, I am the Lord's, and another shall call himself by the name of Jacob.'

Source: F. Kobler (ed.) *Letters of Jews through the Ages* (New York: East and West Library, 1952), vol. I, pp. 194–6.

1.13 JUDAISM AS A 'REVEALED LEGISLATION'
MOSES MENDELSSOHN

Moses Mendelssohn (1729–86) was a German philosopher who increasingly in the latter years of his life devoted his studies to issues relating to Judaism. He produced a German translation of the Pentateuch and is often regarded as the founder of modern Jewish thought.

It is true: I recognise no eternal truths, other than those which can not only be comprehended by human reason, but also demonstrated and verified by the human faculties. However, he is misled by a serious misconception of Judaism if he supposes that I cannot maintain this position without deviating from the religion of my forefathers. On the contrary, I hold that this is an essential point of the Jewish religion, and I believe that this doctrine constitutes a characteristic difference between Judaism and Christianity. To put it in one word: I believe that Judaism knows nothing of revealed religion [*geoffenbarte Religion*], in the sense in which this is understood by Christians. The Israelites possess divine legislation [*göttliche Gesetzgebung*] – laws, commandments, statutes, rules of conduct, instruction in God's will and in how they are to behave in order to attain temporal and eternal felicity. It was these laws and commandments that were revealed to them by Moses in a miraculous and supernatural way, but not dogmas, or saving truths, or universal propositions of reason. These the Eternal reveals to us, as to all other men, at all times through nature and events, never through the spoken or written word . . .

Judaism does not claim to possess the exclusive revelation of eternal truths which are necessary for man's happiness. It does not claim to be revealed religion in the sense in which this term is usually understood. Revealed religion [*geoffenbarte Religion*] is one thing, revealed legislation [*geoffenbarte Gesetzgebung*] another. The voice which was heard at Sinai on that day did not announce: 'I am the Eternal, your God, the necessary, self-existent Being, who is omnipotent and omniscient, and who rewards men in a future life according to their deeds!' This is general religion for all mankind, not Judaism; and the universal religion of mankind, without which men can be neither virtuous nor happy, should not – indeed, fundamentally could not – have been revealed at Sinai. For whom could the thunder-claps and the trumpet-blasts have convinced of these saving doctrines? Certainly not the unthinking animal man who had not yet been led by his own meditations to recognise the existence of an invisible Being who rules the visible world. The thunder-claps would have imparted no concepts to such a person, and so could never have convinced him. Still less would they have convinced the Sophist who has so many doubts and difficulties roaring in his ears that he no longer perceives the voice of sound common sense. He demands rational proofs, not miracles. And even if some great religious teacher were to resurrect from the earth all the dead who ever walked on it, in order to confirm some eternal truth, the sceptic would still say: 'The Teacher has, indeed, raised many dead, but I still know no more about eternal truth than I did before. All I know is that someone is able to perform and to make us hear extraordinary things, but there may exist other, similar beings who simply do not chose to reveal themselves at this moment.' And how far is all this still removed from the infinitely sublime idea of a unique, eternal Deity, who rules this whole universe according to his own absolute will, and who looks into men's innermost thoughts, in order to recompense their works according to their merit, if not here, then in the hereafter! – Anyone who did not already know all this, who was not already convinced of these truths which are necessary for human happiness, and approached the holy mountain unprepared, might have been stunned and overwhelmed by the great and wonderful happenings there, but he would still not have been enlightened as to the truth. No! all this was supposed to be already known; probably during the days of preparation it had been taught and explained, and through human arguments placed beyond all doubt. And now the divine voice announced: 'I am the Eternal, your God, who brought you out of the land of Egypt and freed you from slavery' (Exod. 20:2). It was an historical fact on which the legislation of this particular people was to be founded, and it was laws that were to be revealed there, commandments and ordinances, not eternal truths of religion. 'I am the Eternal, your God, who made a covenant with your forefathers, Abraham, Isaac and Jacob, and swore to them to form from their seed a nation special to myself. The time has at last come when this promise must be fulfilled. To this end I have redeemed you from slavery in Egypt, redeemed you with unheard-of miracles and signs. I am your Redeemer, your Sovereign and King. I now make with you a covenant, and give you laws by which you must live and become a fortunate people in the land which I shall bestow on you.' All these are historical truths which, by their very nature, rest on historical evidence, which must be validated by authority, and can be corroborated by miracles.

According to Judaism miracles and extraordinary signs cannot furnish proof for or against the eternal truths of reason. Hence we are instructed by Scripture itself not to listen to a prophet if he teaches or advises things which are contrary to established truths, even if he confirms his mission by miracles. Indeed, we are bidden to condemn the wonder-worker to death, if he seeks to entice us into idolatry. For miracles can only verify testimonies, support authority, confirm the reliability of witnesses and of those who transmit traditions. But there is no testimony or authority that can overthrow an established truth of reason, or put a doubtful notion beyond doubt or question.

Although that divine book which we have received from Moses is essentially a lawbook, and so contains ordinances, rules of conduct and regulations, it also includes, as is well known, an inexhaustible store of rational truths and religious doctrines, which are so closely bound up with the laws as to constitute with them a single unity. All laws refer to, or are based upon, the eternal truths of reason, or they recall those truths, or arouse us to reflect on them, so that our Rabbis rightly said: 'The laws and the doctrines are related to each other as the body to the soul.' I shall have occasion to say more about this later on. For the moment I shall rest content with simply asserting it as a fact which anyone can verify for himself who examines the laws of Moses, even if only in translation. The experience of many centuries also teaches that this divine lawbook has become for the great part of the human race a source of knowledge from which they derive new ideas, or correct old ones. The more you delve into it, the more astonished you will be at the insights which lie hidden within it. At first glance, indeed, truth presents itself in this book in the plainest garb without any pretension. But the nearer you approach her, and the purer, more innocent, more loving and longing is the look with which you gaze at her, the more she will disclose to you her divine beauty, which she covers with a thin veil, so that it may not be profaned by vulgar and unholy eyes. But all these excellent propositions are addressed to our understanding and laid before us for consideration, without being forced upon our belief. Among all the precepts and ordinances of the Mosaic law there is not one which demands: 'You shall believe!'; or, 'You shall not believe!' Rather, they all say: 'You shall do!'; or, 'You shall not do!' Faith cannot be commanded, for faith accepts no commands other than those which come to it by way of conviction. All the commands of the divine law are addressed to man's will, to his capacity to act. Indeed, the word in Hebrew which is usually translated 'belief', in most cases really means 'trust', 'confidence', 'firm reliance on a pledge or promise': 'Abraham trusted [he'emin] the Eternal and it was reckoned to him for righteousness' (Gen. 15:6); 'The Israelites saw . . . and trusted [vayya'aminu] the Lord and his servant Moses' (Exod. 14:31). Where it is a question of the eternal truths of reason, the text speaks not of 'believing' but of 'understanding' and 'knowing': 'That you might know [la-da'at] that the Eternal is the true God; there is none other beside him' (Deut. 4:35); 'Know [ve-yada'ta], therefore, and lay it to heart, that the Lord is God in heaven above and on the earth beneath: there is none other beside him' (Deut. 4:39); 'Hear, O Israel, the Lord our God, the Lord is One' (Deut. 6:4). Nowhere does it say: 'Believe, O Israel, and you will be blessed! Do not doubt, O Israel, or you will suffer this or that punishment!' Command and prohibition, reward and punishment, apply only to acts, whether of commission or omission, in which a man can exercise free choice, and these acts are affected by our notions of good and evil, and hence also by our hopes and our fears. Belief and doubt, assent and dissent, on the other hand, are governed neither by our volition nor by our hopes and fears, but by our knowledge of what is true or false.

It is for this reason that ancient Judaism has no symbolic books, no articles of faith. No one has to swear to creeds, or give his solemn consent to articles of faith. Indeed, we lack any real concept of what are called 'affirmations of faith', and we must regard such affirmations as incompatible with the spirit of true Judaism. Maimonides was the first to whom the idea occurred of reducing the religion of his forefathers to a fixed number of principles, so that, as he himself explained, religion, like all the other sciences, might have its axioms from which everything else could be deduced. From this purely casual idea arose the thirteen articles of the Jewish catechism to which we are indebted for the morning hymn *Yigdal*, and some fine writings of Hasdai [Crescas], [Joseph] Albo and [Isaac] Abrabanel. But these are the only results which till now Maimonides' articles have produced. They have not yet, thank God!, been forged into fetters for faith. Hasdai disputes some of them and proposes alterations. Albo reduces the number and would recognise only three basic principles, which agree fairly well with those proposed at a later date by Herbert of Cherbury for the catechism. Yet others, particularly [Isaac] Luria and his disciples, the modern Qabbalists, are unwilling to recognise any fixed number of tenets, maintaining that everything in our teaching is fundamental. However, this controversy was conducted, as all such controversies should be, with earnestness and zeal, but without bitterness and rancour. And although Maimonides' Thirteen Principles have been accepted by the large majority of our people, no one, as far as I know, has ever condemned Albo as a heretic, because he reduced their number and wanted to carry them back to more universal axioms. In this matter we have not disregarded the important dictum of our Sages: 'Though this one permits and this one prohibits, nevertheless both teach the words of the living God' [Babylonian Talmud, Eruvin 13b].

Here too everything comes down in the end to the distinction between believing and knowing, between religious doctrine and religious law. All human knowledge can, of course, be reduced to a few basic concepts which are absolutely fundamental. The fewer these are, the stronger will be the superstructure that rests upon them. But laws can tolerate no abridgement. In their case everything is fundamental, and, since this is so, we have good grounds for saying: 'To us all the words of Scripture, all God's commandments and prohibitions, are fundamental.' Should you, nevertheless, wish to know the quintessence of these laws, then listen to how one of our great teachers, Hillel the Elder, who lived before the destruction of the second Temple, defined it. A heathen once said to him: 'Rabbi, teach me the whole law while I stand on one foot!' Shammai, to whom he had previously made this unreasonable request, dismissed him with contempt; but Hillel, famed for his unshakable composure and gentleness, said: 'My son, love your neighbour as yourself. This is the text of the law; all the rest is commentary. Now go and study!' [Babylonian Talmud, Shabbat 31a].

Source: Moses Mendelssohn: 'Judaism as a "revealed legislation"', from P. Alexander (ed. and trans.) *Textual Sources for the Study of Judaism* (Manchester: Manchester University Press, 1984), pp. 143–6.

1.14 THE ROCK OF JUDAISM

S. R. HIRSCH

Samson Raphael Hirsch (1808–88) was a German rabbi and leader of nineteenth-century German Orthodoxy. He was associated with a neo-Orthodoxy that attempted to integrate European culture and learning with traditional Judaism.

But above all what kind of Judaism would that be, if we were allowed to bring it up to date? If the Jew were actually permitted at any given time to bring his Judaism up to date, then he would no longer have any need for it; it would no longer be worthwhile speaking of Judaism. We would take Judaism and throw it out among the other ancient products of delusion and absurdity, and say no more about Judaism and the Jewish religion!

If the Bible is to be for me the word of God, and Judaism and the Jewish law the revealed will of God, am I to be allowed to take my stand on the highway of the ages and the lands and ask every mortal pilgrim on earth for his opinions, born as they are between dream and waking, between error and truth, in order to submit the word of the living God to his approval, in order to mould it to suit his passing whim? And am I to say: 'See here modern, purified Judaism! Here we have the word of the living God, refined, approved and purified by men!'

If the Bible is to be for me God's word, and Judaism and the Jewish law God's revealed will, am I to be allowed to consult my belly, my sensuality and convenience, my casual advantage, to see whether it is also sweet and easy, whether it is also reasonable and pleasant? Am I to be allowed to take religion, my religion which God has given me as the yardstick by which to measure myself, my times and all my actions, and first measure it and adjust it to suit the pettiness, the sensuality and the narrow-mindedness of my passing desires? Am I to be allowed to falsify the divine yardstick in accordance with my passing needs, and then to brag and say: 'See now, up-to-date, purified Judaism. Here we have the word of almighty God, cut down to fit my own weaknesses? See how much in tune with it we are, my times and I!'

Let us not delude ourselves. The whole question is quite simply this. Are the words 'And God spoke to Moses as follows', with which the laws of the Jewish Bible begin, true or false? Do we really and truly believe that the omnipotent, holy God spoke thus to Moses? Are we speaking the truth when, in the presence of our brethren, we lay our hand upon the Torah Scroll and say that God has given us this teaching, his teaching, the teaching of truth, and in so doing has planted eternal life in our midst? If this is to be more than lip service, more than verbiage and deception, then we must keep this Torah and fulfil it without abridgement, without fault-finding, under all circumstances and at all times. This word of God must be for us the eternal rule, superior to all human judgement, to which at all times we must conform ourselves and all our actions, and, instead of complaining that it is not in tune with the age, our one complaint should be that the age is not in tune with it!

And if in fulfilling this word of God we choose to follow the teachings and precepts that have come down to us from the Rabbis, then once again we may and indeed must do so only if and because those teachings (passed down as they are to us by those selfsame generations from whose hand we are prepared to receive as authentic the written word of God) are regarded by us as a tradition *orally* transmitted by God, the selfsame omnipotent, holy God, to Moses, and from Moses to each succeeding generation – a tradition established for the purpose of regulating the practical observance of God's word. This tradition, on the other hand, is for us nothing more than tradition, the word of God passed on *orally*, as Rabbinic Judaism has always taught through the long centuries of its history.

But if this tradition is for us no tradition, but only a mask, a pious fraud by which a priestly caste has foisted its own views on the people as the transmitted word of God; if, in consequence, the fathers have deceived their sons and grandsons, allowing them to live and suffer, to endure and die, for the sake of a deception and delusion; if each of us can be his own oracle and mould the Biblical laws to suit his own views and opinions, then that law is no longer and ought no longer to be God's word; then God did not speak to Moses; then what we have in our hands is not divine teaching; then we, and the whole of humanity whose hopes of salvation are rooted in this word, are all deceivers and deceived, and it is high time openly and freely to get rid of the whole miserable business.

These are the alternatives; there are no others. If Judaism has been established by God, then its business is to teach the age, but not to let itself be taught by the age.

From the beginning God placed Judaism and its adherents in opposition to the age. For thousands of years Judaism was the only protest against a totally pagan world. And if this opposition grew less as the centuries wore on, this was not because Judaism changed to suit the non-Jewish conditions, but because more and more seeds of the Jewish spirit, sparks from the Jewish word of God, found a home in the bosom of the non-Jewish world, and the Jewish word of God more and more fulfilled its silent mission in the world.

For two thousand years at the dawn of history, as the Jewish word of God tells us, things went from bad to worse, the times became ever more godless. Then God spoke to the first Jew, Abraham: 'Dare not to conform to the spirit of the age. Go your own way, far from your native land, your family, your father's house, and let my approval, the approval of the All-Sufficient, be sufficient for you! [cf. Gen. 12:1].' And so among the most cultivated peoples of his time, the Egyptians and the Phoenicians, Abraham wandered alone – with God.

And when the descendants of Abraham had grown in the bitter school of suffering into a people who could be the bearers of God's laws, God placed them once again amongst the most cultured nations of their time, pointed to the Egyptian culture on their left and to the culture of central Asia on their right, and said: 'I have separated you from these peoples; do not walk in their ways. Follow my laws and remain true!'

And when the Jewish state fell in ruins, because Jeroboam in his cleverness had introduced for the first time the principle of adapting Judaism to conform to the times, and Judah once again wandered into strange lands, God addressed to them through the mouth of his prophets this warning valid for all time: 'But what you have in mind will never come to pass, when you say, "We shall be like the peoples of all other lands, worshipping wood and stone"' [Ezek. 20:32]. 'Remember the teaching of Moses my servant which I commanded to him on Horeb for all Israel, even statutes and ordinances' [Mal. 4:4].

All this is abundantly clear from the beginning to the end of the Biblical record, and yet today we make the amazing discovery that Judaism segregates its adherents and makes them appear to the superficial children of every age so out of step with their times!

Yet this segregation is only superficial. There is nothing so well suited as Judaism to inspire in its adherents an all-embracing love, to implant in them a spirit and a heart to which nothing human in the whole wide world is alien, which always shows the most open interest in all human suffering and well-being, which perceives in the darkest events of history God's eternal providence at work. It is the Jew who plants at the grave of the most degenerate profligacy the banner of hope for a future resurrection and return to God, and whose whole strength lies in the consciousness that all men are travelling with him towards the kingdom of God on earth, in which truth and love, justice and salvation will everywhere dwell.

Consider Abraham, the first and most isolated Jew on earth. Was any isolation ever like this? He was unique and alone with God on earth, unique and alone in conflict with the whole of his age. Yet what a heart he carried in his bosom – full of modesty, full of kindness, full of compassion and love for all, even for the most depraved men of his time! When the judgement of God threatened Sodom and Gomorrah, the greatest cess-pit of human depravity ever known, it was Abraham who prayed for Sodom and Gomorrah.

God concluded with him and with his descendants the most separatist of covenants and sealed this covenant with the most separatist of signs, marked on his body and the bodies of his descendants. Yet see how, with this painful sign of separation still fresh on his body, Abraham sits outside his tent in the heat of the sun, keeping watch for weary travellers, inviting wayfarers – strangers and idolators – into his house, and showing compassion and kindness, and the all-embracing love of God, to his fellow men without distinction.

How could it have been any different? Was not this universalism, this broad sympathy, those good deeds done to all without distinction, the essence and object, the reason and meaning of his separation? Was it not this very universalism which set him apart? According to the profound words of our Sages, it was when men, to perpetuate their own fame, had begun to build a tower reaching up to heaven, that God called Abraham to himself. *They* were motivated by selfish pleasure-seeking and ambition. They said: '*Na'seh lanu shem* – Let us make *for ourselves* a name' [Gen. 11:4]. Their famous monument separated and divided men from each other, though it *seemed* to unite them. It was then God said to Abraham: 'You must go another way. Desire nothing for yourself, for your own blessing, for your own fame. In my name call men together, *qara ba-shem* [Gen. 12:8], and be a blessing to them, *heyeh berakhah* [Gen. 12:2], for see, I have destined you to be the father of mankind. Let this be *your* blessing, this *your* fame!'

This remained the fundamental character of Judaism. Abraham was set apart for the sake of mankind, and for the sake of mankind Judaism has to follow its separate path through the ages.

Judaism is the one religion which does *not* say: 'Outside me there is no salvation!' It is Judaism – a religion decried for its supposed particularism – which teaches that the upright of all peoples are journeying towards the same blessed destination. It is the very same Rabbis, so often disparaged for their alleged particularism, who point out that when the prophets and poets predict a glorious new day for humanity they say nothing about priests, Levites and Israelites, but speak only of 'the righteous', 'the just', and 'the honest', and so the righteous, the just and the honest of all peoples are included in the most glorious blessing. And in the darkest hours when the frenzied mob destroyed the Jewish synagogues and tore up the Jewish books, the persecuted, derided Jew always turned to his God and consoled himself by looking forward to the time when even this frenzy would disappear and the name of the one and only God would have implanted justice, truth and peace in every human breast. . . .

But long before this goal is reached, in all his wandering through the ages and the lands, his Judaism has not brought the Jew into such sharp conflict with the ages and the lands. Rather this very Judaism has shown him how to adapt to every age and land through which he has wandered, and taught him to form the friendliest and closest ties with every age and every land.

For he knows that the just and the pure of all societies are working with him for the kingdom of God on earth. He knows, too, that especially during the last two thousand years or so, not only the seeds of a purer humanity which were preserved even in the midst of heathenism, but also the seeds of genuinely Jewish thought, have been germinating and sprouting, and in a variety of spiritual endeavours have contributed to the salvation of mankind. And it is his Judaism – guiding him as it does through the garden of nature and the galleries of history, and summoning him to use his powers fully in the service of God – that encourages him to perceive in each newly discovered truth a welcome contribution to the clearer revelation of God in nature and in history, and to recognise in each new art and science a welcome addition to the means for rendering perfect service to God.

Hence the Jew will not shy away from any science, any art or education, provided that it is truly genuine, truly moral, and truly promotes the good of mankind. He has to test everything by the eternally inviolable touchstone of his divine law. Whatever fails this test, he totally disregards. But the firmer he stands upon the rock of his Judaism, the more thoroughly he is imbued with the consciousness of his Judaism, the more inclined will he be to accept and thankfully appropriate whatever is really true and genuinely good, provided it conforms to the truths of Judaism. No matter in whose mind it originated, no matter who uttered it, he will always be ready *le-qabbel ha-emet mimmi she-amarah* [to accept the truth no matter who speaks it]. Nowhere will he ever sacrifice so much as a thread of his Judaism, nowhere will he ever shape his Judaism to suit the times, but, whenever his age offers him anything consonant with his Judaism, he will gladly make it his own. In every age he will regard it as his duty, from the standpoint of his Judaism, to seek to appreciate the age and its conditions, so that in every age, with whatever new means the age provides and in whatever new circumstances the age creates, he may unfold in ever greater richness the spirit of his ancient Judaism, and fully and totally fulfil the task of his ancient Judaism, in ever greater fullness and with ever-increased fidelity.

Source: S. R. Hirsch: 'The rock of Judaism', from P. Alexander (ed. and trans.) *Textual Sources for the Study of Judaism* (Manchester University Press, 1984), pp. 146–50.

——— ●◆● ———

THE HOLOCAUST AND POST-HOLOCAUST THEOLOGY

— ◆◆◆ —

1.15 YOSSEL RAKOVER'S APPEAL TO GOD
Z. KOLITZ

There was no document written by Yossel Rakover, but there was a Yossel Rakover among those killed in the destruction of the Warsaw ghetto. Zvi Kolitz took the name of Yossel Rakover, a Hasidic Jew, in this reflection on the way in which a Hasidic Jew might address God in the midst of such suffering and inhumanity.

I believe that to be a Jew means to be a fighter, an everlasting swimmer against the turbulent human current. The Jew is a hero, a martyr, a saint. You, our evil enemies, declare that we are bad. I believe that we are better and finer than you, but even if we were worse, I should like to see how you would look in our place!

I am happy to belong to the unhappiest of all peoples of the world, whose precepts represent the loftiest and most beautiful of all morality and laws. These immortal precepts which we possess have now been even more sanctified and immortalised by the fact that they have been so debased and insulted by the enemies of the Lord.

I believe that to be a Jew is an inborn trait. One is born a Jew exactly as one is born an artist. It is impossible to be released from being a Jew. That is our Godly attribute that has made us a chosen people. Those who do not understand this will never understand the higher meaning of our martyrdom. If I ever doubted that God once designated us as the chosen people, I would believe now that our tribulations have made us the chosen one.

I believe in You, God of Israel, even though You have done everything to stop me from believing in You. I believe in Your laws even if I cannot excuse Your actions. My relationship to You is not the relationship of a slave to his master but rather that of a pupil to his teacher. I bow my head before Your greatness, but I will not kiss the lash with which You strike me.

You say, I know, that we have sinned, O Lord. It must surely be true! And therefore we are punished? I can understand that too! But I should like You to tell me whether *there is any sin in the world deserving of such a punishment as the punishment we have received?*

You assert that you will yet repay our enemies? I am convinced of it! Repay them without mercy? I have no doubt of that either! I should like You to tell me, however – *is there any punishment in the world capable of compensating for the crimes that have been committed against us?*

You say, I know, that it is no longer a question of sin and punishment, but rather a situation in which Your countenance is veiled, in which humanity is abandoned to its evil instincts. But I should like to ask You, O Lord – and this question burns in me like a consuming fire – *what more, O, what more must transpire before You unveil Your countenance again to the world?*

I want to say to You that now, more than in any previous period of our eternal path of agony, we, we the tortured, the humiliated, the buried alive and burned alive, we, the insulted, the mocked, the lonely, the forsaken by God and man – we have the right to know *what are the limits of Your forebearance?*

I should like to say something more: Do not put the rope under too much strain, lest, alas, it snaps! The test to which You have put us is so severe, so unbearably severe, that You should – You must – forgive those members of Your people who, in their misery, have turned from You.

Forgive those who have turned from You in their misery, but also those who have turned from You in their happiness. You have transformed our life into such a frightful, perpetual order that the cowards among us have been forced to flee from it; and what is happiness but a place of refuge for cowards? Do not chastise them for it. One does not strike cowards, but has mercy on them. Have mercy on *them*, rather than *us*, O Lord.

Forgive those who have desecrated Your name, who have gone over to the service of other gods, who have become indifferent to You. You have castigated them so severely that they no longer believe that You are their Father, that they have any Father at all.

I tell You this because I do believe in You, because I believe in You more strongly than ever, because now I know that You are my Lord, because after all You are not, You cannot possibly be after all the God of those whose deeds are the most horrible expression of ungodliness!

Source: A. H. Friedlander (ed.) *Out of the Whirlwind* (New York: Union of American Hebrew Congregations, 1968), pp. 396–7.

1.16 THE CONCEPT OF MAN AFTER AUSCHWITZ
J. BEMPORAD

Jack Bemporad, at the time of writing, was director of worship for the Union of American Hebrew Congregations.

Judaism points to the twofoldedness of human nature. Once we recognize that man is by nature neither good nor evil and that both his good and evil are human qualities and that man has the freedom to actualize either good or evil, then we are able to recognize the traditional Jewish teaching with respect to the nature of man.

Judaism recognized that man has much power for good and for evil. It recognizes that man can destroy himself or bring about the Messianic Age. The prophetic doctrine which announces the consequences of destruction through the bold admonition of a day that was darkness and not light also spoke of a day of peace and justice. Judaism believes that man has within him the power to bring about the one or the other. In the book of Deuteronomy Moses spoke to the people and said, 'I have set before thee life and death, the blessing and the curse. Choose life that you may live.' But the blessing and the curse are not in God's hands. It is not something that God is going to take care of for man. Man is to choose and realize life or death, blessing or curse, the Messianic Age or the bomb.

The Midrash to Genesis relates that when God was about to create man, the angels of the service were divided. Love said let him be created for he will do loving deeds. But Truth said let him not be created for he will be all lies. Righteousness said let him be created for he will do righteous deeds. Peace said let him not be created for he will be all quarrelsomeness and discord. What did God do? He took hold of Truth and cast him to the earth. The angels then said, 'Lord of the World, why do You despise the Angel of Truth? Let Truth arise from the earth. As it is said, Truth shall spring from the earth.'

Judaism recognizes that it is man's task to bring forth truth and justice and righteousness and peace. It is a mistake to believe that man is by nature good or evil. Man has the capacity for both and the Holocaust has shown that he can in fact actualize great evil.

The School of Hillel and the School of Shammai fought for many years and there was one question which they fought over very seriously. This question was: Would it have been better for man to have been created, or not to have been created? The School of Shammai said, it would have been better for man not to have been created, and the School of Hillel said, it was better for man to have been created. After all, the Shammaites must have argued, look at all the suffering and tragedy, all that is horrible in the world; it is better off for man not to have been created. So they debated and debated and couldn't agree. After two years of debate they took a vote and the Shammaites won. So they decided that man should examine his past deeds and future deeds. There is a hint as to the meaning of this statement in the Tosafist's comment on this passage and we might expand it as follows: Before a person is born you don't know if it is better if he were created or not. For instance, it certainly would have been much better for Hitler and Stalin never to have been created, and each one of us is never sure whether it would have been better not to be created. Therefore, we interpret the passage to mean, live your life in such a way so that you will be worthy of having been created. This is an important concept. It doesn't mean that when one is born, he is born in a state of original sin, that anything he does will be bad. It doesn't mean that he is born with reason and goodness, and it is only through sheer error that he does anything bad. No, it means that the individual is born with both a potentiality for doing great good and with the potentiality for doing great evil, and it is up to him whether he does one or the other, whether he chooses life and the blessing, or whether he chooses death and the curse. Let us choose life, that we may live.

Source: Friedlander, op. cit., pp. 484–7.

1.17 SURVIVAL AND MEMORY
ITKA FRAJMAN ZYGMUNTOWICZ WITH SARA HOROWITZ

Itka Frajman Zygmuntowicz was born in Poland in 1926. In 1941, her family was forced into the Nowe-Miasto Ghetto and then moved in 1942 to Auschwitz. Before being freed in 1945, she was also held at Ravensbruck and Malchow. She was the only member of her family to survive. Here she is talking with the Holocaust scholar Sara Horowitz.

Four groups of people dramatically influenced my destiny: my beloved family, who knew me and loved me and empowered me with positive energy; the Nazis, who didn't know me but hated me for being born Jewish and in one single day murdered in Auschwitz my entire family; the world that stood silently by, indifferent to my profound level of suffering and grief; and the caring people of the Swedish Red Cross, who didn't know me but liberated me and brought me to a hospital in Lund, Sweden. I am one and the same person, yet four different groups of people viewed me differently and treated me differently. I was loved for who I am, and I was hated for who I am. The more my tormenters tortured me for who I am, the more I became determined never to become like them or to view myself through their eyes. There are those who claim that love is blind, but it seems to me that hatred is blind. Love builds bridges of communication, and hatred builds walls of isolation. Hatred divides us and destroys us, and love protects us and unites us. In union, there is strength, there is brotherhood, there is blessedness, and there is heavenly peace.

I became aware that there is a destiny that others choose for us and a destiny that we choose for ourselves. We can choose how to live, and we can choose to protect life or destroy it. For nearly six years, chronic hunger, terror, and death were my steady companions. I am one of a handful of Jewish Holocaust survivors of Auschwitz concentration camps and the sole survivor of my murdered family of blessed memory. The only member of our household in Ciechanow, Poland, who was privileged to die of old age and have a proper Jewish burial was my maternal widowed grandmother. I was grief stricken when my beloved grandmother died, but now I am grateful that she was spared all the suffering that I had to endure.

All on earth that I loved and held sacred I lost in the Holocaust, including nearly six precious years of my life. All on earth that I had left after liberation from Malchow, Germany, was my skeletal body minus all my hair, minus my monthly cycle, a tattered concentration camp shift dress without undergarments, a pair of beaten up unmatched wooden clogs, plus my 'badge of honor', a large blue number 25673 that the Nazis tattooed on my left forearm on the day of my initiation to Auschwitz inferno. I was homeless, stateless, penniless, jobless, orphaned, and bereaved. I could not speak or understand Swedish, I had no marketable skills and only seven grades of public school and several grades of Hebrew school. Unlike my non-Jewish fellow survivors, I could not go back home to my beloved family, relatives, and friends and resume my former life as they did. Jewish homes, Jewish families, and Jewish communities were destroyed. I was a displaced person, a stranger; alive, but with no home to live in. I had no one to love me, to miss me, to comfort me, or to guide me. My childhood world was gone, but not from my heart and mind. Nothing dies as long as it is remembered and transmitted from person to person, from generation to generation. Or, as my beloved grandmother used to say, 'My child, you only have what you choose to give away!'

Source: Itka Frajman Zygmuntowicz with Sara Horowitz, 'Survival and memory' in E. M. Umansky and D. Ashton (eds) *Four Centuries of Jewish Women's Spirituality – A Sourcebook* (Boston: Beacon Press, 1992), pp. 289–90.

—— ●◆● ——

JUDAISM AND ISRAEL

— ◆ ◆ ◆ —

1.18 THE REDEMPTION OF ISRAEL

Z. H. KALLISCHER

The redemption of Israel, for which we long, is not to be imagined as a sudden miracle. The Almighty, praised be His name, will not suddenly descend from on high and command His people to go forth. He will not send His Messiah from heaven in a twinkling of an eye, to sound the great trumpet for the scattered of Israel and gather them into Jerusalem. He will not surround the Holy City with a wall of fire or cause the Holy Temple to descend from the heavens. The bliss and the miracles that were promised by His servants, the prophets, will certainly come to pass – everything will be fulfilled – but we will not run in terror and flight, for the redemption of Israel will come by slow degrees and the ray of deliverance will shine forth gradually.

My dear reader! Cast aside the conventional view that the Messiah will suddenly sound a blast on the great trumpet and cause all the inhabitants of the earth to tremble. On the contrary, the Redemption will begin by awakening support among the philanthropists and by gaining the consent of the nations to the gathering of some of the scattered of Israel into the Holy Land . . .

Can we logically explain why the Redemption will begin in a natural manner and why the Lord, in His love for His people, will not immediately send the Messiah in an obvious miracle? Yes, we can. We know that all our worship of God is in the form of trials by which He tests us. When God created man and placed him in the Garden of Eden, He also planted the Tree of Knowledge and then commanded man not to eat of it. Why did He put the Tree in the Garden, if not as a trial? . . . When Israel went forth from Egypt, God again tested man's faith with hunger and thirst along the way. . . . Throughout the days of our dispersion we have been dragged from land to land and have borne the yoke of martyrdom for the sanctity of God's name; we have been dragged from land to land and have borne the yoke of exile through the ages, all for the sake of His holy Torah and as a further stage of the testing of our faith.

If the Almighty would suddenly appear, one day in the future, through undeniable miracles, this would be no trial. What straining of our faith would there be in the face of miracles and wonders attending a clear and heavenly command to go up and inherit the land and enjoy its good fruit? Under such circumstances, what fool would not go there, not because of his love of God, but for his own selfish sake? Only a natural beginning of the Redemption is a true test of those who initiate it. To concentrate all one's energy on this holy work and to renounce home and fortune for the sake of living in Zion before 'the voice of gladness' and 'the voice of joy' are heard – there is no greater merit or trial than this . . .

For all this to come about there must first be Jewish resettlement in the Lord; without such settlement, how can the ingathering begin?

Source: Hertzberg, op. cit., pp. 221–2.

1.19 MUSLIMS, JEWS, AND THE WESTERN WORLD – A JEWISH VIEW
RICHARD L. RUBENSTEIN

Richard L. Rubenstein (b. 1924) is an American Jewish theologian and university teacher.

W & I: Islamic scholars and religious leaders say that Islamic fundamentalism is a distortion of real Islam and that it is being used for political purposes. That's one point. Second point: All of the Muslims we have spoken to express a certain bitterness at what they see as the lack of evenhandedness in the West. They claim that America, for example, supposedly stands up for the principle of human rights and the rule of law but that it applies them selectively. It is not applied, for example, to Israeli behavior in Palestine, whereas it is applied to the Iraqi invasion of Kuwait.

R: Here again they are not seeing things straight. As I have tried to show, the Israelis took over the West Bank and Gaza as an act of self-defense in a war in which the joint military forces of Egypt, Syria, Jordan, and Iraq sought to annihilate them. Moreover, whether or not Israeli behavior toward the Palestinians is justified – and it certainly is far less harsh than the behavior of Saddam Hussein and Hafez El Assad toward their domestic opponents – that behavior will not result in a hostile country controlling half of the world's oil supply, whereas if Saddam Hussein's conquest of Kuwait had succeeded, he could have become a worldwide menace. The issue was never oil alone; for Saddam Hussein it was the military power oil wealth could purchase. The real issue for the United States in opposing Iraq's invasion of Kuwait was whether America was going to remain passive while Saddam Hussein gained control of half of the world's oil supply, thereby controlling America's economic destiny. The Israelis never had any interest in doing this; not so Saddam Hussein.

As far as the Arab–Israeli conflict is concerned, I do not believe the Israelis owe the Palestinians much. If the Palestinians had the power to do so, they would drive the Israelis into the sea, no matter what their 'moderates' say, and no one would lift a finger to stop them. The Israelis have no such murderous objectives for the Palestinians. Any people who threaten to drive the Israelis into the sea and who, after the Nazi Holocaust, are in alliance with Saddam Hussein, who promised to gas Jews and turn Tel Aviv into a crematorium, must be seen as a mortal enemy.

W & I: Is it fair to invoke the Nazi Holocaust in this dispute?

R: The Nazi Holocaust was invoked by Saddam Hussein when he promised to gas half of Israel and turned to German corporations that were all too willing to build the poison gas plants to do the job. It didn't take much imagination to determine who Saddam's targets were. Hitler killed millions of Jews with gas, and then Saddam Hussein came along with his German-made gas equipment made available to him by German export permits and said, 'I've got the weapons and I can gas half of Israel out of existence.' That is very, very provocative language, and it was precisely the threat that was bound to create the greatest possible anger and distrust on the part of the Jews everywhere.

W & I: And you interpret his language as deliberately chosen?

R: Absolutely. That man has proven that, if he has a weapon, he will use it if he can. If he is ever in a position to use the gas weapon, he will. The one thing that gave the Israelis any kind of security during the Gulf War was that they knew Saddam Hussein understood that the cost of using gas against Israel would have been so great in terms of the damage the Israelis could have inflicted on his country that he must have had second and third thoughts about using gas. Threats of this kind are not made lightly. Elie Wiesel once observed that Hitler was the only one who kept his promises to the Jews. He promised to kill them and he did. After Hitler, anyone who promises to kill Jews is going to be taken seriously [. . .]

W & I: You speak like an advocate for the Israeli-Jewish side.

R: Of course, I am. As a Jew and a Holocaust theologian, I cannot be indifferent when Jews are threatened with gas after Auschwitz. Nevertheless, I haven't closed the door to a peaceful solution. I would like to see a solution. I would even favor the surrender of territory in Gaza and the West Bank if – and it is a very big if – Israel's security were not thereby seriously compromised. As I have said, I don't see a way out. Nevertheless, there is an enormous difference between not seeing a way out and wanting things to be the way they are. I feel these things very strongly, not as an advocate for one side, but because I have spent much of my life studying Jewish history and the place of Judaism in the modern world.

If you ask me about the conflict with Iraq as distinct from the Palestinian conflict, I must say I am disturbed. To repeat, I see the continuing possibility of a holy war. Saddam Hussein is apparently convinced that, having lost the initial round, he can still win the long-term religio-political conflict, even if he himself has departed from the scene.

I shall never forget an encounter my wife and I had shortly after we checked into that Arab hotel in East Jerusalem at the end of the Six-Day War. We had never been to the Old City. Before the war, Jews couldn't go into East Jerusalem or the Old City. We decided to walk through the Old City, entering by the Damascus Gate. As we entered, a thin, young Palestinian, maybe about twenty years old, came up to me and asked, 'Would you like a guide?' I decided that it would be prudent to have one for the first visit. And, for the next two hours, I heard the most bitter rage and resentment against Israel I have ever heard in my life. The guide assumed that we were Christian because of Betty's blonde hair and blue eyes and because we entered from East Jerusalem. As we listened to him, both of us decided that it was much more important to hear what he had to say than to argue with him. So for two hours I listened attentively. He assured us that the day would come when the Palestinians would drive the Jews into the sea and wipe them out. It was, he said, just a question of time. At the end of the two hours, I paid him the amount we had agreed upon and thanked him, but felt I had to say something in response.

'There is one thing I think you ought to know', I said, 'we're not Christian; we're Jewish.'

He replied, 'Oh, you're Jewish. You Jews have long memories. You remember the destruction of the Temple by the Romans.'

'Yes, we do, and now we have Jerusalem back again.'

'Well, we are your cousins. What makes you think that we have shorter memories? We remember the Crusades.'

'I know you have long memories. That's why there can't be peace between us.'

W & I: Maybe you should learn to forget.

R: A person can only forget a danger when the danger is no longer there. If it is only a fantasy danger, then it is possible, and even desirable, to forget. But when the danger is real, and this one is, then forgetfulness is the height of folly. Don't you understand that for years Saddam Hussein thought in terms of the Crusades and that he did everything he could to get the masses in all Arab countries to think in terms of the Crusades? Listen to his rhetoric. Read his speeches. You can take this man at his word when he promises *jihad*. Keep in mind Elie Wiesel's comment that 'Hitler kept his promises to the Jews.' These are people who have promised to drive the Israelis into the sea, and they still talk like that when they are broadcasting in Arabic even though they have moderated their rhetoric in English. These are promises I simply must take seriously.

W & I: The Islamic religious leaders and scholars tend to say that this is a kind of popular hysteria whipped up for political reasons by unscrupulous politicians and that it is not the real voice of Islam that you are hearing.

R: If you are talking about people like Sheik Zaki Badawi, who lives in London and is a very learned and cultivated man, I would say he is undoubtedly sincere about this. But there are many Islamic scholars in places like Iraq, Iran, Jordan, and even the West Bank who are quite sincere about a less peaceful synthesis of politics and religion. Their point of view is deeply rooted in Muslim history. The Muslims did not conquer faraway lands for the sake of material advantage. They conquered because they were convinced that they alone had the true faith, that they were giving people the true faith. And very few people whom they conquered and converted ever apostatized from their new religion. Islamic political moves always had a religious foundation, and I believe that is still true today.

Source: Richard L. Rubenstein, *After Auschwitz: History, Theology and Contemporary Judaism*, 2nd edn (Baltimore and London: Johns Hopkins Press, 1992), pp. 286–8, 290–2.

1.20 THE CURRENT ROLE OF *HALAKHAH*
DAVID NOVAK

Although *halakhah* is a system of law governing every aspect of personal and communal life, there is no Jewish community in the world today where *halakhah* is the sole basis of governance. This inherent paradox – namely, a total system of law forced by historical reality to share legal authority with another system of law, if not to be actually subordinate to it – has led to a number of tensions both in the state of Israel and in the Diaspora.

Halakhah *in the state of Israel*

In the state of Israel, *halakhah*, as adjudicated by the rabbinical courts, is recognized as the law governing all aspects of public Jewish religious ritual and all areas of marriage and divorce. (The same privilege is extended to the respective systems of law of the various non-Jewish religious communities there.) This political arrangement has led to a number of areas of tension. Thus many secularist Israeli Jews object to having to submit in questions of personal and familial status to the authority of religious courts, whose very religious justification they do not accept. This conflict has manifested itself in the demand by many secularist Israelis for civil marriage and divorce in the state of Israel, something that *halakhah* rejects as unacceptable for Jews. Even more profound is the fact that there is a conflict between *halakhah* and Israeli law on the most basic question of Jewish identity, that is, who is a Jew. According to *halakhah*, anyone born of a Jewish mother or himself or herself converted to Judaism is considered a Jew. According to the Israeli Law of Return (Hoq ha-Shevut), any Jew (with the exception of one convicted of a crime in another country) has the right of Israeli domicile and Israeli citizenship. However, in 1962 in a famous decision the Israeli Supreme Court ruled that Oswald Rufeisen, a Jewish convert to Christianity and a Roman Catholic monk, was not entitled to Israeli citizenship as a Jew because in the popular sense of the term he was not a Jew even though he was one in the technical, halakhic sense. On the other hand, in 1968, in another famous decision, the Israeli Supreme Court ruled that the wife and children of an Israeli Jew, Binyamin Shalit, were not to be considered Jews for purposes of Israeli citizenship because they had not been converted to Judaism, even though they identified themselves as Israeli Jews in the secular sense of the term. In this case, unlike the earlier one, the court accepted a halakhic definition of who is a Jew.

At the present time, furthermore, there is considerable debate in the state of Israel and the Diaspora about what actually constitutes valid conversion to Judaism. All Orthodox and most Conservative halakhists have rejected the conversions performed under Reform auspices because in the great majority of such cases the objective halakhic criteria of conversion – circumcision for males and immersion in a ritual bath (*miqveh*) for both males and females (B.T., *Yev.* 47b) – have not been fulfilled. Even the conversions performed under Conservative auspices, although fulfilling these objective criteria, are also rejected by many Orthodox legalists, who claim that Conservative rabbis lack the requisite commitment to *halakhah* to function as acceptable rabbinical judges. All of this is evidence of the widening division among the branches of contemporary Judaism.

Halakhah *in the Diaspora*

In the Diaspora, where adherence to *halakhah* is a matter of individual choice in practically every country that Judaism may be freely practiced, there is little ability to enforce the communal authority inherent in the halakhic system itself. This has led to a number of vexing problems. For example, the Talmud empowers a rabbinical court to force a man to divorce his wife for a variety of objective reasons that make normal married life impossible. When Jewish communities enjoyed relative internal autonomy, such enforcement could be carried out regularly. However, today, because of the loss of such communal autonomy, such enforcement is impossible, and many Jewish women, although already civilly divorced and no longer living with their former husbands, are still considered married according to *halakhah* and are unable to remarry because of the refusal of their former husbands to comply with the order of a rabbinical court.

This growing problem in societies where mobility and anonymity are facts of life has led to basically three different approaches. Many in the Orthodox community have attempted to resort to legal measures in the civil courts to force compliance with *halakhah*. In addition to a lack of success heretofore, this has raised, especially in the United States, the constitutional issue of governmental interference in private religious matters. On the other hand, the Conservative movement since 1968 has revived the ancient rabbinical privilege of retroactive annulment (B.T., *Git.* 33a) in cases where it is impossible to obtain a Jewish divorce from the husband. The Reform movement, not being bound by the authority of *halakhah*, accepts a civil divorce as sufficient termination of a Jewish marriage. These three widely divergent approaches to a major halakhic problem are further evidence of the growing divisiveness in the Jewish religious community in both the state of Israel and the Diaspora.

Reconstitution of the Sanhedrin

The only chance for effecting any halakhic unanimity among the Jewish people would be the reconstitution of the Sanhedrin in Jerusalem as the universal Jewish legislature and supreme court. This proposal was actually made by the first minister of religious affairs in the state of Israel, Judah Leib Maimon (1875–1962). However, considering the fact that this reconstitution itself presupposes much of the very unanimity it is to effect, it would seem that it is rather utopian, something the Talmud euphemistically called 'messianic *halakhah*' (B.T., *Zev.* 45a).

Source: David Novak, 'The Structure of Halakhah', in Mircea Eliade (ed.) *The Encyclopedia of Religion* (New York: Macmillan, 1989), pp. 164–73.

——— ●◆● ———

TORAH AND COVENANT: RECENT AND CONTEMPORARY VOICES

— ◆◆◆ —

1.21 THE CONCEPT OF TORAH
H. N. BIALIK

Hayyim Nahman Bialik (1873–1934) was a Russian Jewish writer and translator. His poetry and essays celebrate Jewish culture and the literary tradition of Hebrew.

The concept of 'Torah' attained in the esteem of the [Jewish] people an infinite exaltation. For them the Torah was almost another existence, a more spiritual and loftier state, added to or even taking the place of secular existence. The Torah became the center of the nation's secret and avowed aspirations and desires in its exile. The dictum 'Israel and the Torah are one' was no mere phrase; the non-Jew cannot appreciate it, because the concept of 'Torah', in its full national significance, cannot be rendered adequately in any other tongue. Its content and connotations embrace more than 'religion' or 'creed' alone, or 'ethics' or 'commandments' or 'learning' alone, and it is not even just a combination of all these, but something far transcending all of them. It is a mystic, almost cosmic, conception. The Torah is the tool of the Creator; with it and for it He created the universe. The Torah is older than creation. It is the highest idea and the living soul of the world. Without it the world could not exist and would have no right to exist. 'The study of the Torah is more important than the building of the Temple.' 'Knowledge of the Torah ranks higher than priesthood or kingship.' 'Only he is free who engages in the study of the Torah.' 'It is the Torah that magnifies and exalts man over all creatures.' 'Even a heathen who engages in the study of the Torah is as good as a High Priest.'

'A bastard learned in the Torah takes precedence over an ignorant High Priest.' [Quotations are from rabbinic literature.]

Such is the world outlook to which almost seventy generations of Jews have been educated. In accordance therewith their spiritual life was provisionally organized for the interim of the exile. For it they suffered martyrdom and by virtue of it they lived. The Jewish elementary school was established shortly before the destruction of Jerusalem and has survived to this day. As a result of such prolonged training, the nation has acquired a sort of sixth sense for everything connected with the needs of the spirit, a most delicate sense and always the first to be affected, and one possessed by almost every individual. There is not a Jew but would be filled with horror by a cruel decree 'that Jews shall not engage in the Torah'. Even the poorest and meanest man in Israel sacrificed for the teaching of his children, on which he spent sometimes as much as half of his income or more. Before asking for the satisfaction of his material needs, the Jew first prays daily: 'And graciously bestow upon us knowledge, understanding, and comprehension.' And what was the first request of our pious mothers over the Sabbath candles? 'May it be Your will that the eyes of my children may shine with Torah.' Nor do I doubt that if God had appeared to one of these mothers in a dream, as He did once to Solomon, and said, 'Ask, what shall I give unto you?' she would have replied even as Solomon did, 'I ask not for myself either riches or honor, but O Lord of the universe, may it please You to give unto my sons a heart to understand Torah and wisdom to distinguish good from evil' [based on I Kings 3:9–11].

Source: Hertzberg, op. cit., pp. 85–6.

1.22 THE PEOPLE AND THE BOOK
LEO BAECK

When the great test is put to a man, his whole life, all which he has had and has been and which lies before him, enters this one hour. His whole life speaks to him. So, too, is it demanded of a people when it is put to the great test. Its whole history in its journey from the former to the now, from the now to the coming becomes its present. Past and future must pass the test of the now. The now is confronted, and past and future can become vital forces only as they stream into the present.

Only rarely, and then not always as a blessing, did this people have days without spiritual and intellectual strain. Then perhaps the Bible could appear as a book written and in a sense ready at hand, a book that told of what had been, that stated what had been commanded, that announced what the expectation then foresaw. But when the questions pressed and oppressed, when question crowded question, then this Book had to elevate itself and set out on its ceaseless way. As the Book of this people it could only be, to a degree, a book in movement. It had grown together with this people. When the people was reborn, the Book was also reborn, and the rebirth of the Book created the rebirth of the people. Its history runs from present to present.

To designate this unique quality, this dynamic nearness and immediacy of the Book, a special, characteristic expression was coined in early rabbinic times. One said that the Book presented itself in a two-sided manner: as 'Written Torah' and as 'Oral Torah'. It could also be rendered thus: It is a book composed and written down, and it is at the same time a movement, awakened and renewing itself from within. It has its word with which it begins and its word with which it ends. But in reality it never ceases and never ends; ever again it commences and continues. Its word seems to be a word that was spoken once, but it is in reality a task that starts itself again and again. He who believes that he carries it in his hand does not have it; but he who is driven by it, to him has it come. One of the teachers could say: 'The men of this Book can never rest completely [and added with hyperbole], not in this world nor in the world to come.' It is a book in movement, and therefore it belongs to no generation and to no epoch completely. It endures and remains because it takes its way from generation to generation. Therefore it is the 'Written Torah' and the 'Oral Torah'.

Source: Leo Baeck, *This People Israel* (New York: Holt, Rinehart and Winston, 1964), pp. 199–200.

1.23 THE PHARISAIC MOVEMENT
LEO BAECK

One can only speak of a Pharisaic movement, and not of a Pharisaic party, just as the Sadducean group and the Essenic circle, generally compared or contrasted with the Pharisees, should also not be designated as parties. Flavius Josephus, an historian of this people, spoke of them as parties. He wanted to recount the many aspects of his people to the Romans and the Greeks who had to think of parties whenever they thought of differences in a society that had its own internal development. A party wishes to win adherents, to unite them, to lead them to success; but a movement wants to awaken the conscience and effect a change in life. Actually this people was at that time seized by the Pharisaic movement which might even be called the Pharisaic awakening.

To accept in all seriousness the great demand of Sinai, 'And ye shall be unto Me a kingdom of priests, and a holy nation' (Ex. 19:6), to take it seriously always and everywhere, this was the great idea which emanated from this movement. An idea is great and genuine only when it becomes an enduring task; and such a task can only be one which approaches everyone, each exalted and humble soul, in the same manner. The manifold contrasts of caste and divisions of rank basically can be traced to groups which originally or retroactively ascribe to themselves a higher ideal. Upon it they base the claim to set themselves apart from others or look down upon them. The circle of the conqueror, the usurper, the oppressor, is to be considered the domain of the higher idea for whose sake it is to remain protected and secured. The Pharisaic movement, in a decisive manner and with decisive historical success, undertook to bring the higher, the determining ideal to everyone simultaneously, so that they all might come to possess it now, completely. The law of Sinai, with which the true history of this people begins, was rejuvenated, in order to meet changed times and to create for itself new expression and new form. Now each individual was addressed even more strongly; to him, responsibility and through it the right to his place was more firmly given.

Source: Baeck, op. cit., pp. 215–16.

1.24 THE LAW IS NOT A BURDEN
S. SCHECHTER

Solomon Schechter (1847–1915) was a British rabbinic scholar.

It is an illusion to speak of the burden which a scrupulous care to observe six hundred and thirteen commandments must have laid upon the Jew. Even a superficial analysis will discover that in the time of Christ many of these commandments were already obsolete (as for instance those relating to the tabernacle and to the conquest of Palestine), while others concerned only certain classes, as the priests, the judges, the soldiers, the Nazirites, or the representatives of the community, or even only one or two individuals among the whole population, as the King and the High Priest. Others, again, provided for contingencies which could occur only to a few, as for instance the laws concerning divorce or levirate marriages, whilst many – such as those concerning idolatry, and incest, and the sacrifice of children to Moloch – could scarcely have been considered as a practical prohibition by the pre-Christian Jew, just as little as we can speak of Englishmen as lying under the burden of a law preventing them from burning widows or marrying their grandmothers, though such acts would certainly be considered as crimes. Thus it will be found by a careful enumeration that barely a hundred laws remain which really concerned the life of the bulk of the people. If we remember that even these include such laws as belief in the unity of God, the necessity of loving and fearing Him, and of sanctifying His name, of loving one's neighbour and the stranger, of providing for the poor, exhorting the sinner, honouring one's parents and many more of a similar character, it will hardly be said that the ceremonial side of the people's religion was not well balanced by a fair amount of spiritual and social elements. Besides, it would seem that the line between the ceremonial and the spiritual is too often only arbitrarily drawn. With many commandments it is rather a matter of opinion whether they should be relegated to the one category or the other.

Thus the wearing of the Tephillin or phylacteries has, on the one hand, been continually condemned as a meaningless superstition, and a pretext for formalism and hypocrisy. But, on the other hand, Maimonides, who can in no way be suspected of superstition or mysticism, described their importance in the following words: 'Great is the holiness of the Tephillin; for as long as they are on the arm and head of man he is humble and God-fearing, and feels no attraction for frivolity or idle things, nor has he any evil thoughts, but will turn his heart to the words of truth and righteousness.' The view which Rabbi Johanan, a Palestinian preacher of the third century, took of the fulfillment of the Law, will probably be found more rational than that of many a rationalist of today. Upon the basis of the last verse in Hosea, 'The ways of the Lord are right, and the just shall walk in them, but the transgressors shall fall therein', he explains that while one man, for instance, eats his paschal lamb with the purpose of doing the will of God who commanded it, and thereby does an act of righteousness, another thinks only of satisfying his appetite by the lamb, so that his eating it (by the very fact that he professes at the same time to perform a religious rite) becomes a stumbling block for him. Thus all the laws by virtue of their divine authority – and in this there was in the first century no difference of opinion between Jews and Christians – have their spiritual side, and to neglect them implies, at least from the individual's own point of view, a moral offense.

The legalistic attitude may be summarily described as an attempt to live in accordance with the will of God, caring less for what God is than for what He wants us to be. But, nevertheless, on the whole this life never degenerated into religious formalism. Apart from the fact that during the Second Temple there grew up laws, and even beliefs, which show a decided tendency towards progress and development, there were also ceremonies which were popular with the masses, and others which were neglected. Men were not, therefore, the mere soulless slaves of the Law; personal sympathies and dislikes also played a part in their religion. Nor were all the laws actually put upon the same level. With a happy inconsistency men always spoke of heavier and slighter sins, and by the latter – excepting, perhaps, the profanation of the Sabbath – they mostly understood ceremonial transgressions.

Source: Hertzberg, op. cit., pp. 82–4.

1.25 A PRIEST-PEOPLE

K. KOHLER

Kaufmann Kohler (1843–1926) was born in Bavaria but migrated to the United States, where he became a leader of American Reform Judaism.

Undoubtedly the Law, as it embraced the whole of life in its power, sharpened the Jewish sense of duty, and served the Jew as an iron wall of defense against temptations, aberrations, and enticements of the centuries. As soon as the modern Jew, however, undertook to free himself from the tutelage of blind acceptance of authority and inquired after the purpose of all the restrictions of the Law laid upon him, his ancient loyalty to the same collapsed and the pillars of Judaism seemed to be shaken. Then the leaders of Reform, imbued with the prophetic spirit, felt it to be their imperative duty to search out the fundamental ideas of the priestly law of holiness and, accordingly, they learned how to separate the kernel from the shell. In opposition to the orthodox tendency to worship the letter, they insisted on the fact that Israel's separation from the world – which it is ultimately to win for the divine truth – cannot itself be its end and aim, and that blind obedience to the law does not constitute true piety. Only the fundamental idea, that Israel as the 'first-born' among the nations has been elected as a priest-people must remain our imperishable truth, a truth to which the centuries of history bear witness by showing that it has given its life-blood as a ransom for humanity, and is ever bringing new sacrifices for its cause. Only because it has kept itself distinct as a priest-people among the nations could it carry out its great task in history; and only if it remains conscious of its priestly calling and therefore maintains itself as the people of God, can it fulfill its mission. Not until the end of time, when all of God's children will have entered the kingdom of God, may Israel, the high-priest among the nations, renounce his priesthood.

Source: Hertzberg, op. cit., pp. 84–5.

1.26 THE CHOSEN PEOPLE
LOUIS JACOBS

Louis Jacobs (b. 1924) is an English rabbi and scholar in the Orthodox tradition whose writings provoked a controversy with the Chief Rabbi and other sections of the Orthodox community during the 1960s. Jacobs subsequently founded the New London Synagogue.

In view of the importance the doctrine of Israel as God's chosen people assumes in the Bible, its central role in Rabbinic thought and the emphasis placed upon it by many modern Jewish thinkers, it comes as a shock to discover that it features in none of the medieval classifications as a basic principle of the Jewish faith. In all probability the reason for the omission is that the medieval thinkers did not see the chosenness of Israel as a separate dogma but as implied in other principles of the faith, especially those concerning the Torah, which was given to Israel. But it is also very plausible to suggest that the influence of Greek thought, which gave a universalistic cast to medieval thinking, made the doctrine of a chosen people something of an embarrassment. Maimonides, for example, when he does discuss the question of why God revealed His law to one particular nation and at one particular time can only reply that God willed it so. The 'scandal of particularism' is always a problem when this idea of God choosing is examined. The 'oddness' in God's choosing is not in His choice of the Jews but in the choice itself. Why did God have to make a *choice* among peoples, why not convey the truth to all mankind?

It cannot be denied that some Jewish thinkers have interpreted the doctrine to mean that there is a qualitative difference between Jews and other peoples, that the Jews are spiritual supermen, endowed with rare qualities of soul by virtue of their descent from the Patriarchs. In the medieval world the representative of this type of thinking was Judah Ha-Levi. Ha-Levi builds his philosophy on the view that the Jew is not simply a superior type of human being but belongs, in fact, to a different category altogether. The difference between Israel and the other peoples of the world is one of kind, not of degree, just as humans are different from animals, animals from plants, and plants from minerals. Aware of the moral difficulty in such a view,

Ha-Levi observes that since, however, Israel is the 'heart of the nations' it can be the most healthy and the most sick of peoples. A bad Jew is more thoroughly bad than the worst Gentile. Ha-Levi's 'racism' is, of course, limited. He cannot reject the Rabbinic view that Gentiles can be converted to Judaism and hence belong to the Jewish people. But, for Ha-Levi, the higher reaches of the religious life such as prophecy are not possible for those born outside the people of Israel.

In modern times a qualitative interpretation of Jewish chosenness has been advocated by thinkers like Abraham Geiger who believed that the Jewish people has a special genius for religion and is far more sensitive than others to the call of the religious life.

At the opposite extremes are those Jewish thinkers who would reject the whole notion of chosenness as unworthy. On the theological level it has seemed to some to have an inadequate concept of Deity to say that God shows favouritism to any one group and it seems unjust that the children of righteous forebears should be singled out not through any merit of their own but by accident of birth. One of the most vigorous protagonists of the view that all peoples are 'called' by God to fulfil his purpose but none are 'chosen', not even the Jews, is Mordecai Kaplan. Not that Kaplan fails to consider the special nature of Jewish religious forms. Kaplan is a great believer in preserving and furthering the distinctive patterns of Jewish life as enriching and rewarding. But he steadfastly refuses to formulate this in terms of 'chosenness' which suggests privilege. To the stock answer that the 'choice' of Israel is not for privilege but for service, Kaplan retorts that to be chosen for service is the greatest privilege of all. Hugo Bergman, after studying carefully the various moves of modern Jewish thinkers to defend the doctrine of chosenness, finds none of them completely convincing and comes to the conclusion that the doctrine, in whatever form it is presented, is difficult to reconcile with the idea of God's justice.

Between the two extremes is the view, followed here, that while chosenness should not be interpreted in qualitative terms it should not be given up entirely. On the contrary it is still valid and, paradoxical though this may seem, is still the most powerful way of expressing the universal ideal. Jewish history has demonstrated that truths originally the possession of a particular people have become, through the efforts of that people to live by them, the property of millions beyond the confines of the people to whom the truth was originally revealed. Ethical monotheism is the supreme example of this. The rest of this chapter is devoted, then, to a defence of the doctrine of the chosen people always with the *proviso* that the doctrine is conceived of in non-qualitative terms. The following points require especially to be made in defence of the doctrine.

1   The Biblical conception of the election of Israel has nothing in common with the idea of a tribal god protecting his people, responding to their attempts to buy his favour and capable of suffering defeat at the hands of a more powerful deity. The relation of a tribal god to his people is a 'natural one'. He does not 'choose' his people any more than they are members of the tribe by choice. In the Bible it is the universal God who 'chooses'. As I. Heinemann has pointed out, the Biblical references to the choice are in a universalistic framework. 'Now,

therefore, if ye will obey My voice indeed, and keep My covenant, then ye shall be a peculiar treasure unto Me above all people: *For all the earth is Mine'* (Ex. 19:5). 'Why sayest thou, O Jacob, and speakest O Israel, my way is hid from the Lord, and my judgement is passed over from my God? Hast thou not known? hast thou not heard, *that the everlasting God, the Lord, the Creator of the ends of the earth,* fainteth not, neither is weary? there is no searching of His understanding' (Is. 40:27–8). 'Thus saith God the Lord, *He spread the heavens, and stretched them forth, He spread forth the earth and that which cometh out of it, He that giveth bread unto the people upon it, And spirit to them that walk therein*; I the Lord have called thee in righteousness, and have taken hold of thy hand, and kept thee, and set thee for a covenant of the people, For a light of the Nations; to open the blind eyes. To bring out the prisoners from the dungeon. And them that sit in darkness out of the prison-house' (Is. 42:5–7).

2 The doctrine is not of a Herrenvolk whom others must serve but on the contrary of a folk dedicated to the service of others. The prophet Amos declares: 'You only have I known of all the families of the earth, therefore I will visit upon you all your iniquities' (Amos 3:2). The constant castigations of their people by the prophets, their steadfast demands that the people live up to their vocation in which they are failing lamentably, their frequent warnings of divine displeasure, are hardly ideas one associates with divine favouritism. Zangwill once said that the Bible is an anti-Semitic book! In a typical Rabbinic passage we read: 'It is written: "It was not because you were greater than any people that the Lord set His love upon you and chose you for you are the smallest of all peoples" (Deut. 7:7). The Holy One, blessed be He, said to Israel, I love you because even though I bestow greatness upon you, you humble yourselves before Me. I bestowed greatness upon Abraham, yet he said to Me, "I am dust and ashes" (Gen. 18:27); upon Moses and Aaron, yet they said, "And we are nothing" (Ex. 16:8); upon David, yet he said, "But I am a worm and no man" (Ps. 22:7). But with the heathen it is not so. I bestowed greatness upon Nimrod, and he said, "Who is the Lord" (Ex. 5:2); upon Sennacherib, and he said, "Who are they among all the gods of the countries?" (2 Kings 18:35); upon Nebuchadnezzar, and he said, "I will ascend above the heights of the clouds" (Is. 14:14); upon Hiram king of Tyre, and he said, "I sit in the seat of God, in the heart of the seas" (Ezek. 28:2).'

3 The doctrine has no affinity with such notions as that of Aryan racial superiority. Jewish particularism is never exclusive: anyone can become a Jew by embracing the Jewish faith. Some of the greatest of the Rabbis are said to have been descended from converts to Judaism. In one Talmudic passage it is said that the proselyte is dearer to God than the born Israelite. Another passage teaches that Israel was scattered among the nations only that they might make proselytes. The proselyte is regarded as a Jew in every respect. He should recite in his prayers the formula: 'Our God and the God of our fathers', for he is a spiritual child of Abraham. It is strictly forbidden to taunt a proselyte with his background or former behaviour.

4 The choice was reciprocal – God choosing Israel and Israel choosing God. The idea of a covenant between God and Israel is basic to the whole conception.

'Thou has avouched the Lord this day to be thy God, and to walk in His ways, and to keep His statutes, and His commandments and His judgements, and to hearken unto His voice; And the Lord hath avouched thee this day to be His peculiar people, as He hath promised thee, and that thou shouldest keep His commandments' (Deut. 26:17–18). 'And Joshua said unto the people, Ye are witnesses against yourselves that you have chosen you the Lord to serve Him. And they said, we are witnesses' (Josh. 24:22). The Rabbis had something of this in mind when they told of God offering the Torah to all the other nations, who refused it, before giving it to Israel who accepted its yoke and cheerfully proclaimed: 'We will do and we will hear.'

5   If the empirical test is applied it becomes obvious that we are not discussing a dogma incapable of verification but the recognition of sober historical fact. The world owes Israel the idea of the One God of righteousness and holiness. This is how God became known to mankind and clearly God used Israel for this great purpose. When Judaism declares that the covenant is still in force it re-affirms that Israel still has a special role to play.

From what has been said it is clear that the Chosen People idea is not a narrowly exclusive one, that it is universalistic, that it invokes duty rather than bestows privilege, that it is a doctrine of reciprocity, and that it bears the stamp of historical truth.

Yet there is also no doubt that this doctrine, perhaps more than any other, is so easily distorted and may even be dangerous. The suggestion or implication that it means that God is exclusively concerned with Jews or even that they are His special concern is surely at variance with the universalistic doctrine of Judaism that God is the Father of all mankind. Undoubtedly, less worthy interpretations of the doctrine are found in the Jewish sources but the nobler view is also found there and that in abundance.

The Jew of today is the heir to the whole tradition and this means that here, as in other areas, there are tensions with which he has to learn to live. As a powerful spur to Jewish survival, as providing a sense of destiny, as a reaffirmation of the covenant with its demands, responsibilities and obligations, the doctrine of the chosen people still possesses much value. As a temptation to narrowness and exclusiveness it still has its dangers. The modern Jew must learn to avail himself of the values inherent in the doctrine while taking due caution against its degeneration. To attempt to live without such tensions is to deprive life of its creativity. It is altogether right and proper that Jews should be concerned with the difficulties in the doctrine of Israel's chosenness. It may be that the Jew never comes closer to the truth in the doctrine of chosenness than when he is severely critical of why and how God can choose the Jewish people.

Source: Louis Jacobs, *A Jewish Theology* (Darton, Longman and Todd, 1973), pp. 269–75.

1.27 RECLAIMING THE COVENANT: A JEWISH FEMINIST'S SEARCH FOR MEANING

ELLEN M. UMANSKY

Ellen M. Umansky (b. 1950) is a Reform Jew and academic.

Within the last few years, my own struggle to reclaim the Jewish covenant as a bond between God and *all* of the Jewish people – male and female – has been both challenging and frustrating. At times, I have almost abandoned my struggle. The continued exclusion of women from positions of secular and religious leadership within the Jewish community, the extent to which women's spirituality – past and present – is still ignored, the lack of formal ceremonies celebrating important life-cycle events of women, and the liturgical description of God as 'God of our Fathers' (but not our mothers) make me angry and sad. At first, I directed my anger toward Judaism itself, ready to write it off as hopelessly patriarchal. But more recently, I've come to redirect my anger. It's not Judaism itself that angers me but those who seem to have forgotten that Judaism has never been monolithic and that in every period of Jewish history Judaism has developed and grown.

Those who argue that liturgy cannot be changed have lost sight of Judaism as a living religion. How meaningful today are images of God as King, Lord, and Shepherd? And why, if both men and women have been created in God's image, should we not address the Divine as Father *and* Mother, Master and Mistress of Heaven? Martin Buber envisioned Judaism as arising out of a We–Thou dialogue between the Jewish people and God. I'm beginning to suspect, however, that my forefathers did most of the talking. Consequently, Judaism as we now know it was largely fashioned by generations of men who decided what *they* wanted Judaism to be.

Yet even the rabbis of the Talmud admitted that the covenant established at Sinai was given to men *and women*. Perhaps my foremothers were content to live out their membership vicariously, through the rituals and prayers of their fathers, husbands, and sons. Vicarious membership, however, will no longer do. As a feminist, I have begun to reclaim my voice; as a Jew, I am ready to activate my membership within the covenant and to reopen the dialogue with *our* God.

As I think about my spiritual journey, I realize that my search for meaning may never end. What I've learned in the seventeen years since I took my Confirmation vows is that the ground rules are *not* preestablished, that it is my obligation as a Jew to help create a Judaism that is meaningful for my generation. Three thousand years ago, Moses stood at Mt Sinai and received the Ten Commandments from God. When he came down the mountain and saw the Israelites worshipping a golden calf, he broke the tablets in anger. Perhaps he did so not only to warn us against idolatry but also to make it clear that not even God's words are irrevocably carved in stone.

Source: Ellen M. Umansky, 'Reclaiming the covenant: a Jewish feminist's search for meaning', in E. M. Umansky and D. Ashton (eds) *Four Centuries of Jewish Women's Spirituality – A Sourcebook* (Boston: Beacon Press, 1992), p. 234.

1.28 DOMESTIC OBSERVANCES

SHLOMO DESHEN

Besides the synagogue, the home has traditionally been a main focus of religiosity both for the Jewish family as a unit and especially for women. Women were traditionally excluded from the duty of Torah study, which for men was, and to some extent remains, a major focus of spirituality. Moreover, women were not obligated to observe many of the religious practices that bound men. In particular, their place in public synagogue ritual was minimal. Consequently, domestic rituals, and especially those governed by women, are important focuses of their spirituality. For all Jews, certain ritual customs (*minhagim*) and rabbinic laws (*halakhot*) actually require a domestic setting. These rituals may be divided into those that are held on specific occasions of the Jewish calendar and those that are a constant presence in daily life.

Periodic domestic observances

The annual festival cycle begins in the spring with Passover, which focuses on two major domestic activities: the thorough cleaning of the home to remove leavened food, and then the Seder, the Passover eve feast, which has traditionally been led by the father and requires the participation of the children. Shavu'ot, in early summer, is accompanied by only minor domestic customs, such as decorating the home with greenery and partaking of dairy foods. The period of mourning for the destroyed Temple, which follows in midsummer, affects the home in a fashion opposite to that of the festivals: enjoyment of music, food, new clothing, and vacations, and joyfulness in general, are restricted. The fall holy days start with Ro'sh ha-Shanah and Yom Kippur, which are primarily synagogue-centered occasions but which include secondary domestic activities. On Ro'sh ha-Shanah, foods symbolizing good fortune are served at the family meal, and on Yom Kippur, family elders bless the young. During the week-long Sukkot festival the domestic focus is again pronounced. Temporary booths or huts (*sukkot*) are erected near or adjacent to each family home. Meals are eaten there, and some males follow the rabbinic tradition of sleeping in the booths at night. People entertain guests and generally pass time in the family *sukkah*. Hanukkah, in early winter, is focused domestically as well. Lights are ritually kindled in the home, and special holiday foods are prepared. Hanukkah also has indoor child-centered activities (gift-giving and living-room games). In late winter, Purim requires a formal feast at home, and women and children become particularly involved in the traditional sending of gifts of food to friends.

Perennial domestic observances

Besides seasonal events, the Jewish home also has perennial ritual activities, primarily on the Sabbath, when the routine of the home is transformed. Domestic rituals are observed on the Sabbath: candles are lit by the housewife on Sabbath eve; the

Qiddush ('sanctification of the day') is chanted at the first of the three mandatory festive meals; families sing Sabbath songs (*zemirot*) and sometimes study Torah together. Of these customs, candle-lighting is a major rite for women, a virtual symbol of female religious identity. In recent times, with the attenuation of many more burdensome Jewish customs, candle-lighting has remained vital and thus has become more prominent. According to some traditions, parents formally bless their children on Sabbath eve, and Sabbath night is a preferred time for conjugal relations. In the home the Sabbath ends with the ceremony of *havdalah* ('separation' of the Sabbath from the week), which involves the use of wine, spices, and a special braided candle, and at which a new fire is lit. Another perennial domestic ritual element is the display of religious artifacts. Foremost of these is the mandatory *mezuzah* inscription of biblical verses, encased on all doorposts. Brass or silver candelabra, wine goblets, and collections of Judaica books are common in the more prosperous homes. It is a custom to leave a section of wall in the home (about one square foot) unpainted, as a symbol of pain over the destruction of ancient Jerusalem (*zekher le-ḥurban*).

The celebration of rites of passage spills over into the home through the holding of festive meals. Domestically, the most marked rites of passage are mourning rites, which restrict the bereaved to their homes and require them to receive condolence visits. Memorial candles for the dead are lit at home. In the past, marriages in Mediterranean countries were patrilocal and some marriage observances paralleled mourning rites. The bridal couple were restricted to their new home for seven days of festivity, and daily rites were held in the presence of visitors. In our time, owing to the attenuation of patrilocality, the practice among many young Orthodox bridal couples, both in Israel and elsewhere, is to travel distances to visit their kin, and to be hosted in different homes where rites are held for the duration of seven days.

In Orthodox and traditionally observant families, the home is the scene of innumerable daily acts of individual piety: the ritual washing of hands upon arising, before meals and after voiding; the uttering of grace after meals, and of shorter benedictions before and after the partaking of any food. Prayers are recited upon waking and upon retiring at night, and three daily prayer services (*shaḥarit*, in the morning, *minḥah*, in the afternoon, *máariv*, in the evening) are required of all adult males. In recent times, because of the weaker hold of the community, weekday prayers are frequently said at home rather than at the synagogue; hence, the role of the home in daily prayer has increased.

The most pervasive home observances are those that concern food and conjugal relations. Observance of the rules of *kashrut* (maintaining a ritually pure, kosher kitchen), is dependent upon the foods introduced into the home, and on the separation of various categories of foods in the kitchen and dining area. *Kashrut* also requires the services of extra-domestic agents, such as a *shoḥet* (ritual slaughterer), and of manufacturers of kosher foods. The maintenance of 'family purity' (*ṭaharat ha-mishpaḥah*) depends to a greater extent on the privacy of domestic practice. 'Family purity' consists of the maintenance of a monthly schedule of conjugal separation and reunion based on the menstrual cycle, and on the woman's periodic immersion in a *miqveh* (ritual bath). While the availability of an external agent, the *miqveh*, is required here as well, the element of domestic autonomy in this area of intimacy is nonetheless very strong. The autonomy of the home in this area was curtailed in traditional times (in Northern Europe roughly until the mid-nineteenth century, in Mediterranean lands until close to the mid-twentieth century). Decisions concerning the proper timing of immersion were not handled exclusively by the woman then, but rather in conjunction with a circle of elder females, family and neighbors. If there was any physiological irregularity, male rabbis were consulted. In contemporary Orthodoxy, middle-class sensitivities concerning the privacy of sexual matters have eliminated the role of the outside female circle; rabbis are consulted only in the most unusual cases. But it is in the maintenance of *kashrut* that the role of the home has increased most in contemporary times, and has assumed a novel symbolic weight. The affective term 'kosher home' is now commonly used in reference to *kashrut* observance, which has gained much greater prominence in relation to its historical place in Jewish practice and thought. Over time, additional domestic practices have become more prominent (contemporary domestic Sabbath practices are innovations of the late sixteenth century). Most recently in the West, the pressure of Christmastime commercialism has encouraged Jewish families to elaborate the observance of Hanukkah, especially with parties, gift giving, and the decoration of the home, as an ethnic counterpoint to Christian symbols such as the tree and Santa Claus.

There are two major exceptions to this development (i.e., the increasing emphasis on Jewish domestic ritual). One is the virtual disappearance of the *hallah*-separation rite. Married women baking their bread used to separate and burn a small portion of the dough, as a symbol of the tithe that was due the priests in Temple times. *Hallah*-separation used to be a major female responsibility, similar to Sabbath candle-lighting and to the maintenance of family purity (*niddah*). But as bread production has shifted from a domestic to a commercial setting, the rite has become uncommon. Another exception is in practices of the Hasidic movement, which encourages male groups to congregate by themselves, or at the court of the *rebbe*, the sect leader. In these congregations, adult males eat the third of the three required meals together, away from their families, on the Sabbath afternoon. Hasidism also encourages men to spend some of the holy days and Sabbaths at the distant court of the *rebbe*, again separating them from their families.

Source: Shlomo Deshen, 'Domestic observances', in R. M. Seltzer (ed.) *Judaism: A People and its History* (New York: Macmillan, 1989), pp. 251–3.

PART TWO

—◆◆—

CHRISTIANITY

INTRODUCTION

— ● ● ● —

The Christian tradition is founded on the conviction that Jewish prophecies about the coming of the Messiah were fulfilled in the life and death of Jesus of Nazareth. Although the title 'Christ' harks back to traditional Jewish belief in the Messiah as the 'anointed' agent of God, Christians regard Jesus as fully God and view Jesus' death as the outworking of God's plan to redeem humanity. As God in human form, for Christians, Jesus offers human beings the way to salvation and eternal life and his resurrection is seen to be evidence of this. Believing that God has intervened decisively in human history through the person of Jesus, Christians have been vigilant in attempting to ensure that a balance is maintained in their teaching about a being they believe to have been both completely human and perfectly divine. They have been energetic in spreading the gospel, or 'good news', of the saving power of Jesus' life and death, and the church established after the death of Jesus has been the conduit of this energy.

Christianity spread far and wide from its earliest days and by the 4th century CE had been adopted as the official religion of the Roman empire. A little over a thousand years later, Christianity was again the preferred religion of European nations then in the throes of colonial expansion. By the end of the twentieth century, Christianity in its different forms was practised by more people than any other religion and had reaped the benefits of its closeness to the seats of political power and influence for more than a thousand years.

As Christianity has expanded, so have the forms that it has taken. Since the late sixteenth century, the major Christian denominations have been Roman Catholicism, Eastern Orthodoxy and Protestantism. Theological and political disagreements contributed to these schisms, and the historical legacy of these factors is evident in different understandings of the role of the church, the sacraments, and the nature of ecclesiastical authority. This internal diversity has been increased with the proliferation of Protestant churches and sects, and with the growth of informal religious associations.

In parts of the world profoundly affected by European colonialism over the last two hundred years, it has largely been the denomination of the colonisers that has taken root. By the late twentieth century, it was these more recently Christianised regions that contained the largest concentrations of Christians as the appeal of Christianity diminished in its former European strongholds. This change, located in many parts of the world where Christians were facing political oppression, and the claims made by women and gay men and women for full recognition within their churches, promoted new and, at the time, radical theologies.

The readings begin with a statement of the human condition taken from Genesis, one of the books of the Jewish Bible that falls within the Christian canon of the *Old Testament*. The readings that follow from the *New Testament* set out the distinctively Christian understanding of Jesus' work and its significance for humanity. The life of the Christian churches from the days of the early church fathers until the late twentieth century is represented in the remaining readings. Ecumenism, feminist theology and the relationship between religion, politics and the quest for social justice are highlighted as prominent concerns of late twentieth-century Christians.

PASSAGES FROM THE CHRISTIAN BIBLE

— ◆◆◆ —

2.1 CREATION AND THE ORIGINAL CONDITION OF HUMANITY ACCORDING TO THE OLD TESTAMENT

2.1.1

Man's original situation according to Genesis

Then God said, 'Let us make man in our image, after our likeness; and let them have dominion over the fish of the sea, and over the birds of the air, and over the cattle, and over all the earth, and over every creeping thing that creeps upon the earth.' So God created man in his own image, in the image of God he created him; male and female he created them. And God blessed them, and God said to them, 'Be fruitful and multiply, and fill the earth and subdue it, and have dominion over the fish of the sea and over the birds of the air and over every living thing that moves upon the earth . . .'

(Genesis 1:26–8)

2.1.2

Then the Lord God formed man of dust from the ground, and breathed into his nostrils the breath of life; and man became a living being. And the Lord God planted a garden in Eden, in the east; and there he put the man whom he had formed. And out of the ground the Lord God made to grow every tree that is pleasant to the sight and good for food, the tree of life also in the midst of the garden, and the tree of the knowledge of good and evil . . .

(Genesis 2:7–9)

The Lord God took the man and put him in the garden of Eden to till it and keep it. And the Lord God commanded the man, saying, 'You may freely eat of every tree of the garden; but of the tree of the knowledge of good and evil you shall not eat, for in the day that you eat of it you shall die . . .'

(Genesis 2:15–17)

2.1.3

Now the serpent was more subtle than any other wild creature that the Lord God had made. He said to the woman, 'Did God say, "You shall not eat of any tree of the garden"?' And the woman said to the serpent, 'We may eat of the fruit of the trees of the garden; but God said, "You shall not eat of the fruit of the tree which is in the midst of the garden, neither shall you touch it, lest you die."' But the serpent said to the woman, 'You will not die. For God knows that when you eat of it your eyes will be opened, and you will be like God, knowing good and evil.' So when the woman saw that the tree was good for food, and that it was a delight to the eyes, and that the tree was to be desired to make one wise, she took of its fruit and ate; and she also gave some to her husband, and he ate. Then the eyes of both were opened, and they knew that they were naked; and they sewed fig leaves together and made themselves aprons . . .

(Genesis 3:1–7)

The Lord God said to the serpent, 'Because you have done this, cursed are you above all cattle, and above all wild animals; upon your belly you shall go, and dust you shall eat all the days of your life. I will put enmity between you and the woman, and between your seed and her seed; he shall bruise your head, and you shall bruise his heel.' To the woman he said, 'I will greatly multiply your pain in child bearing; in pain you shall bring forth children, yet your desire shall be for your husband, and he shall rule over you.' And to Adam he said, 'Because you have listened to the voice of your wife, and have eaten of the tree of which I commanded you, "You shall not eat of it", cursed is the ground because of you; in toil you shall eat of it all the days of your life; thorns and thistles it shall bring forth to you; and you shall eat the plants of the field. In the sweat of your face you shall eat bread till you return to the ground, for out of it you were taken; you are dust, and to dust you shall return . . .'

(Genesis 3:14–19)

Then the Lord God said, 'Behold, the man has become like one of us, knowing good and evil; and now, lest he put forth his hand and take also of the tree of life and eat, and live forever' – therefore the Lord God sent him forth from the garden of Eden, to till the ground from which he was taken. He drove out the man; and at the east of the garden of Eden he placed the cherubim, and a flaming sword which turned every way, to guard the way to the tree of life.'

(Genesis 3:22–4)

Source: RSV Bible.

2.2 THE KINGDOM OF GOD

2.2.1

And in the days of those kings the God of heaven will set up a kingdom which shall never be destroyed, nor shall its sovereignty be left to another people. It shall break in pieces all these kingdoms and bring them to an end, and it shall stand for ever.

(Daniel 2:44)

2.2.2

How great are his signs, how mighty his wonders!
His kingdom is an everlasting kingdom,
and his dominion is from generation to generation.

(Daniel 4:3)

2.2.3

Thy kingdom come, Thy will be done, On earth as it is in heaven.

(Matthew 6:10)

2.2.4

Jesus came into Galilee, preaching the gospel of God, and saying, 'The time is fulfilled, and the kingdom of God is at hand; repent, and believe in the gospel.'

(Mark 1:14–15)

2.2.5

And if your eye causes you to sin, pluck it out; it is better for you to enter the kingdom of God with one eye than with two eyes to be thrown into hell.

(Mark 9:47)

2.2.6

But if it is by the finger of God that I cast out demons, then the kingdom of God has come upon you.

(Luke 11:20)

2.2.7

He said therefore, 'What is the kingdom of God like? And to what shall I compare it? It is like a grain of mustard seed which a man took and sowed in his garden; and it grew and became a tree, and the birds of the air made nests in its branches.'

(Luke 13:18–19)

2.2.8

The kingdom of God is not coming with signs to be observed; nor will they say, 'Lo, here it is!' or 'There!' for behold, the kingdom of God is in the midst of you (*or*, is within you).

(Luke 17:20–1)

2.2.9

Truly, truly, I say to you, unless one is born anew, he cannot see the kingdom of God.

(John 3:3)

Source: RSV Bible.

2.3 THE SERMON ON THE MOUNT

Seeing the crowds, he went up on the mountain, and when he sat down his disciples came to him. And he opened his mouth and taught them saying:

'Blessed are the poor in spirit, for theirs is the kingdom of heaven. Blessed are those who mourn, for they shall be comforted. Blessed are the meek, for they shall inherit the earth. Blessed are those who hunger and thirst for righteousness, for they shall be satisfied. Blessed are the merciful, for they shall obtain mercy. Blessed are the pure in heart, for they shall see God. Blessed are the peacemakers, for they shall be called sons of God. Blessed are those who are persecuted for righteousness' sake, for theirs is the kingdom of heaven. Blessed are you when men revile you and persecute you and utter all kinds of evil against you falsely on my account. Rejoice and be glad, for your reward is great in heaven, for so men persecuted the prophets who were before you.

You are the salt of the earth; but if salt has lost its taste, how shall its saltness be restored? It is no longer good for anything except to be thrown out and trodden under foot by men. You are the light of the world. A city set on a hill cannot be hid. Nor do men light a lamp and put it under a bushel, but on a stand, and it gives light to all in the house. Let your light so shine before men, that they may see your good works and give glory to your Father who is in heaven.

Think not that I have come to abolish the law and the prophets; I have come not to abolish them but to fulfil them. For truly, I say to you, till heaven and earth pass away, not an iota, not a dot, will pass from the law until all is accomplished. Whoever then relaxes one of the least of these commandments and teaches men so, shall be called least in the kingdom of heaven; but he who does them and teaches them shall be called great in the kingdom of heaven. For I tell you, unless your righteousness exceeds that of the scribes and Pharisees, you will never enter the kingdom of heaven.

You have heard that it was said to the men of old, 'You shall not kill; and whoever kills shall be liable to judgement.' But I say to you that every one who is angry with his brother shall be liable to judgement; whoever insults his brother shall be liable to the council, and whoever says, 'You fool!' shall be liable to the hell of fire. So if you are offering your gift at the altar, and there remember that your brother has something against you, leave your gift there before the altar and go; first be reconciled to your brother, and then come and offer your gift. Make friends quickly with your accuser, while you are going with him to court, lest your accuser hand you over to the judge, and the judge to the guard, and you be put in prison; truly, I say to you, you will never get out till you have paid the last penny.

You have heard that it was said, 'You shall not commit adultery.' But I say to you that every one who looks at a woman lustfully has already committed adultery with her in his heart. If your right eye causes you to sin, pluck it out and throw it away; it is better that you lose one of your members than that your whole body be thrown into hell. And if your right hand causes you to sin, cut it off and throw it away; it is better that you lose one of your members than that your whole body go into hell.

It was also said, 'Whoever divorces his wife, let him give her a certificate of divorce.' But I say to you that every one who divorces his wife, except on the ground of unchastity, makes her an adulteress; and whoever marries a divorced woman commits adultery.

Again you have heard that it was said to the men of old, 'You shall not swear falsely, but shall perform to the Lord what you have sworn.' But I say to you, Do not swear at all, either by heaven, for it is the throne of God, or by the earth, for it is his footstool, or by Jerusalem, for it is the city of the great King. And do not swear by your head, for you cannot make one hair white or black. Let what you say be simply 'Yes' or 'No'; anything more than this comes from evil.

You have heard that it was said, 'An eye for an eye and a tooth for a tooth.' But I say to you, Do not resist one who is evil. But if any one strikes you on the right cheek, turn to him the other also; and if any one would sue you and take your coat, let him have your cloak as well; and if any one forces you to go one mile, go with him two miles. Give to him who begs from you, and do not refuse him who would borrow from you.

You have heard that it was said, 'You shall love your neighbour and hate your enemy.' But I say to you, Love your enemies and pray for those who persecute you, so that you may be sons of your Father who is in heaven; for he makes his sun rise on the evil and on the good, and sends rain on the just and on the unjust. For if you love those who love you, what reward have you? Do not even the tax collectors do the same? And if you salute only your brethren, what more are you doing than others? Do not even the Gentiles do the same?

You, therefore, must be perfect, as your heavenly Father is perfect. Beware of practising your piety before men in order to be seen by them; for then you will have no reward from your Father who is in heaven. Thus, when you give alms, sound no trumpet before you, as the hypocrites do in the synagogues and in the streets, that they may be praised by men. Truly, I say to you, they have their reward. But when you give alms, do not let your left hand know what your right hand is doing, so that your alms may be in secret; and your Father who sees in secret will reward you.

And when you pray, you must not be like the hypocrites; for they love to stand and pray in the synagogues and at the street corners, that they may be seen by men. Truly, I say to you, they have their reward. But when you pray, go into your room and shut the door and pray to your Father who is in secret; and your Father who sees in secret will reward you. And in praying do not heap up empty phrases as the Gentiles do; for they think that they will be heard for their many words. Do not be like them, for your Father knows what you need before you ask him. Pray then like this:

> Our Father who art in heaven,
> Hallowed be thy name.
> Thy kingdom come,
> Thy will be done,
> On earth as it is in heaven.
> Give us this day our daily bread;
> And forgive us our debts,
> As we also have forgiven our debtors;
> And lead us not into temptation,
> But deliver us from evil.

For if you forgive men their trespasses, your heavenly Father also will forgive you; but if you do not forgive men their trespasses, neither will your Father forgive your trespasses.

And when you fast, do not look dismal, like the hypocrites, for they disfigure their faces that their fasting may be seen by men. Truly, I say to you, they have their reward. But when you fast, anoint your head and wash your face, that your fasting may not be seen by men but by your Father who is in secret; and your Father who sees in secret will reward you.

Do not lay up for yourselves treasures on earth, where moth and rust consume and where thieves break in and steal, but lay up for yourselves treasure in heaven, where neither moth nor rust consumes and where thieves do not break in and steal. For where your treasure is, there will your heart be also. The eye is the lamp of the body. So, if your eye is sound, your whole body will be full of light; but if your eye is not sound, your whole body will be full of darkness. If then the light in you is darkness, how great is the darkness!

No one can serve two masters; for either he will hate the one and love the other, or he will be devoted to the one and despise the other. You cannot serve God and mammon. Therefore I tell you, do not be anxious about your life, what you shall eat or what you shall drink, nor about your body, what you shall put on. Is not life more than food, and the body more than clothing? Look at the birds of the air: they neither sow nor reap nor gather into barns, and yet your heavenly Father feeds them. Are you not of more value than they?

And which of you by being anxious can add one cubit to his span of life? And why are you anxious about clothing? Consider the lilies of the field, how they grow; they neither toil nor spin; yet I tell you, even Solomon in all his glory was not arrayed like one of these. But if God so clothes the grass of the field, which today is alive and tomorrow is thrown into the oven, will he not much more clothe you, O men of little faith? Therefore do not be anxious, saying, 'What shall we eat?' or 'What shall we drink?' or 'What shall we wear?' For the gentiles seek all these things; and your heavenly Father knows that you need them all. But seek first his kingdom and his righteousness, and all these things shall be yours as well. Therefore do not be anxious about tomorrow, for tomorrow will be anxious for itself. Let the day's own trouble be sufficient for the day.

Judge not, that you be not judged. For with the judgement you pronounce you will be judged, and the measure you give will be the measure you get. Why do you see the speck that is in your brother's eye, but do not notice the log that is in your own eye? Or how can you say to your brother, 'Let me take the speck out of your eye', when there is the log in your own eye? You hypocrite, first take the log out of your own eye, and then you will see clearly to take the speck out of your brother's eye.

Do not give dogs what is holy; and do not throw your pearls before swine, lest they trample them under foot and turn to attack you. Ask, and it will be given you; seek, and you will find; knock, and it will be opened to you. For everyone who asks receives, and he who seeks finds, and to him who knocks it will be opened. Or what man of you, if his son asks him for bread, will give him a stone? Or if he asks for a fish, will give him a serpent? If you then, who are evil, know how to give good gifts to your children, how much more will your father who is in heaven give good things to those who ask him! So whatever you wish that men would do to you, do so to them; for this is the law and the prophets.

Enter by the narrow gate; for the gate is wide and the way is easy, that leads to destruction, and those who enter by it are many. For the gate is narrow and the way is hard, that leads to life, and those who find it are few. Beware of false prophets, who come to you in sheep's clothing but inwardly are ravenous wolves. You will know them by their fruits. Are grapes gathered from thorns, or figs from thistles? So, every sound tree bears good fruit, but the bad tree bears evil fruit. A sound tree cannot bear evil fruit, nor can a bad tree bear good fruit. Every tree that does not bear good fruit is cut down and thrown into the fire. Thus you will know them by their fruits.

Not every one who says to me, 'Lord, Lord', shall enter the kingdom of heaven, but he who does the will of my Father who is in heaven. On that day many will say to me, 'Lord, Lord, did we not prophesy in your name, and cast out demons in your name, and do many mighty works in your name?'

And then will I declare to them, 'I never knew you; depart from me, you evil-doers.'

Every one then who hears these words of mine and does them will be like a wise man who built his house upon the rock; and the rain fell, and the floods came, and the winds blew and beat upon that house, but it did not fall, because it had been founded on the rock. And every one who hears these words of mine and does not do them will be like a foolish man who built his house upon the sand; and the rain fell, and the floods came, and the winds blew and beat against that house, and it fell; and great was the fall of it.'

And when Jesus finished these sayings, the crowds were astonished at his teaching, for he taught them as one who had authority, and not as their scribes.

(Matthew 5, 6 and 7)

Source: RSV Bible.

2.4 THE RESURRECTION

2.4.1

Now after the sabbath, toward the dawn of the first day of the week, Mary Magdalene and the other Mary went to see the sepulchre. And behold, there was a great earth-quake; for an angel of the Lord descended from heaven and came and rolled back the stone, and sat upon it. His appearance was like lightning, and his raiment white as snow. And for fear of him the guards trembled and became like dead men. But the angel said to the women, 'Do not be afraid; for I know that you seek Jesus who was crucified. He is not here; for he has risen, as he said. Come, see the place where he lay. Then go quickly and tell his disciples that he has risen from the dead, and behold, he is going before you to Galilee; there you will see him. Lo, I have told you.' So they departed quickly from the tomb with fear and great joy, and ran to tell his disciples. And behold, Jesus met them and said, 'Hail!' And they came up and took hold of his feet and worshipped him. Then Jesus said to them, 'Do not be afraid; go and tell my brethren to go to Galilee, and there they will see me.'

While they were going, behold, some of the guard went into the city and told the chief priests all that had taken place. And when they had assembled with the elders and taken counsel, they gave a sum of money to the soldiers and said, 'Tell people, "His disciples came by night and stole him away while we were asleep." And if this comes to the governor's ears, we will satisfy him and keep you out of trouble.' So they took the money and did as they were directed, and this story has been spread among the Jews to this day.

Now the eleven disciples went to Galilee, to the mountain to which Jesus had directed them. And when they saw him they worshipped him; but some doubted. And

Jesus came and said to them, 'All authority in heaven and on earth has been given to me. Go therefore and make disciples of all nations, baptizing them in the name of the Father and of the Son and of the Holy Spirit, teaching them to observe all that I have commanded you; and lo, I am with you always, to the close of the age.'

(Matthew 28)

2.4.2

That very day two of them were going to a village named Emmaus, about seven miles from Jerusalem, and talking with each other about all these things that had happened. While they were talking and discussing together, Jesus himself drew near and went with them. But their eyes were kept from recognizing him. And he said to them, 'What is this conversation which you are holding with each other as you walk?' And they stood still, looking sad. Then one of them, named Cleopas, answered him, 'Are you the only visitor to Jerusalem who does not know the things that have happened there in these days?' And he said to them, 'What things?' And they said to him, 'Concerning Jesus of Nazareth, who was a prophet mighty in deed and word before God and all the people, and how our chief priests and rulers delivered him up to be condemned to death, and crucified him. But we had hoped that he was the one to redeem Israel. Yes, and besides all this, it is now the third day since this happened. Moreover, some women of our company amazed us. They were at the tomb early in the morning and did not find his body; and they came back saying they had seen a vision of angels, who said that he was alive. Some of those who were with us went to the tomb, and found it just as the woman had said; but him they did not see.' And he said to them, 'O foolish men, and slow of heart to believe all that the prophets have spoken! Was it not necessary that the Christ should suffer these things and enter into his glory?' And beginning with Moses and all the prophets, he interpreted to them in all the scriptures the things concerning himself.

So they drew near to the village to which they were going. He appeared to be going further, but they constrained him, saying, 'Stay with us, for it is toward evening and the day is now far spent.' So he went in to stay with them. When he was at table with them, he took the bread and blessed, and broke it, and give it to them. And their eyes were opened and they recognized him; and he vanished out of their sight. They said to each other, 'Did not our hearts burn within us while he talked to us on the road, while he opened to us the scriptures?' And they rose that same hour and returned to Jerusalem; and they found the eleven gathered together and those who were with them, who said, 'The Lord has risen indeed, and has appeared to Simon!' Then they told what had happened on the road, and how he was known to them in the breaking of bread.

As they were saying this, Jesus himself stood among them. But they were startled and frightened, and supposed that they saw a spirit. And he said to them, 'Why are you troubled, and why do questionings rise in your hearts? See my hands and my feet, that it is I myself; handle me, and see; for a spirit has not flesh and bones as you see that I have.' And while they still disbelieved for joy, and wondered, he said to them, 'Have you anything here to eat?' They gave him a piece of broiled fish, and he took it and ate before them.

Then he said to them, 'These are my words which I spoke to you, while I was still with you, that everything written about me in the law of Moses and the prophets and the psalms must be fulfilled.' Then he opened their minds to understand the scriptures, and said to them, 'Thus it is written, that the Christ should suffer and on the third day rise from the dead, and that repentance and forgiveness of sins should be preached in his name to all nations, beginning from Jerusalem. You are witnesses of these things. And behold, I send the promise of my Father upon you; but stay in the city, until you are clothed with power from on high.'

Then he led them out as far as Bethany, and lifting up his hands he blessed them. While he blessed them, he parted from them. And they returned to Jerusalem with great joy, and were continually in the temple blessing God.

(Luke 24:13–53)

2.4.3

But Mary stood weeping outside the tomb, and as she wept she stooped to look into the tomb; and she saw two angels in white, sitting where the body of Jesus had lain, one at the head and one at the feet. They said to her, 'Woman, why are you weeping?' She said to them, 'Because they have taken away my Lord, and I do not know where they have laid him.' Saying this, she turned round and saw Jesus standing, but she did not know that it was Jesus. Jesus said to her, 'Woman, why are you weeping? Whom do you seek?' Supposing him to be the gardener, she said to him, 'Sir, if you have carried him away, tell me where you have laid him, and I will take him away.' Jesus said to her, 'Mary.' She turned and said to him in Hebrew, 'Rabboni!' (which means Teacher). Jesus said to her, 'Do not hold me, for I have not yet ascended to the Father; but go to my brethren and say to them, I am ascending to my Father and your Father, to my God and your God.' Mary Magdalene went and said to the disciples, 'I have seen the Lord'; and she told them that he had said these things to her.

On the evening of that day, the first day of the week, the doors being shut where the disciples were, for fear of the Jews, Jesus came and stood among them and said to them, 'Peace be with you.' When he had said this, he showed them his hands and his side. Then the disciples were glad when they saw the Lord. Jesus said to them again, 'Peace be with you. As the Father has sent me, even so I send you.' And when he had said this, he breathed on them, and said to them, 'Receive the Holy Spirit. If you forgive the sins of any, they are forgiven; if you retain the sins of any, they are retained.'

Now Thomas, one of twelve, called the Twin, was not with them when Jesus came. So the other disciples told him, 'We have seen the Lord.' But he said to them, 'Unless I see in his hands the print of the nails, and place my finger in the mark of the nails, and place my hand in his side, I will not believe.' Eight days later, his disciples were again in the house, and Thomas was with them. The doors were shut, but Jesus came and stood among them, and said, 'Peace be with you.' Then he said to Thomas, 'Put your finger here, and see my hands; and put out your hand, and place it in my side; do not be faithless, but believing.' Thomas answered him, 'My Lord and my God!' Jesus said to him 'Have you believed because you have seen me? Blessed are those who have not seen and yet believe.'

(John 20:11–29)

2.4.4

After this Jesus revealed himself again to the disciples by the Sea of Tiberias; and he revealed himself in this way. Simon Peter, Thomas called the Twin, Nathanael of Cana in Galilee, the sons of Zebedee, and two others of his disciples were together. Simon Peter said to them, 'I am going fishing.' They said to him, 'We will go with you.' They went out and got into the boat; but that night they caught nothing.

Just as day was breaking, Jesus stood on the beach; yet the disciples did not know it was Jesus. Jesus said to them, 'Children, have you any fish?' They answered him, 'No.' He said to them, 'Cast the net on the right side of the boat, and you will find some.' So they cast it, and now they were not able to haul it in, for the quantity of fish. That disciple whom Jesus loved said to Peter, 'It is the Lord!' When Simon Peter heard that it was the Lord, he put on his clothes, for he was stripped for work, and sprang into the sea. But the other disciples came in the boat, dragging the net full of fish, for they were not far from the land, but about a hundred yards off.

When they got out on land, they saw a charcoal fire there, with fish lying on it, and bread. Jesus said to them, 'Bring some of the fish that you have just caught.' So Simon Peter went aboard and hauled the net ashore, full of large fish, a hundred and fifty-three of them; and although there were so many, the net was not torn. Jesus said to them, 'Come and have breakfast.' Now none of the disciples dared ask him, 'Who are you?' They knew it was the Lord. Jesus came and took the bread and gave it to them, and so with the fish. This was now the third time that Jesus was revealed to the disciples after he was raised from the dead.

(John 21:1–14)

2.4.5

For I delivered to you as of first importance what I also received, that Christ died for our sins in accordance with the scriptures, that he was buried, that he was raised on the third day in accordance with the scriptures, and that he appeared to Cephas, then to the twelve. Then he appeared to more than five hundred brethren at one time, most of whom are still alive, though some have fallen asleep. Then he appeared to James, then to all the apostles. Last of all, as to one untimely born, he appeared also to me.

(I Corinthians 15:3–8)

Note: Mark 16:9–20 are not included as by common consent they are not part of the original text of that gospel.

2.4.6

But someone will ask, 'How are the dead raised? With what kind of body do they come?' You foolish man! What you sow does not come to life unless it dies. And what you sow is not the body which is to be, but a bare kernel, perhaps of wheat or of some other grain. But God gives it a body as he has chosen, and to each kind of seed its own body. For not all flesh is alike, but there is one kind for men, another for animals, another for birds, and another for fish. There are celestial bodies and there are terrestrial bodies; but the glory of the celestial is one, and the glory of the terrestrial is another. There is one glory of the sun, and another glory of the moon, and another glory of the stars; for star differs from star in glory. So is it with the resurrection of the dead. What is sown is perishable, what is raised is imperishable. It is sown in dishonour, it is raised in glory. It is sown in weakness, it is raised in power. It is sown a physical body, it is raised a spiritual body. If there is a physical body, there is also a spiritual body. Thus it is written, 'The first man Adam became a living being'; the last Adam became a life-giving spirit. But it is not the spiritual which is first but the physical, and then the spiritual. The first man was from the earth, a man of dust; the second man is from heaven. As was the man of dust, so are those who are of the dust; and as is the man of heaven, so are those who are of heaven. Just as we have borne the image of the man of dust, we shall also bear the image of the man of heaven. I tell you this, brethren: flesh and blood cannot inherit the kingdom of God, nor does the perishable inherit the imperishable. Lo! I tell you a mystery. We shall not all sleep, but we shall all be changed, in a moment, in the twinkling of an eye, at the last trumpet. For the trumpet will sound, and the dead will be raised imperishable, and we shall be changed. For this perishable nature must put on the imperishable, and this mortal nature must put on immortality. When the perishable puts on the imperishable, and the mortal puts on immortality, then shall come to pass the saying that is written: 'Death is swallowed up in victory.' 'Oh death, where is thy victory? Oh death, where is thy sting?' The sting of death is sin, and the power of sin is the law. But thanks be to God, who gives us the victory through our Lord Jesus Christ.

(I Corinthians 15:35–57)

2.4.7

Have this mind among yourselves, which you have in Christ Jesus, who, though he was in the form of God, did not count equality with God a thing to be grasped, but emptied himself, taking the form of a servant, being born in the likeness of men. And being found in human form he humbled himself and became obedient unto death, even death on a cross. Therefore God has highly exalted him and bestowed on him the name which is above every name, that at the name of Jesus every knee should bow, in heaven and on earth and under the earth, and every tongue confess that Jesus Christ is Lord, to the glory of God the Father.

(Philippians 2:5–11)

Source: RSV Bible.

2.5 THE WORK OF CHRIST

2.5.1

Therefore, since we are justified by faith, we have peace with God through our Lord Jesus Christ. Through him we have obtained access to this grace in which we stand, and we rejoice in our hope of sharing the glory of God. More than that, we rejoice in our sufferings knowing that suffering produces endurance, and endurance produces character, and character produces hope, and hope does not disappoint us, because God's love has been poured into our hearts through the Holy Spirit which has been given to us. While we were yet helpless, at the right time Christ died for the ungodly. Why, one will hardly die for a righteous man – though perhaps for a good man one will dare even to die. But God shows his love for us in that while we were yet sinners Christ died for us. Since, therefore, we are now justified by his blood, much more shall we be saved by him from the wrath of God. For if while we were enemies we were reconciled to God by the death of his Son, much more, now that we are reconciled, shall we be saved by his life.

(Romans 5:1–10)

2.5.2

For Christ has entered, not into a sanctuary made with hands, a copy of the true one, but into heaven itself, now to appear in the presence of God on our behalf. Nor was it to offer himself repeatedly, as the high priest enters the Holy Place yearly with blood not his own; for then he would have had to suffer repeatedly since the foundation of the world. But as it is, he has appeared once for all at the end of the age to put away sin by the sacrifice of himself. And just as it is appointed for men to die once, and after that comes judgement, so Christ, having been offered once to bear the sins of many, will appear a second time, not to deal with sin but to save those who are eagerly waiting for him.

(Hebrews 9:24–8)

Source: RSV Bible.

2.6 BAPTISM

2.6.1

And Jesus came and said to them, 'All authority in heaven and on earth has been given to me. Go therefore and make disciples of all nations, baptizing them in the name of the Father and of the Son and of the Holy Spirit, teaching them to observe all that I have commanded you; and lo, I am with you always, to the close of the age.'

(Matthew 28:18–20)

2.6.2

And they were bringing children to him, that he might touch them: and the disciples rebuked them. But when Jesus saw it he was indignant, and said to them, 'Let the children come to me, do not hinder them; for to such belongs the kingdom of God.'

(Mark 10:13–14)

2.6.3

Now when they heard this they were cut to the heart, and said to Peter and the rest of the apostles, 'Brethren, what shall we do?' And Peter said to them, 'Repent, and be baptized every one of you in the name of Jesus Christ for the forgiveness of your sins; and you shall receive the gift of the Holy Spirit.'

(Acts 2:37–8)

2.6.4

Is Christ divided? Was Paul crucified for you? Or were you baptized in the name of Paul? I am thankful that I baptized none of you except Crispus and Gaius; lest any one should say that you were baptized in my name. (I did baptize also the household of Stephanas. Beyond that, I do not know whether I baptized any one else.)

(I Corinthians 1:13–16)

2.6.5

For in Christ Jesus you are all sons of God, through faith. For as many of you as were baptized into Christ have put on Christ.

(Galatians 3:26–7)

Source: RSV Bible.

— ●◆● —

THE CHURCH FATHERS

—— • ◆ • ——

2.7 ORIGEN ON THE BAPTISM OF INFANTS

Origen, theologian and Biblical scholar (*c.* 186–254 CE), was born in
Egypt. He was well versed in Platonic philosophy and used his learning as
an apologist on behalf of the Christian faith.

Can a newborn child have committed sin? Yes, even then it has sin, for which the
[Old Testament] sacrifice is commanded to be offered and from which even he who
is but a day old is said not to be free. It is of this sin that David is supposed to have
said that which we cited earlier, 'In sin did my mother conceive me' (Psalm 51.5),
for there is no mention in the history of any particular sin that his mother had
committed. For this reason the Church received a tradition from the apostles to give
baptism to infants too.

(*Commentary on Romans* 5:9)

Source: K. Aland, *Did the Early Church Baptize Infants?* (London: SCM Press, 1963), p. 47, n. 1.

2.8 ST IGNATIUS ON THE MINISTRY AND SACRAMENTS

St Ignatius (*c.* 37–107 CE) was possibly of Syrian origin and became
Bishop of Antioch. His letter to the Smyrnaeans was one of several letters
written on his way from Antioch to martyrdom in Rome. Anxious to
preserve the church from doctrinal errors, he stresses the role of the
bishop in preserving Christian unity.

Avoid divisions as the beginning of evils. All of you follow the bishop as Jesus Christ
followed the Father, and follow the presbytery as the Apostles; and respect the
deacons as the commandment of God. Let no man perform anything pertaining to
the church without the bishop. Let that be considered a valid Eucharist over which

the bishop presides, or one to whom he commits it. Wherever the bishop appears, there let the people be, just as, wheresoever Christ Jesus is, there is the Catholic Church. It is not permitted either to baptize or hold a love-feast apart from the bishop. But whatever he may approve, that is well-pleasing to God, that everything which you do may be sound and valid.

(Ignatius, Epistle to the Smyrnaeans 8)

Source: Henry Bettenson (ed.) *Documents of the Christian Church*, 2nd edn (OUP, 1963), pp. 63–4.

2.9 ST IRENAEUS ON TRADITION AND SUCCESSION

St Irenaeus (*c.* 130–200 CE) is reputed to have been born in Smyrna and became Bishop of Lyons in *c.* 178 CE. He has been described as the first great Catholic theologian. He opposed Hellenistic Gnosticism and emphasized the tradition of the church and the authority of the Gospels.

Those that wish to discern the truth may observe the apostolic tradition made manifest in every church throughout the world. We can enumerate those who were appointed bishops in the churches by the Apostles, and their successors [*or* successions] down to our own day, who never taught, and never knew, absurdities such as these men produce. For if the Apostles had known hidden mysteries which they taught the perfect in private and in secret, they would rather have committed them to those to whom they entrusted the churches. For they wished those men to be perfect and unblameable whom they left as their successors and to whom they handed over their own office of authority.

(Irenaeus, Against Heresies, 3:3)

Source: Bettenson, op. cit., 1963), p. 68.

——— •◆• ———

THE CHURCHES:
THEIR LIFE AND FAITH

—— ◆◆◆ ——

2.10 THE 'NICENE' OR CONSTANTINOPOLITAN CREED (325 CE)

This creed, which needs to be distinguished from the shorter Nicene Creed,
was approved at the Council of Chalcedon in 451 CE as a creed approved
by church fathers both at Nicaea (325 CE) and at Constantinople (381 CE).
As well as having additional clauses, it lacks the anathemas that formed
part of the Nicene Creed. The 'Nicene' or Constantinopolitan Creed is widely
used in both Eastern and Western churches. The version given below is
the later variant which became popular in the Western church, containing
the contentious phrase 'and the Son' ('filioque') in its reference to the
procession of the Holy Ghost. The Eastern church rejected this addition.

I believe in one God the Father Almighty, Maker of heaven and earth, And of all
things visible and invisible: And in one Lord Jesus Christ, the only begotten Son of
God, Begotten of his Father before all worlds, God of God, Light of Light, Very
God of very God, Begotten, not made, Being of one substance with the Father, By
whom all things were made: Who for us men, and for our salvation came down
from heaven, And was incarnate by the Holy Ghost of the Virgin Mary, And was
made man, And was crucified also for us under Pontius Pilate. He suffered and was
buried, And the third day he rose again according to the Scriptures, And ascended
into heaven, And sitteth on the right hand of the Father. And he shall come again
with glory to judge both the quick and the dead: Whose kingdom shall have no end.

And I believe in the Holy Ghost, the Lord and giver of life, Who proceedeth from
the Father and the Son, Who with the Father and the Son together is worshipped
and glorified, Who spake by the Prophets. And I believe one Catholick and Apostolick
Church. I acknowledge one Baptism for the remission of sins. And I look for the
Resurrection of the dead, And the life of the world to come. Amen.

Source: *The Book of Common Prayer, The Church of England* (Eyre & Spottiswoode, 1968), pp. 291–2.

2.11 THE ATHANASIAN CREED

The Athanasian Creed is also known, from its opening words, as the 'Quicunque Vult'. Although not recognized as a standard of faith by the Eastern churches, it occurs in the Roman Catholic breviary. It is widely used in the Protestant traditions and appears in the Anglican Book of Common Prayer, from where this translation is taken. The date of the creed is disputed, and its traditional attribution to St Athanasius has long been generally abandoned.

Whosoever will be saved: before all things it is necessary that he hold the Catholick Faith.

Which Faith except every one do keep whole and undefiled: without doubt he shall perish everlastingly.

And the Catholick Faith is this: That we worship one God in Trinity, and Trinity in Unity;

Neither confounding the Persons: nor dividing the Substance.

For there is one Person of the Father, another of the Son: and another of the Holy Ghost.

But the Godhead of the Father, of the Son, and of the Holy Ghost, is all one: the Glory equal, the Majesty co-eternal.

Such as the Father is, such is the Son: and such is the Holy Ghost.

The Father uncreate, the Son uncreate: and the Holy Ghost uncreate.

The Father incomprehensible, the Son incomprehensible: and the Holy Ghost incomprehensible.

The Father eternal, the Son eternal: and the Holy Ghost eternal.

And yet they are not three eternals: but one eternal.

As also there are not three incomprehensibles, nor three uncreated: but one uncreated, and one incomprehensible.

So likewise the Father is Almighty, the Son Almighty: and the Holy Ghost Almighty.

And yet they are not three Almighties: but one Almighty.

So the Father is God, the Son is God: and the Holy Ghost is God.

And yet they are not three Gods: but one God.

So likewise the Father is Lord, the Son Lord: and the Holy Ghost Lord.

And yet not three Lords: but one Lord.

For like as we are compelled by the Christian verity: to acknowledge every Person by himself to be God and Lord;

So are we forbidden by the Catholick Religion: to say, There be three Gods, or three Lords.

The Father is made of none: neither created, nor begotten.

The Son is of the Father alone: not made, nor created, but begotten.

The Holy Ghost is of the Father and of the Son: neither made, nor created, nor begotten, but proceeding.

So there is one Father, not three Fathers; one Son, not three Sons: one Holy Ghost, not three Holy Ghosts.

And in this Trinity none is afore, or after other: none is greater, or less than another;

But the whole three Persons are co-eternal together: and co-equal.

So that in all things, as is aforesaid: the Unity in Trinity, and the Trinity in Unity is to be worshipped.

He therefore that will be saved: must thus think of the Trinity.

Furthermore, it is necessary to everlasting salvation: that he also believe rightly the Incarnation of our Lord Jesus Christ.

For the right Faith is, that we believe and confess: that our Lord Jesus Christ, the Son of God, is God and Man;

God, of the Substance of the Father, begotten before the worlds: and Man, of the Substance of his Mother, born in the world;

Perfect God, and perfect Man: of a reasonable soul and human flesh subsisting;

Equal to the Father, as touching his Godhead: and inferior to the Father, as touching his Manhood.

Who although he be God and Man: yet he is not two, but one Christ;

One; not by conversion of the Godhead into flesh: but by taking of the Manhood into God;

One altogether; not by confusion of Substance: but by unity of Person.

For as the reasonable soul and flesh is one man: so God and Man is one Christ;

Who suffered for our salvation: descended into hell, rose again the third day from the dead.

He ascended into heaven, he sitteth on the right hand of the Father, God Almighty: from whence he shall come to judge the quick and the dead.

At whose coming all men shall rise again with their bodies: and shall give account for their own works.

And they that have done good shall go into life everlasting: and they that have done evil into everlasting fire.

This is the Catholick Faith: which except a man believe faithfully, he cannot be saved.

Glory be to the Father, and to the Son: and to the Holy Ghost;

As it was in the beginning, is now, and ever shall be: world without end. Amen.

Source: *The Book of Common Prayer, The Church of England* (Eyre & Spottiswoode, 1968), pp. 68–71.

2.12 A DECLARATION OF THE SECOND VATICAN COUNCIL (1964)

The Eternal Father, by a free and hidden plan of his own wisdom and goodness, created the whole world. His plan was to raise men to a participation of the divine life. God the Father did not abandon men, fallen in Adam, but ceaselessly offered helps to salvation, for the sake of Christ, the Redeemer 'who is the image of the invisible God, the first born of every creature' (Col. 1:15). All the elect, before time began, the Father 'foreknew and predestined to become conformed to the image of his Son, that he should be the first-born among many brethren' (Rom. 8:29). He planned to assemble in the Holy Church all those who would believe in Christ. Already from the beginning of the world the foreshadowing of the Church took place. It was prepared in a remarkable way throughout the history of the people of Israel and by means of the Old Covenant. In the present era of time the Church was constituted and, by the outpouring of the Spirit, was made manifest. At the end of time it will gloriously achieve completion, when, as is read in the Fathers, all the just, from Adam and from Abel the just one, to the last of the elect, will be gathered together with the Father in the universal Church.

The Son therefore, came, sent by the Father. It was in him, before the foundation of the world, that the Father chose us and predestined us to become adopted sons, for in him it pleased the Father to re-establish all things. To carry out the will of the Father, Christ inaugurated the kingdom of Heaven on earth and revealed to us the mystery of that kingdom. By his obedience he brought about redemption. The church, or, in other words, the kingdom of Christ now present in mystery, grows visibly through the power of God in the world. This inauguration and this growth are both symbolised by the blood and water which flowed from the open side of the crucified Jesus (John 19:34), and are foretold in the words of the Lord referring to his death on the cross: 'And I, if I be lifted up from the earth, will draw all things to myself' (John 12:32). As often as the sacrifice of the cross in which Christ our passover was sacrificed (I Cor. 5:7) is celebrated at the altar, the work of our redemption is carried on; and, in the sacrament of the Eucharistic bread, the unity of all believers who form one body in Christ is both expressed and brought about. All men are called to this union with Christ, who is the light of the world, from whom we go forth, through whom we live, and towards whom our whole life tends.

When the work that the Father gave the Son to do on earth was accomplished, the Holy Spirit was sent on the day of Pentecost in order that he might continually sanctify the Church, and thus, all those who believe would have access through Christ in one Spirit to the Father. He is the Spirit of life, a fountain of water springing up to life eternal. To men, dead in sin, the Father gives life through him, until the day when he will bring to life again, in Christ, their mortal bodies.

Source: The Constitution on the Church, *Lumen Gentium*, of the Second Vatican Council; English translation published by Darton, Longman and Todd, 1965.

2.13 ANGLICAN ATTITUDES TO THE CREEDS (1976)

To many members of the Church of England the creeds are a norm of Christian belief, additional to though dependent upon the Bible. For them the creeds not only constitute vital links with the Church's past but also embody the standing truth of the gospel in the present. . . . They find the creeds to be mandatory for them because they have found the contents of the creeds to be true and significant; they do not embrace them simply because they are received as mandatory by others. They know that these verbal formularies, like the Biblical formulations which they more or less directly reflect, circumscribe mysteries whose depth no man can ever plumb. . . . They could not contemplate any replacing or superseding of the historic creeds as official formularies, for in their view it is precisely by the creeds, viewed as classical crystallizations of Biblical faith, that the new thought forms and frameworks, and the assertions which they are used to make, must be measured and tested. They do not wish to clamp down on the exploring of experimental theologies which for the moment might seem to have left the creeds behind. But they do maintain that any significant weakening in the corporate acceptance and use of the creeds would impair the Church of England's catholicity; and they hold therefore, that in Anglicanism the creeds are a norm, and that adherence to them is by Anglican standards essential.

A second approach to Christian belief may be described as on balance traditionalist in its general character; but those who adopt it vary in their detailed reactions to the historic credal formularies. On the negative side they have difficulties about individual clauses in the creeds. Sometimes this problem is resolved by stressing the symbolic character of the words, sometimes by emphasizing their historical context. . . . On the positive side, however, they feel that saying the Nicene Creed, for example, at the Eucharist along with their fellow Christians is one important way of expressing their faith in God through Christ, and of rejoicing in a unity of God's people which transcends time and finds its deepest earthly expression not so much in words as in the bond of the eucharistic action given by that God to whom the words refer.

Thirdly, there is a broad category of Christians whose convictions lead them to approach the creeds in a rather different way. They acknowledge with gratitude that, for those of them at least who were brought up in the Christian community and whose faith in God was fostered and developed there, the creeds have played an important formative part in their lives. But their allegiance now is rather to the continuing Church of God than to any past beliefs and formulations, which they regard as inevitably relative to the culture of the age which produced them. . . . They agree that the creeds are *de facto* without rivals as official formulations of Christian belief, but are in varying degrees unhappy at the thought that they should indefinitely continue to be so. . . . Such Christians would, therefore, like to see the Church investigate all possible ways in which it might testify to its profound concern for truth, leaving open the question whether or not these would be likely to take a credal form of any sort.

Finally, there are Christians for whom the essence of their faith is to be found in a life of discipleship rather than in credal affirmation. Such people may have their own doctrinal interpretation of life, but these doctrines seem to them to be relative to their own culture and temperament rather than permanent statements of their faith. . . . Such people do make theological affirmations but they do so by their lives and through their prayers. They commit themselves to the Reality whom men call God as their creator, their saviour, and their sanctifier; and they commit themselves also to a life of Christian discipleship in the sense of loyalty to Jesus and to his values, attitudes and teaching as depicted in the Gospels. They find in him a key to the truth about God and the world, and an authentic way of life. Commitment to God and to Jesus, understood in this sense, is more important to them than 'provisional' assent to credal propositions of any kind.

Source: 'The Christian and the creeds', in a report entitled *Christian Believing* by the Doctrine Commission of the Church of England (SPCK, 1976), pp. 35–8.

2.14 HYMNS

2.14.1 For Christ's saving death upon the cross

The royal banners forward go,
The cross shines forth in mystic glow;
Where he in flesh, our flesh who made,
Our sentence bore, our ransom paid.

There whilst he hung, his sacred side
By soldier's spear was open'd wide,
To cleanse us in the precious flood
Of water mingled with his blood.

Fulfill'd is now what David told
In true prophetic song of old,
How God the heathen's King should be;
For God is reigning from the tree.

Oh tree of glory, tree most fair,
Ordain'd those holy limbs to bear,
How bright in purple robe it stood,
The purple of a Saviour's blood!

Upon its arms, like balance true,
He weigh'd the price for sinners due,
The price which none but he could pay,
And spoil'd the spoiler of his prey.

To thee, eternal Three in One,
Let homage meet by all be done;
As by the Cross thou dost restore,
So rule and guide us ever more.

      (*Vexilla Regis Proeunt*: original Latin words by Venantius Fortunatus,
      sixth-century; English translation by John Mason Neale and others)

2.14.2 To pay the price of sin

There is a green hill far away,
Without a city wall,
Where the dear Lord was crucified
Who died to save us all.

We may not know, we cannot tell,
What pains he had to bear,
But we believe it was for us
He hung and suffered there.

He died that we might be forgiven,
He died to make us good;
That we might go at last to Heaven,
Saved by the precious blood.

There was no other good enough
To pay the price of sin;
He only could unlock the gate
Of heaven, and let us in.

O, dearly, dearly has he loved,
And we must love him too,
And trust in his redeeming blood,
And try his works to do.

(Cecil Frances Alexander 1818–95)

2.14.3 Love so amazing

When I survey the wondrous Cross,
On which the Prince of glory died,
My richest gain I count but loss,
And pour contempt on all my pride.

Forbid it, Lord, that I should boast
Save in the death of Christ my God;
All the vain things that charm me most,
I sacrifice them to his Blood.

See from his head, his hands, his feet,
Sorrow and love flow mingled down;
Did e'er such love and sorrow meet,
Or thorns compose so rich a crown?

His dying crimson like a robe,
Spreads o'er his body on the Tree;
Then am I dead to all the globe,
And all the globe is dead to me.

Were the whole realm of nature mine,
That were an offering far too small;
Love so amazing, so divine,
Demands my soul, my life, my all.

(Isaac Watts, 1674–1748)

2.14.4 For Christ's Resurrection

Christ the Lord is risen today,
Christians haste your vows to pay;
Offer ye your praises meet
At the Paschal victim's feet;
For the sheep the Lamb hath bled,
Sinless in the sinner's stead,
Christ is risen today we cry,
Now he lives no more to die.

Christ, the victim undefiled,
Man to God hath reconciled;
Whilst in strange and awful strife
Met together death and life;
Christians, on this happy day
Haste with joy your vows to pay,
Christ is risen today we cry,
Now he lives no more to die.

Christ, who once for sinners bled,
Now the first-born from the dead,
Throned in endless might and power,
Lives and reigns for evermore.
Hail, eternal hope on high!
Hail, thou King of victory!
Hail, thou Prince of life adored!
Help and save us, gracious Lord.

(Original Latin words by Wipo, eleventh century; English translation
by Jane E. Leeson)

2.15 A JOINT DECLARATION BY THE ARCHBISHOP OF CANTERBURY AND THE BISHOP OF ROME, 1989

Against the background of human disunity the arduous journey to Christian unity must be pursued with determination and vigour, whatever obstacles are perceived to block the path. We here solemnly re-commit ourselves and those we represent to the restoration of visible unity and full ecclesial communion in the confidence that to seek anything less would be to betray our Lord's intention for the unity of his people.

This is by no means to be unrealistic about the difficulties facing our dialogue at the present time. When we established the Second Anglican-Roman Catholic International Commission in Canterbury in 1982, we were well aware that the Commission's task would be far from easy. The convergences achieved within the report of the First Anglican-Roman Catholic International Commission have happily now been accepted by the Lambeth Conference of the bishops of the Anglican Communion. This report is currently also being studied by the Catholic Church with a view to responding to it. On the other hand, the question and practice of the admission of women to the ministerial priesthood in some Provinces of the Anglican Communion prevents reconciliation between us even where there is otherwise progress towards agreement in faith on the meaning of the Eucharist and the ordained ministry. These differences in faith reflect important ecclesiological differences and we urge the members of the Anglican-Roman Catholic International Commission and all others engaged in prayer and work for visible unity not to minimize these differences. At the same time we also urge them not to abandon either their hope or work for unity. At the beginning of the dialogue established here in Rome in 1966 by our beloved predecessors Pope Paul VI and Archbishop Michael Ramsey, no one saw clearly how long-inherited divisions would be overcome and how unity in faith might be achieved. No pilgrim knows in advance all the steps along the path. Saint Augustine of Canterbury set out from Rome with his band of monks for what was then a distant corner of the world. Yet Pope Gregory was soon to write of the baptism of the English and of 'such great miracles . . . that they seemed to imitate the powers of the apostles' (Letter of Gregory the Great to Eulogius of Alexandria). While we ourselves do not see a solution to this obstacle, we are confident that through our engagement with this matter our conversations will in fact help to deepen and enlarge our understanding. We have this confidence because Christ promised that the Holy Spirit, who is the Spirit of Truth, will remain with us forever (cf. John 14:16–17).

We also urge our clergy and faithful not to neglect or undervalue that certain yet imperfect communion we already share. This communion already shared is grounded in faith in God our Father, in our Lord Jesus Christ, and in the Holy Spirit; our common baptism into Christ; our sharing of the Holy Scriptures, of the Apostles' and Nicene Creeds; the Chalcedonian definition and the teaching of the Fathers; our common Christian inheritance for many centuries. This communion should be cherished and guarded as we seek to grow into the fuller communion Christ wills. Even in the years of our separation we have been able to recognize gifts of the Spirit in each other. The ecumenical journey is not only about the removal of obstacles but also about the sharing of gifts.

As we meet together today we have also in our hearts those other Churches and Ecclesial Communities with whom we are in dialogue. As we have said once before in Canterbury, our aim extends to the fulfilment of God's will for the visible unity of all his people.

Nor is God's will for unity limited exclusively to Christians alone. Christian unity is demanded so that the Church can be a more effective sign of God's Kingdom of love and justice for all humanity. In fact, the Church is the sign and sacrament of the communion in Christ which God wills for the whole of his creation.

Such a vision elicits hope and patient determination, not despair or cynicism. And because such hope is a gift of the Holy Spirit we shall not be disappointed; for 'the power at work within us is able to do far more abundantly than all we ask or think. To him be glory in the Church and in Christ Jesus to all generations, for ever and ever. Amen' (Eph. 3:20–1).

2 October 1989
Pope John Paul II
Robert Runcie, Archbishop of Canterbury

Source: *One in Hope* (London: Church House Publishing and Incorporated Catholic Truth Society, 1989), pp. 7–10.

2.16 THE PRIMACY OF THE BISHOP OF ROME FROM A HOMILY BY POPE JOHN PAUL II, 1989

On Saturday evening, 30 September, the Holy Father presided at First Vespers of the Twenty-Sixth Sunday of the Year in the Church of Saints Andrew and Gregory on the Caelian Hill, in the presence of His Grace Dr Robert Runcie, Archbishop of Canterbury. After the reading of a passage from St Paul's Letter to the Colossians (1:2b–6), John Paul II delivered the following homily.

'Grace to you and peace from God, our Father' (Col. 1:2).

We hear this greeting as we listen to the words of Saint Paul to the community of Colossae, in the reading appointed for the eve of the twenty-sixth Sunday of the year.

These same words I address to you this evening. I greet, first of all, my brother in Christ, the Archbishop of Canterbury; I warmly welcome you, together with the other representatives of the Anglican Communion who accompany you. I welcome you to Rome, the city that was stained with the blood of the Apostles Peter and Paul; I welcome you to this Church of Saint Gregory from which, fourteen hundred years ago, my predecessor Pope Saint Gregory the Great sent Saint Augustine to preach the 'word of truth' (cf. Col. 1:5) to the people of England. [. . .]

In sending Saint Augustine to preach to the Anglo-Saxon people, Saint Gregory was exercising the pastoral and missionary responsibility which is proper to the office of the Bishop of Rome. In his own writings we discover a profound and rich appreciation of the universal primacy entrusted to the Bishop who occupies the See of Peter. He it was who called the Bishop of Rome the *caput fidei* and who described the one who holds this office as the *servus servorum Dei* (Eph. XIII, 39).

It was as Bishop of Rome that seven years ago I myself went to England to visit the Catholic people there. My journey took me also to Canterbury, to the Cathedral Church of Saint Augustine. In making my pilgrimage to the shrine of the martyr, Saint Thomas Becket, I sought to play a part in healing the terrible wounds inflicted on the Body of Christ in the sixteenth century. We prayed together there, Your Grace and I, for that wholeness, that fullness of life in Christ which is God's gift of unity.

My pilgrimage to Canterbury was motivated by obedience to the will of Christ our Lord who, on the night before he died, prayed 'that they all may be one' (John 17:21). Today the divisions among Christians require that the primacy of the Bishop of Rome should also be a primacy in action and initiative in favour of that unity for which Christ so earnestly prayed. I see our celebration of Evening Prayer together as a further moment in that ecumenical pilgrimage that Catholics and Anglicans, together with other Christians, are called to make. Our goal is to discover once more that common inheritance of faith which was shared before the tragic sequence of events which divided Christian Europe four centuries ago. We must find our common roots in that period of a thousand years when Christians in England were united in the faith that had been planted there by Saint Augustine.

In the Common Declaration we signed together at Canterbury, we established the Second Anglican-Roman Catholic International Commission (ARCIC-II) to study the doctrinal differences that still separate us. But as we meet today, we cannot but acknowledge that events in recent years have seriously aggravated the differences between us, making the work of the Commission more difficult. I wish today to confirm the members of the Commission in their arduous task as they study the roots and origins of the differences between us. May they be endowed with hope and courage as they seek to meet the challenge.

The integrity of the apostolic faith as delivered once and for all to the saints in the apostolic Tradition (cf. Jude 3), must be fully preserved if our unity is to be that for which Christ prayed.

Responsibility for discerning the teaching and practice that are part of what Saint Paul calls the deposit which has been entrusted to us and which we must guard (cf. I Tim. 6:20) lies with the teaching authority of the Church. In the words of the Second Vatican Council, 'the task of giving an authentic interpretation of the Word of God, whether in its written form or in the form of Tradition, has been entrusted to the living teaching office of the Church alone' (*Dei Verbum*, 10–CTS Do 361). The specific role of bishops which is to be exercised in communion with the See of Peter in ensuring the unity and continuity of the faith is vital if we are to hand on the faith of Peter, Gregory and Augustine, if we are to evangelize once more the peoples of Europe and to preach the Gospel to the peoples of the world.

Source: *One in Hope* (London: Church House Publishing and Incorporated Catholic Truth Society, 1989), pp. 11–13.

2.17 CONFESSIONS OF FAITH: THE ST HILDA COMMUNITY

The St Hilda Community was formed in Britain by a group of Anglican women in 1986 following the decision taken by the General Synod not to allow women ordained abroad to celebrate Holy Communion. The Community resolved to develop a 'non-sexist' liturgy and to advertise eucharists that would be taken by women priests. It was named after St Hilda of Whitby.

We believe in the presence of God in the world.

She is our mother, source of deep wisdom, who:
> holds and protects us,
> nourishes our bodies,
> comforts our pain,
> hears and accepts our times of failure and success.

She is our lover and is allowed to touch our pain:
> healing and recreating,
> seeking out what is hidden,
> revealing deep, precious mysteries.

She is our friend who stands alongside us:
> working co-operatively for the common good,
> sharing our concerns,
> fiercely criticizing our lack of integrity.

We believe in the presence of God in our world.
We meet her as people met her in Jesus, in countless relationships which are at once human and divine:
> in simple encounters with men, women and children,
> in office and schoolroom, home and supermarket,
> in the community of her people.

We believe in the presence of God in our world,
whose truth is denied, in anguish, like that of Jesus on the cross, whenever:
> food is withheld,
> the earth is poisoned, abused or destroyed,
> people are oppressed, denied dignity and responsibility,
> tortured or killed.

Together we affirm the truth and goodness of God, our mother, lover and friend and commit ourselves to her in following the way of our brother Jesus.

Source: The St Hilda Community, *Women Included* (SPCK, 1991), p. 48.

2.18 ON ABORTION FROM *EVANGELIUM VITAE*

An encyclical letter addressed by Pope John Paul II to the Roman Catholic Church on the value and inviolability of human life, 25 March 1995.

'Your eyes beheld my unformed substance' (Ps 139:16): the unspeakable crime of abortion

Among all the crimes which can be committed against life, procured abortion has characteristics making it particularly serious and deplorable. The Second Vatican Council defines abortion, together with infanticide, as an 'unspeakable crime'.

But today, in many people's consciences, the perception of its gravity has become progressively obscured. The acceptance of abortion in the popular mind, in behaviour and even in law itself, is a telling sign of an extremely dangerous crisis of the moral sense, which is becoming more and more incapable of distinguishing between good and evil, even when the fundamental right to life is at stake. Given such a grave situation, we need now more than ever to have the courage to look the truth in the eye and to *call things by their proper name*, without yielding to convenient compromises or to the temptation of self-deception. In this regard the reproach of the Prophet is extremely straightforward: 'Woe to those who call evil good and good evil, who put darkness for light and light for darkness' (Is 5:20). Especially in the case of abortion there is a widespread use of ambiguous terminology, such as 'interruption of pregnancy', which tends to hide abortion's true nature and to attenuate its seriousness in public opinion. Perhaps this linguistic phenomenon is itself a symptom of an uneasiness of conscience. But no word has the power to change the reality of things: procured abortion is *the deliberate and direct killing, by whatever means it is carried out, of a human being in the initial phase of his or her existence, extending from conception to birth.* [. . .]

Given such unanimity in the doctrinal and disciplinary tradition of the Church, Paul VI was able to declare that this tradition is unchanged and unchangeable. Therefore, by the authority which Christ conferred upon Peter and his Successors, in communion with the Bishops – who on various occasions have condemned abortion and who in the aforementioned consultation, albeit dispersed throughout the world, have shown unanimous agreement concerning this doctrine – *I declare that direct abortion, that is, abortion willed as an end or as a means, always constitutes a grave moral disorder*, since it is the deliberate killing of an innocent human being. This doctrine is based upon the natural law and upon the written Word of God, is transmitted by the Church's Tradition and taught by the ordinary and universal Magisterium.

No circumstance, no purpose, no law whatsoever can ever make licit an act which is intrinsically illicit, since it is contrary to the Law of God which is written in every human heart, knowable by reason itself, and proclaimed by the Church.

Source: *Evangelium Vitae* (Dublin: Veritas, n.d.), pp. 103–4, 112–13.

—— •◆• ——

WOMEN'S VOICES AND FEMINIST THEOLOGY

———— •◆• ————

2.19 GOD AS MOTHER AND FATHER

JULIAN OF NORWICH

Little is known about the life of Mother Julian of Norwich (*c.* 1400). She was a recluse, but whether she became a nun is not certain. It is said that her hermitage was attached to the Benedictine community at Carrow. Her *Revelations of Divine Love* recounts sixteen revelations or 'shewings' experienced in 1373.

In the elect, wickedness is transformed into blessedness by the work of mercy and grace; God's way is to set good against evil by Jesus, our Mother in grace; the most virtuous soul is the most humble; all virtues are grounded in God

All this blessedness is ours through mercy and grace. We would never have had it or known it if goodness (that is, God) had not been opposed. It is because of this that we enjoy this bliss. Wickedness was allowed to rise up against goodness, and the goodness of mercy and grace rose up against wickedness and then turned it all into goodness and honour, at least as far as those who are to be saved are concerned. For it is the way of God to set good against evil. So Jesus Christ who sets good against evil is our real Mother. We owe our being to him – and this is the essence of motherhood! – and all the delightful, loving protection which ever follows. God is as really our Mother as he is our Father. He showed this throughout, and particularly when he said that sweet word, 'It is I.' In other words, 'It is I who am the strength and goodness of Fatherhood; I who am the wisdom of Motherhood; I who am light and grace and blessed love; I who am Trinity; I who am Unity; I who am the sovereign goodness of every single thing; I who enable you to love; I who enable you to long. It is I, the eternal satisfaction of every genuine desire.'

For the soul is at its best, its most noble and honourable, when it is most lowly, and humble, and gentle. Springing from this fundamental source and as part of our natural endowment, are all the virtues of our sensual nature, aided and abetted as they are by mercy and grace. Without such assistance we should be in a poor way!

Our great Father, God almighty, who is Being, knew and loved us from eternity. Through his knowledge, and in the marvellous depths of his charity, together with the foresight and wisdom of the whole blessed Trinity, he willed that the Second Person should become our Mother, Brother, and Saviour. Hence it follows that God is as truly our Mother as he is our Father. Our Father decides, our Mother works, our good Lord, the Holy Spirit, strengthens. So we ought to love our God in whom we have our own being, reverently thanking him, and praising him for creating us, earnestly beseeching our Mother for mercy and pity, and our Lord, the Spirit, for help and grace. For in these three is contained our life: nature, mercy, grace. From these we get our humility, gentleness, patience and pity. From them too we get our hatred of sin and wickedness – it is the function of virtue to hate these.

So we see that Jesus is the true Mother of our nature, for he made us. He is our Mother, too, by grace, because he took our created nature upon himself. All the lovely deeds and tender services that beloved motherhood implies are appropriate to the Second Person. In him the godly will is always safe and sound, both in nature and grace, because of his own fundamental goodness. I came to realize that there were three ways of looking at God's motherhood: the first is based on the fact that our nature is *made*; the second is found in the assumption of that nature – there begins the motherhood of grace; the third is the motherhood of work which flows out over all by that same grace – the length and breadth and height and depth of it is everlasting. And so is his love.

Source: Julian of Norwich, *Revelations of Divine Love*, trans. Clifton Wolters (Penguin Books, 1966), pp. 167–8.

2.20 THE INTIFADA, NONVIOLENCE AND THE BIBLE

JEAN ZARU

The Intifada is the uprising for liberation organized by Palestinians against the Israeli occupation that began in 1987.

As a Christian Palestinian woman, native of the Holy Land, I have been confronted all my life with social, economic, political, and religious structures of injustice that violated my dignity and self-esteem. The Church, as well as my mother, taught me not to resist, for this is not Christian and is not in favor of peace, the way they understood it. Even now, I remember very vividly that the only time my mother ever hit me and was really angry with me (as a child of eight) was when I did not listen to her and climbed the fig tree in our backyard and picked figs. She claimed this made my grandmother angry, and that I should not make her angry. I thought I had a right to the tree, in my father's and grandfather's property, just as my grandmother had. I could not understand why I could not have some of our figs. Peace for my mother meant submission and relinquishment of rights. I have come to see that this results in doing violence to ourselves and others.

The rebel in me started searching, agonizing, and asking questions. I kept asking myself, if we say there is something of God in every person, why is it often so difficult to see that presence of God in others? Why is there so much evil and suffering in our world? For many years I struggled with this Christian truth, that we are made in the image and likeness of God. I was happy to learn that the belief in the divinity seems to be part of all religions. 'The kingdom of God is within you', said Jesus. 'You are the temple of God', wrote St Paul. 'He who knows himself knows God', said the Prophet Mohammed, and this is echoed by many Sufis.

This recognition of our shared brotherhood and sisterhood convinced me that it must lead to the disappearance of injustice, exploitation, oppression, and everything that comes from false beliefs that justify ourselves and degrade others. So, acknowledgment of our true selves is revolutionary. It must lead to great changes and to peace. Thus the search for peace and for the recognition of true reality are identical.

All along, as Palestinians and as women, we were told to be peaceful. This was understood to mean being passive, being nice, allowing ourselves to be walked over. The Israelis talked to us about a 'peace' that was achieved by pounding the opposition into submission, a 'peace' maintained by crushing protest against injustice, a 'peace' for the rulers at the expense of and through the misery of the ruled.

In December 1987 our Intifada started. With it we created an atmosphere of nonviolent action – notice I say 'action' – by which we hoped to resolve our problems of occupation and oppression and to promote peace. We started by affirming one another. All of us felt empowered. [. . .]

The Intifada contradicts the idea that our situation is hopeless and that we are helpless in solving it. We are not helpless, and it is not hopeless. Isn't this also the message of the resurrection?

We live daily as persons and as communities in the midst of violence. We often find ourselves willingly or unwillingly participating in social organizations that practice and embody violence. We may deliberately act in violent or nonviolent ways to promote justice. Can we say to those who have opted for violence against injustice that we would rather see you die than defend yourselves? Who will throw the first stone to condemn them? Who is morally superior? There are many Palestinians who sacrificed their lives so we may have life with dignity and freedom. Isn't this Jesus' message?

As we opt for violence or nonviolence in our revolution, we know that the liberty to choose is not always there. I believe the division between the pacifist and the non-pacifist is not an absolute one. The pacifist and the non-pacifist, both committed to the struggle for a just future, should regard one another as allies on most issues. The conflict is not between them, but between those who support the oppressive structures of the status quo and those on the side of liberation. As Christians, the gospel compels us not to support the oppressive structures. Such an alternative is not possible for us today.

One peculiar strength of nonviolence comes from the dual nature of its approach – the offering of respect and concern, on the one hand, and of defiance and stubborn noncooperation with injustice, on the other. Put into a feminist perspective, non-violence is the merging of our uncompromising rage at patriarchy's brutal destructiveness with a refusal to adopt its ways, a refusal to give in to despair or hate. To rage against, yet refuse to destroy, is a true revolution, not just a shuffle of death-wielding power. [. . .]

We are seeking God's Kingdom, God's will where peace will prevail. Searching for this peace is often a cause for strife. Jesus himself foresaw this. 'Do not think that I have come to bring peace to earth. I have not come to bring peace, but a sword!' Where can we find peace? Many people, including women, think that they can find peace by running away from the world, by doing nothing about it. The churches have become a refuge for tired folk. But this is not the message of the Gospels, for God loved the world, so we should be in the world that God loved and loves. The world is full of strife, and it is our duty as Christians to bring peace. We cannot bring peace only by proclaiming it. We should work. Wherever injustice and wrong exist, we should be there to say, this is not the will of God, this should be changed. But, we cannot fulfill this duty if we are not at peace with ourselves. The saddest thing in our time is that Christians have found it so difficult to live at peace with one another, locally and internationally.

There are many Christians whose theology brings to me, as a Palestinian and a woman, strife and confusion. These Christians are part of the structures of injustice we are facing. An example of this is the phenomenon of Christian fundamentalism in the West. Many of these Western Christians give blind support to Israel. They never question what Israel is doing, because they see the Jews as the 'chosen people' and Israel as a 'fulfillment of prophecy'. Interpretations such as these affect us directly as Palestinians.

For the last two years, our people have been bleeding. Daily we are reminded of life and death, of the crucifixion. We feel the words of Jesus, who said, 'Weep for yourselves and your children' (Luke 23:27–31). We often pray as Jesus did that the bitter cup of death may be taken away. We often shout with a loud voice, God, why have you forsaken us? But, until we surrender to God as Jesus did, and until we reach that stage where we can forgive those who have offended us, we will not have peace, and we will not have liberation.

Source: Ursula King (ed.) *Feminist Theology from the Third World* (London: SPCK/Orbis, 1994), pp. 230–1, 232–3, 234–5.

2.21 MARY AS ONE OF THE BASES OF FEMINIST THEOLOGY

This statement is taken from an ecumenical paper prepared by Asian Christian women at a conference in Singapore, 1987.

Each of us, within our own culture, has found different strengths in the process of reclaiming and redefining Mary. We can look at Mary the mother and see her womb as the place of the action of the Holy Spirit – a place of struggle and suffering which brings new life. The struggle of mothers in the Asia/Pacific context, who struggle with and for their children, to give birth to a new and just reality. Mary is the mother of suffering, of those who suffer.

If we recognize that Mary is a woman of the poor, we must also challenge the lie that depicts her as jeweled and elaborately dressed. Because the good news of the Magnificat is bad news for the rich, we reject Mary's hijacking by a wealthy Church – for the consolation of the rich. This simply reinforces the oppression of the poor. If we understand the virgin birth as the beginning of a new order, in which patriarchy can no longer be the basis of human life, we must hear the angel's greeting, 'Hail, full of grace', as addressed to all of us. We too must participate in changing oppressive relationships and cultural symbols – overcoming patterns of domination and subordination between north and south, rich and poor, male and female, black and white.

The Magnificat is the rallying point for ecumenism, as Christians join together working to liberate the poor and all victims of injustice. It is the liberation song of women, who are, with their children, the poorest of the poor. However, in the context of the indigenous struggles of Aotearoa [the Maori name for New Zealand] and Australia, it is necessary for women of the dominant group to remember that while we are oppressed by patriarchy, we also benefit from institutionalized racism, so our sisterhood is not one of equality. So while we too sing the Magnificat in our countries, we must learn the response of relinquishing power as indigenous women take control of their own lives.

We acknowledge that in Asia and the Pacific the need for economic and political liberation is often used to trivialize women's struggle. However, the struggle of indigenous women is a fight for a people's survival. If feminist theology is concerned only with sexism, and not with the liberation of the whole human race, it too is oppressive. We see feminist Mariology as a liberation theology that gives hope of humanization to all the world.

Our task now is to describe Mary as Asian/Pacific women. This will mean addressing Christology, ecclesiology, sacramental theology, worship, language, music, and symbols from the perspective of suffering women. Our liberation starts within each of us. Let us begin.

Source: Ursula King (ed.) *Feminist Theology from the Third World* (London: SPCK/Orbis, 1994), pp. 273–4.

2.22 THEOLOGICAL PERSPECTIVES OF A RELIGIOUS WOMAN TODAY

SISTER MARY JOHN MANANZAN, OSB

Being a religious woman today is more difficult, less simple, more demanding, but definitely more challenging. When I hear a young woman answer the question 'Why do you want to enter the convent?' with 'Because I want to have peace and quiet', I just smile.

The religious life has come a long way from the *fuga mundi* [flight from the world] principle of the early days of monasticism. Religious women who were particularly the objects of enclosure laws of canon law (because they were not only *religious* but *women*) have emerged from this constraint and have become involved in the burning issues of society, and in some cases have been at the forefront of militant causes.

Personally, I find being a religious woman today in a Third World country a dangerous, but challenging and meaningful, existence. It forces one to go back to the original meaning of the core of the Christian message. Impelled by a sense of urgency because of the lived experience of suffering and oppression, religious women are inspired to a consequent living out of this Christian imperative in the concrete struggles of their world. This in turn gives them an experiential insight into the meaning of the paradox of committed freedom. The religious woman committed to justice becomes truly convinced that to seek her life is to lose it and to lose her life is to gain it, not only for herself but for others – for those who will perhaps see the fulfillment of her vision of a better world, something she will probably not see in her own lifetime.

Source: Ursula King (ed.) *Feminist Theology from the Third World* (London: SPCK/Orbis 1994), p. 349.

—— ● ◆ ● ——

CHRISTIANITY AND SOCIAL JUSTICE

— •◆• —

2.23 AN ATTEMPT AT SYNTHESIS: SOLIDARITY AND POVERTY
GUSTAVO GUTIERREZ

How are we [. . .] to understand the evangelical meaning of the witness of a real, material, concrete poverty? *Lumen gentium*[1] invites us to look for the deepest meaning of Christian poverty *in Christ*: 'Just as Christ carried out the work of redemption in poverty and under oppression, so the Church is called to follow the same path in communicating to men the fruits of salvation. Christ Jesus, though He was by nature God . . . emptied himself, taking the nature of a slave (Phil. 2:6), and being rich, he became poor (II Cor. 8:9) for our sakes. Thus, although the Church needs human resources to carry out her mission, she is not set up to seek earthly glory, but to proclaim humility and self-sacrifice, even by her own example' [. . .]. The Incarnation is an act of love. Christ became man, died, and rose from the dead to set us free so that we might enjoy freedom (Gal. 5:1). To die and to rise again with Christ is to vanquish death and to enter into a new life (cf. Rom. 6:1–11). The cross and the resurrection are the seal of our liberty.

The taking on of the servile and sinful condition of man, as foretold in Second Isaiah, is presented by Paul as an act of voluntary impoverishment: 'For you know how generous our Lord Jesus Christ has been: He was rich, yet for your sake he became poor, so that through his poverty you might become rich' (II Cor. 8:9). This is the humiliation of Christ, his *kenosis* (Phil. 2:6–11). But he does not take on man's sinful condition and its consequences to idealize it. It is rather because of love for and solidarity with men who suffer in it. It is to redeem them from their sin and to enrich them with his poverty. It is to struggle against human selfishness and everything that divides men and enables there to be rich and poor, possessors and dispossessed, oppressors and oppressed.

Poverty is an act of love and liberation. It has a redemptive value. If the ultimate cause of man's exploitation and alienation is selfishness, the deepest reason for voluntary poverty is love of neighbor. Christian poverty has meaning only as a commitment of solidarity with the poor, with those who suffer misery and injustice. The commitment is to witness to the evil which has resulted from sin and is a breach of communion. It is not a question of idealizing poverty, but rather of taking it on as it is – an evil – to protest against it and to struggle to abolish it [. . .] you cannot really be with the poor unless you are struggling against poverty. Because of this solidarity – which must manifest itself in specific action, a style of life, a break with one's social class – one can also help the poor and exploited to become aware of their exploitation and seek liberation from it. Christian poverty, an expression of love, is solidarity *with the poor* and is a protest *against poverty*. This is the concrete, contemporary meaning of the witness of poverty. It is a poverty lived not for its own sake, but rather as an authentic imitation of Christ; it is a poverty which means taking on the sinful condition of man to liberate him from sin and all its consequences.

Luke presents the community of goods in the early Church as an ideal. 'All whose faith had drawn them together held everything in common' (Acts 2:44); 'not a man of them claimed any of his possessions as his own, but everything was held in common' (Acts 4:33). They did this with a profound unity, one 'in heart and soul' (*ibid.*). But [. . .] this was not a question of erecting poverty as an ideal, but rather of seeing to it that there were no poor: 'They had never a needy person among them, because all who had property in land or houses sold it, brought the proceeds of the sale, and laid the money at the feet of the apostles; it was then distributed to any who stood in need' (Acts 4:34–5). The meaning of the community of goods is clear: to eliminate poverty because of love of the poor person. [. . .]

We must pay special attention to the words we use. The term *poor* might seem not only vague and churchy, but also somewhat sentimental and aseptic. The 'poor' person today is the oppressed one, the one marginated from society, the member of the proletariat struggling for his most basic rights; he is the exploited and plundered social class, the country struggling for its liberation. In today's world the solidarity and protest of which we are speaking have an evident and inevitable 'political' character insofar as they imply liberation. To be with the oppressed is to be against the oppressor. In our times and on our continent to be in solidarity with the 'poor', understood in this way, means to run personal risks – even to put one's life in danger. Many Christians – and non-Christians – who are committed to the Latin American revolutionary process are running these risks. And so there are emerging new ways of living poverty which are different from the classic 'renunciation of the goods of this world'.

Only by rejecting poverty and by making itself poor in order to protest against it can the Church preach something that is uniquely its own: 'spiritual poverty', that is, the openness of man and history to the future promised by God.[2] Only in this way will the Church be able to fulfill authentically – and with any possibility of being listened to – its prophetic function of denouncing every injustice to man. And only in this way will it be able to preach the word which liberates, the word of genuine brotherhood.[3]

Only authentic solidarity with the poor and a real protest against the poverty of our time can provide the concrete, vital context necessary for a theological discussion of poverty. The absence of a sufficient commitment to the poor, the marginated, and the exploited is perhaps the fundamental reason why we have no solid contemporary reflection on the witness of poverty.

For the Latin American Church especially, this witness is an inescapable and much-needed sign of the authenticity of its mission.

---

1 *Lumen Gentium* is a constitution (or statement of dogma) resulting from the Second Vatican Council. It sets out the doctrine of the Church, including the Church's concern for social justice and its missionary obligation.

2 The Medellin document on 'Poverty of the Church' distinguishes among three meanings of the term *poverty* and describes the mission of the Church in terms of that distinction. It might be useful to quote here the entire paragraph: '(a) Poverty, as a lack of the goods of this world necessary to live worthily as men, is in itself evil. The prophets denounce it as contrary to the will of the Lord and most of the time as the fruit of the injustice and sin of men. (b) Spiritual poverty is the theme of the poor of Yahweh (cf. Zeph. 2:3; Luke 1:46–55). Spiritual poverty is the attitude of opening up to God, the ready disposition of one who hopes for everything from the Lord (cf. Matt. 5:3). Although he values the goods of this world, he does not become attached to them and he recognizes the higher value of the riches of the Kingdom (cf. Amos 2:6–7; 4:1; Jer. 5:28; Mic. 6:12–13; Isa. 10:2 et passim). (c) Poverty as a commitment, through which one assumes voluntarily and lovingly the conditions of the needy of this world in order to bear witness to the evil which it represents and to spiritual liberty in the face of material goods, follows the example of Christ Who took to Himself all the consequences of men's sinful condition (cf. Phil. 2:5–8) and Who 'being rich became poor' (cf. II Cor. 8:9) in order to redeem us.

'In this context a poor Church: – Denounces the unjust lack of this world's goods and the sin that begets it; – Preaches and lives in spiritual poverty, as an attitude of spiritual childhood and openness to the Lord; – Is herself bound to material poverty. The poverty of the Church is, in effect, a constant factor in the history of salvation' (nos. 4–5).

3 In this regard it is necessary to rethink seriously the meaning of the assistance that the churches of the wealthy countries give to the churches of the poor countries. This assistance could very well be counterproductive as regards the witness to poverty that these poor churches should be giving. Moreover it might lead them into a reformist approach, resulting in superficial social changes which in the long run serve only to prolong the misery and injustice which marginated peoples suffer. This assistance can also provide a satisfied conscience – at low cost – for Christians who are citizens of countries which control the world economy. In this regard see the famous article of Ivan Illich, 'The Seamy Side of Charity', *America* 116, no. 3 (January 21, 1967): 88–91.

Source: G. Gutierrez, 'An attempt at synthesis: solidarity and poverty', *A Theology of Liberation* (London: SCM, 1974), pp. 300–2.

2.24 THE BLACK MESSIAH AND BLACK HUMANITY

ALLAN BOESAK

Having studied theology in the United States and Europe, as well as in South Africa, Allan Boesak developed his own distinctive theology of liberation. It was informed by ecumenical insights and in particular tested the relevance of American black theology to the situation in South Africa during the years of apartheid.

True love and true justice, as I have said, enable persons to realize the full potential of their humanity. In this situation a person can be an authentic person. Humanity is extremely important; it is not a general and empty concept that can be given any content one desires. Humanity is an important concept: it functions in the context of God's activity among us. At the center of this activity of God is the Christ-event.

We confess that Jesus Christ embodies true divinity and true humanity. He was human as God intended humans to be. In him God was in the world. In him God was with humankind. In him our being 'like God', of necessity, took a clear and distinct form. Subsequently there could be no misunderstanding about what God expects from us.

Our being 'like God' has nothing to do with the physical appearance of God. It is meant to indicate how God is God and how we must be what we are. Jesus of Nazareth was the concrete and living image of God. Israel recognized and knew God in God's deeds, in God's 'dealings' with and on behalf of the people. In his 'dealings' with persons Jesus was the true and authentic reflection of the gracious God in action: 'The one who has seen me [in action] has seen the Father [in action]' (John 14:9).

We must raise the following question: What is the meaning of this confession for blacks who are the oppressed of the world? Do we see in Jesus the one to whom we have been introduced through the ages – the romantic preacher who declared a message of submissiveness oriented solely to the future, to heaven? Is Jesus really as 'Western' as the 'civilization' that claims him? Is the Jesus whom thousands of our ancestors learned to know while they worked on plantations as slaves identified with the power and the oppression of whites? If this picture of Jesus is true and real, then Jesus is white and he is unacceptable to blacks. The Jesus who represented the God of the Bible cannot be the same one whose name was carved into the bows of the Dutch slave ships in which Africans were transported to their death. For black Christians, as James Cone has said, the only authentic confession in our age is the confession of Jesus Christ as the black Messiah.

The image of Jesus that the New Testament presents to us is one that identifies him to a remarkable degree with the black experience. He was poor. At the time of his circumcision, his poor parents were not able to bring the sacrifice prescribed in the law. They brought instead the sacrifice of the poor: two turtledoves in place of a year-old lamb (Lev. 12:6–8; Luke 2:21–4). He maintained the humble status of his birth throughout his life. He belonged to a poor, dispossessed people, without rights in its own land, subjected daily to countless humiliations by foreign oppressors. Jesus lived and worked among the poor. His disciples and followers came from among the poor. He lived a life of solidarity with the poor. He felt at home with the 'have-nots' rather than with the 'haves'. All must admit that his message spoke to the condition of the lowly. His message generated hope and trust among them. And they felt at home with *him*. His message had an effect among the poor. It had little or no positive effect among the rich and the privileged.

Jesus made no secret of the fact that he had come for the lowly – the outcasts, the despised ones, those of whom the rich in their 'sophisticated' language would have said, they 'are very primitive. If they were to be given freedom in an amiable fashion, they would not live virtuously and would not know how to govern themselves. But even if they live in wretched circumstances, nevertheless, one can expect them to serve one well.' This is how the Reformed pastor from Coevorden, the Netherlands, Johan Picardt, wrote about the 'kaffirs' in South Africa. But Jesus came for them; not for those who had no need of a physician.

At the very beginning of his public ministry, Jesus made clear what his mission was: 'The Spirit of the Lord is upon me, because he has anointed me to bring the good news to the poor. He has sent me to proclaim release to the captives and recovery of sight to the blind, to set at liberty those who are oppressed, to proclaim the acceptable year of the Lord' (Luke 4:18ff.). This program is one in which there is solidarity between Jesus and those he has come to serve. Jesus the oppressed one came and took sides with the oppressed. He came as the forsaken one without form or appearance, a man of sorrows, bowed down with illness (Isa. 53). He knew what it was to live like a hunted animal. He knew what it was to speak with care at all times so as to evade the clutches of 'informers'. He lived on earth in a way familiar to us blacks. He identified himself completely with us. He is the black Messiah.

In spite of his humble position, however, he still is called Jesus the liberator. He brought a new message to his oppressed people and to everyone who will listen to it: a new message of hope and liberation. He lived among the oppressed with a heavenly radicalism. By so doing he set dynamite to the status quo and to 'law and order'. The lowly had been 'things'. They were without value except insofar as they were useful to the Romans and their accomplices. Jesus told them that he loved them; that they were of greater value than the birds and the flowers, even if it was true that Solomon in all his glory lacked their natural splendor. In a country where the Roman fist was the highest authority, Jesus enthroned the human value of the oppressed.

Nor did Jesus practice a 'Christian sadism' among his followers. When he was alone with the woman who had been accused of adultery, he did not permit her to bow down on the ground to demonstrate her gratitude. She, rather, was able to assume a responsible role immediately: 'Go and from now on sin no more!' (John 8:11).

Jesus protected the lowly from the religious tyranny of the priests and scribes: the person is more important than the Sabbath; the law functions in the service of the people. Herod, the political tyrant and accomplice of the Romans, Jesus called a 'fox'. The self-centered Pharisees he called 'whitened sepulchers', 'hypocrites', 'serpents', 'a brood of adders'. Jesus calls the Pharisees by these names because they 'devoured the houses of widows', but 'for the sake of appearance' they prayed long prayers, and because they ignored 'the weightier' matters of the law: judgement and mercy and fidelity (Matt. 23). He offers liberation to the lowly and establishes their humanity in a radical way. By his royal association with them, he summoned the lowly to claim and to strengthen their own humanity.

We have looked in vain for this Jesus in the preaching of whites. The message we heard there was a completely different message. The message was one of passivity, of glossing over white injustice – a message that assured whites their position always and unconditionally. You need only read the sermons and orations that have been given in South Africa on the 'Day of Promise' to understand why one of the publications of the *Pro Veritate* movement speaks about an 'Afrikaner gospel' (i.e., a white gospel).

I cannot omit reference to one more example of 'gospel proclamation' to emphasize how the ground was prepared for both blacks and whites to view black–white relationships. This example comes from a report of the Dutch pastor M. C. Vos, who migrated to South Africa at the end of the eighteenth century. In his report he tells how he persuaded farmers to permit their slaves to be instructed in the gospel. Keep in mind that he was neither ignorant nor blind to reality:

'It is natural that your slaves will not become worse but, rather, better through education. Let me try to convince you of this. You have slaves, I have noticed, who originally came from a variety of lands. Put yourself in the place of one of them for a few minutes and think in the following way: I am a poor slave, but I was not born in this status. I was taken from my dear parents, my loving wife or husband, from my children, my brothers and sisters, by human thieves who kidnaped me and took me away from my own country. I have no hope that I shall ever see one of my family members again. I have been dragged here to this land by tyrants. On the ride to this place, if I had not been in chains and fetters I would have chosen death in preference to life. Here I was sold as an animal. Now I am a slave. I must do everything which is commanded me even to the point of doing very undesirable work. If I do not do this willingly, then I am beaten severely.'

'Suppose for a few minutes', the pastor continued in his conversation with the farmer, 'that this was the situation in which *you* found yourself. Tell me, if you were to be in that situation, would you have the desire to do your work? Would you not, rather, frequently be despondent, sorrowful, obstinate, and disobedient?'

The man was moved. He said, 'I had never thought about that. If I were in the place of one like the one you have described, who knows to what sort of acts of despair I would be driven.'

'Well', I continued, 'if you permit them to remain stupid and ignorant, upon occasion thoughts of this type will arise and, at times, come to expression in terribly extreme actions. If they are instructed correctly, as they should be, they will be instructed that God rules all things; that nothing happens apart from his rule; that God is a God of order; that in the same way in which they must serve their master and mistress, their master and mistress must serve those who are in positions of authority over them; that those who do not serve obediently are punished either on their body or in their purse. You can make clear to them that that which seems evil to us frequently turns out to our advantage. If they had remained by their friends in their own country, then they would have remained ignorant of the way of salvation until their death; and then, at death, because of this ignorance, they would have been lost forever. Now, however, since they have been brought to a Christian land, they have the opportunity of gaining knowledge of the only Savior who can and shall make them happy through all eternity. When they begin to understand this a bit, the despondent and grieving thoughts will change. Then they will begin to think: if that is the way things are, then I shall be content with my lot and I shall attempt to do my work obediently and joyfully.'

The farmer cried out, 'Why weren't we told these things before? I must confess my ignorance. From now on I shall never dissuade anyone from educating his slaves. I, rather, shall persuade everyone to educate their slaves.'

Today, of course, different arguments are used. We are all more sophisticated. The heart of the matter, however, is unchanged. The calling and responsibility of black theology is to liberate us from this undesirable 'whiteness'. Because our blackness, and only our blackness, is the cause of the oppression of the black community, Cone says, 'the christological importance of Jesus Christ must be found in his blackness. ... Taking our cue from the historical Jesus who is pictured in the New Testament as the Oppressed One, what else, except blackness, could adequately tell us the meaning of his presence today?' Today, just as yesterday, he has taken the sorrow of his people upon himself. He has become for them everything that is necessary for their liberation. For us Jesus is the black Messiah and the irrevocable guarantee of our black humanity.

Source: Allan Boesak, *Black and Reformed*, ed. L. Sweetman (New York: Orbis Books, 1984), pp. 10–15.

2.25 REFLECTIONS ON LIBERATION THEOLOGY
DESMOND TUTU

Archbishop Desmond Tutu (born 1931) is the primatial (chief) Anglican bishop of South Africa. He won the Nobel Peace Prize in 1984 and was an outspoken critic of the apartheid system, calling repeatedly for sanctions against South Africa.

In the recent past, it used to be taken for granted that when you talked about Christian theology, then you were really referring to theology as it had been done or was being done in the great centres of Christanity in Western Christendom. You would be thought to be discussing theology as it was being written, taught or discussed in the UK, North America or on the European Continent, especially in Germany. If you came from a Third World country, you would be expected to study the theologians produced in these great centres, if you yourself aspired to be a theologian who wanted to be taken account of in the future!

But we note that some of the best theologies have come not from the undisturbed peace of a don's study, or his speculations in a university seminar, but from a situation where they have been hammered out on the anvil of adversity, in the heat of battle, or soon thereafter. For too long Western theology has wanted to lay claim to a universality that it cannot too easily call its own. Christians have found that the answers they possessed, were answers to questions that nobody in different situations was asking. New theologies have arisen, addressing themselves to the issues in front of them. Consequently we have in our midst now the theology of Liberation, as developed in Latin America, and Black theology, developed in the USA and Southern Africa.

The perplexity they have to deal with is this: Why does suffering single out black people so conspicuously, suffering not at the hands of pagans or other unbelievers, but at the hands of white fellow Christians who claim allegiance to the same Lord and Master?

A few years ago it became fashionable to say that the world sets the agenda for the Church. This represented a salutary shift of emphasis away from our unhealthy otherworldliness. Christians had wanted to shut themselves in a holy ghetto, almost entirely unmindful of the cries of the hungry, and the anguish of the poor and exploited ones of this world. There was an almost Manichean dread of the material, existent world, and Christians had to deny in an absolute way the world, the flesh and the devil – in order to concentrate on the world to come. Those who reacted against this unsatisfactory state of affairs declaimed approvingly that 'God loved not the Church, but the world'. Such a reminder was important; it represented a positive gain and we must give thanks that it happened. And yet one has the suspicion that the pendulum of reaction might just have swung too far, and that (to change the image) the baby has been thrown out with the bath water. What I am trying to underline is that we cannot denigrate the Church, and devalue it, because we want to enhance the value of the world.

In South Africa, to refer now to some specifics, the Church of God must sustain the hope of a people who have been tempted to grow despondent, because the powers of this world seem to be rampant. It does not appear that significant political change can happen without much bloodshed and violence, and it seems that God does not care, or is impotent. The Church of God must say that despite all appearances to the contrary, this is God's world. He cares and cares enormously, his is ultimately a moral universe that we inhabit, and that right and wrong matter, and that the resurrection of Jesus Christ proclaims that right will prevail. Goodness and Love, Justice and Peace are not illusory, or mirages that forever elude our grasp. We must say that Jesus Christ has inaugurated the Kingdom of God, which is a Kingdom of Justice, Peace and Love, or fullness of life, that God is on the side of the oppressed, the marginalised and the exploited. He is a God of the poor, of the hungry, of the naked, with whom the Church identifies and has solidarity. The Church in South Africa must be the prophetic Church, which cries out 'Thus saith the Lord', speaking up against injustice and violence, against oppression and exploitation, against all that dehumanises God's children and makes them less than what God intended them to be.

Source: Desmond Tutu, *Crying in the Wilderness*, introduced and edited by John Webster, 2nd edn (London and Oxford: Mowbray, 1986), pp. 11–13.

2.26 DECLARATION OF THE HOLY SYNOD OF THE RUSSIAN ORTHODOX CHURCH, APRIL 1990

God-loving archpastors, pastors, and all the faithful children of the Russian Orthodox Church,

In our life, the time has come when everybody must realize their responsibility before the Lord for our Mother Church and its historical destiny.

The rapid changes taking place in the country have not bypassed the church and have posed serious challenges. For decades the church has been artificially separated from the people and largely separated from the life of society, but now it attracts close attention from various social forces and movements. Not infrequently, these forces and movements find themselves bitterly opposed to one another and each would like to see the church among their allies and to have the church support their understanding of the objectives and purposes of the spiritual, political, social, and economic transformation of the country and the solution of ethnic problems. We are called upon to be the guardians of the church tradition and be guided by the will of the First Bishop Tikhon, the Patriarch of All Russia, and other confessors of Christ's faith in our century, and we emphatically state: The Orthodox Church cannot be on the side of any group or party interests; it cannot link our destiny with politics. The church is the mother of all its faithful children, and she embraces all of them, irrespective of their political outlooks, with love, demanding from them the purity of the Orthodox faith and faithfulness to their Christian calling. It is this position that gives the church the right to make a moral evaluation of the developments that are currently taking place and the problems that concern our society. In doing so, the church is guided solely by the word of God and the apostolic tradition that it preserves.

One acute problem involving ethnic conflicts prompted the bishops of our church to convene a council in January of 1990 and to address all the children of the church with an appeal, which we hope has received an appropriate Christian response from you.

But our country is still facing many difficult problems that directly affect all of us: the need for spiritual renewal of society through practical measures of the upbringing of children and youth; the task of reviving our fatherland's culture, whose many monuments have been criminally destroyed or neglected, and calling for immediate measures to save them; the protection of the environment, which is in a catastrophic state in some regions of the country due to barbaric methods of economic management; and, finally, the need to pay attention to the social sphere, which has been greatly damaged by both the economic policy and the heartless attitude of many people. Today, society expects the church to take practical and effective steps to help resolve all these problems in the shortest period of time.

However, we should admit with humility that in many respects our church community, including the hierarchy, the clergy, and the laity, has turned out to be unprepared to respond appropriately to present challenges. The difficult decades have not gone by without leaving their mark. For many years the church was perceived as an ideological force that posed a threat to society. The open reprisals, which began in the difficult years of the Revolution and continued in the 1920s, the 1930s, the late 1950s, and the early 1960s, were all aimed at the church's elimination. During some periods its influence on people was curbed by means of covert encroachments and attempts to compromise it through organized propaganda. The interference of state agencies in the policy of the selection of the leaders of the church and the administration of parishes was also designed to achieve the same objectives. As a result, the church was forced out of the life of society, its activity was limited strictly to performing Divine Services in cathedrals, its testimony was weakened by constant pressure on the clergy, and its material base was severely undermined. Looking back over the past decades and the tragic experience of life and the testimony of our fathers and mothers, brothers and sisters, and attempting to understand our own experience, we can state that the church has survived not by its power or human wisdom, but by the power of its spirit and the gift of Divine Grace. This gift of grace has strengthened the weak forces of hierarchs, clergy, and all the faithful and has helped the church to preserve its faith in Christ and to continue along the road of the cross. Today, some people believe that some who walked along this road did not do as they should have done. With surprising ease judgment is passed on those who were subjected to scorn, open oppression, or covert pressure and who, throughout all those difficult years, tried to remain faithful to their calling as far as their understanding and strength would allow. We should all remember that human judgment is limited to the possibility of analyzing only those facts that are accessible to history, and in this sense even the most just judgment must always be qualified. Only God, who understands all hearts, knows 'the hidden things of darkness', and only he 'will make manifest the councils of the hearts' (1 Cor. 4:1–5). For this reason the evaluation of our church's modern history which is being made in church circles today should be as impartial as it should be ethical. It should serve the spiritual renewal of all of us, it should unite and not divide the children of the church, and it should be Christian in its spirit and its meaning.

But the past, no matter how difficult it was, does not relieve us of responsibility for the results of our service today. It is absolutely clear that many people have grown accustomed to the situation of forced social inactivity and, whether they want it or not, continue to remain aloof from the changes taking place and do not use the possibilities now opening for the church. However, there is another extreme. Church representatives are now taking part in the activities of public organizations and elected bodies of power, speaking in the press and other media, yet not all representatives of the church realize their responsibility and by their statements give cause for passing judgement both in the religious and the secular spheres. It is absolutely clear that there is temptation in the church just as there is very frequently in our secular community to replace deeds with rhetorical statements and posturing designed to produce effect. [. . .]

Nevertheless, it is absolutely clear that under certain conditions the tensions that have emerged inside the body of the church can serve a creative and constructive purpose. They can promote a genuine revival of the mission of the church, the organization of religious and moral education of children and adults, and the cause of charity and the participation of the church is solving problems facing our people today. The most important of these conditions is preserving the canon order and the unity of the church and renouncing the secular political methods of struggle and mutual recriminations and suspicions. We should not repeat the sad history of the religious schisms of the 1920s. Today, as never before in recent years, we must consolidate the efforts of all the healthy forces of the church community. We must resolve the urgent problems of the internal organization of church life without delay.

Source: Igor Troyanovsky (ed.) *Religion in the Soviet Republics* (San Francisco: Harper, 1991), pp. 66–8.

2.27 A STATEMENT IN SUPPORT OF LITHUANIAN INDEPENDENCE, EASTER EVE, 1990

CARDINAL VINCENTAS SLADKEVICIUS

'The church has enabled us to maintain our links with the western world because the church itself and its activity are open to the world. The church cannot be walled off. The Catholic Church of Lithuania is part of the world Church. It has been able to make our people aware of all the sentiments in the world Church. Our nation's most precious values – freedom, a strong yearning for truth, faith in the future, and good – have been inherited from the church. Today the church also shows what we have to strive for and how we should grow.

'Faith has always helped preserve the basis of spirituality. Faith in God has always sustained believers. Even in exile, when there was absolutely no way out, people were not overpowered by hopelessness and despair. They hoped to return home. Every believer knew that if he did not return to Lithuania, he had the road to paradise open for him.

'Geographically, our nation is placed between great peoples. We have always felt the influence of the neighboring cultures and could not isolate ourselves from this influence. Interaction has evolved by itself. With the exception of Poland, the neighboring countries were not Catholic. On the one side, we had Old Believers [Russians], on the other, Protestants. However, we learned to live together with all of them.

'We, Catholics, do not find it difficult to interact with others because the basis for this is in our religion, in the Lord's commandment, "Thou shalt love thy neighbor as thyself." When we were still children living in the countryside, our parents taught us to share bread with a passerby, no matter what language he or she spoke. Today, we can assert that the Lithuanian people have acquired a high level of tolerance through education. We would like other people to reciprocate these sentiments.

'Today, we can say that the affairs of the Catholic Church in Lithuania have advanced positively in all principal questions. There is no question that the main thing for us was teaching the law of God and the religious instruction of the young. In the past, we confronted major obstacles along this path and suffered irreplaceable losses. For years it was alleged that man did not need faith and that it would only harm him. For some time we lost our influence and could make no impact. All that remained to the Catholic Church was the pulpit. We did not have our own publication. In many instances we were unable to take any steps without the blessing and agreement from an official responsible for religious affairs. Outsiders interfered in the appointment of clergymen or the selection of students for a religious seminary. Today, this is no longer the case. The leadership of the republic has radically changed its attitude toward believers and faith itself [. . .]

'We hope that in time everything will work out. All the conditions for this are in place: there is no limit on the number of people entering religious seminaries any more; we are accumulating strength for work with high school students. We are confident that the number of Catholic priests will continue to grow steadily. At the same time, we need not only a large quantity of people but also good quality specialists. It will, most likely, take five or six years for a new generation of Catholic priests to appear.

'The problem with Roman Catholic churches is also being addressed. Some of them have already been returned; others will be returned in the not too distant future. We do not have any major difficulties in constructing new churches. However, it will not be easy for us to solve this question on our own, because our financial resources are rather limited. That is why we try to practice economy and moderation and demand that Roman Catholic priests do the same. Generally speaking, we are convinced that moderation is the clearest sign of wisdom. It reflects God's kindness. The Almighty is generous and kind; however, he takes care of all our needs at the right time and in the right way. This is the sign of divine wisdom. [. . .]

'Although Lithuania is small, our people are few and our land is not rich in natural resources that other nations enjoy and take pride in. We have folk simplicity and pride, sincerity and friendliness, that is, the spiritual values sustained by our faith. We are happy to see the church regain its treasures; however, it is even more significant that the church with all its spiritual wealth is returning to the people. It is coming back with its former influence.

'Easter's main theme is rebirth. It is the source of the greatest joy and a potent force stimulating all people to spiritual renewal and, in a broader context, to the national and spiritual rebirth of the nation. We, believers, are ready to travel Lithuania's road of renewal and to make our contribution toward its rebirth.'

Source: Igor Troyanovsky (ed.) *Religion in the Soviet Republics* (San Francisco: Harper, 1991), pp. 134–6.

PART THREE

—◆◆—

ISLAM

INTRODUCTION

— ◆◆◆ —

Islam recognises a prophetic tradition that has much in common with the lineage traced in Jewish and Christian scriptures. For Muslims, however, that line of prophecy became corrupted over time and thus needed both correction and fulfilment. To be a Muslim, one who accepts the will of God and is at peace with God, is to accept that this task was completed by the revelation of the *Qur'an* to the prophet Muhammad by the one true God, Allah. Muslims believe that the *Qur'an* is the very word of God, existing in eternity until revealed by Allah to his prophet. Just as Muhammad is the 'seal' of the prophets, so too the *Qur'an* constitutes Allah's complete and final guidance for human beings, correcting and perfecting the books given to earlier prophets. Although the *Qur'an* acknowledges certain individuals who had been 'Muslims' before Muhammad, recognising and responding to the divine will on the basis of personal experience, the mission of Muhammad led to the establishment of the first Muslim community. It derived its principles from the *Qur'an* and the precedents set by the Prophet. This was to evolve into a succession of Islamic empires and civilizations through conquest, trade and acculturation, regulated by Islamic legal codes. In the process, internal disputes over the succession to leadership of the Muslim community after the death of the Prophet led to the creation of Shi'ite Islam and Sunni Islam. The former, still very much a minority, look to leaders who claim direct descent from 'Ali, the Prophet's cousin. The latter recognise the authenticity of the line of caliphs ('successors') who ruled after the death of the Prophet, thus claiming to abide by the consensus of the community. Both these broad traditions differ to some extent in their theology, their legal systems and their practices. Shi'ite Islam is further subdivided.

Until the expansion of European colonialism, the experience of the vast majority of Muslims was confined to life within an Islamic culture in which the political institutions, the legal system and educational provision were founded upon the principles of the *Qur'an* and constructed by authoritative exponents of Islamic law. Although Muslims have debated the extent to which religion should be fused with the state and society, life under European colonial powers saw Muslims placed under non-Muslim law and their faith restricted to the personal sphere. After the decline of the Mughal empire in India at the end of the eighteenth century, the disintegrating Turkish Ottoman empire remained the only extensive region where Islam wielded political power. This came to an end after the First World War.

With the end of European colonialism and the growth of oil wealth, many Muslim countries recovered both their independence and their influence during the latter half of the twentieth century. This opened up new opportunities and triggered debates about what kind of state should be established, and whether the predominance of Muslims in a given country should be grounds for creating an Islamic state, one based on the integration of Muslim law with its political and social institutions. In countries such as Libya and Iran, resentment against the previous century of subordination to Europe and the United States brought together a desire to transform existing political structures with a violent rejection of American influence as the standard-bearer of capitalism. Out of this was born what has been popularly called 'Islamic fundamentalism'.

The readings begin with a series of translated passages from the *Qur'an*, which are followed by sections drawn from the mystical and legal traditions within Islam. The final selection of readings address the position of Islam in the late twentieth century from the perspective of the Muslim minority in Europe, a prominent woman commentator, and an academic analysing Islam as a political phenomenon.

FROM THE QUR'AN

——◆◆•——

3.1 II THE COW (EXTRACT)

It is not piety, that you turn your faces
    to the East and to the West.
      True piety is this:
to believe in God, and the Last Day,
the angels, the Book, and the Prophets,
to give of one's substance, however cherished,
    to kinsmen, and orphans,
the needy, the traveller, beggars,
    and to ransom the slave,
to perform the prayer, to pay the alms.
And they who fulfil their covenant
when they have engaged in a covenant,
    and endure with fortitude
    misfortune, hardship and peril,
these are they who are true in their faith,
    these are the truly godfearing.

O believers, prescribed for you is
retaliation, touching the slain;
freeman for freeman, slave for slave,
female for female. But if aught is pardoned
a man by his brother, let the pursuing

be honourable, and let the payment be
with kindliness. That is a lightening
granted you by your Lord, and a mercy;
and for him who commits aggression
after that – for him there awaits
    a painful chastisement.
175   In retaliation there is life for you,
men possessed of minds; haply you
      will be godfearing.

O believers, prescribed for you is
the Fast, even as it was prescribed for
those that were before you – haply you
      will be godfearing –
180   for days numbered; and if any of you
be sick, or if he be on a journey,
then a number of other days; and for those
who are able to fast, a redemption
by feeding a poor man. Yet better
it is for him who volunteers good,
and that you should fast is better for you,
      if you but know;
the month of Ramadan, wherein the Koran
was sent down to be a guidance
to the people, and as clear signs
of the Guidance and the Salvation.
So let those of you, who are present
at the month, fast it; and if any of you
be sick, or if he be on a journey,
then a number of other days; God desires
ease for you, and desires not hardship
for you; and that you fulfil the number, and
magnify God that He has guided you, and haply
      you will be thankful.

And when My servants question thee
concerning Me – I am near to answer
the call of the caller, when he calls
to Me; so let them respond to Me,
and let them believe in Me; haply so
      they will go aright.

Permitted to you, upon the night of
the Fast, is to go in to your wives;
they are a vestment for you, and you are
a vestment for them. God knows that you have been
betraying yourselves, and has turned to you

and pardoned you. So now lie with them,
and seek what God has prescribed for you.
And eat and drink, until the white thread
shows clearly to you from the black thread
at the dawn; then complete the Fast
unto the night, and do not lie with them
while you cleave to the mosques. Those are
God's bounds; keep well within them. So God
makes clear His signs to men; haply they
    will be godfearing.

Consume not your goods between you
in vanity; neither proffer it
to the judges, that you may sinfully
consume a portion of other men's goods,
    and that wittingly.

185   They will question thee concerning
the new moons. Say: 'They are appointed
times for the people, and the Pilgrimage.'

It is not piety to come to the houses
from the backs of them; but piety is
to be godfearing; so come to the houses
by their doors, and fear God; haply so
    you will prosper.

And fight in the way of God with those
who fight with you, but aggress not: God loves
    not the aggressors.
And slay them wherever you come upon them,
and expel them from where they expelled you;
persecution is more grievous than slaying.
But fight them not by the Holy Mosque
until they should fight you there;
then, if they fight you, slay them –
such is the recompense of unbelievers –
but if they give over, surely God is
All-forgiving, All-compassionate.

Fight them, till there is no persecution
and the religion is God's; then if they
give over, there shall be no enmity
    save for evildoers.
190   The holy month for the holy month;
holy things demand retaliation.
Whoso commits aggression against you,

do you commit aggression against him
like as he has committed against you;
and fear you God, and know that God is
        with the godfearing.

And expend in the way of God;
and cast not yourselves by your own hands
into destruction, but be good-doers; God
        loves the good-doers.

Fulfil the Pilgrimage and the Visitation
unto God; but if you are prevented,
then such offering as may be feasible.
And shave not your heads, till the offering
reaches its place of sacrifice. If any
of you is sick, or injured in his head,
then redemption by fast, or freewill offering,
or ritual sacrifice. When you are secure,
then whosoever enjoys the Visitation
until the Pilgrimage, let his offering
be such as may be feasible; or if he
finds none, then a fast of three days
in the Pilgrimage, and of seven when
you return, that is ten completely;
that is for him, whose family are not
present at the Holy Mosque. And fear
God, and know that God is terrible
        in retribution.

The Pilgrimage is in months well-known;
whoso undertakes the duty of Pilgrimage
in them shall not go in to his womenfolk
nor indulge in ungodliness and disputing
in the Pilgrimage. Whatever good you do,
God knows it. And take provision;
but the best provision is godfearing,
so fear you Me, men possessed of minds!
It is no fault in you, that you should seek
bounty from your Lord; but when you press on
from Arafat, then remember God
at the Holy Waymark, and remember Him
as He has guided you, though formerly you
        were gone astray.

195   Then press on from where the people
        press on, and pray for God's forgiveness;
        God is All-forgiving, All-compassionate.

And when you have performed your holy rites
remember God, as you remember your fathers
or yet more devoutly. Now some men
there are who say, 'Our Lord, give to us
in this world'; such men shall have no part
in the world to come.

And others there are who say, 'Our Lord,
give to us in this world good, and good
in the world to come, and guard us against the
chastisement of the Fire';
those – they shall have a portion from
what they have earned; and God is swift
at the reckoning.

And remember God during certain days
numbered. If any man hastens on
in two days, that is no sin in him;
and if any delays, it is not a sin
in him, if he be godfearing. And
fear you God, and know that unto Him
you shall be mustered.

3.2 XVII THE NIGHT JOURNEY (EXTRACT)

Set not up with God
another god, or thou
wilt sit condemned
and forsaken.
Thy Lord has decreed
you shall not serve
any but Him,
and to be good to parents,
whether one or both of them
attains old age with thee;
say not to them 'Fie'
neither chide them, but
speak unto them words
respectful,
25 and lower to them the
wing of humbleness
out of mercy and say,
'My Lord,
have mercy upon them,
as they raised me up
when I was little.'

Your Lord knows very well what is in your hearts
    if you are righteous,
for He is All-forgiving to those who are penitent.
    And give the kinsman his right,
    and the needy, and the traveller;
      and never squander;
    the squanderers are brothers of
    Satan, and Satan is unthankful
      to his Lord.
30   But if thou turnest from them,
    seeking mercy from thy Lord that
    thou hopest for, then speak unto
      them gentle words.
    And keep not thy hand chained
    to thy neck, nor outspread it
    widespread altogether, or thou
      wilt sit reproached
        and denuded.
Surely thy Lord outspreads and straitens His provision
    unto whom He will;
  surely He is aware of and sees His servants.

And slay not your children for fear of poverty;
    We will provide for you and them;
  surely the slaying of them is a grievous sin.
    And approach not fornication;
  surely it is an indecency, and evil as a way.
35   And slay not the soul God has
forbidden, except by right. Whosoever is slain
    unjustly, We have appointed to
his next-of-kin authority; but let him not exceed
    in slaying; he shall be helped.

And do not approach the property of the orphan
save in the fairest manner, until he is of age.
And fulfil the covenant; surely the covenant
    shall be questioned of.
And fill up the measure when you measure, and
weigh with the straight balance; that is better
    and fairer in the issue.
And pursue not that thou hast no knowledge of;
the hearing, the sight, the heart – all of those
    shall be questioned of.
And walk not in the earth exultantly; certainly
thou wilt never tear the earth open, nor attain
    the mountains in height.
40 All of that – the wickedness of it is hateful
    in the sight of thy Lord.

That is of the wisdom thy Lord has revealed to thee:
    set not up with God
    another god, or thou
    will be cast into
    Gehenna, reproached
      and rejected.

3.3 XXIII THE BELIEVERS (EXTRACT)

In the Name of God, the Merciful, the Compassionate

    Prosperous are the believers
    who in their prayers are humble
    and from idle talk turn away
    and at almsgiving are active
5   and guard their private parts
save from their wives and what their right hands own
      then being not blameworthy
    (but whosoever seeks after more than that,
      those are the transgressors)
    and who preserve their trusts
      and their covenant
    and who observe their prayers.
10   Those are the inheritors
    who shall inherit Paradise
    therein dwelling forever.

    We created man of an extraction
      of clay,
then We set him, a drop, in a receptacle
      secure,
    then We created of the drop a clot
    then We created of the clot a tissue
    then We created of the tissue bones
    then We garmented the bones in flesh;
thereafter We produced him as another creature.
So blessed be God, the fairest of creators!
15   Then after that you shall surely die,
    then on the Day of Resurrection you
      shall surely be raised up.
    And We created above you seven ways,
    and We were not heedless of creation.

    And We sent down out of heaven water
    in measure and lodged it in the earth;

and We are able to take it away.
Then We produced for you therewith
gardens of palms and vines
wherein are many fruits for
you, and of them you eat,
20 and a tree issuing from the Mount of Sinai that
bears oil and seasoning
for all to eat.
And surely in the cattle there is a lesson for you;
We give you to drink of
what is in their bellies,
and many uses there are in them for you,
and of them you eat;
and upon them, and on the ships, you are borne.

And We sent Noah to his people;
and he said, 'O my people, serve God!
You have no god other than He.
Will you not be godfearing?'
Said the Council of the unbelievers
of his people, 'This is naught but
a mortal like yourselves, who desires
to gain superiority over you. And
if God willed, He would have sent down
angels. We never heard of this among
our fathers, the ancients.
25 He is naught but a man bedevilled; so
wait on him for a time.'
He said, 'O my Lord, help me,
for that they cry me lies.'
Then We said to him, 'Make thou the Ark
under Our eyes and as We reveal,
and then, when Our command comes
and the Oven boils,
insert in it two of every kind
and thy family – except for him
against whom the word already
has been spoken; and address Me not
concerning those who have done evil;
they shall be drowned.
Then, when thou art seated in the Ark
and those with thee, say, "Praise belongs to
God, who has delivered us from the people
of the evildoers."
30 And say, "O my Lord, do Thou harbour
me in a blessed harbour, for Thou art
the best of harbourers."'

Surely in that are signs, and surely
   We put to the test.

Thereafter, after them, We produced
   another generation,
and We sent amongst them a Messenger
of themselves, saying, 'Serve God!
You have no god other than He.
   Will you not be godfearing?'
Said the Council of the unbelievers
of his people, who cried lies to the
encounter of the world to come,
and to whom We had given ease in the
present life, 'This is naught but
a mortal like yourselves, who eats
   of what you eat
35   and drinks of what you drink.
If you obey a mortal like yourselves,
   then you will be losers.
What, does he promise you that when you are
dead, and become dust and bones, you
   shall be brought forth?
     Away, away
   with that you are promised!
There is nothing but our present life;
we die, and we live, and we shall
   not be raised up.
40   He is naught but a man who has forged
against God a lie, and we will
   not believe him.'
He said, 'O my Lord, help me,
   for that they cry me lies.'
He said, 'In a little they will
   be remorseful.'
And the Cry seized them justly, and We
made them as scum; so away with the people
   of the evildoers!

Thereafter, after them, We produced
   other generations;
45   no nation outstrips its term, nor
   do they put it back.
Then sent We Our Messengers successively;
whenever its Messenger came to a nation
they cried him lies, so We caused some
of them to follow others, and We made them
as but tales; so away with a people
   who do not believe!

Then we sent Moses and his brother
Aaron with Our signs and a manifest
   authority
unto Pharaoh and his Council;
but they waxed proud, and they were
   a lofty people,
and they said, 'What, shall we believe
two mortals like ourselves, whose people
   are our servants?'
50   So they cried them lies, and they were
   among the destroyed.

And We gave Moses the Book, that haply
   they would be guided;
and We made Mary's sons, and his mother,
to be a sign, and gave them refuge
upon a height, where was a hollow
   and a spring:
'O Messengers, eat of the good things
and do righteousness; surely I know
   the things you do.
Surely this community of yours
is one community, and I am your Lord;
   so Fear Me.'
But they split in their affair between them
into sects, each party rejoicing in
   what is with them.
So leave thou them in their perplexity
   for a time.
What, do they think that We succour them with
   of wealth and children
We vie in good works for them? Nay, but
   they are not aware.

Surely those who tremble in fear of their Lord
60   and those who believe in the signs of their Lord
and those who associate naught with their Lord
and those who give what they give, their hearts
quaking that they are returning to their Lord –
those vie in good works, outracing to them.

We charge not any soul save to its capacity,
and with Us is a Book speaking truth, and
   they shall not be wronged.
65   Nay, but their hearts are in perplexity
as to this, and they have deeds besides that
   that they are doing.

Till, when We seize with the chastisement
the ones of them that live at ease,
   behold, they groan.
'Groan not today; surely you shall not be
   helped from Us.
My signs were recited to you, but upon your
   heels you withdrew,
waxing proud against it, talking foolish
   talk by night.'

70   Have they not pondered the saying, or came there
upon them that which came not upon their
   fathers, the ancients?
Or did they not recognise their Messenger
   and so denied him?
Or do they say, 'He is bedevilled'? Nay,
he has brought them the truth, but most of them are
   averse from the truth.
Had the truth followed their caprices,
the heavens and the earth and whosoever
in them is had surely corrupted. Nay, We
brought them their Remembrance, but from their
   Remembrance they turned.
Or dost thou ask them for tribute? Yet the
tribute of thy Lord is better, and He is the
   best of providers.

75   Assuredly thou art calling them
   to a straight path;
and surely they that believe not
in the world to come are deviating
   from the path.
Did We have mercy on them, and remove
the affliction that is upon them,
they would persist in their insolence
   wandering blindly.
We already seized them with the chastisement,
yet they abased not themselves to their Lord
   nor were they humble;
until, when We open against them a door
of terrible chastisement, lo, they are sore
   confounded at it.

80   It is He who produced for you hearing, and eyes, and hearts;
   little thanks you show.
It is He who scattered you in the earth, and to Him
   you shall be mustered.
It is He who gives life, and makes to die, and to Him

belongs the alternation of night and day; what,
  will you not understand?
Nay, but they said the like of what
  the ancients said.
They said, 'What, when we are dead
and become dust and bones, shall we be
  indeed raised up?
85 We and our fathers have been promised this
before; this is naught but the fairy-tales
  of the ancients.'
Say: 'Whose is the earth, and whoso is in it,
  if you have knowledge?'
They will say, 'God's.' Say: 'Will you not
  then remember?'
Say: 'Who is the Lord of the seven heavens
  and the Lord of the mighty Throne?'
They will say, 'God's.' Say: 'Will you not
  then be godfearing?'
Say: 'In whose hand is the dominion of
everything, protecting and Himself unprotected,
  if you have knowledge?'
They will say, 'God's.' Say: 'How then
  are you bewitched?'
Nay, but we brought them the truth, and they
  are truly liars.
God has not taken to Himself any son,
nor is there any god with Him; for then
each god would have taken off that he created
and some of them would have risen up
over others; glory to be God, beyond
  that they describe,
who has knowledge of the Unseen and the
Visible; high exalted be He, above
  that they associate!

95 Say: 'O my Lord, if Thou shouldst show me
  that they are promised,
O my Lord, put me not among the people
  of the evildoers.'
Assuredly, We are able to show thee
  that We promise them.
Repel thou the evil with that which is
fairer. We Ourselves know very well
  that they describe.
And say: 'O my Lord, I take refuge
in Thee from the evil suggestions
  of the Satans,

100 and I take refuge in Thee, O my Lord,
    lest they attend me.'
Till, when death comes to one of them, he says,
    'My Lord, return me;
haply I shall do righteousness in that
I forsook.' Nay, it is but a word
he speaks; and there, behind them,
Is a barrier until the day that they
    shall be raised up.

For when the Trumpet is blown, that day there shall be no
    kinship
any more between them, neither will they question one
    another.
Then he whose scales are heavy – they are the prosperers,
105 and he whose scales are light – they have lost their souls
in Gehenna dwelling forever, the Fire smiting their faces
the while they glower there. 'What, were My signs not recited
to you, and you cried them lies?' They shall say, 'Our Lord,
our adversity prevailed over us; we were an erring people.
Our Lord, bring us forth out of it! Then, if we revert,
110 we shall be evildoers indeed.' 'Slink you into it.'

3.4 XXIV LIGHT (EXTRACT)

35 God is the Light of the heavens and the earth;
    the likeness of His Light is as a niche
        wherein is a lamp
        (the lamp in a glass,
    the glass as it were a glittering star)
        kindled from a Blessed Tree,
    an olive that is neither of the East nor of the West
whose oil wellnigh would shine, even if no fire touched it;
        Light upon Light;
    (God guides to His Light whom He will.)
    (And God strikes similitudes for men,
    and God has knowledge of everything.)
    in temples God has allowed to be raised up,
    and His Name to be commemorated therein;
therein glorifying Him, in the mornings and the evenings,
    are men whom neither commerce nor trafficking
        diverts from the remembrance of God
    and to perform the prayer, and to pay the alms,
fearing a day when hearts and eyes shall be turned about,
that God may recompense them for their fairest works

and give them increase of His bounty;
and God provides whomsoever He will, without reckoning.

And as for the unbelievers,
their works are as a mirage in a spacious plain
    which the man athirst supposes to be water,
till, when he comes to it, he finds it is nothing;
        there indeed he finds God,
and He pays him his account in full; (and God is swift
            at the reckoning.)
40   or they are as shadows upon a sea obscure
            covered by a billow
            above which is a billow
            above which are clouds,
        shadows piled one upon another;
when he puts forth his hand, wellnigh he cannot see it.
    And to whomsoever God assigns no light,
            no light has he.

Hast thou not seen how that whatsoever is in the heavens
        and in the earth extols God,
        and the birds spreading their wings?
Each – He knows its prayer and its extolling; and God knows
            the things they do.
To God belongs the Kingdom of the heavens and the earth,
        and to Him is the homecoming.
Hast thou not seen how God drives the clouds, then composes
    them,
        then converts them into a mass,
then thou seest the rain issuing out of the midst of them?
And He sends down out of heaven mountains, wherein is hail,
so that He smites whom He will with it, and turns it aside
            from whom He will;
wellnigh the gleam of His lightning snatches away the sight.
        God turns about the day and the night;
    surely in that is a lesson for those who have eyes.
        God has created every beast of water,
        and some of them go upon their bellies,
        and some of them go upon two feet,
        and some of them go upon four; God
        creates whatever He will; God is powerful
            over everything.

3.5 XXXVI YA SIN (EXTRACT)

And the Trumpet shall be blown; then behold, they are sliding down
    from their tombs unto their Lord.
They say, 'Alas for us! Who roused us out of our sleeping-place?
This is what the All-merciful promised, and the Envoys spoke truly.'
'It was only one Cry; then behold, they are all arraigned before Us.
So today no soul shall be wronged anything, and you shall not be
recompensed, except according to what you have been doing.
55   See, the inhabitants of Paradise today are busy in their rejoicing,
they and their spouses, reclining upon couches in the shade;
therein they have fruits, and they have all that they call for.
'Peace!' – such is the greeting, from a Lord All-compassionate.
'Now keep yourselves apart, you sinners, upon this day!
60   Made I not convenant with you, Children of Adam, that you
should not serve Satan – surely he is a manifest foe to you –
and that you should serve Me? This is a straight path.
He led astray many a throng of you; did you not understand?
This is Gehenna, then, the same that you were promised;
roast well in it today, for that you were unbelievers!'
65   Today We set a seal on their mouths, and their hands speak to Us,
and their feet bear witness as to what they have been earning.

3.6 LII THE MOUNT (EXTRACT)

Surely the godfearing shall be in gardens and bliss,
    rejoicing in that their Lord has given them;
and their Lord shall guard them against the chastisement of Hell.
    'Eat and drink, with wholesome appetite, for that you were working.'
20   Reclining upon couches ranged in rows;
and We shall espouse them to wide-eyed houris.
And those who believed, and their seed followed them
in belief, We shall join their seed with them, and We
shall not defraud them of aught of their work;
every man shall be pledged for what he earned.
And We shall succour them with fruits and flesh such as they desire
while they pass therein a cup one to another
wherein is no idle talk, no cause of sin,
and there go round them youths, their own,
    as if they were hidden pearls.
25   They advance one upon another, asking each other questions.
They say, 'We were before among our people, ever going in fear,
and God was gracious to us, and guarded us
against the chastisement of the burning wind;
we were before ever calling upon Him; surely
He is the All-benign, the All-compassionate.'

3.7 LVII IRON (EXTRACT)

In the Name of God, the Merciful, the Compassionate

All that is in the heavens and the earth magnifies God;
  He is the All-mighty, the All-wise.
To Him belongs the Kingdom of the heavens and the earth;
He gives life, and He makes to die, and He is powerful
   over everything.
He is the First and the Last, the Outward and the Inward;
  He has knowledge of everything.
  It is He that created the heavens and the earth
   in six days
  then seated Himself upon the Throne.
  He knows what penetrates into the earth,
   and what comes forth from it,
  what comes down from heaven, and what goes up unto it.
   He is with you wherever you are; and God sees
    the things you do.

5 To Him belongs the Kingdom of the heavens and the earth;
   and unto Him all matters are returned.
  He makes the night to enter into the day
  and makes the day to enter into the night.
  He knows the thoughts within the breasts.

Believe in God and His Messenger, and expend of
that unto which He has made you successors. And
those of you who believe and expend shall have
   a mighty wage.
How is it with you, that you believe not in God
seeing that the Messenger is calling you to
believe in your Lord, and He has taken compact
   with you, if you are believers?
It is He who sends down upon His servant signs,
clear signs, that He may bring you forth from
the shadows into the light. Surely God is to you
   All-gentle, All-compassionate.

10 How is it with you, that you expend not in the
way of God, and to God belongs the inheritance
of the heavens and the earth? Not equal is he
among you who spent, and who fought before the
victory; those are mightier in rank than they
who spent and fought afterwards; and unto each
God has promised the reward most fair; and God
   is aware of the things you do.
Who is he that will lend to God a good loan,
and He will multiply it for him, and his shall be
   a generous wage?

Upon the day when thou seest the believers, men and women,
their light running before them, and on their right hands.
'Good tidings for you today! Gardens underneath which
rivers flow, therein to dwell for ever; that is indeed
    the mighty triumph.'
Upon the day when the hypocrites, men and women, shall say
to those who have believed, 'Wait for us, so that we may
borrow your light!' It shall be said, 'Return you back
behind, and seek for a light!' And a wall shall be set up
between them, having a door in the inward whereof is
mercy, and against the outward thereof is chastisement.
They shall be calling unto them, 'Were we not with you?'
They shall say, 'Yes indeed; but you tempted yourselves,
and you awaited, and you were in doubt, and fancies
deluded you, until God's commandment came, and the
Deluder deluded you concerning God. Therefore today
no ransom shall be taken from you, neither from those who
disbelieved. Your refuge is the Fire, that is your master –
    an evil homecoming!'

15 Is it not time that the hearts of those
who believe should be humbled to the
Remembrance of God and the Truth which
He has sent down, and that they should
not be as those to whom the Book was
given aforetime, and the term seemed
over long to them, so that their hearts
have become hard, and many of them
    are ungodly?
Know that God revives the earth after
it was dead. We have indeed made clear
for you the signs, that haply you will
    understand.
Surely those, the men and the women,
who make freewill offerings and have
lent to God a good loan, it shall be
multiplied for them, and theirs shall be
    a generous wage.
And those who believe in God and His
Messengers – they are the just men
and the martyrs in their Lord's sight;
they have their wage, and their light.
But the unbelievers, who have cried lies
to Our signs, they are the inhabitants
    of Hell.
Know that the present life is but a
sport and a diversion, an adornment

and a cause for boasting among you,
and a rivalry in wealth and children.
It is as a rain whose vegetation
pleases the unbelievers; then it
withers, and thou seest it turning
yellow, then it becomes broken orts.
And in the world to come there is a
      terrible chastisement,
20   and forgiveness from God and good pleasure;
and the present life is but the joy
      of delusion.
Race to forgiveness from your Lord,
and a Garden the breadth whereof is
as the breadth of heaven and earth,
made ready for those who believe in
God and His Messengers. That is the
bounty of God; He gives it unto
whomsoever He will; and God is of
      bounty abounding.
No affliction befalls in the earth
or in yourselves, but it is in a
Book, before We create it; that is
      easy for God;
that you may not grieve for what
escapes you, nor rejoice in what has
come to you; God loves not any man
      proud and boastful,
such as are niggardly, and bid men
to be niggardly. And whosoever
turns away, God is the All-sufficient,
      the All-laudable.

25   Indeed, We sent Our Messengers with
the clear signs, and We sent down
with them the Book and the Balance
so that men might uphold justice.
And we sent down iron, wherein is
great might, and many uses for men,
and so that God might know who
helps Him, and His Messengers,
in the Unseen. Surely God is
      All-strong, All-mighty.
And We sent Noah, and Abraham,
and We appointed the Prophecy and
the Book to be among their seed; and
some of them are guided, and many of
      them are ungodly.

Then We sent, following
in their footsteps, Our
Messengers; and We sent,
following, Jesus son of
Mary, and gave unto him
    the Gospel.
And We set in the hearts of those who
followed him tenderness and mercy.

And monasticism they invented – We
did not prescribe it for them – only
seeking the good pleasure of God; but
they observed it not as it should be
observed. So We gave those of them
who believed their wage; and many of
    them are ungodly.

O believers, fear God, and believe
in His Messenger, and He will give you
a twofold portion of His mercy, and
He will appoint for you a light whereby
you shall walk, and forgive you; God is
    All-forgiving, All-compassionate;
that the People of the Book may know
that they have no power over anything
of God's bounty, and that bounty is in
the hand of God; He gives it unto
whomsoever He will; and God is of
    bounty abounding.

3.8 LIX THE MUSTERING (EXTRACT)

O believers, fear God. Let every soul
consider what it has forwarded for the
morrow. And fear God; God is aware of
    the things you do.
Be not as those who forgot God, and so He
caused them to forget their souls, those –
    they are the ungodly.
20   Not equal are the inhabitants of the
Fire and the inhabitants of Paradise.
The inhabitants of Paradise – they
    are the triumphant.

If We had sent down this Koran upon a mountain,
thou wouldst have seen it humbled, split asunder
    out of the fear of God.

And those similitudes – We strike them for men;
    haply they will reflect.

    He is God;
    there is no god but He.
He is the knower of the Unseen and the Visible;
He is the All-merciful, the All-compassionate.

    He is God;
    there is no god but He.
He is the King, the All-holy, the All-peaceable,
    the All-faithful, the All-preserver,
    the All-mighty, the All-compeller,
    the All-sublime.
Glory be to God, above that they associate!

    He is God,
    the Creator, the Maker, the Shaper.
To Him belong the Names Most Beautiful.
All that is in the heavens and the earth magnifies Him;
    He is the All-mighty, the All-wise.

3.9 XC THE LAND

In the Name of God, the Merciful, the Compassionate

    No! I swear by this land,
    and thou art a lodger in this land;
    by the begetter, and that he begot,
    indeed, We created man in trouble.
What, does he think none has power over him,
saying, 'I have consumed wealth abundant'?
    What, does he think none has seen him?

Have We not appointed to him two eyes,
    and a tongue, and two lips,
and guided him on the two highways?
    Yet he has not assaulted the steep;
and what shall teach thee what is the steep?
    The freeing of a slave,
    or giving food upon a day of hunger
    to an orphan near of kin
    or a needy man in misery;
then that he become of those who believe
and counsel each other to be steadfast,
and counsel each other to be merciful.

Those are the Companions of the Right Hand.
And those who disbelieve in Our signs,
they are the Companions of the Left Hand;
over them is a Fire covered down.

3.10 XCI THE SUN

In the Name of God, the Merciful, the Compassionate

By the sun and his morning brightness
and by the moon when she follows him,
and by the day when it displays him
and by the night when it enshrouds him!
By the heaven and That which built it
and by the earth and That which extended it!
By the soul, and That which shaped it
and inspired it to lewdness and godfearing!
Prosperous is he who purifies it,
and failed has he who seduces it.

Thamood cried lies in their insolence
when the most wretched of them uprose,
then the Messenger of God said to them,
'The She-camel of God; let her drink!'
But they cried him lies, and hamstrung her,
so their Lord crushed them for their sin, and levelled them:
and He fears not the issue thereof.

3.11 XCII THE NIGHT

In the Name of God, the Merciful, the Compassionate

By the night enshrouding
and the day in splendour
and That which created the male and the female,
surely your striving is to diverse ends.

As for him who gives and is godfearing
and confirms the reward most fair,
We shall surely ease him to the Easing.
But as for him who is a miser, and self-sufficient,
and cries lies to the reward most fair,
We shall surely ease him to the Hardship;
his wealth shall not avail him when he perishes.

Surely upon Us rests the guidance,
and to Us belong the Last and the First.

Now I have warned you of a Fire that flames,
whereat none but the most wretched shall be roasted,
even he who cried lies, and turned away;
and from which the most godfearing shall be removed,
even he who gives his wealth to purify himself
and confers no favour on any man for recompense,
only seeking the Face of his Lord the Most High;
and he shall surely be satisfied.

3.12 XCIII THE FORENOON

In the Name of God, the Merciful, the Compassionate

By the white forenoon
and the brooding night!
Thy Lord has neither foresaken thee nor hates thee
and the Last shall be better for thee than the First.
Thy Lord shall give thee, and thou shalt be satisfied.

Did He not find thee an orphan, and shelter thee?
Did He not find thee erring, and guide thee?
Did He not find thee needy, and suffice thee?

As for the orphan, do not oppress him,
As for the beggar, scold him not;
and as for thy Lord's blessing, declare it.

3.13 XCIV THE EXPANDING

In the Name of God, the Merciful, the Compassionate

Did We not expand thy breast for thee
and lift from thee thy burden,
the burden that weighed down thy back?
Did We not exalt thy fame?

So truly with hardship comes ease,
Truly with hardship comes ease.
So, when thou art empty, labour,
and let thy Lord be thy Quest.

3.14 XCV THE FIG

In the Name of God, the Merciful, the Compassionate

By the fig and the olive
and the Mount Sinai
and this land secure!
We indeed created Man in the fairest stature
then We restored him the lowest of the low –
save those who believe, and do righteous deeds;
they shall have a wage unfailing.

What then shall cry thee lies as to the Doom?
Is not God the justest of judges?

3.15 XCVI THE BLOOD-CLOT

In the Name of God, the Merciful, the Compassionate

Recite: In the Name of thy Lord who created,
created Man of a blood-clot.
Recite: And thy Lord is the Most Generous,
who taught by the Pen,
taught Man that he knew not.

No indeed; surely Man waxes insolent,
for he thinks himself self-sufficient.
Surely unto thy Lord is the Returning.

What thinkest thou? He who forbids
a servant when he prays –
What thinkest thou? If he were upon guidance
or bade to godfearing –
What thinkest thou? If he cries lies, and turns away –
Did he not know that God sees?

No indeed; surely, if he gives not over,
We shall seize him by the forelock,
a lying, sinful forelock.
So let him call on his concourse!
We shall call on the guards of Hell.

No indeed; do thou not obey him,
and bow thyself, and draw nigh.

3.16 XCVII POWER

In the Name of God the Merciful, the Compassionate

Behold, We sent it down on the Night of Power;
And what shall teach thee what is the Night of Power?
The Night of Power is better than a thousand months;
in it the angels and the Spirit descend,
by the leave of their Lord, upon every command,
Peace it is, till the rising of dawn.

3.17 XCVIII THE CLEAR SIGN

In the Name of God, the Merciful, the Compassionate

The unbelievers of the People of the Book
and the idolaters would never leave off,
till the Clear Sign came to them,
a Messenger from God, reciting pages purified
therein true Books.
And they scattered not, those that were given the Book,
excepting after the Clear Sign came to them.
They were commanded only to serve God,
making the religion His sincerely,
men of pure faith, and to perform
the prayer, and pay the alms – that is
the religion of the True.

The unbelievers of the People of the Book
and the idolaters shall be in the Fire of Gehenna,
therein dwelling forever;
those are the worst of creatures.
But those who believe, and do righteous deeds,
those are the best of creatures;
their recompense is with their Lord –
Gardens of Eden, underneath which rivers flow,
therein dwelling for ever and ever.
God is well-pleased with them, and they are well-pleased with Him;
that is for him who fears his Lord.

3.18 XCIX THE EARTHQUAKE

In the Name of God, the Merciful, the Compassionate

When earth is shaken with a mighty shaking

and earth brings forth her burdens,
and Man says, 'What ails her?'
upon that day she shall tell her tidings
for that her Lord has inspired her.

Upon that day men shall issue in scatterings to see their works,
and whoso has done an atom's weight of good shall see it,
and whoso has done an atom's weight of evil shall see it.

3.19 C THE CHARGERS

In the Name of God, the Merciful, the Compassionate

By the snorting chargers,
by the strikers of fire,
by the dawn-raiders,
blazing a trail of dust,
cleaving there with a host!
Surely Man is ungrateful to his Lord,
and surely he is a witness against that!
Surely he is passionate in his love for good things.
Knows he not that when that which is in the tombs is overthrown,
and that which is in the breasts is brought out –
surely on that day their Lord shall be aware of them!

3.20 CI THE CLATTERER

In the Name of God, the Merciful, the Compassionate

The Clatterer! What is the Clatterer
And what shall teach thee what is the Clatterer?
The day that men shall be like scattered moths,
and the mountains shall be like plucked wool-tufts.

Then he whose deeds weigh heavy in the Balance
shall inherit a pleasing life,
but he whose deeds weigh light in the Balance
shall plunge in the womb of the Pit.
And what shall teach thee what is the Pit?
A blazing Fire!

3.21 CII RIVALRY

In the Name of God, the Merciful, the Compassionate

Gross rivalry diverts you,
even till you visit the tombs,
No indeed; but soon you shall know.
Again, no indeed; but soon you shall know.
No indeed; did you know with the knowledge of certainty,
you shall surely see Hell.
Again, you shall surely see it with the eye of uncertainty
then you shall be questioned that day concerning true bliss.

3.22 CIII AFTERNOON

In the Name of God, the Merciful, the Compassionate

By the afternoon!
Surely Man is in the way of loss,
save those who believe, and do righteous deeds,
and counsel each other unto the truth,
and counsel each other to be steadfast.

3.23 CIV THE BACKBITER

In the Name of God, the Merciful, the Compassionate

Woe unto every backbiter, slanderer,
who has gathered riches and counted them over
thinking his riches have made him immortal!

No indeed; he shall be thrust into the Crusher;
and what shall teach thee what is the Crusher?
The Fire of God kindled
roaring over the hearts
covered down upon them,
in columns outstretched.

3.24 CV THE ELEPHANT

In the Name of God, the Merciful, the Compassionate

Hast thou not seen how thy Lord did with the Men of the Elephant?
Did He not make their guile to go astray?
And He loosed upon them birds in flights,
hurling against them stones of baked clay
and He made them like green blades devoured.

3.25 CVI KORAISH

In the Name of God, the Merciful, the Compassionate

For the composing of Koraish,
their composing for the winter and summer caravan!

So let them serve the Lord of this House
who has fed them against hunger,
and secured them from fear.

3.26 CVII CHARITY

In the Name of God, the Merciful, the Compassionate

Hast thou seen him who cries lies to the Doom?
That is he who repulses the orphan
and urges not the feeding of the needy.

So woe to those that pray
and are heedless of their prayers,
to those who make display
and refuse charity.

3.27 CVIII ABUNDANCE

In the Name of God, the Merciful, the Compassionate

Surely We have given thee abundance;
so pray unto thy Lord and sacrifice.
Surely he that hates thee, he is the one cut off.

3.28 CIX THE UNBELIEVERS

In the Name of God, the Merciful, the Compassionate

Say: 'O unbelievers,

I serve not what you serve
and you are not serving what I serve,
nor am I serving what you have served,
neither are you serving what I serve.

To you your religion, and to me my religion!'

3.29 CX HELP

In the Name of God, the Merciful, the Compassionate

When comes the help of God, and victory
and thou seest men entering God's religion in throngs,
then proclaim the praise of thy Lord, and seek His forgiveness;
for He turns again unto men.

3.30 CXI PERISH

In the Name of God, the Merciful, the Compassionate

Perish the hands of Abu Lahab, and perish he!
His wealth avails him not, neither what he has earned;
he shall roast at a flaming fire
and his wife, the carrier of the firewood,
upon her neck a rope of palm-fibre.

3.31 CXII SINCERE RELIGION

In the Name of God, the Merciful, the Compassionate

Say: 'He is God, One,
God, the Everlasting Refuge,
who has not begotten, and has not been begotten,
and equal to Him is not any one.'

3.32 CXIII DAYBREAK

In the Name of God, the Merciful, the Compassionate

Say: 'I take refuge with the Lord of the Daybreak
from the evil of what He has created,
from the evil of darkness when it gathers,

from the evil of the women who blow on knots,
from the evil of an envier when he envies.'

3.33 CXIV MEN

In the Name of God, the Merciful, the Compassionate

Say: 'I take refuge with the Lord of men,
　　　　the King of men,
　　　　the God of men,
　　from the evil of the slinking whisperer
　　who whispers in the breasts of men
　　　　of jinn and men.'

Source: A. J. Arberry (trans.) *The Koran Interpreted* (Allen & Unwin, 1964), Surahs 2, 17, 23, 24, 36, 52, 57, 90–114.

—— ●◆● ——

THE BEAUTIFUL NAMES

— • ◆ • —

3.34

ABU HAMID AL-GHAZALI

Abu Hamid al-Ghazali (1058–1111 CE) was a renowned Muslim scholar and mystic. Although he never entirely abandoned his life as a scholar and teacher, in 1096 CE he became a Sufi and subsequently followed an ascetic lifestyle. It has been said that it was largely due to the influence of al-Ghazali that Sufism came to be accepted within mainstream Islam. Al-Ghazali is one of several Muslims who has written a commentary on the ninety-nine Beautiful Names of God that are often recited while using a string of ninety-nine beads.

3.34.1 The Great

You must know that the word 'great' was applied to physical bodies in its original coinage. Thus one says: 'This body is great and this body is greater than that body', if it is more extended in respect of length, width and depth.

Then you must know that it is divided into (a) the 'greatness' of which the eye receives an impression and (b) that whose extremities it is inconceivable that vision could grasp completely, such as the earth and the heavens. Thus one says that the elephant is 'great', and the mountain is 'great', and yet vision is able to grasp their extremities completely. Either of these is 'great' in comparison with that which is smaller than it. As far as the earth is concerned, it is inconceivable that vision should be able to grasp its extremities completely, and this is true also of the heavens. It is to these objects in the realm of those things subject to physical vision that the term 'great' is applied in the absolute sense.

You must understand that there is also a difference in respect of those things that are apprehended by the powers of mental perception. Human reason grasps completely the core of the real nature of some of them and falls short in the case of others. That portion of them with reason falls short of completely is divided into (a) that which some may conceivably grasp although the understanding of the majority falls short of it, and (b) into that concerning which reason cannot conceivably grasp the core of its real nature completely. This last one is the absolute 'Great One' who exceeds all the limits of human understanding so that the comprehension of His essential Being is inconceivable. And that One is God most High . . .

An admonition: The 'great' among men are the prophets and the scholars. When the wise man knows something of their attributes, his bosom is filled with veneration and his heart so replete with veneration that no room remains in it for anything else. The prophet is 'great' in respect of his people, the shaikh in respect of his disciple and the teacher in respect of his student, since the reason (of these subordinates) is incapable of comprehending the core of the master's attributes. But if the subordinate equals or surpasses the master, then the latter is no longer 'great' in comparison with the former. Every greatness applied to other than God is deficient and not absolutely 'great', because it manifests itself in relation to one thing and not another – apart from the greatness of God most High. Certainly He is the absolutely 'Great', not only relatively.

3.34.2 The Opener

He is the One by whose concern everything that is closed is opened, and the One by whose guidance everything that is obscure is made manifest. At times He causes kingdoms to be opened (that is, conquered) for His prophets and He takes them out of the hand of their enemies and says: 'Lo! We have given thee (O Muhammad) a signal victory (lit. "opening") that God may forgive thee.' At times He lifts the screen from the hearts of His friends, and He opens to them the gates of the kingdom of His heaven and the beauty of His grandeur. He says: 'That which God openeth unto mankind of mercy, none can withhold it.' The one in whose hand are the keys to the invisible world, as well as the keys to the means of sustenance, he is the one who is truly worthy of being an opener.

An admonition: In order that man might have a portion of the name *Al-Fattāh*, it is necessary that he longs for the time when he will reach the stage where the locks upon the divine problems are opened by his tongue, and those religious and worldly subjects which have been difficult for mankind will become easy by means of his knowledge.

3.34.3 The Forgiving

Al-Ghaffār is the One who makes manifest what is noble and veils what is disgraceful. The sins (of man) are among the disgraceful things which He veils by placing a veil upon them in this world and disregarding their punishment in the hereafter. *Al-Ghafr* means veiling. The first of God's veils for man is to be found in the fact that the opening in the body that has been created for that which his eyes consider ugly has been hidden within him and is concealed within the beauty of his exterior. How great is the difference between the interior of man and his exterior in terms of cleanliness and dirtiness, of ugliness and beauty! Just look at that part of him which God exposes and that part which He covers.

God's second veil for man is the human heart which He has made the seat of his reprehensible thoughts and disgraceful desires so that no one might know about this veil. If mankind were aware of the things that occurred in [a man's] mind, in terms of repeated temptations, thoughts of corruption, deception and evil thinking in general, certainly they would detest him. But behold how his secrets and weaknesses are veiled from all people but himself!

God's third veil for man is the forgiveness of the sins for which he deserved to be disgraced in the sight of mankind. God has promised that He will exchange good deeds for man's misdeeds so that he might cover the repulsive qualities of his sins with the reward of his good deeds when he has proved his faith.

An admonition: Man's portion of this name lies in his veiling for the next man that part of him which needs to be veiled. (Muhammad) said – May the peace of God be upon him: 'The one who veils the imperfections of a believer, his imperfections will God cover on the day of resurrection.' The slanderer, the spy, the avenger, and the one who requites evil with evil, are far removed from this characterisation. However, the one who is characterised by it is the one who does not divulge anything about God's creation except those things which are best in them. There is no creature totally free from perfection and imperfection, from ugliness and beauty. The one who disregards the repulsive qualities and remembers the good ones is the person who possesses a share of this name, even as it is related of Jesus – may peace be upon him – that he and his disciples passed by a dead dog, and the stench of it was overpowering. His disciples exclaimed: 'How this corpse smells!' But Jesus – may peace be upon him – replied: 'How lovely is the white of his teeth!' In this way he pointed out that they ought to mention only that which is good.

3.34.4 The One Who Raises to Honour and Abases

He is the One who gives dominion to whom He wishes and the One who takes it from whom He wishes. True dominion is to be found in liberation from the humiliation of [physical] needs, the subjugation of appetite[s] and the fault of the disgrace of ignorance. Therefore, [in the case of] the one from whose heart the veil is lifted so that he can know the beauty of God's presence, and the one who is granted the ability to be abstemious so that as a result of it he has no need for the things of God's creation, and is provided with strength and support so that by means of them he controls his own attributes, God has raised this man to a position of honour and gives him dominion in this world. God will also raise him to honour in the hereafter in terms of this person's gaining access to Him, and God will call for him, saying: 'O soul at peace, return unto thy Lord.' (Surah 89.27)

The one whom God causes to look at human beings in such a way that he is dependent on them and is so much under the dominion of greediness that he is not content even when he has sufficient to satisfy his needs, and the one who advances by his cunning until he is deceived about himself and (thus) remains in the darkness of ignorance, God abases such a one and dispossesses him. That is the workmanship of God most High, as and when He desires it.

For He is the One of whom it is said: 'Thou exaltest whom Thou wilt and abasest whom Thou wilt.' (Surah 3.26) And this lowly one is the one to whom God speaks and says: 'But you tempted one another, and hesitated, and doubted, and vain desires beguiled you till the ordinance of God came to pass: and the deceiver deceived you concerning God, so this day no ransom can be taken for you.' (Surah 57.14) This is the utmost limit of abasement. Each person who acts by means of his hand and his tongue so as to make the causes of honour easy possesses a portion of this char- acterisation.

3.34.5 The Grand One

Al-Kabīr is the one who possesses grandeur. Grandeur is an expression for the perfec- tion of the essence, by which I mean the perfection of existence. The perfection of existence is traceable to two things. One of them is its perpetuity, both past and future. Every existence is deficient which sooner or later is interrupted by a period of non-existence. For this reason, one says of a man whose period of existence is lengthy that he is a *kabīr*, that is to say, great of age, one who has lived long on this earth, and one does not say that he is *'azīm* of age. *Al-Kabīr* is used in ways in which *al-'azīm* cannot be used. If, then, the being whose period of existence is lengthy, even though its actual duration is limited, is said to be a *kabīr* [i.e. aged] then the one who always will be and always has been eternal, the one in relation to whom non- existence is inconceivable, is more worthy of being called a *kabīr*.

The second is that his existence is the existence from which the existence of all existing things emanates. If the one whose existence is complete in itself is perfect and grand, then the one from whom the existence of all existing things originated is more worthy of being called perfect and grand.

An admonition: *Al-kabīr* among men is the perfect one whose attributes of perfec- tion are not restricted to himself. Rather do they extend to others beside himself. No one sits next to him without pouring out upon the other (one) something of his own perfection. Man's perfection lies in his reason, piety and knowledge. *Al-kabīr* is the God-fearing wise one who leads people, the one who is fit to be a pattern, the one whose lights and knowledge are a fount for others. For this reason Jesus said – may peace be upon him – 'The one who knows and acts accordingly is called mighty (*'azīm*) in the kingdom of the heavens.'

Source: R. C. Stade (trans.) *The Names of God* (Ibadan: The Daystar Press, 1970), pp. 68–9, 36–8, 44–5, 49–50, 75–6.

3.35 Muhyi al-Din Ibn Arabi on the beautiful names

Muhyi al-Din Ibn Arabi (1165–1240 CE) was raised in Spain and travelled widely, including to Mecca, before settling in Damascus, where he died. Stressing the importance of the inner light rather than external authorities, he extolled a pantheistic belief. Although viewed by some of his contemporaries as heretical, Ibn Arabi was one of the most influential Muslim mystical philosophers and has been described as the most systematic thinker among Muslim mystics.

Let us now come to the gifts which flow from the Divine Names. The mercy (*Rahmah*) which God lavishes on His creatures runs wholly through the Divine Names: it is, on the one hand, of pure mercy, like everything that is licit from nourishment and natural pleasures, and which is not tainted with blame on the day of resurrection (conforming to the Quranic word: 'Say, who then would render illicit the beauty which God manifested for His servants and the lawful things of nourishment', say: They are for those who believe, in this world, and will not be subject to reproach on the day of resurrection . . .'): It is these gifts which flow from the Name *Al-Rahmān*, and, on the other hand, of mercy which is mixed with punishment, like medicine which is disagreeable to take, but which is followed by relief.

Such are the Divine gifts. For God (in His personal or qualified aspect) never gives except through the intermediary of one of the guardians of the Temple which are his Names.

Thus, God sometimes gratifies the servant by mediation of the Name 'compassionate' (*Al-Rahmān*) and it is then that the gift is free from any mixture which would be momentarily contrary to the nature of him who receives it, or which would contradict the intention, or anything else (of the petitioner). Sometimes He gives by mediation of the Name, The Inclusive (*Al-Wāsi'*), lavishing his gifts in a global manner. Or he gives by mediation of the Name of the Wise (*Al-Hakīm*) judging by that which is salutary for the servant at the given moment, or by the mediation of the Name of He who gives freely (*Al-Wahhāb*), giving that which is good without the servant who receives it by virtue of this Name, needing to compensate for it by actions of merit or grace. Or He gives by the Name of Him who established the order (*Al-Jabbār*) considering the cosmic environment and that which is necessary to it, or by the Name of the Forgiver (*Al-Ghaffār*), considering the state of him who receives the forgiveness. If he finds him in a state which deserves punishment, He protects him from this punishment, and if He finds him in a state which would not deserve punishment He protects him from a state which would deserve it, and it is in this sense that the servant (or saint) is said to be protected or safeguarded from sin.

The giver is always God, in the sense that He is the treasurer of all possibilities and that He only produces according to a predestined measure and by the hand of a Name concerning that possibility. Thus, He gives to everything its own constitution by virtue of His Name, The Just (*Al-'Adi*) and its brothers, like the Arbitrator (*Al-Hakam*), He who rules (*Al-Walī*) and The Victorious (*Al-Qahhār*).

Although the Divine Names may be infinite as to their multitude (for one knows them by that which flows from them which is equally unlimited), they are nonetheless reducible to a definite number of roots, which are the 'mothers' of the Divine Names, or the Divine presences integrating the Names. In truth, there is but one single, essential Reality (*Haqiqah*) which assumes all the relations and associations which one ascribes to it by the Divine Names. Now, this Reality causes each of these Names which manifest themselves indefinitely to contain an essential truth by which it distinguishes itself from the other Names. It is this distinctive truth, and not that which it has in common with the others, which is the proper determination of the Name. It is in the same way that the Divine gifts distinguish themselves from one another by their personal nature, although they come from the same source. It is, moreover, evident that this one is not that one, the reason, precisely, being the distinction within the Divine Names. Because of His infinity, there is in the Divine Presence nothing that repeats itself, and that is a fundamental truth.

Source: Muhyi al-Din Ibn Arabi, *The Wisdom of the Prophets* (Aldsworth: Beshara Publications, 1975), pp. 27–9.

3.36 FROM *PEARLS OF FAITH*

EDWIN ARNOLD

This verse commentary celebrates the Beautiful Names by drawing upon Qur'anic and other Muslim sources.

3.36.1 Pearl of al-Kabir (The Grand One)

Seven heavens God made: first Paradise,
Next the gate of eternity, the third the house of peace,
The fourth Felicity, the fifth the home of golden light,
The sixth the garden of delight, the seventh the
Footstool of the Throne. And each and every one
Sphere above sphere, and treasure over treasure,
The great decree of God made for reward and pleasure.
Saith the perspicuous Book: 'Look up to heaven! look!
Dost thou see fault or flaw, in that vast vault,
Spangled with silvery lamps of night,
Or gilded with glad light
Of sunrise, or of sunset, or warm noon?
Rounded He well the moon?
Kindled He wisely the red lord of day?
Look twice! look thrice, and say?'
Thy weak gaze fails:
Eyesight is drowned in yon abyss of blue:

Ye see the glory but ye see not through:
God's greatness veils
Its greatness by its greatness – all that wonder
Lieth the lowest of the heavens under,
Beyond which angels view
God and God's mighty works, asunder:
The thronged clouds whisper of it when they thunder.
Allāh Kabīr, in silence we
Meditate on Thy majesty!

3.36.2 Pearl of al-Fattah (The Opener)

Al-Fattāh, praise the Opener and recite
The marvels of that 'Journey of the Night'.
Our Lord Muhammad lay upon the hill
Safe, whereby the holy city stands,
Asleep, wrapped in a robe of camels' wool.

Dark was the night, that Night of grace, and still:
When all the spheres, by God's commands,
Opened unto him, splendid and wonderful.

For Gabriel, softly lighting, touched his side,
Saying: 'Rise, thou enwrapped one, come and see
The things which be beyond. Lo! I have brought
Burāq, the horse of swiftness: mount and ride.'
Milk-white that steed was, with embroidery
Of pearls and emeralds in his long hair wrought.

Hooved like a mule he was, with a man's face:
His eyes gleamed from his forelock, each a star
Of lucent hyacinth: the saddle cloth
Was woven gold, which priceless work did grace:
The lightning goeth not so fast or far
As those broad pinions which he fluttered forth.
One heel he smote on Safa, and one heel
On Sinai, where the dint is to this day.
Next at Jerusalem he neighed. Our Lord,
Descending with the Archangel there, did kneel
Making the midnight prayer: afterwards they
Tethered him to the Temple by a cord.

'Ascend!' spake Gabriel: and behold! there fell
Out of the sky a ladder bright and great,
Whereby, with easy steps, on radiant stairs,

They mounted, past our earth and heaven and hell,
To the first sphere, where Adam kept his gate,
Which was of vaporous gold and silvery squares.

Here thronged the lesser angels: some took charge
To fill the clouds with rain and speed them round.
And some to tend live creatures: for what's born
Hath guardians there in its own shape: a large
Beauteous white cock crowed matins, at the sound
Cocks in a thousand planets hailed the morn.

Unto the second sphere by that white slope
Ascended they, whereof Noah held the key:
And twofold was the throng of angels here,
But all so dazzling glowed its fretted cope,
Burning with beams, Muhammad could not see
What manner of celestial folk was there.

A third sphere lay a thousand years beyond
If thou shouldest journey as the sun-ray doth,
But in one *Fātihah* climbed they thitherward.
David and Solomon in union fond
Ruled at the entrance, keeping Sabaoth
Of ceaseless joy. The void was paven hard
With paven work of rubies if there be

Jewels on earth to liken unto them
Which had such colour as no goldsmith knows.
And here a vast archangel they did see,
'Faithful of God' his name, whose diadem
Was set with peopled stars: wherefrom arose
Lauds to the glory of God, filling the blue
With lovely music, as rose gardens fill
A land with essences and young stars, shaking
Tresses of lovely light, gathered and grew
Under his mighty plumes, departing still
Like ships with crews and treasure, voyage-making.

So came they to the fourth sphere: where there sate
Enoch, who never tasted death: and there
Behind its awful portal Azrael writes:
The shadow of his brows compassionate
Made night across all worlds: our Lord felt fear,
Marking the stern eyes and the hand which smites.
For always on a scroll he sets the names
Of new-born beings, and from off the scroll
He blotteth who must die: and holy tears

Roll down his cheeks, recording all our shames
And sins and penalties: while of each soul
Munkir and Nakir reckon the arrears.

Next, at the fifth sphere's entry, they were 'ware
Of a door built in sapphire, having graven
Letters of flashing fire, the faith unfolding:
'There is no god save God', Aaron sat there
Guarding the region of 'the wrath of heaven'.
And Isrefel behind, his trumpet holding,
His trumpet holding, which shall wake the dead
And slay the living – all his cheek puffed out,
Bursting to blow. For none knows God's time
Nor when the word of judgement shall be said.
And darts and chains of fire lay all around,
Terrible tortures for the ungodly's crime.

When to the sixth sphere passed they, Moses sped
Its bars of chrysoprase, and kissed our Lord,
And spake full sweet: 'Prophet of Allāh, thou
More souls of Ismael's tribes to truth hast led,
Than I of Isaac's.' Here the crystal sword

Of Michael gave the light they journeyed through.
But at the seventh sphere that light which shone
Hath not an earthly name, nor any voice
Can tell its splendour, nay, nor any ear
Learn, if it listened: only he alone
Who saw it, knows how there th'elect rejoice,
'Isa, and Ibrahim, and the souls most dear.
And he, the glorious regent of the sphere,
Had seventy thousand heads: and every head
As many countenances, and each face
As many mouths: and in each mouth there are
Tongues seventy thousand, whereof each tongue said:
Ever and ever: 'Praise be to God, praise!'

Here, at the bound, is fixed that lotus-tree
Sidrah, which none among the angels pass
And not great Gabriel's self might farther wend.
Yet, led by presences too bright to see,
Too high to name, on paths like purple glass,
Our Lord Muhammad journeyed to the end.

Alone, alone, through hosts of Cherubim
Crowding the infinite void with whispering vans,
From splendour unto splendour still he sped,

Across 'the lake of gloom' they ferried him,
And then 'the sea of glory', mortal man's
Heart cannot hold the wonders witnessed.

So to the region of the veils he came,
Which shut all times off from eternity.
The bars of being where thought cannot reach:
Ten thousand thousand are they, walls of flame
Lambent with loveliness and mystery,
Ramparts of utmost heaven, having no breach.
Then he saw God! our prophet saw the Throne!
O God, let these weak words be forgiven!
Thou, the Supreme, 'The Opener', spake at last.
The Throne, the Throne, he saw – our Lord alone!
Saw it and heard! But the verse falls from heaven
Like a poised eagle whom the lightnings blast.

And Gabriel, waiting by the tree, he found,
And Burāq, tethered to the Temple porch.
He loosed the horse, and twixt its wings ascended.
One hoof it smote on Zion's hallowed ground,
One upon Sinai: and the day-star's torch
Was not yet fading when the journey ended.

Al-Fattāh! Opener! we say
Thy Name and worship Thee always.

Source: E. Arnold (trans.) *Pearls of Faith* (Lahore: Orientalis, 1954), pp. 80–1, 41–6.

— ●◆● —

HADITH/SUNNAH

— ◆◆◆ —

3.37 THE LIVING THOUGHTS OF THE PROPHET MUHAMMAD

Hadith (a story or report) is a tradition that records the *sunnah* (custom) of the Prophet Muhammad. The 'customs' of the Prophet provide direction and moral guidance for later generations of Muslims, although a clear distinction is made between guidance derived from the Qur'an and that taken from hadith. Within the Sunni tradition, six collections of hadiths have achieved canonical status. Shi'ite Muslims recognize sources independent of these.

The Prophet said: 'The man who knows most the Book of God shall act as *Imām* of the people. The most virtuous among you shall deliver the *adhān* (call to prayer) and those having most knowledge of the Qur'ān shall act as *Imāms*.'

'Every child conforms to the true religion [lit. human nature]: It is his parents who make him a Jew, a Christian or a Magian.'

'Surely a day will come over Hell, when it will be like a field of corn that has dried up after flourishing for a while – a day when there shall not be a single human being in it.'

Asked about the efficacy of prayer, Muhammad counter-questioned: 'Tell me, if there is a stream at the door of any one of you, in which he bathes five times daily, what do you say, will it leave anything of his dirt?' On receiving a reply in the negative, he continued: 'This is the likeness of the five prayers with which God washes away all faults.' 'When one of you says his prayers, he holds confidential intercourse with his Lord.'

'Thou shouldest worship God as if thou didst see Him: if thou dost not see Him, He surely sees thee.'

'Whoever does the needful for his brother, God does the needful for him. Whoever removes the distress of a Muslim, God removes for him a distress out of the distresses of the day of resurrection.'

'Thou wilt recognise the faithful in their having mercy upon each other and in their love for one another and in their kindness towards one another, like the body – when one member of it ails, the entire body ails.'

'Your slaves are your brethren: God has placed them under your control. So whoever has his brother under his control, he should feed him from what he eats and give him clothes to wear from what he wears. Do not impose on them a task which should overpower them, and if you do impose on them such a task help them in the doing of it.'

'One who manages the affairs of the widow and the needy is like one who exerts himself hard in the way of God, or like one who stands up for prayer in the night and fasts in the day.'

'I, and the man who brings up an orphan, will be in paradise like this.' And he pointed with his two fingers, the forefinger and the middle finger.

'God has no mercy in him who is not merciful to men.'

'He is not of us who does not show mercy to our little ones and respect to our great ones.'

'Be careful of your duty to God regarding these dumb animals. Ride them while they are in fit condition, and eat them while they are in fit condition.'

'Charity is incumbent on every Muslim.'

'Every good deed is charity, and it is a good deed that thou meet thy brother with a cheerful countenance and that thou pour water from thy bucket into the vessel of thy brother.'

'Surely truth leads to virtue, and virtue leads to paradise, and a man continues to speak the truth until he becomes utterly truthful. Surely falsehood leads to vice and vice leads to the fire, and a man who continues to tell lies is written down a great liar with God.'

'The most excellent *jihād* is the uttering of truth in the presence of an unjust ruler.'

'Among the best of you are those who are good in payment of debt. Whoever contracts a debt intending to repay it, God will pay it for him: whoever contracts a debt intending to waste it, God will bring him to ruin.'

'Delaying the payment of a debt by a well-to-do person is injustice. Deferring payment by one who has the means to pay makes his punishment legitimate.'

'If the debtor is in constrained circumstances, then there should be postponement until he is in ease, and if you remit it as alms, it is better for you' (quoting Surah 2.280).

'No one eats better food than that which he eats out of the work of his own hand. God did not raise a prophet but that he pastured goats. Yes! I used to pasture them for the people of Mecca.'

'There are three persons whose adversary in dispute God will be on the day of resurrection: a person who makes a promise in His Name, then acts unfaithfully: a person who sells a free person then devours his price: and a person who employs a servant and receives fully the labour due from him and then does not pay him his remuneration.'

'The Truthful honest merchant is as the prophets and the truthful ones and the martyrs.'

'May God have mercy on the man who is generous when he buys and when he sells and when he demands his due.'

'If they [traders] both speak the truth and make manifest [the defect, if any, in the transaction], their transaction shall be blessed: if they conceal [the defect] and tell lies, the blessing of their transaction shall be obliterated.'

'The taking of oaths makes the commodities sell, but it obliterates the blessing therein.'

'Whoever buys cereals, he shall not sell them until he obtains their possession.'

'There is no Muslim who plants a tree or cultivates land and then bird or man or animal eat of it, but it is a charitable deed for him. Whoever cultivates land which is not the property of anyone has a better title to it.'

'The man who marries perfects half his religion.'

'O assembly of young people, whoever of you has the means to support a wife, he should get married. This is the best means of keeping the looks cast down and of guarding chastity. And he who has not the means let him keep fast, for this will act as restraining of desire.'

'Every one of you is a ruler and everyone shall be questioned about his subjects. The king is a ruler: and the man is the ruler over the people of his house: and the woman is a ruler over the house of her husband and his children.'

'Thy body has a right over thee, and thy soul has a right over thee, and thy wife has a right over thee.'

'Never did God allow anything more hateful to Him than divorce. With God, the most detestable of all things allowed is divorce.'

'To hear and obey [the authorities] is binding, so long as one is not commanded to disobey God. When one is commanded to disobey God, he should neither hear nor obey.' On being appointed Governor of Yemen, Mu'adh was asked by the Prophet as to the rule by which he would abide. 'By the Qur'an', he replied. 'But if you do not find any direction therein, what then?' 'Then I will act according to the *Sunnah* of the Prophet', he responded.

'But, if you do not find any direction in the *Sunnah*, what then?' 'Then I will exercise my judgement and act on that.' The Prophet raised his hands and said: 'Praise be to God Who guides the messenger of His Messenger as He wills.'

'Gather together the righteous from among my community and decide the matter by their counsel and do not decide it by one man's opinion.' [This principle of the corporate mind lies behind the institution of *Ijmā'*, or 'consensus', by which the mind of the community, under the priority of the Qur'an and the *Sunnah*, is held to be indicative of the mind of God.

'Never do a people take counsel but they are guided to the right course in their affair.'

'The authority of the head [of State] should only be disputed if he has committed open acts of unbelief, in which you have a clear argument from God.'

Source: Muhammad 'Ali (ed), *The Living Thoughts of the Prophet Muhammad* (Cassell, 1947), pp. 62, 68, 71, 75, 83–5, 89, 92, 110, 114–15, 117, 123, 125–6, 135–7.

—— ● ◆ ● ——

LAW IN ISLAM

—— ◆◆◆ ——

3.38 ON BIRTH CONTROL

3.38.1
AL-GHAZALI

It is a rule of cohabitation that the emission of semen should not take place outside of the vagina, for what God has decreed must take place. The prophet said likewise. There are differences among the learned class concerning *'azl* or *coitus interruptus*. One group says that *'azl* is lawful in all circumstances while another group says it is unlawful in every circumstance. Another group says it is lawful with the consent of one's wife while another group says it is lawful in the case of female slaves but not in the case of free women. To us, the custom of *'azl* is lawful but it is not commendable for the reason that the merits of ejaculation in the vagina are lost. A similar example is found in the person who sits idly in the mosque without remembering God. The point is that the person is not doing something which is intended to be done in the situation; that is not commendable. There is virtue in producing a child but that is lost in *'azl*. Muhammad said: 'If a man cohabits with his wife, the reward of producing a child is decreed for him – such a child will become a martyr fighting in the way of God.' He said this in consideration of reward, because if a child is born like this, he will get the reward for producing a martyr in the way of God. This is only possible with full intercourse.

That birth control by *'azl* is lawful is supported by legal analogy from the Qur'an. Though there is no clear verse regarding the matter, it can be gathered by analogy such as the following. It is not unlawful to give up marriage or to give up intercourse after marriage or to give up ejaculation of semen after intercourse. It is true that rewards are given up on these actions but absence of actions is not unlawful. There is no difference between these three things. A child is born after ejaculation into the vagina. Before it there are four stages: (1) to marry; (2) to cohabit; (3) to have patience to ejaculate after intercourse; (4) to ejaculate into the vagina and then to stay in that condition until the semen is settled therein. The life of a child coming into existence has a number of stages: (1) semen in the vagina must be mixed with the female egg. If both are mixed, it is a sin to destroy it. There is no sin if they are not allowed to mix; (2) if it is created into a clot of blood and a lump of flesh, it is more hateable to destroy it; (3) if life is infused into that lump of flesh, it is most hateable to destroy it; (4) the last limit of sin is to destroy the child when it is born. If the male semen is mixed with the menstrual blood of a woman, it is condensed, as happens when something is mixed with milk. It is just like proposal and acceptance which constitute an agreement or contract. Both things are necessary for a contract. If there is a proposal but no acceptance, there is no sin in breaking it. The ejaculation of semen is like a proposal and doing that in the vagina is like its acceptance. If it is ejaculated outside the vagina, the proposal is lost. There is no sin in it. Therefore, to ejaculate outside the vagina before the semen is mixed with female egg is not a sin.

Question: if there is no sin in ejaculating outside of the vagina, it must still be considered bad because the object of semen is to produce a child and if that is not done, it is secret polytheism.

Answer: There are four aims of *'azl.* (1) To preserve the beauty and health of one's wife and thus to enjoy her always. If semen is destroyed with this object, then it is not unlawful. (2) To prevent the birth of too many children. It is not unlawful; to maintain too many children is very difficult. The verse in the Qur'an which guarantees maintenance of all creatures means perfection of God-reliance and perfection of merits and rewards but it is no sin to give up the highest stage of merits just as it is no sin to protect one's wealth and properties and to hoard things for a limited period of time. This is the meaning of the verse: *There is no animal in the earth of which the maintenance is not upon God* (Qur'an 11:6). (3) To practise birth control for fear of the birth of daughters. This is unlawful. The Arabs before Islam used to bury their daughters alive and they feared the birth of daughters. This was prohibited in the Qur'an. If with the above object, marriage or intercourse is given up, it will be committing a sin but these actions without that object are not sinful. If semen is ejaculated outside of the vagina with this purpose, then it is unlawful. (4) To protect the honour of a woman, to keep her neat and clean, and to save her from maintaining children. This too is unlawful use of *'azl.*

Source: A. Rippin and J. Knappert (eds and trans.) *Textual Sources for the Study of Islam* (Manchester University Press, 1986), pp. 108–10.

3.38.2

MAULANA MAWDUDI

Maulānā Sayyid Abu al-A'lā Mawdūdī (1903–79) began life as a journalist and became the editor of Indian Muslim publications. He emphasized the need for Muslim societies to return to the Qur'an and hadith and created the Jamā'at-i-Islāmī to provide leadership for the Muslim cause in pre-Independence India. Having emigrated to Pakistan, he continued to press for the creation of a proper Islamic state in Pakistan. His writings and the organization continue to be influential both in South Asia and more widely.

Is birth control compatible with Islam?

If we view the problem in the light of the above discussed fundamental principle of Islam it becomes abundantly clear that the pattern of life that Islam builds can have no place for birth control as a national social policy. The Islamic culture strikes at the roots of the materialistic and sensate view of life and eliminates the motivating forces that make man abstain from fulfilling one of the most fundamental urges of human nature, that is, of procreation. As already seen, birth control is not an unavoidable demand of human nature. He does not need it for the fulfilment of his personality. Instead it is a product of certain cultural forces, of a peculiar social circumstance, of a value-pattern that makes man obsessed with his personal comforts and pleasures, to the neglect of the needs of the society and the race. It is then that procreation is discounted and artificial curtailment of the family gets premium. From this it can be legitimately inferred that if a people have a different socio-cultural set-up, and if the forces and conditions that led to the social movement of birth control in the western society do not obtain amongst them, the occasion for such a movement will not arise. When the motives and the causes are not there, the situation will be different. When the tree is not there, how could the fruits be? Naturally in such a social organisation all inducements to attempt to alter God's scheme, to transgress the limits prescribed by Him, and to violate the course of nature He has laid will cease to operate. This movement can have no place in such a society.

Let us look a little more deeply in the social system of Islam to see how it precludes the possibility of the emergence of tendencies that may give rise to a situation favourable to the movement of birth control or to any other unnatural tendency.

Islam's economic system has struck at the very roots of capitalism and the spirit of acquisitiveness. It forbids usury and interest, disallows monopoly, forbids speculation and gambling, discourages hoarding, and introduces such institutions and policies (*zakat*, an equitable law of succession and inheritance, fair wage, guarantee of basic necessities of life to all people, etc.) as lead to diffusion of wealth and wellbeing. Islam takes these and many other effective measures to remedy the ills that have been responsible for economic dislocation and disparity in the Western society and for raising a system of economic exploitation of the many at the hands of the few.

The social system of Islam has given legal, economic, social, and judicial rights to woman. She has a share, by her own right, in the earnings of man, over and above the right to own and inherit property and invest capital in business and industry under her own name. Islam, however, clearly states that men and women have their own spheres of activities – a scheme of functional division in accord with their respective natural dispositions and inherent physical and physiological qualities and characteristics. Free mixing of the sexes is prohibited through *hijab*. That is how the doors of a number of social and economic ills have been closed, and the errands that might lead men and women away from the function that nature has assigned them have been blocked. The preservation and propagation of life is not left to chance arrangements, instead the entire scheme of social life is so arranged that on the one hand the demands of human nature may be fulfilled and on the other the task of procreation and rearing of new generations be accomplished in the best possible way.

The ethical teachings of Islam require man to lead a simple and morally chaste and unblemished life. Islam declares unlawful all forms of social misbehaviour including drinking, fornication, adultery, and other sexual vices. It discourages idleness and waste of time in useless pursuits and places effective checks on irresponsibility, extravagance, and indulgences in those recreations and enjoyments that result in a care-free life and frittering of wealth on trifles. Islam wants man to live a balanced life – balance between work and rest, effort and enjoyment, material and moral, individual and social aspects of life. *Eat and drink but be not prodigal. Lo! Allah loveth not those who exceed the limits* (Qur'an 7:31), is the Qur'anic injunction. Islam's approach to spending is that wealth is a trust and should be spent only where necessary and up to an extent that is desirable. In the matter of dress, housing, and procuring comforts of life, one should exercise restraint and spend within reasonable limits. That is how not only through moral training and spiritual education but also through a set of social, moral, and economic regulations and directive principles Islam strikes at the roots of immorality, extravagance and insatiable hunger for luxury, and lust – the hall-marks of a society that takes to birth control, as was done in the West.

Islam also inculcates the spirit of mutual love and affection, fellow-feeling and sympathy. It stresses the right of the blood-relations and enjoins a policy of co-operation and help. It insists on compassion for neighbours and ordains *infaq fi sabil Allah*, spending in the way of Allah for the promotion of good and virtue in its widest sense. Islam develops a system of social responsibility and national solidarity and provides for the help of the poor and needy irrespective of their faith, colour, race, creed, religion, or country, and protects them from selfishness, greed, and exploitation by vested interests.

These, in brief, are some of the ways and means that inculcate in each man a sense of responsible individualism as well as develop a healthy and integrated society. It is a moral society for a moral man. Such a morally sublime atmosphere cannot breed any social tendency towards birth control.

Along with these social attitudes and a *modus operandi*, for their operation and flowering, Islam brings about a change in the heart of man – the seat of his personality. It assures that man is not alone in the universe. There is a God, the Creator, the Sustainer, the Lord. To Him it turns his face and thus brings him in line with the way all creation – and creatures – behave. Strive man must, but it should be done with faith and hope. Islam asks man to rely on his Creator and makes him realise that He alone is the Nourisher and the Provider of him as He is of all other organic beings in the universe. This realisation saves man from many a moment of false despondency or arrogance. He relies on himself and his resources; but he relies more on the Lord of the universe.

Summing up, we find that the nature of Islamic faith, its spiritual and moral attitudes, its social laws and regulations, its code of ethical behaviour, and its over-all ideals and mission in life – all have contributed towards mitigating those forces that give rise to the movement of birth control and its adoption as a social policy. Islamic and the Western civilizations, from this viewpoint, are poles apart. A really Islamic society can have no place for birth control as a national policy. If a person is a true Muslim in thought and deed he, in the ordinary course of circumstances, can neither feel any urge towards birth control nor would he be thrown in an amoral situation where violation of nature is forced upon him. He enjoys life by living with restraint. And that is the course most suited to human genius.

Does Islam forbid birth control?

So far we studied the problem in more general terms. We shall now look at the issue more directly and try to find out whether Islam forbids birth control or not.

The Holy Qur'an lays down a fundamental principle that effecting change in the scheme of God is a fiendish act. Changing God's scheme and creation signifies misuse of a thing, its utilisation for a purpose other than the one for which it was intended, or to use it in a manner that its real purpose is defeated. In the light of this fundamental principle let us see as to what is 'God's scheme' in the marital relationship of man and woman, i.e. what is the real natural purpose of this relationship and whether birth control changes it in the other direction. The Qur'an is not silent on this point. It has, on the one hand, forbidden sexual relations outside marriage, and on the other, laid bare the objective which matrimonial relations between men and women are to serve. These objectives are (a) procreation and (b) fostering of love and affection and promoting culture and civilisation. The Qur'an says: *Your wives are a tilth for you, so go into your tilth as you like and do good beforehand for yourselves* (Qur'an 2:223).

This verse expounds the first objective of marriage. The other one is referred to in the following verse: *And one of His signs is that He created mates for you from yourselves that you may find consolation in them and He ordained between you love and compassion* (Qur'an 30:21).

In the first verse by describing women as a tilth an important biological fact has been pointed out. Biologically man is a tiller and a woman a tilth and the foremost purpose of the interrelationship between the two is the procreation of the human race. This is an objective which is common to all – human beings, animals, and the world of vegetation. The tiller of the soil cultivates the land not in vain, but for the produce. Take away this purpose, and the entire pursuit becomes meaningless. Through the parable of the tilth this important fact has been stressed by the Qur'an.

The second verse refers to another purpose of this relationship, viz. the establishment of an organised social life. When husband and wife take up to live together as a family they in fact lay the foundation of culture and civilisation. Herein lies the unique function which man is to perform in God's creation and work towards the flowering of all that has been laid in man. This urge is latent in man's nature and seeks its fulfilment through promptings from within and without.

Source: A. Rippin and J. Knappert (eds and trans.) *Textual Sources for the Study of Islam* (Manchester University Press, 1986), pp. 187–90.

3.39 THE CHARACTER OF ISLAMIC LAW

A. AL-AZMEH

Blasphemy and the character of Islamic law

When in 1608, King James asked the jurist and parliamentarian Sir Edward Coke why it was that law could not be interpreted by any intelligent man in the light of reason, Sir Edward resorted to an argument for the technical nature of legal reason:

> True it is that God has endowed Your Majesty with excellent science, and great endowments of nature; but Your Majesty is not learned in the law of this your realm of England, and causes which concern the life, or inheritance, or goods, or fortune of your subjects, are not to be decided by natural reason, but by the artificial reason and judgement of the law, which law is an art which requires long study and experience before that a man can attain to the cognizance of it.

A response of the same nature could be given by any jurist with technical competence in the field of Islamic law to the claims made for this law by advocates of Islamist political ideologies. These advocates claim to speak for a univocal body of legislation which is not grounded in the vast historical experience of Muslims. They also speak in terms of explicit and demonstrable commands deriving from scriptural statements without the mediation of legal reason. Finally, they give the impression, and sometimes make the utopian presumption, of a universal extra-territoriality which has no grounds in Islamic scriptures or in the historical experience of Muslims.

This may not be surprising. This advocacy is made by ideologues with at best a rudimentary knowledge of Muslim scriptures. In the case of divines with undisputed knowledge of Islamic scripture and legal texts, it arises from the suspension of such knowledge in favour of immediate ideological and political purposes. It is unfortunate that an impression of ferocious crudity and simplicity is being given of Islamic law, an impression which is certainly undeserved by the vast corpus of writings on law and legal methodology (deontic logic, analogical connections, rhetorical methods, philological and lexical procedures) stretching over centuries and vast expanses of territory, the ensemble of which is Islamic law.

The first characteristic feature of Islamic law which ought to be indicated as a corrective concerns its technical nature. Islamic law is highly technical, indeed arcane, to those who have not sought properly to tackle its vast body of literature. Some of the great jurists such as Sarakhsī, the greatest figure in the Hanafite school to which the vast majority of Indian Subcontinent Muslims adhere (along with Afghans, Turks and the Arabs of Syria and Iraq) went to great lengths to demonstrate that his notions and procedures are so technical that they have none but a most tangential connection with ethical or dogmatic considerations. The divine origin of some of the utterances which enter the conveyor belt of legal reason – that is, the text of the Koran – is technically irrelevant to their legal aspect. Infractions of law are punishable in this world, infractions of divine purpose in the next. This must be the first matter to bear in mind today, when ignorance and politics are wilfully confusing Islamic law with the requirements of Islamist ideology.

The second point concerns legal innovation. Contrary to political and ideological pretensions, the historical reality of the practice of Islamic law has been one of wide latitude in opinions over specific points of law (the *ikhtilāf*). The corollary of this, quite naturally, is the mutability of this law in the context of changing circumstances, a mutability which does not accord with the utopian archaism of Islamist politics. And indeed, the reform of Islamic law over the past century has instituted a condition of 'absolute discretion' (*ijtihād muṭlaq*) based on the reinterpretation of scriptural and other foundation texts, in addition to what Islamic legal theory designates as the 'auxiliary' sources of law: custom, public interest and equity. The prevalent trend in Muslim law reform in the present century has indeed been an attempt to generalize the classical precepts in such a manner as to have them merge with a notion of natural law; such has been the achievement of the great reformer Muhammad Abduh. In theoretical terms, Muslim jurists (though not the Shi'a) have adopted a highly sceptical view of the finality of their judgements; hence the readiness mutually to recognize views that may be contradictory. It is recognized – though this recognition is not shared by Islamist ideologues – that it is against natural justice and natural law (which accords with divine will) to foist ordinances of relevance to the seventh century upon the twentieth.

Moreover, Islamic law is not a code. This is why the frequently heard call for its 'application' is meaningless, most particularly when calls are made for the application of *sharī'a* – this last term does not designate law, but is a general term designating good order, much like *nomos* or *dharma*. Islamic law is a repertoire of precedents, cases and general principles, along with a body of well-developed hermeneutical and paralogical techniques. In certain respects, it resembles English law quite strongly. [. . .] This characteristic nature of Islamic law reinforces its legal latitudinarianism, a fact which explains how it emerged and reigned successfully as one of the great legal systems of the world over more than twelve centuries in very different parts of the globe. Little wonder, then, that Islamic law has a predominantly objectivist character. [. . .] This (in marked contrast to French law) reinforces its technical nature and further accentuates its being the preserve of fully trained jurists.

One final point must be mentioned. Islamic law as a corpus is predominantly private: it treats of obligation, contract, personal status (including succession) and other aspects of secular life. These are termed by Islamic jurists *ḥuqūq al-ʿibād*, the rights of persons. A much smaller corpus of public law exists under the rubric *ḥuqūq Allāh*, the rights of God. These concern the obligations incumbent upon properly constituted Islamic polities; they are redundant in the absence of such a polity and have no extraterritorial competence, and a Muslim *in partibus infidelium* is a *mustaʾmin* 'under safe conduct', obliged to follow the laws of his or her country of residence. Substantively, the rights of God concern protecting and maintaining the Muslim body politic through international relations both martial and pacific, and through invigilating its internal integrity by the creation of a *Rechtsstaat* and the suppression of ideological sedition – that is, unbelief, apostasy and the very difficult notion of blasphemy.

Apostasy as a legal notion was questioned in the Middle Ages, abolished in Ottoman territories before the middle of the nineteenth century, and regarded by the famous Muslim reformer of the present century, Muhammad Rashid Rida, as a political matter concerning the seventh century and, as such, of no consequence to the present age; indeed, the Koran states quite unequivocally that there should be no compulsion in matters of religion (*la ikrāha fid-dīn*). Unbelief and blasphemy have had different meanings and accents over the historical experience of Muslims, although there does exist a hard core of dogmas which are universally held, regardless of their historical justification; all traditions harden in this manner. Additionally, all traditions vary, over time and place, in the severity and in the systematic character with which unbelief and dogmatic deviance are pursued. Likewise, most traditions reach a point where doctrinal purity and univocality become redundant. Such is the case with those parts of the world with Muslim majorities, especially in the Arab world, except for subcultural pockets and among political minorities which espouse a fundamentalist primitivism entirely inattentive to the historical experience of Muslims and to the historical character of their law. Islam has, moreover, never had a central authority which determines rectitude and which has exclusive title to the legitimacy which renders its territories the Abode of Islam, and thus the location of the practice of the Islamic legal system. This is especially so in modern times, when the Rights of Persons have been partly incorporated into the civil codes of such countries as Egypt, Syria and Iraq [. . .] but according to modern legal principles. What was not thus incorporated has been forgotten – and even such as was codified has lost its 'Islamic' and taken on an entirely civil character. The Rights of God, on the other hand, though rarely abolished in any explicit manner, have been left in abeyance and relegated for exaction in the next world.

Thus any consideration of the question of blasphemy or of heresy, be it that of Mr Rushdie or of others, must first face the historical irrelevance of his task, and must also be cognizant of its technical impossibility in the very terms of the Islamic legal corpus and system themselves. Calls for the 'application of Islamic law' have no connection with the Muslim legal tradition built upon multivocality, technical competence and the existence of an executive political authority which controls the legal system. It is a political slogan, not a return to a past reality.

Source: Appendix: 'Blasphemy and the character of Islamic law', in A. al-Azmeh, *Islams and Modernities* (London: Verso, 1993), pp. 10–14.

MUSLIM MYSTICS

— ◆◆ —

3.40 'THE BLEMISHES OF THE SOUL'

ABU HAMID AL-GHAZALI (1058–1111 CE)

What ails my soul, that maketh long complaint
to men, but for the fear of God is faint?
Its very plaint forbiddeth its release,
augments its terror, and destroys its peace.
Would it but come with humble love sincere
unto its Master, He would draw it near;
but since it chooseth who His creatures are
above their Fashioner, He keeps it far,
and makes its need yet more: but let it flee
to Him, He'll grant it full satiety.
Unto His creatures it complains, as though
they have the power to work it weal or woe:
but would it lay all matters at His feet
in true sincerity and trust complete,
He would not leave it in its long despairs,
but give it gladness in return for cares.
It angers God, that it seeks man to please:
a curse upon its self-sought miseries!
If it would dare man's anger to attain,
pleasing its Lord, it would His pleasure gain.
I have a soul whose nature I would tell,
that we may know it and its habits well:
hear then my tale thereon, and tell in turn,
that men of wit its mysteries may learn.
It labours after folly as its goal:
alas, the foolish labour of my soul!
I chide it, but it never will obey,

as if I will not well in what I say;
but idly looking at another's sin
forgets the faults it cherishes within.
Its evil manners have corrupted me,
and leave me neither rank nor piety.
At concert with vain talk it fills the air,
has small remembrance of its God at prayer,
receives His favours with scant gratitude,
and, suffering, with less patience is endued:
full slow of foot its remedy to obtain,
but swift to seek the things that are its bane;
finds endless cause its promises to break,
is false in every claim that it doth make;
keen-sighted after evil vanities,
but blind to where its own salvation lies;
grasping at pleasures with alacrity,
at time of meditation sluggardly;
with leaden eye forgets its God to greet
Who fashioned it in symmetry complete;
when all is well, in confidence arrayed,
but in distress most mightily afraid;
in pride and in hypocrisy well-versed,
yea, and by pride corrupted and accursed;
unstinted in approval and appraise
of him who seeks its dignity to raise,
but lavish of opprobrium and blame
when any dares its shortcomings to name;
in eating and in drinking takes delight,
and to repose is eager for the night;
accounts to others where their faults begin,
forgetful of its own account of sin.
How other far that man, who guards his soul
in cleanliness, godfearing, sweet and whole,
teaches it righteousness, keeping it keen,
nurturing it with lawful food and clean.
All night he holds it instant and awake,
washed with the tears that from his eyelids break.
When lusting after passion, with the fear
of God he visits it, and brings it cheer;
with fasting trains it, till it is subdued,
spite all its waywardness and turpitude.
So it remembers God with thankfulness
and love sincere doth secretly confess.
How well by God assisted is that soul
which, seeking refuge, gains in God its goal!
Rank and renown it winneth from its King,
and at the founts of faith finds watering:

it soars to God in loveliness of thought,
by God with love and kindness it is sought,
and if in need unto the Lord it cries
He hears its prayer, and speedily supplies.
He gives it patience in calamity,
and to its call His hand is ever free.
Not so my soul: wildly rebellious,
to orders and restraints impervious,
God's holy ordinance it never heeds;
alas, my soul! Alas, its sinful deeds!
How shall it ever to its Lord repent,
that serves the Devil, and his blandishment?
Whene'er I say, 'My soul, attend my word,
be heedful of the orders of thy Lord',
the truth it will not heed, though hearing all,
as though it were another that I call.
Knew it the purpose of its fashioning,
that knowledge grief and bitter tears would bring;
were it made ware of God in verity
truly sincere would its godfearing be;
but God hath made it ignorant of him,
neglect hath made the light of guidance dim.
And ah, my soul! Alas for it, and woe,
if God abandons it, and lets it go!
Beguiled by this world's pleasure, it knows not
what after death shall be its dreadful lot.
Much I have strained, to make my soul obey,
but for whose sin I had not gone astray;
when I would be obedient, it was faint,
and shewed a strange distaste and unrestraint.
I wrestled with my soul, as with a foe,
it bidding me to err, I saying no;
we were as ancient enemies at large;
I put on patience, to withstand its charge,
with troops of tempting came it forth to fight –
what patience could withstand such reckless might? –
which gave it courage, when its courage quailed,
and reinforcement, when its forces failed.
Now I succeed, now it, in the affray,
yet, when we meet, it ever wins the day.
I love it well, but it opposes me
as if I held it not in amity:
it is an enemy I cannot hate,
a memory I can ne'er obliterate.
Blindly it swims upon its sinful sea,
clutching the hems of its iniquity:
I greatly fear, if it doth still rebel,

its ruin in this life, and, after, Hell!
Wherefore, O Lord, bring its repentance near,
and wash away its sin in founts of fear:
if Thou, my God, its chastener shouldst be,
O whither shall it look for clemency?
Be gracious, then, and all its sins forgive:
Thou art its Lord, for through Thee it doth live.

Source: A. J. Arberry (trans.) 'Uyub al-Nafs' (attributed to al-Ghazali), *The Muslim World Quarterly*, 30 (1940) pp. 140–3 (Hartford, Conn.).

3.41 'POEM OF THE WAY'

IBN AL-FARID

Ibn al-Farid (1182–1235 CE) was born in Cairo. After converting to Sufism, he visited Mecca but returned to die in Cairo. His verse depicts his own mystical experience and is still committed to heart by Sufis in Egypt today.

Thou seest forms of things in every garb
Displayed before thee from behind the veil
Of ambiguity: the opposites
In them united for a purpose wise:
Their shapes appear in each and every guise:
Silent, they utter speech: though still, they move:
Themselves unluminous, they scatter light.
Thou laughest gleefully, as the most gay
Of men rejoices; weep'st like a bereaved
And sorrowing mother, in profoundest grief;
Mournest, if they do moan, upon the loss
Of some great happiness; art jubilant,
If they do sing, for such sweet melody.
Thou seest how the birds among the boughs
Delight thee with their cooing, when they chant
Their mournful notes to win thy sympathy,
And marvellest at their voices and their words
Expressing uninterpretable speech.
Then on the land the tawny camels race
Benighted through the wilderness; at sea
The tossed ships run amid the billowy deep.
Thou gazest on twain armies – now on land,
Anon at sea – in huge battalions
Clad all in mail of steel for valour's sake
And fenced about with points of swords and spears.
The troops of the land-army – some are knights
Upon their chargers, some stout infantry;

The heroes of the sea-force – some bestride
The decks of ships, some swarm the lance-like masts.
Some violently smite with gleaming swords,
Some thrust with spears strong, tawny, quivering;
Some 'neath the arrows' volley drown in fire,
Some burn in water of the flaming flares.
This troop thou seest offering their lives
In reckless onslaught, that with broken ranks
Fleeing humiliated in the rout.
And thou beholdest the great catapult
Set up and fired, to smash the fortresses
And stubborn strongholds. Likewise thou mayst gaze
On phantom shapes with disembodied souls
Cowering darkly in their dim domain,
Apparelled in strange forms that disaccord
Most wildly with the homely guise of men;
For none would call the Jinnis homely folk.
And fishermen cast in the stream their nets
With busy hands, and swiftly bring forth fish;
And cunning fowlers spread their gins, that birds
A-hunger may be trapped there by a grain.
Ravening monsters of the ocean wreck
The fragile ships; the jungle-lions seize
Their slinking prey; birds swoop on other birds
Out of the heavens; in a wilderness
Beasts hunt for other beasts. And thou mayst glimpse
Still other shapes that I have overpassed
To mention, not relying save upon
The best exemplars. Take a single time
For thy consideration – no long while –
And thou shalt find all that appears to thee
And whatsoever thou dost contemplate
The act of one alone, but in the veils
Of occultation wrapt: when he removes
The curtain, thou beholdest none but him,
And in the shapes confusion no more reigns.

Source: A. J. Arberry (trans.) *'Poem of the Way' by Ibn al-Fārid*, Chester Beatty Monographs (London: Emergy Walker, 1952), lines 2137–99.

3.42

SHAIKH ABU-L-ABBAS AL-ALAWI

Shaikh Abu-l-Abbas al-Alawi (1869–1934 CE) was an Algerian Sufi whose spirituality was known beyond north Africa. In the first of these extracts, he offers a vigorous defence to a critic of the way of the 'Folk' or Sufis.

3.42.1 From the newspaper *Al-Balagh*

There is no religious authority or man of learning in Islam who has not a due respect for the path of the Folk, either through direct experience of it in spiritual realization, or else through firm belief in it, except those who suffer from chronic short-sightedness and remissness and lack of aspiration and who *prefer to take what is inferior in exchange for the superior*. As for the believer of high aspiration, his soul by its very nature strains yearningly upwards towards what lies beyond these conditions that surround us, in the hope that he may chance upon some spiritual perfume or holy breath of inspiration which has strayed from the next world and which will be as a lamp in his hand to light him upon his path. God says: *Whoso striveth after Us, verily We shall lead them upon Our paths*, and indeed the true believer looks unceasingly for one who will take him to God, or at the very least he looks for the spiritual gifts which lie hidden within him, that is, for the primordial nature which he has lost sight of and in virtue of which he is human. It is characteristic of man that his soul should tend upwards beyond those inclinations to cleave to the earth which are what connects him with the lower animal species.' [. . .]

'I do not deny, my brother, the existence of many intruders among the Sufis – only too many – who deserve censure, and if you had concentrated on these, no one could have blamed you. Moreover you would have had a good deed to your own credit, while doing us, in particular, a service at the same time. What offended us was your vilification of the way of the Folk altogether, and your speaking ill of its men without making any exceptions, and this is what prompted me to put before you these quotations from some of the highest religious authorities. At the very least they should impel you to consider your brothers the Sufis as members of the community of true believers, every individual of whom both we and you are bound to respect. The Prophet said: "Whoso prayeth our prayer and useth our orientation and eateth of our sacrifices, the same is a Moslem, and he is under a pact of protection from God and His Messenger. So cause not the pact of God to be violated."' [. . .]

'You know, my brother, that every name has an influence which attaches itself to the soul of him who mentions it even if it is not one of the Divine Names. For example, if a man repeat several times the word "death", he will feel an imprint upon his soul owing to the mention of that name, especially if he persists in it, and there is no doubt that this imprint will be different from that which is experienced from mentioning "wealth" or "glory" or "power".

'Any reasonably sensitive man will be conscious of the influence upon his soul of the name that he mentions, and if we admit this, we are bound to believe that the Name of God also produces an influence upon the soul as other names do, each one leaving the particular imprint that corresponds to it. I think you are aware that a name is ennobled with the nobility of him who is named inasmuch as it carries his imprint in the hidden fold of its secret essence and its meaning.' [. . .]

'The question of invocation is of wider scope than you imagine. A sick man lay groaning in the presence of the Prophet and one of the Companions told him to stop and to be patient, whereupon the Prophet said: "Let him groan, for groaning is one of the Names of God in which the sick man may find relief."

'Now suppose that the sick man had been repeating the Name of Majesty *Allāh! Allāh!* instead of *Ah! Ah!*, would that Companion's objection have been justified . . .?'

'This is surely enough to make a man think well of the rememberers, whatever their method of remembrance. But supposing that all I have said so far does not convince you as a logical proof, then it is only fair to say that the question is one about which we must agree to differ. In other words, it is a matter for *ijtihād*, and on what pretext, my brother, would you compel us to accept your way of thinking and subscribe to your *ijtihād* when we have done nothing to compel you to subscribe to ours?' [. . .]

'Abū Ḥāmid al-Ghazālī said: 'First of all I sought to make my way upon the path of the mystics with many litanies and much fasting and prayer. Then when God had proved the sincerity of my purpose, He decreed that I should meet one of His Saints, who said to me: "My son, rid thy heart of all attachment save unto God, and go apart by thyself and say with all thy powers of concentration *Allāh Allāh Allāh*."' He also said, I mean Ghazālī: "When thy thoughts are muddied with other than God, thou hast need of the negation *lā ilāha*. But once thou hast withdrawn from all things in contemplation of Him who is the Lord of all, thou takest thy rest in *Say Allāh, and leave them to their idle prating*." Then he said: "When thou hast finished recalling that which never was and art busied with the remembrance of Him who ever is, thou sayest *Allāh* and takest thy rest from all else." He also said: "Open the door of thy Heart with the key of thy saying *lā ilāha illā' Llāh* and the door of thy Spirit by saying *Allāh*, and lure down the bird of thy Secret by saying *Huwa Huwa*."

3.43.2 Shaikh Abu-l-Abbas al-Alawi remembered by a contemporary

'In his brown jallabah and white turban, with his silver-grey beard and his long hands which seemed when he moved them to be weighed down by the flow of his *barakah* (blessing), he exhaled something of the pure archaic ambiance of Sayyidnā Ibrāhīm al-Khalīl ["Abraham the Friend (of God)"]. He spoke in a subdued, gentle voice, a voice of splintered crystal from which, fragment by fragment, he let fall his words. . . . His eyes, which were like two sepulchral lamps, seemed to pierce through all objects, seeing in their outer shell merely one and the same nothingness, beyond which they saw always one and the same reality – the Infinite. Their look was very direct, almost hard in its enigmatic unwaveringness, and yet full of charity. Often their long ovals would grow suddenly round as if in amazement or as if enthralled by some marvellous spectacle. The cadence of the singing, the dances and the ritual incantations seemed to go on vibrating in him perpetually; his head would sometimes rock rhythmically to and fro while his soul was plunged in the unfathomable mysteries of the Divine Name, hidden in the *dhikr*, the Remembrance. . . . He gave out an impression of unreality, so remote was he, so inaccessible, so difficult to take in on account of his altogether abstract simplicity. . . . He was surrounded, at one and the same time, with all the veneration that is due to saints, to leaders, to the old, and to the dying.'

Source: Martin Lings, *A Sufi Saint of the Twentieth Century*, 2nd edn (London: Allen & Unwin, 1971), pp. 109–14, 117.

— ● ◆ ● —

ISLAM IN THE LATE
TWENTIETH CENTURY

———— ◆◆◆ ————

3.43 A STATEMENT BY THE ISLAMIC COUNCIL OF EUROPE, 1976

'In the name of God, Most Gracious, most Merciful'
'And God invites (you) to the House of Peace'

(al-Qur'an, 10:25)

Man has conquered the seas and the skies; man has harnessed the forces of nature to his service; man has created vast and complex institutions and organizations to administer his affairs; man seems to have reached the pinnacle of material progress!

Man also claims to have deeply reflected upon his position in the universe. He has begun to interpret reality with the sole use of his reason and the knowledge yielded by his senses. With a new found confidence in his own reasoning power and in the powers of science and technology, he has jettisoned his link with tradition, with revealed Truth, indeed with every form of guidance from beyond himself.

From this elevated position he seeks to mould the world according to his whims and fancies. But the 'brave new world' he has created drives an ordinary human being into profound disillusionment. In spite of unprecedented technological advancement and overall material development the condition of man remains highly unsettled. He sees the powerful subjugating the weak, the rich dominating the poor, the 'have-nots' arrayed against the 'haves'; he sees injustice and exploitation at national and international levels; he sees disintegration of the family, alienation of individual from society and its institutions, even from himself; and he sees the abuse of trust and authority in all spheres. Although he has shown his ability to fly in the air like the birds, and to swim in the oceans like the fishes, (but) he has failed to show his ability to live on the earth as good human beings. His failure here brings into doubt his capability to conduct his affairs in society without clear-cut guidelines for human action.

Man finds himself caught in a dilemma. He believes that he has reached the apex of civilization. But on reaching the apex he faces a new and greater void. He finds himself and the civilization he has built threatened with forces of his own creation. He frantically searches for remedies to rid his life of those portents of destruction which threaten to deprive him of his cherished dream of ultimate bliss. He finds that his world-view lacks definitive criteria to help him judge between right and wrong; he finds that his learning and expertise fail to give him universal criteria to distinguish between good and bad; he finds that change and the pace of change have swept him off his feet – nothing tangible and lasting remains. Increasingly man becomes dubious about the direction he is heading for. Inability to conceive a way out of this dilemma leads him to despair and gloom. Man becomes increasingly selfish and unmindful of humanity's collective needs. Man becomes aware of a choice – either he relinquishes all pretences to be anything other than an animal and sadly pronounces himself as the 'naked ape' or strives further to regain and retain his sanity.

His search leads him to the awareness that the fruits of his reason are not in themselves sufficient for comprehending the reality around him. He turns to meditation, to mysticism, to occult practices, to pseudo-spiritualism for gaining further insight and inspiration. His thirst remains unquenched; he fails to find a comprehensive doctrine based on reality and capable of universal application.

Man and the Word of God

At this stage, man needs to discover the Word of God. It informs him of his Creator, informs him of the purpose of his creation, informs him of his place as the 'best of creation', provides him with guidance to lead a fulfilling and rewarding life, tells him of the hereafter, teaches him the value of his fellow beings, makes everything else subservient to the criterion of Truth – in short, enables him to be at peace with himself, with the whole of creation and with the Creator.

The religion of Islam embodies the final and most complete Word of God. It is the embodiment of the code of life which God, the Creator and the Lord of the universe, has revealed for the guidance of mankind. Islam integrates man with God and His creation in such a way that he moves in cooperation with all that exists. Neglect of this dimension has impoverished human life and has made most of man's material conquests meaningless. Over-secularisation has deprived human life of its spiritual significance. But spiritual greatness cannot be achieved by a simple swing of the pendulum to the other extreme. Harmony and equilibrium can be attained only by the integration of the material with the spiritual. This is the approach that Islam brings to bear: it makes the whole of the domain of existence spiritual and religious. It stands for the harmonisation of the human will with the Divine Will – this is how peace is achieved in human life. It is through peace with God that man attains peace in the human order as also peace with nature, outside as well as within him.

The meaning of Islam

Islam is an Arabic word. It is derived from two roots, one *salm*, meaning peace and the other *slm*, meaning submission. Islam stands for 'a commitment to surrender one's will to the Will of God' and as such be at peace with the Creator and all that has been created by Him. It is through submission to the Will of God that peace is produced. Harmonisation of man's will with the Will of God brings about harmonisation of different spheres of life under an all-embracing ideal. Departmentalisation of life into different watertight compartments, religious and secular, sacred and profane, spiritual and material, is ruled out. There is unity of life and unity of the source of guidance. As God is One and indivisible, so is life and man's personality. Each aspect of life is inseparable from one another. Religious and secular are not two autonomous categories; they represent two sides of the same coin. Each and every act becomes related to God and His guidance. Every human activity is given a transcendent dimension; it becomes sacred and meaningful and goal-centred.

Islam is a world-view and an outlook on life. It is based on the recognition of the unity of the Creator and of man's submission to His will. Everything originates from the one God and everyone is ultimately responsible to Him. Thus the unity of the Creator has as its corollary the oneness of His creation. Distinctions of race, colour, caste, wealth and power disappear; man's relation with fellow man assumes total equality by virtue of the common Creator. Henceforth, man's mission becomes dedication to his Creator – worship and obedience of the Creator becomes his purpose in life.

The Creator has not left man without guidance for the conduct of his life. Ever since the beginning of Creation, He has sent down Prophets who conveyed His message to mankind. They are the source for finding God's Will. Thus we have the chain of Prophets beginning with Adam (peace be upon him) and ending with Muhammad (peace be upon him). Noah, John, Zacariah, Moses and Jesus (peace be upon them) all belong to this golden chain of Prophets. Prophets David, Moses, Jesus and Muhammad (may peace be upon them all), brought revealed books of guidance with them. The Qur'an, the Book revealed to the Prophet Muhammad, is the last of these books of guidance.

The Qur'an contains the Word of God and nothing but the Word of God. In it is preserved the divine revelation, unalloyed by human interpolation of any kind, unaffected by any change or loss to the original. In it is distilled the essence of all the messages sent down in the past. In it is embodied a framework for the conduct of the whole of man's life. There are explicit criteria for judging between the right and wrong, there are principles of individual and collective conduct of man. In it are depicted the follies of man in the past; in it are warnings for mankind and in it are assurances for continued guidance for those who seek God's help.

The Qur'an has depicted a path, the Straight Path (*Sirat al-Mustaqim*) which, when followed by man, revolutionises his whole life. It brings about a transformation in man's character and galvanises him into action. This action takes the form of purification of the self, and then unceasing effort to establish the laws of God on earth, resulting in a new order based on truth, justice, virtue and goodness.

Man plays a crucial role in the making of this world. He acts as God's [vicegerent] (*Khalifa*), His deputy and representative on the earth. He is morally prepared to play this role. His success lies in playing it properly: to enjoin what is right and forbid what is wrong, to free man from the bondage of fellow man, to demonstrate that a sound and serene society can only result if one harmonises one's will with the Will of God, makes seeking the Creator's pleasure as one's only purpose in life, treats the whole of Creation as one's partner, raises the concept of human welfare from the level of mere animal needs to seeking what is best in this world and what is best in the hereafter.

This is the Islamic world-view and its concept of man and his destiny. This is epitomised in the *Kalima* – the declaration of Islamic faith: *There is no god except Allah and Muhammad is Allah's prophet.*

Islam is not a religion in the Western understanding of the word. It is a faith and a way of life, a religion and a social order, a doctrine and a code of conduct, a set of values and principles and a social movement to realise them in history. There is no priesthood in Islam, not even an organised 'church'. All men and women who are committed to this ideal are expected to live in accordance with its principles and to strive to establish them in society and history. Those who commit themselves to Truth try to see that Truth prevails. They strive to make a new world in the image of the Truth.

Islam as a system of life prepares man to play this role and provides him with guidelines for the development of a new personality and a new society. For the purification of the self there are prayers (*Salat*), performed five times a day, in the confines of the home and in congregation in the mosques, strengthening man's commitment to God, refreshing his loyalty to truth, reinvigorating him to work for the realisation of his ideals. Prayer is supplemented by fasting (*Sawm*) for the achievement of these objectives. And if prayer and fasting integrate man with God and provide him with the spiritual discipline he needs to become godly in the midst of the rough and tumble of life, *Zakat* commits man's wealth – his worldly resources – to the achievement of divine purposes in the socio-economic realm. *Zakat* is a monetary obligation. Every Muslim who possesses more than a certain minimum amount of wealth has to contribute at least a certain percentage of his total wealth for welfare functions of the society. It is not merely a charity; it is a religious right which the rich owe to the needy and the poor, and to the society at large. But the spirit of this compulsory contribution is that it is paid by the rich as an act of worship and not merely as a tax. This is how all that man has, his soul, his body or his belongings are harnessed for the service of virtue, justice and truth. It is also obligatory on Muslims to visit the *Ka'ba* at least once in their lifetime for *hajj* (pilgrimage). This among others, is an index of the unity of the Muslim community (*Ummah*), a community of faith and a symbol of the unity of mankind. A universal order can come into existence only on the basis of a universal faith and not on the basis of commitment to the gods of race, colour, or region. The ideal of man's brotherhood seeks actualisation in Islam.

Islam in history

Islam is the original religion of man. It began with the first man, who was also the first prophet and who himself submitted to the Will of God and invited others to do the same. The same message was preached by all the prophets of God, who guided man to the Right Path. But man not only veered away from the right path again and again, but also lost or distorted the code of guidance which the prophets handed out to him. That was why other prophets were sent to re-state the original message and guide man to the right path. The last of these prophets was Muhammad (peace be upon him) who presented God's guidance in its final form and also arranged to preserve it for all time. It is this guidance which is now known as Islam and is enshrined in the Qur'an and the life-example of the prophet.

Muhammad (peace be upon him) was born in Makka in 571 C.E. At the age of forty (611 C.E.), he received revelation from God and began his role as God's prophet. He invited those around him to the path of Islam: some responded to his call and became his companions; others rebuked him and subjected him and his companions to all form of persecution. He continued his work undaunted by all storms of opposition and oppression. His noble example won converts from far and near. In the twelfth year of his prophethood (622 C.E.) he migrated from Makka, his own birth-place, to Yathrib, later known as Madinah, as the people of Madinah had accepted his message and invited him as their leader and head of the state to establish the new order he was preaching. The Muslim calendar begins from the day the prophet migrated to Madinah, the day Islam became an established order. The prophet lived another ten years during which the new system was developed in Madinah, from where it spread to the whole of Arabia. When the prophet died in 632 C.E. the warring tribes of Arabia were united under the banner of Islam and were poised to make significant contribution to world history and civilisation. The message of Islam had galvanised the hitherto scattered nomadic Arabs into a powerful community with a mission. Within a short space of time the message of Islam was echoed from the shores of Europe to China. The invitation to accept the sovereignty of One God was overwhelmingly accepted, over eight hundred million Muslims bear testimony to this message today. A new society was established on the basis of an ideology and it was able to have within its embrace people belonging to different races, colours and historical traditions.

A new model of human personality and a new vision of human culture were presented before humanity. Science and technology were developed but they were not directed towards destroying nature and man's abode therein; they added to man's efficiency as much as to life's sublimity. There was a new harmony between man and nature and between man and society. The uniqueness of Islamic culture lies in its values. When Muslims, after an illustrious historical career, became oblivious of this fact and became obsessed with the manifestations of their culture, as against its sources, they could not even fully protect the house they had built. The strength of Islam lies in its ideals, values and principles. And their relevance to man is as great today as it has been in history. The message, the Qur'an that contains the message, the example of the prophet that embodies this message, and the example of his followers who have kept the torch burning throughout history are a living force. The message is timeless and the principles it embodies are of universal application. Man has to grasp the message and follow the example of Muhammad (may peace be upon him) to elevate himself to his true position as God's representative on earth.

Thus man, who has lost his bearings at the very threshold of his material and technological prowess needs the reality of Islam to breathe a new spirit into him; to revive his decaying morality and values; to show him a fresh direction; to prevent him from taking that final suicidal leap into oblivion; to show him the path to happiness and bliss for which he has laboured so much only to find himself on the edge of a precipice – in short, to give him what, deep down within him, he has always wanted, and on which his survival and future development rests.

Source: Published by the Islamic Council of Europe by The Islamic Foundation (Leicester, 1976).

3.44 VEILED THREATS
RANA KABBANI

Rana Kabbani was born in 1958 in Damascus and subsequently has lived and studied in many countries. She has described herself as an 'underground Muslim' until 'forced into the open' by the Salman Rushdie affair and provoked to reflect on her situation as a Muslim living in the West.

Perhaps one of the most contentious issues for the West, particularly Western women, is the place of the veil in Islamic culture. In the popular mind in the United States and Europe, the veil covering the face is the very symbol of Islam. Yet it is worth recalling that it is of Christian origin, and was adopted by the Arabs only when they conquered Syria in the seventh century in imitation of the social elite they found there and displaced. The veil should not be confused with the Islamic *hijab* which covers a woman's hair, considered sexually attractive and arousing. During the Prophet's lifetime even the *hijab* was worn only by his wives in order to distinguish them from other women. It was later taken on by Muslim women in emulation of these 'Mothers of Islam'. The Qur'an enjoins modesty of apparel, so as not to reveal to men outside her family a woman's hair, her naked limbs or her bosom.

Earlier this century, some relaxation of the rules of modesty crept into Muslim practice here and there, particularly in countries with secular governments. But where change occurred, it met with resistance. When the miniskirt came in and I was allowed to wear one, my paternal grandmother, who never appeared in public without a *hijab*, was aghast. 'The knee is shameful', she would mutter. And when, aged ten, on the way to the swimming pool, I once ran into the kitchen at home wearing a bathing costume, our aged cook nearly dropped her pot, exclaiming to my mother, 'Aren't you ashamed to let your daughter appear naked in front of men!' When she got no satisfactory reply, she complained to my father. He calmed her down by reminding her that the Prophet himself had urged Muslims to teach their children, girls and boys alike, to swim, hunt and ride horses.

My paternal grandmother's 'at home' days were occasions when I could observe the rituals of traditional female behaviour. These occasions were the pattern in poor as well as bourgeois homes, where women met together and enjoyed each other's company away from the pressures of their households. The mornings were spent in preparation in my grandmother's house: vats of lemonade were made with grated peel; bowls of custard were laid out to cool in the dark pantry; and everything was cleaned a dozen times: the floors swept and then scrubbed with soap and water, the chests dusted then rubbed with oil to make the marquetry stand out, and the divan covers freshly laundered and starched. Sugared almonds were piled in dishes and *nargilehs* set out for those elderly ladies who smoked and whose disapproving husbands were dead.

The women entered the house by the harem door and, once safely inside the rooms reserved for them, took off their *hijab* and street coats. For the rest of the afternoon that part of the house was strictly out of bounds to men, allowing the guests to relax. Many were wearing their finery, their hair shaped with curling tongs and their eyes ringed with *kohl*. Bare arms and *décolleté* dresses were displayed. Some had brought their unwed daughters, since others had come to find brides for their unmarried sons. The newly betrothed (whether rich or poor) would wear their in-laws' gifts of jewellery for all to admire. Some carried lutes or tambourines to entertain the company while others would sing, dance, or tell stories. The more devout would deliver a religious homily.

My maternal grandmother was a very different story. Her upper-class family wore their religion lightly. Two generations ago, between the two world wars, educated Muslim women like her were flamboyantly tearing off the *hijab*. For maximum publicity, such luminaries of the feminist movement in Egypt as Huda Sha'rawi and Durriya Shafiq dropped their headscarves over the rail of ships or threw them out of the windows of trains as they returned to the Muslim world from Europe. Compared to the secular and scientific West, their own societies seemed stagnant, suffocating and tradition-bound. They had been impressed by the suffragette movement and modelled their own liberation on it.

In the wider political arena, these early Arab feminists agreed with their men that to throw off colonial rule, Western methods had to be adopted because they seemed to hold the key to strength. The most ardent nationalists, those who had suffered most from Western domination, still felt drawn to Western culture.

Across the Arab world, the daughters of this revolutionary generation managed to lead lives not unlike those of Western women of the more affluent classes: going to university, finding jobs in the professions, marrying for love, and bringing up their own families in the modern way. Western fashions were assiduously followed: the New Look was as much 'in' in Damascus as it was in Paris. In the courtyards of the old houses, upper-class men and women danced to the latest tangos and foxtrots on the gramophone; while Western art was admired and studied, influencing style as much as it did in Europe. [. . .]

These trends grew out of a new post-war prosperity, out of the emergence of an educated middle class, out of a widely shared hope that the revolutionary upheavals then shaking the region would lead to political renewal with greater popular partic-ipation. Nasser was the hero of the hour. Whenever he spoke, people across the Arab world would be glued to their radios, and when he nationalised the Suez Canal in 1956, crowds ran shouting with excitement into the streets in a spontaneous cele-bration of the new era.

There was a sense that the whole 'Third World' was awakening and that it had a future which it would fashion itself. Nasser was one of a pantheon which included Nehru, Nkrumah, Sukarno – proud leaders who for the first time represented the interests and aspirations of their people. This was the heyday of nationalism. Algeria's eight-year war of independence against France, a classic armed struggle against colonial rule, aroused enormous passions.

One of the heroines of this struggle was Jamila Bouhired, who had been tortured and scarred by her French captors but had inspired a whole generation of Algerian women to become freedom fighters in the war of a 'million martyrs'. In the early sixties, when the war was over, she paid an official visit to Kuwait, where the Minister of Education and a party of veiled women teachers waited to receive her at the airport. She appeared at the door of the plane – with her hair uncovered. Not wishing to embarrass her, and no doubt infected by the spirit of the times, the Minister turned to the teachers and commanded: 'Quick, take off your *hijab!*'

Much has changed today. It would be inconceivable for an official in a Muslim country to order women to remove their *hijab* without starting a riot. This is not only because of the rise of fundamentalism; it is primarily because the *hijab* is no longer seen as a symbol of an archaic tradition. Rather, it has become a striking affirmation of identity – religious, cultural and political – reflecting the more radical feelings that now prevail.

The adoption of the *hijab* by educated and politicised young women, often from secular families, has in the 1980s become an inescapable phenomenon of life in most Muslim cities. There are many reasons for this, but above all it reflects the disillusion of this generation with the achievements of its elders. In the Arab world, indepen-dence proved an immense disappointment. No new social order founded on justice was created: instead, corruption and repression ruled. Defeat in war led to the loss of yet more lives and land. Despite Arab rhetoric Israeli hegemony, propped up by the West, remained unchallenged. 'Third World' solidarity collapsed. In Arabia and the Gulf, the very areas where oil wealth in independent Arab hands could have made a difference, Western interests rather than Arab aspirations seemed to prevail. Western products of all sorts, cultural as well as material, flooded the marketplace.

Responding to these setbacks, Muslim feminists no longer choose to model them-selves on their Western sisters. The over-permissive West – which they now perceive, perhaps crudely, as exploitive of women, as plagued by drugs and AIDS, and as indifferent to the sufferings of the rest of the world – is to them a less attractive place than it seemed to their grandmothers. At the risk of reiterating what has now become a cliché, it must also be said that the issues which concern them are not those of Western feminists. In the late 1970s a conference was held in Scandinavia on International Women's Day. Among the Arabs present was the Palestinian guerrilla fighter Fatima Barnawi, who had spent long years in Israeli jails, was tortured, and had been forced to watch her father being tortured when no information could be extracted from her. I recall her bewilderment when, newly arrived at the conference, she was exposed to hour-long speeches by European feminists on lesbian rights. Although the importance of debates about sexuality in the context of Western feminism should not be underestimated, the political exigencies of survival in the Middle East could not help but make these issues seem a luxury.

When Arabs today view their society – and much the same could be said for all Muslims – they see a travesty of modernism, neither genuinely Western nor properly Eastern, and certainly not satisfactory. The frenzy of Islamic revivalism must surely be a reaction to this state of affairs. The women who decide to put on the *hijab*, that flag of Islamic commitment, are not retreating from ground won by their grandmothers. Just as it was a political choice fifty years ago to remove the *hijab*, a choice freely made and of great consequence, so the decision today to put it on again is equally momentous and equally political.

These women are not withdrawing to an archaic past, nor do they wish to stay demurely at home. Most often they are professional women, doctors, teachers, pharmacists and lawyers. Politically, they are activists – a sort of Muslim Sisterhood not unlike the Muslim Brotherhood of male militants, but unconnected with it. The wearing of Islamic dress gives these women greater rather than less freedom and mobility, for in such austere garb and with the mentality that accompanies it, they are much less likely to be closely monitored by their families.

Wearing the *hijab* can be a liberation, freeing women from being sexual objects, releasing them from the trap of Western dress and the dictates of Western fashion. Just as feminists in the West have reflected on the connection between 'feminine' clothes and female oppression, so Muslim feminists reject the outward symbols of sexual allure. In favour of the *hijab* it can be said that by distancing its wearer from the world, it enriches spiritual life, grants freedom from material preoccupations, and erases class differences by expressing solidarity with others in the same uniform. Since all women look the same in it, it is a most effective equaliser, and since it camouflages rich clothing, it is in keeping with the Islamic injunction against ostentation. [. . .]

Some practical advantage may be derived from the *hijab*. Western feminists are familiar with the notion of a supportive group of friends, acquaintances and contacts – a female alternative to the exclusive 'old boy' network – and so it is with their Muslim sisters. In most Muslim countries – in Morocco, Algeria, Libya, Tunisia, Egypt, Sudan and Nigeria; in Jordan; in the occupied West Bank and Gaza; in Lebanon and Syria; in the Gulf; in Turkey, Iran, Afghanistan and Pakistan; in Malaysia and Indonesia – something like a women's underground is taking shape, providing an alternative to the apparatus of power and influence which in all these countries belongs to the state and to those most closely associated with it.

Women drawn into this underground are, on the whole, those who have received an education and made their way in life. They are encouraged by friends who are committed Muslims to adopt the *hijab* if they have not already done so. They meet at social gatherings at which something like cells are formed. Soon women discover that this network can provide real advantages – one of its members knows how to obtain a supply of scarce medicines, another can find places for children at an oversubscribed school, a third has a high-placed contact in a ministry. Such connections are extremely useful in developing countries, where life is always something of a struggle and a push by a person of influence is usually necessary to get things done. The network provides an informal matchmaking service, finding husbands for its unmarried members, and also works as a therapeutic group where women can talk about their personal problems and get comfort and advice.

Undoubtedly such coteries can be tainted by fanaticism, by a holier-than-thou exclusiveness, by a blinkered approach to life. Belonging to a Sisterhood and sharing the faith can be attractive but it can also be imprisoning, limiting one's choices on every level. Viewed from the outside such zealotry can be distasteful, as fanaticism is in all religions. But the anger and frustration which fuel it should not be under-estimated.

To the secular Western mind, displays of religious fervour by veiled women – but especially by heavily bearded men of dark skin – are always incomprehensible, disagreeable, even frightening. The spectacle of Muslims in large numbers, demon-strating, shaking their fists, clinging passionately to their religion, renouncing the West, arouses understandable anxiety and a defensive instinct. But it is as well to remember that the threatening crowd often itself feels threatened, and seeks in religious fervour a haven from a hostile world. Loyalty to a creed which bonds them together makes Muslims feel politically less vulnerable, particularly at a time when Arab unity, say, or 'Third World' solidarity, has been revealed as bankrupt. There is of course a real conflict which cannot be disguised between mob passions and the Western ideal of individualism, with its rights and freedoms. But beyond this philo-sophical conflict there is another, more real to Muslims, between a dominating West and a still struggling East. Political and economic frustrations have led to an often worrying increase in religious 'fundamentalism' all over the Muslim world.

Source: R. Kabbani, 'Veiled threats', in *Letter to Christendom* (London: Virago, 1989), pp. 22–8

3.45 DISAGGREGATING 'ISLAM': FOUR GUIDELINES
FRED HALLIDAY

This overview of developments since the 1970s may serve to illustrate some of the features of this international trend, but also to underline the dangers of simplifica-tion with regard to it. In the light of this diversity, and of the record of the past two decades, it is possible to make some general remarks about this current and to place it in some broader perspective. Four of these are especially relevant to any assess-ment of the current stage of Islamic movements.

1 Islamism as politics

The terms 'revival' and 'fundamentalist' are misleading, since both refer to trends *within* a religion. This Islamic current involves not a revival of religious belief, but an assertion of the relevance of this belief, selectively interpreted, to politics. The Islamic movement has had a strong religious character: but it has not involved a movement of conversion, from other religions, or a return to belief by formerly Muslim communities who had abandoned their faith. Rather, it involves the assertion that, in the face of secular, modern, and European ideas, Islamic values should play a dominant role in political and social life and should define the identity of the Islamic peoples. If there is one common thread running through the multiple movements characterized as 'fundamentalist', it is not anything to do with their interpretation of the Islamic 'foundations', i.e. the Qur'an or *hadith* but rather their claim to be able to determine a politics for Muslim peoples. The central concern of Islamist movements is the state, how to resist what is seen as an alien and oppressive state, and how, through a variety of tactics, to obtain and maintain control of the state. In this perspective the rise of Islamist movements in the 1970s and 1980s bears comparison with that of tendencies elsewhere that deploy religious ideology in pursuit of other, nationalist and populist, political goals – in Christianity, Judaism, Hinduism, Buddhism. Given the tendency of both Muslims themselves and those who write about 'Islam' to treat it as both a unitary and unique phenomenon, it would be prudent henceforth to check any generalization about Islam against the practices of those using other, non-Islamic, religions in a similarly political manner.

2 Variants of Islamism

Once this essentially political interpretation becomes clear, then it is more possible to identify and explain the variety of Islamist movements and ideas. For the character of Islamist movements varies according to the political and social context in which these trends arise. Broadly speaking, there are three such contexts. The first is Islamic popular revolt. This is where a popular movement within an Islamic country challenges a secular state, or one that is regarded as insufficiently Islamic, for political power: this was classically the case in Iran in 1978–9, and it also applies in Algeria, Tunisia, Egypt, Turkey and, in very different circumstances, Afghanistan. It involves a popular revolt against the modernizing, centralizing, state. The second form of Islamic politics is where Islam is used by a state itself to legitimate and consolidate its position. Here there exists a spectrum, from the very token invocation of Islamic identity by what are in effect secular rulers (Nasser's Egypt, Morocco, the FLN in Algeria, the Ba'th in Syria and Iraq) through to the use of Islam as a more central part of the state's authority and power. Even this category permits of no simple definition, since regimes that proclaim themselves as legitimated by Islam range across the gamut of political options: military dictatorships (Libya, Pakistan, and now Sudan); tribal oligarchies (Saudi Arabia); clerical dictatorship (Iran). Nothing could make clearer the extent to which Islamic politics is dependent on the pre-existing context and serves as the instrument of state power.

The last variant of Islamic politics is in contexts of confessional or ethnic conflict. Here Islamism serves to articulate the interests and identity of groups that form part of a broader political community that is heterogeneous on religious grounds, i.e.

includes Muslims and non-Muslims, or, even where all are Muslims, includes divergent sects of Islam or different linguistic and ethnic groups. This has received less
attention on the international level, but it is a major part of the picture of Islamic
politics in the contemporary world. Long-established variants of this are the Lebanon
and the Caucasus, and the Islamic–Coptic conflict in Egypt. But modern developments have created new contexts in which such tendencies can develop as part of
conflicts within specific states. This is, after all, the context in which Islamism is
spreading in Western Europe, as part of a self-definition of new communities within
a secular, post-Christian, society. It is equally so in the Balkans: for all the talk, mainly
from Orthodox Christians in Serbia and Greece of a 'Muslim' challenge to the
Balkans, it is the non-Muslims who have accentuated the situation there, and in so
doing led some Muslims, in Bosnia and in Albania, to adopt more fundamentalist
positions. This communal context is part, too, of the explanation for the role of
Islamist ideas amongst the Palestinians, since they are, in effect, a subordinated part
of a broader non-Muslim, in this case Israeli, society. Equally a part of the Islamist
movement in Algeria can be seen in this light, as the expression of Arab hostility to
the Kabyle minority for whom the French language, and a more secular order, provide
an alternative to domination by the Arab majority. The issue of Arabic within Algeria
has, therefore, several layers of significance: as a cultural assertion against French, as
an Islamic assertion against non-Islamic values, and as an Arab assertion against the
Kabyles. The close association of the Arabic language with Islamic identity enables
this campaign for Arabic to bear these multiple, ethnic-religious, meanings. To take
an example from the non-Arab world, that of Malaysia: in a society divided between
Muslim Malays and non-Muslim Chinese, and growing resentment by the former of
the latter, Islamism serves amongst the Malays to express an ethnic and confessional
interest.

3 Contingent interpretations

This picture of the variant roles of Islam in politics can illumine the degree to which
'Islam' itself is open to differing interpretations, how the particular use made of its
traditions and texts is variable, contingent on contemporary, rather more material
and political concerns. In the hypostatization of doctrine this is a point that is too
often obscured in discussions, by Muslims and non-Muslims alike, of the role of
'Islam' itself in these processes. The presupposition upon which much discussion
of the question rests is that there exists one, unified and clear, tradition to which
contemporary believers and political forces may relate. Many of the discussions that
have taken place in the Islamic world have rested on this assumption, of an essential
Islam. This was the case in the 1960s in the debate about whether Islam favoured
capitalism or socialism. It recurred in the 1970s and 1980s in discussions of the place
of women, in analysis of the proper role of the clergy in an Islamic society, in the
debate on Islamic teaching on tolerance after the Rushdie affair and so forth. These
all involve an assumption that there is one 'true' interpretation. Opponents of Islamist
movements tend to reproduce this essentialist assumption in discussing such questions

as whether Islamic societies can ever be democratic, or whether there is some special link between the 'Islamic mind' and terrorism. The reality is that no such essential Islam exists: as one Iranian thinker put it, Islam is a sea in which it is possible to catch almost any fish one wants. It is, like all the great religions, a reserve of values, symbols, and ideas from which it is possible to derive a contemporary politics and social code: the answer as to why this or that interpretation was put upon Islam resides therefore, not in the religion and its texts itself, but in the contemporary needs of those articulating an Islamic politics. These needs are evident, and secular, enough: the desire to challenge or retain state power; the need to mobilize dominated, usually urban, populations for political action; the articulation of a nationalist ideology against foreign domination and those within the society associated with it; the 'need' to control women; the carrying out of social and political reforms designed to strengthen post-revolutionary states.

4 Criteria of 'success'

Once 'Islam' and 'Islamism' are disaggregated in this way, the movements that proclaim their adherence to Islam can be seen both within their own specific contexts and as part of a loose, variegated, and unco-ordinated international system. Moreover, it may become easier to arrive at a yardstick for assessing the impact and success of this phenomenon. The criterion often raised after the Iranian revolution was whether or not there would be a repetition of what happened in Iran: on this criterion, the Iranian revolution has not spread and fundamentalism has been contained. But this criterion is in two major respects an inadequate one. First, it adopts too small a timescale. Revolutionaries themselves, whether Islamic or other, are impatient, and expect other peoples to imitate them immediately: in this sense they become disappointed just as quickly as their opponents become relieved. But in historical perspective it would seem that the timescale for assessing the international impact of revolution is not a few years but several decades: the impact of the French revolution was felt throughout the nineteenth century; it was in the late 1940s, thirty years after 1917, that the USSR enjoyed its greatest external expansion; it took Castro twenty years to secure a revolutionary ally on the Latin American mainland, in Nicaragua. In the case of the Iranian revolution, however, there is a further reason why the criterion of state power is inadequate, namely that the impact of the Islamic upheaval there has been substantial even though no other state has become an Islamic republic. It is only necessary to see the rise in Islamist political consciousness in a range of couuntries to see how far the Iranian model has influenced political behaviour, or to recognize the increased interest amongst young people in Islamic clothing, Islamic literature, mosque attendance, and so forth. It is commonly asserted that Iran lost its following in the Arab world after it became embroiled in the war with Iraq in 1980: but while it was often presented by Arab states as just another example of Persian expansionism and Shiite heterodoxy, a general identification with the Iranian revolution was evident in many countries, and, in some, such as Lebanon, took organized form. Whether or not Islamist forces of the Iranian variety to come to power in the following years or decades, the impact of the revolution and of the broader trend with which it is associated is undeniable.

As was noted earlier, each of the three forms of Islamic interaction with politics has evident relevance to the contemporary international situation, and to the Mediterranean in particular. Thus the movements in Algeria, Tunisia, Egypt, Israel, Lebanon, and Turkey are all variants of the first category, that of populist revolts, from below, against the State: indeed 'Islam' has become the dominant idiom in which such resistance is expressed. Within this category there are also major differences – some are led by clerics, others by lay personnel; some are Sunni, others Shiite. The use of 'Islam' by established regimes to promote their own legitimacy is also widespread: thus in their attempt to pre-empt Islamist revolt from below, Egyptian rulers since Nasser, Sadat, and Mubarak, have presented themselves in Islamic garb. In a more militant form, Qaddafi has also done the same thing: yet Qaddafi's espousal of the Islamic cause can be seen as much as a radical extension of the Nasserite Arab nationalist use of Islam as something involving a clear primacy for Islam. His territorial claims are Arab nationalist – on a par with the Iraqi claim on part of Iran, the Syrian on part of Turkey, the belief that Eritrea and the Canary Islands are 'Arab', or occasional evocations of *malta arabiyya*. Qaddafi has clashed with the clerical and Islamist opposition within his own country, and is widely believed to be responsible for the death of the Lebanese Shiite leader Musa Sadr in 1978. In recent years he has taken to stressing the primary role of the Arabs within Islam and has attacked non-Arab Islamic forces, such as the Jamaat-i-Islami of Pakistan and the *tabligh* movement prevalent amongst Muslims of western Europe. The role of Islam in confessional conflicts, the third broad category, is evident on both sides of the Mediterranean – in Egypt and Lebanon, but also in Yugoslavia and in those western European countries with a larger Islamic population.

Source: F. Halliday, 'Disaggregating "Islam": four guidelines', from 'The politics of Islamic fundamentalism: Iran, Tunisia and the challenge of the secular state', in A. S. Ahmed and H. Donnan (eds) *Islam, Globalization and Postmodernity* (London and New York: Routledge, 1994), pp. 93–8.

PART FOUR

—•••—

HINDUISM

INTRODUCTION

— ◆◆◆ —

It is entirely appropriate that the readings on Hinduism begin with a discussion of the artificial nature of the term 'Hinduism' itself. India has given rise to a number of religious traditions and has also seen the arrival of religions such as Islam and Christianity that have taken their own distinctive forms once in India. European observers created the label 'Hinduism' to refer to the style of indigenous religion, past and present, practised by the majority of India's population and from which other Indian religions such as Buddhism and Jainism consciously distinguish themselves. Without a historical founder and lacking a distinct religious organisation, the many variations under the umbrella of Hinduism have been marked by adherence to a common worldview, and the pervasive influence of the caste system with its related social and ritual duties.

Hinduism does not centre on one manifestation of the divine or one set of beliefs about the nature of ultimate reality. In fact, Hinduism honours many different deities and supernatural beings. It also includes influential schools of thought that posit a non-personal and unified reality of which the deities in their personal forms are but lower and partial manifestations. The influence of early ritual and philosophical traditions, now found within the sacred text known as the Veda, has been felt more directly by the Brahmin caste entrusted with the transmission of the Vedic tradition and by those higher castes for whom the Brahmins act as ritual specialists. For the vast majority of Hindus, however, the religious life has revolved around a relationship with a deity or deities to whom devotion is offered and who may be approached for assistance with problems in the here and now. Hinduism addresses these problems as much as the longer term quest for *moksha*, final liberation from the round of rebirth.

During the last two centuries, a range of religious organisations have developed within Hinduism, which, unlike earlier internal variations, have been founded upon notions of membership. Typically, they have developed from a founding guru or teacher around whom a strong personality cult may have developed. With their own institutions, teachings and literature, many have spread throughout India and abroad. Some of these organisations have admitted those not born into Hindu families and thus into caste. This latitude, and the settlement of Hindu communities beyond India, has added a further dimension to Hinduism, which until relatively recently was largely tied to south Asia and its peoples.

During the campaign for independence from British rule, religious differences became more pronounced. Since Independence, Hinduism within India has become the marker of Indian identity for some Hindus. In the last quarter of the twentieth century, right-wing groups, which previously had limited public support, increased their political influence. The emergence of a more assertive and intolerant expression of Hinduism stands in contrast to its more universalistic tendencies.

The readings attempt to reflect something of the diversity within Hinduism. The day-to-day practice of rural Hindus is represented in selections taken from sociological and anthropological studies of village Hinduism. This is balanced by readings taken from influential texts that have shaped the practice and thought patterns of Hindus familiar with scriptural tradition. The distinctive ideas of a range of modern Hindu thinkers are included, and the section ends with a discussion of the growth of the Hindu right as a political force.

VILLAGE HINDUISM

———— ● ◆ ● ————

4.1 THE CONCEPT 'HINDUISM'
W. CANTWELL SMITH

The term 'Hinduism' is, in my judgement, a particularly false conceptualisation, one that is conspicuously incompatible with any adequate understanding of the religious outlook of Hindus. Even the term 'Hindu' was unknown to classical Hindus. 'Hinduism' as a concept certainly they did not have. And indeed one only has to reflect on the situation carefully to realise that it would necessarily have been quite meaningless to them.

As we have previously observed, the classical Hindus were inhibited by no lack of sophistication or self-consciousness. They thought about what we call religious questions profusely and with critical analysis. But they could not think of Hinduism because that is the name that we give to a totality whatever it might be that they thought, or did, or thought worth doing ...

My objection to the term 'Hinduism', of course, is not on the grounds that nothing exists. Obviously an enormous quantity of phenomena is to be found that this term covers. My point, and I think that this is the first step that one must take towards understanding something of the vision of Hindus, is that the mass of religious phenomena that we shelter under the umbrella of that term, is not a unity and does not aspire to be. It is not an entity in any theoretical sense, let alone any practical one.

'Islam' and 'Christianity', as we shall subsequently consider, are also in fact, in actual practice, internally diverse, and have been historically fluid. They, however, have included a tendency to wish not to be so; this is not how they conceptualise themselves. Many Christians and many Muslims have come to believe that there is one true Christianity and one true Islam. Hindus, on the other hand, have gloried in diversity. One of their basic and persistent affirmations has been that there are as many aspects of the truth as there are persons to perceive it.

Or, if some proclaimed a dogmatic exclusivism, insisting on their own version of the truth over against alternatives, it was always on a sectarian basis, one fraction of the total Hindu complex affirmed against other fractions – not of one transcending Hindu scheme as a whole. Some Hindus have been tolerant of diversity, and indeed have made a principle of it; those who have not, have adhered to a particularist position that thereby segmented the Hindu tradition as a possible theoretic unity. In either case, 'Hinduism' has not been a feasible concept for them in any essentialist sense . . .

What obstructs a definition of Hinduism, for instance, is precisely the richness of what exists, in all its extravagant variety from century to century and from village to village. The empirical religious tradition of the Hindus developing historically in the minds and hearts and institutions and literature and societies of untold millions of actual people is not a form, but a growing congeries of living realities. It is not to be compressed within or eviscerated into or confused with any systematic intellectual pattern.

'Hinduism' refers not to an entity; it is a name that the West has given to a prodigiously variegated series of facts. It is a notion in men's minds – and a notion that cannot but be inadequate. To use this term at all is inescapably a gross oversimplification.

Source: W. Cantwell Smith, *The Meaning and End of Religion*, Mentor Religious Classics (Mentor, 1964), pp. 61, 63 and 130.

4.2 THE PROBLEM OF VILLAGE HINDUISM

U. SHARMA

The theoretical problem and the 'fragmentary' approach

Anyone who studies Hinduism in its village context is liable to be more immediately impressed by the diversity of its local forms than by their unity. In the first place, the pantheon of any particular village is likely to be complex enough; the deities of the place may include gods and goddesses whose cults are sanctioned in the Vedas themselves alongside local godlings whose names are barely heard of outside a restricted area. The rituals used in worshipping these deities may be just as diverse; they will include relatively informal and private acts of worship on the part of individual devotees, whilst on other occasions highly formalised ritual procedure defined in Sanskrit texts must be used. Again, some rites are performed at the initiative of the individual and are directed to ends personal to himself, whilst others are associated with fixed dates in the calendar.

This diversity poses the following problem for the sociologist: to what extent do these various forms of religious activity form any kind of system? How are they related to each other in terms of either common underlying values or consistency of purpose? If Hinduism can indeed be envisaged as a system of social behaviour (as opposed to a mere collection of heterogeneous, and uncoordinated ritual activities, which we associate with each other merely through the force of tradition) then what gives coherence to this system? Hinduism is not sustained as a whole by any ecclesiastical or sectarian organisation; in the absence of such an institutional framework, at what level ought we to seek continuities between the diverse elements of which it is made?

Hitherto, the majority of sociologists who have made field studies of Hinduism have attempted to deal with this bewildering variety of its local forms by trying to arrange them in some scheme of classification, usually according to more or less culturological criteria. The origins of this kind of method can be seen in the pre-occupation of nineteenth-century ethnographers with the distinction between 'Aryan' and 'pre-Aryan' deities but the most prominent example of this type of approach in modern sociology is Srinivas's formulation of the 'Sanskritic'/'non-Sanskritic' dichotomy, and also his distinction between 'all-India' and 'local' Hinduism. Another leading example is Marriott's division of Hindu cultural features into the 'great traditional' and the 'little traditional'. This kind of approach is unsatisfactory in that it tends to deal with the individual elements of Hindu religious behaviour (cults, deities, rites) as discrete cultural traits, capable of being considered in isolation from each other. This is no doubt justifiable if our interest does not go beyond the cultural origins of these features; but for the sociologist it is hardly legitimate to treat them as independent entities, since in doing so he is obliged to lift them from their social context of meaning and purpose. Encumbered by frames of reference more suited to culturological investigation than to sociology, these writers have been able to pay little attention to such questions as whether for the individual Hindu his religious activities have any kind of underlying purpose or rationale integrating their diversity. Because the kind of approach which I have described emphasises, on the contrary, the ways in which the Hindu's religious experience and activity can be broken down and pigeon-holed into different categories I shall term this the 'fragmentary' method.

The most influential exponent of this kind of method has been M. N. Srinivas. In his study of the Coorgs he analyses their religion in terms of the distinction between, on the one hand, those forms which they share with Hindus everywhere in India (all-India Hinduism) and, on the other hand, those which they share only with members of a restricted locality (regional and local Hinduism). There are also forms which are entirely peculiar to themselves as a caste. Besides this formal distinction, Srinivas also distinguishes between those elements in Coorg religion which are Sanskritic (a term which he never adequately or explicitly defines, but by which he seems to mean 'sanctioned in scriptural texts written in Sanskrit') and those which are non-Sanskritic. In practice, for Srinivas, these two dichotomies often amount to one and the same distinction, since on the whole Sanskritic Hinduism and all-India Hinduism are the same thing. The process of Sanskritisation consists of the adoption of Sanskritic cults and practices and the giving up of purely local non-Sanskritic forms. In so far as Sanskritic forms (being associated with the Brahmans and the high castes) bear prestige, they may be copied by castes who wish to improve their status in the local caste hierarchy. The Coorgs, claims Srinivas, have Sanskritised many of their practices in recent times. Their participation in reformist movements such as the Ramakrishna Mission and the Lingayat sect are cited as evidence of this process, also the fact that they have begun to honour their ancestors by observing the annual *shraddha* ritual under the direction of a Brahman priest where before they made offerings of meat and wine to their ancestors through a low caste oracle. Because of his tendency to fragment Coorg religious experience, Srinivas is unable to tell us whether this Sankritisation represents any kind of qualitative change in the mode of Coorg religiosity, or whether it is a purely formal change; that is, when Coorg offer *shraddha* through Brahman priests instead of meat and wine through low-caste oracles, does this mean that they have in any way altered their ideas about the after-life or their attitudes towards their ancestors, or are these simply new manifestations of the same religious attitudes? If their acquaintance with the Lingayat sect has influenced the Coorgs to observe Shivratri and erect images of Shiva's Nandi bull, does this adoption of Sanskritised practice indicate the development of new religious ideas or sentiments, or simply the adoption of different cultural forms of expression? Does it mean that the Coorgs have changed the way in which they view their pantheon, or the relative importance which they give to its various members? Such questions cannot be answered so long as the practices in question are considered separately from Coorg religion in general. Whilst the sociologist ought not to concentrate exclusively on the subjective aspects of religion, Srinivas's over-concentration on ritual (as a self-acknowledged follower of Radcliffe-Brown) leads him to neglect the role of attitudes and values. Hence it is impossible to tell whether or in what way the Sanskritic elements in their religion and the non-Sanskritic elements are related to each other so far as the Coorgs themselves are concerned.

Even supposing that this kind of classification is useful, it still poses many problems of definition. In the absence of any clear statement of what exactly constitutes Sanskritic Hinduism, are we to use the term only to refer to rites sanctioned in the Hindu scriptures? Srinivas seems to imply this. Yet, if by Sanskritic deities we mean scriptural deities, how can we term Bheru (generally identified as a form of Shiva) and Chamunda (a form of Devi) as non-Sanskritic? At other times Srinivas seems to identify Sanskritic Hinduism with the forms of ritual and belief characteristic of the Brahmans as a caste. But if this identification is valid it is hardly consistent to refer to sects which explictly challenge the authority of the traditional Brahman priesthood as agents of Sanskritisation. Mahar describes the Arya Samaj as a Sanskritising influence on the group of sweepers which she studied, yet it is questionable whether such a term ought to be used of a movement which has aroused much bitter opposition from orthodox Brahmans. If we are to apply the term Sanskritic to sects which have rejected the religious value of the Sanskrit language and which have encouraged the development of vernacular religious literature – as Cohn does when he states that the Shiv Narayan sect has assisted the Sanskritisation of a group of Chamars – then we are quite evidently not using the term in a literal sense to mean 'connected with the Sanskrit language' (a point which Cohn does recognise himself).

Srinivas himself cannot, of course, be blamed if others have used the concept which he originated somewhat lavishly and loosely. But the fact that he never gives a strict definition of what the term Sanskritic is supposed to comprise leaves it open to this kind of use, and especially when he himself seems to use it to embrace what is actually quite a heterogeneous group of concepts. Staal makes the same point in his critique of Srinivas's use of the term Sanskritic when he complains that

'Sanskritisation is a complex concept or class of concepts' which covers a wide variety of phenomena. To be useful to the sociologist, therefore, any typology of Hindu religious forms needs a much narrower and better defined set of categories.

An approach to the problem of the diversity of local Hinduism which is very similar to Srinivas's in certain respects is that of McKim Marriott. He distinguishes between those cultural features of a North Indian village which belong to what he calls the great traditional culture (the culture of the wider community of which the village is a part) and those belonging to the little tradition (the parochial culture of a particular locality). Just as Srinivas recognises that there is communication between the Sanskritic and the non-Sanskritic levels of Hinduism (for instance non-Sanskritic deities such as village gods and goddesses may be assimilated to the Sanskritic tradition by being identified with forms of Sanskritic deities), so Marriott recognises that there is continual communication between the great and little traditions. Features of the great tradition develop local peculiarities and accretions and likewise what were once no doubt purely local forms and customs come to have more universal reference and eventually become assimilated to the great tradition. But no more than Srinivas does Marriott make it clear whether these changes have more than formal significance. For instance, if the festival of Charm Tying can be regarded as a great traditional version of the little traditional festival of Saluno (which also celebrates the brother–sister relationship), is the transformation one of cultural form alone or is it accompanied by a reinterpretation of the values and beliefs which Saluno expresses? If, on the other hand, Saluno and Charm Tying are simply different ways of expressing the same set of beliefs and values, why does the more universalised form have an attraction for the villagers when, after all, their own local culture already provided them with an occasion for celebrating the brother–sister bond? What function, if any, does this cultural duplication fulfil? It could be that the adoption of the priestly great traditional form of the festival signifies something about changing attitudes to caste and status rather than to the sibling relationship. But it is impossible to come to any conclusions about what such changes represent in terms of the meaning of the rites for their participants so long as we consider the rites in isolation from the rest of the religious activity of the village. Were Marriott to give us further information about, for instance, local attitudes to the Brahman priesthood, any recent extensions in the villagers' religious knowledge or experience, which may have come about through (for instance) education or greater opportunities for travel, the nature of the brother–sister relationship and any changes which it may have undergone in recent times, we might then be in a position to assess the sociological significance of this transformation. But as long as this festival is treated only as an isolable fragment we are permitted to view it in cultural terms alone.

Some progress towards a more integrated view of Hinduism has been made by E. B. Harper. Describing the 'supernaturals' worshipped by the members of a South Indian village he divides these beings into three groups. First, there are the vegetarian, Sanskritic *devaru*; secondly, there are the meat-eating *devate* or local gods; thirdly, there are the blood-thirsty and demonic *devva*. On the whole the divinities of the first group are worshipped predominantly by the Brahmans and the high castes; on the other hand the Brahmans never participate directly in the non-vegetarian cults of the *devva*. The deities thus form a kind of hierarchy according to the status of their devotees. But Harper recognises that this kind of classification on its own does not explain very much. He therefore further distinguishes the three classes of deity on the basis of the different functions they fulfil in village religion. The *devaru* are primarily viewed as benevolent beings and are worshipped chiefly for the purpose of acquiring spiritual merit. The *devate* are generally worshipped with more this-wordly ends in view; they are believed to be able to use their powers both to help and to harass human beings, and correct worship can persuade them to act bene-volently. The *devva*, on the other hand, are purely hostile beings and never anything but malevolent in disposition. They are worshipped only by way of appeasement in order to avert the terrible results of their displeasure. Harper leaves unanswered the question of whether the villager himself visualises his pantheon as a structured hier-archy in this manner, or how he relates these cults to each other. To this extent he still treats the supernaturals as detachable elements in the religious tradition of the village. But at least he presents these culturally transmitted elements – i.e., beliefs in different kinds of deity – in the context of the purposes and activities associated with them by the members of this tradition.

Harper avoids the fragmentary approach more successfully in a later article in which he describes the same supernaturals as members of a hierarchy of beings which includes both human beings as well as deities and spirits. The 'pure' (vegetarian) deities stand in a similar relationship to the 'impure' (carnivorous) deities as that of the high castes among human beings to the low castes. The services of the members of the level in the cosmic hierarchy are necessary to the members of the next ascending level if the latter are to maintain their superior ritual status. Thus, just as the members of the middle castes are only able to retain their purity if members of the lowest castes perform tasks for them which would be polluting were they to carry them out themselves, so the deities in turn require the services of the priestly (high) caste among men to act as their ritual servants or 'purifiers'. Since on the whole the same kind of things are held to be polluting for the gods as are thought to be polluting to men, the purity–pollution principle provides a theme which does not only relate the different elements in the Hindu's religious life to each other, but also integrates his religious activities as a total system to the rest of his social life.

Some years earlier, Louis Dumont had reached a very similar conclusion on the basis of fieldwork carried out in another part of South India. Writing on the religion of the Pramalai Kallar he observes that the deities worshipped by the Kallar are seldom considered in isolation from each other; where they are represented in temples, it is always as members of a pantheon. Temples contain not one deity but groups of deities – traditionally twenty-one, though sometimes fewer than twenty-one can actually be identified by name. What is important about these temple pantheons, Dumont says, is the fact that they are invariably divided into two sections, the pure deities and the impure deities. The impure (carnivorous) deities are seen as standing in a relationship to the pure (vegetarian) deities which is subordinate and yet comple-mentary. The pure deities are above the impure deities but yet dependent on them both practically (for the services which the impure deities are held to perform as doorkeepers and guardians of the temples) and conceptually (in that purity can only be said to exist in relationship to impurity, and hence the existence of pure beings has no meaning unless impure beings are also held to exist). The division between the pure and the impure deities is reflected both in their separate accommodation in the same temples and in the different kinds of offering made to them, often also in the existence of dual sets of cultic instruments and a dual priesthood. This dichotomy or polar opposition between the pure and the impure at the divine level is for Dumont not just a projection of caste values or an intrusion of secular values into the religious sphere; the principle which activates the caste system is actually identical with that which gives the pantheon its structure. 'La caste mêle les hommes et les dieux . . . le dieu véritable c'est le Brahmane' (Dumont). Herein, according to Dumont, lies the unity of Hindu religious life, since it amounts to a consistent expression of faith in the polarity of the pure and the impure. For the worship of impure deities does not constitute a lower or separate level or tradition of Hinduism which has yet to be assimilated to some more universal or Sanskritic mainstream, but rather an indispensable adjunct to the worship of the pure deities – an inseparable part of the same system of activity.

The objection may be raised, however, that Dumont and Harper no doubt come to these conclusions as a result of the fact that they have both done their fieldwork in South India; it is well-known that in peninsular India the ritual distance between different castes is maintained in a more literal and rigid manner than in other parts of the subcontinent. Thus it is hardly a matter of surprise if we find that South Indian Hindus carry this purity–pollution principle into the religious sphere also. But will we find the same principle operating as an integrating factor in the religion of, say, Punjabi or Pahari Hindus, who observe a much looser system of caste restrictions? Can we argue that the opposition of the pure and the impure is a universally valid principle of Hindu religious experience? I hope to show from some field material of my own that the religious activities of the Hindus of a North Indian hill village can indeed be equally successfully interpreted according to these terms.

Purity and pollution in practice: The case of Ghanyari

Ghanyari lies in District Kangra in the lower ranges of the Himalayan foothills, a few miles from the border dividing Himachal Pradesh from the Punjab. The numerically preponderant and economically dominant caste in the village is a group of Saraswat Brahmans. These Brahmans, however, perform no priestly functions but are mainly engaged in agriculture, working their own landholdings. The other inhabitants of the village are the members of five intermediate service castes and the untouchable Chamars, whose hamlet lies at a little distance from the main settlement area. The difference in ritual status between the Brahmans and the artisan castes is not very conspicuous in everyday activities. There are no strongly marked dietary differences between castes since, unlike Brahmans in most other parts of India, the Brahmans of Ghanyari may eat meat. (Few in fact do, but this is for economic rather than ritual reasons; there is no caste prohibition on their taking meat if they wish to do so.) Brahmans take *pakka* food from members of all the artisan castes and will take *kaccha* food and water from most of them. Only in the case of Chamars is there a very conspicuous emphasis on ritual distance in daily dealings, since none of the other castes in the village will take food of any kind or water from a Chamar. Even physical contact with a Chamar is polluting and strictly avoided, except in cases where it is quite inevitable, such as when men of different castes travel together in a crowded bus or when men of different castes are engaged in work alongside each other (e.g., house construction or harvesting grain). Nevertheless, the purity–pollution principle is certainly not absent. If pollution puts less distance between man and man than in other parts of India, the sources which are held to give rise to ritual pollution are essentially those which other Hindus believe in. Lack of space prevents me from giving a detailed account of how the purity–pollution principle operates in daily life, but in general the ritual idiom is that of what Stevenson calls the 'Hindu Pollution Concept', even if this concept operates somewhat less rigorously compared with the nicety with which it is applied elsewhere. To take but one example, spittle is generally treated as a source of pollution. Srinivas mentions the fact that among the Coorgs it is considered necessary for a person to wash his hands if he has so much as touched his tongue or teeth. Otherwise he is regarded as having fallen from his normal state of ritual purity. In Ghanyari no one, not even the Brahmans, would consider it necessary to wash one's hands after casually putting a finger in one's mouth. But in the context of a mealtime the transmission of food to the mouth is considered to pollute the hands and a person who is in the process of eating food ought not to touch any food or vessels other than his own until he has washed his hands. If he does so, these vessels must be purified before they can be used again by others by being scoured with ashes, and any food or drink they contain should be thrown away. These Hindus therefore observe the same principle as the Coorgs of South India but they apply it in a more narrowly defined set of situations.

Similarly we find that, as among the Coorgs, the Hindus of Ghanyari regard death as a strong source of pollution, especially for members of the family of the dead person. In Coorgs this principle is applied to the extent that relatives of the deceased must avoid even touching other people during the period of mourning. In Ghanyari the restriction on bodily contact is observed only on the day of death itself. During the rest of the mourning period it is only the cooking of food and eating together which is thought to transmit pollution to non-relatives.

In brief, the Hindus of Ghanyari, as in other parts of India, regard themselves as each having a normal ritual status which can be threatened or preserved by certain kinds of contact. They differ from other Hindus only in the degree of detail and rigidity with which they apply these principles of purity and pollution in daily life, and not in the nature of the principles themselves.

The range of religious activity

How then do these rules apply to the religious sphere, and to what extent can they be said to order the diversity of religious activities in Ghanyari? Certainly this diversity is not less apparent here than in other Indian villages for which we have information. We find the same variety of cults, deities, festivals, etc. that other field investigators have reported. However, for descriptive purposes we can divide the religious activities of Ghanyari into two broad categories. Firstly, there are private acts of devotion performed by individuals to deities of their own choice. These acts are carried out without the aid of priests, either in the home or at a shrine or temple. They are usually performed at the initiative of the worshipper on a particular occasion, generally either because he has reason to suppose that the deity in question is troubling him in some way and demands to be appeased with an offering, or because he hopes to seek some positive favour which he believes the deity has in his power to grant. This kind of ritual act of devotion can however also be performed on festival days to the deities to which the feasts are dedicated.

The second main category of religious activity consists of rituals addressed to deities through the offices of a Brahman priest according to forms laid down in Sanskrit texts and accompanied by the chanting of these sacred verses by the priest. The rituals which fall into this class are mainly rites of passage but the preliminary worship which always precedes the reading of a *katha* (scripture recital) is also of this kind.

I should emphasise that this scheme is not exhaustive; there are religious activities (such as for instance the full moon fast which women keep for their husbands' welfare) which cannot conveniently be placed in either of these categories. I must also point out most emphatically that this division is not intended to have any theoretical significance whatsoever; it is a purely ad hoc scheme which I have introduced simply in order to reduce the complexity of the data to proportions manageable in a paper. If I were to ascribe to it more than this empirical significance I might justly be accused of adopting the very 'fragmentary' approach which I have just deplored. However, this division has the virtue of corresponding in fact roughly with some of the typologies made by other sociologists and hence is useful for comparative purposes. The 'individual' rites are mainly addressed to what Srinivas would call non-Sanskritic deities and belong to what Marriott would call the little tradition. 'Priestly' rites are Sanskritic and great traditional, and are furthermore confined to the upper castes since Chamars are unable to hire Brahman priests to serve them and depend on ritual specialists of their own caste to perform their life-cycle rites for them. If therefore, we can show that there is a common theme or set of values which integrate these two types of religious activity we shall also have demonstrated the continuity between the levels of Hinduism which other writers have distinguished.

I therefore propose now to describe first an example of an individual ritual of worship and then an example of priestly ritual. We shall then be in a position to see whether they truly express different kinds of religious value or tradition.

Individual ritual and the structure of the pantheon

Villagers assert that their deities number thirty-three crore but this is more an expression of the general belief that *devatas* (deities) are legion than the outcome of any kind of divine census-taking. The number of *devatas* which are actually worshipped or of whom the villagers have a detailed knowledge is much smaller. The *devatas* with whom any one villager will have regular dealings of any kind will rarely exceed about a dozen in number and he may know about a dozen more by repute. These *devatas*, it is often asserted, are but forms of the Supreme Spirit, Paramatma or Bhagvan. God, the villagers say, is really above these manifestations of his, but in fact practically no institutionalised religious activities are directed purely to God conceived as Bhagvan. The various *devatas* are held to have various characteristics ranging from the generally benevolent (such as the local saint Baba Ludru) via the mildly annoying (exemplified by the mountain spirit Baba Sindhu) to the downright dangerous (such as the Chamar *devata* Siddh Channo). But all the *devatas* are considered to be both potentially troublesome if their wishes are ignored and potentially helpful if their goodwill is solicited in the right manner. The correct way to avert their anger as well as to seek their active aid in a particular project or dilemma is to make offerings to them accompanied by the performance of certain simple ritual acts. (The orientation of these cults is therefore decidedly pragmatic rather than directed to any species of other-worldly salvation.) The making of such offerings is the most commonly observed form of religious activity in the village and such acts are undertaken by individuals according to their own needs and circumstances. A *devata* may be worshipped in order to secure a good harvest for the next year, to seek a cure for some troublesome disease, to obtain offspring, or in thanksgiving for some fortunate event such as the birth of a child or the passing of an examination. Not being directed by a priest, nor carried out with reference to any written text, the details of the worship can be varied by the individual worshipper; he is at liberty to omit certain acts and to include others at least to a limited extent; but the general pattern which these rites follow is fairly constant and is exemplified adequately in the case I shall describe.

I shall give an account of the ritual acts carried out by Ratno, a Tarkhan woman, on the occasion of the maize harvest of 1966. She worshipped the *devata* Baba Balak Nath in thanksgiving for the help which she believed him to have given in ensuring that the harvest was a good one, and in the hope that a pleasing offering would induce him to render the same aid in future years. I shall outline the ritual acts which she performed in the sequence in which they took place.

1   Ratno rises early and takes a bath. She puts on clean clothes and begins a fast which she keeps until the ritual of worship has been completed.
2   She replasters her kitchen floor and hearth with cowdung. On the newly plastered hearth she prepares a quantity of *karah* – a kind of sweet pudding which is to be used as the offering.
3   She takes out an image of Baba Balak Nath from the inner room where it is generally kept. She smears a small area of the verandah floor with the same plaster of cowdung which she used in the kitchen. She sets up the image on a small wooden stool placed on this area. No one in the household now approaches this area unless they have first removed their shoes.
4   Ratno removes her shoes before she bathes the image with fresh water.
5   She bows before the image and offers flowers and incense before it. She takes a quantity of red powder and applies it to the 'forehead' of the *devata* in the

form of a *tika*. She ties a length of the sacred red thread known as *moli* round the 'waist' of the image.

6   Finally she offers a small quantity of the pudding before the image, pressing a little of it to the 'mouth' of the *devata*.

7   She distributes the remaining portion of the food prepared for the offering – which is now known as *prasad*, i.e. the transmitter of the grace of the *devata* – amongst the members of her household and to a few close neighbours who happen to be around. She then sets the rest aside. It is later offered to other friends and relatives who happen to call at the house during the course of the day. Great care is taken that no crumb of this *prasad* should fall to the ground or be left where it might accidentally come into contact with any impure substance, such as leather shoes.

8   Later in the day Ratno removes the image and puts it away. She clears the area where the worship has been carried out of its ritual debris. The remains of the items offered are taken and thrown into a nearby stream.

The *devata* to whom this worship was addressed may be described as belonging to the regional Hinduism of Punjab and Himachal Pradesh. Baba Balak Nath is said to have been born on earth in a Brahman family some hundreds of years ago and to have lived the life of an ascetic at Shah Talai, a village some twenty miles from Ghanyari. After completing the span of his mortal life on earth he achieved a state of liberation from the body through his asceticism and saintliness. The god Shiva then conferred upon him the gift of immortality, whereupon he attained the status of a *devata* himself. He is well known to the villagers of this region, many of whom have visited his cult centre at Shah Talai. Those who are literate will have read, and may perhaps own, copies of the popular booklets relating the story of his life, his exploits, the miracles he is supposed to have performed and the words of hymns sung in his praise. These booklets are obtainable at stalls selling religious literature, almanacs, etc. in many towns of the Punjab and District Kangra. His cult is not recorded in Sanskrit literature as far as I know, however, and the rituals which are carried out in his honour (whether at home or at the village shrines dedicated to him) do not need the services of a Brahman, or indeed of any kind of ritual specialist. Members of any caste may and do worship him in the way described, and according to my observation he is not worshipped by members of any particular caste more than others.

Unlike the Pramalai Kallar, the villagers of Ghanyari do not rank the members of their pantheon explicitly in any kind of hierarchy. The vegetarian/non-vegetarian distinction in any case hardly exists there. I was told that goats used to be sacrificed to certain *devatas* but that this practice has been discontinued for the past forty years or more. Interestingly enough, goats are still presented to Baba Balak Nath at his shrine at Shah Talai, but they are never killed nowadays. They are simply offered live before the image of the *devata*, and once the latter has shown his approval of the gift by causing the animal to shiver and tremble it is then released. Therefore the pure–impure dichotomy cannot be applied to the pantheon of this village at the present time, whatever the case might once have been. What, however, one does find is that villagers tend to rank their *devatas* after a fashion, according to the strength of the powers they believe them to have. Thus some of the *devatas*, mainly the great traditional deities like Vishnu, Shiva and Durga, are attributed more universal power than the lesser local, or little traditional deities such as Baba Balak Nath himself. Certain more educated villagers sometimes dismiss the latter class of deity, not as having no existence, but as having little power to influence the lives of men (with the implication that their worship is therefore a waste of time if not a positive distraction from the true path to salvation, which consists of doing good *karma* and revering Bhagvan through inner prayer). The point which I am trying to emphasise here is that the pantheon of Ghanyari can only with difficulty be divided into Sanskritic and non-Sanskritic, pure and impure, great and little traditional levels; but to the extent that any such distinction can be made, or is in fact made by the villagers themselves, we are obliged to classify the cult of Baba Balak Nath as belonging to the inferior (non-Sanskritic, little traditional) level.

Priestly ritual: Public worship

In contrast to the ritual which I have just described, let us now look at a rite which can only be classified as Sanskritic and great traditional (no matter how we choose to define these terms). A popular form of religious activity in the village is the *katha*, or scripture recital. This consists of a reading by a Brahman priest of some story of moral import taken from the scriptures. The text is recited in Sanskrit and then expounded line by line in the vernacular by the priest. The reading itself is preceded by a formal rite of worship in which the householder who is sponsoring the reading worships Ganesh and the nine planets and seeks their blessing for the meritorious act which he is about to have performed. This ritual is carried out under the direction of the priest who has been hired to read the *katha*. I shall describe here the form of this ritual as carried out by a Braham farmer, Ramanand, when he held a *katha* to celebrate the completion of the new house he had been building. However, there is, as far as I could observe at least, almost no variation in the way this ritual is performed on different occasions (as there can be in the case of individual rites of worship) for the very reason that it depends on a written text. This text is regarded as sacred and hence any intentional variation is not even envisaged, let alone approved.

The acts constituting the ritual of worship on this occasion were as follows:

1   On returning from the fields on the evening of the day when the *katha* is to be held (the auspicious day and time has been ascertained beforehand from the Brahman priest who has consulted his almanac for the purpose) Ramanand takes a bath and changes into clean clothes.

2   Ramanand's wife replasters her kitchen hearth and the place in the main room of the house where the worship is to be offered by resmearing them with cowdung. She then prepares the *prasad* which is to be distributed after the *katha* (in this case a kind of sweet made from flour fried in *ghi* and sweetened with crude sugar).

3   The priest arrives. He has also bathed and changed his clothes before leaving his house and on arrival once more washes his hands. He then begins to prepare a *mandala*, that is a sacred diagram, on the area of the floor which Ramanand's wife has previously replastered. This diagram consists of symbolic representation of the nine planets and other deities or sacred beings. These include Ganesh, Tridev (Vishnu, Shiva and Brahman), Suraj Devata (the sun), Shesh Nag (the serpent who upholds the world), the sixty-four Yoginis (the wives of the deity Bhairon) and Onkar (the sacred syllable Om conceived as a divine being). The symbols of these deities are traced on the floor in white flour.

4   The invited guests begin to arrive. The priest blows a blast on his conch shell to signify that the worship is about to begin. He bids Ramanand sit down beside him before the *mandala* which he has prepared. He ties a length of red *moli* to Ramanand's wrist and tufts of the sacred kusha grass to the third finger of each of his hands.

5   The priest recites the appropriate lines from the Sanskrit text which he has opened in front of him as he directs Ramanand in the worship of the symbols represented in the *mandala*. To each in turn various substances are offered: water, rice, flowers, incense. Ritual gestures, such as bowing with folded hands, are made to the various symbols.

6   After this the reading itself begins. The priest chants the Sanskrit verses and then explains what they mean to his listeners. The text includes various anecdotes concerning the sage Narada which illustrate the effectiveness of righteous conduct and the diligent observance of fasting and other ritual practices as means of obtaining salvation. After the reading is completed the *prasad*, which has been placed beside the *mandala*, is distributed to all present. Great care is taken that no portion of the *prasad* should be trodden under foot.

7   After the guests have departed, Ramanand's wife scrapes up what is left of the sacred diagram and the items offered to it and puts them by on a tray. They are removed later by Ramanand and thrown into a stream.

In certain striking respects this ritual quite obviously belongs to a different strand of the Hindu tradition from the private ritual carried out by Ratno to Baba Balak Nath, and fulfils a different kind of religious function. The ritual has a fixed form, as has been pointed out, and depends on a written text. Moreover this text is not written in the vernacular but in a language which is incomprehensible to the ordinary villager. The services of a Brahman priest are essential to the villager for this kind of ritual, not merely because only the priest has the requisite training to understand the directions for worship contained in the text, but also because only a Brahman is considered fit, by virtue of his special ritual status, to utter and expound the holy verses in question. The ritual therefore cannot take place without his aid, or at least without the presence of a Brahman who can read enough Sanskrit to stumble through the text. (One *katha* which I attended was read by a Brahman villager, who had a little education, when the priest who had been invited failed to turn up.)

Furthermore, the ritual preceding a *katha*, unlike the rite conducted by Ratno in her home, is public. It is carried out in the presence of guests formally invited, whose attendance is considered essential as witnesses that the ritual has been carried out in the proper manner. The rite is performed by the head of the household on behalf of his whole family. Individual rites of worship may be carried out in order to further aims which are of interest or benefit to the whole household, as indeed was Ratno's worship of Baba Balak Nath; but in such cases the worshipper is still acting on his own individual initiative and not because of his structural position in the kinship group. In such cases any member of the family may equally legitimately perform the worship. Priestly rituals seldom involve women (except in cases such as weddings and naming rites, when the bride and the mother of the new baby have a certain part to play). A *katha* could, I was told, be sponsored by a woman in the last resort in the absence of any male member of the household, but no one could recall such an occasion. Normally a woman's inferior ritual status debars her from taking part in this kind of ritual. One priest said, 'A woman can never be as pure as a man and therefore if there is a man in her household, he should perform the necessary rites.' Individual acts of worship to *devatas* can be performed by members of either sex with equal legitimacy and effectiveness.

The deities worshipped through priestly ritual also tend to belong to a different category. Whilst Shiva, Vishnu and Ganesh are sometimes worshipped through individual rites of the type described already, the other divinities depicted on the *mandala* which Ramanand worshipped are not worshipped by individual villagers privately. Indeed many of them are only known to the villagers at all because they feature in the worship effected at weddings, namely rites, *kathas* and other priestly rituals. If they are known outside these contexts at all it is as scriptural figures, but as most of the villagers are illiterate this means that these beings belong to a literary tradition to which they have little direct access. Deities like Baba Balak Nath, on the other hand, belong to the oral traditions of the place and knowledge of them does not depend on written sources (although written sources in the forms of books and pamphlets may amplify the villager's information concerning them if he is literate).

There is also, as I have mentioned, a functional difference between the two kinds of rite. Individual rites are oriented towards the attainment of highly specific and this-worldly ends rather than towards the attainment of salvation (in the sense of liberation from this world). Priestly rites, to be sure, certainly have a this-worldly reference also; *kathas* can be held (as Ramanand's was) to celebrate the achievement of some material or this-worldly end, and life cycle rites such as weddings obviously have a this-worldly reference. But the completion of these rituals is also conceived as a worthy end in itself, and an aid on the path to salvation. Life cycle rites should be performed duly and correctly, since this is fulfilment of one's *dharma* and hence a religious necessity. As for *kathas*, one informant told me, 'In former times, in the Sat Yug, a man who sponsored a *katha* accumulated so much merit through the deed that he was not reborn in mortal form for thousands of years; even now there is great merit in performing a *katha*.' Individual rites of worship are obviously directed to much more immediate ends.

Continuities and common principles

Having outlined the differences between the two classes of religious activity which I have described I ought now, if I am to fulfil the intention which I expressed in the beginning of this paper, to point out where the continuities between them lie. If we choose to analyse Hinduism in terms of types or levels then the two rituals which I have described certainly belong to different levels of the religious culture of Ghanyari. But it is not difficult to find a definite consistency in the idiom they employ if we examine the ritual procedure followed in either case. Obvious similarities, for instance, can be seen in the fact that in both kinds of ritual the main participant(s) had first to bathe themselves and change their clothes; in both rituals the site where worship was to take place was first smeared with cowdung; in both rituals this area was not approached without shoes being first removed; in either case the ritual equipment used was disposed of after the worship was over by being immersed in running water; in both cases certain precautions were observed in the disposal of the *prasad*. When we take into account both these regularities in practice and the statements which villagers make in explanation of these practices, it becomes clear that there is a basic likeness in the rules observed in both contexts which underlies the more conspicuous differences in their content and purpose.

The rules which govern both kinds of ritual alike can be summarised according to the following scheme:

(a) Rules which maintain or maximise the purity of the worshipper(s)

These comprise the taking of a preliminary ritual bath, changing clothes, washing hands, fasting. (Fasting can be seen as a means of purification in that the consumption of food always conveys a certain degree of pollution, and by avoiding eating one is also avoiding an occasion for pollution.)

(b) Rules directed towards maintaining or preserving the purity of the deity or deities to be worshipped

These include smearing the site of worship with cowdung, removing shoes before coming near this area, bathing the image with water. All these acts can be interpreted in terms of the preservation of the purity of the gods (or more specifically the images and symbols which are used to represent their presence). Indeed they are so interpreted by the villagers themselves.

(c) Rules governing the purity of the offering

These include the obligation on the woman who is to cook the *prasad* to take a bath (whether or not she will participate in the ritual worship herself), the purification of the hearth before the cooking takes place, and the precautions taken about the disposal of the *prasad* after it has been presented to the gods. Under this heading we may also include the practice of immersing the remains of the other offerings in running water; this is also explicitly described by villagers as being carried out in order to ensure that the substances offered to and accepted by the gods should not become defiled accidentally by being left lying about where they might come into contact with sources of pollution.

It is clear that the substances which are considered to be sources of pollution in this context (whether it is the purity of the deity which they threaten or that of his worshipper) are no different from those which are thought to transmit pollution in other contexts. For instance, leather (especially in the form of footwear) is polluting and should not be brought near the area where worship is to take place. Exactly the same principle is at work when villagers remove their shoes before entering a kitchen or cooking area, except that in the latter case it is the purity of the household's cooking utensils and foodstuffs which is at stake rather than purity of a deity or his devotee. And the same rule is in operation when villagers place ritual distance between themselves and the low caste Chamars, whose traditional work is the preparation of leather from the hides of dead cattle.

Similarly the substances which are conceived as purifiers in the religious context are also those which are used for purificatory purposes in non-religious contexts. Cowdung, as the product of that extraordinarily pure animal, the cow, is used to purify the area where the image or symbols of the deities are to be placed for worship and to purify the hearth where *prasad* is to be prepared. When a housewife smears her kitchen floor and hearth with cowdung as a regular practice, even when no ritual is to take place, or when a new mother is made to drink cow's urine after the birth of her child in order to remove the pollution which the very act of parturition brings upon her, the very same principle is being observed. Likewise there is consistency between the religious and non-religious use of water as an agent of purification. Villagers bathe themselves and the images of their gods with water and immerse the remains of their offerings in water in order that everything associated with the divine should remain pure. In accordance with the same principle, a villager will purify himself by bathing in clean water if he ever becomes polluted through accidental contact with a person of unclean caste. Bathing is also used as a means of purification when a birth or death in the household involves its members in pollution of another kind.

Now that I have made them, these remarks may seem rather obvious – especially to anyone who has spent any time in an Indian village. But it has been necessary to make them in order to counter the effects of the 'fragmentary' approach which has hitherto dominated the study of Hindu religion in its village context. I hope I have shown that in spite of the distinctions which can be made between the different types of Hindu religious activity on the basis of their different cultural origins or their different functions, there is also an underlying consistency of idiom. The purity–pollution principle is applied in the conduct of religious rituals of all types in exactly the same manner.

The cosmic hierarchy

It should also be obvious from material I have presented that there is in addition a consistency between application of the purity–pollution principle in the religious sphere and its application in the non-religious context. The evidence from Ghanyari tends to confirm the ideas expressed by Harper and Dumont, namely that the Hindu pantheon can be viewed as an upwards extension of the caste system. In Ghanyari, as in the South Indian villages which these writers studied, the man–*devata* relationship emerges as being of a similar character to the low caste–high caste relationship in certain important respects. The rules of ritual procedure followed in the examples I have described are in both cases oriented to the maintenance of the superior ritual purity of the *devata(s)*. The purity of the worshipper is instrumental in this context, not an object in itself, for the villagers state that only if the worshipper makes himself pure will his worship be acceptable to the deities he addresses. More than this, in both kinds of ritual the intrusion of any source of pollution may even excite the anger of the offended *devata*. The purity of the *prasad* is interpreted by the villagers as being necessary also in order to make it an acceptable offering to the gods, a principle which is consistent with the fact that in the human sphere only food which is pure can be passed from ritual inferior to ritual superior (in so far as men can accept food from their ritual inferiors at all). Thus only a ritual inferior will accept polluted food; only Chamars will accept the scraps left over from the plates of members of the higher castes. The exclusion of leather articles from the area of worship can be compared with the custom according to which (at least until about forty years ago) Chamars were not allowed to enter the main settlement area of the village where the other castes lived unless they first removed their shoes as a mark of respect. Even nowadays a Chamar will not enter the courtyard of a member of the higher castes without first leaving his shoes at the gate or entrance. There are obvious parallels here between the way a low-caste man treats a high-caste man and the way a worshipper treats the deity he worships.

   Theoretically attractive, the analogy between caste relationships and man–*devata* relationships does have certain common-sense limitations in actual practice. For instance, a Brahman (unlike a *devata*) can take certain measures himself to maintain his normal ritual status, by avoiding contacts with members of low castes. (He can move away if a Chamar approaches him; if he has to give food to an untouchable he can insist that the latter provide his own vessels.) Of course, it is doubtful whether a Brahman could protect himself effectively from a deliberate attempt to pollute him on the part of a low-caste man who was quite bent on seeing him ritually degraded. However, I imagine such a flagrant and calculated effort to violate a ritual superior's ritual purity would be a rather rare occurrence, at least on the part of persons very low in the hierarchy, because any such step could be met with punishment; the ritual superior is usually also superior in political and economic status and thus has effective sanctions at his disposal.

   Even so, unlike the *devata*'s worshipper, the low-caste man might even be said to have a certain interest in reducing his superior's ritual status to the extent that if the ritual distance between them is diminished he may be able to obtain recognition of a higher rank for himself in the hierarchy. (The worshipper has no possible interest in changing his *devata*'s status.) Thus where members of a caste which is ritually low, but on the ascendant in socio-economic terms, succeed in inducing members of a higher caste to take food from them where there had been no inter-dining before, this might pave the way for confirmation of a shift in their relative ritual positions. But the literature on village Hinduism suggests that it is far more common for a mobile caste to try to pull themselves up the ritual ladder by purifying their own customs – giving up meat, liquor, etc. – than by making deliberate assaults on the purity of their superiors such that the latter would find hard to avoid.

A *devata* – in spite of the greater power with which he is credited to shape the progress of events and fortunes at a more general level – can only react passively by punishing the person who violates his purity after the offence has been committed; punishment is within his power but not active avoidance (although of course this power to punish should not be underestimated as a form of sanction).

To summarise this discussion, which is admittedly somewhat of a digression from our main argument, we could perhaps say that the main limitation to our analogy is that in caste relationships both sides are active agents and both can help to effect readjustments in the ritual distance which separates them, especially over periods of time. In particular, the ritual superior may lose out to his inferior, the more so if he loses the economic and political power which enabled him to punish the low-caste man for breaches of caste etiquette and get away with it. The man–*devata* relationship is asymmetrical in that the superior partner is partly passive; he can punish but not forestall or avoid outrages to his purity. The relationship is a simpler one in a sense, for it is not complicated by the economic and political considerations which are the secular concomitants of the ritual side of caste relationships.

It must also be stressed that villagers recognise the superior purity of their *devatas* only indirectly and implicitly. That is, when asked to describe their pantheon, they will make statements such as 'the *devatas* are powerful' rather than 'the *devatas* are pure'. But when asked to account for the details of the worship they offer to these *devatas* act by act, they will state, for example, 'we bathe to make ourselves pure' or 'we remove our shoes because they are made of leather and are not pure'.

Conclusions

It is only with certain qualifications, therefore, that we can agree with Harper and Dumont as regards the similarity between the application of the purity–pollution principle in the religious sphere and in the caste context. However, this does not prejudice our agreement with these authors concerning the importance of this principle as an integrator of the Hindu's experience and activity within the religious sphere. The villager is, as we have seen, acting on similar principles whether he worships some local little traditional *devata* privately or whether he sits beside his *purohit* to perform some *puja* before a *mandala* prepared by the priest. Whether the little tradition is a parochialised version of the great tradition, or whether the great tradition is a more generalised version of a prior folk culture – this is a matter for the cultural historian to decide and need not concern us here. What the sociologist has to determine is the relationship of these strands of cultural activity to each other in the context of modern social organisation. For the practical purposes of description I have found it necessary to divide religious activity in the village into two broad categories, and indeed the villager himself sometimes makes such a distinction between priestly and non-priestly ritual. But, as I have shown, the differences between these two kinds of activities, or 'traditions' (if one wishes to use the term) is greater in terms of their mode of transmission and superficial style than in terms of thematic content and underlying values. The hierarchical aspect of the purity–pollution principle is emphasised again and again – from the explicit exhortation to fast and be pure contained in the priestly *kathas* to the practical regard for the *devatas'* purity implicit in the villager's very action as he worships his domestic *devatas*. Indeed the need to mark off the pure from the impure not only pervades the Hindu's social and religious life but also his attitudes to all the members of his cosmos. Within almost any category which he distinguishes, the Hindu will rank some items as more pure than others. Thus among animals the cow is most pure; among trees the *pipal* and the *bor* are pure and the *lasura* is impure – a 'Musulman' tree, too polluted to be used for timber. Among vegetables, carrot and turnips are less pure than pumpkins and potatoes, which is why it is permissible to eat the latter on fast days but not the former. Of beverages, milk and clean water (especially Ganges water) are pure, and alcoholic drinks are impure. These distinctions are not of equal practical significance, although of course, the distinctions among foodstuffs are of considerable importance in the ritual sphere. But they are all of potential religious importance in that during worship the devotee wishes to exclude what is not pure and to include what is pure as far as he is able. On the conceptual level these distinctions illustrate the broad dominion of the purity–pollution principle which we have been discussing. A detailed study of the cosmology of popular Hinduism and the way in which the Hindu villager frames his world view might reveal further elaboration of the purity–pollution theme and would be a rewarding subject for further research. However our conclusions in this paper must be limited to the religious sphere, and we can summarise them by stating that we find in Ghanyari, just as others have found in South India, that the link between the different cultural levels of religious tradition and activity lies in the consistent application of the rules of purity and pollution to the relationship between man and the forces which he reveres as divine.

Source: Ursula Sharma, *Contributions to Indian Sociology* (Vikas Publishing House, 1973), pp. 1–21.

4.3 CASTE, FOOD AND COMMENSALITY

L. DUMONT

A local example (Central India)

In order to take an accurate view of the way in which the hierarchical principle is expressed in the caste system, one must obviously study what happens at a given place among the actual castes which co-exist there. On the other hand, it will have been noticed that the rules which lay down for the members of each caste from whom they may or may not accept such and such a kind of food, or simply drinking-water, without degradation, are one of the most convenient manifestations of the hierarchical principle from the point of view of recording and observing. I say 'recording and observing', for it is not enough to list the rules which the witnesses recite. One must also know if and under what circumstances these presumptive rules are applied in practice. In the first period of inquiries into these questions, people were too often content to ask informants and reproduce the rules which they mentioned. But what can a rule like the following signify: 'I may, or may not, take water from X', if the witness cannot cite a single moment in his life when the question has really arisen for him? From this point of view, there are different kinds of food which, as McKim Marriott has rightly said, are suitable for different situations: ordinary everyday food based, according to region, on wheat cakes or boiled rice, is essentially for the family, and is accepted only by servants of a distinctly inferior rank, and so on this level is food for service. By contrast, food fried in butter (or certain equivalent foods) is the food of feasts: its greater purity, or rather, its greater resistance to impurity, enables a greater number of castes than in the preceding case to accept it, and it is thus suitable for banquets to which one invites neighbours; if these include superiors, it is advisable that the cook should himself be of high caste. Akin to this type are certain special preparations which can be called food for travelling; these too are relatively resistant to impurity in virtue of their composition and preparation, and they make it possible to eat in circumstances where it is preferable not to have to do any cooking. Finally, if one remunerates a superior – a Brahman, say – in food, this will be raw food which is immune from pollution and which he will cook himself (*sīdhā*); Marriott rightly calls this the food of gifts. Our aim here was not to study food in itself, but to throw just as much light on the question as is required in order to use the corresponding rules for the study of caste ranking.

A good study of this topic is available: Mayer's book[1] about a village in Southern Malwa (Central India). Perhaps it is not perfect, but one must take into account the complexity of the phenomena and the difficulty of recording them correctly, which is what this writer has done. He cannot be reproached for not having pursued his analysis far enough, for it is open to the reader to do so. The village includes twenty-three castes, and their relationships will be studied under three headings: use of the same pipe, and the provision of ordinary food, called *kachā*, and of perfect food, called *pakkā*. In the north-west of India, men of castes of similar status are wont to meet round a hookah (*hukkā*), which is smoked in turn. This would be inconceivable in the south in view of the contact between the lips, and hence saliva, and the mouthpiece of the pipe, even if a cloth or a hand is placed between. Here the pipe smoked is of clay without a tube (*cilam*), and a cloth is interposed between lips and mouthpiece. The pipe is shared among roughly the same castes as those from whom one accepts water, and there is considerable tolerance. The data are to be found in figure 1b. Higher castes share the pipe with almost all castes excluding, apart from the Untouchables (F), only four other castes (Mayer's category 4, category E here) and, in a varying way, certain of the lower castes included (D). In some cases, a different

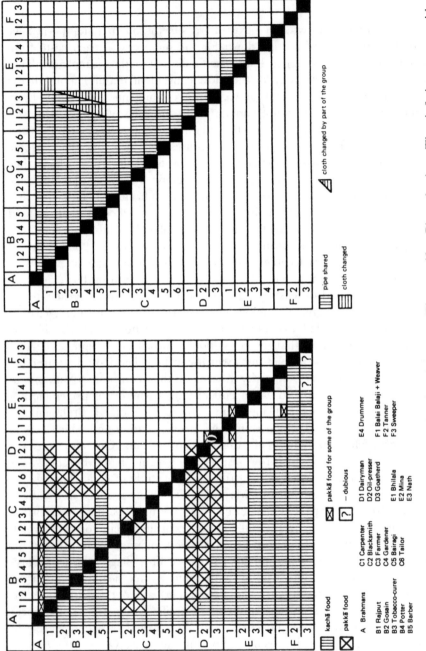

Figure 1a Status ranking on the basis of exchange of food in a Malwa village (from the data in A. C. Mayer, *Caste and Kinship*, pp. 33–40). For each caste (■), the castes from whom it accepts such-and-such a food are read horizontally, those who accept the food from it are read vertically.

Legend:
- kachā food
- pakkā food
- pakkā food for some of the group
- ? – dubious

A Brahmans

B1 Rajput
B2 Gosain
B3 Tobacco-curer
B4 Potter
B5 Barber

C1 Carpenter
C2 Blacksmith
C3 Farmer
C4 Gardener
C5 Bairagi
C6 Tailor

D1 Dairyman
D2 Oil-presser
D3 Goatherd

E1 Bhilala
E2 Mina
E3 Nath
E4 Drummer

F1 Balai Balaji + Weaver
F2 Tanner
F3 Sweeper

Figure 1b Pipe sharing. The inferior castes with whom a given caste will share a pipe are read horizontally, starting from the caste in question (■). Same locality. [Castes and categories as detailed under Figure 1a]

Legend:
- pipe shared
- cloth changed
- cloth changed by part of the group

cloth must be placed between the pipe and the lips of the smoker. Briefly, between twelve and sixteen castes smoke together; in the first place, this is very remarkable by comparison with other regions, and in the second it indicates a cleavage which is higher than that marked by Untouchability, and is obviously important. Let us also note that lower castes either do not share the pipe (these are Untouchables, and their exclusiveness is not exceptional), or else do so only with one or two castes immediately below (the two castes of my category E).

For the rest, and to see it more clearly, we must arrange Mayer's material in a hierarchical way. The facts about the food for feasts, pakkā, are not essential, for it is not really used in its true function in this locality. Indeed, one reads that at a banquet the food was partly kachā and party pakkā: in such a case the pakkā has no more than a gastronomic significance since all those who could eat pakkā alone but not kachā could obviously not partake of it. There remains the ordinary food, kachā. There are two ways in which it may be considered here: from whom do I accept kachā, and who accepts it from me. The two are not necessarily connected, for I may be punctilious in my acceptance, and yet at the same time possess other characteristics which make others refuse kachā from me. The essential thing here is the common opinion which others have of me, and not my own opinion of them. Hence we shall take as the essential criterion for the order in which we shall rank the castes: *what castes accept kachā from the caste in question?* Thus we obtain the table (Figure 1a) in which the caste under consideration is placed on the diagonal; the castes which take kachā from it are read vertically, forming a kind of ladder from left to right at the bottom of the diagram; the castes from which it accepts kachā are read horizontally.

The choice of our main criterion leads to a slight modification of the grouping proposed by Mayer, namely, to the division of category 2 into B and D. For the rest, his 3 corresponds to our C, his 4 becomes our E and his 5 our F (Untouchables). Still considering only kachā, it will be seen from the table that the castes of category B have a peculiarity which distinguishes them from all the others; the other castes, except the very last, F, will accept (horizontally) kachā only from very superior castes. By contrast, the castes of category B form a compact rectangle in this respect: B1, B2, B3, B4, B5 eat the ordinary food together! Now B1 represents the Rajputs, the dominant caste, which in this instance may be called the royal caste, and group B as a whole represents what Mayer calls as a result the 'allied castes'. The commensality of the group is even more remarkable because it includes 'serving' castes like the potters, B4, who accept kachā from a caste outside the group, the carpenters, and especially the barbers, B5, who, as a necessary result of their domestic functions, accept it from four of the castes in category C, which are themselves very exclusive. This is in general an admission of inferiority, and one might expect to see the B castes dissociate themselves from B5 in order to preserve their status. This is far from the case, and one may even observe that an inferior caste, D3, makes no distinction between them and accepts kachā from the barbers, B5, just as from the other members of B. Further, castes of category C, who accept kachā only from the Brahmans, are classed by three castes (D3, E1, E2) below the barber (except for the carpenter, C1, who is thought inferior only by D3). Now the C castes are vegetarian, while the B castes eat meat. Hence in this case the promiscuity of meat eaters prevails over the separatism of vegetarians in public esteem (the esteem not only of inferiors, but even of the Brahmans, who accept pakkā only up to and including C2). Here, to all appearances, the principle of the pure and the impure is in abeyance. In this form the fact is, I believe, unique up to this date. To understand it, it must be remembered that the B castes are united around the power caste, B1. (Moreover, some of them are dominant in neighbouring villages.) This is the point at which, in the manner we have already hinted at, power participates in purity, although the latter negates it in theory; in other words, this is the point at which the solidarity between the first two varnas reveals itself.

Consideration of the purer food, pakkā, brings out two points: (1) as has been mentioned, it is not used here in its full capacity as food for festivals, which should normally allow for the commensality between the B castes and the C castes which are close in status; (2) the distinctive feature of the exclusiveness of C castes is that they refuse almost all pakkā as well as kachā (which is absurd), while by contrast the B castes generally accept pakkā from the C castes (C4 seems to be inferior to the other C castes, but I do not intend to make any modifications in detail to the order given by the author); the D castes, on the contrary, behave normally in accepting pakkā from all the superior categories; pakkā is scarcely used among the E and F castes.

In short, the main lesson of this investigation concerns the opposition of the B and C castes, whose behaviour must be seen together. Faced with the 'allied castes', allied around power, who here display exceptional carefreeness and solidarity, the C castes seem to exaggerate the reserve and self-containment of vegetarians, to such a degree that even the Brahmans scarcely take them seriously. We are told that the B castes are lavish and freely invite other castes to their family ceremonies, followed in this by the carpenters (C1). By contrast, the farmers (C3) are niggardly and scarcely invite any except members of their own caste; at the same time, they pose as puritans, if they are invited they insist on receiving raw food and cooking it in their own homes. That it is a question of asserting themselves in face of the B castes is the more clear in that in other villages this same caste is part of the group of 'allies'.

We have seen how, in an actual situation, power may victoriously offset purity. In a less spectacular form this is a very widespread phenomenon. This is why we have been at pains to indicate above how the theory of varnas opens the road to this possibility.

---

1 *Caste and Kinship*, pp. 33–40.

Source: Louis Dumont, *Homo Hierarchicus* (Weidenfeld & Nicolson, 1972), pp. 123–9.

4.4 STATUS EVALUATION IN THE HINDU CASTE SYSTEM
H. N. C. STEVENSON

Conclusions

The following tentative hypotheses emerge from this survey of Hindu status evaluation:

1 There are two categories of status – secular status and ritual status – each derived from different sources and socially manifested in different ways.

2 Whereas secular status is derived from such criteria as skill, education, wealth, land ownership and economic 'lines of demarcation' in occupation, ritual status is derived from behaviour patterns linked with mystical beliefs, of which the most important are those subsumed under the title 'The Hindu Pollution Concept'.

3 The principal constituent beliefs of the Pollution Concept are: (i) that group behaviour patterns establish group-derived natal ritual status; (ii) that this group ritual status cannot be altered so long as the person concerned conforms to the group pattern of behaviour; (iii) that there is another category of ritual status – personal ritual status – which is derived from personal rather than group conduct, and which provides the individual with the means of achieving higher natal ritual status in subsequent rebirths; (iv) that a rise or fall in personal ritual status above or below the level of group ritual status involves deviation from the group pattern of behaviour.

4 The main principles governing evaluation of natal status through group behaviour are: (i) that the life principle is sacred, and that destruction of life for a living (as in oil-seed-crushing) is polluting; (ii) that death and decay are polluting and therefore occupational association with them is polluting; (iii) that all human emissions are polluting, and therefore occupational association with these, too, is polluting; (iv) that the cow is sacred above all creatures, and that killing it, or flaying it, or dealing in skins or eating its flesh is sinful, and therefore polluting; (v) that certain other creatures – some monkeys, cobras, squirrels, etc. – are also sacred in varying degrees or in some localities, and that killing or eating them is polluting; and (vi) that the drinking of alcohol is polluting.

5 Pollution may be permanent or temporary, being subdivisible into voluntary pollution, the result of wrong behaviour, and involuntary pollution, the result of such natural crises as birth, death and menstruation. Pollution may also be subdivided into external and internal pollution, the latter being much the less easily expunged.

6 Permanent pollution is a function of the relations between commensal and endogamous groups; between man and the phenomena of the natural world, and among these phenomena themselves.

7 Temporary pollution is situational, and in general is a function of the relations between an individual and the commensal, endogamous and local groups of which he or she is a member.

8 Group ritual status is socially manifested mainly through ritual avoidances which may arise from: (i) social activation of a single group (or category, e.g. *sannyasis*) by one or more beliefs; or, (ii) social activation of a number of groups – from the family through its associated endogamous and commensal groups to the caste system as a whole – by one or more beliefs.

9 There is no fixed hierarchy of 'castes' and 'sub-castes'. Group status – both secular and ritual – is *variable* and *relative* in time, space and interaction. Relativity and fission are the characteristics which make possible the status mobility of endogamous groups. Observance of different combinations of status principles makes possible fine differentiations of status at all levels.

10 Change of group ritual status by endogamous groups may be both upward and downward, upward change being secured only by generations of conformation to behaviour patterns which avoid pollution, and by severing marital and commensal relations with any non-conforming section.

11 Ritual status is of different orders at different structural levels. (i) *At the level of endogamous and commensal groups*, group ritual status vis-à-vis like groups can be changed, and is evaluated on the basis of (a) the observance of certain standards of behaviour, mainly concerning occupation, diet and marriage, by reference to the Pollution Concept; (b) the right to perform certain rites, of which the most important is the orthodox initiation rite of *upanayana*, which divides the *duija*, or 'twice-born' groups, from the lower orders. (ii) *At the level of exogamous groups*, group ritual status vis-à-vis like groups cannot be changed, and is evaluated according to (a) the ritual status of the endogamous group to which the exogamous group belongs; (b) mythical origin; (c) difference in protecting deities. (iii) *At the level of the individual*, group-derived ritual status vis-à-vis the whole Hindu system is inherited and cannot be changed except by deviation from the group behaviour pattern of the endogamous group to which the individual belongs. It is evaluated (a) within the caste system, according to the status of the endogamous and commensal groups to which the individual belongs; (b) within the endogamous group, according to the exogamous group to which the individual belongs; (c) within the local community, according to ritual roles undertaken by his status group in local group ritual. On the other hand, personal ritual status, achieved through such deviations from the group pattern of behaviour as asceticism or breach of pollution rules, is variable upwards and downwards. A permanent rise or fall in personal ritual status involves severance of social ties with the natal group.

Source: H. N. C. Stevenson, *Proceedings of the Royal Anthropological Institute of Great Britain and Ireland* (1954) pp. 63–4.

4.5 THEODICY AND THE DOCTRINE OF KARMA
U. SHARMA

In this article I shall take as my starting point the general problem of the need for a cultural resolution for the problem of suffering, which Max Weber terms the need for 'theodicy'; in particular I shall examine the ways in which this need is fulfilled in popular Hinduism, using data from a field study carried out in a Himachal Pradesh village.

The idea that religion can primarily be seen as a means of comfort (spurious or genuine, according to one's view) in a world of suffering is not a new one. One of the earlier sociological versions of this idea was suggested by Marx; religion reconciles the oppressed to their uncomfortable roles in this life by dignifying their suffering and promising spiritual rewards in a world to come. But apart from the psychological problem, the existence of suffering also poses a cognitive problem, albeit in practice the two are often closely related or even confused with each other. Religion does not only have to provide the promise of some kind of escape or salvation from suffering but also some kind of moral vindication of its distribution in this world.

> Thou art indeed just, Lord, if I contend
> With thee; but, sir, what I plead is just.
> Why do sinners' ways prosper? and why must
> Disappointment all I endeavour end?

(Gerard Manley Hopkins)

Geertz suggests that 'the strange opacity of events, the dumb senselessness of intense or inexorable pain, and the enigmatic unaccountability of gross iniquity all raise the uncomfortable suspicion that perhaps the world, and hence man's life in the world, has no genuine order at all – no empirical regularity, no emotional form, no moral coherence'.[1] Religion provides a solution for this problem, since it offers 'a formulation by means of symbols, of an image of such a genuine order of the world which will account for, and even celebrate, the perceived ambiguities, puzzles and paradoxes in human experience'. Geertz's presentation of the problem implies that it is a universal function of religion to provide such an answer to the problematic nature of the world around us, since suffering is a universal fact, and in no place is it distributed entirely according to merit (allowing for the different interpretations which we may place upon the word 'merit'). On the whole, Geertz says, the religious answers to this problem do not try to deny that the just suffer sometimes, in spite of their righteousness, but only deny that their suffering is inexplicable, or without either value or meaning – even if that meaning is not fully accessible to human comprehension.

If this kind of approach to religion is less popular amongst anthropologists (perhaps still embarrassed by early attempts to explain the origins of religion as a kind of primitive and speculative substitute for science), it has established a respectable position in the sociological camp, where Weber and (latterly) Parsons[2] have been its main exponents. Weber takes as given the need for an explanation of the distribution of fortune – what he calls the 'ineradicable need for a theodicy' – and shows how different religious systems have offered contributions to a solution of this problem. They have supplied different sorts of answer according to the kinds of evil which men have seen as being in most need of explanation, and where they have failed to satisfy these needs, often new religious movements have risen. Often, for instance, the theory which has satisfied the privileged strata of society has failed to meet the needs of the depressed and poor, and hence redemption religions have appealed to the latter, giving a positive evaluation to their sufferings (e.g. Weber[3]). The provision of a theodicy according to such views, then, would by implication appear to be a functional necessity, if not from the point of view of the survival of the entire society in question, then at least so far as the persistence of the religious system itself is concerned. Thus it has sometimes been argued that failure to satisfy the need for a theodicy could well be one of the factors accounting for the failure of Christianity to maintain its hold in countries like Britain, where participation in institutionalised forms of religion is low. Weber himself cites the evidence gathered from German workers which showed that the 'rejection of the God idea was motivated not by scientific arguments but by the difficulty in reconciling the idea of providence with the injustice and imperfections of the social order'.[4] If this has really been an important factor in the general movement away from religion in its institutionalised form, at least in modern Europe, it is difficult to see why it did not take effect earlier since injustice and suffering have not been limited to any particular period.

Interesting as this question is, however, it is somewhat of a red herring so far as my main argument here is concerned, my contention being that the problem of suffering, which Weber, Geertz, Parsons and others have presented as central to the relationship between doctrine and religious needs, is itself a complex one; rather it involves two, or maybe three, connected problems.

Obeyesekere recognises this fact when he points out that Weber has in fact used the term theodicy in more than one sense. He uses it to refer to the 'existential need to explain suffering and evil; and . . . to mean the resolution of these needs in statements of moral meaning'.[5] But the 'classical' sense of the term is a vindication of the goodness and mercy of God in the face of suffering and misery in the world he is said to have created. The need for a theodicy in this sense only exists in those dogmatically monotheistic religions for which the ethical righteousness of God is an indispensable dogma – for only in such systems is the tension pronounced between observed reality (an imperfect world) and *a priori* assumptions (a perfect God). It follows from this that there are really three aspects to the problem of evil and suffering which must be resolved in every religious interpretation of the world. There is (1) the cognitive problem (why does the sinner prosper and the good man suffer?); there is (2) the psychological problem (assurance of comfort, or perhaps ultimate termination of suffering); and (3) the theological problem just referred to in the case of certain monotheistic religions. (Let us refer to these as problems 1, 2 and 3 to avoid repetition.) But if problem 3 is confined only to those religions in which the goodness and omnipotence of God are both essential dogmas, then even problem 1, the cognitive problem, is not a universal one. For as Obeyesekere points out, if a man once accepts a theory like that of *karma* then the need for a theodicy in this sense will never arise; if all suffering is the result of past sins then no suffering can be unjust. The rationally closed belief systems which Weber describes as the only three truly rational theodicies (*karma*, dualism and predestination) suppress problem 2 altogether. But if they preclude the rise of any intellectual problem because of their extreme theoretical consistency, does it follow that they are satisfactory from the psychological point of view, that is, do they provide workable answers to problem 2? Obeyesekere refers to this problem when he states that 'even more important is the fact that *karma*, as a theory of causation, is *psychologically* indeterminate. The past determines the present which (combined with the past) determines the future.'[6] Not knowing what his actions have been in past lives, the individual is therefore in the dark so far as his future is concerned. 'Anything could happen to me; sudden changes or alternations of fortune are to be expected for my present existence is determined by past *karma* regarding which I know nothing. Today I may be in perfect health, but tomorrow I may be suddenly struck down by fatal disease. It is my fault that it is so, but my conscious experience cannot tell me what this fault is.'[7] At least, this is the case if he really does accept the doctrine of *karma* in its scriptural form as, say, expounded in the *Bhagavad Gita*. I add this word of precaution since, as M. S. A. Rao has pointed out, there is nothing more dangerous for the sociologist than what he calls the 'hypothetico-deductive approach'.[8] We should not, he says, assume that once a particular belief is held it will have a determining effect on behaviour. (Indeed we should not assume that it is held at all merely on the strength of its existence in ancient texts.) We cannot understand the meaning of a particular belief if we depend only upon scriptural statements, or any other cultural expression of creed, until we have discovered its position in the total belief system of its adherents and seen how it operates in its social context. If we expect the sacred literature of Hinduism to supply us with the context of beliefs we are expecting something which it cannot provide and are liable to further confusion, for as Dumont has pointed out, the scriptures record the ideas and the experiences of the renouncer rather than those of the 'man-in-the-world'.[9]

According to Rao, we cannot judge the consequences of the adherence to the doctrine of *karma* for the individual believer until we know, for instance, whether the notion of *karma* enters the thought process as a cause of action or as a rationalising after-thought. 'More often when a person fails to succeed in business he rationalises his failure in terms of *karma* rather than think of it in advance. Conversely, when he achieves success, he hardly attributes it to *karma*. Hence it is difficult to trace the causal relationship between beliefs and human motivations for what is presented as a cause might well be treated as a justification.'[10] We would be rash then to assert that the problem of *karma must* cause the Hindu to feel anxious or uncomforted about his future without conducting empirical investigation to ascertain whether this is really so. However, we could go so far as to say that such a hypothesis would be worth testing.

So far, my discussion of the problem may seem to be somewhat abstract, theological rather than sociological. But I think such a discussion must form a necessary preliminary to the study of the problem of theodicy in Hinduism. For one thing, as should be abundantly clear by now, the particular form which the problem of suffering takes will vary in different societies. Whilst problem 2 (psychological) in some form could be assumed to be universal, the nature and magnitude of problem 1 (cognitive) and the very existence or non-existence of problem 3 (theological) depend on the kind of solution given to problem 2. Thus the precise nature of the questions to be resolved has to be reformulated in each cultural case. In Hinduism, as we have seen, problem 3 would hardly seem to arise, for as Weber has pointed out, the doctrine of *karma* is one of the most rational of all possible theodicies at the theological level. But problem 2 might be assumed to be fairly acute. Secondly, the fact that in reality Hindus very often do not behave quite as we should expect them to behave if they were to hold strictly to such scriptural beliefs as *karma*, *dharma* etc., suggests that we should not make assumptions in the first place as to what they really do believe as adherents of the Hindu religion. Indeed, some empirical studies show that some Hindus quite definitely claim that they do not accept certain beliefs like *karma* or the existence of a supreme deity. Individuals may reject certain 'orthodox' beliefs, or at any rate adhere to modified forms or idiosyncratic interpretations of these beliefs. (I record here my reservations about the terms 'modified' and 'interpretations', as they imply that the scripturally 'orthodox' beliefs existed *first* and that villagers and other laymen having once received, then subsequently adapted them to suit their own tastes. I shall return to this point later.) Indeed, it would seem that sociologists were naïve to assume that there would be any less diversity of belief and cosmology among Hindu peasants than among educated Christian Europeans.

Both the points I have raised here indicate that further progress will not be made unless we conduct empirical (and preferably numerous) studies of what Hindus of various types actually do believe about such problems as the causes of misfortune and the relationship of misfortune to behaviour. I will therefore forbear from further theoretical dalliance and present the information which I was able to gather in Ghanyari, a Himachal Pradesh village, during the course of fieldwork carried out in 1966 and 1967. I do not think it will be necessary for me to give a preliminary account of this village except to mention a couple of salient points. First, the dominant caste there is a group of Brahmins; they do not practise priestcraft, being chiefly engaged in agriculture as a full-time source of livelihood. Secondly, the district in which the village lies, whilst not 100 per cent Hindu, has a very strong Hindu majority and has been relatively little exposed to the belief systems of Islam, Sikhism, Christianity or Buddhism. There is only one Muslim family in Ghanyari, which has a population of roughly 350, and is thus large by local standards. The Muslims in this area share many customs with their Hindu neighbours and even celebrate some Hindu festivals. Indeed, being a somewhat isolated area with a very low level of literacy, there has been little possibility for the exposure to any external intellectual influences until recently.

How, then, do villagers account for misfortune and the distribution of suffering in the world? When speaking in general terms, that is, without reference to any particular instance of good or bad fortune, informants invariably explained the distribution of good and bad fortune in terms of the *karma* theory in its familiar form. The universe is peopled with beings in different stages of spiritual advancement; those who do meritorious deeds in this life will be reborn in favourable circumstances, and similarly those who are sinful will be punished by being reborn in wretched circumstances or as some low form of life. Every deed, good or bad, will eventually bear its fruits, and the individual cannot escape from them. He is thus totally responsible for his fate. The concepts of merit (*pun*) and sin (*pap*), it should be noted, are very broad categories and include ritual conformity and ritual offences respectively, although, as we shall see, this does not mean that ethical and ritual offences are confused, since the distinction between them is clearly made in other contexts. Sometimes the *karma* theory is elaborated in such a way as to personalise the process of judgement and retribution; thus the dead person's soul is judged by Dharmraj, the Lord of the Dead, who assigns to it whatever future status it deserves. Before his soul is reborn in mundane form, one who has done excessive evil may be condemned by Dharmraj to spend some time in whichever of the various hells is appropriate to his offence. Similarly, one whose virtue has been outstanding may dwell for a time in *svarg*, or heaven, before resuming the round of mundane birth and rebirth. These elaborations of the basic theory, however, do not in any way negate the idea that merit is automatically rewarded and sin automatically punished.

Considered thus *in abstracto*, the process of karmic retribution is generally seen as a long-term affair. As one Brahmin priest explained, 'If a man has led a very wicked life he may be happy enough at first, but he will certainly be reborn as a snake or a *bhut* (malevolent ghost) or a dog after his death. He may have to undergo rebirth in such a dreadful form several times before he can expiate his sin and be born in some more auspicious form.' Could he not escape this by being a very good dog, snake, etc., I asked? No, the priest replied, because these creatures have no *dharma* (religious duty attached to their status or condition). Only human beings have *dharma* and if they do not fulfil it, they may take several rebirths in lower non-human forms before they are sufficiently punished for their omissions. Though this informant's view that only men have *dharma* may have been idiosyncratic, his recognition that the operation of *karma* may not be immediate was typical of the views of other villagers whom I questioned on the subject.

Next, let us examine some actual instances in which the theory of *karma* was explicitly invoked to account for misfortune. Here again we find some variations, as it were, on the scriptural themes. For instance, *karma* is sometimes described as not merely the total result of a person's actions – good and bad – for himself (the actor), but as a kind of influence which attaches to his person by virtue of these actions, and which can affect others also. When a boat crowded with pilgrims bound for the shrine of a local saint sank in a lake near to Ghanyari, and all the passengers were drowned, one informant remarked that there must have been some very sinful person aboard for such a terrible disaster to have occurred. When a youth who had been born with a slight deformity of the leg, so that he walked with a limp, found difficulty in getting a bride because of this disability, his father said that this trouble must have been due to the bad *karma* of *both father and son* in past lives. In another family the eldest son of Atma Ram had died in his early twenties, leaving a widow still in her teens, but no children; Atma Ram's cousin commented that this trouble must have been due to the bad *karma* of someone in the household (not necessarily the boy himself). In yet another case a Brahmin, Basala, who had been very much feared and disliked during his lifetime, died, leaving two sons and a married daughter. A series of misfortunes beset the family during the years following his death. First of all the younger son died quite suddenly when he was only sixteen. The elder son married, but his first child died within a few days of birth. Various quarrels took place within the household, both between the Brahmin's two widows (he had married twice, as his first wife had borne no children), and between the elder widow and the son. As a result of these troubles the son and his young wife attempted to commit suicide by drowning themselves in the lake, but were rescued by passers-by. Several neighbours attributed these misfortunes and domestic strife to the bad *karma* of the dead Brahmin which was causing suffering in his family even after his decease.

When I asked a Brahmin priest to explain the concept of *karma* he stated quite explicitly that the *karma* of one person could affect another, and used a well-known story to illustrate this idea. In this story, a professional burglar is teaching his son the best way to break into a rich man's house. The father points out a house where every window is bright with light from within and where all the inhabitants seem to be enjoying themselves, dressed in fine garments and eating good food, and he remarks to his son that he has burgled this house many a time. But the son observes that the inmates of the house which has provided them with their livelihood appear prosperous and happy in spite of the father's depredations, while their own house remains a gloomy and miserable place. This makes the father think again and he comes to the conclusion that his past life has indeed been futile and sinful, and that the joylessness of his life is due to his wickedness. He takes heed of his son's words and reforms his ways, albeit late in life. This, explained the priest, illustrates how the good *karma* of the son affected that of the father for the virtue and wisdom of the son (expressions of his arrival at a superior stage of karmic evolution) counteracted the sin of the father, enabling the latter to reform before he was inextricably ensnared in the effects of his own bad *karma*.

It will be noted that many of the instances I have cited refer to members of the same household or kin group being affected by each other's *karma*. In this connection it may be worth noting that many villagers expressed the idea that when a couple marry the wife will henceforth tend to reap the results of her husband's *karma* as well as her own. That is, if he is generous in almsgiving or diligent in keeping fasts, some of the good *karma* he acquires will accrue to the wife, and similarly she would automatically be affected by his bad deeds. The converse, however, did not hold, for her own deeds affect her own fate alone, and would not become part of the *karma* of her husband.

If bad *karma* can exert an influence on those associated with or related to the doer, so also can good *karma* affect others. For example, one villager described how he had been riding in one of a convoy of trucks during the monsoon season. One of the trucks had been swept into the churning waters of a river when the bridge it had been crossing collapsed. But the truck in which he himself had been riding arrived safely at the far side of the bridge just at the very moment before this disaster occurred, and he observed that someone among the company must have had very good *karma* to counteract the danger of the situation.

In the above instances, *karma* has usually been referred to as a general influence, having its origin in unspecified and indeed unknown offences (or good deeds) in the past lives of individuals. Very often, however, misfortunes are seen as the karmic consequences of some known, and usually fairly recent offence in this life.

An interesting example was that of an elderly Brahmin who had been living for some time with the widow of a washerman. His caste fellows had disowned him for associating with such a low-caste woman, and had ceased to eat, drink or smoke with him when he refused to give her up. More than once I heard Brahmins in the village explain the blindness which afflicted his latter years as a punishment for his breach of caste rules. His metaphorical blindness (failure to perceive or take account of caste differences) had become, as it were, a real physical disease. This idea can be compared with the widespread belief that lameness may be the result of having kicked either a cow or a Brahmin in some past life. There are also various legends and stories in which wrongdoers are punished in ways explicitly appropriate to their crimes in some future rebirth.

A similar example of ritual offence being punished with physical disease was the case of another villager, Ramanand, who suffered from such severe rheumatism that he was virtually bed-ridden. His neighbours attributed this to the fact that the year before he had felled a *pipal* tree growing on his land in order to extend one of his meadows (the *pipal* tree being regarded as sacred). Misfortunes suffered by entire groups of people can similarly be attributed to offences or omissions for which they were collectively responsible, as in the case of a *jag*, or feast, organised for the whole village in honour of the deity Thakur, the lord of the rains, during a period of severe drought. The rite failed. The rain which the rite was expected to procure did not fall, or at least not as soon as expected, and this was explained by some as being due to the fact that some of the Chamars (low-caste leather workers) had been turned away rather brusquely by the men in charge of the distribution of the food. The drought itself, incidentally, was regarded by some as a punishment dealt to the village as a whole for its general wickedness, and in particular the quarrelling and disunity of its Brahmin members.

Specific offences, ritual or otherwise, are not related to misfortunes solely retrospectively. Sometimes the commission of a particular offence would give rise to the expectation that some misfortune or disaster would overtake the wrongdoer. For example two brothers cut down a *pipal* tree in order to clear a site for their new house. They satisfied themselves by performing a ritual of worship before the tree before actually taking the axe to it, but their neighbours did not consider this to be a sufficient precaution (as one man remarked, 'what difference does it make to the *pipal* whether you have worshipped it or not when you begin to lop its branches?') and expressed the opinion that some kind of trouble was surely in store for the brothers by way of retribution for this offence.

So far we have been dealing with explanations of misfortune in terms of the moral consequences of offences of an ethical or ritual nature, either specific and known (committed in this life) or putative and unknown (committed in some past life). But perhaps the commonest mode of accounting for misfortunes, especially illness or injury, is not in terms of *karma*, but of the malice of some other person, deity or personalised agent. Thus physical ailments which are chronic or do not respond to treatment are readily attributed to the sorcery (*tuna*) of a near kinsman or affine, and resort may be made to a *chela*, a ritual specialist who will attempt to detect the origin of the trouble and suggest protective measures (such as wearing special charms or amulets). Much more could be said about the techniques used in the practice and cure of sorcery and about the role of the *chela* as diviner, but I will not go into further detail as we are concerned here with the intellectual status of the theory of *tuna* as used to explain misfortune. Alternatively, the afflicted person may view his suffering as due to the anger (*khota*) of some deity or spirit, but here the misfortune is not so readily seen as the result of undeserved or unprovoked spite. Deities as a general rule only send illness or misfortune to those who offend them in some way. A deity may be offended by an individual's failure to worship him, his failure to fulfil vows he has made to the deity or otherwise neglecting the cult. These offences may be specific and known or only presumed.

These kinds of explanation of suffering are rather different from that which appeals to the principle of *karma* pure and simple, without the involvement of any other agent, as they interpret the individual's suffering in such a way as to indicate some positive and immediate steps which he can take to attempt to remove his troubles – to consult the diviner if he suspects *tuna*, to restore good relations with any deity he feels he has offended or neglected, in whatever may be the appropriate way.

A villager who is suffering from some chronic ailment or trouble which is particularly persistent may invoke both *tuna* and *khota* to explain his problems, either simultaneously or consecutively. For instance one Brahmin woman suffered from some kind of skin disease which would not respond to medication. This convinced her that her sufferings were traceable to more than mere physical causes, but sometimes she favoured the idea that her sister-in-law was causing her sufferings through *tuna* (the two women were not on very good terms at the time) and at others considered the displeasure of the goddess Durga a more likely cause. She was aware of having made a vow to donate charitable gifts to unmarried girls in honour of Durga (a common means of fêting the goddess) which she had not yet been in a position to fulfil, and recalled several dreams she had had in which the goddess had appeared to her, angry and accusing. To cover the possibility of *tuna* she ceased to take food in her sister-in-law's house (*tuna* can often, according to villagers' accounts, be performed by putting magical objects in a person's food which are then consumed without his being aware of the fact). But she also arranged to conduct rites in honour of Durga as soon as was practicable, so as to take care of the possibility of this goddess's anger being the prime cause of her troubles. Whilst taking these ritual precautions, she did not give up her attempts to find an effective medical treatment, as she continued to try out numerous different kinds of medication and folk remedy.

Usually explanations of suffering in terms of *tuna* and *khota* are used only by the sufferer himself to explain his own misfortune, and not as a means to account for the misfortune of others. After all, family tensions and jealousies or violations of good relations with particular deities are matters known best to the individual concerned. But in some cases this kind of explanation is used to rationalise the sufferings of another, as in the case of Sibbi, an elderly woman who had become sick and senile. Her mind had begun to wander and she behaved in a very eccentric way, causing her family much embarrassment. Her neighbours attributed her sufferings to the fact that she was apparently known to have made a vow to Gugga, a local saint, to make an offering of Rs.10 at his shrine if her daughter-in-law was safely delivered of a son. In fact two sons were born during the next five years, but Sibbi still had not fulfilled her promise and therefore Gugga was causing her suffering to remind her of this vow.

This would seem a suitable point to summarise some points which emerge from the material presented so far.

1 The theory of *karma* in its classical form, at least, is not the only concept used to rationalise the occurrence of suffering. Variants of this theory as well as other theories, apparently unconnected, may be used.
2 These theories imply differing degrees of responsibility on the part of the subject, and where responsibility is implied, the offence which is thought to have provoked the affliction in question may be more or less remote in time, more or less specific, known or unknown to the subject.
3 The explanation for particular events or misfortunes given by the afflicted person and by those amongst whom he lives may not be identical in every case.

What does all this tell us about the ways in which Hinduism as practised provides solutions to the cognitive and psychological problems of suffering?

I suggested earlier that whilst Hinduism certainly provides an answer to the cognitive problem of suffering (indeed a multiplicity of possible answers at the popular level, as my material shows) it might be supposed that the kind of answer it provides would intensify rather than resolve the psychological problem, i.e. that of providing comfort and justification for the suffering. In theory, Hinduism teaches that suffering is deserved, therefore the sufferer is afflicted by both misfortune *and* guilt. In practice, our material shows that the kinds of explanation given for various kinds of misfortune can be placed on a hypothetical continuum, according to the degree of responsibility allowed to the sufferer, and the immediacy of the responsibility:

karma; known offence in this life
khota; known offence against deity
khota; unintentional or unknown offence against deity
karma; of others and generalised *karma*
tuna; sorcery.

Where a misfortune is attributed to the retributive karmic effect of some offence committed in this life, in theory the maximum responsibility is borne by the actor. Where his troubles are attributed to *tuna* his responsibility would be minimal since it is in no way necessarily his fault if he has jealous or malicious kinsmen or neighbours. It is only in the first three instances listed above that we should expect the question of moral guilt to complicate the problem of actual suffering seriously. In practice, as we have seen, there are ways in which individuals can protect themselves from the psychological consequences which might be presumed to follow from such moral propositions.

First, as my material should make clear, there are cases in which the explanation given by the actual sufferer differs from that given by others who witness his suffering in such a way as to remove the responsibility from himself to a degree, or altogether. Thus Ramanand's neighbours attributed his problems to the fact that he had felled a *pipal* tree; but Ramanand himself merely attributed them to generalised bad *karma*, earned in some previous incarnation. One cannot give more than subjective impressions in matters like this, but I should say that villagers do not show signs of deep anxiety or acute remorse over unknown offences committed in past lives. Such offences were theoretically committed by the same self incarnated in a different body, but in practice villagers seem to feel immediate responsibility only for offences committed in the present incarnation. Past incarnations are in theory the same self, but it is a rather remote kind of self, differently constituted. Thus Ramanand did not appear to be unduly anxious about the presumed offences which had earned him bad *karma*, on the principle that one can hardly feel guilt about offences that one is unaware of. This kind of multiple explanation is also found in other kinds of case. For instance in the case of Sibbi, whilst her neighbours explained her illness in terms of her responsibility for an offence against a deity, Sibbi herself was more inclined to either a straightforward explanation in mundane physical terms, or in terms of *tuna* practised by her daughter-in-law, thus removing direct moral responsibility from herself. We may add that where villagers use ideas of ritual offence or omission to explain particular troubles, this does not necessarily imply a burden of guilt being placed upon the offender. Whilst it would be untrue to say that ritual errors or omissions are morally entirely neutral, a clear distinction is made between the kind of ethical or ritual offence which is knowingly committed (telling lies, felling a *pipal* tree) and the kind of ritual error which can be made unwittingly, such as omitting some ritual act expected by the deity in question. (This distinction is maintained in practice in spite of the fact that both kinds of offence are subsumed under the concept of *pap*.) This kind of omission is a familiar theme in legend and folk stories. For instance there is a story current in Ghanyari concerning a blacksmith who was afflicted with nightmares and sickness because he had used a large boulder, in which (unknown to him) the deity Thakur had chosen to reside, as a weight to secure the jute stems which he was soaking in a local stream. Fortunately Thakur revealed his offence to him in a dream, and he was able to make good his error by building a shrine to the deity in which the stone in question was given a place of honour. In a case like this, unintentional ritual offence implies no moral opprobrium and therefore an individual might own to having (presumably) committed some such error without implying any moral culpability on his own part. Again, where the bad deeds of some member of the family – known (as in the case of Basala) or unknown (as in the case of Atma Ram) – are involved the acceptance of the working of *karma* does not oblige the sufferer to accept disturbing guilt feelings, since he himself has not committed the acts which provoked the karmic retribution. The effects of karmic retribution have, as it were, become diffused to include him through no direct fault of his own. Occasionally we even hear villagers employ the Islamic term *kismet*, to account for events and fortunes, thus approaching a purely fatalistic interpretation. Also, it is not uncommon to hear villagers account for events by saying 'It is God's will', although I believe that this is more often proffered as a kind of conventional consolation to, for example, someone suffering from a bereavement, rather than a thought-out explanation of the misfortune in question.

From observation, therefore, we may say that whilst the concept of *karma* is accepted in theory by the villagers, in actual operation it is either supplemented by other notions of causation, or it is implemented in such a way that the afflicted person is protected from a heavy sense of responsibility or feelings of anxiety about past deeds. I do not mean that the Hindu villager has side-stepped the problem of moral guilt altogether, or that due to some sort of intellectual cheating he never feels this emotion; I mean that for him it does not constitute a *special* problem, such as a naïve view of the existence of the *karma* theory as an explanation of suffering might lead us to expect.

But what about the future? Does not the Hindu feel insecure in whatever good fortune he may enjoy, by virtue of the fact that he may yet have to receive punishment for unknown offences in past lives? In practice, I would say that this does not seem to be a subject which causes the villager to lose much sleep. The very 'supplementary' theories of causation which he used to explain suffering imply, as I have already observed, techniques for attempting to improve one's lot in future or averting trouble and suffering, and on the whole it is the fairly immediate future with which the villager concerns himself. Thus the idea of *khota* is balanced by the idea that deities can also be placated and won over by offerings and worship to provide positive good fortune to their devotees. If ritual offences bring misfortune, the punctilious observance of fasts and other religious rituals ensure[s] happiness and welfare. If neighbours and relatives can cause trouble through the practice of *tuna* then the diviner and his various skills are there to be used to counteract this. So the villager does not by any means see himself as helpless in the face of fortune, even though according to a strict interpretation of the *karma* theory he is in fact highly vulnerable to the effects of deeds committed in this and other lives.

It will be noticed that the words 'in theory' and 'in practice' are continually juxtaposed and contrasted. I have mentioned the existence of 'supplementary' theories – supplementary, that is, to the scriptural notion of *karma*. What is the status of that theory if it is frequently negated in practice, and apparently competes with other theories?

On the face of it, it would seem that to claim in the first place that *karma* accounts for the differential distribution of good and bad fortune, and then to explain a particular misfortune in terms of, say, *tuna*, would amount to a logical inconsistency. If the individual is ultimately responsible for his own fate, how can the will of others influence this fate for good or ill? The operative word here, however, is 'ultimately'. When I put this question to villagers directly they answered that explanations of bad fortune in terms of one's relationships with the deities or one's kinsmen do not negate the theory of *karma*. One might suffer from some illness on account of the machinations of some jealous kinsman who practised sorcery, to be sure, but this was only an explanation in terms of immediate causes. If the sufferer's *karma* had been good, he would not have succumbed to his kinsman's *tuna*. To put it another way, it must be the *karma* of the individual which explains why he in particular is fated to be the victim of such malice. Again, a person might suffer from financial troubles or ill health because of his neglect of a particular deity, but in the final analysis it is the *karma* which he has accumulated in this and previous lives which determines the degree to which he is successful in his dealings with the gods. In short, we encounter here the familiar distinction between the 'cause' and the 'meaning' of misfortune.

The practice of astrology would also appear to imply a rejection of the principle of karmic determination, for if the events in one's life are determined by the conjunction of stars at one's birth, how can they also be shaped by one's moral activity in previous lives? But, I was told, this is only a contradiction at the superficial level; the very moment of one's birth is determined by one's past *karma*, so that if a person is born at an astrologically inauspicious time this must be because of his sinfulness in a past life. The stars therefore *predict* a man's future rather than *determine* it. I have not dwelt on the phenomenon of astrology because whilst the horoscope is of great importance at weddings (when the horoscopes of the bride and groom must be matched and found compatible), I did not find that particular instances of misfortune were often attributed to inauspicious planetary influences. For one thing, horoscopes and astrological predictions seldom foretell good or bad events in a very specific way; the fact that some kind of trouble is predicted in a person's horoscope may diminish the surprise element when trouble eventually occurs, but some other more precise explanation is generally sought in addition, if the trouble is felt to be problematic.

The admission of immediate causes of suffering for which the victim is not directly responsible should not therefore be taken as a denial of his long-term responsibility for his fate according to the principle of *karma*. The various types of explanation given for suffering and misfortune have not been integrated by the villagers into a tidy and logically coherent system of metaphysics, but they should not therefore be regarded as entirely discrete and unrelated. The principle of *karma* is prior to the others in several senses. First, it is logically prior to all other possible explanations in the sense that the latter can be reduced to or made compatible with the *karma* doctrine in the final analysis. Secondly, whilst the *karma* principle need not be the theory which the villager turns to first of all in his search for a meaning for the misfortune he suffers, it is generally the last which he will abandon. By this I mean that he is more likely to express scepticism towards the cult of the gods or towards the idea of *tuna* than he is explicitly to reject the doctrine of *karma*. This at least was the impression I received when talking to some of the more educated and sophisticated members of the village.

As we have seen, in times of stress or trouble, a villager is more likely to act on the assumption that his suffering is not inevitable and that it can be dealt with by applying whichever of the other possible kinds of explanations seems appropriate, or even more than one theory simultaneously. Since the logical paramountcy of the *karma* theory does not in any way preclude the existence of other beliefs, it is tempting to treat these beliefs as distinct and incongruent bodies of theory, especially in view of the fact that the philosophy of *karma* is elaborated in some of the Hindu texts, whereas the other theories receive less authoritative treatment or none at all. The temptation to treat the theories as disparate or conflicting is the greater in view of the fact that each kind of theory is associated with its own system of ritual practice or 'technology' and its separate set of specialists. To the level of ultimate karmic explanation belongs all that body of ritual (*kathas*, fasts, charitable donations, feeding of Brahmins) which is directed to improving one's store of personal merit and thereby warding off the misfortunes which may arise from bad *karma*. To the more immediate level of explanation (in terms of malevolent deities) correspond the cults of the gods with all their priests and ritual paraphernalia, all the ritual designed to improve a person's fortune by ensuring that the gods are well-disposed towards him. At a more mundane level there are explanations of misfortune in terms of the sufferer's relationship with other human beings; associated with this kind of belief we find the institution of the *chela* and the remedies for the effects of *tuna* which he can prescribe. Alongside all these 'supernatural' kinds of belief and procedure there are all the various kinds of material technology available to the villager through which he can try to better his lot and ward off misfortune, including at least three different systems of medicine known and practised locally. (This may seem an obvious point, but it would be misleading if our interest in religious and philosophical interpretations of misfortune were to lead us to assume that the Hindu himself is only interested in this kind of explanation and ignores the various material techniques of cure and prevention which are at his disposal.)

Having made these distinctions, the anthropologist may be further tempted to regard the well-known 'classical' version of the *karma* theory as 'orthodox', from which it will follow that the various other kinds of explanation which I have described must be regarded as heterodox variations of, or even departures from, the basic theory. The temptation is especially acute for the educated western observer whose prior knowledge of Hinduism before he arrives in the field may largely be derived from scriptural texts which he has read in translation. Yet in Ghanyari it is very difficult to talk about orthodoxy. For one thing whilst the Brahmin priest certainly has a monopoly in the performance of some key rituals and may be regarded as having a special competence to pronounce on matters of doctrine, he cannot be said to have final authority in the case of the latter. Respect for his judgement is based on his superior learning (although most priests in the area are not particularly erudite) rather than on his authority *qua* priest.

Secondly, whilst the theory of *karma* may be expounded by the priests when they recite the Sanskrit texts at scripture recitals and other religious occasions, it is my impression that the doctrine does not depend on this channel of information for its survival and propagation. In practice the individual receives the concept of *karma* as part of a living folk tradition which includes equally the other ideas which I have described, such as those concerning the pantheon, or the effects of *tuna*. In other words, the villager is not much concerned with the different sources of authority for these various strands in local Hindu thought. Indeed, far from regarding the *karma* concept in any passive way, the villager, as we have seen, is liable to elaborate or reinterpret the theory actively, resulting in variations and idiosyncrasies of interpretation. (This applies equally to the Brahmin priest.) The existence of scriptural expositions of the kind of idea which we have been discussing cannot simply be left out of account, since the villager is aware of their existence and prestige even though he is not very likely to have read them; the scriptures are constantly referred to in a vague manner as the epitome of Hindu metaphysics and law, even though few have a very precise idea of their contents. On the other hand, the villager does not let this interfere with his right to reinterpret received doctrines in the light of his own personal ideas and experiences. This, at least, is true of Ghanyari, although I am aware that a different situation might obtain, in, say, an area where there were influential groups of learned Brahmins or sectarian scholars, or centres of traditional Hindu learning and culture.

The problem of the relationship of the *karma* theory to other theories used to interpret suffering and misfortune is not peculiar to the Hindu world. In fact it has been studied more extensively with reference to Buddhism. The Buddhists of south and south-east Asia have in common with the Hindus of Ghanyari both a belief in *karma* (albeit in a slightly different form), and a religious tradition which is conductive to heterogeneity, being decentralised and multi-stranded. In Thailand, Tambiah notes that the merit-making ceremonies which are associated with scriptural beliefs in *karma* coexist with the cults addressed to deities which are also believed to be capable of influencing the affairs of men. At first sight an inconsistency would seem to exist in the religious thinking of these Buddhists, for Tambiah comments that 'if the doctrine of *karma* gives an explanation for present suffering and squarely puts the burden of release on individual effort then the doctrine that supernatural agents can cause or relieve suffering and that relief can come through propitiating them contradicts the karma postulate'.[11] But Tambiah goes on to say that it is not helpful to regard these two theories as being, as it were, in competition with each other, for 'while this categorical opposition is present in Thailand I see it as one which operates within a total field that expresses other relations as well of complementarity and hierarchical ordering between Buddhism and the spirit cults. To emphasise one aspect at the expense of others seems to me to be a partial analysis; to go further and assert that there are in fact two contradictory religions in uneasy coexistence appears to me to be a misunderstanding.'[12] Tambiah is referring here to Spiro's study of Buddhism in Burma where Buddhism and the cult of the *nats* (powerful and often malevolent spirits capable of causing illness and misfortune to humans) provide answers to different kinds of moral or personal crises. To the extent that they seem to embody different moral values, Spiro regards them as being in conflict and points out that his Burmese informants themselves were aware of the tension between the values of the two cults. But we may concur with Tambiah that this does not justify the assertion that there are two distinct religions. Presumably it might be possible for Burmese Buddhists to square their performance of *nat* rituals with the belief in the operation of the moral law of *karma*, much as the Hindus of Ghanyari are capable of ironing out the inconsistencies between their worship of the Hindu deities and their belief in the Hindu version of *karma*. But unlike Tambiah's Thai Buddhists, Spiro's informants seemed to be acutely aware of their dilemma and entertained a highly ambivalent attitude to the *nat* cults. The more educated especially deprecated them as being not really 'religion' at all, yet in spite of professed scepticism few omitted to propitiate them, including the educated sceptics. Thus, for these Burmese Buddhists the problem of the discontinuities in their belief system is a real one, and not simply an academic one manufactured by the anthropologist. But in this respect Spiro's material would seem to differ from the other studies discussed here; as Tambiah points out, it is more common for the anthropologist to take as his starting point the scriptural expressions of the *karma* theory and then note how these differ from the 'popular' religion. This orientation dictates its methodology and shapes the final conclusions, for the analyst accordingly seeks to see how 'non-doctrinal' facts are adapted, modified, and rationalised in relation to 'doctrinal' ideas.

Gombrich has tackled the same problem in Ceylon. There, as in Ghanyari, the effects of a rigorous interpretation of the *karma* doctrine are mitigated by a number of practices which would seem to imply modification of the strict *karma* theory. For instance, to make a *prarthana* religious wish – for instance to wish that all the hearers of a particular sermon may attain nirvana – would seem to contradict the *karma* theory; at least this would be the case if the maker of the wish had any faith in the efficacy of his prayer really to affect the spiritual fortunes of others. How can the hearers of a sermon attain nirvana except by their own efforts? 'This is not strictly in contradiction to *karma* theory because it can be said that the wish will only be fulfilled if the *karma* is good enough, and the merit gained just before a *prarthana* is made should ensure this. However, there is little doubt that affectively the donor feels that he is achieving a certain result by a certain action in an automatic, magical way.'[13] So for Gombrich's Buddhists, the real tensions lie not between the various intellectual expressions of their religious ideas, since notions which on the face of it appear undoctrinal can generally be assimilated to canonical doctrines, albeit sometimes with difficulty. The important tensions lie between what Gombrich calls 'cognitive' religion (what people say about their beliefs and practices) and 'affective' religion (the religion of the heart, the ideas that are implied by actual behaviour).

Whilst a comparison with Buddhist cases is obviously interesting here, we must not lose sight of certain important differences between the religious organisations of Buddhism and Hinduism. Here I return to the points I made earlier about orthodoxy. As Gombrich shows, it does make sense to talk about 'canonical' Buddhism provided that we understand that this does not mean that there is any enforcement of intellectual conformity, merely a body of scriptures which are agreed to be authoritative above all others. But of Hinduism one could only say that of the great body of religious literature, some texts are better known and regarded as more authoritative than others, or are regarded as authoritative for certain sects only. Yet as Gombrich shows, some of the tensions between affective and cognitive religion are present within canonical Buddhism itself. Certainly it would not be legitimate to characterise some of the popular ideas and practices which he describes as being in any way heterodox departures from canonical doctrine since, as he points out, some of the very ideas and practices which he refers to would seem to date back to the very beginning of Buddhist history and are even mentioned in early Buddhist writings. They reflect the inevitable tension between the cognitive propositions of Buddhism and the affective needs of the Buddhist rather than the heterodoxy of the latter. This is an important point since it has always been a besetting sin of western scholars (and indeed of some oriental ones) to impute to Buddhism and Hinduism a stronger and more rigid sense of orthodoxy than actually exists, and therefore to regard very readily the latitude with which the uneducated Buddhist or Hindu interprets received religious ideas as departures from 'orthodoxy'. The very term 'orthodoxy' can, I feel, be applied to Indian Hinduism only in certain very specific contexts, as for instance, when we are speaking of the doctrines of particular monastic orders or sects. I hope I have demonstrated this satisfactorily already so far as Ghanyari itself is concerned.

What the Buddhist material which I have mentioned does illustrate very clearly, I think, is that when we set out to discover the relationship between doctrinal tenets and affective needs, we are not by any means creating a pseudo-problem. The danger of creating 'pseudo-problems' is an ever-present one, especially where a 'hypothetico-deductive' approach is used. The study of belief systems is particularly difficult because it is all too easy for the anthropologist to assume that beliefs *are* arranged in systems, instead of feeling obliged to demonstrate that this is in fact the case. Discontinuities or inconsistencies among the ideas expressed by the subject then become a problem to the researcher even though they may not be at all problematic to the subject. Most human beings, after all, seem able to tolerate some areas of uncertainty or confusion in their belief systems, though obviously the problems which appear to need precise resolution and those which can safely be left unresolved or even imperfectly formulated will vary in different societies. Yet, if the questions posed at the beginning of this article were perhaps formulated in an ethnocentric manner, I do not think that they were foolish ones. Approaching the question of theodicy solely in terms of the possible doctrinal conflict between the various theories put forward to explain suffering would not seem to be the most appropriate method of approach in the case of Hinduism, as the material shows, since intellectual conformity is not a matter of great concern to the Hindu villager. It was found more appropriate to define the question in terms of 'tensions' rather than 'conflict' or 'contradiction'. But the very diversity and complexity of the various resolutions to the problem of suffering which can be found within Buddhist and Hindu villages, even such a small and isolated village as Ghanyari, are surely of great interest, not to mention the more general questions about the structure of belief systems which are raised by these studies of Hinduism and Buddhism.

Appendix: Karma and caste

Mention may be made here of the role of the *karma* theory in interpreting the social order. Low-caste status may be conceived as a special form of misfortune or suffering, entailing as it does a position of ritual and frequently economic disprivilege. In Hindu writings the idea is often expressed that low-caste status is to be accounted for by sins in a past life, and sociologists have often assumed that this theory is in fact current as a rationale for the caste system (e.g. Weber). Studies of particular low castes such as those conducted by Cohn, Mahar and others show (not surprisingly) that members of low castes do not in fact use this theory to explain their own low-caste status. Rather they explain it in secular or historical terms (e.g. that they are really descended from a high-caste person who contracted a misalliance, they were outcasted unjustly, etc.). Of the sweepers whom she studied, Kolenda says that their 'conception of why they have a low-caste status protects them from anxiety which would result if they accepted the full *karma* theory with its requirements that members of the lowest caste must have been those who were most sinful in past incarnations'.[14] So far, my experiences in Ghanyari would confirm this observation, for the untouchable castes there used similar mythical explanations for the status of their caste. What is interesting is the fact that when asked to account for the existence of the caste system, Brahmins also tended to explain it primarily in secular terms, usually in terms of the need for a division of labour in society. For instance, one Brahmin farmer said, 'caste arose because one man alone cannot do all the work himself. One person cannot do the work of a teacher, farmer, priest, smith, soldier – he would never have time. Therefore different castes were created to perform these different tasks.' Another Brahmin explained the system in terms of the differential prestige of various occupations. 'Low castes came into existence because some tasks, like sweeping out latrines or skinning dead animals, are dirty and repulsive; ordinary people do not wish to associate with those who do such work, and therefore separate castes were formed.' Responses of a secular kind were given by both high and low caste persons to the question as to why the caste system exists. But when asked to account for a particular individual's birth in a low-caste family, villagers answered in terms of past *karma* and here again, I noticed no great differences between the responses given by members of high or low castes. A member of a low caste said to me, 'You are dressed in fine clothes and are seated upon a chair wherever you go. I am dressed in rags and people only bid me sit on the floor because I am of low caste; surely it must all be due to *karma* in our past life.' This informant did not seem to feel the suggestion that she had been sinful in her past life unacceptable, presumably because – as I have shown – unknown offences committed in a past life are regarded as too remote from the individual who is presumed to have committed them to activate very acute feelings of guilt or responsibility. The theory of *karma* need not therefore pose any greater problem to low castes than it does to anyone else who feels that his situation is unenviable or unfortunate.

---

1 C. Geertz, 'Religion as a cultural system', in *Anthropological Approaches to the Study of Religion*, ed. M. Banton (Assoc. Social Anthrop. Monogr.) London: Tavistock 1966.

2 T. Parsons, 'The theoretical development of the sociology of religion', in *Essays in Sociological Theory, Pure and Applied*, Glencoe: Free Press 1949, pp. 52–66.

3 M. Weber, *The Sociology of Religion*, London: Associated Book Publishers 1966, p. 107.

4 M. Weber, 'The social psychology of the world religions', in *From Max Weber*, eds. H. H. Gerth and C. Wright Mills, London: Routledge and Kegan Paul 1948, p. 276.

5 G. Obeyesekere, 'Theodicy, sin and salvation in a sociology of Buddhism', in *Practical Religion*, ed. E. R. Leach, Cambridge University Press 1968, p. 11.

6 G. Obeyesekere, *op. cit.* p. 21.

7 *Ibid.*

8 M. S. A. Rao, 'Religion and economic development', in *Tradition, Rationality and Change*, Bombay: Popular Prakashan 1972, p. 630.

9 L. Dumont, *Religion, Politics and History in India*, The Hague: Mouton 1970, p. 41.

10 M. S. A. Rao, *op. cit.* p. 66.

11 S. J. Tambiah, *Buddhism and the Spirit Cults in North East Thailand*, Cambridge University Press 1970, p. 41.

12 *Ibid.*

13 R. I. Gombrich, *Precept and Practice*, Oxford: Clarendon Press 1971, p. 220.
14 P. M. Kolenda, 'Religious anxiety and Hindu fate', in *Journal of Asian Studies*, No. 23, pp. 71–9.

Source: U. Sharma, 'Theodicy and the doctrine of karma', *Man* 8(3) (1973): 347–64.

—— ●◆● ——

HINDU PATTERNS OF LIBERATION

— ◆ ◆ —

4.6 FROM THE UPANISHADS

4.6.1 The *Isha Upanishad*

1   This whole world is to be dwelt in by the Lord,
        whatever living being there is in the world.
    So you should eat what has been abandoned;
        and do not covet anyone's wealth.

2   Just performing works in this world,
        you should desire to live your hundred years.
    Thus, and not otherwise, in fact,
        does work not smear off on you.

3   'Demonic' are those worlds called,
        in blind darkness they are cloaked;
    Into them after death they go,
        all those people who kill the self.

4   Although not moving, the one is swifter than the mind;
        the gods cannot catch it, as it speeds on in front.
    Standing, it outpaces others who run;
        within it Mātariśvan places the waters.

5   It moves – yet it does not move
        It's far away – yet it is near at hand!

It is within this whole world – yet
    it's also outside this whole world.

6   When a man sees all beings
        within his very self,
        and his self within all beings,
    It will not seek to hide from him.

7   When in the self of a discerning man,
        his very self has become all beings,
    What bewilderment, what sorrow can there be,
        regarding that self of him who sees this oneness.

8   He has reached the seed – without body or wound,
        without sinews, not riddled by evil.
    Self-existent and all-encompassing,
        the wise sage has dispensed objects
        through endless years.

9   Into blind darkness they enter,
        people who worship ignorance;
    And into still blinder darkness,
        people who delight in learning.

10 It's far different from knowledge, they say,
    Different also from ignorance, we're told –
        so have we heard from wise men,
        who have explained it to us.

11 Knowledge and ignorance –
        a man who knows them both together,
    Passes beyond death by ignorance,
        and by knowledge attains immortality.

12 Into blind darkness they enter,
        people who worship non-becoming;
    And into still blinder darkness,
        people who delight in becoming.

13 It's far different from coming-into-being, they say,
    Different also from not coming-into-being, we're told –
        so have we heard from wise men,
        who have explained it all to us.

14 The becoming and the destruction –
        a man who knows them both together;
    Passes beyond death by the destruction,
        and by the becoming attains immortality.

15 The face of truth is covered
        with a golden dish.
   Open it, O Pūsan, for me,
        a man faithful to the truth.
   Open it, O Pūsan, for me to see.

16 O Pūsan, sole seer!
   Yama! Sun! Son of Prajāpati!
        Spread out your rays!
        Draw in your light!
   I see your fairest form.
   That person up there,
        I am he!

17 The never-resting is the wind,
        the immortal!
   Ashes are this body's lot.
        OM!
   Mind, remember the deed!
        Remember!
   Mind, remember the deed!
        Remember!

18 O Fire, you know all coverings;
   O god, lead us to riches,
        along an easy path.
   Keep the sin that angers,
        far away from us;
   And the highest song of praise,
        we shall offer to you!

Source: Patrick Olivelle (trans.) *Upanishads* (OUP, 1996), pp. 249–51.

4.6.2 The *Chandogya Upanishad*

1 There was one Śvetaketu, the son of Āruṇi. One day his father told him: 'Śvetaketu, take up the celibate life of a student, for there is no one in our family, my son, who has not studied and is the kind of Brahmin who is so only because of birth.'
   ² So he went away to become a student at the age of 12 and, after learning all the Vedas, returned when he was 24, swell-headed, thinking himself to be learned, and arrogant. ³ His father then said to him: 'Śvetaketu, here you are, my son, swell-headed, thinking yourself to be learned, and arrogant; so you must have surely asked about that rule of substitution by which one hears what has not been heard of before, thinks of what has not been thought of before, and perceives what has not been perceived before?'
   ⁴ 'How indeed does that rule of substitution work, sir?'

'It is like this, son. By means of just one lump of clay one would perceive everything made of clay – the transformation is a verbal handle, a name – while the reality is just this: "It's clay."

[5] 'It is like this, son. By means of just one copper trinket one would perceive everything made of copper – the transformation is a verbal handle, a name – while the reality is just this: "It's copper."

[6] 'It is like this son. By means of just one nail-cutter one would perceive everything made of iron – the transformation is a verbal handle, a name – while the reality is just this: "It's iron."

'That, son, is how this rule of substitution works.'

[7] 'Surely, those illustrious men did not know this, for had they known, how could they have not told it to me? So, why don't you, sir, tell me yourself?'

'All right, son,' he replied.

2 'In the beginning, son, this world was simply what is existent – one only, without a second. Now, on this point some do say: "In the beginning this world was simply what is non-existent – one only, without a second. And from what is non-existent was born what is existent."

[2] 'But, son, how can that possibly be?' he continued. 'How can what is existent be born from what is non-existent? On the contrary, son, in the beginning this world was simply what is existent – one only, without a second.

[3] 'And it thought to itself: "Let me become many. Let me propagate myself." It emitted heat. The heat thought to itself: "Let me become many. Let me propagate myself." It emitted water. Whenever it is hot, therefore, a man surely perspires; and thus it is from heat that water is produced. [4] The water thought to itself: "Let me become many. Let me propagate myself." It emitted food. Whenever it rains, therefore, food becomes abundant; and thus it is from water that foodstuffs are produced.

3 'There are, as you can see, only three sources from which these creatures here originate: they are born from eggs, from living individuals, or from sprouts.

[2] 'Then that same deity thought to itself: "Come now, why don't I establish the distinctions of name and appearance by entering these three deities here with this living self (ātman), [3] and make each of them threefold." So, that deity established the distinctions of name and appearance by entering these three deities here with this living self (ātman), [4] and made each of them threefold.

'Learn from me, my son, how each of these three deities becomes threefold.

4 'The red appearance of a fire is, in fact, the appearance of heat, the white, that of water, and the black, that of food. So vanishes from the fire the character of fire – the transformation is a verbal handle, a name – while the reality is just, "It's the three appearances."

[2] 'The red appearance of the sun is, in fact, the appearance of heat, the white, that of water, and the black, that of food. So vanishes from the sun the character of sun – the transformation is a verbal handle, a name – while the reality is just, "It's the three appearances."

[3] 'The red appearance of the moon is, in fact, the appearance of heat, the white, that of water, and the black, that of food. So vanishes from the moon the character of moon – the transformation is a verbal handle, a name – while the reality is just, "It's the three appearances."

[4] 'The red appearance of lightning is, in fact, the appearance of heat, the white, that of water, and the black, that of food. So vanishes from lightning the character of lightning – the transformation is a verbal handle, a name – while the reality is just, "It's the three appearances."

[5] 'It was, indeed, this that they knew, those extremely wealthy and immensely learned householders of old, when they said: "Now no one will be able to spring something upon us that we have not heard of or thought of or understood before." For they derived that knowledge from these three – [6] when they noticed anything that was reddish, they knew: "That is the appearance of heat"; when they noticed anything that was whitish, they knew: "That is the appearance of water"; when they noticed anything that was blackish, they knew: "That is the appearance of food"; [7] and when they noticed anything that was somehow indistinct, they knew: "That is a combination of these same three deities".

'Learn from me, son, how, when they enter a man, each of these three deities become threefold.

5 'When one eats food it breaks down into three parts. The densest becomes faeces, the medium becomes flesh, and the finest becomes mind. [2] When one drinks water it breaks down into three parts. The densest becomes urine, the medium becomes blood, and the finest becomes breath. [3] When one eats heat it breaks down into three parts. The densest becomes bones, the medium becomes marrow, and the finest becomes speech. [4] For the mind is made up of food, son; breath, of water; and speech, of heat.'

'Sir, teach me more.'

'Very well, son.'

6 'When one churns curd, its finest part rises to the top and becomes butter. [2] In the same way, son, when one eats food its finest part rises to the top and becomes mind; [3] when one drinks water its finest part rises to the top and becomes breath; [4] and when one eats heat its finest part rises to the top and becomes speech. [5] For the mind is made up of food, son; breath, of water; and speech, of heat.'

'Sir, teach me more.'

'Very well, son.

7 'A man, my son, consists of sixteen parts. Do not eat for fifteen days, but drink water at will. Breath is made of water; so it will not be cut off if one drinks.'

[2] Śvetaketu did not eat for fifteen days. Then he came back to his father and said: 'What shall I recite, sir?'

'The Ṛg verses, the Yajus formulas, and the Sāman chants.'

'Sir, I just can't remember them,' he replied. [3] And his father said to him:

'It is like this, son. Out of a huge fire that one has built, if there is left only a single ember the size of a firefly – by means of that the fire thereafter would not burn all that much. Likewise, son, you are left with only one of your sixteen parts; by means of that at present you don't remember the Vedas.

'Eat, and then you will learn from me.'

[4] He ate and then came back to his father. And he answered everything that his father asked. [5] And the father said to him:

'It is like this, son. Out of a huge fire that one has built, if there is left only a single ember the size of a firefly and if one were to cover it with straw and set it ablaze – by means of that, the fire thereafter would burn very much. [6] Likewise, son, you were left with only one of your sixteen parts, and when you covered it with food, it was set ablaze – by means of that you now remember the Vedas, for the mind, son, is made up of food; breath, of water; and speech, of heat.'

And he did, indeed, learn it from him.

8 Uddalāka Āruni said to his son, Śvetaketu: 'Son, learn from me that nature of sleep. When one says here: "The man is sleeping", son, then he is united with the existent; into himself (*sva*) he has entered (*apīta*). Therefore, people say with reference to him: "He is sleeping" (*svapiti*), for then he has entered into himself.

[2] 'It is like this. Take a bird that is tied with a string. It will fly off in every direction and, when it cannot find a resting-place anywhere else, it will alight back upon the very thing to which it is tied. Similarly, son, the mind flies off in every direction and, when it cannot find a resting-place anywhere else, it alights back upon the breath itself; for the mind, my son, is tied to the breath.

[3] 'Son, learn from me about hunger and thirst. When one says here: "The man is hungry", then the water drives away with what he has eaten. So, just as one calls someone a "cattle-driver", or a "horse-driver", or a "man-driver", similarly one calls water "hunger" – the "food-driver".

'With regard to this, son, you should recognize this as a bud that has come out. It cannot be without a root, [4] and what could its root be if not food? Likewise, son, with food as the bud, look to water as the root; with water as the bud, look to heat as the root; and with heat as the bud, look to the existent as the root. The existent, my son, is the root of all these creatures – the existent is their resting-place, the existent is their foundation.

[5] 'When, moreover, one says here: "The man is thirsty", then the heat drives away with what he has drunk. So, just as one calls someone a "cattle-driver", or a "horse-driver", or a "man-driver", similarly one calls heat "thirst" – the "water-driver".

'With regard to this, son, you should recognize this as a bud that has come out. It cannot be without a root, [6] and what could its root be if not water? Likewise, son, with water as the bud, look to heat as the root; and with heat as the bud, look to the existent as the root. The existent, my son, is the root of all these creatures – the existent is their resting-place, the existent is their foundation.

'I have already explained to you, son, how, when they enter a man, each of these three deities become threefold.

'When a man is dying, my son, his speech merges into his mind; his mind, into his breath; his breath, into heat; and heat, into the highest deity.

[7] 'The finest essence here – that constitutes the self of this whole world; that is the truth; that is the self (*ātman*). And that's how you are, Śvetaketu.'

'Sir, teach me more.'

'Very well, son.

9 'Now, take the bees, son. They prepare the honey by gathering nectar from a variety of trees and by reducing that nectar to a homogeneous whole. [2] In that state the nectar from each different tree is not able to differentiate: "I am the nectar of that tree", and "I am the nectar of this tree". In exactly the same way, son, when all these creatures merge into the existent, they are not aware that: "We are merging into the existent." [3] No matter what they are in this world – whether it is a tiger, a lion, a wolf, a boar, a worm, a moth, a gnat, or a mosquito – they all merge into that.

[4] 'The finest essence here – that constitutes the self of this whole world; that is the truth; that is the self (*ātman*). And that's how you are, Śvetaketu.'

'Sir, teach me more.'

'Very well, son.

10 'Now, take these rivers, son. The easterly ones flow towards the east, and the westerly ones flow towards the west. From the ocean, they merge into the very ocean; they become just the ocean. In that state they are not aware that: "I am that river", and "I am this river". [2] In exactly the same way, son, when all these creatures reach the existent, they are not aware that: "We are reaching the existent". No matter what they are in this world – whether it is a tiger, a lion, a boar, a work, a moth, a gnat, or a mosquito – they all merge into that.

[3] 'The finest essence here – that constitutes the self of this whole world; that is the truth; that is the self (*ātman*). And that's how you are, Śvetaketu.'

'Sir, teach me more.'

'Very well, son.

11 'Now, take this huge tree here, son. If someone were to hack it at the bottom, its living sap would flow. Likewise, if someone were to hack it in the middle, its living sap would flow; and if someone were to hack it at the top, its living sap would flow. Pervaded by the living (*jīva*) essence (*ātman*), this tree stands here ceaselessly drinking water and flourishing. [2] When, however, life (*jīva*) leaves one of its branches, that branch withers away. When it leaves a second branch, that likewise withers away, and when it leaves a third branch, that also withers away. When it leaves the entire tree, the whole tree withers away.

[3] 'In exactly the same way,' he continued, 'know that this, of course, dies when it is bereft of life (*jīva*); but life itself does not die.

'The finest essence here – that constitutes the self of this whole world; that is the truth; that is the self (*ātman*). And that's how you are, Śvetaketu.'

'Sir, teach me more.'

'Very well, son.

12 'Bring a banyan fruit.'

'Here it is, sir.'

'Cut it up.'

'I've cut it up, sir.'

'What do you see there?'

'These quite tiny seeds, sir.'

'Now, take one of them and cut it up.'

'I've cut one up, sir.'

'What do you see there?'

'Nothing, sir.'

[2] Then he told him: 'This finest essence here, son, that you can't even see – look how on account of that finest essence this huge banyan tree stands here.

'Believe, my son: [3] the finest essence here – that constitutes the self of this whole world; that is the truth; that is the self (*ātman*). And that's how you are, Śvetaketu.'

'Sir, teach me more.'

'Very well, son.

13 'Put this chunk of salt in a container of water and come back tomorrow.' The son did as he was told, and the father said to him: 'The chunk of salt you put in the water last evening – bring it here.' He groped for it but could not find it, [2] as it had dissolved completely.

'Now, take a sip from this corner,' said the father. 'How does it taste?'

'Salty.'

'Take a sip from the centre. – How does it taste?'

'Salty.'

'Take a sip from that corner. – How does it taste?'

'Salty.'

'Throw it out and come back later.' He did as he was told and found that the salt was always there. The father told him: 'You, of course, did not see it there, son; yet it was always right there.

[3] 'The finest essence here – that constitutes the self of this whole world; that is the truth; that is the self (*ātman*). And that's how you are, Śvetaketu.'

'Sir, teach me more.'

'Very well, son.

14 'Take, for example, son, a man who is brought here blindfolded from the land of Gandhāra and then left in a deserted region. As he was brought blindfolded and left there blindfolded, he would drift about there towards the east, or the north, or the south. [2] Now, if someone were to free him from his blindfold and tell him, "Go that way; the land of Gandhāra is in that direction", being a learned and wise man, he would go from village to village asking for directions and finally arrive in the land of Gandhāra. In exactly the same way in this world when a man has a teacher, he knows: "There is a delay for me here only until I am freed; but then I will arrive!"

[3] 'The finest essence here – that constitutes the self of this whole world; that is the truth; that is the self (*ātman*). And that's how you are, Śvetaketu.'

'Sir, teach me more.'

'Very well, son.

15 'Take, for example, son, a man gravely ill. His relatives gather around him and ask: "Do you recognize me?" "Do you recognize me?" As long as his voice does not merge into his mind; his mind, into his breath; his breath, into heat; and heat, into the highest deity, he recognizes them. [2] When, however, his voice merges into his mind; his mind, into his breath; his breath, into heat; and heat, into the highest deity, then he no longer recognizes them.

[3] 'The finest essence here – that constitutes the self of this whole world; that is the truth; that is the self (*ātman*). And that's how you are, Śvetaketu.'

'Sir, teach me more.'

'Very well, son.

16 'Take, for example, son, a manacled man brought here by people shouting: "He's a thief! He has committed a theft! Heat an axe for him!" Now, if he is guilty of the crime, then he turns himself into a lie; uttering a falsehood and covering himself in falsehood, he takes hold of the axe and gets burnt, upon which he is executed. [2] If, on the other hand, he is innocent of the crime, then he turns himself into the truth; uttering the truth and covering himself with the truth, he takes hold of the axe and is not burnt, upon which he is released.

[3] 'What on that occasion prevents him from being burnt – that constituents the self of this whole world; that is the truth; that is the self (*ātman*). And that's how you are, Śvetaketu.'

And he did, indeed, learn it from him.

Source: Patrick Olivelle (trans.) *Upanisads* (OUP, 1996), pp. 153–6.

4.7 FROM THE *BHAGAVAD GITA*

Chapter I

Dhrtaraṣṭra said:
1. In the Field of Right, the Kuru-field,
    Assembled ready to fight,
    My men and the sons of Pāṇḍu as well,
    What did they do, Saṃjaya?

Saṃjaya said:
2. Seeing however the host of the sons of Pāṇḍu
    Arrayed, Duryodhana then
    Approached the Teacher (Droṇa),
    And spoke a word, the prince:

3. Behold of Pāṇḍu's sons this
    Great host, O Teacher!

Arrayed by Drupada's son,
    Thy skilful pupil.

4.   Here are heroes, great archers,
      Like unto Bhīma and Arjuna in battle,
    Yuyudhāna, and Virāṭa,
      And Drupada of the great car;

5.   Dhṛṣṭaketu, Cekitāna,
      And the heroic king of Benares,
    Purujit, and Kuntibhoja,
      And the Śibi-king, bull of men;

6.   Yudhāmanyu the valorous,
      And Uttamaujas the heroic,
    The son of Subhadrā, and the sons of Draupadī,
      All, aye all, men of great cars.

7.   But of our men, who are the most distinguished
      Learn from me, best of brahmans –
    Who are the leaders of my host;
      To name them, I declare them to thee.

8.   Thy good self, and Bhīṣma, and Karṇa,
      And battle-winning Kṛpa,
    Aśvatthāman, and Vikarṇa,
      And the son of Somadatta too;

9. And many other heroes,
      Giving up life for my sake;
    With various weapons and arms,
      All skilled in conflict.

10. (Altho) insufficient (in number) this our
      Host is protected by (the wise) Bhīṣma;
    On the other hand, (while) sufficient, this their
      Host is protected by (the unskilled) Bhīma.

11. And (so) in all movements,
      Stationed in your several places,
    Guard Bhīṣma above all,
      Each and every one of you.

12. Producing joy in his heart,
      The aged grandsire of the Kurus

Roared a lion's roar on high,
  And blew his conch-shell, full of valor.

13. Then conch-shells and drums,
  Kettle-drums, cymbals and trumpets,
 All at once were sounded;
  The sound was tremendous.

14. Then on the white-horse-yoked
  Mighty car standing,
 Mādhava (Kṛṣṇa) and the son of Pāṇḍu (Arjuna)
  Blew their wondrous conch-shells:

15. Hṛṣīkeśa (Kṛṣṇa) blew Pāñcajanya,
  Dhanaṃjaya (Arjuna) blew Devadatta,
 The great shell Pauṇḍra blew
  Wolf-belly (Bhīma) of terrible deeds.

16. (The shell) Anantavijaya (blew) the king
  Yudhiṣṭhira, Kuntī's son;
 Nakula and Sahadeva
  (Blew) Sughoṣa and Maṇipuṣpaka.

17. And the king of Benares, supreme archer,
  And Śikhaṇḍin, of the great car,
 And Dhṛṣṭadyumna and Virāṭa,
  And the unconquered Sātyaki,

18. Drupada and the sons of Draupadī,
  All together, O king,
 And the great-armed son of Subhadrā,
  Blew their conch-shells severally.

19. That sound Dhṛtarāṣṭra's men's
  Hearts did rend;
 And both sky and earth
  It made to resound, swelling aloft.

20. Then seeing arrayed
  Dhṛtarāṣṭra's sons, the ape-bannered (Arjuna),
 When the clash of arms had already begun,
  Lifted up his bow, the son of Pāṇḍu,

21. And to Hṛṣīkeśa then words
  Like these spoke, O king.

Between the two armies
  Halt my chariot, O unshaken one,

22. Until I espy these
  That are drawn up eager to fight,
(And see) with whom I must fight
  In this warlike enterprise.

23. I will see those who are going to fight,
  Who are here assembled,
For Dhṛtarāṣṭra's ill-minded son
  Eager to do service in battle.

24. Hṛṣīkeśa, thus addressed
  By Guḍākeśa, O son of Bhārata,
Between the two armies
  Halted the excellent car,

25. In front of Bhīṣma and Droṇa
  And all the kings,
And said: Son of Pṛthā, behold these
  Assembled Kurus!

26. There the son of Pṛthā saw stationed
  Fathers and grandsires,
Teachers, uncles, brothers,
  Sons, grandsons, and comrades too,

27. Fathers-in-law and friends as well,
  In both the two armies.
The son of Kuntī, seeing them,
  All his kinsmen arrayed,

28. Filled with utmost compassion,
  Despondent, spoke these words:
Seeing my own kinsfolk here, Kṛṣṇa,
  That have drawn near eager to fight,

29. My limbs sink down,
  And my mouth becomes parched,
And there is trembling in my body,
  And my hair stands on end.

30. (The bow) Gāṇḍīva falls from my hand,
  And my skin, too, is burning,

And I cannot stand still,
  And my mind seems to wander.

31. And I see portents
    That are adverse, Keśava;
  And I foresee no welfare,
    Having slain my kinsfolk in battle.

32. I wish no victory, Kṛṣṇa,
    Nor kingdom nor joys;
  Of what use to us were kingdom, Govinda,
    Of what use enjoyments or life?

33. For whose sake we desire
    Kingdom, enjoyments, and happiness,
  They are drawn up here in battle,
    Giving up life and wealth;

34. Teachers, fathers, sons,
    Grandsires as well,
  Uncles, fathers-in-law, grandsons,
    Brothers-in-law, and (other) kinsfolk.

35. Them I do not wish to slay,
    Even tho they slay (me), O slayer of Madhu,
  Even for three-world-rulerships'
    Sake; how much less for the sake of the earth!

36. Having slain Dhṛtarāṣṭra's men, to us
    What joy would ensue, Janārdana?
  Evil alone would light upon us,
    Did we slay these (our would-be) murderers.

37. Therefore we should not slay
    Dhṛtarāṣṭra's men, our own kinsfolk.
  For how, having slain our kinsfolk,
    Could we be happy, Mādhava?

38. Even if they do not see,
    Because their intelligence is destroyed by greed,
  The sin caused by destruction of family,
    And the crime involved in injury to a friend,

39. How should we not know enough
    To turn back from this wickedness,

The sin caused by destruction of family
    Perceiving, O Janārdana?

40. Upon the destruction of the family, perish
    The immemorial holy laws of the family;
When the laws have perished, the whole family
    Lawlessness overwhelms also.

41. Because of the prevalence of lawlessness, Kṛṣṇa,
    The women of the family are corrupted;
When the women are corrupted, O Vṛṣṇi-clansman,
    Mixture of caste ensues.

42. Mixture (of caste) leads to naught but hell
    For the destroyers of the family and for the family;
For their ancestors fall (to hell),
    Because the rites of (giving) food and water are interrupted.

43. By these sins of family-destroyers,
    (Sins) which produce caste-mixture,
The caste laws are destroyed,
    And the eternal family laws.

44. When the family laws are destroyed,
    Janārdana, then for men
Dwelling in hell certainly
    Ensues: so we have heard (from the Holy Word).

45. Ah woe! 'Twas a great wickedness
    That we had resolved to commit,
In that, thru greed for the joys of kingship,
    We undertook to slay our kinsfolk.

46. If me unresisting,
    Weaponless, with weapons in their hands
Dhṛtarāṣṭra's men should slay in battle,
    That would be a safer course for me.

47. Thus speaking Arjuna in the battle
    Sat down in the box of the car,
Letting fall his bow and arrows,
    His heart smitten with grief.

Chapter II

Saṃjaya said:
1. To him thus by compassion possessed,
    His eyes tear-filled, blurred,
Despondent, this word
    Spoke the Slayer of Madhu.

The Blessed One said:
2. Whence to thee this faintheartedness
    In peril has come,
Offensive to the noble, not leading to heaven,
    Inglorious, O Arjuna?

3. Yield not to unmanliness, son of Pṛthā;
    It is not meet for thee.
Petty weakness of heart
    Rejecting, arise, scorcher of the foe!

Arjuna said:
4. How shall I in battle against Bhīṣma,
    And Droṇa, O Slayer of Madhu,
Fight with arrows,
    Who are both worthy of reverence, Slayer of Enemies?

5. For not slaying my revered elders of great dignity
    'Twere better to eat alms-food, even, in this world;
But having slain my elders who seek their ends, right in this world
    I should eat food smeared with blood.

6. And we know not which of the two were better for us,
    Whether we should conquer, or they should conquer us;
What very ones having slain we wish not to live,
    They are arrayed in front of us, Dhṛtarāṣṭra's men.

7. My very being afflicted with the taint of weak compassion,
    I ask Thee, my mind bewildered as to the right:
Which were better, that tell me definitely;
    I am Thy pupil, teach me that have come to Thee (for instruction).

8. For I see not what would dispel my
    Grief, the witherer of the senses,
If I attained on earth rivalless, prosperous
    Kingship, and even overlordship of the gods.

Saṃjaya said:

9. Thus speaking to Hṛṣīkeśa,
    Guḍākeśa the Slayer of the Foe
'I'll not fight!' to Govinda
    Said, and was silent.

10. To him spoke Hṛṣīkeśa,
    With a semblance of a smile, son of Bhārata,
Betwixt the two armies
    As he was despondent, these words:

The Blessed One said:

11. Thou hast mourned those who should not be mourned,
    And (yet) thou speakest words about wisdom!
Dead and living men
    The (truly) learned do not mourn.

12. But not in any respect was I (ever) not,
    Nor thou, nor these kings;
And not at all shall we ever come not to be,
    All of us, henceforward.

13. As to the embodied (soul) in this body
    Come childhood, youth, old age,
So the coming to another body;
    The wise man is not confused herein.

14. But contacts with matter, son of Kuntī,
    Cause cold and heat, pleasure and pain;
They come and go, and are impermanent;
    Put up with them, son of Bhārata!

15. For whom these (contacts) do not cause to waver,
    The man, O bull of men,
To whom pain and pleasure are alike, the wise,
    He is fit for immortality.

16. Of what is not, no coming to be occurs;
    No coming not to be occurs of what is;
But the dividing-line of both is seen,
    Of these two, by those who see the truth.

17. But know that that is indestructible,
    By which this all is pervaded;
Destruction of this imperishable one
    No one can cause.

18. These bodies, come to an end,
     It is declared, of the eternal embodied (soul),
Which is indestructible and unfathomable.
     Therefore fight, son of Bhārata!

19. Who believes him a slayer,
     And who thinks him slain,
Both these understand not:
     He slays not, is not slain.

20. He is not born, nor does he ever die;
     Nor, having come to be, will he ever more come not to be.
Unborn, eternal, everlasting, this ancient one
     Is not slain when the body is slain.

21. Who knows as indestructible and eternal
     This unborn, imperishable one,
That man, son of Pṛthā, how
     Can he slay or cause to slay – whom?

22. As leaving aside worn-out garments
     A man takes other, new ones,
So leaving aside worn-out bodies
     To other, new ones goes the embodied (soul).

23. Swords cut him not,
     Fire burns him not,
Water wets him not,
     Wind dries him not.

24. Not to be cut is he, not to be burnt is he,
     Not to be wet nor yet dried;
Eternal, omnipresent, fixed,
     Immovable, everlasting is he.

25. Unmanifest he, unthinkable he,
     Unchangeable he is declared to be;
Therefore knowing him thus
     Thou shouldst not mourn him.

26. Moreover, even if constantly born
     Or constantly dying thou considerest him,
Even so, great-armed one, thou
     Shouldst not mourn him.

27. For to one that is born death is certain,
     And birth is certain for one that has died;

Therefore, the thing being unavoidable,
    Thou shouldst not mourn.

28. The beginnings of things are unmanifest,
    Manifest their middles, son of Bhārata,
Unmanifest again their ends:
    Why mourn about this?

29. By a rare chance one may see him,
    And by a rare chance likewise may another declare him,
And by a rare chance may another hear (of) him;
    (But) even having heard (of) him, no one whatsoever knows him.

30. This embodied (soul) is eternally unslayable
    In the body of every one, son of Bhārata;
Therefore all beings
    Thou shouldst not mourn.

31. Likewise having regard for thine own (caste) duty
    Thou shouldst not tremble;
For another, better thing than a fight required of duty
    Exists not for a warrior.

32. Presented by mere luck,
    An open door of heaven –
Happy the warriors, son of Pṛthā,
    That get such a fight!

33. Now, if thou this duty-required
    Conflict wilt not perform,
Then thine own duty and glory
    Abandoning, thou shalt get thee evil.

34. Disgrace, too, will creatures
    Speak of thee, without end;
And for one that has been esteemed, disgrace
    Is worse than death.

35. That thou hast abstained from battle thru fear
    The (warriors) of great chariots will think of thee;
And of whom thou wast highly regarded,
    Thou shalt come to be held lightly.

36. And many sayings that should not be said
    Thy ill-wishers will say of thee,
Speaking ill of thy capacity:
    What, pray, is more grievous than that?

37. Either slain thou shalt gain heaven,
    Or conquering thou shalt enjoy the earth.
    Therefore arise, son of Kuntī,
    Unto battle, making a firm resolve.

38. Holding pleasure and pain alike,
    Gain and loss, victory and defeat,
    Then gird thyself for battle:
    Thus thou shalt not get evil.

39. This has been declared to thee (that is found) in Reason-method,
    This mental attitude: but hear this in Discipline-method,
    Disciplined with which mental attitude, son of Pṛthā,
    Thou shalt get rid of the bondage of action.

40. In it there is no loss of a start once made,
    Nor does any reverse occur;
    Even a little of this duty
    Saves from great danger.

41. The mental attitude whose nature is resolution
    Is but one in this world, son of Kuru;
    For many-branched and endless
    Are the mental attitudes of the irresolute.

42. This flowery speech which
    Undiscerning men utter,
    Who take delight in the words of the Veda, son of Pṛthā,
    Saying that there is nothing else,

43. Whose nature is desire, who are intent on heaven,
    (The speech) which yields rebirth as the fruit of actions,
    Which is replete with various (ritual) acts
    Aiming at the goal of enjoyment and power –

44. Of men devoted to enjoyment and power,
    Who are robbed of insight by that (speech),
    A mental attitude resolute in nature
    Is not established in concentration.

45. The Vedas have the three Strands (of matter) as their scope;
    Be thou free from the three Strands, Arjuna,
    Free from the pairs (of opposites), eternally fixed in goodness,
    Free from acquisition and possession, self-possessed.

46. As much profit as there is in a water-tank
    When on all sides there is a flood of water,

No more is there in all the Vedas
    For a brahman who (truly) understands.

47. On action alone be thy interest,
    Never on its fruits;
Let not the fruits of action be thy motive,
    Nor be thy attachment to inaction.

48. Abiding in discipline perform actions,
    Abandoning attachment, Dhanaṃjaya,
Being indifferent to success or failure;
    Discipline is defined as indifference.

49. For action is far inferior
    To discipline of mental attitude, Dhanaṃjaya.
In the mental attitude seek thy (religious) refuge;
    Wretched are those whose motive is the fruit (of action).

50. The disciplined in mental attitude leaves behind in this world
    Both good and evil deeds.
Therefore discipline thyself unto discipline;
    Discipline in actions is weal.

51. For the disciplined in mental attitude, action-produced
    Fruit abandoning, the intelligent ones,
Freed from the bondage of rebirth,
    Go to the place that is free from illness.

52. When the jungle of delusion
    Thy mentality shall get across,
Then thou shalt come to aversion
    Towards what is to be heard and has been heard (in the Veda).

53. Averse to traditional lore ('heard' in the Veda)
    When shall stand motionless
Thy mentality, immovable in concentration,
    Then thou shalt attain discipline.

      Arjuna said:
54. What is the description of the man of stabilized mentality,
    That is fixed in concentration, Keśava?
How might the man of stabilized mentality speak,
    How might he sit, how walk?

      The Blessed One said:
55. When he abandons desires,
    All that are in the mind, son of Pṛthā,

> Finding contentment by himself in the self alone,
>> Then he is called of stabilized mentality.

56. When his mind is not perturbed in sorrows,
>> And he has lost desire for joys,
> His longing, fear, and wrath departed,
>> He is called a stable-minded holy man.

57. Who has no desire towards any thing,
>> And getting this or that good or evil
> Neither delights in it nor loathes it,
>> His mentality is stabilized.

58. And when he withdraws,
>> As a tortoise his limbs from all sides,
> His senses from the objects of sense,
>> His mentality is stabilized.

59. The objects of sense turn away
>> From the embodied one that abstains from food,
> Except flavor; flavor also from him
>> Turns away when he has seen the highest.

60. For even of one who strives, son of Kuntī,
>> Of the man of discernment,
> The impetuous senses
>> Carry away the mind by violence.

61. Them all restraining,
>> Let him sit disciplined, intent on Me;
> For whose senses are under control,
>> His mentality is stabilized.

62. When a man meditates on the objects of sense,
>> Attachment to them is produced.
> From attachment springs desire,
>> From desire wrath arises;

63. From wrath comes infatuation,
>> From infatuation loss of memory;
> From loss of memory, loss of mind;
>> From loss of mind he perishes.

64. But with desire-and-loathing-severed
>> Senses acting on the objects of sense,
> With (senses) self-controlled, he, governing his self,
>> Goes unto tranquillity.

65. In tranquillity, of all griefs
    Riddance is engendered for him;
For of the tranquil-minded quickly
    The mentality becomes stable.

66. The undisciplined has no (right) mentality,
    And the undisciplined has no efficient-force;
Who has no efficient-force has no peace;
    For him that has no peace how can there be bliss?

67. For the senses are roving,
    And when the thought-organ is directed after them,
It carries away his mentality,
    As wind a ship on the water.

68. Therefore whosoever, great-armed one,
    Has withdrawn on all sides
The senses from the objects of sense,
    His mentality is stabilized.

69. What is night for all beings,
    Therein the man of restraint is awake;
Wherein (other) beings are awake,
    That is night for the sage of vision.

70. It is ever being filled, and (yet) its foundation remains unmoved –
    The sea: just as waters enter it,
Whom all desires enter in that same way
    He attains peace; not the man who lusts after desires.

71. Abandoning all desires, what
    Man moves free from longing,
Without self-interest and egotism,
    He goes to peace.

72. This is the fixation that is Brahmanic, son of Pṛthā;
    Having attained it he is not (again) confused.
Abiding in it even at the time of death,
    He goes to Brahman-nirvāṇa.

Chapter VII

    The Blessed One said:
1. With mind attached to Me, son of Pṛthā,
    Practising discipline with reliance on Me,

Without doubt Me entirely
   How thou shalt know, that hear!

2. Theoretical knowledge to thee along with practical
      I shall now expound completely;
   Having known which, in this world no other further
      Thing to be known is left.

3. Among thousands of men
      Perchance one strives for perfection;
   Even of those that strive and are perfected,
      Perchance one knows Me in very truth.

4. Earth, water, fire, wind,
      Ether, thought-organ, and consciousness,
   And I-faculty: thus My
      Nature is divided eight-fold.

5. This is My lower (nature). But other than this,
      My higher nature know:
   It is the Life (soul), great-armed one,
      By which this world is maintained.

6. Beings spring from it,
      All of them, be assured.
   Of the whole world I am
      The origin and the dissolution too.

7. Than Me no other higher thing
      Whatsoever exists, Dhanaṃjaya;
   On Me all this (universe) is strung,
      Like heaps of pearls on a string.

8. I am taste in water, son of Kuntī,
      I am light in the moon and sun,
   The sacred syllable (ōm) in all the Vedas,
      Sound in ether, manliness in men.

9. Both the goodly odor in earth,
      And brilliance in fire am I,
   Life in all beings,
      And austerity in ascetics am I.
10. The seed of all beings am I,
      The eternal, be assured, son of Pṛthā;
   I am intelligence of the intelligent,
      Majesty of the majestic am I.

11. Might of the mighty am I, too,
        (Such as is) free from desire and passion;
    (So far as it is) not inconsistent with right, in creatures
        I am desire, O best of Bhāratas.

12. Both whatsoever states are of (the Strand) goodness,
        And those of (the Strands) passion and darkness too,
    Know that they are from Me alone;
        But I am not in them; they are in Me.

13. By the three states (of being), composed of the Strands,
        These (just named), all this world,
    Deluded, does not recognize
        Me that am higher than they and eternal.

14. For this is My divine strand-composed
        Trick-of-illusion, hard to get past;
    Those who resort to Me alone
        Penetrate beyond this trick-of-illusion.

15. Not to Me do deluded evil-doers
        Resort, base men,
    Whom this illusion robs of knowledge,
        Who cleave to demoniac estate.

16. Fourfold are those that worship Me,
        (All) virtuous folk, Arjuna:
    The afflicted, the knowledge-seeker, he who seeks personal ends,
        And the possessor of knowledge, bull of Bhāratas.

17. Of these the possessor of knowledge, constantly disciplined,
        Of single devotion, is the best;
    For extremely dear to the possessor of knowledge
        Am I, and he is dear to Me.

18. All these are noble;
        But the man of knowledge is My very self, so I hold.
    For he with disciplined soul has resorted
        To Me alone as the highest goal.

19. At the end of many births
        The man of knowledge resorts to Me;
    Who thinks 'Vāsudeva (Kṛṣṇa) is all',
        That noble soul is hard to find.

20. Deprived of knowledge by this or that desire,
        Men resort to other deities,

Taking to this or that (religious) rule,
　　Constrained by their own nature.

21. Whatsoever (divine) form any devotee
　　　With faith seeks to worship,
　　For every such (devotee), faith unswerving
　　　I ordain that same to be.

22. He, disciplined with that faith,
　　　Seeks to propitiate that (divine being),
　　And obtains therefrom his desires,
　　　Because I myself ordain them.

23. But finite fruition for them
　　　That becomes, (since) they are of scant intelligence;
　　The worshipers of the gods go to the gods,
　　　My devotees go to Me also.

24. Unmanifest, as having come into manifestation
　　　Fools conceive Me,
　　Not knowing the higher essence
　　　Of Me, which is imperishable, supreme.

25. I am not revealed to every one,
　　　Being veiled by My magic trick-of-illusion;
　　'Tis deluded and does not recognize
　　　Me the unborn, imperishable – this world.

26. I know those that are past,
　　　And that are present, Arjuna,
　　And beings that are yet to be,
　　　But no one knows Me.

27. It arises from desire and loathing,
　　　The delusion of the pairs (of opposites), son of Bhārata;
　　Because of it all beings to confusion
　　　Are subject at their birth, scorcher of the foe.

28. But those whose sin is ended,
　　　Men of virtuous deeds,
　　Freed from the delusion of the pairs,
　　　Revere Me with firm resolve.
29. Unto freedom from old age and death
　　　Those who strive, relying on Me,
　　They know that Brahman entire,
　　　And the over-soul, and action altogether.

30. Me together with the over-being and the over-divinity,
     And with the over-worship, whoso know,
     And (who know) Me even at the hour of death,
     They (truly) know (Me), with disciplined hearts.

Chapter XI

         Arjuna said:
1. As a favor to me the supreme
        Mystery, called the over-soul,
     The words which Thou hast spoken, thereby
        This delusion of mine is dispelled.

2. For the origin and dissolution of beings
        Have been heard by me in full detail
     From Thee, Lotus-petal-eyed One,
        And also (Thine) exalted nature unending.

3. Thus it is, as Thou declarest
        Thyself, O Supreme Lord.
     I desire to see Thy form
        As God, O Supreme Spirit!

4. If Thou thinkest that it can
        Be seen by me, O Lord,
     Prince of mystic power then do Thou to me
        Reveal Thine immortal Self.

         The Blessed One said:
5. Behold My forms, son of Pṛthā,
        By hundreds and by thousands,
     Of various sorts, marvelous,
        Of various colors and shapes.

6. Behold the Ādityas, Vasus, Rudras,
        The Aśvin-pair and the Maruts too;
     Many before-unseen
        Marvels behold, son of Bhārata.

7. Here the whole world united
        Behold today, with moving and unmoving things,
     In My body, Guḍākeśa,
        And whatsoever else thou wishest to see.

8. But thou canst not see Me
        With this same eye of thine own;

I give thee a supernatural eye:
    Behold My mystic power as God!

    Saṃjaya said:
9. Thus speaking then, O king,
    Hari (Viṣṇu), the great Lord of Mystic Power,
Showed unto the son of Pṛthā
    His supernal form as God:

10. Of many mouths and eyes,
    Of many wondrous aspects,
Of many marvelous ornaments,
    Of marvelous and many uplifted weapons;

11. Wearing marvelous garlands and garments,
    With marvelous perfumes and ointments,
Made up of all wonders, the god,
    Infinite, with faces in all directions.

12. Of a thousand suns in the sky
    If suddenly should burst forth
The light, it would be like
    Unto the light of that exalted one.

13. The whole world there united,
    And divided many-fold,
Beheld in the God of Gods'
    Body the son of Pāṇḍu then.

14. Then filled with amazement,
    His hair standing upright, Dhanaṃjaya
Bowed with his head to the God,
    And said with a gesture of reverence:

    Arjuna said:
15. I see the gods in Thy body, O God,
    All of them, and the hosts of various kinds of beings too,
Lord Brahmā sitting on the lotus-seat,
    And the seers all, and the divine serpents.

16. With many arms, bellies, mouths, and eyes,
    I see Thee, infinite in form on all sides;
No end nor middle nor yet beginning of Thee
    Do I see, O All-God, All-formed!

17. With diadem, club, and disc,
    A mass of radiance, glowing on all sides,

I see Thee, hard to look at, on every side
    With the glory of flaming fire and sun, immeasurable.

18. Thou art the Imperishable, the supreme Object of Knowledge;
    Thou art the ultimate resting-place of this universe;
Thou art the immortal guardian of the eternal right,
    Thou art the everlasting Spirit, I hold.

19. Without beginning, middle, or end, of infinite power,
    Of infinite arms, whose eyes are the moon and sun,
I see Thee, whose face is flaming fire,
    Burning this whole universe with Thy radiance.

20. For this region between heaven and earth
    Is pervaded by Thee alone, and all the directions;
Seeing this Thy wondrous, terrible form,
    The triple world trembles, O exalted one!

21. For into Thee are entering yonder throngs of gods;
    Some, affrighted, praise Thee with reverent gestures;
Crying 'Hail!' the throngs of the great seers and perfected ones
    Praise Thee with abundant laudations.

22. The Rudras, the Ādityas, the Vasus, and the Sādhyas,
    All-gods, Aśvins, Maruts, and the Steam-drinkers ('fathers'),
The hosts of heavenly musicians, sprites, demons, and perfected ones,
    Gaze upon Thee, and all are quite amazed.

23. Thy great form, of many mouths and eyes,
    O great-armed one, of many arms, thighs and feet,
Of many bellies, terrible with many tusks –
    Seeing it the worlds tremble, and I too.

24. Touching the sky, aflame, of many colors,
    With yawning mouths and flaming enormous eyes,
Verily seeing Thee (so), my inmost soul is shaken,
    And I find no steadiness nor peace, O Viṣṇu!

25. And Thy mouths, terrible with great tusks,
    No sooner do I see them, like the fire of dissolution (of the world),
Than I know not the directions of the sky, and I find no refuge;
    Have mercy, Lord of Gods, Thou in whom the world dwells!
26. And Thee yonder sons of Dhṛtarāṣṭra,
    All of them, together with the hosts of kings,
Bhīṣma, Droṇa, and yonder son of the charioteer (Karṇa) too,
    Together with our chief warriors likewise,

27. Hastening enter Thy mouths,
     Frightful with tusks, and terrifying;
   Some, stuck between the teeth,
     Are seen with their heads crushed.

28. As the many water-torrents of the rivers
     Rush headlong towards the single sea,
   So yonder heroes of the world of men into Thy
     Flaming mouths do enter.

29. As moths into a burning flame
     Do enter unto their destruction with utmost impetuosity,
   Just so unto their destruction enter the worlds
     Into Thy mouths also, with utmost impetuosity.

30. Devouring them Thou lickest up voraciously on all sides
     All the worlds with Thy flaming jaws;
   Filling with radiance the whole universe,
     Thy terrible splendors burn, O Viṣṇu!

31. Tell me, who art Thou, of awful form?
     Homage be to Thee: Best of Gods, be merciful!
   I desire to understand Thee, the primal one;
     For I do not comprehend what Thou hast set out to do.

          The Blessed One said:
32. I am Time (Death), cause of destruction of the worlds, matured
     And set out to gather in the worlds here.
   Even without thee (thy action), all shall cease to exist,
     The warriors that are drawn up in the opposing ranks.

33. Therefore arise thou, win glory,
     Conquer thine enemies and enjoy prospered kingship,
   By Me Myself they have already been slain long ago;
     Be thou the mere instrument, left-handed archer!

34. Droṇa and Bhīṣma and Jayadratha,
     Karṇa too, and the other warrior-heroes as well,
   Do thou slay, (since) they are already slain by Me; do not hesitate!
     Fight! Thou shalt conquer thy rivals in battle.
          Saṃjaya said:
35. Hearing these words of Keśava,
     Making a reverent gesture, trembling, the Diademed (Arjuna)
   Made obeisance and spoke yet again to Kṛṣṇa,
     Stammering, greatly affrighted, bowing down:

Arjuna said:

36. It is in place, Hṛṣīkeśa, that at Thy praise
    The world rejoices and is exceeding glad;
    Ogres fly in terror in all directions,
    And all the hosts of perfected ones pay homage.

37. And why should they not pay homage to Thee, Exalted One?
    Thou art greater even than Brahman; Thou art the First Creator;
    Of infinite Lord of Gods, in whom the world dwells,
    Thou the imperishable, existent, non-existent, and beyond both!

38. Thou art the Primal God, the Ancient Spirit,
    Thou art the supreme resting-place of this universe;
    Thou art the knower, the object of knowledge, and the highest station,
    By Thee the universe is pervaded, Thou of infinite form!

39. Vāyu, Yama, Agni, Varuṇa, the moon,
    Prajāpati art Thou, and the Greatgrandsire;
    Homage, homage be to Thee a thousand fold,
    And again be yet further homage, homage to Thee!

40. Homage be to Thee from in front and from behind,
    Homage be to Thee from all sides, Thou All!
    O Thou of infinite might, Thy prowess is unmeasured;
    Thou attainest all; therefore Thou art All!

41. Whatever I said rashly, thinking Thee my boon-companion,
    Calling Thee 'Kṛṣṇa, Yādava, Companion!',
    Not knowing this (truth, namely) Thy greatness,
    Thru careless negligence, or even thru affection,

42. And if I treated Thee disrespectfully, to make sport of Thee,
    In the course of amusement, resting, sitting, or eating,
    Either alone, O unshaken one, or in the presence of those (others),
    For that I beg forgiveness of Thee, the immeasurable one.

43. Thou art the father of the world of things that move and move not,
    And Thou art its revered, most venerable Guru;
    There is no other like Thee – how then a greater?
    Even in the three worlds, O Thou of matchless greatness!

44. Therefore, bowing and prostrating my body,
    I beg grace of Thee, the Lord to be revered:
    As a father to his son, as a friend to his friend,
    As a lover to his beloved, be pleased to show mercy, O God!

45. Having seen what was never seen before, I am thrilled,
  And (at the same time) my heart is shaken with fear;
 Show me, O God, that same form of Thine (as before)!
  Be merciful, Lord of Gods, Abode of the World!

46. Wearing the diadem, carrying the club, with disc in hand,
  Just (as before) I desire to see Thee;
 In that same four-armed shape
  Present Thyself, O Thousand-armed One, of universal form!

  The Blessed One said:
47. By Me showing grace towards thee, Arjuna, this
  Supreme form has been manifested by My own mysterious power;
 (This form) made up of splendor, universal, infinite, primal,
  Of Mine, which has never been seen before by any other than thee.

48. Not by the Vedas, by acts of worship, or study, or gifts,
  Nor yet by rites, nor by grim austerities,
 In the world of men can I in such a form
  Be seen by any other than thee, hero of the Kurus.

49. Have no perturbation, nor any state of bewilderment,
  Seeing this so awful form of Mine;
 Dispel thy fear; let thy heart be of good cheer; again do thou
  Behold that same (former) form of Mine: here!

  Saṃjaya said:
50. Having thus spoken to Arjuna, Vāsudeva
  Again revealed his own (natural) form,
 And comforted him in his fright
  By once more assuming his gracious aspect, the Exalted One.

  Arjuna said:
51. Seeing this human form
  Of Thine, gracious, O Janārdana,
 Now I have become
  Possessed of my senses, and restored to normal state.

  The Blessed One said:
52. This form that is right hard to see,
  Which thou hast seen of Mine,
 Of this form even the gods
  Constantly long for the sight.

53. Not by the Vedas nor by austerity,
  Nor by gifts or acts of worship,
 Can I be seen in such a guise,
  As thou hast seen Me.

54. But by unswerving devotion can
    I in such a guise, Arjuna,
Be known and seen in very truth,
    And entered into, scorcher of the foe.

55. Doing My Work, intent on Me,
    Devoted to Me, free from attachment,
Free from enmity to all beings,
    Who is so, goes to Me, son of Pāṇḍu.

Chapter XVIII

Arjuna said:
1. Of renunciation, great-armed one,
    I desire to know the truth,
And of abandonment, Hṛṣīkeśa,
    Severally, Slayer of Keśin.

The Blessed One said:
2. The renouncing of acts of desire
    Sages call renunciation.
The abandonment of all action-fruits
    The wise call abandonment.

3. That it must be abandoned as sinful, some
    Wise men say of action;
That actions of worship, gift, and austerity
    Must not be abandoned, say others.

4. Hear my decision in this matter
    Of abandonment, best of Bhāratas;
For abandonment, O man-tiger,
    Is reputed to be threefold.

5. Actions of worship, gift, and austerity
    Must not be abandoned, but rather performed;
Worship, gift, and austerity
    Are purifiers of the wise.

6. However, these actions
    With abandonment of attachment and fruits
Must be performed: this, son of Pṛthā, is My
    Definite and highest judgment.

7. But abandonment of a (religiously) required
    Action is not seemly;

Abandonment thereof owing to delusion
  Is reputed to be of the nature of darkness.

8. Just because it is troublesome, what action
    One abandons thru fear of bodily affliction,
  Such a man performs an abandonment that is of the nature of passion;
    By no means shall he get any fruit of (this) abandonment.

9. Simply because it ought to be done, when action
    That is (religiously) required is performed, Arjuna,
  Abandoning attachment and fruit,
    That abandonment is held to be of goodness.

10. He loathes not disagreeable action,
    Nor does he cling to agreeable (action),
  The man of abandonment who is filled with goodness,
    Wise, whose doubts are destroyed.

11. For a body-bearing (soul) cannot
    Abandon actions without remainder;
  But he who abandons the fruit of action
    Is called the man of (true) abandonment.

12. Undesired, desired, and mixed –
    Threefold is the fruit of action
  That ensues after death for those who are not men of abandonment,
    But never for men of renunciation.

13. O great-armed one, these five
    Factors learn from Me,
  Which are declared in the reason-method doctrine
    For the effective performance of all actions.

14. The (material) basis, the agent too,
    And the instruments of various sorts,
  And the various motions of several kinds,
    And just Fate as the fifth of them.

15. With body, speech, or mind, whatever
    Action a man undertakes,
  Whether it be lawful or the reverse,
    These are its five factors.

16. This being so, as agent herein
    Whoso however the self alone
  Regards, because his intelligence is imperfect,
    He does not see (truly), the fool.

17. Whose state (of mind) is not egoized,
    Whose intelligence is not stained,
  He, even tho he slays these folk,
    Does not slay, and is not bound (by his actions).

18. Knowledge, the object of knowledge, the knower,
    Form the threefold impellent cause of action;
  Instrument, action, and the agent,
    Form the threefold summary of action.

19. Knowledge, and action, and the agent
    Are of just three kinds, according to difference of Strands;
  So it is declared in the theory of the Strands;
    Hear of them also, how they are.

20. Whereby in all beings one
    Unchanging condition men perceive,
  Unmanifold in the manifold,
    Know that that knowledge is of goodness.

21. But what knowledge in various fashion
    Different conditions of various sorts
  Sees in all beings,
    Know that that knowledge is of passion.

22. But what knowledge to one – as it were all –
    Thing to be done is attached, unconcerned with causes,
  Not dealing with the true nature of things, and insignificant,
    That is declared to be of darkness.

23. Obligatory, free from attachment,
    Done without desire or loathing,
  By one who seeks no fruit from it, action
    Such as this is called of goodness.

24. But action which by one seeking desires,
    Or again by one who is selfish,
  Is done, with much weary labor,
    That is declared to be of passion.

25. Consequences, loss, injury (to others),
    And (one's own) human power disregarding,
  Owing to delusion, when action is undertaken,
    It is declared to be of darkness.

26. Free from attachment, not talking of himself,
    Full of steadfastness and energy,

Unchanged in success or failure,
     Such an agent is called one of goodness.

27. Passionate, seeking the fruits of action,
       Greedy, injurious, impure,
     Full of joy and grief, such an agent
       Is celebrated as one of passion.

28. Undisciplined, vulgar, arrogant,
       Tricky, dishonest, lazy,
     Despondent, and procrastinating,
       Such an agent is said to be of darkness.

29. The distinction of intelligence and of firmness also,
       Threefold according to the Strands, hear
     Fully expounded
       In their several forms, Dhanaṃjaya.

30. Activity and cessation from it,
       Things to be done and not to be done, danger and security,
     Bondage and release, that which knows these
       Is the intelligence that is of goodness, son of Pṛthā.

31. Whereby right and unright,
       And things to be done and not to be done,
     Are understood incorrectly,
       That intelligence, son of Pṛthā, is of passion.

32. Right as unright what
       Conceives, obscured by darkness,
     And all things contrary (to the truth),
       That intelligence, son of Pṛthā, is of darkness.

33. The firmness with which one holds fast,
       The activities of the mind, life-breaths, and senses,
     And which is unswerving in discipline,
       That firmness is of goodness, son of Pṛthā.

34. But when to religion, love, and wealth
       With firmness he holds fast, Arjuna,
     With attachment, desirous of the fruits,
       That firmness is of passion, son of Pṛthā.

35. Whereby sleep, fear, sorrow,
       Despondency, and pride,
     The foolish man does not let go,
       That firmness is of darkness, son of Pṛthā.

36. But now the threefold happiness
      Hear from Me, bull of Bhāratas.
   That in which he comes to delight thru long practice (only),
      And comes to the end of suffering,

37. Which in the beginning is like poison,
      But in maturity like nectar,
   That is called the happiness of goodness,
      Sprung from serenity of soul and of intellect.

38. (Springing) from union of the senses and their objects,
      That which in the beginning is like nectar,
   In maturity like poison,
      That happiness is recorded as of passion.

39. Which both in the beginning and in its consequence
      Is a happiness that deludes the self,
   Arising from sleep, sloth, and heedlessness,
      That is declared to be of darkness.

40. There is no thing, whether on earth,
      Or yet in heaven, among the gods,
   No being which free from the material-nature-born
      Strands, these three, might be.

41. Of brahmans, warriors, and artisans,
      And of serfs, scorcher of the foe,
   The actions are distinguished
      According to the Strands that spring from their innate nature.

42. Calm, (self-) control, austerities, purity,
      Patience, and uprightness,
   Theoretical and practical knowledge, and religious faith,
      Are the natural-born actions of brahmans.

43. Heroism, majesty, firmness, skill,
      And not fleeing in battle also,
   Generosity, and lordly nature,
      Are the natural-born actions of warriors.

44. Agriculture, cattle-tending, and commerce
      Are the natural-born actions of artisans;
   Action that consists of service
      Is likewise natural-born to a serf.

45. Taking delight in his own special kind of action,
      A man attains perfection;

Delighting in one's own special action, success
    How one reaches, that hear!

46. Whence comes the activity of beings,
    By whom this all is pervaded –
Him worshipping by (doing) one's own appropriate action,
    A man attains perfection.

47. Better one's own duty, (even) imperfect,
    Than another's duty well performed.
Action pertaining to his own estate
    Performing, he incurs no guilt.

48. Natural-born action, son of Kuntī,
    Even tho it be faulty, one should not abandon.
For all undertakings by faults
    Are dimmed, as fire by smoke.

49. His mentality unattached to any object,
    Self-conquered, free from longings,
To the supreme perfection of actionlessness
    He comes thru renunciation.

50. Having attained perfection, how to Brahman
    He also attains, hear from Me,
In only brief compass, son of Kuntī;
    Which is the highest culmination of knowledge.

51. With purified mentality disciplined,
    And restraining himself with firmness,
Abandoning the objects of sense, sounds and the rest,
    And putting away desire and loathing.

52. Cultivating solitude, eating lightly,
    Restraining speech, body, and mind,
Devoted to the discipline of meditation constantly,
    Taking refuge in dispassion,

53. From egotism, force, pride,
    Desire, wrath, and possession
Freed, unselfish, calmed,
    He is fit for becoming Brahman.

54. Having become Brahman, serene-souled,
    He neither grieves nor longs;
Alike to all beings,
    He attains supreme devotion to Me.

55. Thru devotion he comes to know me,
      What My measure is, and who I am, in very truth;
    Then, knowing Me in very truth,
      He enters into (Me) straightway.

56. Even tho all actions ever
      He performs, relying on Me,
    By My grace he reaches
      The eternal, undying station.

57. With thy thoughts all actions
      Casting upon Me, devoted to Me,
    Turning to discipline of mentality,
      Keep thy mind ever fixed on Me.

58. If thy mind is on Me, all difficulties
      Shalt thou cross over by My grace;
    But if thru egotism thou
      Wilt not heed, thou shalt perish.

59. If clinging to egotism
      Thou thinkest 'I will not fight',
    Vain is this thy resolve;
      (Thine own) material nature will coerce thee.

60. Son of Kuntī, by thine own natural
      Action held fast,
    What thru delusion thou seekest not to do,
      That thou shalt do even against thy will.

61. Of all beings, the Lord
      In the heart abides, Arjuna,
    Causing all beings to turn around
      (As if) fixed in a machine, by his magic power.

62. To Him alone go for refuge
      With thy whole being, son of Bhārata;
    By his grace, supreme peace
      And the eternal station shalt thou attain.

63. Thus to thee has been expounded the knowledge
      That is more secret than the secret, by Me;
    After pondering on it fully,
      Act as thou thinkest best.

64. Further, the highest secret of all,
      My supreme message, hear.

Because thou art greatly loved of Me,
    Therefore I shall tell thee what is good for thee.

65. Be Me-minded, devoted to Me;
    Worshipping Me, revere Me;
And to Me alone shalt thou go; truly to thee
    I promise it – (because) thou art dear to Me.

66. Abandoning all (other) duties,
    Go to Me as thy sole refuge;
From all evils I thee
    Shall rescue: be not grieved!

67. This on thy part to no one not endowed with austerity,
    Nor ever to one not devoted,
Nor to one not obedient, must be told,
    Nor to one who murmurs against Me.

68. Whoso this supreme secret
    Shall make known to My devotees,
Showing utmost devotion to Me,
    Shall go just to Me, without a doubt.

69. And not than he among men
    Is there any who does things more pleasing to Me;
Nor shall there be than he to Me
    Any other dearer on earth.

70. And whoso shall study this
    Colloquy on duty between us two,
By him with knowledge – worship I
    Would be worshipped: so I hold.

71. With faith, and not murmuring against it,
    What man even hears it,
He too shall be released, and the fair worlds
    Of men of virtuous deeds shall he attain.

72. Has this been heard, son of Pṛthā,
    By thee with concentrated thought?
Has the confusion of ignorance
    In thee been destroyed, Dhanaṃjaya?

    Arjuna said:
73. Destroyed the confusion; attention (to the truth) is won,
    By Thy grace, on my part, O Changeless One;

I stand firm, with doubts dispersed;
    I shall do Thy word.

        Saṃjaya said:
74. Thus I of Vāsudeva
    And the exalted son of Pṛthā
This colloquy have heard,
    Marvelous and thrilling.

75. By the grace of Vyāsa have I heard
    This supreme secret,
This discipline, from Kṛṣṇa the Lord of Discipline,
    Speaking it Himself in very person.

76. O king, as I recall again and again
    This marvelous colloquy,
And holy, of Keśava and Arjuna,
    I thrill with joy at every moment.

77. And as I recall again and again that
    Most wondrous form of Hari,
Great is my amazement, O king,
    And I thrill with joy again and again.

78. Where is Kṛṣṇa the Lord of Discipline,
    And where is the Bowman, the son of Pṛthā,
There fortune, victory, prosperity,
    And statecraft are firmly fixed, I ween.

Source: Franklin Edgerton (trans.) *The Bhagavad Gîtā* (New York: Harper & Row, 1944), pp. 2–8, 9–16, 38–41, 55–61, 83–91.

4.8. FROM *THE LAWS OF MANU*: DUTIES OF HUSBAND AND WIFE

Chapter IX

[1] I will tell the eternal duties of a man and wife who stay on the path of duty both in union and in separation. [2] Men must make their women dependent day and night, and keep under their own control those who are attached to sensory objects. [3] Her father guards her in childhood, her husband guards her in youth, and her sons guard her in old age. A woman is not fit for independence. [4] A father who does not give her away at the proper time should be blamed, and a husband who does not have sex with her at the proper time should be blamed; and the son who does not guard his mother when her husband is dead should be blamed.

[5] Women should especially be guarded against addictions, even trifling ones, for unguarded (women) would bring sorrow upon both families. [6] Regarding this as the supreme duty of all the classes, husbands, even weak ones, try to guard their wives. [7] For by zealously guarding his wife he guards his own descendants, practices, family, and himself, as well as his own duty. [8] The husband enters the wife, becomes an embryo, and is born here on earth. That is why a wife is called a wife (*jāyā*), because he is born (*jāyate*) again in her. [9] The wife brings forth a son who is just like the man she makes love with; that is why he should guard his wife zealously, in order to keep his progeny clean.

[10] No man is able to guard women entirely by force, but they can be entirely guarded by using these means: [11] he should keep her busy amassing and spending money, engaging in purification, attending to her duty, cooking food, and looking after the furniture. [12] Women are not guarded when they are confined in a house by men who can be trusted to do their jobs well; but women who guard themselves by themselves are well guarded. [13] Drinking, associating with bad people, being separated from their husbands, wandering about, sleeping, and living in other people's houses are the six things that corrupt women. [14] Good looks do not matter to them, nor do they care about youth; 'A man!' they say, and enjoy sex with him, whether he is good-looking or ugly. [15] By running after men like whores, by their fickle minds, and by their natural lack of affection these women are unfaithful to their husbands even when they are zealously guarded here. [16] Knowing that their very own nature is like this, as it was born at the creation by the Lord of Creatures, a man should make the utmost effort to guard them. [17] The bed and the seat, jewellery, lust, anger, crookedness, a malicious nature, and bad conduct are what Manu assigned to women. [18] There is no ritual with Vedic verses for women; this is a firmly established point of law. For women, who have no virile strength and no Vedic verses, are falsehood; this is well established.

[19] There are many revealed canonical texts to this effect that are sung even in treatises on the meaning of the Vedas, so that women's distinctive traits may be carefully inspected. Now listen to the redemptions for their (errors).

[20] 'If my mother has given in to her desire, going astray and violating her vow to her husband, let my father keep that semen away from me.' This is a canonical example. [21] If in her mind she thinks of anything that the man that married her would not wish, this is said as a complete reparation for that infidelity.

[22] When a woman is joined with a husband in accordance with the rules, she takes on the very same qualities that he has, just like a river flowing down into the ocean. [23] When Akṣamālā, who was born of the lowest womb, united with Vasiṣṭha, and Sārangī, the bird-woman, with Mandapāla, they became worthy of honour. [24] These and other women of vile birth in this world were pulled up through the particular auspicious qualities of their own husbands.

[25] The ordinary life of a husband and wife, which is always auspicious, has thus been described. Now learn the duties regarding progeny, which lead to future happiness both here on earth and after death.

[26] There is no difference at all between the goddesses of good fortune who live in houses and women who are the lamps of their houses, worthy of reverence and

greatly blessed because of their progeny. [27] The wife is the visible form of what holds together the begetting of children, the caring for them when they are born, and the ordinary business of every day. [28] Children, the fulfilment of duties, obedience, and the ultimate sexual pleasure depend upon a wife, and so does heaven, for oneself and one's ancestors. [29] The woman who is not unfaithful to her husband but restrains her mind-and-heart, speech, and body reaches her husband's worlds (after death), and good people call her a virtuous woman. [30] But a woman who is unfaithful to her husband is an object of reproach in this world; (then) she is reborn in the womb of a jackal and is tormented by the diseases (born) of (her) evil.

Source: Wendy Doniger with Brian K. Smith (trans.) *The Laws of Manu* (Penguin, 1991), pp. 197–200.

── ●◆● ──

THE MODERN PERIOD

— ◆◆ —

4.9 THE MEANING OF *MOKSHA* IN CONTEMPORARY HINDU THOUGHT AND LIFE

K. SIVARAMAN

I have been asked to discuss *moksha*, the Hindu counterpart of salvation, and its meaning for the 'contemporary' Hindu. In view of my specialised interest and supposed competence, my approach will be from the perspective of 'theistic' Hinduism. Accordingly, I wish first to comment briefly on 'contemporaneity' and, at more length, on 'theism' in relation to Hinduism. My comments will of course bear on the theme of *moksha*. I shall then analyse the implication of *moksha* by a bold appropriation of terms and ideas to which I have been exposed.

I

Does *moksha* have any meaning for the thought and life of the present-day Hindu? The normal attitude is to treat it as part of traditional Hindu culture and therefore as accepted today, if at all, out of sheer cultural habit. It is true that many Hindus in their scholarly discussions exhibit this attitude. As in the rest of the world many Hindus too have no kind of contact with any form of religion or its modes of thought. They grow up as strangers to the terms and meaning of religion. If Hinduism as a living religion interests them little, its transcendent claims focused in a concept like *moksha* interest them even less.

But we do not have to search for a greatest or lowest common measure of acceptance in order to justify the claim of meaningfulness. To those to whom it is meaningful it is profoundly meaningful. To them, *moksha* is a living reality of their experience. The contemporary Hindu may not be exercised to the extent of prophesying about religious problems being the principal problem of the end of the century. But he certainly values *moksha*, whether actively or implicitly, and seeks to find a place for it in his view of human life and purposes. To many it presents itself as an 'esoteric' possibility open through submission to the rigour of spiritual discipline and discipleship. To some it is a kind of transient mystical ecstasy that is induced as the culmination of devotion, group-singing, meditation, etc. To the philosophically lettered, *moksha* is an abstract, formal, intellectual possibility and despite its abstractness, that is as something that one has not yet 'had', its real value is still assumed as a possible experience for oneself.

All this is interesting as information but I do not think that these are the points which really concern us. What matters for contemporary Hindu thought is the Hindu self-understanding of his tradition in terms of growth and regeneration in response to the requirements of modern living and thinking. The contemporary Hindu is heir to systems of ideas of the Hindu East and of the non-Hindu West, both of which serve as sources of his way of looking at things. He achieves assimilation of the foreign not by a rejection of his own standpoint or ideal but by a deepening of it with increasing reverence through infinite patience and humility until what was foreign reveals its kinship with his own. The outcome is a reassessment of his heritage and a continual recreation or renewal of his faith. What remains 'traditional' about the tradition is its continuity, not its conservatism. Hindu tradition is a continuous process of evolution by a free use of reason and experience. This is how a Hindu, today, 'liberated' from his native medievalism, looks at his own faith. It is in this spirit that my personal reflections and reassessments of the meaning of *moksha*, quickened by closeness to a particular phase of Hinduism, are offered in this paper and made to pass for 'contemporary' views.

I now pass on to 'theistic' Hinduism. The theistic–absolutistic polarisation of standpoints is one of the significant features of Hindu thought and life, and to accord recognition to this is to take a major step towards truly encountering Hinduism. Present from the very dawn of its history, this polarisation emerged with greater self-consciousness and philosophic sophistication under the stimulus of the challenge of Buddhism.

The great divide between Hinduism and Buddhism seems to be, to put it in relation to our present concern, between the point of view according to which the love of a personal God is the very crown of the experience of liberation from bondage to which man has been subject, and a point of view where the love of God is acclaimed only as a preparation, even if a necessary one, for realising the goal of such liberation. In both, it may be noted, liberation or deliverance stands for the ultimate goal of life's endeavour. The difference is in respect of what is entailed by the two standpoints, theoretically and also in practice. For the theist, spiritual liberation is identified with the love which becomes central and persuasive in the sphere of experience. God, none other than love itself (cf. the oft-quoted Tamil verse 'Love is God'), is the exact expression of perfect deliverance. God's self-revelation and man's liberation from self-estrangement coincide in the moment of the experience of love. The love of God means avowedly a corresponding love towards the concrete, individual, unique here and now. It is in the meeting of these two that *moksha* liberates and enlarges human existence. In contrast, the absolutist sees 'liberation' as, unequivocally, liberation from time, from the world and all that is conditioned by time.

Spiritual liberation, itself no doubt a positive experience as the perfect expression of self or self-hood, is negative in respect of all those values associated with human life: history, personality, freedom, community, progress, etc. Self is, precisely, 'not this, not this'.

II

What gives a real edge to the 'absolutist' Hindu attitude is his severely theoretical veto of everything that is 'not-self'. Falsity – this is his key-concept – includes within its sweep the worlds of nature and of culture alike. The latter is denied not merely as a value. For the theistic world-view also devalues the world on account of its evanescence. The absolutist denies it as a real given. Lapse of value means lapse of reality. As one of the Hindu classics puts it, 'the snake is false at the very place and in the very moment that it appeared, substituting as it did, demonically, for the rope'.

One of the outcomes of this attitude, of great consequence for Hindu thought and life as a whole, is to view reality not horizontally but as a pyramid of levels succeeding each other in a vertical direction, according to their degree of value and of their consequent power of being. The world's encountered diversities and pluralities, its change, all that goes with freedom and action are all alike 'levelled' as belonging together under a common verdict. Unity, however, stands on a 'higher' level not contradicted by but contradicting diversity, so that movement is possible from below to above but not vice versa. 'From death to immortality' is the pattern. Not the other way round. Again, in the asymmetrical movement from one level to another, there is no organic transition implied in so far as the higher does not literally 'fulfil' the lower. *Telos* or fulfilment does not have a horizontal sense of lying at the end of the road. It is vertical, involving an 'ascent' or leap. 'Liberation', comparable to waking up from a dream, is an essential possibility present for man always, and at no time in particular. It is not, strictly, accomplishing something. Indeed, it is waking up from the illusion of accomplishment.

The model of 'waking from dream' likewise contains implicit answers to the problems of individuality, community or social obligation. When I 'wake up' from a dream I realise that all the individuals I saw in the dream were 'false', but I also realise that the person I call myself, with the body and behaviour I had in the dream, was equally 'false'. There is illusion, there is freedom from illusion, but individuals are not freed from illusion. Individuals are the products of illusion. Individuality is itself precisely the illusion from which we seek to be freed. You and I differ in our bodies, in the minds and egos associated with bodies, but we do not differ in self. It is by falsely identifying the self with the body that we suffer the illusion of individuality. The self is in the world as the sleeper is in his dream-world; he is not really in it, he only seems to be. Similarly, the ethical problem simply does not arise for the 'liberated'. While dreaming, the dreamer has moral obligations to the persons in the dream. But after he wakes up from his dream he feels no obligation to go back to sleep in order to recover his dream and help those persons further, because he knows that they no longer exist – in fact they never did exist.

I have dwelt at some length on the absolutist's uncompromising views only to set off negatively the Hindu theist's frame of reference. Theistic Hinduism of all shades stands defined by its repudiation of the theory of falsity, and of the distinction of levels implied by it. In effect it may be said to affirm freedom, love, personality, community, history and moral obligation, and to rediscover their deeper spiritual significance for man. Their positive role in the service of man's freedom from the thraldom of unfreedom can be duly appreciated once man is 'liberated' from the penumbra of falsity. There is a spiritual purpose in history: to reclaim man estranged from himself and from others in consequence of his estrangement from the ground of his very being. God's cosmic functions are, to generalise the theology of Hindu theism, to help us to grow into full spiritual manhood. History as the sphere of man's conscious, deliberate and collective striving is what makes possible the realisation of his values, though this is not itself viewed as 'accomplishment' but as an aspect of cosmic history.

Two kinds of eschatologies – under the categories of 'bondage' and 'liberation' – are used. In contrast to the generality of absolutistic thought, theism is sensitive of the continuity between the two. Bondage, or *samsara*, includes the conception of an 'after-life' which remains on the same level as the present life, and though comprising all forms of life, sub-human and super-human alike, is typified in regard to moral responsibility uniquely by human life. The corollary to this 'after-life' concept is *karma*. The individual continues from life to life in an embodied existence, the contents and forms of his life dependent on what the individual has performed in former lives, yet affording some scope for growth and gradual perfection by the performance of meritorious actions. This is the sphere of *dharma*.

The second eschatology consists of the assumption of a 'liberation' (*moksha*), from bondage into unending embodied existence. Negatively, it is the de-conditioning of the individual, subject to multiple conditionings or bonds; positively, it is unhindered conformity to the gracious will of God, not in spite of but in due compliance with the individual's freedom, and a consequent experience of blessedness in the wake of fulfilment and freedom.

Cosmic action on the part of the divine will is conceived imaginatively to consist of two phases. The initial phase involves the self-veiling of God, even while He is witness to the obstructing function of human ignorance. God is thus not only the ground but the hidden meaning and motive of history. The endless sequence of life and death, of wakefulness and sleep, of memory and oblivion, of creation and destruction, is really the grand work of God's construction, in free complicity with man obstructed in his vision and constricted in his action. History is not a series of meaningless recurrences of the 'natural' world but a process pointing and moving toward a fuller disclosure and realisation of life's essential meaning. That this is so becomes apparent retrospectively in the experience of *moksha*. This marks the second phase of God's cosmic function. This is the self-revelation of God coinciding with the termination of bondage, which is of the nature of revelation. The entire sweep of man's existence thus stands in relation to God and as a preparation for *moksha*. No special religious sphere need be set apart from the secular world. Ordinary life as such takes on religious meaning. *Dharma* and *moksha* are continuous, the continuity of course being perceptible only from the perspective of the second.

It is also to be noted here that though bondage and liberation from bondage are alike 'caused' for man from without man, the decision however rests with man and depends on his preparation. Full scope is thus provided for man's being motivated to exert himself individually and collectively toward the common goal of liberation.

The essence of Hindu religiosity is often thought to be the immanent conception of Truth. Truth is something which cannot be introduced from without in time but is within the individual. The individual's task is accordingly to strive to appropriate the God within. This is the 'infinite resignation' of the ascetic who renounces the temporal for the sake of the eternal. Even the teacher cannot directly teach but only serve as a stimulus or occasion for the individual to help himself. He can, to use Socrates' words, stimulate but not 'beget'.

This view can, however, bear reassessment and reconstruction in the light of the reoriented understanding of the problem in Hindu theism, which conceives the individual to be transcendentally conditioned, as the being primordially divided from the truth by an infinite qualitative gulf. He neither has the truth nor is he able to acquire it. The teacher must supply the condition as well as the truth. This particular teacher can only be God. He acts in history, confronting man as the 'thou', exemplifying personal relationship and investing time with decisive significance. His action gives the temporal eternal significance. Man, tied to the temporal, is redeemed in time, 'at the appropriate moment' which is filled with the significance of the eternal.

Lastly, *moksha*, contrary to the belief that it cries halt to all dynamism, may be interpreted with the support of the authentic theistic tradition as implying the eternal conquest of the negative. *Eternal* blessedness involves the presence of three factors: the 'giver' and the 'enjoyer' and the 'occasioner'. By 'occasioner' is meant the negative factor which also paradoxically contributes to and even constitutes the experience of blessedness. An example may be useful. Light dispels darkness. But does the latter become nonexistent? When the light is withdrawn the darkness returns. This shows that darkness continues to exist even in the presence of the light. The latter continuously prevails against the continuously existent darkness by continuously dispelling it. Bondage is 'privation' of one's will, a thwarting of compliance with one's own unrestrained will which fulfils itself by conforming to Divine will. Liberation is a privation of this privation, a thwarting of the thwarting of will or, positively, a free unhampered exercise of will as in 'Thy will be done', which is joy itself. Even after attaining to the highest, life receives its content by 'repetition' or forward recollection. As Augustine says, commenting on the Psalm 'Seek His Face ever more', 'Finding should not end that seeking by which love is testified but with the increase of love, the seeking of the found one should also increase.'

III

The basic polarity which colours the meaning of *moksha* is the polarity of its negative and positive aspects. Liberation is liberation from pain, suffering and loss. From estrangement of every kind. From the dubious and vulnerable character of human existence. Yet for the precise theistic sense, one must also look into its positive aspect.

It is liberation or freedom *to do*. The free man, religiously speaking, is one who is unhindered in his freedom of volitional conformity or coincidence with the Divine. It is the freedom of enjoying union with God. Freedom to enjoy is another way of saying freedom from any sort of engagement or impediment that stands in the way of fulfilling one's will to enjoy. It is freedom from impediments of both commission and omission. Again, the expression 'free from' suggests that one is happy and *relieved* to be without those things one is freed from. A set of circumstances become constraining only when one wants to do something that these circumstances prevent. The world is a bondage to the extent that the circumstances of worldly existence hinder the accomplishment of the desire for freedom to enjoy. Without the implication of will to enjoy we should hardly know the meaning of freedom. Bondage is a thwarting of one's will and liberation is a thwarting of bondage. The liberating agent merely arrests the arresting of the constraint or opposes its opposing.

The second polarity of meaning that gives substance to the theistic understanding of *moksha* is the polarity of the Divine and the human. The factors involved are Divine grace and human freedom. Acknowledging either without the other leads to the partial emphasis of *moksha* as a prize to be won by one's efforts or as a gift freely given but not earned. This conflict runs through the entire Indian culture and is present in the West too, in the form of opposition between grace and self-reliance.

Grace supplies the essential transcendent element but it does not present itself as a total stranger; rather as a welcome guest whose appearance was not only awaited but intensively aspired or craved with the whole of our centred self.

Theistic Hinduism affirms the paradox that in affirming God man affirms his self-hood. It is genuine self-affirmation rather than self-negation that is entailed by God-affirmation. Saving knowledge is of the form of overcoming of alienation. One becomes aware of the sense of alienation, of being lost to oneself and consequently to the world, paradoxically, in the God-consciousness which at the same time involves the overcoming of this alienation.

To acknowledge a polar relation between self-effort and grace as a feature characteristic of *moksha* enables the avoidance of the extremes of moral legalism and graceless moralism on the one side and amoral lawlessness and a supra-ethical mysticism on the other. It is the affirmation of moral conscience but as having a more than moral foundation. Being precedes action in everything that is, including man, although in man as the bearer of freedom previous action determines present being. *Moksha*, therefore, phenomenologically at least, understood strictly from the self-restricted perspective of the striving seeker, is not exclusively God's work utterly apart from man's latent resources and endowment. The latter must be utilised, transformed and transmuted. God must accept us if we are to accept God. This is not so much an external necessity placed upon God as the inner logic of the situation in which man stands before God, the situation presupposed by the distinction of bondage and freedom from bondage.

Hindu spirituality is thus able to appreciate the theme of how God's 'forgiveness' concretely comes to the fore, because it itself acknowledges Divine initiative in the sphere of knowledge and being, an initiative which does not contradict human freedom but rather assumes it and builds upon it. Hindus will simply add that man's real freedom to be himself comes by the surrender of all claims to isolated independence and self-willedness. Precisely this is what man contributes to his own deliverance which he must 'work out by fear and trembling', for the very reason that 'deliverance' belongs to God. We become aware that this is so in so far as we make ourselves open to the power of God which God makes available to us. Accepting God's acceptance of us, love answering love – this is also the profound theme of Hindu theism. *This* is liberation. Overcoming of suffering, escaping the round of rebirth, all these are circumstantial to it.

The words of Irenaeus about Christ 'as God becoming what we are that he might make us what he himself is' is also exactly the note of praise and prayer addressed by the pupil to his spiritual Master:

> I have seen His mercy's feet
> Seen His roseate Feet this earth hath trod
> Seen Him, even I have known the Blessed one
> Seen in grace He made me His.

(*Thiruvacakam*, a Tamil classic)

I shall close by briefly referring to two other sets of polarities of meaning in respect of *moksha*, the polarity of means and end and the polarity of the individual and the universal. These are what makes *moksha* a *spiritual* experience; in the secular world there can only be conflict between them. The concept of the spiritual involves the identity of means and end. This is the paradox of spiritual realisation. Realisation is eternal realisation. The goal of spiritual life is also a kind of life – life eternal, life divine or life universal, call it by any name. It involves no change in the modes of existence or even in the behaviour of the 'liberated' man. What he has been doing with a sense of 'ought' he now does spontaneously. The example that is given is significant. Milk is taken by the convalescent as a means of nourishment, and also by the healthy for conserving health. *Moksha* is also an eternal conservation of spiritual value, and is continuous with its means. Conversely, knowledge, work, devotion are all involved in the accomplished character of *moksha*. The dawn of saving faith is itself in principle coincident with the advent of *moksha*.

The polarity is also exemplified by the equation of Revelation with liberation. The history of Divine self-disclosure and the 'history' of man's liberation from bondage are one and the same history. The bestowal of revelatory grace is *moksha*, just as the veiling of it is bondage. Lastly, 'liberation' does not imply fulfilment of the individual in isolation. A limited fulfilment of separate individuals would not be fulfilment at all, not even for the individuals, for no person is separated from other persons and from the whole of reality in such a way that he could be 'liberated' apart from the liberation of everyone and everything. This is the polarity of individual and universal.

This demand is implicitly present in classical Hinduism and becomes explicitly articulated in medieval and modern Hinduism, thus giving a religious urgency to community and institutional life. *Moksha* is conceived as an 'empire' where one's autonomy is truly regained. It is an empire of emperors in complete possession of their empire which is only to say: of themselves in conscious conformity with God.

There is complete transparency of everything for the divine to shine through, so that there is no tension of claim and counterclaim. Just as *moksha* may be conceived as life that finally triumphs over what restricts it (death), it can also be viewed as a Divine universe or kingdom, triumphing over the demonic power structure that is the world.

In this paper, I have purposefully highlighted those areas of interest in connection with a discussion on the meaning of *moksha* that will be of significance for dialogue between Hindu and Christian religions. Even at the risk of a certain measure of over-simplification and blurring of distinctions, to which charge I shall plead guilty, I have striven to indicate certain structural affinities between the ideas of 'Salvation in history' and 'Liberation from bondage'. The convergences and divergences which follow should provide the grist for fruitful dialogue.

Source: S. J. Samartha (ed.) *Living Faiths and Ultimate Goals* (Geneva: World Council of Churches, 1974), pp. 2–11.

4.10 THE UNITY OF RELIGIONS

4.10.1 Each religion as a path to God
SRI RAMAKRISHNA

The name of Sri Ramakrishna Paramahamsa (1834–1886 CE) has become associated with a message of tolerance towards all religions. A Bengali rural *brahman* and religious ecstatic devoted to Kali, Ramakrishna gathered a core of young disciples and urban householders as disciples. After his death, these followers under the leadership of Swami Vivekananda created the Ramakrishna Math and Mission to perpetuate a philosophy of service to humanity and tolerance of all religions that was increasingly presented in more exclusively Advaitin terms.

MASTER: 'It is not good to feel that one's own religion alone is true and all others are false. God is one only, and not two. Different people call on Him by different names: some as Allāh, some as God, and others as Krishna, Śiva, and Brahman. It is like the water in a lake. Some drink it at one place and call it "jal", others at another place and call it "pāni", and still others at a third place and call it "water". The Hindus call it "jal", the Christians "water", and the Mussalmāns "pāni". But it is one and the same thing. Opinions are but paths. Each religion is only a path leading to God, as rivers come from different directions and ultimately become one in the one ocean.

'The Truth established in the Vedas, the Purānas, and the Tantras is but one Satchidānanda. In the Vedas It is called Brahman, in the Purānas It is called Krishna, Rāma, and so on, and in the Tantras It is called Śiva. The one Satchidānanda is called Brahman, Krishna, and Śiva.'

The devotees were silent.

A VAISHNAVA DEVOTEE: 'Sir, why should one think of God at all?'

MASTER: 'If a man really has that knowledge, then he is indeed liberated though living in a body.

'Not all, by any means, believe in God. They simply talk. The wordly-minded have heard from someone that God exists and that everything happens by His will; but it is not their inner belief.

'Do you know what a worldly man's idea of God is like? It is like the children's swearing by God when they quarrel. They have heard the word while listening to their elderly aunts quarrelling.

'Is it possible for all to comprehend God? God has created the good and the bad, the devoted and the impious, the faithful and the sceptical. The wonders that we see all exist in His creation. In one place there is more manifestation of His Power, in another less. The sun's light is better reflected by water than by earth, and still better by a mirror. Again, there are different levels among the devotees of God: superior, mediocre, and inferior. All this has been described in the *Gītā*.'

VAISHNAVA: 'True, sir.'

MASTER: 'The inferior devotee says, "God exists, but He is very far off, up there in heaven." The mediocre devotee says, "God exists in all beings as life and consciousness." The superior devotee says: "It is God Himself who has become everything; whatever I see is only a form of God. It is He alone who has become māyā, the universe, and all living beings. Nothing exists but God."'

VAISHNAVA: 'Does anyone ever attain that state of mind?'

MASTER: 'One cannot attain it unless one has seen God. But there are signs that a man has had the vision of God. A man who has seen God sometimes behaves like a madman: he laughs, weeps, dances, and sings. Sometimes he behaves like a child, a child five years old – guileless, generous, without vanity, unattached to anything, not under the control of any of the gunas, always blissful. Sometimes he behaves like a ghoul: he doesn't differentiate between things pure and things impure; he sees no difference between things clean and things unclean. And sometimes he is like an inert thing, staring vacantly: he cannot do any work; he cannot strive for anything.'

Was the Master making a veiled reference to his own states of mind?

MASTER (*to the Vaishnava devotee*): 'The feeling of "Thee and Thine" is the outcome of Knowledge; "I and mine" comes from ignorance. Knowledge makes one feel: "O God, Thou art the Doer and I am Thy instrument. O God, to Thee belongs all – body, mind, house, family, living beings, and the universe. All these are Thine. Nothing belongs to me."

'An ignorant person says, "Oh, God is there – very far off." The man of Knowledge knows that God is right here, very near, in the heart; that He has assumed all forms and dwells in all hearts as their Inner Controller.'

Source: From the teaching of Sri Ramakrishna, *The Gospel of Ramakrishna*, trans. Swami Nikhilananda (Madras: Sri Ramakrishna Math, 1981), pp. 264–6.

4.10.2 Hinduism – The mother of religions

SWAMI VIVEKANANDA

Swami Vivekananda (1863–1902 CE) was Sri Ramakrishna's most prominent disciple and the architect of the Ramakrishna Math and Mission. After travelling to the West in 1893, however, Vivekananda became more widely known for his attempts to defend and propagate Hindu ideas in the West. These two readings illustrate the value Vivekananda placed on Hinduism and his personal understanding of Advaita philosophy.

Addresses at the Parliament of Religions

Response to welcome

At the World's Parliament of Religions, Chicago, 11th September, 1893

Sisters and Brothers of America,

It fills my heart with joy unspeakable to rise in response to the warm and cordial welcome which you have given us. I thank you in the name of the most ancient order of monks in the world; I thank you in the name of the mother of religions; and I thank you in the name of millions and millions of Hindu people of all classes and sects.

My thanks, also, to some of the speakers on this platform who, referring to the delegates from the Orient, have told you that these men from far-off nations may well claim the honour of bearing to different lands the idea of toleration. I am proud to belong to a religion which has taught the world both tolerance and universal acceptance. We believe not only in universal toleration, but we accept all religions as true. I am proud to belong to a nation which has sheltered the persecuted and the refugees of all religions and all nations of the earth. I am proud to tell you that we have gathered in our bosom the purest remnant of the Israelites, who came to Southern India and took refuge with us in the very year in which their holy temple was shattered to pieces by Roman tyranny. I am proud to belong to the religion which has sheltered and is still fostering the remnant of the grand Zoroastrian nation. I will quote to you, brethren, a few lines from a hymn which I remember to have repeated from my earliest boyhood, which is every day repeated by millions of human beings: '*As the different streams having their sources in different places all mingle their water in the sea, so, O Lord, the different paths which men take through different tendencies, various though they appear, crooked or straight, all lead to Thee.*'

The present convention, which is one of the most august assemblies ever held, is in itself a vindication, a declaration to the world of the wonderful doctrine preached in the Gita: '*Whosoever comes to Me, through whatsoever form, I reach him; all men are struggling through paths which in the end lead to me.*' Sectarianism, bigotry, and its horrible descendant, fanaticism, have long possessed this beautiful earth. They have filled the earth with violence, drenched it often and often with human blood, destroyed civilisation and sent whole nations to despair. Had it not been for these horrible demons, human society would be far more advanced than it is now. But their time is come; and I fervently hope that the bell that tolled this morning in honour of this convention may be the death-knell of all fanaticism, of all persecutions with the sword or with the pen, and of all uncharitable feelings between persons wending their way to the same goal.

Source: From the teaching of Swami Vivekananda, *The Complete Works of Swami Vivekananda*, vol. 1 (Calcutta: Advaita Ashrama, 1989), pp. 3–4.

4.11 A MODERN INTERPRETATION OF ADVAITA
SWAMI VIVEKANANDA

According to the Advaita philosophy, then, this differentiation of matter, these phenomena, are, as it were, for a time, hiding the real nature of man; but the latter really has not been changed at all. In the lowest worm, as well as in the highest human being, the same divine nature is present. The worm form is the lower form in which the divinity has been more overshadowed by Maya; that is the highest form in which it has been least overshadowed. Behind everything the same divinity is existing, and out of this comes the basis of morality. Do not injure another. Love everyone as your own self, because the whole universe is one. In injuring another, I am injuring myself; in loving another, I am loving myself. From this also springs that principle of Advaita morality which has been summed up in one word – self-abnegation. The Advaitist says, this little personalised self is the cause of all my misery. This individualised self, which makes me different from all other beings, brings hatred and jealousy and misery, struggle and all other evils. And when this idea has been got rid of, all struggle will cease, all misery vanish. So this is to be given up. We must always hold ourselves ready, even to give up our lives for the lowest beings. When a man has become ready even to give up his life for a little insect, he has reached the perfection which the Advaitist wants to attain; and at that moment when he has become thus ready, the veil of ignorance falls away from him, and he will feel his own nature. Even in this life, he will feel that he is one with the universe. For a time, as it were, the whole of this phenomenal world will disappear for him, and he will realise what he is. But so long as the Karma of this body remains, he will have to live. This state, when the veil has vanished and yet the body remains for some time, is what the Vedantists call the Jivanmukti, the living freedom. If a man is deluded by a mirage for some time, and one day the mirage disappears – if it comes back again the next day, or at some future time, he will not be deluded. Before the mirage first broke, the man could not distinguish between the reality and the deception. But when it has once broken, as long as he has organs and eyes to work with, he will see the image, but will no more be deluded. That fine distinction between the actual world and the mirage he has caught, and the latter cannot delude him any more. So when the Vedantist has realised his own nature, the whole world has vanished for him. It will come back again, but no more the same world of misery.

The prison of misery has become changed into Sat, Chit, Ânanda – Existence Absolute, Knowledge Absolute, Bliss Absolute – and the attainment of this is the goal of the Advaita Philosophy.

Source: *The Complete Works of Swami Vivekananda*, vol. 1 (Calcutta: Advaita Ashrama, 1989), pp. 364–5.

4.12 THE COMING OF A SPIRITUAL AGE: SRI AUROBINDO AND AUROVILLE

4.12.1 Integral perfection

SRI AUROBINDO

A Yoga of integral perfection regards man as a divine spiritual being involved in mind, life and body; it aims therefore at a liberation and a perfection of his divine nature. It seeks to make an inner living in the perfectly developed spiritual being his constant intrinsic living and the spiritualised action of mind, life and body only its outward human expression. In order that this spiritual being may not be something vague and indefinable or else but imperfectly realised and dependent on the mental support and the mental limitations, it seeks to go beyond mind to the supramental knowledge, will, sense, feeling, intuition, dynamic initiation of vital and physical action, all that makes the native working of the spiritual being. It accepts human life, but takes account of the large supraterrestrial action behind the earthly material living, and it joins itself to the divine Being from whom the supreme origination of all these partial and lower states proceeds so that the whole of life may become aware of its divine source and feel in each action of knowledge, of will, of feeling, sense and body the divine originating impulse. It rejects nothing that is essential in the mundane aim, but enlarges it, finds and lives in its greater and its truer meaning now hidden from it, transfigures it from a limited, earthly and mortal thing to a figure of intimate, divine and immortal values.

The integral Yoga meets the religious ideal at several points, but goes beyond it in the sense of a greater wideness. The religious ideal looks, not only beyond this earth, but away from it to a heaven or even beyond all heavens to some kind of Nirvana. Its ideal of perfection is limited to whatever kind of inner or outer mutation will eventually serve the turning away of the soul from the human life to the beyond. Its ordinary idea of perfection is a religio-ethical change, a drastic purification of the active and the emotional being, often with an ascetic abrogation and rejection of the vital impulses as its completest reaching of excellence, and in any case a supra-terrestrial motive and reward or result of a life of piety and right conduct. In so far as it admits a change of knowledge, will, aesthesis, it is in the sense of the turning of them to another object than the aims of human life and eventually brings a rejection of all earthly objects of aesthesis, will and knowledge. The method, whether it lays stress on personal effort or upon divine influence, on works and knowledge or upon grace, is not like the mundane a development, but rather a conversion; but in the end the aim is not a conversion of our mental and physical nature, but the putting on of a pure spiritual nature and being, and since that is not possible here on earth, it looks for its consummation by a transference to another world or a shuffling off of all cosmic existence.

But the integral Yoga founds itself on a conception of the spiritual being as an omnipresent existence, the fullness of which comes not essentially by a transference to other worlds or a cosmic self-extinction, but by a growth out of what we now are phenomenally into the consciousness of the omnipresent reality which we always are in the essence of our being. It substitutes for the form of religious piety its completer spiritual seeking of a divine union. It proceeds by a personal effort to a conversion through a divine influence and possession; but this divine grace, if we may so call it, is not simply a mysterious flow or touch coming from above, but the all-pervading act of a divine presence which we come to know within as the power of the highest Self and Master of our being entering into the soul and so possessing it that we not only feel it close to us and pressing upon our mortal nature, but live in its law, know that law, possess it as the whole power of our spiritualised nature. The conversion its action will effect is an integral conversion of our ethical being into the Truth and Right of the divine nature, of our intellectual into the illumination of divine knowledge, our emotional into the divine love and unity, our dynamic and volitional into a working of the divine power, our aesthetic into a plenary reception and a creative enjoyment of divine beauty, not excluding even in the end a divine conversion of the vital and physical being. It regards all the previous life as an involuntary and unconscious or half-conscious preparatory growing towards this change and Yoga as the voluntary and conscious effort and realisation of the change, by which all the aim of human existence in all its parts is fulfilled, even while it is transfigured. Admitting the supracosmic truth and life in worlds beyond, it admits too the terrestrial as a continued term of the one existence and a change of individual and communal life on earth as a strain of its divine meaning.

To open oneself to the supracosmic Divine is an essential condition of this integral perfection; to unite oneself with the universal Divine is another essential condition. Here the Yoga of self-perfection coincides with the Yogas of knowledge, works and devotion; for it is impossible to change the human nature into the divine or to make it an instrument of the divine knowledge, will and joy of existence, unless there is a union with the supreme Being, Consciousness and Bliss and a unity with its universal Self in all things and beings. A wholly separative possession of the divine nature by the human individual, as distinct from a self-withdrawn absorption in it, is not possible. But this unity will not be an inmost spiritual oneness qualified, so long as the human life lasts, by a separative existence in mind, life and body; the full perfection is a possession, through this spiritual unity, of unity too with the universal Mind, the universal Life, the universal Form which are the other constant terms of cosmic being. Moreover, since human life is still accepted as a self-expression of the realised Divine in man, there must be an action of the entire divine nature in our life; and this brings in the need of the supramental conversion which substitutes the native action of spiritual being for the imperfect action of the superficial nature and spiritualises and transfigures its mental, vital and physical parts by the spiritual ideality. These three elements, a union with the supreme Divine, unity with the universal Self, and a supramental life action from this transcendent origin and through this universality, but still with the individual as the soul-channel and natural instrument, constitute the essence of the integral divine perfection of the human being.

Source: Sri Aurobindo, *Birth Centenary Library* (Pondicherry: Sri Aurobindo Ashram, 1972–5, vol. 24, pp. 594–6.

4.12.2 Man a transitional being
SRI AUROBINDO

Man's greatness is not in what he is, but in what he makes possible. His glory is that he is the closed place and secret workshop of a living labour in which superman-hood is being made ready by a divine Craftsman. But he is admitted too to a yet greater greatness and it is that, allowed to be unlike the lower creation, he is partly an artisan of this divine change; his conscious assent, his consecrated will and partici-pation are needed that into his body may descend the glory that will replace him. His aspiration is earth's call to the supramental creator.

If earth calls and the Supreme answers, the hour can be even now for that immense and glorious transformation.

But what shall be the gain to be won for the Earth-consciousness we embody by this unprecedented ascent from mind to supermind and what the ransom of the supramental change? To what end should man leave his safe human limits for this hazardous adventure?

First consider what was gained when Nature passed from the brute inconscience and inertia of what seems inanimate Matter to the vibrant awakening of sensibility of plant range. Life was gained; the gain was the first beginnings of a mite groping and involved, reaching a consciousness that stretches out dumbly for growth, towards sense vibration, to a preparation for vital yearnings, a living joy and beauty. The plant achieved a first form of life but could not possess it, because this first organised life-consciousness had feeling and seeking but was blind, dumb, deaf, chained to the soul and involved in its own nerve and tissue; it could not get out of them, could not get behind its nerve self as does the vital mind of the animal; still less could it turn down from above upon it to know and realise and control its own motions as does the observing and thinking mind in man. This was an imprisoned gain, for there was still a gross oppression of the first Inconscience which had covered up with the brute phenomenon of Matter and of Energy of Matter all signs of the Spirit. Nature could in no wise stop here, because she held much in her that was still occult, potential, unexpressed, unorganised, latent; the evolution had perforce to go farther. The animal had to replace the plant at the head and top of Nature.

And what then was gained when Nature passed from the obscurity of the plant kingdom to the awakened sense, desire and emotion and the free mobility of animal life? The gain was liberated sense and feeling and desire and courage and cunning and the contrivance of the objects of desire, passion and action and hunger and battle and conquest and the sex-call and play and pleasure, and all the joy and pain of the conscious living creature. Not only the life of the body which the animal has in common with the plant but a life-mind that appeared for the first time in the earth-story and grew from form to more organised form till it reached in the best the limit of its own formula.

The animal achieved a first form of mind, but could not possess it, because this first organised mind-consciousness was enslaved to a narrow scope, tied to the full functioning of the physical body and brain and nerve, tied to serve the physical life and its desires and needs and passions, limited to the insistent uses of the vital urge, to material longing and feeling and action, bound in its own inferior instrumentation, its spontaneous combinings of association and memory and instinct. It could not get away from them, could not get behind them as man's intelligence gets behind them to observe them; still less could it turn down on them from above as do human reason and will to control, enlarge, re-order, exceed, sublimate.

At each capital step of Nature's ascent there is a reversal of consciousness in the evolving spirit. As when a climber turns on a summit to which he has laboured and looks down with an exalted and wider power of vision on all that was once above or on a level with him but is now below his feet, the evolutionary being not only transcends his past self, his former now exceeded status, but commands from a higher grade of self-experience and vision, with a new apprehending feeling or a new comprehending sight and effectuating power in a greater system of values, all that was once his own consciousness but is now below him and belongs to an inferior creation. This reversal is the sign of a decisive victory and the seal of a radical progress in Nature.

The new consciousness attained in the spiritual evolution is always higher in grade and power, always larger, more comprehensive, wider in sight and feeling, richer and finer in faculties, more complex, organic, dominating than the consciousness that was once our own but is now left behind us. There are greater breadth and space, heights before impassable, unexpected depths and intimacies. There is a luminous expansion that is the very sign-manual of the Supreme upon his work.

Mark that each of the great radical steps forward already taken by Nature has been infinitely greater in its change, incalculably vaster in its consequences than its puny predecessor. There is a miraculous opening to an always richer and wider expression, there is a new illuminating of the creation and a dynamic heightening of its significances. There is in this world we live in no equality of all on a flat level, but a hierarchy of ever-increasing precipitous superiorities pushing their mountain shoulders upwards towards the Supreme.

Because man is a mental being, he naturally imagines that mind is the one great leader and actor and creator or the indispensable agent in the universe. But this is an error; even for knowledge mind is not the only or the greatest possible instrument, the one aspirant and discoverer. Mind is a clumsy interlude between Nature's vast and precise subconscient action and the vaster infallible superconscient action of the Godhead.

There is nothing mind can do that cannot be better done in the mind's immobility and thought-free stillness.

When mind is still, then Truth gets her chance to be heard in the purity of the silence.

Truth cannot be attained by the Mind's thought but only by identity and silent vision. Truth lives in the calm wordless Light of the eternal spaces; she does not intervene in the noise and cackle of logical debate.

Source: Sri Aurobindo, *Birth Centenary Library* (Pondicherry: Sri Aurobindo Ashram, 1972–5), vol. 17, pp. 9–11.

4.12.3 A dream
THE MOTHER [OF THE SRI AUROBINDO ASHRAM]

There should be somewhere upon earth a place that no nation could claim as its sole property, a place where all human beings of good will, sincere in their aspiration, could live freely as citizens of the world, obeying one single authority, that of the supreme Truth, a place of peace, concord, harmony, where all the fighting instincts of man would be used exclusively to conquer the causes of his sufferings and miseries, to surmount his weakness and ignorance, to triumph over his limitations and incapacities; a place where the needs of the spirit and the care for progress would get precedence over the satisfaction of desire and passions, the seeking for material pleasures and enjoyment. In this place, children would be able to grow and develop integrally without losing contact with their soul. Education would be given not with a view to passing examinations and getting certificates and posts but for enriching the existing faculties and bringing forth new ones. In this place titles and positions would be supplanted by opportunities to serve and organise. The needs of the body will be provided for equally in the case of each and everyone. In the general organisation intellectual, moral and spiritual superiority will find expression not in the enhancement of the pleasures and powers of life but in the increase of duties and responsibilities. Artistic beauty in all forms, painting, sculpture, music, literature, will be available equally to all, the opportunity to share in the joys they give being limited solely by each one's capacities and not by social or financial position. For in this ideal place money would be no more the sovereign lord. Individual value would have a greater importance than the value due to material wealth and social position. Work would not be there as the means for gaining one's livelihood, it would be the means whereby to express oneself, develop one's capacities and possibilities, while doing at the same time service to the whole group, which on its side would provide for each one's subsistence and for the field of his work. In brief, it would be a place where the relations among human beings, usually based almost exclusively upon competition and strife, would be replaced by relations of emulation for doing better, for collaboration, relations of real brotherhood.

The earth is certainly not ready to realise such an idea, for mankind does not yet possess the necessary knowledge to understand and accept it nor the indispensable conscious force to execute it. That is why I call it a dream.

Yet, this dream is on the way to becoming a reality. That is exactly what we are seeking to do at the Ashram of Sri Aurobindo on a small scale, in proportion to our modest means. The achievement is indeed far from being perfect but it is progressive; little by little we advance towards our goal, which, we hope, one day we shall be able to hold before the world as a practical and effective means of coming out of the present chaos in order to be born into a more true, more harmonious new life.

4.12.4 To be a true Aurovillian

THE MOTHER [OF THE SRI AUROBINDO ASHRAM]

1   The first necessity is the inner discovery by which one learns who one really is behind the social, moral, cultural, racial and hereditary appearances.

At our inmost centre there is a free being, wide and knowing, who awaits our discovery and who ought to become the acting centre of our being and our life in Auroville.

2   One lives in Auroville in order to be free of moral and social conventions; but this liberty must not be a new slavery to the ego, its desires and its ambitions.

The fulfilment of desires bars the route to the inner discovery which can only be attained in peace and the transparency of a perfect disinterestedness.

3   The Aurovillian must lose the proprietary sense of possession.

For our passage in the material world, that which is indispensable to our life and to our action is put at our disposal according to the place we should occupy there. The more conscious our contact is with our inner being, the more exact are the means given.

4   Work, even manual work, is an indispensable thing for the inner discovery. If one does not work, if one does not inject his consciousness into matter, the latter will never develop. To let one's consciousness organise a bit of matter by way of one's body is very good. To establish order, around oneself, helps to bring order within oneself.

One should organise life not according to outer, artificial rules, but according to an organised, inner consciousness because if one allows life to drift without imposing the control of a higher consciousness, life becomes inexpressive and irresolute. It is to waste one's time in the sense that matter persists without a conscious utilisation.

5   The whole earth must prepare itself for the advent of the new species, and Auroville wants to consciously work towards hastening that advent.

6   Little by little it will be revealed to us what this new species should be, and meanwhile the best measure to take is to consecrate oneself entirely to the Divine.

4.12.5 No religion

THE MOTHER [OF THE SRI AUROBINDO ASHRAM]

Auroville is for those who want to live a life essentially divine but who renounce all religions whether they be ancient, modern or future.

It is only in experience that there can be knowledge of the truth. No one ought to speak of the Divine unless he has had experience of the Divine. Get experience of the Divine, then alone will you have the right to speak of it.

The objective study of religions will be a part of the historical study of the development of human consciousness.

Religions make up part of the history of mankind and it is in this guise that they will be studied at Auroville – not as beliefs to which one ought or ought not to fasten, but as part of a process in the development of human consciousness which should lead man towards his superior realisation.

Program:

Research through experience of the
Supreme Truth
A Life Divine
but
NO RELIGIONS

Source: *The Mother* [of the Sri Aurobindo Ashram], *Auroville: Cradle of a New World* (Pondicherry: Sri Aurobindo Ashram, 1972), pp. 1–6.

4.13 M. K. GANDHI'S EXPERIMENTS WITH TRUTH

4.13.1 Experiments with Truth

M. K. GANDHI

This argument had some effect on me. But it is not my purpose to attempt a real autobiography. I simply want to tell the story of my numerous experiments with truth, and as my life consists of nothing but those experiments, it is true that the story will take the shape of an autobiography. But I shall not mind, if every page of it speaks only of my experiments. I believe, or at any rate flatter myself with the belief, that a connected account of all these experiments will not be without benefit to the reader. My experiments in the political fields are now known, not only to India, but to a certain extent to the 'civilized' world. For me, they have not much value; and the title of 'Mahatma' that they have won for me has, therefore, even less. Often the title has deeply pained me; and there is not a moment I can recall when it may be said to have tickled me. But I should certainly like to narrate my experiments in the spiritual field which are known only to myself, and from which I have derived such power as I possess for working in the political field. If the experiments are really spiritual, then there can be no room for self-praise. They can only add to my humility. The more I reflect and look back on the past, the more vividly do I feel my limitations.

What I want to achieve – what I have been striving and pining to achieve these thirty years – is self-realization, to see God face to face, to attain *moksha*.[1] I live and move and have my being in pursuit of this goal. All that I do by way of speaking and writing, and all my ventures in the political field, are directed to this same end. But as I have all along believed that what is possible for one is possible for all, my experiments have not been conducted in the closet, but in the open; and I do not think that this fact detracts from their spiritual value. There are some things which are known only to oneself and one's Maker. These are clearly incommunicable. The experiments I am about to relate are not such. But they are spiritual, or rather moral; for the essence of religion is morality.

Only those matters of religion that can be comprehended as much by children as by older people will be included in this story. If I can narrate them in a dispassionate and humble spirit, many other experiments will find in them provision for their onward march. Far be it from me to claim any degree of perfection for these experiments. I claim for them nothing more than does a scientist who, though he conducts his experiments with the utmost accuracy, forethought and minuteness, never claims any finality about his conclusions, but keeps an open mind regarding them. I have gone through deep self-introspection, searched myself through and through, and examined and analysed every psychological situation. Yet I am far from claiming any finality or infallibility about my conclusions. One claim I do indeed make and it is this. For me they appear to be absolutely correct, and seem for the time being to be final. For if they were not, I should base no action on them. But at every step I have carried out the process of acceptance or rejection and acted accordingly. And so long as my acts satisfy my reason and my heart, I must firmly adhere to my original conclusions.

If I had only to discuss academic principles, I should clearly not attempt an auto-biography. But my purpose being to give an account of various practical applications of these principles, I have given the chapters I propose to write the title of *The Story of My Experiments with Truth.* These will of course include experiments with non-violence, celibacy and other principles of conduct believed to be distinct from truth. But for me, truth is the sovereign principle, which includes numerous other principles. This truth is not only truthfulness in word, but truthfulness in thought also, and not only the relative truth of our conception, but the Absolute Truth, the Eternal Principle, that is God. There are innumerable definitions of God, because His manifestations are innumerable. They overwhelm me with wonder and awe and for a moment stun me. But I worship God as Truth only I have not yet found Him, but I am seeking after Him. I am prepared to sacrifice the things dearest to me in pursuit of this quest. Even if the sacrifice demanded be my very life, I hope I may be prepared to give it. But as long as I have not realized this Absolute Truth, so long must I hold by the relative truth as I have conceived it. That relative truth must, meanwhile, be my beacon, my shield and buckler. Though this path is strait and narrow and sharp as the razor's edge, for me it has been the quickest and easiest. Even my Himalayan blunders have seemed trifling to me because I have kept strictly to this path. For the path has saved me from coming to grief, and I have gone forward according to my light. Often in my progress I have had faint glimpses of the Absolute Truth, God, and daily the conviction is growing upon me that He alone is real and all else is unreal. Let those, who wish, realize how the conviction has grown upon me; let them share my experiments and share also my conviction if they can.

---

1 Literally freedom from birth and death. The nearest English equivalent is 'salvation'.

Source: M. K. Gandhi, *An Autobiography, or The Story of my Experiments with Truth* (Harmondsworth: Penguin, 1982), pp. 14–16.

4.13.2 Gandhi's mission

I do not consider myself worthy to be mentioned in the same breath with the race of prophets. I am a humble seeker after truth. I am impatient to realise myself, to attain *moksha* in this very existence. My national service is part of my training for freeing my soul from the bondage of flesh. Thus considered, my service may be regarded as purely selfish. I have no desire for the perishable kingdom of earth. I am striving for the Kindom of Heaven which is *moksha*. To attain my end it is not necessary for me to seek the shelter of a cave. I carry one about me, if I would but know it. A cave-dweller can build castles in the air whereas a dweller in a palace like Janak has no castles to build. The cave-dweller who hovers round the world on the wings of thought has no peace. A Janak though living in the midst of 'pomp and circumstance' may have peace that passeth understanding. For me the road to salvation lies through incessant toil in the service of my country and therethrough of humanity. I want to identify myself with everything that lives. In the language of the Gītā I want to live at peace with both friend and foe. Though therefore a Mussulman or a Christian or a Hindu may despise me and hate me, I want to love him and serve him even as I would love my wife or son though they hate me. So my patriotism is for me a stage in my journey to the land of eternal freedom and peace. Thus it will be seen that for me there are no politics devoid of religion. They subserve religion. Politics bereft of religion are a deathtrap because they kill the soul.

4.13.3 Gandhism

There is no such thing as 'Gandhism', and I do not want to leave any sect after me. I do not claim to have originated any new principle or doctrine. I have simply tried in my own way to apply the eternal truths to our daily life and problems. There is, therefore, no question of my leaving any code like the *Code of Manu*. There can be no comparison between that great lawgiver and me. The opinions I have formed and the conclusions I have arrived at are not final. I may change them tomorrow. I have nothing new to teach the world. Truth and non-violence are as old as the hills. All I have done is to try experiments in both on as vast a scale as I could do.

In doing so I have sometimes erred and learnt by my errors. Life and its problems have thus become to me so many experiments in the practice of truth and non-violence. By instinct I have been truthful, but not non-violent. As a Jain *muni* once rightly said I was not so much a votary of *ahimsa* as I was of truth, and I put the latter in the first place and the former in the second. For, as he put it, I was capable of sacrificing non-violence for the sake of truth. In fact it was in the course of my pursuit of truth that I discovered non-violence. Our scriptures have declared that there is no *dharma* (law) higher than Truth. But non-violence they say is the highest duty. The word *dharma* in my opinion has different connotations as used in the two aphorisms.

Well, all my philosophy, if it may be called by that pretentious name, is contained in what I have said. You will not call it 'Gandhism'; there is no *ism* about it. And no elaborate literature or propaganda is needed about it.

4.13.4 On the Gita

QUESTIONER: I am told you recite the Bhagavadgita daily?

GANDHI: Yes, we finish the entire Gītā reading once every week.

QUESTIONER: But at the end of the Gītā Krishna recommends violence.

GANDHI: I do not think so. I am also fighting. I should not be fighting effectively if I were fighting violently. The message of the Gītā is to be found in the second chapter of the Gītā where Krishna speaks of the balanced state of mind, of mental equipoise. In nineteen verses at the close of the second chapter of the Gītā, Krishna explains how this state can be achieved. It can be achieved, he tells us, after killing all your passions. It is not possible to kill your brother after having killed all your passions. I should like to see that man dealing death – who has no passions, who is indifferent to pleasure and pain, who is undisturbed by the storms that trouble mortal man. The whole thing is described in language of beauty that is unsurpassed. These verses show that the fight Krishna speaks of is a spiritual fight.

QUESTIONER: To the common mind it sounds as though it was actual fighting.

GANDHI: You must read the whole thing dispassionately in its true context. After the first mention of fighting, there is no mention of fighting at all. The rest is a spiritual discourse.

QUESTIONER: Has anybody interpreted it like you?

GANDHI: Yes. The fight is there, but the fight as it is going on within. The Pandavas and Kauravas are the forces of good and evil within. The war is the war between Jekyll and Hyde, God and Satan, going on in the human breast. The internal evidence in support of this interpretation is there in the work itself and in the Mahabharata of which the Gītā is a minute part. It is not a history of war between two families, but the history of man – the history of the spiritual struggle of man.

QUESTIONER: Is the central teaching of the Gītā selfless action or non-violence?

GANDHI: I have no doubt that it is *anasakti* – selfless action. Indeed I have called my little translation of the Gītā Anasaktiyoga. And anasakti transcends ahimsa. He who would be *anasakta* (selfless) has necessarily to practise non-violence in order to attain the state of selflessness. Ahimsa is, therefore, a necessary preliminary, it is included in anasakti, it does not go beyond it.

QUESTIONER: Then does the Gītā teach himsa and ahimsa both?

GANDHI: I do not read that meaning in the Gītā. It is quite likely that the author did not write it to inculcate ahimsa, but as a commentator draws innumerable interpretations from a poetic text, even so I interpret the Gītā to mean that if its central theme is anasakti, it also teaches ahimsa. Whilst we are in the flesh and tread the solid earth, we have to practise ahimsa. In the life beyond there is no himsa or ahimsa.

QUESTIONER: But Lord Krishna actually counters the doctrine of ahimsa. For Arjuna utters this pacifist resolve:

> Better I deem it, if my kinsmen strike,
> To face them weaponless, and bear my breast
> To shaft and spear, than answer blow with blow.

And Lord Krishna teaches him to 'answer blow with blow'.

GANDHI: There I join issue with you. Those words of Arjuna were words of pretentious wisdom. 'Until yesterday', says Krishna to him, 'you fought your kinsmen with deadly weapons without the slightest compunction. Even today you would strike if the enemy was a stranger and not your own kith and kin!' The question before him was not of non-violence but whether he should slay his nearest and dearest.

4.13.5 Ashram vows

Gandhi sent during 1930 a series of weekly discourses from Yeravda Jail (which he called *mandir* or temple) to members of his Ashram at Sabarmati. Four of these, dealing with the Ashram vows of Truth, Nonviolence, Chastity and Non-possession, are given here. The remaining seven vows of the Ashram are: Control of the Palate, Non-stealing, Fearlessness, Removal of Untouchability, Bread Labour, Equality of Religions and Swadeshi. Gandhi's discourses on these also will be found in the booklet *From Yeravda Mandir* (published by the Navajivan Press, Ahmedabad).

Importance of vows

Taking vows is not a sign of weakness, but of strength. To do at any cost something that one ought to do constitutes a vow. It becomes a bulwark of strength. One, who says that he will do something 'as far as possible', betrays either his pride or his weakness. I have noticed in my own case, as well as in the case of others, that the limitation 'as far as possible' provides a fatal loophole. To do something 'as far as possible' is to succumb to the very first temptation. There is no sense in saying that one would observe truth 'as far as possible'. Even as no businessman will look at a note in which a man promises to pay a certain amount on a certain date 'as far as possible', so will God refuse to accept a promissory note drawn by one, who would observe truth 'as far as possible'.

God is the very image of the vow. God would cease to be God if He swerved from His own laws even by a hair's breadth. The sun is a great keeper of observances; hence the possibility of measuring time and publishing almanacs. All business depends upon men fulfilling their promises. Are such promises less necessary in character-building or self-realisation? We should therefore never doubt the necessity of vows for the purpose of self-purification and self-realisation.

Truth

I deal with Truth first of all, as the Satyagraha Ashram owes its very existence to the pursuit and the attempted practice of Truth.

The word *Satya* (Truth) is derived from *Sat*, which means 'being'. Nothing is or exists in reality except Truth. That is why *Sat* or Truth is perhaps the most important name of God. In fact it is more correct to say that Truth is God, than to say that God is Truth. But as we cannot do without a ruler or a general, names of God such as 'King of Kings' or 'the Almighty' are and will remain generally current. On deeper thinking, however, it will be realised, that *Sat* or *Satya* is the only correct and fully significant name for God.

And where there is truth, there also is knowledge which is true. Where there is no Truth, there can be no true knowledge. That is why the word *Chit* or knowledge is associated with the name of God. And where there is true knowledge, there is always bliss (*Ananda*). There sorrow has no place. And even as Truth is eternal, so is the bliss derived from it. Hence we know God as *Sat-chit-ananda*, One who combines in Himself Truth, Knowledge and Bliss.

Devotion to this Truth is the sole justification for our existence. All our activities should be centred in Truth. Truth should be the very breath of our life. When once this stage in the pilgrim's progress is reached, all other rules of correct living will come without effort, and obedience to them will be instinctive. But without Truth it would be impossible to observe any principles or rules in life.

Generally speaking, observation of the law of Truth is understood merely to mean that we must speak the truth. But we in the Ashram should understand the word *Satya* or Truth in a much wider sense. There should be Truth in thought, Truth in speech, and Truth in action. To the man who has realised this Truth in its fulness, nothing else remains to be known, because all knowledge is necessarily included in it. What is not included in it is not Truth, and so not true knowledge; and there can be no inward peace without true knowledge. If we once learn how to apply this never-failing test of Truth, we will at once be able to find out what is worth doing, what is worth seeing, what is worth reading.

But how is one to realise this Truth, which may be likened to the philosopher's stone or the cow of plenty? By single-minded devotion (*abhyasa*) and indifference to all other interests in life (*vairagya*) – replies the *Bhagavadgita*. In spite, however, of such devotion, what may appear as truth to one person will often appear as untruth to another person. But that need not worry the seeker. Where there is honest effort, it will be realised that what appear to be different truths are like the countless and apparently different leaves of the same tree. Does not God Himself appear to different individuals in different aspects? Yet we know that He is one. But Truth is the right designation of God. Hence there is nothing wrong in every man following Truth according to his lights. Indeed it is his duty to do so. Then if there is a mistake on the part of any one so following Truth, it will be automatically set right. For the quest of Truth involves *tapas* – self-suffering, sometimes even unto death. There can be no place in it for even a trace of self-interest. In such selfless search for Truth nobody can lose his bearings for long. Directly he takes to the wrong path he stumbles, and is thus redirected to the right path. Therefore the pursuit of Truth is true *bhakti* (devotion). It is the path that leads to God. There is no place in it for cowardice, no place for defeat. It is the talisman by which death itself becomes the portal to life eternal.

Ahimsa *or love*

We saw last week how the path of Truth is as narrow as it is straight. Even so is that of *ahimsa*. It is like balancing oneself on the edge of a sword. By concentration an acrobat can walk on a rope. But the concentration required to tread the path of Truth and *ahimsa* is far greater. The slightest inattention brings one tumbling to the ground. One can realise Truth and *ahimsa* only by ceaseless striving.

But it is impossible for us to realise perfect Truth so long as we are imprisoned in this mortal frame. We can only visualise it in our imagination. We cannot, through the instrumentality of this ephemeral body, see face to face Truth which is eternal. That is why in the last resort we must depend on faith.

It appears that the impossibility of full realisation of Truth in this mortal body led some ancient seeker after Truth to the appreciation of *ahimsa*. The question which confronted him was: 'Shall I bear with those who create difficulties for me, or shall I destroy them?' The seeker realised that he who went on destroying others did not make headway but simply stayed where he was, while the man who suffered those who created difficulties marched ahead, and at times even took the others with him. The first act of destruction taught him that the Truth which was the object of his quest was not outside himself but within. Hence the more he took to violence, the more he receded from Truth. For in fighting the imagined enemy without, he neglected the enemy within.

We punish thieves, because we think they harass us. They may leave us alone; but they will only transfer their attentions to another victim. This other victim however is also a human being, ourselves in a different form, and so we are caught in a vicious circle. The trouble from thieves continues to increase, as they think it is their business to steal. In the end we see that it is better to endure the thieves than to punish them. The forbearance may even bring them to their senses. By enduring them we realise that thieves are not different from ourselves, they are our brethren, our friends, and may not be punished. But whilst we may bear with the thieves, we may not endure the infliction. That would only induce cowardice. So we realise a further duty. Since we regard the thieves as our kith and kin, they must be made to realise the kinship. And so we must take pains to devise ways and means of winning them over. This is the path of *ahimsa*. It may entail continuous suffering and the cultivating of endless patience. Given these two conditions, the thief is bound in the end to turn away from his evil ways. Thus step by step we learn how to make friends with all the world; we realise the greatness of God – of Truth. Our peace of mind increases in spite of suffering; we become braver and more enterprising; we understand more clearly the difference between what is everlasting and what is not; we learn how to distinguish between what is our duty and what is not. Our pride melts away, and we become humble. Our wordly attachments diminish, and the evil within us diminishes from day to day.

Ahimsa is not the crude thing it has been made to appear. Not to hurt any living thing is no doubt a part of *ahimsa*. But it is its least expression. The principle of *ahimsa* is hurt by every evil thought, by undue haste, by lying, by hatred, by wishing ill to anybody. It is also violated by our holding on to what the world needs. But the world needs even what we eat day by day. In the place where we stand there are millions of micro-organisms to whom the place belongs, and who are hurt by our presence there. What should we do then? Should we commit suicide? Even that is no solution if we believe, as we do, that so long as the spirit is attached to the flesh, on every destruction of the body it weaves for itself another. The body will cease to be only when we give up all attachment to it. This freedom from all attachment is the realisation of God as Truth. Such realisation cannot be attained in a hurry. The body does not belong to us. While it lasts, we must use it as a trust handed over to our charge. Treating in this way the things of the flesh, we may one day expect to become free from the burden of the body. Realising the limitations of the flesh, we must strive day by day towards the ideal with what strength we have in us.

It is perhaps clear from the foregoing, that without *ahimsa* it is not possible to seek and find Truth. *Ahimsa* and Truth are so intertwined that it is practically impossible to disentangle and separate them. They are like the two sides of a coin, or rather of a smooth unstamped metallic disc. Who can say, which is the obverse, and which is the reverse? Nevertheless *ahimsa* is the means; Truth is the end. Means to be means must always be within our reach, and so *ahimsa* is our supreme duty. If we take care of the means, we are bound to reach the end sooner or later. When once we have grasped this point, final victory is beyond question. Whatever difficulties we encounter, whatever apparent reverses we sustain, we may not give up the quest for Truth which alone is, being God Himself.

Brahmacharya *or chastity*

The third among our observances is *brahmacharya*. As a matter of fact all observances are deducible from Truth, and are meant to subserve it. The man, who is wedded to Truth and worships Truth alone, proves unfaithful to her, if he applies his talents to anything else. How then can he minister to the senses? A man, whose activities are wholly consecrated to the realisation of Truth, which requires utter selflessness, can have no time for the selfish purpose of begetting children and running a household. Realisation of Truth through self-gratification should, after what has been said before, appear a contradiction in terms.

If we look at it from the standpoint of *ahimsa* (non-violence), we find that the fulfilment of *ahimsa* is impossible without utter selflessness. *Ahimsa* means Universal Love. If a man gives his love to one woman, or a woman to one man, what is there left for all the world besides? It simply means, 'We two first, and the devil take all the rest of them.' As a faithful wife must be prepared to sacrifice her all for the sake of her husband, and a faithful husband for the sake of his wife, it is clear that such persons cannot rise to the height of Universal Love, or look upon all mankind as kith and kin. For they have created a boundary wall round their love. The larger their family, the farther are they from Universal Love. Hence one who would obey the law of *ahimsa* cannot marry, not to speak of gratification outside the marital bond.

Then what about people who are already married? Will they never be able to realise Truth? Can they never offer up their all at the altar of humanity? There is a way out for them. They can behave as if they were not married. Those who have enjoyed this happy condition will be able to bear me out. Many have to my knowledge successfully tried the experiment. If the married couple can think of each other as brother and sister, they are freed for universal service. The very thought that all the women in the world are his sisters, mothers or daughters will at once ennoble a man and snap his chains. The husband and wife do not lose anything here, but only add to their resources and even to their family. Their love becomes free from the impurity of lust and so grows stronger. With the disappearance of this impurity, they can serve each other better, and the occasions for quarrel become fewer. There are more occasions for quarrelling where the love is selfish and bounded.

If the foregoing argument is appreciated, a consideration of the physical benefits of chastity becomes a matter of secondary importance. How foolish it is intentionally to dissipate vital energy in sensual enjoyment! It is a grave misuse to fritter away for physical gratification that which is given to man and woman for the full development of their bodily and mental powers. Such misuse is the root cause of many a disease.

Brahmacharya, like all other observances, must be observed in thought, word and deed. We are told in the *Gītā*, and experience will corroborate the statement, that the foolish man, who appears to control his body, but is nursing evil thoughts in his mind, makes a vain effort. It may be harmful to suppress the body, if the mind is at the same time allowed to go astray. Where the mind wanders, the body must follow sooner or later.

It is necessary here to appreciate a distinction. It is one thing to allow the mind to harbour impure thoughts; it is a different thing altogether if it strays among them in spite of ourselves. Victory will be ours in the end, if we non-cooperate with the mind in its evil wanderings.

Non-possession or poverty

Possession implies provision for the future. A seeker after Truth, a follower of the law of Love, cannot hold anything against tomorrow. God never stores for the morrow; He never creates more than what is strictly needed for the moment. If therefore we repose faith in His providence, we should rest assured, that He will give us every day our daily bread, meaning everything that we require. Saints and devotees, who have lived in such faith, have always derived a justification for it from their experience. Our ignorance or negligence of the Divine Law, which gives to man from day to day his daily bread and no more, has given rise to inequalities with all the miseries attendant upon them. The rich have a superfluous store of things which they do not need, and which are therefore neglected and wasted; while millions are starved to death for want of sustenance. If each retained possession only of what he needed, no one would be in want, and all would live in contentment. As it is, the rich are discontented no less than the poor. The poor man would fain become a millionaire, and the millionaire a multi-millionaire. The rich should take the initiative in dispossession with a view to a universal diffusion of the spirit of contentment. If only they keep their own property within moderate limits, the starving will be easily fed, and will learn the lesson of contentment along with the rich. Perfect fulfilment of the idea of Non-possession requires, that man should, like the birds, have no roof over his head, no clothing and no stock of food for the morrow. He will indeed need his daily bread, but it will be God's business, and not his, to provide it. Only the fewest possible, if any at all, can reach this ideal. We ordinary seekers may be repelled by the seeming impossibility. But we must keep the ideal constantly in view, and in the light thereof, critically examine our possessions, and try to reduce them. Civilisation, in the real sense of the term, consists not in the multiplication, but in the deliberate and voluntary reduction of wants. This alone promotes real happiness and contentment, and increases the capacity for service. Judging by this criterion, we find that in the Ashram we possess many things, the necessity for which cannot be proved, and we thus tempt our neighbours to thieve.

From the standpoint of pure Truth, the body too is a possession. It has been truly said, that desire for enjoyment creates bodies for the soul. When this desire vanishes, there remains no further need for the body, and man is free from the vicious cycle of births and deaths. The soul is omnipresent; why should she care to be confined within the cagelike body, or do evil and even kill for the sake of that cage? We thus arrive at the ideal of total renunciation, and learn to use the body for the purpose of service so long as it exists, so much so that service, and not bread, becomes with us the staff of life.

HINDUISM —— •♦• —— 314

4.13.6 Sanatana Dharma

I have asserted my claim to being a *Sanatani* Hindu, and yet there are things which are commonly done in the name of Hinduism, which I disregard. I have no desire to be called a *Sanatani* Hindu or any other if I am not such. It is therefore necessary for me once for all distinctly to give my meaning of *Sanatana* Hinduism. The word *Sanatana* I use in its natural sense.

I call myself a *Sanatani* Hindu, because,

1   I believe in the *Vedas*, the *Upanishads*, the *Puranas* and all that goes by the name of Hindu scriptures, and therefore in *avataras* and rebirth;
2   I believe in the *varnashrama dharma* in a sense, in my opinion, strictly *Vedic* but not in its present popular and crude sense;
3   I believe in the protection of the cow in its much larger sense than the popular;
4   I do not disbelieve in idol-worship.

The reader will note that I have purposely refrained from using the word divine origin in reference to the *Vedas* or any other scriptures. For I do not believe in the exclusive divinity of the *Vedas*. I believe the Bible, the Quran, and the Zend Avesta to be as much divinely inspired as the *Vedas*. My belief in the Hindu scriptures does not require me to accept every word and every verse as divinely inspired. Nor do I claim to have any first-hand knowledge of these wonderful books. But I do claim to know and feel the truths of the essential teaching of the scriptures. I decline to be bound by any interpretation, however learned it may be, if it is repugnant to reason or moral sense. I do most emphatically repudiate the claim (if they advance any such) of the present *Shankaracharyas* and *shastris* to give a correct interpretation of the Hindu scriptures. On the contrary I believe that our present knowledge of these books is in a most chaotic state. I believe implicitly in the Hindu aphorism, that no one truly knows the *shastras* who has not attained perfection in Innocence (*ahimsa*), Truth (*satya*) and Self-control (*brahmacharya*) and who has not renounced all acquisition or possession of wealth. I believe in the institution of *gurus*, but in this age millions must go without a *guru*, because it is a rare thing to find a combination of perfect purity and perfect learning. But one need not despair of ever knowing the truth of one's religion, because the fundamentals of Hinduism, as of every great religion, are unchangeable, and easily understood. Every Hindu believes in God and His oneness, in rebirth and salvation.

I can no more describe my feeling for Hinduism than for my own wife. She moves me as no other woman in the world can. Not that she has no faults. I dare say she has many more than I see myself. But the feeling of an indissoluble bond is there. Even so I feel for and about Hinduism with all its faults and limitations. Nothing elates me so much as the music of the *Gītā* or the *Ramayana* by Tulsidas, the only two books in Hinduism I may be said to know. When I fancied I was taking my last breath the *Gītā* was my solace. I know the vice that is going on today in all the great Hindu shrines, but I love them in spite of their unspeakable failings. There is an interest which I take in them and which I take in no other. I am a reformer through and through. But my zeal never takes me to the rejection of any of the essential things of Hinduism. I have said I do not disbelieve in idol-worship. An idol does not excite any feeling of veneration in me. But I think that idol-worship is part of human nature. We hanker after symbolism. Why should one be more composed in a church than elsewhere? Images are an aid to worship. No Hindu considers an image to be God. I do not consider idol-worship a sin.

It is clear from the foregoing, that Hinduism is not an exclusive religion. In it there is room for the worship of all the prophets of the world. It is not a missionary religion in the ordinary sense of the term. It has no doubt absorbed many tribes in its fold, but this absorption has been of an evolutionary imperceptible character. Hinduism tells every one to worship God according to his own faith or *dharma*, and so it lives at peace with all the religions.

That being my conception of Hinduism, I have never been able to reconcile myself to untouchability. I have always regarded it as an excrescence. It is true that it has been handed down to us from generations, but so are many evil practices even to this day. I should be ashamed to think that dedication of girls to virtual prostitution was a part of Hinduism. Yet it is practised by Hindus in many parts of India. I consider it positive irreligion to sacrifice goats to Kali and do not consider it a part of Hinduism. Hinduism is a growth of ages. The very name, Hinduism, was given to the religion of the people of Hindustan by foreigners. There was no doubt at one time sacrifice of animals offered in the name of religion. But it is not religion, much less is it Hindu religion. And so also it seems to me, that when cow-protection became an article of faith with our ancestors, those who persisted in eating beef were excommunicated. The civil strife must have been fierce. Social boycott was applied not only to the recalcitrants, but their sins were visited upon their children also. The practice which had probably its origin in good intentions hardened into usage, and even verses crept into our sacred books giving the practice a permanence wholly undeserved and still less justified.

Whether my theory is correct or not, untouchability is repugnant to reason and to the instinct of mercy, pity or love. A religion that establishes the worship of the cow cannot possibly countenance or warrant a cruel and inhuman boycott of human beings. And I should be content to be torn to pieces rather than disown the suppressed classes. Hindus will certainly never deserve freedom, nor get it, if they allow their noble religion to be disgraced by the retention of the taint of untouchability. And as I love Hinduism dearer than life itself, the taint has become for me an intolerable burden. Let us not deny God by denying to a fifth of our race the right of association on an equal footing.

Source: M. K. Gandhi, *Hindu Dharma* (Ahmedabad: Navajivan Publishing House, 1950). The extracts make use of pages in the following order: p. 13; p. 3; pp. 158–60; pp. 220–8; pp. 6–9.

4.14 'HINDU-NESS'

V. D. SAVARKAR

Vinayak Damodar Savarkar (1883–1966 CE) early on in life
developed a deep hostility towards Indian Muslims, as the enemies of
Hinduism, and the British as India's rulers. A fierce critic of Gandhi's policy
of non-violent opposition to British rule, Savarkar published his influential
essay on *Hindutva*, or 'Hindu-ness', in 1923. His ideas have subsequently
exercised considerable influence over those who have promoted Hinduism
as the national tradition of India over and against the claims of
Muslims and other Indian minorities.

A country, a common home, is the first important essential of stable strong nationality; and as of all countries in the world our country can hardly be surpassed by any in its capacity to afford a soil so specially fitted for the growth of a great nation; we Hindus, whose very first article of faith is the love we bear to the common Fatherland, have in that love the strongest talismanic tie that can bind close and keep a nation firm and enthuse and enable it to accomplish things greater than ever.

The second essential of *Hindutva* puts the estimate of our latent powers of national cohesion and greatness yet higher. No country in the world, with the exception of China again, is peopled by a race so homogeneous, yet so ancient and yet so strong both numerically and vitally. [. . .] Mohammedans are no race nor are the Christians. They are a religious unit, yet neither a racial nor a national one. But we Hindus, if possible, are all the three put together and live under our ancient and common roof. The numerical strength of our race is an asset that cannot be too highly prized. [. . .]

The ideal conditions, therefore, under which a nation can attain perfect solidarity and cohesion would, other things being equal, be found in the case of those people who inhabit the land they adore, the land of whose forefathers is also the land of their Gods and Angels, of Seers and Prophets; the scenes of whose history are also the scenes of their mythology.

The Hindus are about the only people who are blessed with these ideal conditions that are at the same time incentive to national solidarity, cohesion, and greatness. [. . .]

Thus the actual essentials of *Hindutva* are, as this running sketch reveals, also the ideal essentials of nationality. If we would we can build on this foundation of *Hindutva*, a future greater than what any other people on earth can dream of – greater even than our own past; provided we are able to utilize our opportunities! For let our people remember that great combinations are the order of the day. The leagues of nations, the alliances of powers, Pan-Islamism, Pan-Slavism, Pan-Ethiopism – all little beings are seeking to get themselves incorporated into greater wholes, so as to be better fitted for the struggle for existence and power. Those who are not naturally and historically blessed with numerical or geographical or racial advantages are seeking to share them with others. Woe to those who have them already as their birthright and know them not; or worse, despise them! The nations of the world are desperately trying to find a place in this or that combination for aggression: – can any one of you, Oh Hindus! whether Jain or Samāji or Sanātani or Sīkh or any other subsection, afford to cut yourselves off or fall out and destroy the ancient, the natural, and the organic combination that already exists? – a combination that is bound not by any scraps of paper nor by the ties of exigencies alone, but by the ties of blood and birth and culture? Strengthen them if you can; pull down the barriers that have survived their utility, of castes and customs, of sects and sections. What of interdining? But intermarriages between provinces and provinces, castes and castes, be encouraged where they do not exist. But where they already exist as between the Sīkhs and Sanātanies, Jains and Vaishnavas, Lingayats and Non-Lingayats – suicidal be the hand that tries to cut the nuptial tie. Let the minorities remember they would be cutting the very branch on which they stand. Strengthen every tie that binds you to the main organism, whether of blood or language or common festivals and feasts or culture love you bear to the common Motherland. Let this ancient and noble stream of Hindu blood flow from vein to vein . . . till at last the Hindu people get fused and welded into an indivisible whole, till our race gets consolidated and strong and sharp as steel . . .

Thirty crores of people, with India for their basis of operation, for their Fatherland and for their Holyland, with such a history behind them, bound together by ties of a common blood and common culture can dictate their terms to the whole world. A day will come when mankind will have to face the force.

Equally certain it is that whenever the Hindus come to hold such a position whence they could dictate terms to the whole world – those terms cannot be very different from the terms which [the] *Gītā* dictates or the Buddha lays down. A Hindu is most intensely so, when he ceases to be a Hindu; and with a Kabir claims the whole earth for a Benares . . . or with a Tukaram exclaims: 'My country? Oh brothers, the limits of the Universe – there the frontiers of my country lie.'

Source: V. D. Savarkar, *Hindutva* (1923), in S. Hay (ed.) *Sources of Indian Tradition*, vol. 2, (New York: Columbia University Press, 1988), pp. 292–5.

4.15 A MODERN HINDU PHILOSOPHER'S UNDERSTANDING OF CASTE

S. RADHAKRISHNAN

Sarvepalli Radhakrishnan (born in 1888 CE) was a Hindu philosopher who taught both in India and at the University of Oxford. A Vedantin through personal conviction, he became a prominent apologist on behalf of Hinduism. In the period following Indian Independence, he served as a diplomat and eventually became the President of India.

The system of caste insists that the law of social life should not be cold and cruel competition, but harmony and co-operation. Society is not a field of rivalry among individuals. The castes are not allowed to compete with one another. A man born in a particular group is trained to its manner, and will find it extremely hard to adjust himself to a new way. Each man is said to have his own specific nature (*svabhāva*) fitting him for his own specific function (*svadharma*), and changes of dharma or function are not encouraged. A sudden change of function when the nature is against its proper fulfilment may simply destroy the individuality of the being. We may wish to change or modify our particular mode of being, but we have not the power to effect it. Nature cannot be hurried by our desires. The four castes represent men of thought, men of action, men of feeling, and others in whom none of these is highly developed. Of course, these are the dominant and not the exclusive characters, and there are all sorts of permutations and combinations of them which constitute adulterations (*sankara*) and mixture (*miśra-jāti*). The author of the *Bhagavadgītā* believes that the divisions of caste are in accordance with each man's character and aptitude. Karma is adapted to *guṇa*, and our qualities in nature can be altered only gradually. Since we cannot determine in each individual case what the aptitudes of the individuals are, heredity and training are used to fix the calling. Though the functions were regarded as hereditary, exceptions were freely allowed. We can learn even from lowly persons. All people possess all qualities though in different degrees. The Brahmin has in him the possibilities of a warrior. The *ṛṣis* [sages] of old were agriculturists and sometimes warriors too.

The caste idea of vocation as service, with its traditions and spiritual aims, never encouraged the notion of work as a degrading servitude to be done grudgingly and purely from the economic motive. The perfecting of its specific function is the spiritual aim which each vocational group set to itself. The worker has the fulfilment of his being through and in his work. According to the *Bhagavadgītā*, one obtains perfection if one does one's duty in the proper spirit of non-attachment. The cant of the preacher who appeals to us for the deep-sea fishermen on the ground that they daily risk their lives, that other people may have fish for their breakfasts, ignores the effect of the work on the worker. They go to sea not for us and our breakfasts but for the satisfaction of their being. Our convenience is an accident of their labours. Happily the world is so arranged that each man's good turns out to be the good of others. The loss of artistic vitality has affected much of our industrial population. A building craftsman of the old days had fewer political rights, less pay and less comfort too, but he was more happy as he enjoyed his work. Our workers who enjoy votes will call him a slave simply because he did not go to the ballot-box. But his work was the expression of his life. The worker, whether a mason or a bricklayer, blacksmith or carpenter, was a member of a great co-operative group initiated into the secrets of his craft at an impressionable age. He was dominated by the impulse to create beauty. Specialization has robbed the worker of pride in craft. Work has now become business, and the worker wants to escape from it and seeks his pleasure outside in cinemas and television. While the social aspirations of the working classes for a fuller life are quite legitimate, there is unfortunately an increasing tendency to interpret welfare in terms of wealth. The claims of materialism are more insistent in the present vision of social betterment. The improvement of human nature is the true goal of all endeavour, though this certainly requires an indispensable minimum of comfort to which the worker is entitled.

We are now face to face with class conflicts. There has grown up an intense class consciousness with elements of suspicion and hatred, envy and jealousy. We are no more content to bring up our children in our own manner of life, but are insisting that all doors must be opened to those equipped with knowledge. The difficulties are due to the fact that some occupations are economically more paying, and all wish to knock at the paying doors. Democracy is so interpreted as to justify not only the very legitimate aspiration to bring about a more equitable distribution of wealth, but also the increasing tendency for a levelling down of all talent. This is not possible. There will always be men of ability who lead and direct, and others who will obey and follow. Brains and character will come to the top, and within the framework of democracy we shall have an aristocracy of direction. It is not true that all men are born equal in every way, and everyone is equally fit to govern the country or till the ground. The functional diversities of workers cannot be suppressed. Every line of development is specific and exclusive. If we wish to pursue one we shall have to turn our attention away from others. While we should remove the oppressive restrictions, dispel the ignorance of the masses, increase their self-respect, and open to them opportunities of higher life, we should not be under the illusion that we can abolish the distinctions of the genius and the fool, the able organizer and the submissive worker. Modern democracies tend to make us all mere 'human beings', but such beings exist nowhere.

India has to face in the near future the perils of industrialism. In factory labour where men are mechanized, where they have little to do with the finished product, and cannot take any pleasure in its production, work is mere labour, and it does not satisfy the soul. If such mechanical work cannot be done by machines, if men have to do it, the less of it they have to do the better for them. The more the work tends to become mechanical and monotonous, the more necessary it is that the worker should have larger leisure and a better equipment for the intelligent use of it. The standard of employment must be raised not merely in wages, but in welfare. Mechanical work should be economically more paying than even that of the artist or the statesman. For in the latter case work is its own reward. In ancient India the highest kind of work, that of preserving the treasures of spiritual knowledge, was the least paid. The Brahmin had no political power or material wealth. I think there is some justice in this arrangement, which shows greater sympathy for those whose work is soul-deadening. We have also to remember that the economic factor is not the most important in a man's life. A man's rank is not to be determined by his economic position. Gambling peers are not higher than honest artisans. The exaltation of the economic will lead to a steady degradation of character. Again, we should not forget that the individuals who constitute the nation cannot all pursue the one occupation of political leadership or military power, but will be distributed into many employments, and these will tend to create distinctive habits and sympathies. Though there may be transfers from one group to another, they are not likely to be numerous.

We are not so certain today as we were a century ago that the individualistic conception of society is the last word in social theory. The moral advantages of the spiritual view of society as an organic whole are receiving greater attention. A living community is not a loose federation of competing groups of traders and teachers, bankers and lawyers, farmers and weavers, each competing against all the rest for higher wages and better conditions. If the members of the different groups are to realize their potentialities, they must share a certain community of feeling, a sense of belonging together for good or evil. There is much to be said from this point of view for the system of caste which adheres to the organic view of society and substitutes for the criterion of economic success and expediency a rule of life which is superior to the individual's interests and desires. Service of one's fellows is a religious obligation. To repudiate it is impiety.

Source: S. Radhakrishnan, *The Hindu View of Life* (London: George Allen & Unwin, 1927), pp. 79–82.

4.16 NEW WINE, OLD SKINS: THE SANGH PARIVAR AND THE TRANSFORMATION OF 'HINDUISM'

JAMES G. LOCHTEFELD

Sangh Parivar refers to the 'family' of organizations that have developed from the Rashtriya Svayamsevak Sangh, or RSS (The National Volunteer Corps), and which have been held to have been responsible for the growth of 'political Hinduism' in twentieth-century India.

The Hindu Right has risen from virtual obscurity to become a significant force in modern India. The major agent for this has been the Rashtriya Svayamsevak Sangh (RSS) and its affiliates, particularly the Vishva Hindu Parishad (VHP). The Sangh 'family' emphasis has been empowering Hindus and affirming Hindu identity, exemplified by their struggle to construct the Ram Janam Bhumi temple in Ayodhya. Yet even though the Sangh family claims to speak for all Hindus, and characterizes its platform as 'Hindu-ness' (*Hindutva*), its goals and assumptions often diverge sharply from traditional Hindu ideas. Despite the rhetoric of reclamation, it is redefining what it 'means' to be Hindu.

Introduction

The past ten years have seen the rapid, sometimes explosive growth of Hindutva, and the equally vehement criticism of its opponents, some of whom have characterized it as a 'fascist' movement. Whether or not one agrees with Hindutva ideas and methods, its recent prominence makes it all the more important to examine and genuinely address. Labeling it 'fascism' (or any other name) may reflect the perception of these critics, and perhaps give them emotional satisfaction, but this does little to help us understand its recent success, after nearly fifty years as a marginal force in Indian life. Nor does this indicate its prospects for further success, or the ways that its influence is shaping modern Indian life and understandings of India's past.

This shaping stems directly from its affirmations on Hindu identity and religion, and has been most pronounced in two dimensions. On one hand, it has attempted to transform the term 'Hindu' into signifying political rather than religious identity, (somewhat as the U.S. religious right has appropriated 'Christian'), and explicitly equate this Hindu identity with Indian nationalism. At the same time, it has also been actively reshaping the tradition's religious forms, to cement this identity by providing new symbols, images, ceremonies, and institutions. These new forms have been carefully chosen, often delivered in highly innovative ways, and have usually been introduced using the rhetoric of reclaiming the past, to disguise how much of this identity has been newly constructed. This understanding reflects definite changes in what it means to 'be' a Hindu, and critics have charged that this rhetoric of recla- mation masks an attempt to impose an arbitrary (and artificial) systematization, hier- archy and order on the tradition. None of this has taken place in a vacuum, and in assessing these changes one must consider a variety of issues, including the Hindutva movement's increasingly international character.

Major players

The major players in the contemporary Hindutva movement are all members of the so-called Sangh 'family' (*parivār*). The 'parent' organization is the Rashtriya Svayamsevak Sangh ('National Volunteer Corps', hereafter RSS), which was founded in Nagpur in 1925. The RSS is an unabashedly elitist organization, whose self- proclaimed mission is to produce the leaders for a renascent Hindu India. It is highly autocratic, run by a single leader (the *sārsanghcālak*) whose decisions are never ques- tioned, who is appointed by the previous *sārsanghcālak*, and who normally holds this position for life.[1] RSS training stresses obedience, discipline, loyalty, and ideological formation; one observer notes that the last relies not on mastering any text, but is 'preached in a style that deliberately avoids complexities and debates, and inculcated simultaneously via a whole battery of rituals and symbols'.[2]

Since its inception the RSS has been almost exclusively an urban phenomenon, whose membership has largely been drawn from 'the salaried lower middle-class and small-scale shopkeepers . . . groups whose social and economic aspirations are under- mined by inflation, by scarcity of job opportunities, and by their relative inability to influence the political process'.[3] At the local level its greatest attraction seems to have been its ability to create a sense of community among such alienated (and often newly urbanized) people, and for many these personal relationships are their strongest tie to the organization.[4]

Throughout its history the RSS has shunned overt political activity – claiming that its mission was cultural and character-building – but has exercised considerable influence through its affiliated organizations. At present there are at least 19 such affiliates, ranging from trade and student unions to charitable and educational societies, for which the RSS provides the leadership cadre.[5] This cadre is disciplined, dedicated, spartan in lifestyle, energetic, and mobile; the hierarchical structure of the RSS also tends to promote what one writer describes as 'the social skills of the company man', who can work productively with others in varying capacities.[6]

The most important affiliates in the recent Hindutva resurgence are the Bharatiya Janata Party (BJP), a political party, and the Vishva Hindu Parishad (VHP), whose mandate has been more explicitly religious issues.[7] Both are committed to the RSS world view, but their different functions have given them different imperatives, which occasionally creates tension between them. Because it aspires to govern, the BJP strives to project an image of discipline, stability, and responsibility; it must also respond to its constituents' needs.[8] More recently, the BJP has also been constrained by court judgments limiting the party's ability to invoke religious issues for political ends, or for BJP candidates to appeal to religious loyalties during elections.[9] The threat of legal sanctions or disqualification of its candidates has forced the BJP to modify its tone considerably, as have its internal needs to be perceived as more than a single-issue party.

The VHP is not bound by any of these concerns, and can therefore take a much harder line, particularly in its disdain for the rule of law, as shown most clearly by its role in demolishing the Babri Masjid in December 1992. Whereas the BJP's most visible figures are politicians, the front men for the VHP are mainly ascetics. The VHP also has its own affiliate, the Bajrang Dal, whose primary function is to support the VHP's campaigns by supplying manpower and muscle.

In theory these are completely separate organizations – which allows them to shift responsibility to the others – but in practice their interests, actions, and even personnel coincide: leaders for both the BJP and VHP have long-standing ties with the RSS; BJP parliamentarians include officials from the Bajrang Dal and the VHP, and the VHP is the only RSS affiliate in which the RSS chief sits on the board, providing further evidence of their links.[10] They are all members of the same 'family', and as in any idealized extended family, have only the interests of the family at heart. Much of what follows will be focused on the VHP, but these interconnections make it virtually impossible to discuss any one of them in isolation. [. . .]

Hindutva *ideology*

The word *Hindutva* literally means 'Hindu-ness', the quality of being Hindu. It began with the writings of Veer Savarkar, whose central thesis was that the Hindus were a nation, despite their linguistic, social, and regional differences. Savarkar defined a Hindu as anyone regarding India as fatherland and holy land, and to this day these remain the litmus test.[11] This defines the Hindu nation on cultural criteria – as a people united by a common cultural heritage – and from the start Hindutva proponents have insisted that the word 'Hindu' refers to a cultural rather than a religious community.[12]

Hindutva is sometimes presented as a simple majoritarian argument: Hindus are 85 per cent of India's population, and therefore India is a Hindu nation, just as Great Britain is a 'Christian nation'.[13] Although no one can deny that the Hindu ethos has an unmistakable presence in Indian life, the Hindutva claim is not ultimately about numbers, but about value. It projects Hindu culture and values as India's sole cultural foundation, and the only appropriate model for national life. This explicitly rejects the 'composite culture' idea – the notion that Indian culture grew from a variety of sources – which was one of Nehru's fundamental assumptions.[14]

By seeking the lowest common denominator, Savarkar's definition can accommodate almost anyone, a decided advantage in a tradition so diverse and decentralized to render any criteria for Hindu identity problematic.[15] Critics charge that disregarding such sharp differences imposes a facade of Hindu unity on communities with nothing in common, and it is interesting that certain groups who fit these criteria, such as the Sikhs, vehemently deny that they are Hindus. This definition's lack of real substance also makes it difficult to discover meaningful connections when one gets to concrete individuals and communities. The Sangh's response to this, as we shall see, has been to cement this Hindu identity by creating new symbols and rituals that do not compete with established ones, allowing people to take on their new 'Hindu' identity without unduly disturbing their present one.

One must also look at who this definition excludes. Savarkar's definition of a Hindu is plastic enough to include everyone in a notoriously polyform tradition, but the condition that one regard India as the holy land largely excludes both Muslims and Christians. This definition equates Hindu identity and Indian nationalism, meaning that religious minorities are not only 'aliens', but because of their 'extra-territorial loyalties' (to holy lands in Arabia and Israel) they are also potential traitors.[16] [. . .]

The most potent symbol of Hindu oppression has been the Ram Janam Bhumi – first in the oft-repeated claim that Muslim invaders destroyed the original temple at Ram's birthplace, and erected the Babri Masjid in its place as a visible symbol of their conquest. This has been reinforced by various governments' efforts to protect the Babri Masjid, particularly in November 1990, when police fired upon a crowd attempting to storm and destroy it. In addition to the Ram Janam Bhumi, there have also been periodic demands for the restoration of sites in Benares and Mathura, as well as the more general call for restoring thousands of temples claimed to have been destroyed or converted into mosques.

Reasons for Hindutva success

None of this would have mattered had there not been other factors extraneous to the Sangh. The most important cause for the advent of Hindutva has been the pervasive conviction that Nehruvian socialism has been an utter failure, which even the Congress(I) has implicitly admitted by its recent economic policies.[17] Indians have an overwhelming sense that the government has failed to deliver, a sense of failure heightened by pervasive corruption, by the social and economic dislocation since Independence, by the internal instability in various regions, and by comparisons with other, newly prosperous Asian countries.

This disaffection is particularly strong in the educated urban poor, who behold the abyss between their expectations and their possibilities. In bad economic times people look for scapegoats, and those who provide them will receive a measure of support, whether or not these targets are the actual root of the problem. Like Ross Perot, the Sangh has successfully tapped this vein of popular discontent, and their well-formed world view provides people with quick and easy answers. This economic disaster has also eroded the Congress Party's political standing, allowing them to be displaced by other forces all over North India.

Yet another factor in legitimating Hindutva has been the Congress(I)'s own amoral flirtation with it for electoral gain. In her last years Indira Gandhi followed a 'soft Hinduism' strategy aimed at winning Hindu support without completely alienating Muslims, a strategy that included building informal bridges with the RSS.[18] In his quest for votes Rajiv Gandhi was even willing to adopt Hindutva rhetoric [. . .].[19]

The Sangh did not control the actions of the Congress(I) leaders, or the track record of their governments, although it has used these factors to its advantage. Yet one of the strongest factors for its steadily growing support has been the way that the Sangh Parivār, for which the VHP has been the most visible agent, has selected and manipulated images to implant, uphold, and reinforce its world view, showing a media mastery and an eye for symbols that would put most ad agencies to shame.

A look at the VHP's first successful campaign reveals the care to correlate the images presented with the target population. After the Meenakshipuram conversions, the VHP responded by crisscrossing Tamil Nadu in two vans converted into mobile temples. These so-called 'Jnana Rathams' ('Wisdom Chariots') were intended to counter caste discrimination, by allowing low-caste people to bathe the images of Murugan in the vans.[20] Murugan was an astute choice for the environment – he is an important regional deity whose six major shrines span the Tamil country, thus appealing to Tamil pride and identity.[21] The Jnana Rathams were an innovative and unusual way to bring these images directly to the people, and especially in small villages the novelty alone would ensure a ready audience. They provided an opportunity for a public denial of caste, at least in ritual matters, and the publicity successfully enhanced the VHP's public image.

This was followed by the 1983 Ekatmata Yajna ('Sacrifice for Unity'), which transposed several of these elements to an All-India level. Here too the symbols presented, the Ganges and Mother India, were carefully chosen to appeal to Hindus across the spectrum. The Ganges is the paradigmatic sacred river, to which many other Indian rivers are homologized, yet it is seldom a devotee's primary object of worship.[22] In the same way, although many people can feel loyalty to the notion of Mother India, in everyday worship she is nobody's goddess.[23] In both cases, people could easily assimilate these symbols by simply layering them over their existing loyalties, with which these symbols did not conflict.

The Yajna's focus was three caravans carrying Ganges water: one from Kathmandu to Rameshvaram, one from Ganga Sagar to Somnath, and one from Hardwar to Kanyakumari. The caravans traveled across the continent on pilgrimage routes, converging at midpoint in Nagpur, the headquarters of the RSS. Along the way the Ganges water carried by the caravans was mixed with water from local rivers, to demonstrate symbolically the country's unity. The Yajna went smoothly, in large part through massive support by RSS volunteers; it was conducted amid extensive publicity, and sales of Ganges water along the way generated considerable revenue.[24]

These are very evocative symbols, but hardly conform to traditional ritual. Rather, they are a shorthand symbolism with tremendous emotional appeal to India's television generation.[25] Each of these carefully structured campaigns has been accompanied by a media blitz, portraying these campaigns as an upwelling of Hindu unity, and a rebellion against the 'oppression' of Hindus.

Aside from using new and unconventional symbols, another break with tradition has been de-emphasizing brahmin ritual privilege, as the Jnana Rathams clearly showed. The RSS has historically condemned untouchability as a pernicious practice dividing Hindu society, and in keeping with the Sangh emphasis on publicity, the VHP has demonstrated this in highly visible places. [. . .]

Aside from creating and manipulating new symbols, the VHP has also used traditional strategies to reinforce its legitimacy and spread its message. Ascetics have been a visible part of the VHP since its inception in 1964, and as the VHP's 'front men' they have been an important presence in legitimating its claim to speak for the Hindu community. The most prominent ascetics provide the sound bites and photo opportunities that promote the Sangh's message in a national forum. At the grass-roots level its (reportedly) 25,000 ascetic members spread the Sangh's messages in their travels through village India, playing on their traditional status as teachers and authorities.

Yet despite this conspicuous presence, one could legitimately question whether ascetics have any genuine clout. Both of the VHP's General Secretaries have been RSS men, and in 1993 the 51-member Governing Council had only one *sanyāsī*, Swami Chinmayanand, who died that August.[26] Equally instructive is what sort of ascetics the VHP has managed to attract. Most of them are independents or small-time *mahants*, characterized by one source as 'a more pliable second line of the Hindu religious leadership'.[27] Many of these are ascetics without significant personal position or resources, for whom the VHP has provided both status and patronage.

Festivals have been another important element in the VHP strategy, both as a vehicle for transforming itself into a source of patronage, and as a setting to promote more explicit political goals. In doing so, they are clearly taking a cue from the RSS, whose six annual festivals coincide with festivals in the Hindu calendar, but which have been reinterpreted to serve their own ends.[28] The VHP has carefully cultivated relationships with festival organizers, which are then used to get more desirable spots for its supporters, thus transforming the VHP into a source of patronage.[29] Festivals have also been used as a theater for explicit political goals [. . .] festivals have provided the VHP with a highly visible arena in which to carry out their activities, and to publicize concerns on their larger agenda.

This paper was originally delivered at the 1993 annual meeting of the AAR/SBL in Washington, D.C. Since that time it has been revised and expanded, in the course of which I owe thanks to Dr A. M. Shah, Ivan Strenski, Lise McKean, and an anonymous reviewer.

1 The first two *sārsanghcālaks* held the position for life. The third stepped down in March 1994, citing failing health.
2 Tapan Basu (1993, p. 36 and ff.). This training is one of the features that prompts comparisons to fascism; a second is that M. S. Golwalker, the second *sārsanghcālak*, has been portrayed as an admirer of Hitler (see Yechury, 1993, p. 14). Even though the latter assertion seems credible, it does not follow that modern RSS leaders would express similar admiration, and Andersen & Damle (see 3–5) (1987, pp. 82–3) note some of the differences between the RSS and European fascism.

3 Andersen & Damle (1987, p. 248).

4 Andersen & Damle (1987, pp. 7, 248); Masud (1984, p. 18).

5 Andersen & Damle (1987, pp. 108–44).

6 Gold (1991, p. 562).

7 The Bharatiya Janata Party and Vishva Hindu Parishad can be translated respectively as 'Indian People's Party' and 'World Hindu Organization'.

8 Tarun Basu (1993, p. 4); Chhaya (1993, p. 4).

9 Agha *et al.* (1994, pp. 34, 36). In upholding the dismissal of four BJP governments after the destruction of the Babri Masjid, the Supreme Court asserted that secularism was an integral part of the Indian Constitution, and that anti-secular acts by a state government could be grounds for dismissal.

10 Andersen & Damle (1987, p. 154, note 109).

11 Andersen & Damle (1987, p. 34); Datta (1991, p. 2517) notes that Savarkar adds native land and realm for action (*karmabhūmi*), and that these four criteria were quoted by an RSS *pracārak*.

12 See, for example, Deshmukh (1990, p. 9).

13 In fact, many minorities would claim that this has already happened. Duara (1991, p. 44) notes that official government language is highly Sanskritized, which many religious minorities see as imposing Hindu culture upon them. One could also point to the televised *Ramayana* and *Mahabharata*; even if one views them for pure entertainment, their origins and messages are still Hindu.

14 It is interesting that even though Hindutva proponents consider Partition the 'rape' of the Motherland, they essentially bear out Jinnah's 'two-nation' theory – that Muslims are not secure in a Hindu majority nation, and therefore need their own country.

15 One solution has been to define Hindus by exclusion – they are Indians who are not by religion Muslims, Christians, Parsis, or Jews – and as Derrett notes (1963, p. 18) this is one of the ways Hindus have been defined according to modern Indian law. Of course, knowing who Hindus are not gives little indication who they are, and why, and the other legal definition Derrett mentions, 'being Hindu by religion', does nothing to clarify these issues.

16 For instance, see Goradia (1991, p. 7) or Sharma's interview with Ashok Singhal (11/18/90, p. 13).

17 Lourdusamy (1990, p. 126) notes that since Independence India's position in the world economy has deteriorated steadily.

18 See Thakur (1984).

19 This was a transparent attempt to attract the Hindu vote, and it backfired badly – Hindus sympathetic to the appeal were already more likely to vote for the BJP, while Muslims deserted the Congress(I) wholesale.

20 McKean (1992, p. 99).

21 See Clothey (1972).

22 For instance, the Cauvery is referred to as the 'Southern Ganges', as is the Godavari.

23 The image of Mother India is a well-known RSS symbol, see Andersen & Damle (1987, p. 77).

24 McKean (1992, pp. 107–13). Estimates on the number of pots of Ganges water sold range from 60,000 (L. McKean, personal communication) to 1.5 million (Sonalkar, 1984); at ten rupees per pot this would have raised between 600,000 to 15 million rupees.

25 Tapan Basu (1993, pp. 62–3). In doing so they have not been shy about breaking established traditions, such as selling Ganges water.

26 Tapan Basu (1993, p. 63). Chinmayanand was one of the founding members of the VHP, which may have accounted for his presence. I do not know whether more *sanyāsīs* have been named to the Governing Council since then.

27 Staff Writer (1994).

28 Gold (1991, p. 548). For instance, the Dussehra festival emphasizes not the victory of Ram

over Ravana, but a 'martial tone, with . . . military exercises and the worship of weapons associated with Shivaji'.
29 McKean (1992, p. 100).

Bibliography

Agha, Z. *et al.*, 'Groping for direction', *India Today* 6/30/94 (1994), pp. 34–6.

Andersen, W. K. & Damle, S., *The Brotherhood In Saffron*. New Delhi, Vistaar Publications 1987.

Basu, Tapan, *et al.*, *Khaki Shorts and Saffron Flags*. New Delhi, Orient Longman Limited 1993.

Basu, Tarun, 'A 3-year surge to national status', *India Abroad* 4/23/93 (1993), p. 4.

Chhaya, Mayank, 'BJP softens its strident image', *India Abroad* 8/6/93 (1993), p. 4.

Clothey, F. 'Pilgrimage centers in the Tamil cultus of Murukan', *JAAR* 40 (1972), pp. 79–95.

Datta, P., 'VHP's Ram at Ayodhya', *Economic And Political Weekly* 11/2/91 (1991), pp. 2517–26.

Derrett, J. D. M., *Introduction To Modern Hindu Law*. Bombay, Indian Branch, Oxford University Press 1963.

Deshmukh, N., 'Secularism – a fresh look', *Organiser* 12/2/90 (1990), pp. 9–10.

Duora, P., 'The new politics of Hinduism', *Wilson Quarterly* Summer (1991), pp. 42–50.

Gold, Daniel, 'Organized Hinduisms: from Vedic truth to Hindu nation', in *Fundamentalisms Observed*, ed. Martin Marty and R. Scott Appleby. Chicago, University of Chicago Press, 1991, pp. 531–93.

Goradia, P., 'Focus on extra-territorial loyalty', *Organiser* 2/10/91 (1991), p. 70.

Lourdusamy, S., 'Religious fundamentalism as political weapon', *Journal of Dharma* 15 (1990), pp. 125–34.

McKean, L., 'Towards a politics of spirituality: Hindu religious organizations and Indian Nationalism', Ph.D. Dissertation. University of Sydney 1992.

Sharma, M., 'Free India's worst brutalities perpetrated in Ayodhya on Nov. 2', *Organiser* 11/18/90 (1990), pp. 13–14.

Sonalkar, S., 'In search of a Hindu identity', *The Illustrated Weekly of India* 1/8/84 (1984).

Staff Writer, 'Top court holds off on Ayodhya', *India Abroad* (1994), p. 4.

Thakur, J., 'Mrs Gandhi's Hindu connection', *The Illustrated Weekly of India* (1984), pp. 32–5.

Yechury, S., *What Is This Hindu Rashtra?* Madras, Frontline Publications 1993.

Source: James G. Lochtefeld, 'New wine, old skins', *Religion*, 26(2) (April 1996): 101–7, 113–15, 116–17.

PART FIVE

— •◆• —

BUDDHISM

INTRODUCTION

———— •◆• ————

Siddhartha Gautama, the Buddha, or 'Awakened One', was raised within the religious environment of northern India. Reflecting on his experience, he became determined to seek his own path to enlightenment. His testing of ways of indulgence and asceticism led him to the 'Middle Way', which he eventually decided to teach to others. This Middle Way, with the Four Noble Truths and the Noble Eightfold Path at its core, is the raft that the Buddha has offered his followers to enable them to cross the stormy seas of existence. According to Buddhist theory, Siddhartha was not the first or only Buddha, but he is of unique significance because he was born within a historical timespan that embraces the present age and thus his teaching remains accessible. These 'Awakened Ones', who realise the same unchanging truths about the nature of existence and the human condition, are seen but rarely. The legacy of their teaching (the *dharma*) becomes corrupted or is lost with the passing of the ages until revived by the coming of another Buddha.

The purpose of the Middle Way is to bring the aspirant to enlightenment or awakening and, from its earliest days, Buddhism regarded the monastic community as the ideal setting for this purpose. Although nuns were known in early Buddhism, throughout the greater part of Buddhist history, the monastic community has been made up of men. The Buddhist community (*sangha*) thus comprises both a monastic *sangha* and a lay *sangha*. The former take on more religious responsibilities, including teaching and guiding the laity, while the latter, who are not prevented from pursuing spiritual goals, also provide material support for the monks. The Buddha, the teaching and the community are referred to as the 'three jewels' of Buddhism.

As Buddhism spread beyond India, early differences in understanding the *dharma* became more pronounced and were compounded by the assimilation of regional cultural and religious characteristics. It is customary today to distinguish between Southern, Northern and Eastern forms of Buddhism. Southern Buddhism, dominant in south and south-east Asia, practises Theravāda Buddhism. Northern and Eastern Buddhism follow varieties of Mahayana Buddhism, and are to be found respectively in the Himalayan region and in east Asia. The underlying distinction between Theravāda and Mahayana Buddhism is rooted in early debates about the Buddha's teaching, the significance of the Buddha, and the extent to which lay people could participate in the quest for enlightenment.

Like the other religions covered in this volume, over the last century or so Buddhism has become established in countries where previously it had no foothold, for example, in the United States and Europe. It has also been embroiled in the political struggles that have taken place in parts of Asia where it has long been a major presence, and it has been subjected to persecution in China, Tibet and elsewhere. These bitter conflicts have prompted reflection on Buddhist attitudes to non-violence and political and social activism. Its appeal in materially developed and secular countries of the West has also led Buddhists to examine what is central to Buddhism as distinct from its different cultural forms.

The readings have been selected to reflect the richness of Buddhism, as well as to give an indication of its doctrinal heritage. They begin with extracts from the textual canons of the Theravāda and Mahayana traditions. The next group of readings indicates the nature and diversity of Buddhist practices. Finally there is a selection of writings about recent and contemporary Buddhist concerns, including the transfer of Buddhism to the West and the role of social action.

FROM THE SUTTAS (DISCOURSES) AND VINAYA (DISCIPLINE) OF THE THERAVĀDA TRADITION

— ◆ ◆ ◆ —

5.1 THE BUDDHA

5.1.1 The great renunciation

Monks. I was delicately nurtured, exceeding delicately nurtured, delicately nurtured beyond measure. For instance, in my father's house lotus-pools were made thus: one of blue lotuses, one of red, another of white lotuses, just for my benefit. No sandal-wood powder did I use that was not from Kāsi: of Kāsi cloth was my turban made: of Kāsi cloth was my jacket, my tunic and my cloak. By night and day a white canopy was held over me, lest cold or heat, dust or chaff or dew, should touch me. Moreover, monks. I had three palaces: one for winter, one for summer, and one for the rainy season. In the four months of the rains I was waited on by min-strels, women all of them. I came not down from my palace in those months. Again, whereas in other men's homes broken rice together with sour gruel is given as food to slave-servants, in my father's home they were given rice, meat and milk-rice for their food.

To me, monks, thus blest with much prosperity, thus nurtured with exceeding delicacy, this thought occurred: Surely one of the uneducated manyfolk, though himself subject to old age and decay, not having passed beyond old age and decay, when he sees another broken down with age, is troubled, ashamed, disgusted, forgetful that he himself is such an one. Now I too am subject to old age and decay, not having passed beyond old age and decay. Were I to see another broken down with old age, I might be troubled, ashamed and disgusted. That would not be seemly in me. Thus, monks, as I considered the matter, all pride in my youth deserted me.

Again, monks, I thought: One of the uneducated manyfolk, though himself subject to disease, not having passed beyond disease, when he sees another person diseased, is troubled, ashamed and disgusted, forgetful that he himself is such an one. Now I too am subject to disease. I have not passed beyond disease. Were I to see another diseased, I might be troubled, ashamed, disgusted. That would not be seemly in me. Thus, monks, as I considered the matter, all pride in my health deserted me.

Again, monks, I thought: One of the uneducated manyfolk . . . when he sees another person subject to death . . . is disgusted and ashamed, forgetful that he himself is such an one. Now I too am subject to death. I have not passed beyond death. Were I to see another subject to death, I might be troubled. . . . That would not be seemly in me. Thus, monks, as I considered the matter, all pride in my life deserted me.

Source: F. L. Woodward (trans.) *The Aṅguttara Nikāya* in *Gradual Sayings Vol. I* (Oxford: Pali Text Society, 1932), pp. 128–129.

5.1.2 The Buddha's enlightenment

I, by severe austerity, do not reach states of further-men, the excellent knowledge and vision befitting the ariyans. Could there be another way to awakening?'

This, Aggivessana, occurred to me: 'I know that while my father, the Sakyan, was ploughing, and I was sitting in the cool shade of a rose-apple tree, aloof from pleasures of the senses, aloof from unskilled states of mind, entering on the first meditation, which is accompanied by initial thought and discursive thought, is born of aloofness, and is rapturous and joyful, and while abiding therein, I thought: 'Now could this be a way to awakening?' Then, following on my mindfulness, Aggivessana, there was the consciousness: This is itself the Way to awakening. This occurred to me, Aggivessana: 'Now, am I afraid of that happiness which is happiness apart from sense-pleasures, apart from unskilled states of mind?' This occurred to me, Aggivessana: 'I am not afraid of that happiness which is happiness apart from sense-pleasures, apart from unskilled states of mind.'

This occurred to me, Aggivessana: 'Now it is not easy to reach that happiness by thus subjecting the body to extreme emaciation. Suppose I were to take material nourishment – boiled rice and sour milk?' So I, Aggivessana, took material nourishment – boiled rice and sour milk. Now at that time, Aggivessana, five monks were attending me and (they thought): 'When the recluse[1] Gotama wins *dhamma* he will announce it to us.' But when I, Aggivessana, took material nourishment – boiled rice and sour milk – then these five monks turned on me in disgust, saying: 'The recluse Gotama lives in abundance, he is wavering in his striving, he has reverted to a life of abundance.'

But when I, Aggivessana, had taken some material nourishment, having picked up strength, aloof from pleasures of the senses, aloof from unskilled states of mind, I entered on and abided in the first meditation which is accompanied by initial thought and discursive thought, is born of aloofness, and is rapturous and joyful. But yet, Aggivessana, the pleasurable feeling, arising in me, persisted without impinging on my mind. By allaying initial thought and discursive thought, with the mind subjectively tranquillised and fixed on one point, I entered on and abided in the second meditation which is devoid of initial and discursive thought, is born of concentration, and is rapturous and joyful. But yet, Aggivessana, the pleasurable feeling, arising in me, persisted, without impinging on my mind. By the fading out of rapture I dwelt with equanimity, attentive and clearly conscious, and I experienced in my person that joy of which the ariyans say: 'Joyful lives he who has equanimity and is mindful,' and I entered on and abided in the third meditation. But yet, Aggivessana, the pleasurable feeling, arising in me, persisted without impinging on my mind. By getting rid of joy and by getting rid of anguish, by the going down of former pleasures and sorrows, I entered into and abided in the fourth meditation which has neither anguish nor joy and which is entirely purified by equanimity and mindfulness. But yet, Aggivessana, the pleasurable feeling, arising in me, persisted without impinging on my mind.

With the mind composed thus, quite purified, quite clarified, without blemish, without defilement, grown soft and workable, fixed, immovable, I directed my mind to the knowledge and recollection of former habitations.[2] Thus do I remember divers former habitations in all their modes and details. This, Aggivessana, was the first knowledge attained by me in the first watch of the night; ignorance was dispelled, knowledge arose, darkness was dispelled, light arose, even as I abided diligent, ardent, self-resolute. But yet, Aggivessana, the pleasurable feeling, arising in me, persisted without impinging on my mind.

With the mind composed thus, quite purified, quite clarified, without blemish, without defilement, grown soft and workable, fixed, immovable, I directed my mind to the knowledge of the passing hence and arising of beings. . . . Thus with the purified *deva*-vision surpassing that of men, do I see beings as they pass hence, as they arise,[3] I comprehend that beings are mean, excellent, fair, foul, in a good bourn, in a bad bourn according to the consequences of their deeds. This, Aggivessana, was the second knowledge attained by me in the middle watch of the night; ignorance was dispelled, knowledge arose, darkness was dispelled, light arose, even as I abided diligent, ardent, self-resolute. But yet, Aggivessana, the pleasurable feeling, arising in me, persisted without impinging on my mind.

With the mind composed thus, quite purified, quite clarified, without blemish, without defilement, grown soft and workable, fixed, immovable, I directed my mind to the knowledge of the destruction of the cankers. . . . When I knew thus, saw thus, my mind was freed from the canker of sense-pleasures and my mind was freed from the canker of becoming and my mind was freed from the canker of ignorance. In freedom the knowledge came to be that I was freed, and I comprehended: Destroyed is birth, brought to a close is the Brahma-faring, done is what was to be done, there is no more of being such or such. This, Aggivessana, was the third knowledge attained by me in the third watch of the night; ignorance was dispelled, knowledge arose . . . even as I abided . . . self-resolute. But yet, Aggivessana, the pleasurable feeling, arising in me, persisted without impinging on my mind.

---

1 Renunciate.
2 Former lives.
3 I.e. death and rebirth according to Karma.

Source: I. B. Horner (trans.) *Mahāsaccakasutta* in *The Middle Length Sayings Vol. I* (Oxford: The Pali Text Society, 1967), pp. 301–303.

5.1.3 The Buddha hesitates to teach the profound Dhamma

Then as the Lord was meditating in seclusion a reasoning arose in his mind thus: 'This *dhamma*, won to by me, is deep, difficult to see, difficult to understand, peaceful, excellent, beyond dialectic, subtle, intelligible to the learned. But this is a creation delighting in sensual pleasure, delighted by sensual pleasure, rejoicing in sensual pleasure. So that for a creation delighting in sensual pleasure, delighted by sensual pleasure, rejoicing in sensual pleasure, this were a matter difficult to see, that is to say causal uprising by way of cause. This too were a matter very difficult to see that is to say the calming of all the habitual tendencies, the renunciation of all attachment, the destruction of craving, dispassion, stopping, nirvana. And so if I were to teach *dhamma* and others were not to understand me, this would be a weariness to me, this would be a vexation to me.'

And further, these verses not heard before in the past occurred spontaneously to the Lord:

> 'This that through many toils I've won –
> Enough! Why should I make it known?
> By folk with lust and hate consumed
> This *dhamma* is not understood.
> Leading on against the stream,
> Subtle, deep, difficult to see, delicate,
> Unseen 'twill be by passion's slaves
> Cloaked in the murk of ignorance.'

In such wise, as the Lord pondered, his mind inclined to little effort and not to teaching *dhamma*. Then it occurred to Brahmā Sahampati, knowing with his mind the reasoning in the Lord's mind: 'Alas, the world is lost, alas, the world is destroyed, inasmuch as the mind of the Truth-finder, the perfected one, the fully awakened one, inclines to little effort and not to teaching *dhamma*.'

Then as a strong man might stretch forth his bent arm or might bend back his outstretched arm, even so did Brahmā Sahampati, vanishing from the Brahma-world, become manifest before the Lord.

Then Brahmā Sahampati, having arranged his upper robe over one shoulder, having stooped his right knee to the ground, having saluted the Lord with joined palms, spoke thus to the Lord: 'Lord, let the Lord teach *dhamma*, let the Well-farer teach *dhamma*; there are beings with little dust in their eyes who, not hearing *dhamma*, are decaying, (but if) they are learners of *dhamma*, they will grow.'

Thus spoke Brahmā Sahampati; having said this, he further spoke thus:

> 'There has appeared in Magadha before thee
> An unclean *dhamma* by impure minds devised.
> Open this door of deathlessness, let them hear
> *Dhamma* awakened to by the stainless one.
> As on a crag on crest of mountain standing
> A man might watch the people far below,
> E'en so do thou, O Wisdom fair, ascending,
> O Seer of all, the terraced heights of truth,
> Look down, from grief released, upon the peoples
> Sunken in grief, oppressed with birth and age.
> Arise, thou hero! Conqueror in the battle!
> Thou freed from debt! Man of the caravan!
> Walk the world over, let the Blessed One
> Teach *dhamma*. They who learn will grow.'

When he had spoken thus, the Lord spoke thus to Brahmā Sahampati: 'Brahmā, it occurred to me: 'This *dhamma* penetrated by me is deep . . . that would be a vexation to me.' And further, Brahmā, these verses not heard before in the past occurred spontaneously to me: 'This that through many toils I've won . . . cloaked in the murk of ignorance.' In such wise, Brahmā, as I pondered, my mind inclined to little effort and not to teaching *dhamma*.'

Then a second time did Brahmā Sahampati speak thus to the Lord: 'Lord, let the Lord teach *dhamma* . . . if they are learners of *dhamma*, they will grow.' Then a second time did the Lord speak thus to Brahmā Sahampati: 'But, Brahmā, it occurred to me: . . . my mind inclined to little effort and not to teaching *dhamma*.'

Then a third time did Brahmā Sahampati speak thus to the Lord: 'Lord, let the Lord teach *dhamma* . . . if they are learners of *dhamma*, they will grow.' Then the Lord, having understood Brahmā's entreaty and, out of compassion for beings, surveyed the world with the eye of an awakened one. As the Lord was surveying the world with the eye of an awakened one, he saw beings with little dust in their eyes, with much dust in their eyes, with acute faculties, with dull faculties, of good dispositions, of bad dispositions, docile, indocile, few seeing fear in sins and the worlds beyond.

Even as in a pond of blue lotuses or in a pond of red lotuses or in a pond of white lotuses, a few blue or red or white lotuses are born in the water, grow in the water, do not rise above the water but thrive while altogether immersed; a few blue or red or white lotuses are born in the water, grow in the water and reach to the surface of the water; a few blue or red or white lotuses are born in the water, grow in the water, and stand up rising out of the water, undefiled by the water.

Even so, did the Lord, surveying the world with the eye of an awakened one, see beings with little dust in their eyes, with much dust in their eyes, with acute faculties, with dull faculties, of good dispositions, of bad dispositions, docile, indocile, few seeing fear in sins and the worlds beyond. Seeing Brahmā Sahampati, he addressed him with verses:

> 'Open for those who hear are the doors of deathlessness;
>   let them renounce their faith.
> Thinking of useless fatigue, I have not preached, Brahmā, the
>   sublime and excellent *dhamma* to men.'

Then Brahmā Sahampati, thinking: 'The opportunity was made by me for the Lord to teach *dhamma*,' greeting the Lord, keeping his right side towards him, vanished then and there.

Source: I. B. Horner (trans,) *Mahāvagga I* in *The Book of the Discipline Vol. IV* (London: Luzac, 1971), pp. 7–10.

5.1.4 From the Buddha's last days

2.23. And during the Rains the Lord was attacked by a severe sickness, with sharp pains as if he were about to die. But he endured all this mindfully, clearly aware and without complaining. He thought: 'It is not fitting that I should attain final Nibbāna without addressing my followers and taking leave of the order of monks. I must hold this disease in check by energy and apply myself to the force of life.' He did so, and the disease abated.

2.24. Then the Lord, having recovered from his sickness, as soon as he felt better, went outside and sat on a prepared seat in front of his dwelling. Then the Venerable Ānanda came to him, saluted him, sat down to one side and said: 'Lord, I have seen the Lord in comfort, and I have seen the Lord's patient enduring. And, Lord, my body was like a drunkard's. I lost my bearings and things were unclear to me because of the Lord's sickness. The only thing that was some comfort to me was the thought: "The Lord will not attain final Nibbāna until he had made some statement about the order of monks."'

2.25. 'But, Ānanda, what does the order of monks expect of me? I have taught the Dhamma, Ānanda, making no "inner" and "outer": the Tathāgata has no "teacher's fist" in respect of doctrines. If there is anyone who thinks: "I shall take charge of the order", or "The order should refer to me", let him make some statement about the order, but the Tathāgata does not think in such terms. So why should the Tathāgata make a statement about the order?

'Ānanda, I am now old, worn out, venerable, one who has traversed life's path, I have reached the term of life, which is eighty. Just as an old cart is made to go by being held together with straps, so the Tathāgata's body is kept going by being strapped up. It is only when the Tathāgata withdraws his attention from outward signs, and by the cessation of certain feelings, enters into the signless concentration of mind, that his body knows comfort.

2.26. 'Therefore, Ānanda, you should live as islands unto yourselves, being your own refuge, with no one else as your refuge, with the Dhamma as an island, with the Dhamma as your refuge, with no other refuge. And how does a monk live as an island unto himself,. . . with no other refuge? Here, Ānanda, a monk abides contemplating the body as body, earnestly, clearly aware, mindful and having put away all hankering and fretting for the world, and likewise with regard to feelings, mind and mind-objects,. . . with no other refuge. And those who now in my time or afterwards live thus, they will become the highest, if they are desirous of learning.' . . .

5.7. 'Lord, formerly monks who had spent the Rains in various places used to come to see the Tathāgata, and we used to welcome them so that such well-trained monks might see you and pay their respects. But with the Lord's passing, we shall no longer have a chance to do this.'

5.8. 'Ānanda, there are four places the sight of which should arouse emotion in the faithful. Which are they? "Here the Tathāgata was born" is the first. "Here the Tathāgata attained supreme enlightenment" is the second. "Here the Tathāgata set in motion the Wheel of Dhamma" is the third. "Here the Tathāgata attained the Nibbāna-element without remainder" is the fourth. And, Ānanda, the faithful monks and nuns, male and female lay-followers will visit those places. And any who die while making the pilgrimage to these shrines with a devout heart will, at the breaking-up of the body after death, be reborn in a heavenly world.

5.9. 'Lord, how should we act towards women?' 'Do not see them, Ānanda.' 'But if we see them, how should we behave, Lord?' 'Do not speak to them, Ānanda.' 'But if they speak to us, Lord, how should we behave?' 'Practise mindfulness, Ānanda.'

5.10. 'Lord, what shall we do with the Tathāgata's remains?' 'Do not worry yourselves about the funeral arrangements, Ānanda. You should strive for the highest goal, devote yourselves to the highest goal, and dwell with your minds tirelessly, zealously devoted to the highest goal. There are wise Khattiyas, Brahmins and householders who are devoted to the Tathāgata: they will take care of the funeral.'. . .

6.1. And the Lord said to Ānanda: 'Ānanda, it may be that you will think: "The Teacher's instruction has ceased, now we have no teacher!" It should not be seen like this, Ānanda, for what I have taught and explained to you as Dhamma and discipline will, at my passing, be your teacher.

6.2. 'And whereas the monks are in the habit of addressing one another as "friend", this custom is to be abrogated after my passing. Senior monks shall address more junior monks by their name, their clan or as "friend", whereas more junior monks are to address their seniors either as "Lord" or as "Venerable Sir".

6.3. 'If they wish, the order may abolish the minor rules after my passing.

6.4. 'After my passing, the monk Channa is to receive the Brahma-penalty.' 'But, Lord, what is the Brahma-penalty?' 'Whatever the monk Channa wants or says, he is not to be spoken to, admonished or instructed by the monks.'

6.5. Then the Lord addressed the monks, saying: 'It may be, monks, that some monk has doubts or uncertainty about the Buddha, the Dhamma, the Sangha, or about the path or the practice. Ask, monks! Do not afterwards feel remorse, thinking: "The Teacher was there before us, and we failed to ask the Lord face to face!"' At these words the monks were silent. The Lord repeated his words a second and a third time, and still the monks were silent. Then the Lord said: 'Perhaps, monks, you do not ask out of respect for the Teacher. Then, monks, let one friend tell it to another.' But still they were silent.

6.6. And the Venerable Ānanda said: 'It is wonderful, Lord, it is marvellous! I clearly perceive that in this assembly there is not one monk who has doubts or uncertainty . . .' 'You, Ānanda, speak from faith. But the Tathāgata knows that in this assembly there is not one monk who has doubts or uncertainty about the Buddha, the Dhamma or the Sangha or about the path or the practice. Ānanda, the least one of these five hundred monks is a Stream-Winner, incapable of falling into states of woe, certain of Nibbāna.'

6.7. Then the Lord said to the monks: 'Now, monks, I declare to you: all conditioned things are of a nature to decay – strive on untiringly.' These were the Tathāgata's last words.

6.8. Then the Lord entered the first jhāna. And leaving that he entered the second, the third, the fourth jhāna. Then leaving the fourth jhāna he entered the Sphere of Infinite Space, then the Sphere of Infinite Consciousness, then the Sphere of No-Thingness, then the Sphere of Neither-Perception-Nor-Non-Perception, and leaving that he attained the Cessation of Feeling and Perception.

Then the Venerable Ānanda said to the Venerable Anuruddha: 'Venerable Anuruddha, the Lord has passed away.' 'No, friend Ānanda, the Lord has not passed away, he has attained the Cessation of Feeling and Perception.'

6.9. Then the Lord, leaving the attainment of the Cessation of Feeling and Perception, entered the Sphere of Neither-Perception-Nor-Non-Perception, from that he entered the Sphere of No-Thingness, the Sphere of Infinite Consciousness, the Sphere of Infinite Space. From the Sphere of Infinite Space he entered the fourth jhāna, from there the third, the second and the first jhāna. Leaving the first jhāna, he entered the second, the third, the fourth jhāna. And, leaving the fourth jhāna, the Lord finally passed away.

6.10. And at the Blessed Lord's final passing there was a great earthquake, terrible and hair-raising, accompanied by thunder. And Brahmā Sahampati uttered this verse:

> 'All beings in the world, all bodies must break up:
> Even the Teacher, peerless in the human world,
> The mighty Lord and perfect Buddha's passed away.'

And Sakka, ruler of the devas, uttered this verse:

> 'Impermanent are compounded things, prone to rise and fall,
> Having risen, they're destroyed, their passing truest bliss.'

And the Venerable Anuruddha uttered this verse:

> 'No breathing in and out – just with steadfast heart
> The Sage who's free from lust has passed away to peace.

With mind unshaken he endured all pains:
By Nibbāna the Illumined's mind is freed.'

And the Venerable Ānanda uttered this verse:

'Terrible was the quaking, men's hair stood on end,
When the all-accomplished Buddha passed away.'

And those monks who had not yet overcome their passions wept and tore their hair, raising their arms, throwing themselves down and twisting and turning, crying: 'All too soon the Blessed Lord has passed away, all too soon the Well-Farer has passed away, all too soon the Eye of the World has disappeared!' But those monks who were free from craving endured mindfully and clearly aware, saying: 'All compounded things are impermanent – what is the use of this?'

6.11. Then the Venerable Anuruddha said: 'Friends, enough of your weeping and wailing! Has not the Lord already told you that all things that are pleasant and delightful are changeable, subject to separation and to becoming other? So why all this, friends? Whatever is born, become, compounded is subject to decay, it cannot be that it does not decay. The devas, friends, are grumbling.'

Source: M. Walshe (trans.) *Mahāparinibbāna Sutta* in *The Long Discourses of the Buddha (Dīgha Nikāya)* (Boston: Wisdom, 1995), pp. 244–245, 263–264, 269–272.

5.1.5 The Buddha in a previous life

Birth-Story of the Sandy Desert

Once upon a time when Brahmadatta was reigning in Benares in the kingdom of Kāsi, the Bodhisatta took re-linking[1] in a caravan leader's family. When he was grown up he used to tour about trading with five hundred carts. On one occasion he entered on a waterless desert sixty leagues in extent. In this desert the sand was so fine that if taken up in a closed fist it would not remain in the hand, and from sunrise onwards was so hot, like a heap of burning embers, one could not tread on it. In consequence, those entering on (this desert) used to take firewood, water, oil, husked rice and so on in their carts and, travelling only by night, would arrange the carts in a circle at dawn and spread an awning overhead. In the morning they would get ready the food they would need and then spend the day sitting in the shade. When the sun had set and they had eaten their evening meal and the ground had become cool, they harnessed their carts and travelled on. Such travelling was like voyaging on the sea; a desert-pilot as he was called, would help the caravan across by his knowledge of the stars.

At that time and in this manner this caravan-leader was also travelling over this desert. When he had gone for fifty-nine leagues he thought: 'Now, after one more night we shall get out of this waterless desert', and having eaten the evening meal and used up all the firewood and water, he had the carts harnessed and went on his way. The pilot, having had his mattress spread in the leading cart, then looked at the stars in the sky and saying: 'Drive on from here', lay down and fell asleep, exhausted from having gone without sleep for a long time. So he did not realise that the bullocks had turned round and were taking the very way they had come by. All night the bullocks went on. The pilot woke at dawn and observing the constellations, shouted out: 'Turn the carts round, turn them round.' By the time they had turned them round and were forming them into line, the sun was rising. The men said: 'This is the exact place where we made camp yesterday, but our firewood and water are exhausted. We are done for now.' And when they had unyoked the carts and arranged them in a circle and spread the awning overhead, each man lay down despairing under his own cart.

The Bodhisatta thought: 'If I slacken in energy they will all perish', and roaming about in the cool of the early morning he saw a clump of coarse grass. He reasoned that it must be growing there because there was running water underneath, and on having had a spade brought he had that ground dug up. When they had dug to the depth of sixty cubits, the spade struck against a rock and was broken. And even as it struck they all gave up hope. But the Bodhisatta thought the water must be beneath the rock, so he got down on it and, standing there, bent down and applied his ear, listening for a sound. Catching the sound of water flowing beneath, he came up and said to his young attendant: 'My lad, if you don't do your utmost we shall all perish, so don't give in but take this iron hammer, get down into the hole and strike this rock a (hard) blow.' Obedient to his bidding, and not giving in although the others had done so, he went down into the hole and struck the rock such a (hard) blow that, splitting down the middle, it crashed down and came to rest in the stream it had been damming. Up surged the gushing water as high as the trunk of a palm-tree. When everyone had drunk of the water, they bathed. Then they chopped up their spare axles and yokes and so on, cooked conjey and rice, and when they had eaten their meal they fed the bullocks. After the sun had set they hoisted a flag near the water-hole and went on to their desired destination.

There they traded merchandise for twice and four times its value. Then, taking the proceeds they had acquired, each man went back to his own home. Remaining there for the rest of their lives, they fared on according to kamma. The Bodhisatta too, having done good: (given) gifts and so on, fared on even according to kamma.

. . . Identifying the Birth-Story, the Teacher said: 'At that time this monk who relaxed in energy (and about whom the monks had been telling the Buddha) was the young attendant who, not relaxing in energy, split the rock and was the giver of water to the multitude. The rest of the (caravan-) company are now the Buddha-company; and I myself was the chief caravan-leader.'

---

1 Rebirth.

Source: I. B. Horner (trans.) 'Energy' in *Ten Jātaka Stories*, (Bangkok: Mahāmakut Rājavidyālaya Press, 1974), pp. 37–41.

5.2 THE DHAMMA

5.2.1 The four-noble truths

Then the Lord addressed the group of five monks, saying: 'These two (dead) ends, monks, should not be followed by one who has gone forth. Which two? That which is, among sense-pleasures, addiction to attractive sense-pleasures, low, of the villager, of the average man, unariyan, not connected with the goal; and that which is addiction to self-torment, ill, unariyan, not connected with the goal. Now, monks, without adopting either of these two (dead) ends, there is a middle course, fully awakened to by the Truthfinder[1], making for vision, making for knowledge, which conduces to calming, to super-knowledge, to awakening, to nirvana.

'And what, monks, is this middle course fully awakened to by the Truthfinder, making for vision, making for knowledge, which conduces to calming, to super-knowledge, [of the four truths] to awakening, to nirvana? It is this ariyan eightfold Way itself, that is to say: right view, right thought, right speech, right action, right mode of living, right endeavour, right mindfulness, right concentration. This, monks, is the middle course, fully awakened to by the Truthfinder, making for vision, making for knowledge, which conduces to calming, to super-knowledge, to awakening, to nirvana.

'And this, monks, is the ariyan truth of ill. Birth is ill, and old age is ill and disease is ill and dying is ill, association with what is not dear is ill, separation from what is dear is ill, not getting what one wants is ill – in short the five groups[2] of grasping are ill.

'And this, monks, is the ariyan truth of the uprising of ill: that which is craving connected with again-becoming, accompanied by delight and passion, finding delight in this and that, that is to say: craving for sense-pleasures, craving for becoming, craving for de-becoming.

'And this, monks, is the ariyan truth of the stopping of ill: the utter and passionless stopping of that very craving, its renunciation, surrender, release, the lack of pleasure in it.

'And this, monks, is the ariyan truth of the course leading to the stopping of ill: this aryan eightfold Way itself, that is to say: right view . . . right concentration.

On thinking, 'This is the ariyan truth of ill', among things not heard before by me, monks, vision arose, knowledge arose, wisdom arose, higher knowledge arose, light arose. On thinking, 'Now that which is the ariyan truth of ill must be completely known' . . . 'Now that which is the ariyan truth of ill is completely known', among things not heard before by me, monks, vision arose, knowledge arose, wisdom arose, higher knowledge arose, light arose.

'On thinking, "This is the ariyan truth of the uprising of ill" . . . light arose. On thinking, 'Now that which is this ariyan truth of the uprising of ill must be given up' . . . ". . . is given up" . . . light arose.

'On thinking, "This is the ariyan truth of the stopping of ill" . . . light arose. On thinking, "Now that which is this ariyan truth of the stopping of ill must be realised" . . . ". . . is realised" . . . light arose.

'On thinking, "This is the ariyan truth of the course going to the stopping of ill" ... light arose. On thinking, "Now that which is this ariyan truth of the course leading to the stopping of ill must be made to become" ... ". . . is made to become" ... light arose.

'And so long, monks, the vision of knowledge of these four ariyan truths, with the three sections and twelve modes as they really are, was not well purified by me, so long was I, monks, not thoroughly awakened with the supreme full awakening as to the world with its *devas*, with its Māras, with its Brahmās, with its recluses and brahmans, its creatures with *devas* and men. This I knew.

'But when, monks, the vision of knowledge of these four ariyan truths, with the three sections and twelve modes as they really are, was well purified by me, then was I, monks, thoroughly awakened with the supreme full awakening as to the world ... with its recluses and brahmans, its creatures with *devas* and men. This I knew.

'Moreover, the vision of knowledge arose in me: "Freedom of mind is for me unshakeable, this the last birth, there is not now again-becoming." Thus spoke the Lord; delighted, the group of five monks rejoiced in the Lord's utterance. Moreover, while this discourse was being uttered, *dhamma*-vision, dustless, stainless, arose to the venerable Koṇḍañña that 'whatever is of the nature to uprise, all that is of the nature to stop.'

And when the Lord had rolled the *dhamma*-wheel, the earth *devas* made this sound heard: 'The supreme *dhamma*-wheel rolled thus by the Lord at Benares in the deer-park at Isipatana cannot be rolled back by a recluse or brahmin or *deva* or by Māra or by Brahmā or by anyone in the world.' Having heard the sound of the earth *devas*, the *devas* of the Four Great Kings made this sound heard ... the Thirty *devas* ... Yama's *devas* ... the Happy *devas* ... the *devas* who delight in creation ... the *devas* who delight in the creation of others ... the *devas* of Brahmā's retinue made this sound heard: 'The supreme *dhamma*-wheel rolled thus by the Lord at Benares in the deer-park at Isipatana cannot be rolled back by a recluse or brahmin or *deva* or by Māra or by Brahmā or by anyone in the world.'

In this wise in that moment, in that second, in that instant, the sound reached as far as the Brahma-world, and the ten thousandfold world-system trembled, quaked, shook violently and a radiance, splendid, measureless, surpassing the *devas*' own glory, was manifest in the world. Then the Lord uttered this solemn utterance: 'Indeed, Koṇḍañña has understood, indeed, Koṇḍañña has understood.' Thus it was that Aññāta Koṇḍañña became the venerable Koṇḍañña's name.

Then the venerable Aññāta Koṇḍañña, having seen *dhamma*, attained *dhamma*, known *dhamma*, plunged into *dhamma*, having crossed over doubt, having put away uncertainty, having attained without another's help to full confidence in the teacher's instruction, spoke thus to the Lord: 'May I, Lord, receive the going forth in the Lord's presence, may I receive ordination?'

---

1 Tathāgatha
2 i.e. objects of grasping

Source: I. B. Horner (trans.) *Mahāvagga I* in *The Book of the Discipline Vol. IV* (London: Luzac, 1971), pp. 15–16.

5.2.2 The senses are burning

Then the Lord, having stayed at Uruvelā for as long as he found suiting, set out on tour for Gayā Head together with a large Order of monks, with all those same thousand monks who had formerly been matted hair ascetics. Then the Lord stayed near Gayā at Gayā Head together with the thousand monks.

And there the Lord addressed the monks, saying: 'Monks, everything is burning. And what, monks, is everything that is burning? The eye, monks, is burning, material shapes[1] are burning, consciousness through the eye is burning, impingement on the eye is burning, in other words the feeling which arises from impingement on the eye, be it pleasant or painful or neither painful nor pleasant, that too is burning. With what is it burning? I say it is burning with the fire of passion, with the fire of hatred, with the fire of stupidity[2]; it is burning because of birth, ageing, dying, because of grief, sorrow, suffering, lamentation and despair.

'The ear is burning, sounds are burning . . . the nose is burning, odours are burning . . . the tongue is burning, tastes are burning . . . the body is burning, tangible objects are burning . . . the mind is burning, mental states are burning, consciousness through the mind is burning, impingement on the mind is burning, in other words the feeling which raises through impingement on the mind, be it pleasant or painful or neither painful nor pleasant, that too is burning. With what is it burning? I say it is burning with the fire of passion, with the fire of hatred, with the fire of stupidity; it is burning because of birth, ageing, dying, because of grief, sorrow, suffering, lamentation and despair.

'Seeing this, monks, the instructed disciple of the ariyans disregards[3] the eye and he disregards material shapes and he disregards consciousness through the eye and he disregards impingement on the eye, in other words the feeling which arises from impingement on the eye, be it pleasant or painful or neither painful nor pleasant, that too he disregards. And he disregards the ear and he disregards sounds, and he disregards the nose and he disregards odours, and he disregards the tongue and he disregards tastes, and he disregards the body and he disregards tangible objects, and he disregards the mind and he disregards mental states and he disregards consciousness through the mind and he disregards impingement on the mind, in other words the feeling that arises from impingement on the mind, be it pleasant or painful or neither painful nor pleasant, that too he disregards; disregarding, he is dispassionate; through dispassion he is freed; in freedom the knowledge comes to be, 'I am freed', and he comprehends: Destroyed is birth, lived is the Brahma-faring, done is what was to be done, there is no more of being such or such.'

And while this discourse was being uttered, the minds of these thousand monks were freed from the cankers without grasping.

---

1 I.e. Visual forms.
2 I.e. Delusion.
3 I.e. Turns away from; lets go of.

Source: I. B. Horner (trans.) *Mahāvagga I* in *The Book of the Discipline Vol. IV* (London: Luzac, 1971), pp. 45,46.

5.2.3 Questions unconnected with the goal

Thus have I heard: At one time the Lord was staying near Sāvatthī in the Jeta Grove in Anāthapiṇḍika's monastery. Then a reasoning of mind arose to the venerable Māluṅkyāputta as he was meditating in solitary seclusion, thus: 'Those (speculative) views that are not explained, set aside and ignored by the Lord: The world is eternal, the world is not eternal, the world is an ending thing, the world is not an ending thing; the life-principle is the same as the body, the life-principle is one thing, the body another; the Tathāgata is after dying, the Tathāgata is not after dying, the Tathāgata both is and is not after dying, the Tathāgata neither is nor is not after dying – the Lord does not explain these to me. That the Lord does not explain these to me does not please me, does not satisfy me, so I, having approached the Lord, will question him on the matter. If the Lord will explain to me either that the world is eternal or that the world is not eternal or that the world is an ending thing . . . or that the Tathāgata neither is nor is not after dying, then will I fare the Brahma-faring under the Lord. But if the Lord will not explain to me either that the world is eternal or that the world is not eternal . . . or that the Tathāgata neither is nor is not after dying, then will I, disavowing the training, revert to secular life.'

Then the venerable Māluṅkyāputta, emerging from solitary meditation towards evening, approached the Lord; having approached, having greeted the Lord, he sat down at a respectful distance. As he was sitting down at a respectful distance, the venerable Māluṅkyāputta spoke thus to the Lord: 'Now, revered sir, as I was meditating in solitary seclusion, a reasoning of mind arose to me thus: "Those (speculative) views that are not explained, set aside, ignored by the Lord: The world is eternal . . . or that the Tathāgata neither is nor is not after dying, then will I, disavowing the training, revert to secular life." If the Lord knows that the world is eternal, let the Lord explain to me that the world is eternal. If the Lord knows that the world is not eternal, let the Lord explain to me that the world is not eternal. If the Lord does not know whether the world is eternal or whether the world is not eternal, then, not knowing, not seeing, this would be honest, namely to say: "I do not know, I do not see." If the Lord knows that the world is an ending thing . . . (*repeated in the case of each view as above*) . . . . . . If the Lord does not know whether the Tathāgata neither is nor is not after dying, then, not knowing, not seeing, this would be honest, namely to say: "I do not know, I do not see."'

'But did I ever speak thus to you, Māluṅkyāputta: "Come you, Māluṅkyāputta, fare the Brahma-faring under me and I will explain to you either that the world is eternal or that the world is not eternal . . . or that the Tathāgata neither is nor is not after dying?"'

'No, revered sir.'

'Or did you speak thus to me: "I, revered sir, will fare the Brahma-faring under the Lord if the Lord will explain to me either that the world is eternal or that the world is not eternal . . . or that the Tathāgata neither is nor is not after dying"?'

'No, revered sir.'

'So it is agreed, Māluṅkyāputta, that neither did I say: 'Come you, Māluṅkyāputta, fare the Brahma-faring under me and I will explain to you either that the world is eternal or that the world is not eternal ... or that the Tathāgata neither is nor is not after dying'; and that neither did you say: 'I, revered sir, will fare the Brahma-faring under the Lord if the Lord will explain to me either that the world is eternal ... or that the Tathāgata neither is nor is not after dying.' This being so, foolish man, who are you that you are disavowing?

Whoever, Māluṅkyāputta, should speak thus: 'I will not fare the Brahma-faring under the Lord until the Lord explains to me whether the world is eternal or whether the world is not eternal ... or whether the Tathāgata neither is nor is not after dying' – this man might pass away, Māluṅkyāputta, or ever this was explained to him by the Tathāgata. Māluṅkyāputta, it is as if a man were pierced by an arrow that was thickly smeared with poison and his friends and relations, his kith and kin, were to procure a physician and surgeon. He might speak thus: 'I will not draw out this arrow until I know of the man who pierced me whether he is a noble or brahman or merchant or worker.' He might speak thus: 'I will not draw out this arrow until I know the name and clan of the man who pierced me.' He might speak thus: 'I will not draw out this arrow until I know of the man who pierced me whether he is tall or short or middling in height.' He might speak thus: 'I will not draw out this arrow until I know of the man who pierced me whether he is black or deep brown or golden skinned.' He might speak thus: 'I will not draw out this arrow until I know of the man who pierced me to what village or market town or town he belongs.' He might speak thus: 'I will not draw out this arrow until I know of the bow from which I was pierced whether it was a spring-bow or a cross-bow.' He might speak thus: 'I will not draw out this arrow until I know of the bow-string from which I was pierced whether it was of swallow-wort or of reed or sinew or hemp or a tree.' He might speak thus: 'I will not draw out this arrow until I know of the shaft by which I was pierced whether it was of reeds of this kind or that.' He might speak thus: 'I will not draw out this arrow until I know of the shaft from which I was pierced what kind of feathers it had: whether those of a vulture or heron or hawk or peacock or some other bird.' He might speak thus: 'I will not draw out this arrow until I know of the shaft from which I was pierced with what kind of sinews it was uncased: whether those of a cow or buffalo or deer or monkey.' He might speak thus: 'I will not draw out this arrow until I know of the arrow by which I was pierced whether it was an (ordinary) arrow or some other kind of arrow.' Māluṅkyāputta, this man might pass away or ever this was known to him. In the same way, Māluṅkyāputta, whoever should speak thus: 'I will not fare the Brahma-faring under the Lord until the Lord explains to me either that the world is eternal or that the world is not eternal ... or that the Tathāgata neither is nor is not after dying,' this man might pass away, Māluṅkyāputta, or ever it was explained to him by the Tathāgata.

The living of the Brahma-faring, Māluṅkyāputta, could not be said to depend on the view that the world is eternal. Nor could the living of the Brahma-faring, Māluṅkyāputta, be said to depend on the view that the world is not eternal. Whether there is the view that the world is eternal or whether there is the view that the world is not eternal, there *is* birth, there is ageing, there is dying, there are grief, sorrow, suffering, lamentation and despair, the suppression of which I lay down here and now. (*The same is repeated for each of the other speculative views: that the world is an ending thing, not an ending thing; that the life-principle and the body are the same and that they are different; that after dying the Tathāgata is, is not, both is and is not, neither is nor is not*) . . . The living of the Brahma-faring, Māluṅkyāputta, could not be said to depend on the view that the Tathāgata both is and is not after dying. The living of the Brahma-faring, Māluṅkyāputta, could not be said to depend on the view that the Tathāgata neither is nor is not after dying. Whether there is the view that the Tathāgata both is and is not after dying, or whether, Māluṅkyāputta, there is the view that the Tathāgata neither is nor is not after dying, there *is* birth, there is ageing, there is dying, there are grief, sorrow, suffering, lamentation and despair, the suppression of which I lay down here and now.

Wherefore, Māluṅkyāputta, understand as not explained what has not been explained by me, and understand as explained what has been explained by me. And what, Māluṅkyāputta, has not been explained by me? That the world is eternal has not been explained by me, Māluṅkyāputta; that the world is not eternal . . . that the world is an ending thing . . . that the world is not an ending thing . . . that the life-principle and the body are the same . . . that the life-principle is one thing and the body another thing . . . that after dying the Tathāgata is . . . is not . . . both is and is not . . . neither is nor is not has not been explained by me, Māluṅkyāputta. And why, Māluṅkyāputta, has this not been explained by me? It is because it is not connected with the goal, is not fundamental to the Brahma-faring, and does not conduce to turning away from, nor to dispassion, stopping, calming, super-knowledge, awakening nor to nibbāna. Therefore it has not been explained by me, Māluṅkyāputta. And what has been explained by me, Māluṅkyāputta? 'This is anguish' has been explained by me, Māluṅkyāputta. 'This is the arising of anguish' has been explained by me. 'This is the stopping of anguish' has been explained by me. 'This is the course leading to the stopping of anguish' has been explained by me. And why, Māluṅkyāputta, has this been explained by me? It is because it is connected with the goal, is fundamental to the Brahma-faring, and conduces to turning away from, to dispassion, stopping, calming, super-knowledge, awakening and nibbāna. Therefore it has been explained by me. Wherefore, Māluṅkyāputta, understand as not explained what has not been explained by me, and understand as explained what has been explained by me.'

Thus spoke the Lord. Delighted, the venerable Māluṅkyāputta rejoiced in what the Lord had said.

Source: I. B. Horner (trans.) *Cuḷa- Māluṅkyāsutta* in *The Middle Length Sayings Vol. II* (Oxford: Pali Text Society, 1989), pp. 97–101.

5.2.4 Testing the teachings

Thus have I heard: On a certain occasion the Exalted One, while going his rounds among the Kosalans with a great company of monks, came to Kesaputta, a district of the Kosalans.

Now the Kālāmas of Kesaputta heard it said that Gotama the recluse, the Sakyans' son who went forth as a wanderer from the Sakyan clan, had reached Kesaputta.

And this good report was noised abroad about Gotama, that Exalted One, thus: He it is, the Exalted One, Arahant, a Fully Enlightened One, perfect in knowledge and practice, and so forth. . . . It were indeed a good thing to get sight of such arahants!

So the Kālāmas of Kesaputta came to see the Exalted One. . . . Then as they thus sat the Kālāmas of Kesaputta said this to the Exalted One:

'Sir, certain recluses and brāhmins come to Kesaputta. As to their own view, they proclaim and expound it in full: but as to the view of others, they abuse it, revile it, depreciate and cripple[1] it. Moreover, sir, other recluses and brāhmins, on coming to Kesaputta, do likewise. When we listen to them, sir, we have doubt and wavering as to which of these worthies is speaking truth and which speaks falsehood.'

'Yes, Kālāmas, you may well doubt, you may well waver. In a doubtful matter wavering does arise.

Now look you, Kālāmas. Be ye not misled by report or tradition or hearsay. Be not misled by proficiency in the collections,[2] nor by mere logic or inference, nor after considering reasons, nor after reflection on and approval of some theory, nor because it fits becoming,[3] nor out of respect for a recluse (who holds it). But, Kālāmas, when you know for yourselves: These things are unprofitable, these things are blameworthy, these things are censured by the intelligent; these things, when performed and undertaken, conduce to loss and sorrow, – then indeed do ye reject them, Kālāmas.

Now what think ye, Kālāmas? When greed arises within a man, does it arise to his profit or to his loss?'

'To his loss, sir.'

'Now, Kālāmas, does not this man, thus become greedy, being overcome by greed and losing control of his mind, – does he not kill a living creature, take what is not given, go after another's wife, tell lies and lead another into such a state as causes his loss and sorrow for a long time?'

'He does, sir.' . . .

'So then, Kālāmas, as to my words to you just now: "Be ye not misled by report or tradition or hearsay. Be not misled by proficiency in the collections, nor by mere logic or inference, nor after considering reasons, nor after reflection on and approval of some theory, nor because it fits becoming, nor out of respect for a recluse (who holds it). But, Kālāmas, when you know for yourselves: These things are unprofitable, these things are blameworthy, these things are censured by the intelligent, these things, when performed and undertaken, conduce to loss and sorrow, – then indeed do ye reject them," such was my reason for uttering those words.

Come now, Kālāmas, be ye not . . . so misled. But if at any time ye know of yourselves: These things are profitable, they are blameless, they are praised by the intelligent: these things, when performed and undertaken, conduce to profit and happiness, – then, Kālāmas, do ye, having undertaken them, abide therein.

1 Renunciate.
2 Knowledge of religious texts.
3 seems that it ough to be true.

Source: F. L. Woodward (trans.) '*Kālāma Sutta*' in *Gradual Sayings Vol I* (Oxford: Pali Text Society, 1989) pp. 170–173.

5.2.5 A teaching about Nirvana (Nibbana)

Next was the brahmin student Kappa:

1 'Sir', he said, 'there are people stuck midstream in the terror and the fear of the rush of the river of being, and death and decay overwhelm them. For their sakes, Sir, tell me where to find an island, tell me where there is solid ground beyond the reach of all this pain.'

2 'Kappa', said the Master, 'for the sake of those people stuck in the middle of the river of being, overwhelmed by death and decay, I will tell you where to find solid ground.

3 There is an island, an island which you cannot go beyond. It is a place of nothingness, a place of non-possession and of non-attachment. It is the total end of death and decay, and this is why I call it Nibbāna [the extinguished, the cool].

4 There are people who, in mindfulness, have realized this and are completely cooled here and now. They do not become slaves working for Māra, for Death; they cannot fall into his power.'

Source: H. Saddhatissa, *Kappa's Question* in *The Sutta-Nipāta* (London: Curzon, 1985), p. 126.

5.2.6 King Milinda's questions

Then King Milinda approached the venerable Nāgasena; having approached, he exchanged greetings with the venerable Nāgasena; and, having exchanged greetings of friendliness and courtesy, he sat down at a respectful distance. And the venerable Nāgasena greeted him in return so that he gladdened the heart of King Milinda. Then King Milinda spoke thus to the venerable Nāgasena:

'How is the revered one known? What is your name, revered sir?'

'Sire, I am known as Nāgasena; fellow Brahma-farers address me, sire, as Nāgasena. But though (my) parents gave (me) the name of Nāgasena or Sūrasena or Vīrasena or Sīhasena, yet it is but a denotation, appellation, designation, a current usage, for Nāgasena is only a name since no person is got at here.'

Then King Milinda spoke thus: 'Good sirs, let the five hundred Bactrian Greeks and the eighty thousand monks hear me: This Nāgasena speaks thus: "Since no person is got at here." Now, is it suitable to approve of that?' And King Milinda spoke thus to the venerable Nāgasena:

'If, revered Nāgasena, the person is not got at, who then is it that gives you the requisites of robe-material, almsfood, lodgings and medicines for the sick, who is it

that makes use of them; who is that guards moral habit, practises (mental) development, realizes the Ways, the fruits, nibbāna; who is it that kills a living thing, takes
what has not been given, goes wrongly amid the sense-pleasures, speaks lyingly, drinks
toddy; and who commits the fivefold kamma (the fruit of which comes with) no
delay? Therefore there is not skill, there is not unskill, there is not one that does or
makes another do deeds that are skilled or unskilled, there is no fruit or ripening
of deeds well or ill done. If, revered Nāgasena, someone killed you there would
be no onslaught on creatures for him. Also, revered Nāgasena, you have no teacher,
no preceptor, no ordination. If you say: 'Fellow Brahma-farers address me, sire, as
Nāgasena,' what here is Nāgasena? Is it, revered sir, that the hairs of the head are
Nāgasena?'

'O no, sire.'

'That the hairs of the body are Nāgasena?'

'O no, sire.'

'That the nails . . . the teeth, the skin, the flesh, the sinews, the bones, the marrow,
the kidneys, the heart, the liver, the membranes, the spleen, the lungs, the intestines,
the mesentery, the stomach, the excrement, the bile, the phlegm, the pus, the blood,
the sweat, the fat, the tears, the serum, the saliva, the mucus, the synovic fluid, the
urine, or the brain in the head are (any of them) Nāgasena?'

'O no, sire.'

'Is Nāgasena material shape, revered sir?'

'O no, sire.'

'Is Nāgasena feeling . . . perception . . . the habitual tendencies? Is Nāgasena
consciousness?'

'O no, sire.'

'But then, revered sir, is Nāgasena material shape and feeling and perception and
habitual tendencies and consciousness?'

'O no, sire.'

'But then, revered sir, is there Nāgasena apart from material shape, feeling, perception, the habitual tendencies and consciousness?'

'O no, sire.'

'Though I, revered sir, am asking you repeatedly, I do not see this Nāgasena.
Nāgasena is only a sound, revered sir. For who here is Nāgasena? You, revered sir,
are speaking an untruth, a lying word. There is no Nāgasena.'

Then the venerable Nāgasena spoke thus to King Milinda: 'You, sire, are a noble
delicately nurtured, exceedingly delicately nurtured. If you, sire, go on foot at noon-
time on the scorching ground and hot sand, trampling on sharp grit and pebbles
and sand, your feet hurt you, your body wearies, your thought is impaired, and tactile
consciousness arises accompanied by anguish. Now, did you come on foot or in a
conveyance?'

'I, revered sir, did not come on foot, I came in a chariot.'

'If you, sire, came by chariot, show me the chariot. Is the pole the chariot, sire?'

'O no, revered sir.'

'Is the axle the chariot?'

'O no, revered sir.'

'Are the wheels the chariot?'

'O no, revered sir.'

'Is the body of the chariot the chariot . . . is the flag-staff of the chariot the chariot . . . is the yoke the chariot . . . are the reins the chariot . . . is the goad the chariot?'

'O no, revered sir.'

'But then, sire, is the chariot the pole, the axle, the wheels, the body of the chariot, the flag-staff of the chariot, the yoke, the reins, the goad?'

'O no, revered sir.'

'But then, sire, is there a chariot apart from the pole, the axle, the wheels, the body of the chariot, the flag-staff of the chariot, the yoke, the reins, the goad?'

'O no, revered sir.'

'Though I, sire, am asking you repeatedly, I do not see the chariot. Chariot is only a sound, sire. For what here is the chariot? You, sire, are speaking an untruth, a lying word. There is no chariot. You, sire, are the chief rājah in the whole of India. Of whom are you afraid that you speak a lie? Let the five hundred worthy Bactrian Greeks and the eighty thousand monks listen to me: This King Milinda speaks thus: 'I have come by chariot.' But on being told: 'If you, sire, have come by chariot, show me the chariot,' he does not produce the chariot. Is it suitable to approve of that?'

When this had been said, the five hundred Bactrian Greeks, applauding the venerable Nāgasena, spoke thus to King Milinda: 'Now do you, sire, speak if you can.' Then King Milinda spoke thus to the venerable Nāgasena:

'I, revered Nāgasena, am not telling a lie, for it is because of the pole, because of the axle, the wheels, the body of a chariot, the flag-staff of a chariot, the yoke, the reins, and because of the goad that 'chariot' exists as a denotation, appellation, designation, as a current usage, as a name.'

'It is well; you, sire, understand a chariot. Even so is it for me, sire, because of the hair of the head and because of the hair of the body . . . . . . and because of the brain in the head and because of material shape and feeling and perception and the habitual tendencies and consciousness that 'Nāgasena' exists as a denotation, appellation, designation, as a current usage, merely as a name. But according to the highest meaning the person is not got at here. This, sire, was spoken by the nun Vajirā face to face with the Lord:

> Just as when the parts are rightly set
> The word 'chariot' is spoken,
> So when there are the *khandhā*
> It is the convention to say 'being'.'

'It is wonderful, revered Nāgasena, it is marvellous, revered Nāgasena. The explanations of the questions that were asked are very brilliant. If the Buddha were still here he would applaud. It is good, it is good, Nāgasena. The explanations of the questions that were asked are very brilliant.

Source: I. B. Horner (trans.) *Milinda's Questions*, (Oxford: Pali Text Society 1990), pp. 34–38.

5.2.7 Extracts from the *Dhammapada*

1. Mental phenomena are preceded by mind, have mind as their leader, are made by mind. If one acts or speaks with an evil mind, from that sorrow follows him, as the wheel follows him, as the wheel follows the foot of the ox.

2. Mental phenomena are preceded by mind, have mind as their leader, are made by mind. If one acts or speaks with a pure mind, from that happiness follows him, like a shadow not going away.

3. 'He abused me, he struck me, he overcame me, he robbed me'. Of those who wrap themselves up in it hatred is not quenched.

4. 'He abused me, he struck me, he overcame me, he robbed me'. Of those who do not wrap themselves up in it hatred is quenched.

5. For not by hatred are hatreds ever quenched here, but they are quenched by non-hatred. This is the ancient rule.

21. Carefulness is the place of the death-free; carelessness is the place of death. The careful do not die; the careless are as though (already) dead.

23. Meditating, persevering, constantly making a firm effort, those wise ones attain nibbāna, supreme rest from exertion.

24. Of one who exerts himself, is mindful, does pure deeds, acts considerately, is restrained, lives according to the law, is careful, the fame increases.

25. By exertion, by carefulness, by restraint and self-control, a wise man would make an island, which a flood does not overwhelm.

26. Fools, stupid people, apply themselves to carelessness; but a wise man guards his carefulness as his best treasure.

96. Of him properly released by knowledge, calm, of such a kind, the mind is calm, the voice is calm and also the deed.

100. If there were a thousand utterances made up of meaningless words, better is one word of meaning, which hearing one becomes calm.

103. If a man were to conquer in battle a thousand times a thousand men, but conquer one, himself, he indeed is the best conqueror in battle.

129. All tremble at violence; all fear death. Comparing (others) with oneself, one should not kill or cause to kill.

130. All tremble at violence; to all life is dear. Comparing (others) with oneself, one should not kill or cause to kill.

131. Whoever injures with violence creatures desiring happiness, seeking his own happiness he does not gain happiness when he has passed away.

132. Whoever does not injure with violence creatures desiring happiness, seeking his own happiness he gains happiness when he has passed away.

165. By the self alone is evil done; by the self is one defiled. By the self is evil not done; by the self alone is one purified. Purity and impurity concern the individual. One man may not purify another.

183. The avoidance of all evil; the undertaking of good; the cleansing of one's mind; this is the teaching of the awakened ones.

222. One who indeed could control his anger when it arises, like a chariot gone astray, him I call a charioteer. The other people are merely rein-holders.

223. One should conquer anger by non-anger; one should conquer bad by good; one should conquer miserliness by giving, and one speaking falsehood by truth.

276. You must show energy. The tathāgatas are (only) teachers. Those who have entered (on the path), meditative, will be released from Māra's fetter.

Source: K. R. Norman. *The Word of the Doctrine.* (Oxford: Pali Text Society, 1997), pp. 1, 4, 14, 16, 20, 24, 28, 34, 40.

5.3 THE SANGHA

5.3.1 Control of admission to the monastic Sangha

Now at that time ordained monks were to be seen who were afflicted by leprosy and boils and eczema and consumption and epilepsy. They told this matter to the Lord. He said:

'I allow you, monks, when one is being ordained to ask him about the things which are stumbling blocks for him. And thus, monks should he be asked:

Have you diseases like this: leprosy, boils, eczema, consumption, epilepsy?

(*There was a danger of infection where monks were living together.*)

Are you a human being?

(*Stories were told of non-humans who tried to enter the Sangha by taking human form.*)

Are you a man?

(*These are the admission rules for monks; nuns followed a different set of rules.*)

Are you a freeman?

(*Slaves needed to be released by their masters before they could enter the order.*)

Are you without debts?

(*The Sangha was not designed as a haven for debtors.*)

Are you not in the royal service?

(*It was important that military and political stability be maintained and that rulers should have no complaint against the Sangha*)

Have you your parents consent?

(*Monks were encouraged to show courtesy to their families when entering the Sangha.*)

Are you full twenty tears of age?

(*Novices were admitted to the Sangha from age 7 or 8 but 20 was the normal age at which full-ordination was given.*)

Are you complete as to bowls and robes?

(*Monks, their families or supporters had to supply these requisites.*)

What is your name?

(*It was necessary to know the identity of new monks although it was common practice for an ordination name to be given.*)

What is the name of your preceptor?'

(A monk's preceptor or teacher, was responsible for ensuring that he had been correctly prepared.)

Source: I. B. Horner (trans.) *Mahāvagga I* in *Book of Discipline Vol. IV* (London: Luzac, 1971), p. 120.

5.3.2 Training precepts for novices

Then it occurred to the novices: 'Now, how many rules for training are there for us and in which we are to train?' They told this matter to the Lord. He said:

'Monks, I allow ten rules for training for novices and novices to train in these: restraint from onslaught on creatures, restraint from taking what is not given, restraint from unchastity,[1] restraint from lying, restraint from the occasion of sloth (induced by) fermented liquor, spirits and strong drink, restraint from eating at the wrong time, restraint from seeing shows of dancing, singing and music, restraint from the occasion of using garlands, scents, unguents and wearing finery, restraint from using high beds, large beds, restraint from accepting gold and silver. I allow, monks, these ten rules for training for novices and novices to train in these.'

---

1 i.e. complete sexual abstinence

Source: I. B. Horner (trans.) *Mahāvagga 1* in *The Book of the Discipline Vol.IV* (London: Luzac, 1971), p. 105–106.

5.3.3 The monastic rules entailing defeat

1. Whatever monk should indulge in sexual intercourse is one who is defeated, he is no longer in communion.'

2. 'Whatever monk should take by means of theft what has not been given to him, in such manner of taking as kings, catching a thief in the act of stealing, would flog him or imprison him or banish him, saying: 'You are a robber, you are foolish, you are wrong, you are a thief,' – even so a monk, taking what is not given him, is also one who is defeated, he is not in communion.'

3. 'Whatever monk should intentionally deprive a human being of life or should look about so as to be his knife-bringer, or should praise the beauty of death, or should incite (anyone) to death, saying, 'Hullo there, my man, of what use to you is this evil, difficult life? Death is better for you than life,' or who should deliberately and purposefully in various ways praise the beauty of death or should incite (anyone) to death: he also is one who is defeated, he is not in communion.'

4. Whatever monk should boast, with reference to himself of a state of further-men, sufficient ariyan knowledge and insight, though not knowing it fully, and saying: 'This I know, this I see,' then if later on, he, being pressed or not being pressed, fallen, should

desire to be purified, and should say: 'Your reverence, I said that I know what I do not know, see what I do not see, I spoke idly, falsely, vainly,' apart from the undue estimate of himself, he also is one who is defeated, he is not in communion.'

Source: I. B. Horner (trans.) *The Book of the Discipline Vol. I Suttavibhanga.* (London: Luzac, 1970), pp. 38, 72, 125–126, 159.

5.3.4 The founding of the nuns order and the eight important rules

At one time the Awakened One, the Lord, was staying among the Sakyans at Kapilavatthu in the Banyan monastery. Then the Gotamid, Pajāpatī the Great, approached the Lord; having approached, having greeted the Lord, she stood at a respectful distance. As she was standing at a respectful distance, the Gotamid, Pajāpatī the Great, spoke thus to the Lord:

'Lord, it were well that women should obtain the going forth from home into homelessness in this *dhamma* and discipline proclaimed by the Truth-finder.'

'Be careful, Gotami, of the going forth of women from home into homelessness in this *dhamma* and discipline proclaimed by the Truth-finder.' And a second time. . . . And a third time did the Gotamid, Pajāpatī the Great speak thus to the Lord: 'Lord, it were well. . . .'

'Be careful, Gotami, of the going forth of women from home into homelessness in this *dhamma* and discipline proclaimed by the Truth-finder.'

Then the Gotamid, Pajāpatī the Great, thinking: 'The Lord does not allow women to go forth from home into homelessness in the *dhamma* and discipline proclaimed by the Truth-finder,' afflicted, grieved, with a tearful face and crying, having greeted the Lord, departed keeping her right side towards him.

Then the Lord having stayed at Kapilavatthu for as long as he found suiting, set out on tour for Vesālī. Gradually, walking on tour, he arrived as Vesālī. The Lord stayed there in Vesālī in the Great Grove in the Gabled Hall. Then the Gotamid, Pajāpatī the Great, having had her hair cut off, having donned saffron robes, set out for Vesālī with several Sakyan women, and in due course approached Vesālī, the Great Grove, the Gabled Hall. Then the Gotamid, Pajāpatī the Great, her feet swollen, her limbs covered with dust, with tearful face, and crying, stood outside the porch of the gateway.

The venerable Ānanda saw the Gotamid, Pajāpatī the Great, standing outside the porch of the gateway, her feet swollen, her limbs covered with dust, with tearful face and crying; seeing her, he spoke thus to the Gotamid, Pajāpatī the Great:

'Why are you, Gotami, standing . . . and crying?'

'It is because, honoured Ānanda, the Lord does not allow the going forth of women from home into homelessness in the *dhamma* and discipline proclaimed by the Truth-finder.'

'Well now, Gotami, stay here a moment, until I have asked the Lord for the going forth of women from home into homelessness in the *dhamma* and discipline proclaimed by the Truth-finder.'

Then the venerable Ānanda approached the Lord; having approached, having greeted the Lord, he sat down at a respectful distance. As he was sitting down at a respectful distance, the venerable Ānanda spoke thus to the Lord:

'Lord, this Gotamid, Pajāpatī the Great, is standing outside the porch of the gateway, her feet swollen, her limbs covered with dust, with tearful face and crying, and saying that the Lord does not allow the going forth of women from home into homelessness in the *dhamma* and discipline proclaimed by the Truth-finder. It were well, Lord, if women might obtain the going forth from home . . . by the Truth-finder.'

'Be careful, Ānanda, of the going forth of women from home . . . by the Truth-finder.' And a second time. . . . And a third time the venerable Ānanda spoke thus to the Lord: 'It were well, Lord, if women might obtain the going forth . . . proclaimed by the Truth-finder.'

'Be careful, Ānanda, of the going forth of women from home into homelessness in the *dhamma* and discipline proclaimed by the Truth-finder.' Then the venerable Ānanda, thinking:

'The Lord does not allow the going forth of women from home into homelessness in the *dhamma* and discipline proclaimed by the Truth-finder. Suppose now that I, by some other method, should ask the Lord for the going forth of women from home into homelessness in the *dhamma* and discipline proclaimed by the Truth-finder.' Then the venerable Ānanda spoke thus to the Lord:

'Now, Lord, are women, having gone forth from home into homelessness in the *dhamma* and discipline proclaimed by the Truth-finder, able to realise the fruit of stream-attainment or the fruit of once-returning or the fruit of non-returning or perfection?'[1]

'Women, Ānanda, having gone forth . . . are able to realise . . . perfection.'

'If, Lord, women, having gone forth . . . are able to realise . . . perfection – and, Lord, the Gotamid, Pajāpatī the Great, was of great service: she was the Lord's aunt, foster-mother, nurse, giver of milk, for when the Lord's mother passed away she suckled him – it were well, Lord, that women should obtain the going forth from home into homelessness in the *dhamma* and discipline proclaimed by the Truth-finder.'

'If, Ānanda, the Gotamid, Pajāpatī the Great, accepts eight important rules, that may be ordination for her:

'A nun who has been ordained (even) for a century must greet respectfully, rise up from her seat, salute with joined palms, do proper homage to a monk ordained but that day. And this rule is to be honoured, respected, revered, venerated, never to be transgressed during her life.

'A nun must not spend the rains in a residence where there is no monk. This rule too is to be honoured . . . during her life.

'Every half month a nun should desire two things from the Order of monks: the asking (as to the date) of the Observance day, and the coming for the exhortation. This rule too is to be honoured . . . during her life.

'After the rains a nun must 'invite' before both Orders in respect of three matters: what was seen, what was heard, what was suspected. This rule too is to be honoured . . . during her life.

'A nun, offending against an important rule, must undergo *mānatta* (discipline) for half a month before both Orders. This rule too must be honoured . . . during her life.

'When, as a probationer, she has trained in the six rules for two years, she should seek ordination from both Orders. This rule too is to be honoured . . . during her life.

'A monk must not be abused or reviled in any way by a nun. This rule too is to be honoured . . . during her life.

'From to-day admonition of monks by nuns is forbidden, admonition of nuns by monks is not forbidden. This rule too is to be honoured, respected, revered, venerated, never to be transgressed during her life.

'If, Ānanda, the Gotamid, Pajāpatī the Great, accepts these eight important rules, that may be ordination for her.'

Then the venerable Ānanda, having learnt the eight important rules from the Lord, approached the Gotamid, Pajāpatī the Great; having approached, he spoke thus to the Gotamid, Pajāpatī the Great:

'If you, Gotami, will accept eight important rules, that will be the ordination for you: a nun who has been ordained (even) for a century. . . . From to-day admonition of monks by nuns is forbidden . . . never to be transgressed during your life. If you, Gotami, will accept these eight important rules, that will be the ordination for you.'

'Even, honoured Ānanda, as a woman or a man when young, of tender years, and fond of ornaments, having washed (himself and his) head, having obtained a garland of lotus flowers or a garland of jasmine flowers or a garland of some sweet-scented creeper, having taken it with both hands, should place it on top of his head – even so do I, honoured Ānanda, accept these eight important rules never to be transgressed during my life.'

Then the venerable Ānanda approached the Lord: having approached, having greeted the Lord, he sat down at a respectful distance. As he was sitting down at a respectful distance, the venerable Ānanda spoke thus to the Lord: 'Lord, the eight important rules were accepted by the Gotamid, Pajāpatī the Great.'

'If, Ānanda, women had not obtained the going forth from home into homelessness in the *dhamma* and discipline proclaimed by the Truth-finder, the Brahma-faring, Ānanda, would have lasted long, true *dhamma* would have endured for a thousand years. But since, Ānanda, women have gone forth . . . in the *dhamma* and discipline proclaimed by the Truth-finder, now, Ānanda, the Brahma-faring will not last long, true *dhamma* will endure only for five hundred years.

'Even, Ānanda, as those households which have many women and few men easily fall a prey to robbers, to pot-thieves, even so, Ānanda in whatever *dhamma* and discipline women obtain the going forth from home into homelessness, that Brahma-faring will not last long.

'Even, Ānanda, as when the disease known as mildew attacks a whole field of rice that field of rice does not last long, even so, Ānanda, in whatever *dhamma* and discipline women obtain the going forth . . . that Brahma-faring will not last long.

'Even, Ānanda, as when the disease known as red rust attacks a whole field of sugar-cane, that field of sugar-cane does not last long, even so, Ānanda, in whatever *dhamma* and discipline . . . that Brahma-faring will not last long.

'Even, Ānanda, as a man, looking forward, may build a dyke to a great reservoir so that the water may not overflow, even so, Ānanda, were the eight important rules for nuns laid down by me, looking forward, not to be transgressed during their life.'

---

1 Arahatship.

Source: I. B. Horner (trans.) *Cullavagga X* in *The Book of the Discipline Vol. V* (London: Luzac, 1963), pp. 352–356.

— ●◆● —

FROM THE MAHAYANA TEXTS

— ● ◆ ● —

5.4 THE MAHAYANA

5.4.1 The Bodhisattva vows

'Imbued with these ways of purifying the stages, enlightening beings are well established in the stage of Extreme Joy. Once established in this stage, enlightening beings undertake great vows, great resolutions, great undertakings such as the following: They undertake a first great vow to make offerings to each and every buddha, in the best of forms, with the highest purity of faith, as extensively as the cosmos, to the furthest reaches of space, throughout all time. They undertake a second great vow to maintain the eye of the teachings spoken by all buddhas, to associate with all buddhas and enlightening beings, to preserve the teachings of all complete buddhas, to take in all truths, to the extent of the cosmos, to the furthest reaches of space, throughout all time, without ceasing, in all eons for as many buddhas as appear in the world. They undertake a third great vow to go to all places in all worlds where buddhas appear – from their existence in the heaven of satisfaction, descending into the human world, entry into the womb, abiding in the womb, birth, youthful enjoyments, married life, renunciation, practice of austerities, conquering demons, enlightenment, being requested to teach, setting the wheel of the great teaching in motion, and entry into great absolute nirvana – to go to all places at once, taking the lead in making offerings, receiving the teaching, and applying it in practice, to the extent of the cosmos, to the farthest reaches of space, throughout all time, without ceasing in all eons for as many buddhas as appear in the world, until the attainment of great absolute nirvana. They undertake a fourth vow to bring forth the determination to disseminate instruction in the accomplishment of means of purification of the ways of transcendence, accurate explanation of the path of the stages, the practices of all enlightening beings, bringing forth their total and particular aspects, with consideration of their common and distinctive features, as they are formed and dissolved, the many extensive immeasurable holistic practices of all buddhas and enlightening beings contained in the ways of transcendence, purifying all the stages of enlightening beings, vowing to call forth this aspiration to the extent of the cosmos, to the furthest reaches of space, throughout all time. They undertake a fifth great vow to fully develop all beings, corporeal or immaterial, thinking, nonthinking, or neither, born of eggs, wombs, moisture, or spontaneously, in all realms contained in the worlds of desire, forms, and formlessness, bound to the six paths of mundane existence in all places of birth, caught up in names and forms – to develop them to lead them into the Buddha teaching, to free them from all mundane groupings, to establish them in omniscience, to develop and mature all beings forever, to the extent of the cosmos, throughout the reaches of space, for all time, for as many eons and beings as there be. They undertake a sixth great vow for direct knowledge of the unnumerable distinctions in all the worlds of the ten directions, variously reflecting one another, subtle and gross, upside-down, inverted, and upright, their appearance and consolidation – they vow to comprehend the distinctions of worlds, to the extent of the cosmos, throughout the reaches of space, for all time. They undertake a seventh great vow, to show all beings the purification of all lands in one land and one land in all lands, the adornment of innumerable buddha-lands with arrays of light, entering into the supreme realm of buddhas from which all afflictions are removed, completely purified and filled with wise beings, showing this to all beings to please them in accord with their mentalities, vowing to thoroughly purify all buddha-lands, to the extent of the cosmos, to the farthest reaches of space, throughout all time, unceasing for as many eons and buddha-lands as there may be. They undertake an eighth great vow, to work with the same one determination as all enlightening beings, to build up roots of goodness without opposition, to be equally focused on the same one object as all enlightening beings, to be in concert with all enlightening beings, to manifest appearances of Buddha as desired, to attain the knowledge of the powers of the Enlightened at will, to attain ever-present mystic knowledge, to travel to all worlds, to appear in the circles of all buddhas, to adapt to all situations, to attain realization of the inconceivable great vehicle, to continue to carry out the practices of enlightening beings, vowing to enter the great vehicle, to the extent of the cosmos, to the furthest reaches of space, throughout all time, unceasing for as many eons and practices as there may be. They undertake a ninth great vow to carry out the practice of enlightening beings, riding on the wheel that never rolls backward, by means of fruitful words, thoughts, and deeds, so that those who see them will surely realize buddhahood, those who hear what they say will attain knowledge, and so that those who have pure faith will be freed from afflictions – they vow to attain a state like a master physician, to attain embodiment of magical fulfillment of aspirations, to carry out the practices of enlightening beings as extensively as the cosmos, to the farthest reaches of space, throughout all time, unceasing for as many eons and as many practices as there be, that their deeds not be in vain. They undertake a tenth great vow, to awaken completely to unexcelled perfect enlightenment in all worlds, to show at every point – without leaving one place – birth, leaving home, transfiguration, austere practice, conquering demons, sitting at the pinnacle of enlightenment, turning the wheel of the teaching, and final absolute nirvana, to attain the knowledge of power of the vast realm of buddhahood and in each instant show all sentient beings the emergence of a buddha in accordance with their mentalities so that they may attain enlightenment and perfect peace, to universally realize the nirvana of all phenomena by one perfect enlightenment, to please all beings according to their mentalities with a single utterance, to show great ultimate nirvana without cutting off the power of practice, to show the construction of all teachings of the stages of great knowledge, to pervade all worlds by the mystic power of the knowledge of truth and the mystic knowledge of illusoriness, vowing to bring forth great knowledge to the extent of the cosmos, to the farthest reaches of space, throughout all time, never ceasing for all eons, for all true enlightenments.

'Thus, having brought to the fore such great aspirations, great purposes, great undertakings, through ten great vows, enlightening beings stationed in the stage of Extreme Joy undertake countless consummate vows, which they undertake in ten ultimate terms: that is, to the ultimate extent of living beings, to the ultimate extent of worlds, to the ultimate extent of space, to the ultimate extent of the cosmos, to the ultimate extent of the realm of nirvana, to the ultimate extent of the emergence of buddhas, to the ultimate extent of enlightened knowledge, to the ultimate extent of realms of mental objects, to the ultimate extent of entries of knowledge into the sphere of buddhas, to the ultimate extent of the courses of worlds, the courses of teachings, and the courses of knowledge. Enlightening beings vow that their undertakings shall be coterminous with living beings, worlds, space, the cosmos, nirvana, the emergence of buddhas, enlightened knowledge, mental objects, entries of knowledge into the sphere of buddhas, the courses of worlds, the courses of teachings, and the courses of knowledge; and that just as all of these are endless, so shall the enlightening beings' roots of goodness be endless.

Source: T. Cleary (trans.) *The Flower Ornament Scripture* (Boston & London: Shambhala, 1993), pp. 704–707.

5.4.2 The six perfections of a Bodhisattva

(a) The perfection of giving:
Sariputra: What is the worldly, and what is the supramundane perfection of giving?

Subhuti: The worldly perfection of giving consists in this: The Bodhisattva gives liberally to all those who ask, all the while thinking in terms of real things.[1] It occurs to him: 'I give, that one receives, this is the gift. I renounce all my possessions without stint. I act as the Buddha commands. I practise the perfection of giving. I, having made this gift into the common property of all beings, dedicate it to supreme enlightenment, and that without apprehending anything. By means of this gift and its fruit, may all beings in this very life be at their ease, and may they one day enter Nirvana!' Tied by three ties he gives a gift. Which three? A perception of self, a perception of others, a perception of the gift.

The supramundane perfection of giving, on the other hand, consists in the three-fold purity. What is the threefold purity? Here a Bodhisattva gives a gift, and he does not apprehend a self, a recipient, a gift; also no reward of his giving. He surrenders that gift to all beings, but he apprehends neither beings nor self. He dedicates that gift to supreme enlightenment, but he does not apprehend any enlightenment. This is called the supramundane perfection of giving.

(b) The Perfection of morality.
The Lord: An irreversible Bodhisattva observes the ten ways of wholesome action. He himself observes, and he instigates others to observe, abstention from taking life, abstention from taking what is not given, abstention from wrong conduct as regards sensuous pleasures, abstention from intoxicants as tending to cloud the mind, absten-tion from lying speech, abstention from malicious speech, abstention from harsh speech, abstention from indistinct prattling, abstention from covetousness, abstention from ill-will, abstention from wrong views. Even in his dreams he never commits offences against those ten precepts, and he does not nurse such offences in his mind. Even in his dreams an irreversible Bodhisattva keeps the ten wholesome paths of action present in his mind.

The Lord: A Bodhisattva progresses to perfect purity of morality, i.e. he pays no attention to the ideas of the Disciples or Pratyekabuddhas, nor to any other dharmas which make for bad behaviour or which could cause delays on the road to enlight-enment.

(c) The Perfection of patience.
The Lord: A Bodhisattva is firmly grounded in the power of patience when his atti-tude towards all beings is free from ill-will and a desire to harm them.

The Lord: A Tathagata's perfection of patience is really no perfection. Because, Subhuti, when the king of Kalinga cut my flesh from every limb, at that time I had no notion of a self, or of a being, or of a soul, or of a person, nor had I any notion or non-notion. And why? If, Subhuti, at that time I had had a notion of self, I would also have had a notion of ill-will at that time. If I had had a notion of a being, of a soul, of a person, then I also would have had a notion of ill-will at that time. And why? By my superknowledge I know the past, five hundred births, and how I have been the Rishi, 'Preacher of Patience'. Then also I have had no notion of a self, or a being, or a soul, or a person. Therefore then, Subhuti, a Bodhisattva, a great being should, after he has got rid of all notions, raise his thought to the supreme enlight-enment. Unsupported by form a thought should be produced, unsupported by sounds, smells, tastes, touchables or mind-objects a thought should be produced, unsupported by dharma a thought should be produced, unsupported by no-dharma a thought should be produced, unsupported by anything a thought should be produced. And why? What is supported has no support.

(d) The Perfection of Vigour
Purna: Here a Bodhisattva, who courses towards enlightenment and who has stood in the perfection of giving, gives gifts, not for the sake of a limited number of beings,

but, on the contrary, for the sake of all beings. And so for the other perfections. When a Bodhisattva puts on the great armour, he does not circumscribe beings and say, 'so many beings I will lead to Nirvana, so many beings I will not lead to Nirvana; so many beings will I introduce to enlightenment, so many beings I will not introduce to enlightenment'. But, on the contrary, it is for the sake of all beings that he puts on the great armour, and he reflects: 'I myself, I will fulfil the perfection of giving, and also on all beings will I enjoin the perfection of giving'. And so for the other perfections.

(e) The Perfection of Concentration

Purna: If a Bodhisattva, although he enters the trances, the Unlimited, the formless attainments, does not gain rebirth through them, does not even relish them, is not captivated by them, that is his perfection of concentration.

The Lord: When he practises the perfection of meditation for the sake of other beings his mind becomes undistracted. For he reflects that 'even worldly meditation is hard to accomplish with distracted thoughts, how much more so is full enlightenment. Therefore I must remain undistracted until I have won full enlightenment'. . . . Moreover, Subhuti, a Bodhisattva, beginning with the first thought of enlightenment, practises the perfection of meditation. His mental activities are associated with the knowledge of all modes when he enters into meditation. When he has seen forms with his eye, he does not seize upon them as signs of realities which concern him, nor is he interested in the accessory details. He sets himself to restrain that which, if he does not restrain his organ of sight, might give occasion for covetousness, sadness or other evil and unwholesome dharmas to reach his heart. He watches over the organ of sight. And the same with the other five sense-organs, – ear, nose, tongue, body, mind.

Whether he walks or stands, sits or lies down, talks or remains silent, his concentration does not leave him. He does not fidget with his hands or feet, or twitch his face; he is not incoherent in his speech, confused in his senses, exalted or uplifted, fickle or idle, agitated in body or mind. Calm is his body, calm is his voice, calm is his mind. His demeanour shows contentment, both in private and public. . . . He is frugal, easy to feed, easy to serve, of good life and habits; though in a crowd he dwells apart; even and unchanged, in gain and loss; not elated, not cast down. Thus in happiness and suffering, in praise and blame, in fame and disrepute, in life or death, he is the same unchanged, neither elated nor cast down. And so with foe or friend, with what is pleasant or unpleasant, with holy or unholy men, with noises or music, with forms that are dear or undear, he remains the same unchanged, neither elated nor cast down, neither gratified nor thwarted. And why? Because he sees all dharmas as empty of marks of their own, without true reality, incomplete and uncreated.

(f) The Perfection of Wisdom

Subhuti: What is the supramundane perfection of wisdom? Through the fact that neither self, nor being, nor gift, nor enlightenment have been apprehended, and through the three-fold purity, he cleanses the perfection of giving for the sake of enlightenment. Through the fact that neither self nor being nor morality nor enlightenment have been apprehended, he cleanses the perfection of morality for the sake of enlightenment. And so with the other perfections. For the sake of enlightenment he dedicates all wholesome roots to the supreme enlightenment, by means of an undifferentiated dedication, by means of a dedication which is supreme, which equals the unequalled, which is unthinkable, incomparable and measureless. This is called the supramundane perfection of wisdom.

---

1 Literally: leaning on something.

Source: E. Conze (trans.) *Selected Sayings from the Perfection of Wisdom* (London: The Buddhist Society, 1968), pp. 66–70.

5.4.3 The qualities of the Bodhisattva Avalokiteśvara

At that time the bodhisattva Inexhaustible Mind (Akṣayamati) straightway rose from his seat and, baring his right shoulder and facing the Buddha with palms joined, said: 'O World-Honored One! For what reason is the bodhisattva He Who Observes the Sounds of the World (Avalokiteśvara) called Observer of the Sounds of the World?' The Buddha declared to the bodhisattva Inexhaustible Mind, 'Good man, if incalculable hundreds of thousands of myriads of millions of living beings, suffering pain and torment, hear of this bodhisattva He Who Observes the Sounds of the World and single-mindedly call upon his name, the bodhisattva He Who Observes the Sounds of the World shall straightway heed their voices, and all shall gain deliverance.

'If there is one who keeps the name of this bodhisattva He Who Observes the Sounds of the World, even if he should fall into a great fire, the fire would be unable to burn him, thanks to the imposing supernatural power of this bodhisattva.

'If he should be carried off by a great river and call upon this bodhisattva's name, then straightway he would find a shallow place.

'If a hundred thousand myriads of millions of living beings enter the great sea in quest of gold, silver, vaiḍūrya, giant clamshell, agate, coral, amber, pearl, and other such gems, even if a black wind blows their ship away, carrying it off and plunging it into the realm of the rākṣasa-ghosts, if there is among them but one man who calls upon the name of the bodhisattva He Who Observes the Sounds of the World, those men shall be delivered from the troubles [caused by] the rākṣasas. It is for this reason that he is called Observer of the Sounds of the World.

'If, again, a man who is about to be murdered calls upon the name of the bodhisattva He Who Observes the Sounds of the World, then the knives and staves borne by the other fellow shall be broken in pieces, and the man shall gain deliverance.

'If there should be a thousand-millionfold world of lands filled with yakṣas and rākṣasas who wish to come and do harm to others, if they should but hear the name of the bodhisattva He Who Observes the Sounds of the World, these malignant ghosts would not be able even to look upon those others with an evil eye, how much the less to inflict harm on them!

'Even if there is a man, whether guilty or guiltless, whose body is fettered with stocks, pillory, or chains, if he calls upon the name of the bodhisattva He Who Observes the Sounds of the World, they shall all be severed and broken, and he shall straightway gain deliverance.

'If in a thousand-millionfold world of lands full of malicious bandits there is a merchant chief whose men are carrying precious gems over a road by a steep drop, if there is among them one man who makes this proclamation: 'Good men, do not let terror take possession of you! You all must single-mindedly call upon the name of the bodhisattva He Who Observes the Sounds of the World. For that bodhisattva can confer fearlessness upon living beings. If you all call upon his name, then from these malicious bandits you shall contrive to be delivered'; and if the multitude of merchants, hearing this, speak these words in unison, saying, 'Namo bodhisattvāya He Who Observes the Sounds of the World!'; then, by the mere calling upon his name, they shall forthwith gain deliverance.

'Inexhaustible Mind, the imposing, supernatural power of the bodhisattva He Who Observes the Sounds of the World is as sublime as this!

'If there are beings of much lust who are constantly mindful of and humbly respectful to the bodhisattva He Who Observes the Sounds of the World, they shall straightway contrive to be separated from their lust. If those with much anger are constantly mindful of and humbly respectful to the bodhisattva He Who Observes the Sounds of the World, they shall straightway contrive to be separated from their anger. If those of much folly are constantly mindful of and humbly respectful to the bodhisattva He Who Observes the Sounds of the World, they shall straightway contrive to be separated from their folly. Inexhaustible Mind! Such imposing supernatural power has the bodhisattva He Who Observes the Sounds of the World, so many are the benefits he confers! For this reason the beings should ever bear him in mind.

'If there is a woman, and if she is desirous and hopeful of having a son, making worshipful offerings to the bodhisattva He Who Observes the Sounds of the World, she shall straightway bear a son of happiness, excellence, and wisdom. If she be desirous and hopeful of having a daughter, she shall straightway bear a daughter, upright and endowed with proper marks, one who has previously planted wholesome roots, who is loved and honored by a multitude of men. O Inexhaustible Mind, such is the power of the bodhisattva He Who Observes the Sounds of the World!

'If there are beings who in humble reverence worship the bodhisattva He Who Observes the Sounds of the World, their happiness shall not be vainly cast aside,

'For this reason the beings must all receive and keep the name of the bodhisattva He Who Observes the Sounds of the World. Inexhaustible Mind! If there is anyone who receives and keeps the names of bodhisattvas as numerous as the sands of sixty-two million Ganges rivers, also exhausting his whole physical being in offering food and drink, clothing, bedding, and medicine, in your thinking how shall it be? Shall the merit of this good man or good woman be much or not?'

Inexhaustible Mind said, 'Very much, O World-Honored One!'

The Buddha said, 'If again there is a man who receives and keeps the name of the bodhisattva He Who Observes the Sounds of the World, making worshipful offerings to it but once, the happiness of these two shall be equal and undifferentiated, not to be exhausted in a hundred thousand myriads of millions of kalpas. Inexhaustible Mind! One who accepts and keeps the name of the bodhisattva He Who Observes the Sounds of the World shall gain the benefit of merits as incalculable and as limitless as these!'

Source: L. Hurvitz (trans.) *Scripture of the Lotus Blossom of the Fine Dharma* (Kumarajiva's version) (New York: Columbia University Press, 1976), pp. 311–313.

5.4.4 The illusion of self-hood

Subhūti, what do you think? Let no one say the Tathāgata cherishes the idea 'I must liberate all living beings.' Allow no such thought, Subhūti. Wherefore? Because in reality there are no living beings to be liberated by the Tathāgata. If there were living beings for the Tathāgata to liberate, he would partake in the idea of self-hood, personality . . . and separate individuality.

Subhūti, though the common people accept self as real, the Tathāgata declares that self is not different from non self. Subhūti, those whom the Tathāgata referred to as 'common people' are not really common people; such is merely a name.

Source: A. F. Price and Wong Mou-Lam (trans.) Chapter 25 *The Diamond Sutra* in *The Diamond Sutra and the Sutra of Hui-Neng* (Boston: Shambhala, 1990), p. 46 [slightly amended].

5.4.5 Praise of the awakening mind

1 In adoration I make obeisance to the Sugatas and their sons, and to their bodies of Dharma, and to all those worthy of praise. In brief, and in accordance with scripture, I shall describe the undertaking of the observance of the sons of the Sugatas.

2 Nothing new will be said here, nor have I any skill in composition. Therefore I do not imagine that I can benefit others. I have done this to perfume my own mind.

3 While doing this, the surge of my inspiration to cultivate what is skilful increases. Moreover, should another, of the very same humours as me, also look at this, then he too may benefit from it.

4 This opportune moment is extremely hard to meet. Once met, it yields the welfare of mankind. If the advantage is neglected now, how will this meeting come again?

5 At night in darkness thick with clouds a lightning flash gives a moment's brightness. So, sometime, by the power of the Buddha, the mind of the world might for a moment turn to acts of merit.

6 This being so, the power of good is always weak, while the power of evil is vast and terrible. What other good could conquer that, were there not the perfect Awakening Mind?

7 This is the benefit, seen by the Lords of the Sages meditating for many aeons, whereby deep-welling happiness elates immeasurable masses of beings, though happiness alone.

8 Those who long to transcend the hundreds of miseries of existence, who long to relieve creatures of the sorrows, who long to enjoy many hundreds of joys, must never abandon the Awakening Mind.

9 When the Awakening Mind has arisen in him, a wretch, captive in the prison of existence, he is straightway hailed son of the Sugatas, to be revered in the worlds of gods and men. . . .

15 The Awakening Mind should be understood to be of two kinds; in brief: the Mind resolved on Awakening and the Mind proceeding towards Awakening.

16 The distinction between these two should be understood by the wise in the same way as the distinction is recognized between a person who desires to go and one who is going, in that order.

17 Even in cyclic existence great fruit comes from the Mind resolved on Awakening, but nothing like the uninterrupted merit that comes from that resolve when put into action.

18 From the moment that he takes on that Mind to release the limitless realm of beings, with a resolve that cannot be turned back.

19 From that moment on, though he may doze off or be distracted many times, uninterrupted streams of merit like the bursting sky continuously pour forth.

20 This is what the Tathāgata himself explained with proof in the *Question of Subāhu*, for the benefit of beings who are disposed toward the inferior path.

21 Immeasurable merit took hold of the well-intentioned person who thought 'Let me dispel the headaches of beings'.

22 What then of the person who longs to remove the unequalled agony of every single being and make their virtue infinite?

23 Whose mother or father ever has such a desire for their welfare as this, what deities or sages or Brahmās have it?

24 Those beings did not conceive this desire before, even for their own sake, even if a dream. How could they have it for the sake of others?

25 Such a being, unprecedented, an excellent jewel, in whom there is born a concern for the welfare of others such as others have not even for themselves, how is he born?

26 That jewel, the Mind, which is the seed of pure happiness in the world and the remedy for the suffering of the world, how at all can its merit be measured?

27 Worship of the Buddha is surpassed merely by the desire for the welfare of others; how much more so by the persistent effort for the complete happiness of every being?

28 Hoping to escape suffering, it is to suffering that they run. In the desire for happiness, out of delusion, they destroy their own happiness, like an enemy.

29 It satisfies with every happiness those starved of happiness, and cuts away oppressions from those oppressed in many ways.

30 It also drives off delusion. How could there be a holy man its equal, how such a friend, or how such merit?

31 Even if someone returns a favour, he is praised. What, then, can be said of the Bodhisattva, who does good without obligation?

32 People honour someone who gives alms to a few people, saying, 'He does good', because he contemptuously supports their life for half a day with a moment's gift of mere food.

33 What then of the one who offers to a limitless number of beings, throughout limitless time, the fulfilment of all desires, unending until the end of the sky and those beings?

34 The Protector has said that one who harbours in his heart a turbid thought against such a lord of gifts, a son of the Conqueror, dwells in hells for aeons as numerous as the moments of that turbid thought.

35 But fruit outweighing that flows forth for one whose mind becomes serenely confident. For evil action against the sons of the Conqueror requires great force, while pure action comes effortlessly.

36 I bow down to the bodies of those in whom that excellent jewel, the Mind, has arisen, and towards whom even harm will lead to happiness. To those mines of happiness, I go for refuge.

Source: K. Crosby & A. Skilton (trans.) *The Bodhicaryāvatāra* (Oxford: Oxford University Press, 1995, pp. 5–8).

5.4.6 The Dragon Princess

Mañjuśrī said, 'There is the daughter of the dragon king Sāgara, whose years are barely eight. Her wisdom is sharp-rooted, and well she knows the faculties and deeds of the beings. She has gained dhāraṇī. The profound treasure house of secrets preached by the Buddhas she is able to accept and to keep in its entirety. She has profoundly entered into dhyāna-concentration, and has arrived at an understanding of the dharmas. In the space of a *kṣaṇa* [moment] she produced bodhi-thought, and has attained the point on nonbacksliding. Her eloquence has no obstructions, and she is compassionately mindful of the beings as if they were her babies. Her merits are perfect. What she recollects in her mind and recites with her mouth is subtle and broad. She is of good will and compassionate, humane and yielding. Her will and thought are harmonious and refined, and she is able to attain to bodhi.'

The bodhisattva Wisdom Accumulation said, 'I have seen the Thus Come One of the Śākyas throughout incalculable kalpas tormenting himself by doing what is hard to do, piling up merit and heaping up excellence, seeking the Path of the bodhisattva and never resting. When I look at the thousand-millionfold world, there is no place, not even the size of a mustardseed, where the bodhisattva did not cast away body and life for the beings' sakes, and only then did he achieve the Way of bodhi. I do not believe that this girl in the space of a moment directly and immediately achieved right, enlightened intuition.'

Before he had finished speaking, at that very time the daughter of the dragon king suddenly appeared in front [of them], and, doing obeisance with head bowed, stood off to one side and spoke praise with gāthās, saying:

> Having profoundly mastered the marks of sin and merit,
>> Universally illuminating all ten directions,
> The subtle and pure Dharma-body
>> Has perfected the marks thirty-two,
> Using the eighty beautiful features
>> As a means of adorning the Dharma-body.
> The object of respectful obeisance for gods and men,
>> It is reverently honored by all dragons and spirits.
> Of all varieties of living beings,
>> None fails to bow to it as an object of worship.
> I have also heard that, as for the achievement of bodhi,
>> Only the Buddha can know it by direct witness.
> I, laying open the teachings of the Great Vehicle,
>> Convey to release the suffering beings.

At that time, Śāriputra spoke to the dragon girl, saying, 'You say that in no long time you shall attain the unexcelled Way. This is hard to believe. What is the reason? A woman's body is filthy, it is not a Dharma-receptacle. How can you attain unexcelled bodhi? The Path of the Buddha is remote and cavernous. Throughout incalculable kalpas, by tormenting oneself and accumulating good conduct, also by thoroughly cultivating the perfections, only by these means can one then be successful. Also, a woman's body even then has five obstacles. It cannot become first a Brahmā god king, second the god Śakra, third King Māra, fourth a sage-king turning the Wheel, fifth a Buddha-body. How can the body of a woman speedily achieve Buddhahood?'

At that time, the dragon girl had a precious gem, whose value was the [whole] thousand-millionfold world, which she held up and gave to the Buddha. The Buddha straightway accepted it. The dragon girl said to the bodhisattva Wisdom Accumulation and to the venerable Śāriputra, 'I offered a precious gem, and the World-Honored One accepted it. Was this quick or not?'

He answered, saying, 'Very quick!'

The girl said, 'With your supernatural power you shall see me achieve Buddhahood even more quickly than that!'

At that time, the assembled multitude all saw the dragon girl in the space of an instant turn into a man, perfect bodhisattva-conduct, straightway go southward to the world-sphere Spotless, sit on a jeweled lotus blossom, and achieve undifferentiating, right, enlightened intuition, with thirty-two marks and eighty beautiful features setting forth the Fine Dharma for all living beings in all ten directions. At that time, in the Sahā world-sphere bodhisattvas, voice-hearers, gods, dragons, the eightfold assembly, humans and nonhumans, all from a distance seeing that dragon girl achieve Buddhahood and universally preach Dharma to the men and gods of the assembly of that time, were overjoyed at heart and all did obeisance from afar. Incalculable living beings, hearing the Dharma and understanding it, attained to nonbacksliding. Incalculable living beings were enabled to receive a prophecy of the Path. The Spotless world-sphere trembled in six different ways, and in the Sahā world-sphere three thousand living beings dwelt on the ground from which there is no backsliding. Three thousand living beings opened up the thought of bodhi and were enabled to receive prophecies. The bodhisattva Wisdom Accumulation, as well as Śāriputra and all the assembled multitude, silently believed and accepted.

Source: L. Hurvitz (trans.) *Scripture of the Lotus Blossom of the Fine Dharma* (Kumarajiva's version) (New York: Columbia University Press, 1976), pp. 199–201.

5.4.7 From the shorter Pure Land Sutra (*Sukhavativyuha*)

The Land of Bliss

Then, the Blessed One addressed the reverend Shariputra, saying: 'To the west of us, Shariputra, a hundred thousand million buddha-fields from where we are, there is a world called the Land of Bliss. At this very moment, the tathagata, arhat, perfect and full buddha called Amitayus lives in that buddha-field; he abides and remains there, and even now continues to teach the Dharma in that field.

'Now, what do you think, Shariputra: Why is that world called the "Land of Bliss"? Shariputra, physical and mental pain are unknown to the living beings that inhabit the world called the "Land of Bliss"; on the contrary, they only experience conditions of boundless happiness. This is why that world is called the "Land of Bliss."

'Furthermore, Shariputra, the world known as the Land of Bliss is adorned and enclosed on every side by seven railings and seven rows of palm trees, all decked with nets of tinkling bells. It is made colorful and attractive by four precious substances, namely, gold, silver, emerald, and rock crystal.

'This is how that buddha-field is adorned, Shariputra, with such a panoply of the wondrous qualities of buddha-fields.

'Furthermore, Shariputra, in the world known as the Land of Bliss there are lotus ponds, all made of seven precious substances, namely, gold, silver, emerald, rock crystal, red pearl, sapphire, and mother of pearl as the seventh. These ponds are brimming with water that is cool, clear, sweet, light, soft, free from odor, free from disease, refreshing, and invigorating. In each of these ponds the bottom slopes gently along the shore, so that the water reaches the right depth in every bathing spot and a crow could drink from the edge of the pond. The bottom of each pond is covered with golden sand. And all around on each of the four sides of these lotus ponds four sets of stairways descend into the pools. These stairways are colorful, elegant, and made of four precious substances, namely, gold, silver, emerald, and rock crystal. And on every side of these lotus ponds grow gem trees, colorful and graceful, made from seven precious substances, namely, gold, silver, emerald, rock crystal, red pearl, sapphire, and mother of pearl as the seventh.

'And in those lotus ponds grow lotus flowers. Some are blue – intensely blue, or with a blue sheen, or with a tinge of blue. Some are yellow – intensely yellow, or with a yellow sheen, or with a tinge of yellow. Some are red – intensely red, or with a red sheen, or with a tinge of red. Some are white – intensely white, with a white sheen, or with a tinge of white. Some are multicolored – intensely multicolored, with a sheen of many colors, or with a tinge of many colors. And these lotus blossoms are as wide as chariot wheels.

'This is how that buddha-field is adorned, Shariputra, with such a panoply of the wondrous qualities of buddhe-fields.

'Furthermore, Shariputra, in that buddha-field one hears heavenly musical instruments constantly being played. And the ground all around is golden in color, pleasant to look at. And in that buddha-field a shower of heavenly coral-tree blossoms pours down three times every day and three times every night. And the living beings who are born there travel before their forenoon meal to other worlds, where they worship a hundred thousand million buddhas, and then return to their own world, the Land of Bliss, in time for the afternoon nap, having showered a hundred thousand million flowers upon each one of those buddhas.

'This is how that buddha-field is adorned, Shariputra, with such a panoply of the wondrous qualities of buddha-fields.

'Furthermore, Shariputra, in that buddha-field wild geese, curlews, and peacocks gather three times every night and three times every day to sing in chorus, each singing with a different voice. And as they sing, one hears that their voices proclaim Buddhist virtues, such as the five spiritual faculties, the five spiritual powers, and the seven elements of awakening. When human beings in that world hear these sounds, their thoughts turn to the Buddha, their thoughts turn to the Buddha's teaching, the Dharma, and their thoughts turn to the Buddha's Order, the Sangha.

'Now, Shariputra, what do you think? Are these birds born from other birds? You could not consider this possible. Why? Because even the names of the hells, the names of animal rebirths, and the name 'Realm of Yama, the King of Death' are unknown in that buddha-field – let alone actual birth in any of these forms. Rather, those flocks of birds gather there to sing with the voice of the Dharma only because they have been created magically by the Buddha who presides in that field, the Tathagata Amitayus.

'This is how that buddha-field is adorned, Shariputra, with such a panoply of the wondrous qualities of buddha-fields.

'Furthermore, Shariputra, when the rows of palm trees and nets of tinkling bells in that buddha-field sway in the wind, a sweet and enrapturing sound issues from them. This concert of sounds is, Shariputra, like a set of heavenly cymbals, with a hundred thousand million playing parts – when these cymbals are played by expert musicians, a sweet and enrapturing sound issues from them. In exactly the same way, a sweet and enrapturing sound proceeds from those rows of palm trees and those nets of tinkling bells when they sway in the wind. When human beings in that world hear this sound, they remember the Buddha and feel his presence in their whole body, they remember the Dharma and feel its presence in their whole body, and they remember the Sangha and feel its presence in their whole body.

'This is how that buddha-field is adorned, Shariputra, with such a panoply of the wondrous qualities of buddha-fields.'

The Buddha Presiding over the Land of Bliss

'Now, what do you think, Shariputra? Why is that tathagata called Amitayus, or 'Measureless Life-span'? Now, Shariputra, the length of that tathagata's life and of the human beings in that buddha-field is immeasurable. This is why that tathagata is called Amitayus, 'Measureless Life-span.'

'And ten cosmic ages have passed, Shariputra, since this tathagata awoke to unsurpassable, perfect, and full awakening.

'What do you think, Shariputra? Why is this tathagata called Amitabha, or 'Measureless Light'? Now, Shariputra, the light of this tathagata spreads unimpended over all buddha-fields. This is why this tathagata is called Amitabha, 'Measureless Light.'

The Inhabitants of the Land of Bliss

'And, Shariputra, this tathagata is surrounded by an immeasurable assembly of disciples, who are all pure arhats and whose number is impossible to count.

'This is how that buddha-field is adorned, Shariputra, with such a panoply of the wondrous qualities of buddha-fields.'

'Furthermore, Shariputra, those sentient beings who are reborn in the buddha-field of the Tathagata Amitayus as pure bodhisattvas who will not fall back and will be separated from awakening by only one birth – the number of these bodhisattvas, Shariputra, is not easy to reckon. One can only approximate their numbers by saying that they are immeasurable and countless.

Exhortation

'Now, Shariputra, sentient beings should set their minds on rebirth in that buddha-field. Why? Because there they will meet persons like themselves, who practise the good. For, Shariputra, living beings are not reborn in that buddha-field of the Tathagata Amitayus as the result of an inferior root of merit.

'Shariputra, those sons or daughters of good families who will hear the name of the blessed Amitayus, the Tathagata, and then will bring it to mind, and will keep it in mind without distraction for one night, or two, or three, four, five, six, or seven nights – they will be met by the Tathagata at the moment of their death. When the moment of death approaches for one of these sons or daughters of good families, Amitayus the Tathagata, surrounded by an assembly of disciples and at the head of a host of bodhisattvas, will stand before this son or daughter, and his son or daughter will die with a mind that is free from distorted views. After they die, they will be reborn in the Land of Bliss, in the buddha-field of Amitayus the Tathagata.'

Therefore, Shariputra, as I understand well the meaning of this, I declare: 'Sons and daughters of a good family should direct their thoughts earnestly towards rebirth in that buddha-field.'

Source: L. O. Gomez (trans.), *Land of Bliss* (Honolulu: University of Hawaii 1996), pp. 16–19.

5.4.8 The benefits of the Lotus Sutra

If one wishes to dwell in the Buddha Path
    And achieve the knowledge born of itself,
One must ever strive to make offerings
    To those who receive and keep the Dharma Blossom.
If there is anyone who wishes quickly to attain
    Knowledge of all modes,
He must receive and keep this scripture
    And make offerings to its bearers.
If there is anyone who can receive and keep
    The Scripture of the Blossom of the Fine Dharma,
Be it known that he was dispatched by the Buddha
    In his merciful mindfulness of the living beings.
Those who can receive and keep
    The Scripture of the Blossom of the Fine Dharma,
Having forsaken their pure lands,
    Have been reborn here out of pity for the multitude.
Be it known that a man such as this,
    Having the power to be reborn wherever he chooses,
Is able in this evil age
    To preach broadly the unexcelled Dharma.
One must with the perfume of divine flowers
    And with garments adorned with divine jewels,
As well as with clusters of the divine jewels themselves,
    Make offerings to one who preaches Dharma.
One who after my extinction, in an evil age,
    Is able to bear this scripture
Is to be worshiped with palms joined,
    As if offerings were being made to a World-Honored One.
With supreme delicacies and many sweetmeats,
    As well as varieties of garments,
Shall [the beings] make offerings to this Buddha's son,
    Hoping to be able to hear him even for a moment.
If there is one who in the latter age can
    Receive and keep this scripture,
I will send him into the midst of men,
    Where he shall do the Thus Come One's business.
If anyone throughout one kalpa,

Ever harboring unwholesome thoughts
And flushed in color, shall malign the Buddha,
  He shall incur incalculably grave guilt.
If there be any who read, recite, and keep
  This Scripture of the Dharma Blossom
Anyone who for a moment heaps abuse on them
  Shall incur guilt exceeding even this.
If there is a man who, in his quest for the Buddha Path,
  Shall throughout one kalpa,
Joining palms in my presence,
  Praise me with numberless gāthās,
By reason of this praise of the Buddha
  He shall gain incalculable merit;
But he who shall praise the bearers of this scripture
  Shall have merit that exceeds even that.
One who throughout eighty millions of kalpas
  With the finest colors and sounds,
As well as scents, flavors, and touches,
  Makes offerings to the bearers of the scripture –
Having made offerings in this way,
  If he can hear it for but a moment,
Shall himself experience delight,
  Thinking, 'I have now gained a great advantage!'
Medicine King, I now proclaim to you
  The scriptures that I preach;
And among these scriptures
  The Dharma Blossom is foremost.

Source: L. Hurvitz (trans.) *Scripture of the Lotus Blossom of the Fine Dharma* (The Lotus Sūtra), (Kumārajīva's version) (New York: Columbia University Press, 1976), pp. 176–178.

5.5 MAHĀYĀNA PHILOSOPHY

5.5.1 The Heart Sutra from the Perfection of Wisdom Texts (*Prajnaparamita* Texts)

Thus did I hear at one time. The Transcendent Victor was sitting on Vulture Mountain in Rājagṛha together with a great assembly of monks and a great assembly of Bodhisattvas. At that time the Transcendent Victor was absorbed in a samādhi on the enumerations of phenomena called 'perception of the profound.' Also at that time, the Bodhisattva, the Mahāsattva, the Superior Avalokiteśvara was contemplating the meaning of the profound perfection of wisdom and he saw that those five aggregates also are empty of inherent existence. Then, by the power of the Buddha, the venerable Śāriputra, said this to the Bodhisattva, the Mahāsattva, the Superior Avalokiteśvara, 'How should a son of good lineage train who wishes to practise the profound perfection of wisdom?'

The Bodhisattva, the Mahāsattva, the Superior Avalokiteśvara said this to the venerable Śāriputra: Śāriputra, a son of good lineage or a daughter of good lineage who wishes to practice the profound perfection of wisdom should view [things] in this way: They should correctly view those five aggregates[1] also as empty of inherent existence. Form is emptiness; emptiness is form. Emptiness is not other than form; form is not other than emptiness. In the same way, feeling, discrimination, compositional factors, and consciousness are empty. Śāriputra, in that way, all phenomena are empty, that is, without characteristic, unproduced, unceased, stainless, not stainless, undiminished, unfilled. Therefore, Śāriputra, in emptiness, there is no form, no feeling, no discrimination, no compositional factors, no consciousness, no eye, no ear, no nose, no tongue, no body, no mind, no form, no sound, no odor, no taste, no object of touch, no phenomenon. There is no eye constituent, no mental constituent, up to and including no mental consciousness constituent. There is no ignorance, no extinction of ignorance, up to and including no aging and death and no extinction of aging and death. Similarly, there are no sufferings, no origins, no cessations, no paths, no exalted wisdom, no attainment, and also no non-attainment.

Therefore, Śāriputra, because Bodhisattvas have no attainment, they depend on and abide in the perfection of wisdom; because their minds are without obstructions, they are without fear. Having completely passed beyond all error they go to the completion of nirvāṇa. All the Buddhas who abide in the three times have been fully awakened into unsurpassed, perfect, complete enlightenment through relying on the perfection of wisdom.

Therefore, the mantra of the perfection of wisdom is the mantra of great knowledge, the unsurpassed mantra, the mantra equal to the unequalled, the mantra that thoroughly pacifies all suffering. Because it is not false, it should be known to be true. The mantra of the perfection of wisdom is stated:

tadyathā oṃ gate gate pāragate pārasaṃgate bodhi svāhā

Śāriputra, Bodhisattva Mahāsattvas should train in the profound perfection of wisdom in that way.

Then the Transcendent Victor rose from that samādhi and said to the Bodhisattva, the Mahāsattva, the Superior Avalokiteśvara, 'Well done. Well done, well done, child of good lineage, it is just so. Child of good lineage, it is like that; the profound perfection of wisdom should be practised just as you have taught it. Even the Tathāgatas admire this.' The Transcendent Victor having so spoken, the venerable Śāriputra, the Bodhisattva, the Mahāsattva, the Superior Avalakiteśvara, and all those surrounding and those of the world, the gods, humans, demigods, and *gandharvas* were filled with admiration and praised the words of the Transcendent Victor.

---

1 The five aggregates are the five skandhas; form is the first of these.

Source: D. S. Lopez (trans.) *The Heart Sūtra Explained: Indian and Tibetan Commentaries.* (New York: SUNY, 1988), pp. 19–20.

5.5.2 The meaning of 'empty' in Madhyamaka philosophy

[An opponent argues:]

1. If everything is empty, there can be no arising or passing away, and it follows that the Four Noble Truths [which involve the arising and passing away of suffering] do not exist.

2. And because the Four Noble Truths do not exist, there can be no understanding [of the truth of suffering], no abandonment [of the cause of suffering], no practice [of the Path], no realization [of nirvāṇa].

3. Nor, without these, can there be any knowledge of the four fruits [of the Path: stream-winner, once-returner, nonreturner, and arhat-ship]; and without these, there can be no individuals who are established in the four fruits, and none who are on the four paths toward them.

4. And if these eight kinds of individuals do not exist, there can be no sangha. And since the Four Noble Truths do not exist either, no true Dharma can be found.

5. And if neither the sangha nor the Dharma exists, how can there be a Buddha? Thus, in speaking of emptiness, you contradict the Three Jewels [Buddha, Dharma, and Sangha].

6. And you deny the reality of the fruits, of good and bad, and of all worldly conventions.

[Nāgārjuna replies:]

7. To this we say that you do not know what emptiness is all about. You are therefore distressed by emptiness and [what you wrongly see as the] implications of emptiness.

8. In teaching the Dharma, Buddhas resort to two truths: worldly conventional truth and ultimate truth.

9. Those who do not know the distinction between these two truths do not understand the deep reality in the Buddha's Teaching.

10. The ultimate cannot be taught without resorting to conventions; and without recourse to the ultimate, one cannot reach nirvāṇa.

11. Emptiness, poorly perceived, destroys those of slight intelligence, like a snake badly grasped or magical knowledge misapplied.

12. That is why the Buddha was at first averse to teaching the Dharma; he thought that it would be difficult for those of slight intelligence to fathom it.

13. You have repeatedly objected to emptiness, but your faulty condemnation has nothing to do with our views, and does not apply to what is empty.

14. What is linked to emptiness is linked to everything; what is not linked to emptiness is linked to nothing.

15. You, putting off onto us your own deficiencies, are like someone who mounts a horse and then forgets he is on it.

16. If you view the true existence of existing things from the perspective of each thing having] its own inherent self-existence [svabhāva], you will necessarily see those existing things as having neither cause nor condition, [as being totally unconnected to anything].

17. And you will deny cause and effect as well as [the possibility of there being] a doer, a deed, a doing, an origin, a cessation, or a fruit [of the Path].

18. Interdependent origination – that is what we call emptiness. That is a conventional designation. It is also the Middle Way.

19. There can be found no element of reality [dharma] that is not inter-dependently originated; therefore, there can be found no element of reality whatsoever that is *not* empty.

20. If everything were *not* empty, there could be no arising or passing away, and it would follow that the Four Noble Truths [which involve the arising and passing away of suffering] did not exist.

21. How could suffering *not* be interdependently originated? Indeed, suffering is said to be impermanent; thus it cannot be found to exist if it has its own [permanent] inherent self-existence.

22. And furthermore, how could there be an arising of suffering having its own inherent self-existence? Because for one who denies emptiness, there is no arising.

23. Nor could a cessation of suffering having its own inherent self-existence be found to exist; by insisting on the notion of inherent self-existence, you deny cessation.

24. Finally, if there is such a thing as inherent self-existence, there can be no practice of the Path. But that Path is cultivated, so it cannot be found to have its own inherent self-existence. [. . .]

31. According to your view, it follows that the Enlightened One is independent of his enlightenment, and enlightenment is independent of the Enlightened One!

32. According to your view, people who, by virtue of their own inherent self-existence, are [defined as being] unenlightened, will never attain enlightenment, even by means of the practices of a bodhisattva.

33. And no good or bad will be done by anyone, for what can be done by what is not-empty? That which has its own inherent self-existence does not act.

34. Indeed, according to your view, a fruit would be found to exist without [reference to having been brought about by] a good or bad deed, because for you a fruit is not found to be fashioned by good or bad deeds.

35. But if according to your view, a fruit *is* fashioned by good or bad deeds, how can that fruit that has *originated* from a good or bad deed not be empty?

36. When you deny emptiness, which is interdependent origination, you deny all worldly transactions.

37. For one who denies emptiness, there would be nothing at all to be done, doing would never get started, and a doer would not be doing.

38. According to the theory of inherent self-existence, the world should be [unchanging]: neither coming into being nor ceasing, utterly uniform and devoid of varying situations.

39. In the absence of emptiness, there could not be found to exist either the attainment of what has not yet been attained, or the bringing to an end of suffering, or the abandonment of all defilements.

40. One who perceives interdependent origination also perceives this: suffering, the origination of suffering, the cessation of suffering, as well as the path to the cessation of suffering.

Source: J. W. de Jong (trans.) Chapter 24, Nāgārjuna's *Mūlamadhyamakakārikaḥ*. In J. S. Strong, *The Experience of Buddhism: Sources and Interpretations* (Belmont CA, 1995), pp. 145–147.

5.5.3 A Yogacara treatise

1.   The imagined,
The other-dependent,
The absolutely accomplished:
These are the three natures,
Which should be thoroughly known by the wise.

2.   That which appears is the other-dependent,
For it depends on causal conditions;
The form in which it appears is the imagined,
For it is merely an imagination.

3.   The perpetual absence of the form
In which the other-dependent appears,
Is to be understood as
The absolutely accomplished nature,
For it is never otherwise.

4.   What is it that appears?
It is the imagination of the non-existent.
How does it appear?
In the form of duality.
What will result from its non-existence?
There will be the state of non-duality.

5.   What is meant by the imagination of the non-existent?
Is it thought,
For by it [the subject-only duality] is imagined.
The form in which it imagines a thing
Never at all exists as such.

6.   The *citta* takes on two modes, as cause and effect,
It is then respectively called
The store-consciousness and the active consciousness,
The latter being seven-fold.

7.   The first is called *citta*, meaning 'collected',
Because in it are collected the seeds
Of defilements and habits;
The second, however, is called *citta*,
Because it acts in diverse ways.

8. Collectively [i.e. as a collection of store-consciousness
and seven active consciousnesses]
It is the imagination of the unreal forms [of
subjectivity and objectivity];
That, too, is said to be three-fold:
Maturing, caused and phenomenal.

9. Of them, the first, [namely the maturing one],
Is the basic consciousness,
Because its nature is to become matured;
The others, [namely the caused and the phenomenal ones],
Are the active consciousness,
For, the latter for its reality, depends
On the knowledge of the perceived-perceiver distinction.

10. The profundity of the three natures
Is indeed recognized, because
The defiled and the pure are each
Existent as well as non-existent,
Dual as well as unitary;
Also because
The three natures are not mutually different
In definition.

11. The imagined nature is said
To be defined both as existent and as non-existent,
For on the one hand it is grasped as existent,
While, on the other,
It is totally non-existent.

12. The other-dependent nature is said
To be defined both as existent and as non-existent,
For, it exists as an illusion,
It does not exist, though, in the form in which it appears.

13. The absolutely accomplished nature is said
To be defined both as existent and as non-existent,
For, it exists as a state of non-duality,
It is also the non-existence of duality.

14. The nature that is imagined by the ignorant is said
To be both dual and unitary,
For, as it is imagined
A thing has two forms,
But as those two forms do not exist,
It is unitary.

15. The other-dependent nature is said
    To be dual as well as unitary,
    For, it appears in dual form,
    While it has an illusory unity as well.

16. The absolutely accomplished nature is said
    To be dual as well as unitary,
    For, on the one hand,
    It is by nature the absence of duality,
    And, on the other hand,
    It is in the nature of unity without duality.

17. What is to be known as being defined
    As defilement are the imagined and the other-dependent natures,
    While the absolutely accomplished nature
    Is recognized as the definition of purity.

18. The absolutely accomplished nature
    Is to be understood
    As not different in definition from the imagined nature,
    For, the latter being in the nature of unreal duality,
    Is by nature the absence of that duality.

19. The imagined nature, too,
    Is to be understood
    As not different in definition from the absolutely accomplished one,
    For, the latter being in the nature of non-duality,
    Is by nature the absence of duality.

20. The absolutely accomplished nature
    Is to be understood
    As not different in definition from the other-dependent nature,
    For, the latter being non-existent in the form in which it appears,
    Is by nature the non-existence of that form.

21. The other-dependent nature, too,
    Is to be understood
    As not different in definition from the absolutely accomplished one,
    For, the former being in the nature of non-existent duality,
    Is by nature non-existent in the form in which it appears.

22. For the sake of proficiency
    A particular order of the natures
    Is recommended, which takes into account
    The conventions [about them], and
    How one understands them.

23.   The imagined nature is essentially of conventional values,
      The other, [namely the other-dependent nature],
      Is essentially that which brings about such conventional values,
      And the third, [namely the absolutely accomplished nature],
      Is the nature freed of all conventional values.

24.   First, the other-dependent nature,
      Which is essentially the absence of duality
      Is understood;
      Then, the unreal duality,
      Namely the duality that is mere imagination,
      Is understood.

25.   Then is understood
      The absolutely accomplished nature,
      Which is positively the absence of duality,
      For, that very nature is then said
      To be both existing and non-existing.

26.   All these three natures
      Depend for the definition
      On [the concept of] non-duality;
      For, [with reference to the imagined nature],
      There is the unreality of duality,
      [With reference to the other-dependent nature],
      It is not in the dual form in which it appears,
      And, [with reference to the absolutely accomplished nature],
      It is by its very nature the absence of that duality.

27.   It is like the magical power,
      Which by the working of incantations
      Appears in the nature of an elephant;
      There is altogether no elephant at all
      But only its form.

28.   The elephant stands for the imagined nature,
      Its form for the other-dependent nature,
      And, that which remains when the elephant has been negated,
      Stands for the absolutely accomplished nature.

29.   So, the imagination of the unreal
      By the working of the basic thought
      Appears in the nature of duality;
      There is altogether no duality at all,
      But only its form.

30. The basic consciousness is like the incantations,
    Suchness is like the piece of wood,
    The [subject-object] discrimination is like the form of the elephant
    And the duality is like the elephant.

31. In comprehending the truth of things
    All three definitions have to be taken together,
    [Although methods of] knowledge, rejection and attainment
    Are to be employed respectively.

32. There, knowledge is non-perception,
    Rejection/destruction is non-appearance,
    Attainment, effected by perception,
    Is direct realization.

33. By the non-perception of duality
    The form of duality disappears;
    The non-duality resulting from its disappearance
    Is then attained.

34. It is just as the case of magic,
    In which the non-perception of the elephant,
    The disappearance of its form, and the perception of the piece of wood,
    Take place all at once.

35. The attainment of liberation becomes effortless
    By getting rid of misunderstanding,
    Intellectually seeing the meaninglessness,
    And following the threefold knowledge.

36. Through the perception
    That there is only thought,
    There arises the non-perception of knowable things;
    Through the non-perception of knowable things,
    There arises the non-perception of thought, too.

37. From the non-perception of duality
    There arises the perception of the essence of reality;
    From the perception of the essence of reality
    There arises the perception of unlimitedness.

38. The wise man, having perceived the unlimitedness,
    And seeing the meaning of oneself and others,
    Attains the unsurpassed enlightenment,
    Which is in the nature of the three bodies.[1]

1 I.e. the three bodies of the Buddha.

Source: T. A. Kochumuttom (trans.) *A Treatise on the Three Natures* by Vasubandhu, in *A Buddhist Doctrine of Experience* (Delhi: Motilal Banarsidass, 1982), pp. 247–253.

5.5.4 The Tathagata–garbha doctrine

'World-Honored One, the Tathāgata-embryo is permanent and indestructible. Therefore, World-Honored One, the Tathāgata-embryo is the base, the support, and the foundation of the wisdom of liberation. It is also the base, the support, and the foundation of all conditioned dharmas.

'World-Honored One, if there were no Tathāgata-embryo, there would be no abhorrence of suffering and no longing for nirvāṇa. Why? The seven dharmas – the six consciousnesses and their objects – are momentary and nonabiding, and therefore cannot retain the experience of suffering. Hence, they are unable to abhor suffering or aspire to nirvāṇa. The Tathāgata-embryo has no beginning, neither arises nor ceases, and can retain the experience of suffering. It is the cause of [sentient beings'] renunciation of suffering and aspiration for nirvāṇa.

'World-Honored One, the Tathāgata-embryo is not a self, a personal identity, a being, or a life. The Tathāgata-embryo is not in the domain of sentient beings who believe in a real self, whose thinking is confused, or who cling to the view of emptiness.

'World-Honored One, the Tathāgata-embryo is the store of the dharma-dhātu, the store of the Dharma-body, the store of the supramundane, and the store of intrinsic purity.

'This intrinsically pure Tathāgata-embryo, as I understand it, is always the inconceivable state of the Tathāgata even if contaminated by defilements, the adventitious dust. Why? World-Honored One, the mind, whether virtuous or non-virtuous, changes from moment to moment, and it cannot be contaminated by defilements, the adventitious dust. Why? Defilements are not in contact with the mind; the mind is not in contact with defilements. How can anything that is not in contact with the mind contaminate the mind? Yet, World-Honored One, because there are defilements there is a defiled mind. It is extremely difficult to know and understand contamination by defilements. Only the Buddha, the World-Honored One, who is the eye, the wisdom, the root of the Dharma, the guide, and the foundation of the true Dharma, can know and see it as it is.'

Source: G. C. C. Chang (trans.) From *The True Lion's Roar of Queen Śrīmālā* (University Park & London: Pennsylvania State University, 1983), pp. 380–381.

5.5.5 Nine examples which illustrate how the Buddha Nature is obscured

The first analogy is that of a small buddha statue concealed within a withering lotus flower. As long as it remains hidden by the shriveled petals, we cannot know it is there, yet when the petals are shed the buddha's image is instantly revealed. At present, our own buddha nature is obscured by the veil of disturbing emotions.

The second metaphor is honey. Honey is sweet and delicious to eat, but if the honey is covered with a cluster of bees, it's impossible to even taste it. Nevertheless, once the bees are dispelled we can enjoy the honey's natural goodness.

The next example is a grain of rice. Most people like rice, but when it is covered by the husk, it is inedible. Whether the grain of rice remains within the husk or is extracted, the quality of the grain itself does not suffer in the least. It's still just rice, but for the one who eats it there's a very big difference in whether or not the rice has been husked.

The fourth analogy compares the enlightened essence to a lump of gold covered with dirt. Imagine that a few thousand years ago someone dropped a big lump of gold into a ditch. Slowly, it became completely encrusted with soil and debris so that no one could see it laying there. The gold itself couldn't call out, 'Hey, I'm here! Please take me out and clean me.' So, there it stayed. Finally, one day a clairvoyant person happened by who could clearly see the gold laying in the ditch. He told people, 'Look! There's gold here! Dig it up, wash away the impurities, and use the gold for whatever you like.' Likewise, when the enlightened essence is recognized and purified, it is invaluable. Even unrecognized, it is still priceless.

The fifth example describes a cache of precious gems hidden under the floor in a poor man's house. Though a treasure of jewels lies unseen just beneath his feet, the fellow hasn't realized this and so undergoes the terrible suffering of deprivation. Unless he uncovers this store of wealth, it won't help him at all. Likewise, although all sentient beings possess the enlightened potential, they will continue to undergo needless suffering until the buddha nature is realized.

The seed of the tree comprises the sixth metaphor. Even a tiny seed can grow into a tree many meters high. Despite close examination, we are unable to perceive the potential tree intrinsic to the seed because it isn't actualized yet. Nonetheless, the seed definitely possesses this latent capacity. Similarly, many qualities lie dormant within the enlightened essence, yet at present they are not actualized.

The seventh example describes the image of a buddha wrapped in old rags and therefore undetectable. Our enlightened essence is, in the same way, temporarily obscured by defilements so that we are unable to recognize it.

Eighth is the example of a destitute woman who carries in her womb a child destined to become a great king. The woman is completely impoverished and living under difficult conditions, perhaps even sick. She has no enjoyments whatsoever. Yet, she carries a child who will later become a great ruler. At this time, no one knows of her unseen possession. Even she herself is unaware. In just this way, all sentient beings 'carry' within them the enlightened essence which need only be realized.

Though now imperceptible, when this essence is realized and fully actualized, the buddha qualities will be immediately evident.

Lastly, the sugatagarbha can be likened to a complete buddha statue which, though perfectly cast, remains yet within the mold. According to the age-old tradition, a statue of wax is melted away within a clay mold before pouring the gold inside. Later, the mold is broken and the golden statue removed. However, in our example, the mold hasn't been removed yet. This precious statue is made of pure gold and, having just the right proportions, is exquisite to behold. Nevertheless, since the rough clay mold still envelops it, we cannot discern the beautiful statue within. Likewise, shrouded by obscurations, the enlightened essence is imperceptible to ordinary sentient beings.

Obviously, the general meaning of all nine examples is that the enlightened essence is obscured by defilement. Therefore, we may think, 'Why are so many examples given if there's only a single idea to comprehend?' But each of the nine examples has a particular inner message and illustrates a definite point. Let's look at these examples, again.

First, we are told the enlightened essence is similar to a statue of the buddha concealed within a wilting lotus blossom. A fresh lotus flower is very appealing to the eye, but as the days go by the flower loses its freshness and grows less and less attractive. By the third or fourth day, the petals begin to dry out and fall off. Likewise, at first the object of our desire seems fascinating yet, as time passes, sooner or later the fascination wears off. The withering lotus is used to illustrate the defilement of desire because attachment clouds the sugatagarbha.

The example of the bees portrays the buddha nature masked by aggression. The honey itself is sweet and delicious, but bees are easily irritated. When angered, they sting and cause suffering. Likewise, anger or aggression hurts one's own mind and brings suffering to others.

The example of rice within the husk symbolizes ignorance. Rice is an important staple. It sustains beings, keeping them alive and nourished. But if the rice remains enveloped by a very hard and unpleasant husk, it is inedible and therefore useless. Like grain encased by husk, sentient beings are totally enveloped by ignorance, unknowing.

Defilements can either be latent or manifest. The fourth example, a lump of gold embedded in filth, represents manifest defilements. The manifest defilements of attachment, aggression, stupidity, and so forth constitute impurities that obstruct our perception of the enlightened essence.

Latent defilements are quite dense and also completely obscure our perception of the buddha nature. The fifth example depicts riches buried under one's house Though it would be easy to reach such a treasure, the earth is dense and one is unable to detect anything hidden below ground. In the same way, though easy to purify, our latent defilements are quite dense and obscuring.

Previously, we mentioned 'that which is abandoned when attaining the *path of seeing*' and 'that which is abandoned when attaining the *path of cultivation*.'

Once a seed is planted, it naturally grows into a tree. In the same way, once the wisdom of the path of seeing has taken birth within oneself, defilements and obscurations are naturally cast away.

Ragged clothes concealing a lovely buddha image are easily stripped away. Likewise, that which is to be abandoned at the path of cultivation is very easily discarded.

The eighth and ninth examples describe a nation's ruler still within his mother's womb and a magnificent statue still within its clay mold. Yet in time this future king, who already exists as an embryo, will take birth; the statue, already finished and perfect, will be gradually freed of its encasement.

The first seven of the ten bodhisattvas levels are called the *seven impure bhumis* while the last three are termed the *three pure bhumis*. The first seven are called 'impure' because some ego-clinging lingers whereas ego-clinging has been totally purified upon reaching the three highest levels.

Source: Thrangu Rinpoche, *Buddha Nature* (Kathmandu: Rangjung Yeshe Publications, 1988), pp. 72–75.

——— ●◆● ———

BUDDHIST PRACTICES

— ◆◆◆ —

5.6 THERAVADA SOURCES

5.6.1 *Anapanasati* meditation – 'mindfulness of breathing'

Meditation is the way of developing the mind so that it may be a base for the arising of wisdom. Here the breath is a physical foundation. We call it Ānāpānasati or 'mindfulness of breathing'. Here we make breathing our mental object. We take this object of meditation because it's the simplest and because it has been the heart of meditation since ancient times.

When a good occasion arises to do sitting meditation, sit cross-legged: right leg on top of the left leg, right hand on top of the left hand. Keep your back straight and erect. Say to yourself, 'Now I will let go of all my burdens and concerns.' You don't want anything that will cause you worry. Let go of all concerns for the time being.

Now fix your attention on the breath. Then breathe in and breathe out. In developing awareness of breathing, don't intentionally make the breath long or short. Neither make it strong or weak. Just let it flow normally and naturally. Mindfulness and self-awareness, arising from the mind, will know the in-breath and the out-breath.

Be at ease. Don't think about anything. No need to think of this or that. The only thing you have to do is fix your attention on the breathing in and breathing out. You have nothing else to do but that! Keep your mindfulness fixed on the in- and out-breaths as they occur. Be aware of the beginning, middle and end of each breath. On inhalation, the beginning of the breath is at the nose tip, the middle at the heart, and the end in the abdomen. On exhalation, it's just the reverse: the beginning of the breath is in the abdomen, the middle at the heart, and the end at the nose tip. Develop the awareness of the breath: 1, at the nose tip; 2, at the heart; 3, in the abdomen. Then in reverse: 1, in the abdomen; 2, at the heart; and 3, at the nose tip.

Focusing the attention on these three points will relieve all worries. Just don't think of anything else! Keep your attention on the breath. Perhaps other thoughts will enter the mind. It will take up other themes and distract you. Don't be concerned. Just take up the breathing again as your object of attention. The mind may get caught up in judging and investigating your moods, but continue to practise, being constantly aware of the beginning, middle and the end of each breath.

Eventually, the mind will be aware of the breath at these three points all the time. When you do this practice for some time, the mind and body will get accustomed to the work. Fatigue will disappear. The body will feel lighter and the breath will become more and more refined. Mindfulness and self-awareness will protect the mind and watch over it.

We practise like this until the mind is peaceful and calm, until it is 'one'. 'One' means that the mind will be completely absorbed in the breathing, that it doesn't separate from the breath. The mind will be unconfused and at ease. It will know the beginning, middle and end of the breath and remain steadily fixed on it.

Then when the mind is peaceful, we fix our attention on the in-breath and out-breath at the nose tip only. We don't have to follow it up and down to the abdomen and back. Just concentrate on the tip of the nose where the breath comes in and goes out.

This is called 'calming the mind', making it relaxed and peaceful. When tranquillity arises, the mind 'stops'; it 'stops' with its single object, the breath. This is what's known as making the mind peaceful so that wisdom may arise.

Source: Ajahn Chah, *Bodhinyāna* (Rajathani, Thailand: The Sangha, Bung Wai Forest Monastery, 1980).

5.6.2 Two *paritta* chants

Metta Sutta: Loving-kindness

In praise of love and goodwill towards all beings

1 He who is skilled in welfare, who wishes to attain that calm state [Nibbāna], should act thus: he should be able, upright, perfectly upright, of noble speech, gentle and humble.

2 Contented, easily supported, with few duties, of light livelihood, with senses calmed, discreet, not impudent, not greedily attracted to families.

3 He should not pursue the slightest thing for which otherwise men might censure him. May all beings be happy and secure, may their hearts be wholesome!

4–5 Whatever living beings there be: feeble or strong, tall, stout or medium, short, small or large, without exception; seen or unseen, those dwelling far or near, those who are born or those who are to be born, may all beings be happy!

6 Let none deceive another, not despise any person whatsoever in any place. Let him not wish any harm to another out of anger or ill-will.

7 Just as a mother would protect her only child at the risk of her own life, even so, let him cultivate a boundless heart towards all beings.

8 Let his thoughts of boundless love pervade the whole world: above, below and across without any obstruction, without any hatred, without any enmity.

9 Whether he stands, walks, sits or lies down, as long as he is awake, he should develop this mindfulness. This they say is the noblest living here.

10 Not falling into wrong views, being virtuous and endowed with insight, by discarding attachment to sense desires, never again is he reborn.

Mahā-Mangala Sutta: The Auspicious Performance

The definition of the highest blessing

Thus have I heard: Once the Buddha was living near Sāvatthi in the Jeta Grove at Anāthapindika's monastery. Then, one beautiful night, a certain devatā,[1] having illumined the whole Jeta Grove with surpassing splendour, came to the Buddha and, making salutations, stood on one side and addressed the Buddha in [the following] verse:

1 Many gods and men, wishing for well-being, have pondered over those things that constitute auspicious performances. Tell us what is the highest auspicious performance. The Buddha:

2 Not to associate with fools, but to associate with the wise and to honour those who are worthy of honour; this is the most auspicious performance.

3 To reside in a congenial environment, to have done meritorious deeds in the past and to set oneself in the right course; this is the most auspicious performance.

4 A good, all-round, education, [appreciation of] the Arts, a highly-trained discipline and pleasant speech; this is the most auspicious performance.

5 Supporting one's father and mother, cherishing wife and children and a peaceful occupation; this is the most auspicious performance.

6 Liberality, dutiful conduct, the helping of relatives and blameless actions; this is the most auspicious performance.

7 Ceasing and abstaining from evil, abstention from intoxicating drinks and diligence in virtue; this is the most auspicious performance.

8 Reverence, humility, contentment, gratitude and timely hearing of the Dhamma; this is the most auspicious performance.

9 Forbearance, obedience, association with exemplars of the Dhamma-life and participation in religious discussions; this is the most auspicious performance.

10 Self-control, perception of the Noble Truths and the realization of Nibbāna; this is the most auspicious performance.

11 If one's mind is sorrowless, stainless and secure [in Nibbāna] and is not disturbed when affected by worldly vicissitudes; this is the most auspicious performance.

12 Those who thus acting are everywhere unconquered, attain happiness everywhere – to them these are the most auspicious performances.

---

1 God, illustrious divine being.

Source: *Metta Sutta* and *Mahā-Mangala Sutta* from H. Saddhatissa (trans.) *The Sutta-Nipāta* (London: Curzon, 1985), pp. 15–16, 29–30.

5.6.3 Vinaya rules on food

27. I shall accept alms-food appreciatingly: this is a training to be done. (1)

28. I shall accept alms-food with attention on the bowl: this is a training to be done. (2)

29. I shall accept alms-food with other foods in proportion (that is, in the proportion of one part in four to the rice): this is a training to be done. (3)

30. I shall accept alms-food level with the edge (of the bowl): this is a training to be done. (4)

31. I shall eat the alms-food appreciatingly: this is a training to be done. (5)

32. I shall eat the alms-food with attention on the bowl: this is a training to be done. (6)

33. I shall eat the alms-food evenly: this is a training to be done. (7)

34. I shall eat the alms-food with curries in proportion: this is a training to be done. (8)

35. I shall not eat the alms-food working down from the top: this is a training to be done. (9)

36. I shall not hide curries and other foods with rice out of desire to get more: this is a training to be done. (10)

37. I shall not unless sick ask for curry or rice for my own benefit and eat it: this is a training to be done. (11)

38. I shall not look finding fault with another's bowl: this is a training to be done. (12)

39. I shall not make up an extra-large mouthful: this is a training to be done. (13)

40. I shall make up a round mouthful: this is a training to be done. (14)

41. I shall not open the mouth when the mouthful is not brought to it: this is a training to be done. (15)

42. I shall not put all the fingers into the mouth when eating: this is a training to be done. (16)

43. I shall not speak with the mouth full: this is a training to be done. (17)

44. I shall not eat tossing up (into the air) a lump of food: this is a training to be done. (18)

45. I shall not eat biting upon a lump of rice: this is a training to be done. (19)

46. I shall not eat stuffing out (the cheeks): this is a training to be done. (20)

47. I shall not eat shaking the hand about: this is a training to be done. (21)

48. I shall not eat scattering rice about: this is a training to be done. (22)

49. I shall not eat putting the tongue out: this is a training to be done. (23)

50. I shall not eat making a champing sound: this is a training to be done. (24)

51. I shall not eat making a sucking sound: this is a training to be done. (25)

52. I shall not eat cleaning (or licking) the hand: this is a training to be done. (26)

53. I shall not eat cleaning (or scraping) the bowl (with the finger): this is a training to be done. (27)

54. I shall not eat cleaning (licking) the lips (with the tongue): this is a training to be done. (28)

55. I shall not accept a drinking-water pot with a hand soiled by food: this is a training to be done. (29)

56. I shall not in an inhabited area throw away bowl-washing water which has rice grains in it: this is a training to be done. (30)

Source: Ven. Ñāṇamoli Thera (trans.) *The Pāṭimokkha 227 Fundamental Rules of a Bhikkhu,* (Bangkok: Mahāmakuṭarājavidyālaya, 1969), pp. 124–128.

5.6.4 From the *Therīgāthā*, the elder nuns' verses

On going deep into a wood, the tempter-god Māra comes to Soma to make her afraid and so desist from meditation. Māra insinuates:

That vantage-ground (i.e. Arahatship) to be attained by sages is hard to win. With her two-finger-intelligence, no woman is able to attain that.

Somā recognizes Māra, though, and replies:

What (difference) should a woman's state make, when the mind is well concentrated, when knowledge is rolling on, when she rightly has insight into *Dhamma*? To one for whom the question arises, 'am I a woman or am I a man (in these matters)?' or 'what indeed am I?'. To such a one is Māra fit to talk!

Source: P. Harvey, *An Introduction to Buddhist Ethics* (Cambridge: Cambridge University Press 2000), p. 359.

5.6.5 Promoting the Dharma – Asoka's Rock Edict IV

For many hundreds of years in the past, slaughter of animals, cruelty to living creatures, discourtesy to relatives, and disrespect for priests and ascetics have been increasing.

But now, because of King Priyadarśī's practice of Dharma, the sound of war drums has become the call to Dharma [rather than to war], summoning the people to exhibitions of the chariots of the gods, elephants, fireworks, and other divine displays.

King Priyadarśī's inculcation of Dharma has increased, beyond anything observed in many hundreds of years, abstention from killing animals and from cruelty to living beings, kindliness in human and family relations, respect for priests and ascetics, and obedience to mother and father and elders.

The practice of Dharma has been promoted in this and other ways. King Priyadarśī will continue to promote the patience of Dharma. His sons, grandsons, and great-grandsons to the end of time will ever promote the practice of Dharma; standing firm themselves in Dharma, they will instruct the people in Dharma and moral conduct.

For instruction in Dharma is the best of actions. The practice of Dharma is impossible for the immoral man. To increase this practice, even to forestall its diminution, is laudable.

The edict has been inscribed in order to inspire my descendants to work for the promotion and to prevent the decline of Dharma. King Priyadarśī commanded this record to be made twelve years after his coronation.

Source: N. A. Nikam & R. McKeon (trans.) 'The Objectives of Inculcation of Dharma' in *The Edicts of Asoka* (London & Chicago: Chicago University Press, 1959), pp. 31,32.

5.7 MAHAYANA SOURCES

5.7.1 Chinese sources relating to Ch'an Buddhism

The Ultimate Reality and the rest

No-Thought is Absolute Reality, in which the Mind ceases to act.

(Fa-Yung)

Void and Being are not seen as two: this is the Middle Way.

(Fa-Yung)

Fa Yung (594–657 CE) was an early Chinese Ch'an (Zen in Japanese) master, although the school that he founded is not one of the acknowledged Ch'an schools.

Substance and action are unimpededly interfused; this is the essence of Ch'an.

(Tung-shan Liang-chieh)

He is the same as me. Yet I am not he.

(Tung-shan Lyang-chieh)

Tung-shan Liang-chieh (807–69 CE) was one of the founders of the Ts'ao-tung (Soto in Japanese) school of Ch'an/Zen Buddhism.

The methods of meditation

You should not search *through others*, lest the Truth recede further from You. When alone I proceed through myself, I meet him wherever I go.

(Tung-shan Liang-chieh)

To *talk* about names and manifestations is useless, but a direct approach easily reaches it. No-Mind is that which is in action; it is that constant action which does not act. The no-Mind of which I speak is not separate from the Mind.

(Fa-Yung)

Do not abide in an excess of Void (sunyata) but illuminate the non-being in being.

(Fa-Yung)

As there is no self and no others, how can one speak of degrees of intimacy? You should not lecture from assembly to assembly, since words do not lead directly to the Truth.

(P'ang-Yun)

P'ang-Yun (740–808/11 CE), also known as Layman P'ang, was the most famous Chinese lay practitioner of Ch'an/Zen. His recorded dialogues and exchanges have a place with those of the great Chinese Ch'an masters.

I have my secret. I look at You with twinkling eye. If You do not understand this, do not call Yourself a monk.

(Hsiang-yen)

Hsiang-yen Chih-hsien (d. 898 CE) was a Chinese Ch'an master.

Koan (enigmas as meditation-topics)

1 If I have nothing, what should I do? Throw it away!
2 You are not allowed to travel at night, but You must arrive before day-break.
3 The bridge flows, the water does not.
4 What is the sound of ONE hand clapping?
5 If You run away from the Void, You can never be free of it. If You search for the Void, You can never reach it.

5.7.2 Japanese sources relating to Zen Buddhism

The Ultimate Reality

There is a Reality, even prior to Heaven and earth.
Indeed it has no form, much less a name . . .
To call it Mind (mind-only, cittamatra) or Buddha violates its nature.

For then it becomes like the mirage of a flower in the air.
It is not Mind, nor Buddha.
Absolutely quiet, and yet illuminating in a mysterious way,
It allows itself to be perceived only by the clear-eyed.
It is a Reality (Dharma) truly beyond form and sound.
It is a Way-Tao, having nothing to do with words.

(Daito Kokushi)

Daito Kokushi, or Kosen Daito Kokushi, was a posthumous
title conferred on Myocho Shuho (1282–1338 CE), a Rinzai Zen master
who founded Daitoku-ji, one of the most important Japanese Zen
monasteries. 'Kokushi', or 'teacher of the nation', was a title given to
the Buddhist teacher of an emperor.

Method

If you desire to listen to the thunderous voice of the Dharma,
Exhaust your words, empty your thoughts,
For then You may come to recognize this one essence.

(Daito Kokushi)

As regards meditation practised in the Mâhayâna,
We have no words to praise it fully:
The virtues of perfection such as benevolence, morality, etc.,
And the invocation of the Buddha's name, confession, ascetic discipline,
And many other good deeds of merit,
All these issue from the practice of meditation.

(Hakuin)

Hakuin (1689–1769), a Rinzai Zen master, is sometimes referred
to as the father of modern Rinzai Zen. He systematized Zen training
through the use of koan, enigmatic and paradoxical statements or verses
used to direct meditation, and zazen, seated meditation.

5.7.3 Militant Buddhism: the determination of Nichiren

Nichiren (1222–82 CE) was the founder of a tradition of Japanese
Buddhism that has emphasized the exclusive power of the Lotus Sutra to
bring humans to liberation. He believed that his mission was to bring
Japan to this realization and so challenged both Japan's rulers and other
Buddhist sects to heed his message. His uncompromising style of
Buddhism brought both persecution and periods of exile.

Already over two hundred years have passed since the world entered the Latter Day of the Law. I was born in a remote land far from India, a person of low station and a priest of humble learning. During my past lifetimes through the six paths, I have perhaps at times been born as a great ruler in the human or heavenly worlds, and have bent the multitudes to my will as a great wind bends the branches of the small trees. And yet at such times I was not able to become a Buddha.

I studied the Hinayana and Mahayana sutras, beginning as an ordinary practitioner with no understanding at all and gradually moving upward to the position of a great bodhisattva. For one kalpa, two kalpas, countless kalpas I devoted myself to the practices of a bodhisattva, until I had almost reached the state where I could never fail to attain Buddhahood. And yet I was dragged down by the powerful and overwhelming influence of evil, and I never attained Buddhahood. [. . .]

While one is practising the teachings of the Lotus Sutra, he may surmount all kinds of difficulties occasioned by the evil forces of worldly life, or by the persecutions of rulers, non-Buddhists, or the followers of the Hinayana sutras. And yet he may encounter [. . .] monks who seemed thoroughly conversant with the teachings of the provisional and the true Mahayana sutras but who were in fact possessed by devils. Such men seem to praise the Lotus Sutra most forcefully, but in fact they belittle the people's ability to understand it, claiming that 'its principles are profound but human understanding is slight'. They mislead others by saying, 'Not a single person has ever attained Buddhahood through that sutra' or 'Not one person in a thousand [can reach enlightenment through its teachings].' Thus, over a period of countless lifetimes, men are deceived more often than there are sands in the Ganges, until they [abandon their faith in the Lotus Sutra and] descend to the teachings of the provisional Mahayana sutras, abandon these and descend to the teachings of the Hinayana sutras, and eventually abandon even these and descend to the teachings and scriptures of the non-Buddhist doctrines. I understand all too well how, in the end, men have come in this way to fall into the evil states of existence.

I, Nichiren, am the only person in all Japan who understands this. But if I utter so much as a word concerning it, then parents, brothers, and teachers will surely criticize me and the government authorities will take steps against me. On the other hand, I am fully aware that if I do not speak out, I will be lacking in compassion. I have considered which course to take in the light of the teachings of the Lotus and Nirvana sutras. If I remain silent, I may escape harm in this lifetime, but in my next life I will most certainly fall into the hell of incessant suffering. If I speak out, I am fully aware that I will have to contend with the three obstacles and the four devils. But of these two courses, surely the latter is the one to choose.

If I were to falter in my determination in the face of government persecutions, however, I would not be able to fulfill my course. In that case, perhaps it would be better not to speak out. [. . .] Persons like myself who are of paltry strength might still be able to lift Mount Sumeru and toss it about; persons like myself who are lacking in spiritual powers might still shoulder a load of dry grass and yet remain unburned in the fire at the end of the kalpa of decline; and persons like myself who are without wisdom might still read and memorize as many sutras as there are sands in the Ganges. But such acts are not difficult, we are told, when compared to the difficulty of embracing even one phrase or verse of the Lotus Sutra in the Latter Day of the Law. Nevertheless, I vowed to summon up a powerful and unconquerable desire for the salvation of all beings, and never to falter in my efforts.

It is already over twenty years since I began proclaiming my doctrines. Day after day, month after month, year after year I have been subjected to repeated persecutions. Minor persecutions and annoyances are too numerous even to be counted, but the major persecutions number four. Among the four, twice I have been subjected to persecutions by the government itself. The most recent one has come near to costing me my life. In addition, my disciples, my lay followers, and even those who have merely listened to my teachings have been subjected to severe punishment and treated as though they were guilty of treason. [. . .]

Thus the Buddha decided the time [when the votary of the Lotus Sutra should appear], describing it as a 'fearful and evil age', 'a latter age', 'a latter age when the Law will disappear', and 'the final five hundred years', as attested by both the two Chinese versions of the Lotus Sutra, *Shō-hokke Kyō* and *Myōhō-renge-kyō*. At such a time, if the three powerful enemies predicted in the Lotus Sutra did not appear, then who would have faith in the words of the Buddha? If it were not for Nichiren, who could fulfill the Buddha's prophecies concerning the votary of the Lotus Sutra? The three schools of southern China and seven schools of northern China, along with the seven great temples of Nara, were numbered among the enemies of the Lotus Sutra in the time of the Middle Day of the Law. How much less can the Zen, Ritsu, and Nembutsu priests of the present time hope to escape a similar label?

With this body of mine, I have fulfilled the prophecies of the sutra. The more the government authorities rage against me, the greater is my joy. For instance, there are certain Hinayana bodhisattvas, not yet freed from delusion, who draw evil karma to themselves by their own compassionate vow. Thus, if one of them sees that his mother and father have fallen into hell and are suffering greatly, he will deliberately create the appropriate karma in hopes that he too may fall into hell and take their suffering upon himself. To suffer for the sake of others is a joy to him. It is the same with me in fulfilling the prophecies. Though at present I must face trials that I can scarcely endure, I rejoice when I think that in the future I will escape being born into the evil paths.

And yet the people doubt me, and I too have doubts about myself. Why do the gods not assist me? Heavenly gods and other guardian deities made their vow before the Buddha. Even if the votary of the Lotus Sutra were an ape rather than a man, if he announced that he was a votary of the Lotus Sutra, then I believe the gods should rush forward to fulfill the vow they made before the Buddha.

Source: B. Watson *et al.* (trans.), edited with introduction by P. Yampolsky, *Selected Writings of Nichiren* (New York: Columbia University Press, 1990), pp. 78–81, 84.

5.8 VAJRAYANA SOURCES

5.8.1 Meeting spiritual friends

Although you may possess the most perfect working basis, but are not urged on by spiritual friends as a contributary cause, it is difficult to set out on the path towards enlightenment, because of the power of inveterate propensities due to evil deeds committed repeatedly in former times. Therefore you have to meet spiritual friends. This necessity is outlined in the following index:

> Five headings refer to the meeting with spiritual friends:
> Reason, classification,
> Primary characteristics of each group,
> The method of meeting them and the benefits.

There are three reasons for meeting them, scriptural authority, necessity and simile. 'Scriptural authority' is found in the ''Phags.pa sdud.pa'

> Virtuous disciples having respect for the Guru
> Should always be in touch with wise Gurus
> Because from them the virtues of a wise man spring.

And in the ''Phags.pa brGyad.stoṅ.pa'

> Thus a Bodhisattva Mahāsattva who wishes to attain unsurpassable
> enlightenment must first approach, then meet and honour spiritual friends.

'Necessity' means that you who have the quality of being an individual able to attain omniscience, must meet with spiritual friends, because you yourself do not know how to accumulate merits and how to tear the two veils of conflicting emotions and primitive beliefs about reality. This is indisputable. In general, the Buddhas of the past, present and future make it clear why friends are necessary, while the Pratyekabuddhas illustrate the fact that without friends the ultimately real remains unattainable. And so for people like ourselves who intend to attain perfect Buddhahood it is necessary to accumulate all those merits which are subsumed under merit proper and spiritual awareness, but the means of accumulating them depends on spiritual friends; and it is equally necessary to tear the two veils of conflicting emotions and primitive beliefs about reality, but the means of doing so again depends on these friends.

The 'similes' are that spiritual friends are like a guide when we travel in unknown territory, an escort when we pass through dangerous regions and a ferry-man when we cross a great river.

As to the first, when we travel guideless in unknown territory there is the danger of going astray and getting lost. But if we go with a guide then there is no such danger, and without missing a single step we reach the desired place. So also, when we have set out on the path towards unsurpassable enlightenment and are going towards the spiritual level of the Samyaksambuddha, if there is no spiritual friend belonging to the Mahāyāna way of life to act as our guide, then there is danger of losing our way in paths of the Non-Buddhists, of going astray in the way of life of the Srāvakas, and of getting lost on the paths of the Pratyekabuddhas. But if we walk with a spiritual friend as our guide, then there is no danger and we arrive at the city of the Omniscient One. This is stated in the 'dPal.'byuṅ.gi rnam.thar':

> Spiritual friends are like guides, because they set us on the path of the
>   perfections.

In the second simile dangerous regions are haunted by thieves and robbers, wild beasts and other noxious animals. When we go there without an escort, there is the danger of losing our body, life or property; but when we have a strong escort we reach the desired place without loss. So also, when we have set out on the path towards enlightenment, accumulated merits and spiritual awareness and are about to go to the city of the Omniscient One, if there is no spiritual friend to act as an escort, there is danger of losing our stock of merits either from within ourselves, by preconceived idea and emotional instability, or from outside, by demons, wrong guides and other treacherous people, and there is also the danger that we may be robbed of our life which is approaching pleasurable forms of existence. As has been stated:

> When the crowd of robber-like emotions,
> Gets a chance to do so, it will steal the good one has acquired
> And even take the life is on its way towards pleasurable forms of
>   existence.

But if we have spiritual friends to escort us, we do not suffer the loss of our stock of the good and wholesome, are not robbed of our lives that are approaching pleasurable forms of existence, and we arrive at the city of the Omniscient One. This is affirmed in the 'dPal.'byuṅ.gi rnam.thar':

> All the merits of a Bodhisattva are guarded by spiritual friends.

And in the 'dGe.sñen.ma Mi.g'yo.ba'i rnam.thar':

> Spiritual friends are like an escort, because they conduct us to the city of
>   the Omniscient One.

Finally in the third simile when we cross a great river, if we have boarded a boat without a boatman, we are either drowned or carried away by the current and do not reach the other shore; but if there is a boatman we land safely by his efforts. So also, when we cross the ocean of Saṃsāra, if there are no spiritual friends to act as boatmen, though we have boarded the ship of the Noble Doctrine, we are either drowned in Saṃsāra or carried away by its current. As has been said:

> One does not reach the other shore without an oarsman in the boat;
> Although one may have all qualities complete, without a Guru one does
>   not arrive at the end of the world.

Therefore, when we are in touch with spiritual friends who are like boatmen, we reach the dry shore of Nirvāṇa, the other side of Saṃsāra. This is expressed in the 'sDoṅ.po bkod.pa'i mdo'

> Spiritual friends are like a boatman, because they make us cross the great
>   river of Saṃsāra.

And so we must meet with spiritual friends who are like a guide, an escort and a boatman.

The classification of these friends is fourfold: (i) in the form of an ordinary human being, (ii) as a Bodhisattva living on a high level of spirituality, (iii) the Nirmāṇakāya, and (iv) Sambhogakāya of the Buddha. These four types are related to our spiritual standing in life.

Since at the beginning of our career it is impossible to be in touch with the Buddhas or with Bodhisattvas living on a high level of spirituality, we have to meet with ordinary human beings as spiritual friends. As soon as the darkness caused by our deeds has lightened, we can find Bodhisattvas on a high level of spirituality. Then when we have risen above the Great Preparatory Path we can find the Nirmāṇakāya of the Buddha. Finally, as soon as we live on a high spiritual level we can meet with the Sambhogakāya as a spiritual friend.

Should you ask, who among these four is our greatest benefactor, the reply is that in the beginning of our career when we are still living imprisoned by our deeds and emotions, we will not even see so much as the face of a superior spiritual friend. Instead we will have to seek an ordinary human being who can illumine the path we have to follow with the light of his counsel, whereafter we shall meet superior ones. Therefore the greatest benefactor is a spiritual friend in the form of an ordinary human being.

Source: H. V. Guenther (trans.) *The Jewel Ornament of Liberation* by sGam.po.pa (Boston & London: Shambhala, 1986), pp. 30–33.

5.8.2 Searching for reincarnated Lamas

The business of identifying *tulkus* is more logical than it may at first appear. Given the Buddhist belief that the principle of rebirth is fact, and given that the whole purpose of reincarnation is to enable a being to continue its effort on behalf of all suffering sentient beings, it stands to reason that it should be possible to identify individual cases. This enables them to be educated and placed in the world so that they can continue their work as soon as possible.

Mistakes in this identification process can certainly be made, but the lives of the great majority of *tulkus* (of whom there are presently a few hundred known, although in Tibet before the Chinese invasion there were probably a few thousand) are adequate testimony of its efficacy.

As I have said, the whole purpose of reincarnation[1] is to facilitate the continuity of a being's work. This fact has great implications when it comes to searching for the successor of a particular person. For example, whilst my efforts in general are directed towards helping my fellow Tibetans. Therefore, if I die before Tibetans regain their freedom, it is only logical to assume that I will be born outside Tibet. Of course, it could be that by then my people will have no use for a Dalai Lama, in which case they will not both to search for me. So I might take rebirth as an insect, or an animal – whatever would be of most value to the largest number of sentient beings.

The way that the identification process is carried out is also less mysterious than might be imagined. It begins as a simple process of elimination. Say, for instance, we are looking for the reincarnation of a particular monk. First it must be established when and where that monk died. Then, considering that the new incarnation will usually be conceived a year or so after the death of its predecessor – these lengths of time we know from experience – a timetable is drawn up. Thus, if Lama X dies in year Y, his next incarnation will probably be born around eighteen months to two years later. In the year Y plus five, the child is likely to be between three and four years old: the field has narrowed already.

Next, the most likely place for the reincarnation to appear is established. This is usually quite easy. First, will it be inside or outside Tibet? If outside, there are a limited number of places where it is likely – the Tibetan communities of India, Nepal or Switzerland, for example. After that, it must be decided in which town the child is most likely to be found. Generally this is done by referring to the life of the previous incarnation.

Having narrowed the options and established parameters in the way I have shown, the next step is usually to assemble a search party. This need not necessarily mean that a group of people is sent out as if they were looking for treasure. Usually it is sufficient to ask various people in the community to look out for a child of between three and four who might be a candidate. Often there are helpful clues, such as unusual phenomena at the time of the child's birth; or the child may exhibit peculiar characteristics.

Sometimes two or three or more possibilities will emerge at this stage. Occasionally, a search party is not required at all because the previous incarnation has left detailed information right down to the name of his successor and the name of his successor's parents. But this is rare. Other times, the monk's followers may have clear dreams or visions about where to find his successor. On the other hand, one high lama recently directed that there should be no search for his own rebirth. He said that whoever seemed likely to serve the Buddha *Dharma* and his community best should be installed as his successor, rather than for anyone to worry about an accurate identification. There are no hard and fast rules.

If it happens that several children are put forward as candidates, it is usual for someone well known to the previous incarnation to conduct a final examination. Frequently, this person will be recognised by one of the children, which is strong evidence of proof, but sometimes marks on the body are also taken into consideration.

In some cases, the identification process involves consulting one of the oracles or someone who has powers of *ngon shé* (clairvoyance). One of the methods that these people use in *Ta*, whereby the practitioner looks into a mirror in which he or she might see the actual child, or a building, or perhaps a written name. I call this 'ancient television'. It corresponds to the visions that people had at Lake Lhamoi Lhatso, where Reting Rinpoché saw the letters *Ah*, *Ka* and *Ma* and the views of a monastery and a house when he began the search for me.

Sometimes, I myself am called upon to direct the search for a reincarnation. In these circumstances it is my responsibility to make the final decision on whether a given candidate has been correctly chosen. I should say here that I have no powers of clairvoyance. I have had neither the time nor the opportunity to develop them, although I have reason to believe that the Thirteenth Dalai Lama did have some ability in this sphere.

As an example of how I do this, I will relate the story of Ling Rinpoché, my Senior Tutor. I always had the greatest respect for Ling Rinpoché, although when I was a child I only had to see his servant to become afraid – and whenever I heard his familiar footsteps, my heart missed a beat. But, in time, I came to value him as one of my greatest and closest friends. When he died not long ago, I felt that life without him at my side would be very difficult. He had become a rock on which I could lean.

I was in Switzerland, in the late summer of 1983, when I first heard of his final illness: he had suffered a stroke and become paralysed. This news disturbed me very much. Yet, as a Buddhist, I knew there was not much use in worrying. As soon as I could, I returned to Dharamsala, where I found him still alive, but in a bad physical state. Yet his mind was as sharp as ever, thanks to a lifetime of assiduous mental training. His condition remained stable for several months before deteriorating quite suddenly. He entered a coma from which he never emerged and died on 25 December 1983. But, as if any further evidence of his being a remarkable person were needed, his body did not begin to decay until thirteen days after he was pronounced dead, despite the hot climate. It was as if he still inhabited his body, even though clinically it was without life.

When I look back at the manner of his demise, I am quite certain that Ling Rinpoché's illness, drawn out as it was over a long period, was entirely deliberate, in order to help me get used to being without him. However, that is only half the story. Because we are speaking of Tibetans, the tale continues happily. Ling Rinpoché's reincarnation has since been found, and he is presently a very bright and naughty boy of three. His discovery was one of those where the child clearly recognises a member of the search called the person by name and went forward to him, smiling. Subsequently he correctly identified several other of his predecessor's acquaintances.

When I met the boy for the first time, I had no doubts about his identity. He behaved in a way that made it obvious he knew me, though he also showed the utmost respect. On that first occasion, I gave little Ling Rinpoché a large bar of chocolate. He stood impassively holding on to it, arm extended and head bowed all the time he was in my presence. I hardly think any other infant would have kept something sweet untasted and remained standing so formally. Then, when I received the boy at my residence and he was brought to the door, he acted just as his predecessor had done. It was plain that he remembered his way round. Moreover, when he came into my study, he showed immediate familiarity with one of my attendants, who was at the time recovering from a broken leg. First, this tiny person gravely presented him with a *kata* and then, full of laughter and childish giggles, he picked up one of Lobsang Gawa's crutches and ran round and round carrying it as if it were a flagpole.

Another impressive story about the boy concerns the time he was taken, at the age of only two, to Bodh Gaya, where I was due to give teachings. Without anyone telling him of its whereabouts, he found my bedroom, having scrambled on his hands and knees up the stairs, and laid a *kata* on my bed. Today, Ling Rinpoché is already reciting scriptures, those it remains to be seen whether, when he has learned to read, he will turn out to be like some of the young *tulkus* who memorise texts at astonishing speed, as if they were simply picking up where they had left off. I have known a number of small children who could declaim many pages with ease.

Certainly there is an element of mystery in this process of identifying incarnations. But suffice to say that, as a Buddhist, I do not believe that people like Mao or Lincoln or Churchill just 'happen'.

---

1 For advanced bodhisattvas. Normal rebirth/reincarnation has no purpose – it just happens.

Source: Tenzin Gyatso The Fourteenth Dalai Lama, *Freedom in Exile* (London: Cardinel, 1991), pp. 236–240.

5.8.3 An Avalokitesvara tantric liturgy:
For All Beings Throughout Space

First take refuge

> On the crown of my head
> And that of all sentient beings throughout space
> Is a white lotus and a moon [-shaped seat].
> On top of that is [the syllable] *hrīh*
> From which [appears]
> The precious, noble Avalokiteśvara.
> He is white and luminous
> And he radiates light rays of five colors.
> He is beautiful and smiling
> And he sees with compassionate eyes.
> Of his four hands,

The palms of the upper two are held together.
In the lower two
He holds a crystal rosary and a white lotus.
Silks and precious ornaments adorn him.
He wears the hide of an antelope across his chest,
And a crown ornamented by Amitābha.
Seated with his two legs in the crossed thunderbolt position,
He leans his back against a pure moon.
He is, by nature, the epitome of all refuges.

Think that I and all sentient beings are praying to him, in one voice:

Lord,
You are unmarred by fault,
And white in body hue.
The perfect buddha ornaments your crown,
And you see beings with compassionate eyes.
I bow to you, Avalokiteśvara.

Recite that three, seven, or as many times as possible.

As a result of this one-pointed prayer,
Light beams radiate out
From the body of the noble one,
And purify defiled karmic appearances and confusion.
The outer container becomes the Land of Bliss.[1]
The inner contents – the body, speech, and mind of beings –
Become the perfected form, teachings, and heart-mind of Avalokiteśvara.
Appearance and sound turn into indivisible awareness-emptiness.

While meditating on that, recite the six syllables [the mantra *oṃ maṇi padme hūṃ*]. At the end, remain absorbed in the own-state of no-conception about the three circles [doer, done-to, or deed].

My and others' bodies are the perfected form of the noble one.
Voices and sounds are the rhythm of the six syllables.
Memories and thoughts are the expanse of great primal consciousness.
Through the merit resulting [from performing this visualization]
May I quickly come to achieve [identification with] Avalokiteśvara,
And then may I establish every single being without exception in that
    state.

---

1 I.e. The Pure Land of Amitabha Buddha, etc.

Source: J .Gyatso (trans.) 'An Avalokiteśvara Sādhana' in *Religions of Tibet in Practice* D.S.Lopez, Jr. (ed.) (Princeton: Princeton University Press, 1997), pp. 269–270.

5.8.4 Tantric 'weather' practices

People expected storms that summer. When the thunder began, I did this protective concentration: first, I visualized my surroundings as a perfect Buddhafield, in the center of which the immeasurably vast, four-storeyed Mount Meru emerged, composed entirely of jewels and precious stones. On the top was a thousand-pronged iron vajra; its thousand lower prongs reached the solid gold ground below; the central knob rested at the level of the top plateau, and its upper thousand prongs projected into space.

I then visualized myself as Vajrapani seated at the heart of the vajra, and above the topmost prongs I visualized a thousand-spoked golden wheel, resting horizontally. In the hub was seated the Buddha. On the spokes, seated in the defending and protecting posture, the 1,002 Buddhas of this fortunate aeon generated from their hearts a thousand white lions that appeared at the spoke-ends and roared fiercely in the ten directions. Terrified and silenced, the thunder-dragons withdrew and took flight.

Several times, while I was concentrating on this visualization and recited the mantra of Vajrapani, the thunder stopped completely, so I thought that my visualization practice was going quite well.

During this time a drought occurred. The local people asked me to bring rain. I said I did not know how to make rain, but that I would pray to the guru and the Three Jewels. Then I went to a lovely nearby meadow facing south. In the middle, at the foot of a juniper tree, flowed a spring. I performed the consecration of the ground, the invitation to the Buddhas, the cleansing ritual, the offering of the *Hundred Tormas*, and the *torma* offering to the nagas. Then I made this prayer:

'By the blessings of all the Buddhas of the ten directions, the merits gathered by all our mother-sentient beings, and by the good fortune I may have gathered through performing virtuous deeds and meditating with pure motivation, when rain is needed, may the sky fill with clouds and as much rain as desired fall.

'When warmth is needed, may a warm, gentle sun shine and ripen the crops. When hail threatens, may the air turn into a great fire and melt the hail into a welcome downpour of rain. When hoarfrost threatens, may it be prevented by a gathering of warming clouds. May all the birds, rabbits, and insects that destroy the crops and damage the trees be diverted.

'May every year be an excellent one, and may harvests be so abundant that jars are filled to the brim with grain and overflow into inexhaustible heaps, ensuring prosperity and happiness for everyone, day and night, as in the golden age.'

After making this prayer, I returned to my hermitage and visualized first a vast empty sky, then this sky becoming filled with huge clouds. Within a few moments, it began to rain heavily. Since the year thus turned into a good one, people's faith grew, and they kept on bringing me offerings and provisions.

Source: M. Ricard et al. (trans.) *The Life of Shabkar* (New York: SUNY, 1994), pp. 112, 263.

—— ◆ ◆ ● ——

RECENT AND CONTEMPORARY BUDDHIST CONCERNS

—— • ◆ • ——

5.9 THE BENEFITS OF NICHIREN'S TEACHING
JOSEI TODA

Josei Toda (1900–58) was the second president of Soka Gakkai,
a lay-Buddhist movement in the Nichiren school of Japanese Buddhism.

When I view the situation in this world, I find rich people and I find poor people. There are families in which man and wife live happily together; in others there are always quarrels. There are homes in which the members all enjoy good health and a happy life. There are homes full of sick people. There are healthy people, and there are unhealthy people. Why is this?

No Occidental philosophy has been able to account for this. It has been explained only by the Buddhist philosophy of the Orient. Its conclusion is that our life is eternal and that we may die in this world, but we must be reborn in this world again. Just as a man who lived yesterday lives today too, a person who lives in his present life will have to be reborn. Just as we must recognize the existence of our next life, we must recognize our past life. This is the basis of the Oriental Buddhist philosophy. Whether you know it or not, it is the fact of life.

Therefore a person who is healthy today gave cause in his past life for his present good health. A person who is rich today gave cause for it in his past life. This is the Buddhist explanation of the fact that there are people who are noble and humble, rich and poor, happy and unhappy. If any one of you here is poor or suffering because of lack of money, it means that you, according to Buddhism, were a burglar in your past life. I think there may be many ex-burglars here now. 'Not me. It must be my neighbor,' you might say. But then you tell yourself there isn't much you can do about this life. But you can be a rich man in your next life and have a good husband or have a good child.

For that, you must do good deeds now to make sure that your next life will be what you want. This is the basis of Buddhist theory.

But just think for a moment. Everyone wants to overcome his destiny. A poor man, no matter how foolish, would not think he should be content with his status. A sick man would not say he is content with being sick. He wants to be cured; he wants to be healthy. A poor man wants to be a rich man. This is quite natural. Yet the law preached by the Buddha is inexorable.

It holds that you cannot change your life now; you must wait until your next reincarnation. This is a problem indeed, isn't it? But if this is the only solution Buddhism can offer, then I would not like to be a Buddhist. No, thanks. Because I couldn't tell if I could have it my way in my next life.

But the Buddhist law of [Nichiren Daishonin] is better than that of the Buddha. That's the reason why we shout: 'We are not pupils of the Buddha. Buddha's law is of no use. It's got to be Daishonin's Buddhist law.' Daishonin said: 'I am making a thing called a *gohonzon*.[1] If you recite "Nam-myoho Renge-kyo" in front of this *gohonzon*, I will endow you with the condition you failed to create in your past life, enabling you to overcome your destiny instantly.' This is a wonderful thing for which we must be grateful. . . .

If there is a poor man among you, all you must do is to believe in this *gohonzon* and carry out *shakubuku*[2] in earnest. Then you will begin to have the good luck with which you did not come into this world. . . .

When I hold a question-and-answer session at Taiseki-ji,[3] I hear many questions. The two simplest ones are how a poor man can become rich and how a man suffering from tuberculosis can be cured. A man in the primary stage of tuberculosis can definitely be cured. I think there are many people who want to have a lot of money. But they can't get money by wishing, I think. I want you to become rich by having a firm faith in a *gohonzon*. How about it? Do you mind that?

Suppose the Tokyo University Hospital invented a medicine that would be sure to make you rich if only you had it injected into you between the hours of six and seven in the morning. I am sure everyone would get up early in the morning and go to the hospital. And they would get the shots even though they might have to wait for one or two hours. And if the medicine was so effective that if you continued to take it for one year you would make hundreds of thousands of yen, and if you continued this for two years you would make millions of yen, and for three years so many more millions of yen, and if a doctor could really do this, then I think there would be a long line of people in front of his clinic. You too would go there, I am sure.

Now, you can get the same result without having to go to the Tokyo University Hospital but by sitting in your own home for only thirty minutes in the morning.

You don't have to spend a single yen for train or tram fare. The only thing you would need would be candles and incense sticks. Isn't this a cheap investment? People who don't do this, I say, are fools. Do it in the morning and in the evening. Don't ever doubt the *gohonzon*. Keep faith. If you doubt, it will be no good . . .

If you do as I tell you, and if things don't work out as you want by the time I come to Niigata next time, then you may come up here and beat me and kick me as much as you want. With this promise, I conclude my talk for tonight.

---

1 *Gohonzon* is the mandala inscribed by Nichiren.
2 *Shakubuku* is a vigorous technique of conversion practised by followers of Soka Gakkai.
3 Taiseki-ji was formerly the main sanctuary and headquarters of Soka Gakkai.

Source: K. Murata, *Japan's New Buddhism* (New York and Tokyo: Walker/Weatherhill, 1969), pp. 108–10.

5.10 ZEN HARDSHIP VERSUS 'INSTANT ENLIGHTENMENT'

Z. SHIBAYAMA

Zenkei Shibayama, abbot of Nanzenji Monastery in Kyoto, became involved in 1965 in efforts to promote Zen Buddhism in the United States.

The aim of Zen training is to die while alive, that is, to actually become the self of no-mind, and no-form, and then to revive as the True Self of no-mind and no-form. In Zen training, therefore, what is most important is for one to revive from the abyss of unconsciousness. Zen training is *not* the emotional process of just being in the state of oneness, nor is it just to have the 'feeling' of no-mind. *Prajna* wisdom (true wisdom) has to shine out after breaking through the extremity of the Great Doubt, and then still further training is needed so that one can freely live the Zen life and work in the world as a new man. At any rate, such deep spiritual experience has a great significance which we should not ignore in developing the spiritual culture of mankind today and in the future.

Hard training is carried on at Zen monasteries today with the purpose of reproducing in a novice the similar inner processes the old Zen Masters experienced. We have to be careful and serious in strictly and correctly adopting the training methods used.

In studying Zen, therefore, those who want to appreciate it as a cultural value, or as religious philosophy, can very well do so from such perspectives. Those, however, who want to experience it in themselves should be prepared to go through the hardship, and should never be tempted to follow an easy shortcut. Recently there have been people who talk about instant enlightenment, or those who take drugs in an attempt to experience *satori*. Whatever claims they may make, I declare that such approaches are not authentic, true Zen at all.

I should like to add a few last words here. True as it may be that Zen is really a supreme way to the Truth, it is obvious that not everyone can be expected to have the training required for attainment of the exquisite moment of *satori*. We have to admit that basic Zen is a very difficult way and only a handful of religiously endowed people under favourable conditions can attain *satori*.

There has to be another way of Zen open for ordinary people to follow even though it may be a secondary approach. In this way people can learn the teachings of old Zen Masters and can make the religious living attitudes of the old Masters the guiding principles of their lives. Thus they can try to follow the examples of Zen life as much as possible under the circumstances in which they live. This might be called the Zen life based on faith. I should like to discuss in more detail this Zen life for ordinary people, but will have to leave it to some other occasion.

Source: Z. Shibayama, *A Flower does not Talk – Zen Essays* (Vermont and Tokyo: Charles E. Tuttle Company, 1970), pp. 46–8.

5.11 WESTERN CLOTHES FOR ZEN BUDDHISM?

C. HUMPHREYS

Christmas Humphreys initially expressed his commitment to Buddhism through membership of the Theosophical Society. An eminent lawyer and judge, he became a pioneer in the development of Buddhist organizations in Britain and, in particular, was closely involved in fostering the practice of Zen Buddhism in Britain.

'Western Buddhism' has passed from the condition of an idle phrase, and is becoming a visible fact. Whether there should be such a thing is beside the point; it is born and it is growing, and it means that the Buddhism of Europe will not be the Buddhism of Ceylon, or of China or Tibet, which are very different in form; nor will its Zen be entirely the Zen Buddhism of Japan.

But the Buddhism of the West will be still more different from that of the East than those of Ceylon and Tibet, for example, are from each other. The Eastern approach to Truth is [. . .] total and intuitive; that of the West is analytic/synthetic and mainly intellectual. Its starting point is the vaunted 'scientific' approach to phenomena, whether objective or in the mind. It moves from the particular to the general, from visible material to intellectual hypotheses; it believes in believing nothing until it must. It follows that a definitely Western Buddhism must in time emerge, and be none the less Buddhism for being Western. The same applies to Zen. The aim of Zen Buddhism is the direct approach to Non-Duality, and nothing less. All else is secondary, including morality, doctrine, and every kind of ritual. Zen Buddhism was born in China of Bodhidharma and Tao, with Indian Buddhism as its reincarnating 'source-material'. It passed to Japan, and is now associated with the culture which it built among that highly cultured people. Now the Japanese offer the West its history, its theory and doctrine, its practice in monasteries and in daily life, and its records of achievement.

These we have imported through the books of Dr D. T. Suzuki, whose name is all but coterminous with Zen as known and practised in the West. But we shall not import these goods and leave them permanently foreign, as Chinese restaurants, French fashions and American films. Rather we shall receive them, study them, test them, digest them, absorb their spirit and then reclothe them in our own idiom of thought and practice. Only in this way will they become the product and expression of our own minds, and thus a useful set of 'devices' to enable us to find and express 'our' Zen, that is, Zen as we shall find it.

Or shall we lose the thing we want in making Western clothes for it? Will Zen in the West be so intellectualised, not only in the approach to it but the thing when found, that it may be splendid but will not be Zen? The answer will depend on our power to achieve it for what it is, if not by Oriental technique then by something more appropriate, though we shall not lightly discard a method which has served the millions of the East for fifteen hundred years. It is true that Carl Jung and others have stressed the folly of the West attempting to import the spiritual technique of the East by the process of intellectual adoption, for in this way it is not grafted on to the individual unconscious so as to present a vital and natural growth. But as the great writer points out, [. . .] in spiritual affairs 'everything depends on the man and little or nothing on the method', which is only 'the way laid down by the man that his action may be the true expression of his nature'. If some in the West, therefore, find the Japanese technique a way which aptly expresses their own search for Reality, let them use it. Those dissatisfied can seek or create their own.

Source: C. Humphreys, *Zen Comes West* (London: Curzon, 1977), pp. 28–30.

5.12 HELPING OTHERS

T. DESHIMARU

A Soto Zen monk, Taisen Deshimaru (died 1982) studied in Japan and, after his master's death, travelled to Paris, from where he promoted the practice of Zen in Europe, North and South America and North Africa.

What is compassion?

There are many degrees and forms of love. Universal love is the deepest. If we really feel sorry for someone we are not just conscious of the person's physical or emotional suffering, their distress. We must become like them, have the same state of mind as they. *Then how should we act, to help, comfort, heal?* We must, always, see things not from our own subjective point of view but by becoming the other, without duality. We must not just love but become identical with the other mind. In love we are always two. Compassion, or *jihi*, is unity.

When I meet you I become you. 'How are you? Not so bad?'

Somebody gave me a present yesterday. I must give him twice as much in return. Often, with love, it is impossible to do that, so in the end you escape. True compassion is genuine sympathy. We must forget ourselves and become the other. But compassion must always go hand in hand with wisdom. And wisdom with compassion. A great deal has been written on this subject in China and Japan. The whole world proclaims it, in fact, but in Buddhism it has become a powerful force.

In love there is always duality, opposition between partners. But in compassion the two beings are only one. Love is relative. Compassion is total communion between two beings. But without wisdom love is blind. Nowadays many parents love their children with egotistical attachment, and so the children want to escape. Too much attachment is not true love, true compassion.

You say that Zen wants to reach the highest wisdom and the deepest love, but some people think zazen produces indifference to others, they say it is the opposite of the active charity taught by Christianity. How would you say that zazen develops an attitude of love?

The ultimate dimension, in the very depths of being, the supreme dimension of life, is universal consciousness and love. Each cannot exist without the other. *Truth and love are one and the same thing.* So you can say that the active charity taught by Christianity is included in that dimension and is a direct emanation of it.

Zen Buddhism is also a religion of love because it is the religion of the bodhisattvas who abandon everything to help others, to work for the salvation of others before their own salvation (and in that practice, it goes even further than Christianity). And the first of the precepts is *fuse* – charity – which means more than a material gift; it means giving morally as well, a sacrifice. Not just giving to somebody but giving oneself and giving to God, to Buddha.

But where is the source of this active charity to be found, if not in the knowledge of one's own heart, of one's profound ego, which is that of every other existence, acquired through meditation?

Zen also teaches harmony, harmonizing with others – chanting the sutras together, meditating together, cultivating harmony together.

In Japanese, to be a monk means to harmonize.

Inner spiritual solitude is good but one must always harmonize with, turn toward, others too.

'All go together, beyond the beyond, to the other shore.'

Isn't a personal quest for inner freedom selfish in comparison with the quest for freedom for all?

Both are necessary. If I can't solve my own problems I will not be able to help other people solve theirs. I have to free myself of my own problems before I can help other people to free themselves. So both are necessary.

Westerners always want to help other people. Roman Catholics, too, want to help people for their salvation and for their own good. Mahayana Buddhism is the same, except that first we must understand ourselves.

You often say that practicing zazen solves the problem of life and death. But how can it solve the suffering of other people?

First you must solve your own suffering, because if your own brain is not in a normal condition you cannot help other people. You would make them even more complicated than they already are. One day you yourself told me that *samu* (physical labor) helped you to solve your sufferings. 'Before I used to suffer a great deal. The poison in my body and mind is now gone.' If you practice zazen you can help other people. There's no need to think about it consciously. Practice zazen. Don't complicate things. Then you will be able to solve the sufferings of others. It takes wisdom to be able to help.

How can one help others concretely?

What does 'help' mean?
Having no object, no goal is better. If you think, during zazen, 'I must help So-and-So and practice zazen now for that purpose', your zazen is not good. To practice zazen with a mushotoku-mind, 'no-profit', that is what is most important; beyond any goal, the highest zazen. It's not worth telling yourself, 'My zazen must be profound so that I can help other people.' Shikantaza means just sitting, without any object. Practice zazen automatically, naturally, unconsciously, and its influence will become infinite. Dogen wrote that if one person practices zazen only one hour, that person influences all the people in the whole world. It is not easy to help other people. Giving them money is not enough.

What matters most is always to remain beyond categories, otherwise one becomes narrow, narrower and narrower.

Hishiryo consciousness is infinite.

What does the sentence, 'Give to the rich and take from the poor,' mean?

Wealthy people are always afraid that someone is going to ask them for something. It's a psychological phenomenon. On the other hand, it will certainly be a pleasant surprise for them if somebody gives them something. Are you rich or poor?

Poor.

If, being poor, you give something, then that is true charity. Rich people can always make presents, but for you it is a true *fuse*, a gift of great value, of great price.

At Nara in Japan there is a very great temple called Todai-ji. In that temple there is an enormous statue of Buddha. Master Genjo, its founder, was asked by the emperor to build a big temple; so the priest went to a bridge under which lived many, many beggars. After bowing down to them he asked them for alms. They were completely bewildered and taken aback. And then they felt very proud.

Every day Genjo came to perform *sampai*, prostrate himself before them; and every day they gave him a little money. Some gave more. And so he began to build the temple. He told them what the statue was to be like and explained that by contributing to the building they would be remembered by history. The statue is of Buddha sitting on a lotus flower.

So the beggars gave him a lot of money and talked about it all day long. Before, they had always been beseeching and complaining, 'I'm sick, help me, please.'

Afterwards, they became truly wise and their words grew profound. They gave away half of everything they begged to build the temple, and they went on giving until it was finished.

Source: T. Deshimaru, *Questions to a Zen Master*, edited and translated by N. Amphoux (London: Rider, 1985), pp. 29–33.

5.13 BUDDHIST GRASS-ROOTS ACTIVISM

K. JONES

By the end of the 1960s it was clear that [. . .] Buddhist socialist modernism [. . .] had failed to engage effectively with the political and social process, notwithstanding the promise it had shown at the high noon of post-colonialism. However, by the 1960s another and very different kind of Buddhist activism was evident in South-East Asia, which may aptly be described as a *transcendental radicalism*. Although it took different forms in Sri Lanka, Thailand and Vietnam it does nevertheless display certain common characteristics, and these suggest the following working principles for a Buddhist radical activism. [. . .]

Sri Lanka

Sarvodaya, which means 'the awakening and welfare of all', refers to spiritually inspired, rural self-development movements in India and Sri Lanka. The Sarvodaya movement of post-colonial India attempted unsuccessfully to implement the Gandhian ideal of a network of autonomous village commonwealths, and Gandhi's heir, Jayaprakash Narayan, followed his example of mass civil disobedience when the Congress government frustrated that ideal. By contrast, the Sri Lanka movement evolved in the Asokan tradition of a just relationship between village communities on the one hand and on the other a State which was perceived to be comparatively benevolent.[1]

Sarvodaya began in Sri Lanka in 1958, when a young teacher, A. Y. Ariyaratne, encouraged his students to organize a fortnight 'holiday work camp' in a destitute village. The students worked closely with the villagers and were concerned to learn what they themselves perceived as their needs and problems. Other schools and colleges followed this example, and a village self-help movement emerged, outside the official rural development programme. During the 1970s training centres for community co-ordinators and specialists were established with help from overseas aid agencies. These schemes included a programme for the systematic training and involvement of Buddhist monks, who traditionally are highly influential in village life. Over two and a half million people, living in 7,000 of Sri Lanka's 23,000 village communities, are now involved in Sarvodaya, aided by some 2,000 monks. The Village Awakening Councils enjoy programme and budget autonomy, but receive much specialist support from area and regional centres backed by extensive training programmes. Projects include roads, irrigation works, preschool facilities, community kitchens, retail co-operatives and the promotion of village handicrafts (though impact on agriculture appears to have been disappointing). Joanna Macy describes the typical *shramadana* or voluntary co-operative work project as being 'like a combination of road gang, town meeting, vaudeville show and revival service – and these many facets build people's trust and enjoyment of each other'.[2]

Ariyaratne, now the movement's President, emphasizes that 'The chief object-ive of Sarvodaya is personality awakening.'[3] The root problem of poverty is seen as being a sense of personal and collective powerlessness. And 'awakening' is to take place not in isolation but through social, economic and political interaction. Personal awakening is seen as being interdependent with the awakening of one's local community, and both play a part in the awakening of one's nation and of the whole world.

The spiritual precondition for all-round social development is kept in the fore-front through Sarvodaya's creative interpretation of traditional Buddhist teachings in forms which can be understood and experienced by people collectively and in social terms. Thus, the shared suffering of a community, the poverty, disease, exploita-tion, conflict and stagnation, is explored together by the members as is also the suffering experienced by each one of them. But, crucially, this suffering is shown to have its origins in individual egocentricity, distrust, greed and competitiveness, which demoralizes and divides the community and wastes its potential. In place of the corrupted traditional meaning of kamma as 'fate', Ariyaratne emphasizes the original Buddhist teaching. 'It is one's own doing that reacts on one's own self, so it is possible to divert the course of our lives. . . . [Once we understand that] inactivity or lethargy suddenly transforms into activity leading to social and economic devel-opment.'[4]

Similarly, each of the practices comprising the traditional Buddhist Eightfold Path is amplified socially. For example, Macy quotes a Sarvodaya trainer:

> Right Mindfulness – that means stay open and alert to the needs of the village. . . . Look to see what is needed – latrines, water, road. . . . Try to enter the minds of the people, to listen behind their words. Practise mindfulness in the shramadana camp: is the food enough? are people getting wet? are the tools in order? is anyone being exploited?[5]

The traditional Buddhist virtues and precepts provide guidelines for joint endeavour and a significant vocabulary in the open discussions which are the lifeblood of the movement. Thus, *dana* had come to be identified with monastic alms-giving, but Sarvodaya extends it back to its original wider meaning of sharing time, skills, goods and energy with one's community and demonstrates the liberating power of sincere and spontaneous generosity to dissolve barriers between individuals and groups. Similarly, the meaning of the 'Four Sublime Abodes' has been extended socially without, however, losing their original spirit. So, *metta* (loving-kindness) refers also to the active concern for others and refraining from any kind of coercion. *Karuna* (compassion) refers to active and selfless giving of energy in the service of others. *Mudita* (rejoicing in others' good fortune) refers to the feeling of well-being experienced when one has been able to make a tangible contribution to one's community. *Upekkha* (equanimity) refers to independence from the need to achieve results and obtain recognition. It is the Buddhist remedy against burn-out of campaigning energies. Macy quotes a District Co-ordinator: '*Upekkha* is dynamite. It is surprising the energy that is released when you stop being so attached. . . . You discover how much you can accomplish when nothing is expected in return.'[6] [. . .]

Ariyaratne claims that 'the Sarvodaya Movement, while originally inspired by the Buddhist tradition, is active throughout our multi-ethnic society, working with Hindu, Muslim and Christian communities and involving scores of thousands of Hindu, Muslim and Christian co-workers. Our message of awakening transcends any effort to categorize it as the teaching of a particular creed.'[7]

As to Sarvodaya's relations with the State, Ariyaratne claims that 'when some aspects of the established order conform with the righteous principles of the Movement, the Movement co-operates with those aspects. When they become unrighteous, in those areas the Movement does not co-operate and may even extend non-violent non-co-operation [though so far it has never done so – KJ]. In between these two extremes there is a vast area . . . in which establishments like the government and the Sarvodaya Movement can co-operate.'[8] [. . .]

Since the late 1970s Sarvodaya has been subjected to new pressures which have raised controversial questions about its character and its future.[9]

In the first place, the growth in size and complexity of Sarvodaya has led to what Kantowsky calls 'the routinization of charisma' in a bureaucracy, arising not least from the need to channel large amounts of foreign aid (which amounted at one time to eighty per cent of income). Although problems of bureaucracy, paternalism and communication undoubtedly persist, they have arguably been reduced by organizational decentralization (since 1980) and by the effects of cutbacks in foreign aid. At the same time Sarvodaya's self-reliance has been increased by initiating a number of local projects.

In the second place, the increasing scale of Sarvodaya's support and activities and the growth of its influence have made it more difficult for it to continue to confine itself to relatively uncontroversial areas. New and pressing questions about the future direction of the movement have also arisen as a consequence of two major developments.

[. . .] From 1978 the government of Sri Lanka embarked on a classic capitalistic development policy, on the grounds that the economy would have broken down and social services would have become unsustainable had the island remained closed to foreign investment.

The only alternative, it was claimed, would have been some kind of austere totalitarian socialism. However, the social values implicit in the government's modernization projects are the antithesis of Sarvodaya's. International capital is now co-operating with the Sri Lankan élite in the creation of a competitive consumer society promoting a secular, materialist and Westernized culture. [. . .] Already, Kantowsky claimed, 'some of the really devoted workers and some of the younger monks have begun to question the Movement's co-operation with the government.'[10] [. . .]

Another factor which could push Sarvodaya towards the radical alternative is the eruption in recent years of inter-racial conflict which already, at the time of writing, was beginning to overshadow all other issues.

At the time of the 1983 riots Sarvodaya acted promptly to give what security it could to Tamils fleeing from Sinhalese mobs, and it subsequently provided refugee camps for many thousands. In a Declaration on National Peace and Harmony Ariyaratne blamed the conflict on the destruction of the Sri Lankan value system 'founded on the ancient Hindu–Buddhist Code of Ethics', and he outspokenly maintained that the Sinhalese community had the 'onus of responsibility' for redeeming the situation.[11]

One result of the crisis was to give Sarvodaya a higher and more controversial public profile. It earned the respect and support of a significant number of people in both communities who might previously have been inclined to dismiss it as just an innocuous movement of dogooders. [. . .] And it has remained the only voluntary national organization in which Sinhalese and Tamils continue to work together. Elsewhere, however, the Sarvodaya response has aroused anger and suspicion from the emergent current of Sinhalese racist nationalism (which includes many highly placed monks). And 'Tamil separatists, as well as some foreign observers and even donors to the Movement, have charged the Movement with not giving adequate attention to Tamil claims and grievances. They point to the clear allegiance, expressed in Ariyaratne's Declaration of Peace and Harmony, to the concept of a 'unitary state', thereby rejecting any serious consideration of secession. Subsequent statements by the Sarvodaya leadership, they also point out, refrain from specifically denouncing oppressive government policies or indiscriminate acts of retaliation by Sinhalese police and military forces.'[12]

The polarizing and destabilizing effects of the ongoing communal conflict have thus to some extent obliged Sarvodaya to bear public witness to its beliefs, even at the risk of antagonizing powerful forces in Sri Lankan society. The future direction of the movement, however, is still in question. It remains arguably the largest and most comprehensive example of socially engaged Buddhism in the world today. [. . .] For Buddhists Sarvodaya offers a still promising democratic updating of the Asokan ideal of a pluralist society, founded on a spiritual perspective of self-cultivation through open learning and dedication to radical social change. Even for spiritually inspired radicals working in different kinds of social situation, Sarvodaya offers a case study in the many problems and dilemmas which have to be worked through. Furthermore, both Kantowsky and Macy argue for Sarvodaya action on a global scale, 'uniting and empowering people in both under-developed and mal-developed (i.e. industrial) countries'.[13] For Sarvodaya principles 'cannot be expected to work in a few backward regions of the Third World while the industrialized countries continue their aggressive expansion'.[14] [. . .]

Vietnam

The third of the sources in recent South-East Asian history which contributes to the formulation of a Buddhist transcendental radicalism is the tragic Vietnam experience, involving Buddhists in both the Mahayana and Theravada traditions. Here the struggle for national independence combined with a struggle between capitalism and communism, in which foreign powers were deeply involved.

As in Burma and Ceylon, Buddhist monks were active from the end of the nineteenth century in the movements to gain independence from the colonial power. And during the 1960s, in the long and bloody struggle between governments in North and South Vietnam, the Unified Buddhist Church inspired an historic campaign of mass nonviolence for a 'third way', for a neutral Vietnam which would cherish its own cultural identity (1967 Programme of the Buddhist Socialist Bloc).

The Buddhist movement sought allies in people of other faiths and beliefs who were willing to work for peace and independence, and, in particular, large numbers of Catholics made common cause with the Buddhists. When, on 16 May 1967, a young Buddhist, Nhat Chi Mai, made of herself 'a torch in the dark night', it was a leading Catholic intellectual, Father Nguyen Ngoc Lan, who undertook the dangerous work of publishing her letters and poems.

The movement for peace was linked with action for social justice and social revolution. From the two radical Buddhist bases of Van Hanh University and the School of Youth for Social Service young people went into the country to work alongside the peasants on rural development projects, and a number of unions and other organizations were formed which also embraced urban workers, women, youth and students. An extensive anti-war literature flourished, of poetry, satire, song and prayer.

The importance of the national cultural identity was emphasized, and the Buddhist and humanistic cultural tradition of Vietnam did much to shape the nonviolent character of the 'Third Way' movement. Zen Master *Thich* Nhat Hanh, who played a leading part, stressed that 'the struggle of the Vietnamese people is not only for peace and independence. *The struggle of the Vietnamese people is to remain Vietnamese.* That is why the means of the struggle cannot be those that will destroy the Vietnamese character and the humanistic values that are so dear to the Vietnamese people. We cannot accept inhuman means that will change the Vietnamese nature. In accepting many of these means we have already permitted foreign powers to come and destroy our land.'[15]

In the annals of historic mass nonviolent movements the Vietnamese episode ranks with those of Gandhi to free India of British rule and of Martin Luther King to rid the United States of racial segregation. Two Saigon dictatorships were toppled – Diem's in 1963 and Khanh's in 1964 – and the Ky-Thieu government would also have been brought down in 1966 had not the United States flown Ky's forces into the centre of the movement (Hué) and exerted other pressures. The writings of perceptive participants like Nhat Hanh[16] can do much to deepen our insight into the character of nonviolence as a positive and compassionate force.

Today the work of the Unified Buddhist Church and its allies for religious freedom and other human rights continues in the face of much persecution, and organizations and individuals all over the world have rallied to the support of the 'prisoners of conscience' – monks, nuns, writers, artists and academics.

1   For the account which follows I am particularly indebted to Joanna R. Macy, *Dharma and development: religion as resource in the Sarvodaya self-help movement*, West Hartford (Conn.): Kumarian Press, revised edn. 1985.
2   Ibid., p. 95.
3   Ibid., p. 32.
4   Ibid., p. 76.
5   Ibid., p. 37.
6   Ibid., p. 39.
7   Ibid., p. 15.
8   Detlef Kantowsky, *Sarvodaya: the other development*, New Delhi: Vikas, 1980, p. 67.
9   For a very fair discussion, see Denis Goulet, *Survival With Integrity: Sarvodaya at the crossroads*, Colombo: Marga Institute, 1981.
10 Kantowsky, op. cit. (note 220), p. 216.
11 Macy, op. cit. (note 212), p. 102.
12 Ibid., p. 104.
13 Ibid., p. 91.
14 Kantowsky, op. cit. (note 220), p. 154.
15 *Thich* Nhat Hanh, *Love in Action: the non-violent struggle for peace in Vietnam*, Paris: The Vietnamese Buddhist Peace Delegation, n.d., p. 5.
16 For example, *Thich* Nhat Hanh, *The Cry of Vietnam*, Greensboro (N. Carolina): Unicorn Press, 1971.

Source: K. Jones, *The Social Face of Buddhism – An Approach to Political and Social Activism* (London: Wisdom Publications, 1989), pp. 240–51, 260–1, 398–400.

5.14 SARVODAYA: SELF-HELP IN SRI LANKA

A. T. ARIYARATNE

Dr A. T. Ariyaratne is the leader of Sarvodaya, a self-help village development scheme that he started in Sri Lanka in 1958.

Ancient Ceylon [now Sri Lanka], in the centuries before the colonial powers came, was known as the Land of Plenty and the Isle of Righteousness. Beside the vast network of irrigation canals and reservoirs (or tanks) that made the island the 'Granary of the East', rose great temples and stupas of the Buddhist order. Those sacred edifices were constructed from the earth excavated for the canals and tanks, whose construction and maintenance were supervised by the monks. That history lives today in the minds of those Sri Lankans who speak of the inherent relationship between 'temple and tank', or between religion and development.

Sarvodaya signifies the awakening or liberation of one and all, without exception. *Sabbe satta sukhi hontu*, 'May all beings be well and happy', is the Buddhist wish, in contrast to the Hegelian[1] concept of the welfare of the majority. In a world where greed, hatred, and ignorance are so well organized, is it possible for this thought of the well-being of all to be effectively practised for the regeneration of the individual and society? The answer to that question lies in the lives of hundreds of thousands of village people in Sri Lanka who have embraced the Sarvodaya way to development.

Since 1958, Sarvodaya has grown from a small group of young pioneers, working alongside the outcaste poor, to a people's self-help movement that is now active in over 4,000 towns and villages, operating programmes for health, education, agriculture, and local industry.

The Sarvodaya movement has been able to attain such scope and vitality because it has not tried to apply any ready-made solutions or development schemes from above; instead it has gone to the people to draw forth the strength and intelligence that are innate in them and that are encouraged by their age-old traditions.

Some development experts would argue that in our fast-changing world, preparing briskly for industrialization and modernization, tradition has no meaningful role; but the initiators of Sarvodaya believe that, without the understanding of tradition, no new theory or programme forced on the people, however ingenious it may be, will reap the desired results. No programme will be effective if it tries to separate the economic aspect of life from the cultural and spiritual aspects, as do both the capitalist and socialist models of development. With their sole emphasis on the production of goods, they neglect the full range of human well-being. For his or her well-being, the needs of the whole person must be met, needs that include satisfying work, harmonious relationships, a safe and beautiful environment, and a life of the mind and spirit, as well as food, clothing, and shelter.

To meet these needs Sarvodaya has committed itself to a dynamic non-violent revolution which is not a transfer of political, economic or social power from one party or class to another, but the transfer of all such power to the people. For that purpose, the individual as well as society must change. Each person must awaken to his or her true needs and true strengths if society is to prosper without conflict and injustice. From the wisdom embodied in our religious traditions we can find principles for that kind of personal and collective awakening. That is what Sarvodaya has done – listening to the villagers, who constitute 80 per cent of our country, and creating a challenge for them in terms of the ideals they still revere and in words that make sense to them.

Any understanding of Sarvodaya needs to recognize the resources that our movement has drawn from the spiritual and cultural traditions of our people.

In the Buddha's teachings, as much emphasis is given to community awakening and community organizational factors as to the awakening of the individual. This fact was unfortunately lost from view during the long colonial period when Western powers attempted to weaken the influence of the Sangha (the Order of Monks) and to separate the subjugated people from the inspiration to dignity, power, and freedom which they could find in their tradition.

Buddhist traditions and nature

In Buddhist culture, particularly in Sri Lanka, nature was considered sacred. It had been very close to the Buddha in all the important occasions of his life: he was born in a garden; he attained Buddhahood and passed away from this world under the trees; he preached his first sermon in a deer park and from then on nearly always taught outdoors in the shade of trees. On one occasion, when internal dissent divided the community of monks, the Buddha spent his time peacefully in the forest with the wild animals.

Sri Lankans' respect for life resulted not only in the preservation of animals, birds and other creatures but also plants and trees. The popular ritual of Bodhi Pooja, or paying respect to the Bodhi tree under which the Buddha attained Enlightenment by pouring water onto the foot of the tree, has extended to other species of trees. In times of drought, trees were kept alive by the practical ritual.

In one of the well-known suttas the Buddha speaks of the 'happiness of living in an appropriate environment' (*Patirupa des vasoca*). The environment, whether village, forest, valley or hill, is beautified when the right kind of people live there. There should be a perfect balance between the people who live in a place and the place itself. This is achieved when people live with nature without disturbing the flora and fauna; without breaking and injuring the rhythm of life. The idea is beautifully expressed by the description of a Buddhist saint (*arahant*) who is said to go about in the manner of a bee collecting nectar from flowers but not harming them in any way.

The Buddha often used examples from nature to teach. A mind, flickering, difficult to guard, is compared to 'a fish drawn out of water'. A fish taken away from its watery home jumps here and there. It reaches its end quickly. On the one hand the simile evokes the fickle condition of the mind and on the other it suggests the sad end of the fish snatched away from its environment.

In Buddhist stories, the plant and animal world is treated as part of our own inheritance. The stories tell how animals and plants could once talk and respond to human beings. The healthy rapport between plants, animals and humans, underlined by boundless compassion, was the basis of Buddhist life.

Compassion creates the foundation for a balanced view of the entire world and of the environment in which we live. It is only by exercising loving compassion toward all that a human being can perfect him- or herself and become a cherisher and sustainer of life. This teaching is immortalized in the story of young Prince Siddhartha (the Buddha before he renounced his worldly life) saving a swan shot down with an arrow by his cousin. Because Prince Siddhartha saved the bird it was judged as belonging to him.

> If life be aught, the saviour of a life
> Owns more the living thing than he can own
> Who sought to slay – the slayer spoils and wastes,
> The cherisher sustains, give him the bird.

Nothing in nature should be spoiled or wasted for wanton destruction upsets the vital balance of life. Destroying natural resources is physical pollution, but psychological pollution can also afflict any society, affecting both human beings and the environment. Buddhist teachings explain how this occurs. If a king or ruler is overcome by feelings of hatred, excessive desire and ignorance, his ministers and officials are affected and infected by it. This travels down infecting everyone in the power hierarchy until it reaches the common people. From there it affects the environment in which they live, plants, trees and living creatures, until all are destroyed. Such is the power of psychological or spiritual pollution.

Let us be clear, however, that when we speak of tradition and its role in development, we do not limit our understanding to Buddhism. The example and relevance of Sarvodaya would be very restricted if we thought it had meaning only for Buddhist societies. The Sarvodaya movement, while originally inspired by the Buddhist tradition, is active throughout our multi-ethnic society, working with Hindu, Muslim and Christian communities and involving tens of thousands of Hindu, Muslim and Christian co-workers. Our message of awakening cannot be labelled as the teaching of one particular creed. Through the philosophy of Sarvodaya – based on loving-kindness, compassionate action, altruistic joy and equanimity, as well as on sharing, pleasant speech, constructive work, and equality – people of different faiths and ethnic origins are motivated to carve out a way of life and a path of development founded on these ideals.

Dr A. T. Ariyaratne
Sarvodaya President

---

1 Hegel was an early nineteenth-century German philosopher. He believed that the views and needs of the individual could only be allowed a voice in society if they were in accord with the interests of society as a whole. In other words, the good of the many took precedence over the good of the few.

Source: M. Batchelor and K. Brown (eds) *Buddhism and Ecology* (London: Cassell, 1992), pp. 78–82.

5.15 SEE THE SUFFERING

THICH NHAT HANH

Thich Nhat Hanh is a Vietnamese Buddhist monk of the Tiep Hien Order. He was nominated for the Nobel Peace Prize in 1967.

In the Tiep Hien Order which we founded in Vietnam during the war, we follow fourteen precepts. These are also helpful in enabling us to remain mindful of our own thoughts and actions as well as the plight of others throughout the day.

The fourth of these precepts reads: 'Do not avoid contact with suffering or close your eyes before suffering. Do not lose awareness of the existence of suffering in the life of the world. Find ways to be with those who are suffering by all means, including personal contact and visits, images, sound. By such means, awaken yourself and others to the reality of suffering in the world.'

Some meditation teachers tell us not to pay attention to the problems of the world like hunger, war, oppression, social injustice, ecological problems, etc. We should only practise. These teachers have not truly understood the meaning of the Mahayana. Of course, we should not neglect practices like counting the breath, meditation, and sutra study, but what is the purpose of doing these things? Meditation's purpose is to be aware of what is going on in ourselves and in the world. What is going on in the world can be seen within ourselves and vice versa. Once we see this clearly, we cannot refuse to take a position and act. When a village is being bombed and children and adults are suffering from wounds and death, can a Buddhist sit still in his unbombed temple? Truly, if he has wisdom and compassion, he will be able to practise Buddhism while helping other people. To practise Buddhism, it is said, is to see into one's own nature and to become a Buddha. If we are unable to see what is going on around us, how can we expect to see into our own nature? Is there not some relationship between the self-nature of a Buddhist and the self-nature of suffering, injustice and war? In fact, to see the true nature of nuclear weapons is to see our own true nature.

The fifth precept says: 'Do not accumulate wealth while millions are hungry. Do not take as the aim of your life fame, profit, wealth or sensual pleasure. Live simply and share time, energy and material resources with those who are in need.'

How can we have time to live the Buddhist ideal if we are constantly pursuing wealth and fame? If we do not live simply, we must work all the time to pay our bills and there will be little or no time for practice. In the context of modern society, simple living also means to remain as free as possible from the destructive momentum of the social and economic machine, to avoid modern diseases such as life stress, depression, high blood pressure and heart disease. We must be determined to oppose the type of modern life filled with pressures and anxieties that so many people now live. The only way out is to consume less. We must discuss this with others who have similar concerns. Once we are able to live simply and happily, we will be better able to help others. We will have more time and energy to share. Sharing is difficult if you are wealthy. Bodhisattvas who practise living a simple life are able to give both their time and energy to others.

And the eleventh precept offers the following encouragement: 'Do not live with a vocation that is harmful to humans and nature. Do not invest in companies that deprive others of their chance to live. Select a vocation which helps realize your ideal of compassion.'

Right livelihood implies practising a profession that harms neither nature nor humans, either physically or morally. Practising mindfulness in our work helps us discover whether our livelihood is right or not. We live in a society where jobs are hard to find and it is difficult to practise right livelihood. Still if it happens that our work entails harming life, we should try our best to secure new employment. We should not allow ourselves to drown in forgetfulness. Our vocation can nourish our understanding and compassion, or it can erode them. Therefore, our work has much to do with our practice of the Way.

Source: M. Batchelor and K. Brown (eds) *Buddhism and Ecology* (London: Cassell, 1992), pp. 107–9.

5.16 Sake, ancestors and meditation:
a visit to a Zen temple

IAN READER

Some years ago I spent a few days at a Sōtō Zen Buddhist temple in Nagano prefecture in the mountains of central Japan. It was one of the sect's recognised training centres where those who had taken a Buddhist monastic ordination could spend time studying Buddhist thought, rituals and meditation, either as training for further meditative practice or – as is most common – as a step on the path of qualifying as a fully trained Buddhist priest able to take over and run a Buddhist temple and perform all the rituals associated with it, including the death rituals and memorial services for the ancestors. I had been staying at various Sōtō Zen temples during that year in the course of my research and had been invited to this one by the head-priest, a noted scholar and teacher, so that I could, at first-hand, study the workings of the temple, talk to the trainees and talk over some questions concerning my research.

Arriving late on a cold December afternoon I almost immediately found myself in a car with the head-priest and three young trainees. As it was the death anniversary of a member of one of the households that had long been affiliated to the temple, the priests were going to perform a memorial service at the family *butsudan* and I was being taken along to see what went on. When we arrived at the house, the head-priest explained to the family who I was and that I was going to participate in the service: by then I had already had various items of Buddhist regalia draped about my person and had had a book of Buddhist chants thrust in my hand. The family did not seem at all taken aback, accepting my presence in the open way to which I have become accustomed in the Japanese religious world.

We all knelt before the *butsudan* and chanted for perhaps an hour. The older members of the family sat with us the whole time, mostly keeping up with the chants, while the younger members, including a couple of children, seemed to drift in and out, putting in an appearance rather than participating. It was a typical Japanese memorial service in that those most overtly involved were the older generation (presumably those who best remembered the deceased), while those ostensibly farthest removed from the processes of death, the young, were the least interested. After the service a splendid meal was laid out for us, along with plenty of sake (Buddhist priests in Japan are not forbidden to drink alcohol), and we all ate and drank while sharing in a general conversation about all manner of things, from local gossip to aspects of Buddhism. It was late before we returned to the temple and went to sleep.

Traditionally, Zen temple life starts very early with one or more periods of meditation, and we were all in the meditation hall the next day at 4 a.m., doing *zazen*, seated Zen meditation, in which the legs are crossed in the lotus[1] position, the back is kept straight, the hands are rested one on the other just below the navel with the thumbs lightly touching, the eyes half open, the mouth firmly closed, and the breath inhaled and exhaled slowly and deeply through the nose. The meditation hall was unheated, lit only by candles, and we sat still and silent in the freezing cold of the early morning, each exhalation of breath turning into a stream of mist, for 90 minutes

– two periods of seated meditation of 40 minutes and a short walking period in between, in which we walked slowly in single file, allowing our legs some respite but maintaining our deep breathing and meditative state.

From the meditation hall we proceeded to the main hall of the temple where, kneeling on the floor, we chanted prayers and Buddhist texts for half an hour, followed by a round of the temple complex, chanting at various Buddhist images. After this we gathered buckets and cloths and washed the cold wooden floors rigorously. One monk prepared breakfast, a sparce meal of rice gruel, pickles and green tea that we finally ate, after a long prayer, in silence at around 7.30 a.m. A short rest period after breakfast was followed by a long talk by the head-priest on points of Buddhist thought and action, after which there was a longer period of work in which we swept the temple grounds, cleaned parts of the graveyard, chopped some logs for fuel and carried out other physical tasks. The rest of the day continued along similar lines, with more meditation and chanting, some periods of relaxation and a question and answer session with the head-priest about Buddhism. Later on, two of the young trainee priests went out to chant prayers at the altar of another of the temple's affiliated households while the rest of us went back to the meditation hall for another 90-minute session in the evening.

The life of the temple thus encompassed austere meditation and rites for the dead, striving for self-awareness and pastoral care for others. Seeking for enlightenment in life, which is the focus of the whole of Zen temple life and practice, operates in tandem with the aim of caring for others, including the spirits of the dead, and transferring the spiritually enlightened powers of Buddhism to others including the ancestors to enable them to attain peace and enlightenment after death. As a training centre for Zen priests the daily routine at this particular temple contained far more in the way of meditation and spiritual training than would most temples, the vast majority of which are run by one priest and his family (marriage has been the norm for Japanese Buddhist priests since the Meiji Restoration) and deal almost entirely with the issue of death and the ancestors. . . .

This is not something limited to Zen, which is by no means the only form of Buddhism to have taken root and flourished in Japan. Others include Tendai Buddhism, with its combination of scholastic and textual learning with esoteric rituals and various spiritual and ascetic practices, Shingon Buddhism, focused specifically on esoteric practices, the various branches of Pure Land Buddhism, with their focus on devotion, faith and salvation, and the militantly nationalist and salvationist Nichiren Buddhism with its devotion to the major Buddhist text the Lotus Sūtra. All encompass similar themes in that they have their own spiritual disciplines that combine with various ritual practices concerning death and the ancestors: Zen is no different from any of the others in this.

---

1 In this posture the legs are crossed, with the right foot placed on the inside of the left thigh and the left foot on the right thigh. The half lotus, in which only one of the legs is placed on the opposite thigh, and the other tucked under it, is also a common meditation posture.

Source: Reader, I. *Religion in Contemporary Japan* (London: Macmillan, 1991), pp. 78–80.

PART SIX

— •◆• —

SIKHISM

INTRODUCTION

—— ◆◆◆ ——

The study of Sikhism was impeded for a considerable period by the persistent image of it being nothing more than a variant of Hinduism. The growth in the number of Sikh communities settled beyond India during the last half of the twentieth century, and the widely reported campaign for an independent Sikh state in the nineteen-eighties led to a more balanced appreciation of Sikhism's distinctive qualities.

Acknowledging one formless God as the true Guru, or spiritual illuminator, Sikhs have been the disciples of the human teachers who revealed the divine teaching and of the sacred book that became the repository of these teachings. The word 'Sikh' means 'disciple'. Beginning with Guru Nanak (b. 1469CE), Sikhism evolved under the guidance of ten historical gurus. The shift of authority to the sacred book, the *Guru Granth Sahib*, and the creation of the distinctive Sikh social institution of the Khalsa are attributed to the last of these teachers, Guru Gobind Singh (d. 1708CE). For many Sikhs to this day, Khalsa Sikhism represents normative Sikhism.

The meditative religion of Guru Nanak attracted a community during Nanak's lifetime. Guru Nanak's emphasis upon the interior spiritual quest made him critical of formalised religion and its divisive effects. The earliest community of his followers probably followed a pattern of prayer that he prescribed and offered hospitality to all who would eat together, a practical affirmation of the unity of human beings. Under successive gurus, however, the Sikh community struggled to maintain its distinctiveness and independence, and gradually more complex institutions, obligations and rituals were introduced to foster a distinctive Sikh identity. Under less religiously tolerant Mughal emperors, Sikhs increasingly took to bearing arms to protect their community and so took on a political as well as religious identity. The creation of the Khalsa in 1699 was the culmination of this gradual process, leading to initiated Sikhs of both sexes adopting the names, dress and obligations that outwardly mark an observant Sikh to this day.

Sikhs have worked to maintain their distinctive identity during the latter half of the twentieth century both in India and elsewhere. In India, largely concentrated in Punjab, Sikhs constitute a small minority within India's population as a whole. The struggle to ensure government recognition of Sikh needs led some Sikhs to campaign for a separate homeland as the only way in which to guarantee their rights. For Sikh communities scattered around the world, their minority status has also led to challenges, and in particular difficulties in retaining the distinctive symbols of their faith, such as the turban, in societies ignorant or intolerant of Sikh practice.

The readings begin with selections from the *Guru Granth Sahib*, which reveal something of the character of Guru Nanak's thought, and from the *Dasam Granth* of Guru Gobind Singh, which also is used in Sikh worship. The historical development of Sikhism as a regulated way of life is reflected in a statement from an influential code of Sikh conduct and analysed in a scholarly discussion of the contradictions revealed by the growth of formalised Sikhism. Sikhism's struggle to survive as a distinctive entity both under the British and in post-independence India is considered in *Khalistan and Sikh Identity* where the readings are taken from different spokespersons within Sikhism and commentators on the growth of Sikh militancy.

The final reading is a reflection by a Sikh woman on the meaning of the outward symbols of Sikhism.

GURU NANAK AND GURU GOBIND SINGH

— ◆ ◆ —

6.1 A SELECTION OF THE HYMNS OF GURU NANAK

Japji

A long poem, from 6.1.1 to 6.1.23

6.1.1

ik omkār

God is One,
He is the True Name,
The Maker and All-pervading Spirit
Fearing nothing, hating no one,
A Being beyond time,
Self-existent beyond birth,
Revealed by the grace of the Guru.

Jap

Before all things existed He was Truth,
In the beginning of all things He was Truth,

Today He is Truth, Nānak,
And Truth He will ever be.

6.1.2

Though I think a hundred thousand thoughts of God, thought alone
  cannot reach Him.

Though I remain in deep and silent meditation, such meditation alone
  cannot achieve the divine Silence.

Though I hunger for Him my hunger does not depart if I am filled only
  with this world's goods.

Though I possess a hundred thousand worldly devices not one avails for
  this task.

How then can I be true?
How can the barrier of untruth be demolished?

By obeying the pre-ordained Will of the Lord, Nānak.

6.1.3

Through His Will things come to be,
His Will is indescribable.
Through His Will souls come to be,
Through His Will excellence is obtained.

Through His Will some are high born, others low;
Through His pre-ordained Will some receive pain, others pleasure.
One through His Will receives blessing,
The other through His Will must ever wander.

His Will applies to all,
None shall escape His Will,
Nānak, he who knows His Will
Cannot glory in his own self.

6.1.4

Some who have the power sing of His might.
Some sing of His gifts, who know His signs.

Some sing of His attributes, His excellent greatness.
Some sing of His knowledge, His deepest thought.
Some sing of His creation of the body and of its dissolution to dust.
Some sing of His taking life and of its restoration.
Some sing of His apparent distance from us,
Some sing of His nearness, beholding us face to face.

Discourses and expositions are endless,
Millions of sermons by millions of preachers.
The giver gives and the receiver wearies of receiving,
Age upon age man is refreshed and replenished.
The Sovereign by His Will has ordered man's path.
He remains happy, Nānak, in His contentment.

6.1.5

The Lord is Truth, His Righteousness is true, His language is
    infinite love.
We pray and beg, 'Give us, give us', and the Giver gives.
What then can we offer Him that we may see His Court?
What words should we utter that He might show us love?
At fragrant dawn reflect on the True Name and His greatness.
Past actions determine our garment, His Grace gives us the door of
    salvation.
Know this, Nānak, that this is the way to know that the True One is
    everything.

6.1.6

He cannot be made and installed like an idol,
He Himself of Himself is self-existent.
Those who have served Him have received honour.
Nānak, praise the Lord, the Treasury of virtues.
Sing and hear and retain His love in your heart,
Thus will sorrow flee and joy shall dwell in its place.
The Guru's voice is the eternal sound, the Guru's voice is the Veda, the
    Guru's voice is all-pervading.
The Guru is Ishwar,[1] the Guru is Gorakh[2] and Brahma, the Guru is
    Parvati[3] and the Mother-goddess.[4]
If I know Him should I not tell His story, but He cannot be described by
    words.

The Guru has explained one thing to me:
There is but one Giver of all life, let me never forget Him.

6.1.7

I would pilgrimage to a holy river if I thought I would gain His love,
But without it the ablutions are useless.
I behold all created beings,
But without grace what can they obtain?
The mind is filled with gems and precious stones
If we listen to just one item of the Guru's teaching.

The Guru has explained one thing to me:
There is but one Giver of all life, let me never forget Him.

6.1.8

Though a man's life spanned the four ages or ten times more,
Or his reputation spread to nine continents and everyone followed him,
Or his name were praised and his renown known in all the world,
If His Grace does not descend on him then he is as someone ignored.
He becomes a worm among worms, even the sinful accuse him of sin.

Nānak, those lacking virtue God makes virtuous, even the virtuous were
    given their virtue by Him.
I cannot think of anyone else who could grant them virtue.

6.1.9

He who hears *the Word* becomes like Ishwar,[5] Brahma and Indra.[6]
He who hears, though he be of low estate, will be filled with praise.
He who hears discovers the way of yoga and the secrets of the body.
He who hears understands the Shastras,[7] Smritis[8] and Vedas.[9]
Nānak, the *bhagats*[10] are always happy.
For him who hears, sorrow and sin are destroyed.

6.1.10

Innumerable His names and innumerable His dwellings,
Inaccessible and incomprehensible His innumerable realms.
It is folly even to say that they are innumerable.
In letters we spell His Name, in letters we sing His praise,
In letters are spelt His Wisdom, in letters are His praises sung and His
    virtues known,
In letters we write down the spoken word,
In letters is a man's destiny inscribed on his brow;

But they are not found on the head of Him who inscribed them.
As he ordains so shall man receive.
As great is creation, so great is His Name.
There is no corner without His Name.
What power of thought have I to describe His creation?
I am not worthy to be sacrificed to Him even once.

Whatever pleases Thee is a good deed.
Thou dost endure always, Formless One.

6.1.11

When hands, feet and the body are dirty,
Water washes the dirt away.
When your clothing is soiled,
With the use of soap it is washed clean.
When the mind is polluted by sin,
It is cleansed by delighting in the Lord's Name.
Purity and sin are not mere words,
Rather are they actions with effective results.
A man eats what he sows.
Nānak, by God's Will we come and go.

6.1.12

Pilgrimage, penance, compassion and the giving of alms
Are given the least honour;[11]
He who hears, obeys and loves God in his heart,
Bathes in a place of pilgrimage within himself.
All virtues are Thine, Lord. I have none.
But without virtue, devotion to Thee is impossible.
Hail to Thee who created Maya, the Word and Brahma,
Thou art Truth and Beauty, whose heart is ever filled with delight.

At what time, at which moment, what day of the month or week,
What was the season, what was the month, when it all took
    shape?
The pandits did not discover the time or it would be in the
    Puranic texts.
The qazis did not discover the time or they would have written it in the
    Qur'an.
Nor did the yogis or anyone else know the season or the month or
    the day of the month or week.
He who created the world alone knows when he did it;

How shall we address Thee, praise Thee, describe Thee or know Thee,
 Lord?
Nānak, all speak about Him, each man wiser than the next.
Great is the Lord, great is His Name, whatever He wills comes to pass.
Nānak, he who thinks himself something will not be honoured in the life
 hereafter.

6.1.13

There are hundreds of thousands of worlds below and heavens above.
Men have wearied themselves searching limitless bounds; but the Vedas
 say the Spirit is one.
The *Katebā*[12] says there are 18,000 worlds but that Reality is one
 principle.
If description were possible then it would have been written; but men
 have exhausted themselves.
Nānak, call Him Great. Only He knows Himself.

6.1.14

There's no limit to God's praise, to His glorification no limit.
There's no limit to His works, to His giving no limit.
We cannot limit Him by our seeing or by our hearing.
We cannot know the limit of the secret of His heart.
We cannot know the limit of His created world.
We cannot know the limit of His own accepted limits.
How many cry out to know His limits?
But His limits cannot be discerned.
This limit no one can know.
The more that is described the more remains.
Great is the Lord, His throne is exalted.
Higher than the highest is His Name.
If anyone were to be as highly exalted as He,
Then he would know His exaltation.
But God alone knows how great He is.
Nānak, what we receive is the result of Grace.

6.1.15

Make contentment thine earrings, spiritual endeavour thy begging bowl
 and wallet, and meditation thy sacred ash.
Wear death like sackcloth, in manner of life let thy body be that of a
 virgin and faith in God be thy staff.

Let communion with all men be thy holy order, control of the mind
   means control of the world.
Hail, Hail to Him!
The First, the Pure, the One without beginning, the Indestructible,
   from age to age retaining the same vesture.

6.1.16

The union of the One with the Mother[13] gave birth to three approved
   disciples.
One the world's Creator, one its Sustainer, and the third its Judge.[14]
According to God's pleasure they perform their duties.
He watches over them, but they behold Him not. What a great marvel!
   Hail, Hail to Him!
The First, the Pure, the One without beginning, the Indestructible, from
   age to age retaining the same vesture.

6.1.17

Let my single tongue become hundreds of thousands twenty times over,
So would I repeat the Name of the Lord of Creation endlessly.
Thus would I ascend the stairs to the Lord and become one with Him.
The sound of heavenly things makes the lowest want to rise.
Nānak, by Grace is God attained, the rest is false boasting.

6.1.18

God created the night, the seasons, days of the month and week.
He created the wind, water, fire and the worlds below.
In their midst he set the world as the sphere of *dharma*.
In it he placed animals of various species and colour,
Their names are many and endless.
Each one is judged according to his deeds.
The Lord Himself is True and His Court is true,
There the elect rejoice in their acceptance.
They bear the sign of grace and mercy.
There the bad and the good are separated.
Nānak, when we go there this will be manifest.

6.1.19

Such is the stage of Religious Duty.
Now I shall describe the activity of the stage of Knowledge.
How many are the winds, waters and fires, how many the Krishnas and
    Sivas!
How many the Brahmas who created worlds, of many forms and colours
    and vestures!
How many worlds of *karma* and mountains like Meru, how many
    Dhruvas under instruction!
How many Indras, moons and suns, how many universes and countries!
How many Siddhas, Buddhas and Nāths, how many goddesses in
    different forms!
How many gods, demons and ascetics, how many jewels and seas![15]
How many sources of life, how many languages, how many royal
    dynasties!
How many approaches to God and servants of God! Nānak, the process is
    endless.

6.1.20

In the stage of Knowledge divine wisdom shines forth;
It is the realm of the eternal sound, giving countless joys and
    pleasures.
In the next stage of Spiritual Striving the language is perfection;
There, things are fashioned in an incomparable way.
What goes on there cannot be described.
Whoever tries must later feel ashamed.
There inner consciousness, intellect, mind and wisdom are shaped.
There the state of being a sage and a Siddha is achieved.

6.1.21

In the stage of Grace, man is so filled with spiritual power
That nothing more can be added to him.
There are found very great warriors and heroes,
Whom the great Lord[16] fills completely.
They are inextricably woven into the greatness of the Lord;
Such is their beauty it cannot be described.
They do not die neither are they deceived,
Those in whose hearts the Lord abides.
There also dwell communities of bhagats;
They live in bliss, the True One in their hearts.

In the stage of Truth, the Formless One resides.
He, the Creator, beholds His creation and looks upon it with grace.
Here there are continents, worlds and universes.
Who can describe a boundless bound?
Here there are worlds within worlds and endless forms.
Whatever God wills, that they do freely.
God beholds His creation and rejoices.
Nānak, to describe it is iron hard.

6.1.22

Let chastity be your furnace, patience your goldsmith.
Let understanding be your anvil, divine knowledge your tools.
Let the fear of God be your bellows, penance your fire.
Let the love of God be your crucible, in which *amrit* is smelted.
In this mint of Truth, the Word is coined.
This is the practice of those on whom God looks graciously.
Nānak, the Gracious One makes glad the heart of those upon whom He
   looks with favour.

6.1.23

The air is the Guru, water our father, the great earth our mother.
Day and night are the male and female nurses, in whose care the whole
   world plays.
Good deeds and bad will be read in the presence of the Righteous One.
According to the operation of karma, some will be near and some afar
   off.
Those who have meditated on the Name and have departed, their toil
   completed,
Their faces, Nānak, will be bright and many will be released along with
   them.

Here follows a series of short poems, from 6.1.24 to 6.1.38.

Sohila Arti

6.1.24

There are six schools of philosophy, six teachers and six doctrines,
But the Guru of gurus is one, though he has many appearances.
Father, the school in which the Creator is praised,

That school protect, it is for Thy greatness.
Just as there are seconds, minutes, watches of the day, lunar days, week-
    days and months,
And many seasons depending on the one sun,
So, Nānak, the one Creator manifests many aspects.

(Rag Asa, Adi Granth, p. 12)

6.1.25

The heaven is Thy salver, the sun and moon Thy lamps,
The stars in their paths are Thy scattered pearls.
The fragrance of sandalwood is Thine incense,
The wind is Thy *chown*[17] and all the forests thy flowers, Lord of Light!
What worship[18] this is! This is Thy worship, Destroyer of rebirth!
The unstruck Word is Thy temple drums.

Thousands are Thine eyes, yet Thou hast no eye.
Thousands are Thine images, yet Thou hast no form.
Thousands are Thy pure feet, yet Thou hast no foot.
Thousands are Thy fragrances, yet Thou hast no fragrance.
This play fascinates me.

In all there is light. Thou art that Light.
The brilliance which is from Him shines in all hearts.
By the Guru's teaching the Light is manifested.
Whatever pleases Him, that is *ārati*.

My heart is attracted by the lotus feet of God as the bee is by the honey,
    night and day I thirst for them.
Give to Nānak, the *sārang*,[19] the water of Thy mercy, so that he may abide
    ever in Thy Name.

(Rag Dhanasri, Adi Granth, p. 663)

6.1.26

If I were to live for millions and millions of years,
If I were to exist on air as my food and drink,
If I were to live in a cave deprived of the sun and moon and never dream
    of sleeping.
Still I would not be able to estimate Thy worth
Nor say how great Thy Name is.

True is the Formless One and unique.
Hearing and hearing one repeatedly proclaims.

If it pleases Him, only He can grant us awareness of Him.
If I were slashed and cut in pieces and ground into a pulp,
If I were consumed by fire and my ashes scattered,
Even then I would not be able to estimate Thy worth
Nor say how great Thy Name is.

If I were to become a bird and fly through a hundred skies,
If I were to vanish completely and exist without drinking or eating,
Still I would not be able to estimate Thy worth,
Nor say how great Thy Name is.

Nānak, had I thousands of tons of books and read them diligently,
Could my pen write with the speed of the wind and the ink never dry,
Even so I would not be able to estimate Thy worth
Nor say how great Thy Name is.

(Sri Rag, Adi Granth, p. 14)

6.1.27

Forgetting the Beloved even for an instant means great sickness in the
   soul.
How can honour be achieved in His Court if the Lord does not dwell in
   the soul?
By meeting the Guru happiness is achieved, the fire is quenched in His
   virtue.
My Soul! day and night repeat the virtues of the Lord.
Those who do not forget the Name for the briefest moment, such men
   are rare in this world.
When our light meets the Light and our wisdom is joined with Wisdom,
Violence and self-interest flee, doubt and sorrow are no more.
The gurmukh[20] in whose heart the Lord dwells, is united by the Guru.
If I give my body as a bride the Lord, the Bridegroom, will take me.
Do not make love with him who is merely passing through.
The gurmukh like a chaste bride enjoys the Bridegroom's couch.
The four fires[21] are quenched and extinguished in the gurmukh by
   pouring the water of the Lord.
Thus the heart, like the lotus, shall blossom; it shall be filled to the brim
   with amrit.
Nānak, make the *Satguru*[22] thy friend, achieve Truth and enter His Court.

(Sri Rag, Adi Granth, p. 21)

6.1.28

Thou, Lord, art the River, knowing all, seeing all.
How can I, the fish, know Thy limits?

Wherever I look Thou art there,
Removed from Thee I perish and die.
I do not know the fisherman nor do I recognize the net.
When pain besets me then I call to Thee.

Thou pervadest all things, I thought you were far off.
Whatever I do, it is always in Thy presence.
Thou seest all yet I deny my actions,
I am unworthy of Thee and therefore cannot glorify Thy Name.

Whatever Thou givest I eat.
There is no other door, to whose door should I go?
Nānak has one petition, accept my body and soul.

The Lord Himself is near, He is also far off and He fills the in-between.
He beholds all, He hears all, by His power He created the world.
Whatever pleases Him, Nānak, it comes to pass according to His Will.

(Sri Rag, Adi Granth, p. 25)

6.1.29

The fish did not recognize the net in the salty and unfathomable sea;
It was very clever and beautiful, why and whence its confidence?
Because of its action it was caught, death does not pass it by.

Brother, know that likewise death hovers over your head.
As with the fish, so with man, the net falls unexpectedly.
The whole world is in bondage to Death, without the Guru death is
    unchallengeable.
Those who are immersed in Truth are saved, leave doubt and vices
    behind.
May I be a sacrifice to the truthful who repose in the Court of Truth.

Birds at the mercy of the hawk and the nets in the hunter's hands are
    parables.
Those whom the Guru cares for are saved, the rest are caught with the
    bait.
Without the Name they are taken and cast aside, without companionship
    and without friends.

In truth we proclaim the Truth, the true realm is Truth.
Those who honour the True One have Truth in their hearts.
He who is pure of mind and speech and has knowledge is a gurmukh.

Pray before the Satguru and you will meet your Beloved.
Happiness results from meeting the Beloved and the angels of death take
    poison and die.
May I dwell in the Name and the Name will abide in my heart.
Without the Guru darkness prevails, without the Word wisdom is lost.
By the Guru's word divine light shines and we are absorbed in Truth.
Death does not enter there and our light blends with the Light.

Thou art the Beloved, Thou art wise, Thou art the agent of union.
Through the Word of the Guru we praise Thee, Thou who art Infinite.
Death cannot reach where the Word of the Guru is supreme.

By His Will all is created.
By His Will all deeds are done.
By His Will some are doomed to die.
By His Will some are united in the Truth.
Nānak, whatever pleases Him comes to pass,
Men are powerless to do anything.

(Sri Rag, Adi Granth, p. 55)

6.1.30

My Soul, let your love of the Lord be like that of the lotus for the water,
Overcome by waves, it still flowers in love.
Living things created in the water, if taken out of the water, die.
My Soul, how can you be saved without love?
The Lord dwells in the heart of the gurmukh, to him he gives a treasure
    of devotion.

My Soul, let your love of the Lord be like that of the fish for the water,
The more water the more happiness and peace of mind and body.
Without water, even for an instant, it cannot live,
And God knows the suffering of its separation . . .

True love cannot be broken if the Satguru is present.
Access to the gift of Knowledge gives insight into the three worlds.
The pure Name is not forgotten if our trade is in virtue . . .

Without the Guru Love is not born, the stain of self-interest does not go
    away.
He who perceives God within himself knows the Word and is satisfied.
When the gurmukh understands himself, what more is there to do?

Why try to unite those who are already united in Him? Having received
    the Word they are satisfied.

The *manmukh*[23] cannot achieve understanding, in his alienation he suffers
  punishment.
Nānak, there is one door to the house of the Lord, there is nowhere else
  to go.

(Sri Rag, Adi Granth, p. 59)

6.1.31

The bhagats adore Him with love, they thirst for the Truth with great
  affection.
Those who plead and pray with tears receive happiness and much love in
  affection.

My Soul, repeat the Name of God and seek His refuge.
The ocean of life is crossed by a boat, namely the repetition of God's
  name as a rule of life.

My Soul, death becomes a well-wisher when you delight in the Word of
  the Lord.
The mind is filled with real and beneficial Knowledge when it is imbued
  with the precious Name of God . . .

This world is lost in temptation and attachment and is in great pain of
  birth and death.
Hasten to Satguru's sanctuary, repeat God's Name in your heart and be
  saved . . .

By fear, love and devotion and fixing the mind on the feet of God man
  crosses the terrible ocean.
Lord, let thy holy and loving Name be in my heart, I have come to Thy
  sanctuary.

The waves of avarice and greed are overcome by the pre-eminence of
  God's Name in the soul.
Chasten my soul, Pure Lord, Nānak seeks Thy protection.

(Gujri Ashtapadi, Adi Granth, p. 505)

6.1.32

There are five adversaries,[24] I am alone. How shall I protect my mortal
  house, my soul?
Time and again they attack and plunder me. To whom shall I appeal?
Utter the Name of the Lord God, my soul.
Before you is the army of death, powerful and numerous.

God has built this temple of many doors, and has installed a woman.
The maid, thinking herself immortal, plays away her life, while the five
    adversaries plunder her.

The temple is burned down and plundered; the maid, all alone, is taken
    captive.
Death bludgeons her, her neck is chained, the five adversaries flee.

The woman wants gold and silver, friends desire good eating.
Nānak, he who sins for the sake of such things, will go bound to the city
    of death.

                     (Rag Gauri Cheti, Adi Granth, p. 155)

6.1.33

The Lord God is King,
He beholds all the world he created.
He sees, understands and knows every little thing.
He is all-pervading.

               (Rag Asa Patti, 24, Adi Granth, p. 433)

6.1.34

Black deer, hear me. Why are you attracted by that enclosed garden?
The sweetness of forbidden fruit lasts but four days; then it becomes bitter.
What you long for most becomes most bitter; without the Name great
    fever ensues.
It is like a ripple on the sea or the lightning's sudden flash.
Without the Lord there is no protector and you have forgotten Him.
Nānak speaks the truth; consider it my Soul, black deer, you will die . . .

My soul, you alien in this world, why do you fall victim to it?
When the True Lord dwells in your soul, why should you be snared in
    death's net?
The fish is separated from the water with tearful eyes when the fisherman
    has cast his net,
The world of maya is a sweet attraction, in the end the delusion is
    exposed.
Make devotion, apply consciousness to God and rid yourself of mental
    apprehension.
Nānak speaks the truth, consider it my Soul, you foreigner soul.
Rivers which separate along different channels hardly come together
    again.
In each succeeding age what appears sweet is in fact full of poison, so a

rare yogi affirms.

Those who experience ultimate union realize God the Satguru and contemplate Him.

Without God's Name we stray as fools in deception and are destroyed.

Those who do not devote themselves to the Name of God, who do not have truth in their hearts, end up in anguish and remorse.

Nānak speaks the truth, through the true Word, those long separated souls unite with Him.

(Rag Asa, Adi Granth, p. 438)

6.1.35

The drop is in the ocean and the ocean in the drop. Who can understand this secret? He who knows the ways of the Lord.

The One who created the world, He Himself knows the meaning.

He who meditates on this Knowledge attains the perfect state through liberation.

The day is in the night and the night in the day; the same is true of heat and cold.

No other knows His condition and extent, without the Guru this understanding is not attained.

The male is in the female and the female in the male, the Divine Teacher knows it.

In the Word is concentration, in concentration there is knowledge, through the grace of the Guru an untold tale.

The soul is in the Light and the Light in the soul, the five senses join as the Guru's brethren,

Nānak says: 'I am a sacrifice to those who have set their heart on the Lord!'

(Rag Ramkali, Adi Granth, p. 878)

6.1.36

Questions from a Yogi

What is the basis of your teaching?

What period is your thought?

Who is your Guru, to whom are you a disciple?

What exposition keeps you in detachment?

Tell us what we want to hear, child Nānak.

Nanak answers

The basis of my teaching is the first breath.
My thought belongs to the age of the Satguru.
The Word is my Guru, I am a disciple of the sound of meditation;
The exposition of the Inexplicable keeps me in detachment.
Nānak, in each succeeding age the Guru is God.[25]
I meditate on the exposition of the One Word,
For the gurmukh, self-interest is consumed in its fire.

> (Rag Ramkali, Adi Granth, p. 942)

6.1.37

For millions of ages there was thick darkness;
There was no earth, no sky, only the Will of the Infinite.
There was no day or night, no moon or sun, only He alone sitting in
  unmoving trance.

No existent matter or speech, no air and no water,
No creation, no destruction, no coming or going,
No continents, no worlds below, no surging ocean or flowing river.

There were no higher, middle or lower levels of existence;
There was no heaven and no hell, neither was there death.
There was no hell and no heaven, no birth or death, no coming or going.

There was no Brahma, Vishnu or Mahesh;[26]
No other was to be seen, only the One.
There was no female or male, no caste and no birth and no-one to suffer
  pain or pleasure . . .

There was no karma or dharma or maya.
Caste and birth were not seen with the eye;
There was no snare of affection, death stalked no head,
There was nothing to meditate on . . .

There was no caste or religious division, no Brahman or Khatri;
No god, no temple, no cow or *Gayatri*.[27]
There was no living sacrifice, no bathing in holy places, no-one to
  perform worship . . .[28]

There were no Vedas, no Kateba, no Smritis, no Shastras.
There was no reading of the Purānas at sunrise and sunset;
The unseen Lord was both subject and object of devotion, the unique
  One Himself perceived all.

When He willed it, then He created the world and He set the
  unsupported firmament.
He created Brahma, Vishnu and Mahesh; and maya and temptation.

A few rare persons are enabled to hear the Guru's Word.
By His will He created all and watches over it.
He founded continents, the universe, the worlds below, the Unmanifest
  manifested Himself.

No one knows His limits;
The Perfect Guru provides understanding.
Nānak, those who are filled with Truth wonder, they delight in singing
  praise to the Guru.

(Rag Maru, Adi Granth, p. 1035)

6.1.38

Where self-interest exists Thou art not.
Where Thou art, self-interest cannot exist.
Gyāni[29] try to unravel this mystery.
This description of the Indescribable must lodge in the soul.
Without the Guru this principle is not discovered, that the Unseen One
  dwells in the soul.
When the Satguru is met, the Name and the Word dwell in the soul.
When the Self is overcome, then doubt and fear are also overcome and
  the sorrow of death and rebirth removed.
The teaching of the Guru makes the Unmanifest manifest, by His perfect
  wisdom we are saved.
Nānak, repeat the formula: 'He is me, I am He.' The three levels of
  existence are summed up in that.

(Rag Maru, Adi Granth, p. 1092)

---

1 Shiva.
2 Vishnu.
3 Wife of Shiva.
4 Lakshmi, wife of Vishnu.
5 See 6.1.6 above.
6 Vedic god of the Heavens.
7 Scriptures.
8 Lit. 'things remembered', i.e. the traditions, texts based on the Vedas.
9 The most ancient scriptures of the Hindus.
10 Or *Bhaktas*, those who adopted the discipline of *bhakti*, or pious devotion to a personal
   God. The hymns of some *bhagats* like Kabir and Namder are included in the Guru
   Granth Sahib though they were not Sikh gurus.
11 Lit. 'as much as a sesamum seed'.
12 The Muslim scriptures.

13   Maya.
14   The triad, Brahma, Vishnu and Shiva.
15   May refer to the myth of the ocean of milk which, when it was churned up, produced jewels, one of which was Lakshmi, goddess of wealth.
16   Rām.
17   An object made of animal hair fixed to a handle and used for fanning important persons like royalty. It is used in the Sikh *gurdwārā* over the Guru Granth Sahib or Holy Book.
18   *Ārati* – a form of worship in which a tray with lights is waved before the object of worship.
19   Hawk-cuckoo, which according to legend drinks only rain water.
20   The spiritual man as opposed to the worldly man (*manmukh*).
21   The four are cruelty, worldly love, anger and avarice, Macauliffe, *The Sikh Religion* Vol. 1 p. 264, New Delhi 1963.
22   The True Guru, a name for God.
23   See 6.1.27, n. 20 above.
24   Lit. 'five others'; lust, anger, greed, attachment and pride.
25   Gopal.
26   Shiva.
27   Sacred verse from *Rig Veda* used by the Hindu in his daily dawn devotions.
28   Lit. puja, i.e. ritual worship.
29   Religious teacher.

Source: Translation by D. A. T. Thomas in W. Foy, *The Religious Quest* (London and New York: Routledge/Open University, 1978), pp. 267–86.

6.2 FROM THE DASAM GRANTH OF GURU GOBIND SINGH

The Dasam Granth ('the Holy Book of the Tenth Master')
contains the compositions of Guru Gobind Singh (1661–1708 CE) and
was compiled after the death of the Guru. It contains both details of his
life and devotional compositions including both the *Jap*
(not to be confused with the *Japji* of Guru Nanak) and
Akal Ustat, which are recited regularly by Sikhs.

6.2.1 The Jap: By the Grace of the Eternal One, the True Guru

He has no visible sign, neither caste nor lineage; || None may describe his form, neither features nor attire. || He is the Eternal One, self-enlightened and of infinite power. || God of Gods, the King of kings; Master of the three worlds, the Lord of creation; ruler of all beings, demon, human and divine; || His nature affirmed by the mantle of the forest, his infinity proclaimed by every blade of grass. || Who can recount your names, O Lord? By your deeds alone can you be known.

Hail to the Eternal One, hail to the Lord of Grace! Hail to the Formless One, incomparable, unique.

Hail to him the invisible Lord, immune from judgement's writ. Hail to him the incorporeal, beyond the cycle of birth and death. || Hail to him the imperishable One, to the One beyond destruction or decay. Hail to him the nameless One, to the One no single place can hold.

The poem continues in this manner through a total of 199
brief stanzas, each naming a cluster of divine features or qualities.
The result is a lengthy catalogue of descriptive terms, some designating
negative concepts but most expressed as positive attributes. Epithet is
heaped on epithet as the Guru develops his extended statement of God's
nature and being. God is formless, uncreated and deathless, fearless, pure
and beyond all desire. He is immanent, infinite, resplendent, unbound.
Absolute in power he is yet benign and merciful, wholly just and
supremely generous. The Light of Truth, he is also the
ultimate mystery. The paean concludes:

Invincible, immortal, fearless, unchanging.
Without beginning, unborn, eternal, all-pervading.
Invulnerable, unyielding, ineffable, self-sustaining.
Timeless, merciful, inexpressible, unbound.
Nameless, without desire, beyond comprehending, unyielding.
Subject to none, destroyer of all; free from the cycle of birth and death, from
    the need to observe any vows of silence.
Wholly detached, without colour, form or sign.
Untrammelled by karma, unhindered by doubt, enduring for ever, beyond all
    power of telling.

Hail to the One who is worthy of reverence, hail to him the Destroyer of all. ||
Hail to him the Invincible Lord, the Nameless One, dwelling within. || Hail to the
One free from passion's control, our dearest treasure, immanent in all. || Scourge
of the wicked, cherished guardian of the obedient, hail all hail to him.

    Eternally true, eternally blissful, Destroyer of all who challenge his might. ||
Bestower of blessing, Maker of all things, Creator Lord pervading all. || Awesome
in wealth, the dread of his enemies. || Destroyer, Creator, compassionate Lord.

    Around us lies God's dwelling-place, his joyous presence on every side. ||
Self-existent and supremely beautiful, he dwells as a presence immanent in all
creation. || Birth and death are abolished by his power, by the grace made
manifest in his being. || Eternally present within all humanity he reigns in glory
for ever.

6.2.2 In praise of the Eternal One (*Akal Ustat*)

The nature of this poem is clearly indicated by its title. Guru Gobind
Singh's *Akal Ustat* is a sustained hymn of praise, one which expounds a
doctrine of God in terms which repeatedly stress the splendour of his
many attributes. Following a brief invocation the poem immediately takes
up its central theme.

The Eternal One is my Protector, all-powerful Lord in steel incarnate. || Master of
Death and Lord of Steel, my Shield, my eternal Protector.

I bow before the Primal One, | | Immanent in sea, in earth, in sky; | | The Primal Being, formless and everlasting, | | Whose light illumines all creation.

Dwelling within both elephant and ant, | | Viewing alike both king and pauper; | | The One unique, beyond our comprehending, | | Yet knowing the secrets of every heart.

Ineffable, eternal, formless and thus devoid of raiment, | | Devoid of passion, colour, shape or lineament, | | Needing no sign to designate his caste, | | The Primal One, alone, without spot or stain.

Immune from caste and the marks which proclaim it; | | Neither father nor mother, friend nor foe; | | Distant from all yet close beside them, | | Immanent in sea, in earth, in sky.

Infinite his form and soundless his speech; | | At his feet even Durga finds refuge. | | Neither Brahma nor Vishnu encompass his bounds. | | 'Not this, not this', Brahma declares.

Thousands of gods has he created, thousands of Indras and deities of lesser power. | | Brahma and Shiv are his creation, both of them created and both to be destroyed. | | The fourteen worlds are the products of his pleasure, | | All to be drawn within him again.

Countless demons, gods, divine serpents – all are the works of his creation | | Celestial musicians and Kuber's attendants,[1] wondrous examples of the beauty he confers. | | All that can happen is known to him, the past, the present, the future yet to come. | | All this he knows and all that lies within, reading the deepest secrets of every human heart.

He has no parents, neither caste nor lineage, | | No single mood ordains the pattern of his deeds. | | Present within the light which lightens every soul, | | Behold him immanent in every place, visible to all.

Beyond the reach of death, immortal; | | Beyond our comprehending, formless and detached; | | Unmarked by symbols designating caste or family line, | | The eternal Lord, for ever true.

Destroyer of all, Creator of all, | | He who disperses illness, grief and guilt. | | Reflect on him for a fleeting moment, | | And thus escape death's snare.

These opening stanzas comprise the first of the poem's eleven cantos. The cantos vary in length from ten to thirty stanzas and employ a variety of poetic forms, but all carry forward the same fervent message of praise to the Eternal One. Insistently they repeat that there is but one God, all-powerful yet supremely merciful, dwelling immanent in his own creation. The third canto stresses the futility of traditional doctrines and rituals as means of finding God or of satisfying him. Other portions of the poem lay particular emphasis on the eirenic belief that the differences which divide men are in reality meaningless. They are meaningless because all people are fundamentally the same and because all are under the same Lord. A famous sequence from the seventh canto gives pointed expression to this view. These verses also declare God to be both the source and ultimate resting place of all mankind, and reinforce the claim that the practices of traditional piety are useless as a means of access to him.

If self-inflicted suffering leads to the Lord of peace and tranquillity, what then of the blows received by the wounded? || If repeating sacred words can bring one to the ineffable Lord, why not the warbler's constant *tuhi* cry?[22] || If God be found by roaming the skies, what then of the bird which remains for ever on the wing? || If burning oneself is the means of liberation, freed is the widow who mounts her husband's pyre; and if it be attained by living beneath the ground then blessed indeed is the snake!

Some shave their heads and become sanyasis, others adopt the style of the yogi; some abstain from connubial pleasure, or claim to be totally chaste. || Some are called Hindus, others are Muslims, members of sects such as Shia or Sunni. Let it be known that mankind is one, that all men belong to a single humanity. || So too with God, whom Hindu and Muslim distinguish with differing names. Let none be misled, for God is but one; he who denies this is duped and deluded. || Worship the One who is Master of all; worship and serve him alone. See him present in all creation, a single form, an all-pervading light.

There is no difference between a temple and a mosque, nor between the prayers of a Hindu or a Muslim. Though differences seem to mark and distinguish, all men are in reality the same. || Gods and demons, celestial beings, men called Muslims and others called Hindus – such differences are trivial, inconsequential, the outward results of locality and dress. || With eyes the same, the ears and body, all possessing a common form – all are in fact a single creation, the elements of nature in a uniform blend. || Allah is the same as the God of the Hindus, Puran and Qur'an are one and the same. All are the same, none is separate; a single form, a single creation. [. . .] || Many dwell by the Ganga, in Mecca or Medina; others follow the ascetic way, roaming the world as renunciants. || Many are sawn apart, others are buried, interred in the ground alive. Others prefer to be skewered on stakes, enduring the pain of impalement. || Many fly in the skies above, others live in the water. Vain is their effort without knowledge of the truth; fire is the fate which awaits them.

The gods have failed in their quest for perfection, the demons in their rebellion. Wise men have failed in their search for wisdom, the devout in their hope of contentment. || Preparing and dabbing on sandal paste, sprinkling the fragrance of attar, worshipping idols, offering sweets – all are futile and worthless. || Visiting graves, seeking comfort from tombs, piously smearing walls, plastering on them auspicious symbols – none can achieve its end. || The music-makers of the gods have failed, those who sing and those who dance. Pundits have failed, ascetics have failed; none knows the way to God.

> The remaining cantos continue the themes already
> enunciated, maintaining the same stress on the manifold glories of
> the eternal, all-pervading bountiful Creator Lord. Such wonders are beyond
> the wit or understanding of even the mightiest of sages. Failure
> must inevitably await any who seek to circumscribe the
> boundless or give expression to the ineffable.

He has no beginning, no middle, no end; no past, no present, no future. || He is the Master of all four ages, Lord of all that they span. || The deepest meditation of the noblest ascetics, the songs of the numberless heavenly host, || All have failed, all are defeated, for none can encompass the infinite.

Countless sages of mighty stature, the rishis Narad and Vyas, || Practised meditation and fearsome austerities, yet in the end tired of their task. || With them have failed the celestial musicians, those who sing and those who dance. || Mighty gods have struggled in vain, ignorant still of the answer.

---

1 Kuber is the god of wealth in Hindu mythology.
2 This cry resembles the words 'tu hi', 'Thee only'.

Source: W. H. McLeod (ed. and trans.) *Textual Sources for the Study of Sikhism* (Manchester: Manchester University Press, 1984), pp. 93–4, 55–8.

The Editor is grateful to Professor McLeod for permission to include selections from his earlier translations from the Dasam Granth. At the time of this volume going to press, it was not possible to incorporate Professor McLeod's new and significantly amended translations of these and other scriptures. In order to compare the translations of Sikh Scriptures in this Reader with more recent translations, see Professor McLeod's 1997 volume *Sikhism* (Harmondsworth, Penguin Books) and Nikky-Guninder Kaur Singh (trans.) (1995) *The Name of my Beloved: Verses of the Sikh Gurus* (The Sacred Literature series) Harper, San Francisco.

—— ●◆● ——

THE SIKH TRADITION

— ◆ ◆ ◆ —

6.3 SIKHISM

H. McLEOD

Although Sikhism is generally understood to be a simple faith, the definitions which are offered to describe it can be widely and confusingly divergent. Four such definitions are commonly encountered. All four relate primarily to the origins of the faith, each reflecting a distinctive range of predilection.

For the strictly orthodox Sikh the faith which by preference he calls *Gurmat* (in contrast to the western term 'Sikhism') can be regarded as nothing less than the product of direct revelation from God. *Gurmat* means 'the Guru's doctrine'. God, the original Guru, imparted his message to his chosen disciple Nānak who, having intuitively apprehended the message, thereby absorbed the divine spirit and became himself the Guru. This same divine spirit passed at Nānak's death into the body of his successor, Guru Angad, and in this manner dwelt successively within a series of ten personal Gurus. At the death of the tenth Guru, Gobind Singh, the divine spirit remained present within the sacred scripture and the community of the Guru's followers. He who accepts the teachings of the Gurus as recorded in the scripture (*granth*) or expressed in the corporate will of the community (*panth*) is truly a Sikh. In its more extreme form this interpretation holds that the actual content of *Gurmat* is wholly original, owing nothing of primary significance to the environment within which it emerged.[1]

As one would expect, the three remaining definitions all dispute this claim to uniqueness, emphasising instead the features which Sikhism so patently holds in common with other religious traditions in India. Many Hindu commentators, stressing the elements common to Sikh and Hindu tradition, have maintained that Sikhism is properly regarded merely as one of the many Hindu reform movements which have appeared from time to time in Indian history. In like manner there have been Muslim claims, based upon such doctrines as the oneness of God and the brotherhood of believers, to the effect that Sikhism is an offshoot of Islam.[2] Finally, there is the interpretation popular in Western textbooks, that Sikhism must be understood as the product of a consciously eclectic intention, an attempt to fuse Hindu and Muslim belief within a single irenic system.

Two of these definitions can be summarily dismissed. Both the Muslim and the eclectic interpretations are based upon partial and superficial readings of Sikh sources. Indications of Muslim influence do appear in the recorded utterances of the Gurus and in subsequent Sikh tradition, but in so far as they constitute significant elements of Sikh belief they normally do so in direct contradiction to the Muslim influence.[3] The eclectic interpretation depends primarily upon a misreading of certain passages which appear in the works of Nānak and of a cryptic reference recorded in the traditional narratives of his life.[4] Guru Nānak does indeed look to a faith transcending both Hindu and Muslim notions, but for him the required pattern of belief and practice is one which spurns rather than blends.

The two remaining definitions require more careful attention. Even if one is unable to accept a doctrine of divine inspiration, there remains an obligation to consider the teachings of Nānak and his successors in terms of genuine originality. Having acknowledged this measure of originality we must also pay heed to those features of Sikhism which so obviously derive from sources within contemporary Indian society. This must be done in the light of the complete range of Sikh history, from the period of Nānak to the present day. The conclusion which will follow is that Sikhism is indeed a unique phenomenon, but that this uniqueness derives more from its later development than from its earliest forms of custom and belief.

Sikhism is generally held to derive from the teachings of the first Guru Nānak (1469–1539). In a sense this is true, for there can be no doubt that the doctrines which he taught survive within the community to this day. Moreover, there can be no doubt that a direct connection links the community of today with the group of disciples who first gathered around Nānak in the Panjāb during the early years of the sixteenth century. In another sense, however, the claim is open to obvious objections. An analysis of the teachings of Nānak will demonstrate that the essential components of his thought were already current in the Indian society of his period. Nānak taught a doctrine of salvation through the divine Name. Others were already preaching this doctrine, and a comparison of their beliefs with those of the early Sikh community plainly shows that Nānak taught from within a tradition which had already developed a measure of definition.

This was the *Nirguna Sampradāya*, or Sant tradition of northern India, a devotional school commonly regarded as a part of the tradition of Vaishnava *bhakti*. A connection between the Sants and the Vaishnavas does indeed exist, but there are distinctive features of Sant doctrine which distinguish it from its Vaishnava antecedents. Most of these can be traced to its other major source, Tantric Yoga. The most prominent of the Sants prior to Nānak was Kabīr, and it is no doubt due to the obvious similarities in their teachings that Nānak has sometimes been represented as a disciple of his predecessor. Although there is no evidence to support this supposition, the measure of doctrinal agreement which links them is beyond dispute.[5]

This debt to the earlier Sant tradition must be acknowledged if there is to be any understanding of the antecedents of Nānak's thought. It is, however, necessary to

add that, as far as can be judged from surviving Sant works, Nānak raised this inheritance to a level of beauty and coherence attained by none of his predecessors. From
the quality of [these] Panjābī verses and the clarity of the message expressed in them
it is easy to appreciate why this particular man should have gathered a following of
sufficient strength to provide the nucleus of a continuing community. The evidence
suggests that Nānak inherited a theory of salvation which was at best incomplete
and commonly naïve in its insistence upon the adequacy of a simple repetition of a
particular divine name. Kabīr, master of the pithy epigram, was certainly not naïve,
nor yet does he appear to have been altogether clear and consistent. These are qualities which one cannot always expect to find in a mystic, and there can be no doubt
that in Kabīr it was the mystical strain which predominated. For Nānak also salvation was to be found in mystical union with God, but Nānak evidently differed in
that he recognised the need to explain in consistent terms the path to the ultimate
experience. It is in the coherence and the compelling beauty of his explanation that
Nānak's originality lies.

The thought of Nānak begins with two groups of basic assumptions. The first
concerns the nature of God, who in an ultimate sense is unknowable. God, the One,
is without form (nirankār), eternal (akāl), and ineffable (alakh). Considerable stress is
thus laid upon divine transcendence, but this alone does not express Nānak's understanding of God. If it did there would be, for Nānak, no possibility of salvation. God
is also gracious, concerned that men should possess the means of salvation and that
these means should be abundantly evident to those who would diligently seek them.
There is, Nānak insists, a purposeful revelation, visible to all who will but open their
eyes and see. God is sarab viāpak, 'everywhere present', immanent in all creation, both
within and without every man.

The second group of assumptions concerns the nature of man. Men are by nature
wilfully blind, shutting their eyes to the divine revelation which lies about them. They
commonly appreciate the need for salvation, but characteristically seek it in ways
which are worse than futile because they confirm and strengthen humanity's congen-
ital blindness. The Hindu worships at the temple and the Muslim at the mosque.
Misled by their religious leaders they mistakenly believe that external exercises of
this kind will provide access to salvation. Instead they bind men more firmly to the
transmigratory wheel of death and rebirth, to a perpetuation of suffering rather than
to the attainment of bliss.

This, for Nānak, is māyā. In Nānak's usage the term does not imply the ultimate
unreality of the world itself, but rather the unreality of the values which it represents. The world's values are a delusion. If a man accepts them no amount of piety
can save him. They must be rejected in favour of alternative values. Salvation can
be obtained only through a recognition of the alternative, and through the faithful
exercise of a discipline which demonstrably produces the desired result.

Nānak's teachings concerning the way of salvation are expressed in a number of
key words which recur constantly in his works. God, being gracious, communicates
his revelation in the form of the sabad (sabda, 'word') uttered by the guru (the
'preceptor'). Any aspect of the created world which communicates a vision or glimpse
of the nature of God or of his purpose is to be regarded as an expression of the

sabda. The guru who expresses, or draws attention to, this revelation is not, however, a human preceptor. It is the 'voice' of God mystically uttered within the human heart. Any means whereby spiritual perception is awakened can be regarded as the activity of the guru.

Duly awakened by the guru, the enlightened man looks around and within himself and there perceives the *hukam* (the divine 'order'). Like its English equivalent, the term *hukam* is used by Nānak in two senses, but it is the notion of harmony which is fundamental. Everywhere there can be perceived a divinely-bestowed harmony. Salvation consists in bringing oneself within this pattern of harmony.

This requires an explicit discipline, the practice of *nām simaran* or *nām japan*. The word *nām* ('name') signifies all that constitutes the nature and being of God; and the verb *simaranā* means 'to hold in remembrance'. The alternative verb *japanā* means, literally, 'to repeat', and for many of the Sants a simple, mechanical repetition of a chosen name of God (e.g. Rām) was believed to be a sufficient method. For Nānak much more is required. The pattern which he sets forth consists of a regular, disciplined meditation upon the *nām*. The essence of the *nām* is harmony and through this discipline the faithful devotee progressively unites himself with the divine harmony. In this manner he ascends to higher and yet higher levels of spiritual attainment, passing eventually into the condition of mystical bliss wherein all disharmony is ended and, in consequence, the round of transmigration is at last terminated. The proof of this is the experience itself. Only those who have attained it can know it.

For most people a reference to Sikhism will at once evoke an impression of beards, turbans and martial valour. It rarely suggests doctrines of salvation through patient meditation upon the divine Name. Both, however, belong to Sikhism. In order to understand how they united it is necessary to trace the history of the Sikh community since the time of Nānak.

Concerning Nānak himself relatively little can be known with assurance, apart from the content of his teachings. Hagiographic narratives abound (the *janam-sākhīs*), but their considerable importance relates principally to the later period within which they evolved. It seems certain that Nānak was born in 1469, probably in the village of Talvandī in the central Panjāb. During his early manhood he was evidently employed in the town of Sultānpur near the confluence of the Beās and Satluj rivers. This was followed by a period visiting pilgrimage centres within and perhaps beyond India, a period which figures with particular prominence in the *janam-sākhī* narratives. Eventually he settled in the village of Kartārpur above Lāhore on the right bank of the Rāvī river and there died, probably in 1539.

The pattern of teaching through the composition and communal singing of hymns was continued by Nānak's first four successors and reached a climax in the work of Arjan, the fifth Guru (died 1606). During the time of the third Guru, Amar Dās (died 1574), a collection was made of the hymns of the first three Gurus and of other writers (Sants and Sūfīs) whose works accorded with the teachings of Nānak. To this collection Guru Arjan added his own compositions and those of his father, Guru Rām Dās. The new compilation, recorded in a single volume in 1603–4, became the primary scripture of the community (the *Adi Granth*, later known as the *Guru*

Granth Sahib). Notable amongst Guru Arjan's own compositions is the lengthy hymn entitled *Sikhmani*, an epitome of the teachings of the Gurus.

In this respect the first four successors followed Nānak's example, faithfully reproducing his teachings in language of sustained excellence. There were, however, significant changes taking place within the community of their followers. The more important of these developments appear to have emerged during the period of the third Guru. Whereas Guru Nānak had laid exclusive emphasis upon the need for inner devotion, Guru Amar Dās, faced by the problems of a growing community, introduced features which served to maintain its cohesion. Distinctively Sikh ceremonies were instituted, a rudimentary system of pastoral supervision was begun, three Hindu festival-days were appointed for assemblies of the faithful, and the Guru's own town of Goindvāl became a recognised pilgrimage centre.

An even more significant development, one which should probably be traced right back to the period of Guru Nānak, concerns the caste constituency of the growing community. Whereas all the Gurus belonged to the urban-based mercantile Khatrī caste, most of their followers were rural Jats. This preponderance of Jats, which continues to the present day, is of fundamental importance in the later development of the community. Many of the features which distinguish the modern community from that of Nānak's day can be traced, as we shall see, to the pressure of Jat ideals.

Signs of Jat influence became apparent during the period of the sixth Guru, Hargobind (died 1644), an influence which is perhaps discernible even earlier, during the years under Guru Arjan. It was during this period that the community first entered into overt conflict with the Mughal administration. According to tradition it was Guru Hargobind who first decided to arm his followers, a decision which he is said to have reached following the death of his father Arjan in Mughal custody. There can be no doubt that the followers of Guru Hargobind did bear arms (three skirmishes were fought with Mughal detachments between 1628 and 1631), yet it is difficult to accept that the martial Jats would have spurned the use of arms prior to this period.

These martial traditions received further encouragement within the community as a result of Guru Hargobind's decision to withdraw to the Shivālik hills in 1634. During their actual tenure of the office of Guru, all four of his successors spent most of their time in the Shivāliks. The move was significant in that it exposed the developing community to the influence of the dominant *Sakti* culture of the hills area. This did not produce a transformation, but such features as the exaltation of the sword which emerge prominently during the period of the tenth Guru should probably be traced to Shivālik influences.

It was during the lifetime of the tenth Guru, Gobind Singh (died 1788), that the conflict with Mughal authority assumed serious proportions. Sikh tradition ascribes to this period and to Guru Gobind Singh the features which distinguish the later community from its precursor. It is said that Guru Gobind Singh, confronted by the evident weaknesses of his followers, decided to transform them into a powerful force which would wage war in the cause of righteousness. This he did by inaugurating a new brotherhood, the Khālsā, in 1699.

To this decision and its fulfilment are traced almost all the distinctive features of contemporary Sikhism. All who joined the Khālsā (both men and women) were to accept baptism and swear to obey a new code of discipline. Prominent amongst the requirements of this new code were an obligation to bear the *panj kakke*, or 'Five K's', and to refrain from various *kurahit*, or 'prohibitions'. The five K's comprised the *keś* (uncut hair), the *kanghā* (comb), *kirpān* (dagger, or short sword), *karā* (bangle), and *kachh* (a variety of breeches which must not reach below the knee). The prohibitions included abstinence from tobacco, from meat slaughtered in the Muslim fashion (*halāl*), and sexual intercourse with Muslim women. A change of name was also required of the initiate. All men who accepted baptism into the Khālsā brotherhood were thereafter to add Singh to their names, and all women were to add Kaur.

Sikh tradition also relates to the period and intention of Guru Gobind Singh another of the distinctive features of the later Sikh community. Immediately prior to his death in 1708 Guru Gobind Singh is said to have declared that with his demise the line of personal Gurus would come to an end. Thereafter the function and the authority of the Guru would vest jointly in the scripture (the *granth*, which accordingly comes to be known as the *Guru Granth Sāhib*) and in the corporate community (the *panth*, or *Khālsā Panth*).

Tradition thus accords to the period and to the deliberate purpose of Guru Gobind Singh almost all the characteristic features which outwardly distinguish the modern Sikh community. It is a tradition which must in some measure be qualified. There can be no doubt that something did in fact happen in 1699 and no reason exists for questioning the claim that Guru Gobind Singh instituted some kind of brotherhood during his lifetime. Beyond this, however, it is still difficult to proceed with assurance, for there is evidence which suggests that particular features of the Khālsā code must have emerged subsequent to the death of Guru Gobind Singh in response to pressures independent of his intention.

Two of these pressures deserve particular emphasis. There is, first, the continuing impact of Jat ideals upon the community, which numerically the Jats dominated. During the period of the Gurus influence would have been minimised although, as the events of Guru Hargobind's period indicate, it was by no means without effect. With the termination of the personal authority of the Guru in 1708 the pressure to incorporate features derived from Jat cultural patterns evidently became much stronger. The confused political circumstances of eighteenth-century Panjāb further enhanced this Jat ascendancy, for periods of military strife would be handled with much greater success by the martial Jats than by any other group in Panjāb society. Their ascendancy was by no means complete (three of the prominent leaders of this period were not Jats), but it was nevertheless extensive and it left its imprint upon the evolving community. The militant attitude of the Sikh community must be traced to this source, together with particular features such as the Five K's.

The second of the important eighteenth-century influences also concerns the battles of that century. Because Ahmad Shāh Abdālī chose to represent his invasions as a Muslim crusade, the Sikh resistance developed a pronounced anti-Muslim aspect.[6] To this development can be traced the three examples of the Five Prohibitions cited above.

It was also during this critically important century and the early decades of its successor that the Sikh doctrine of the Guru emerged in its modern form. For Nānak the guru, the voice of God spoke mystically within the human heart. Because Nanak was believed to give utterance to the divine message the title was conferred upon him, and upon his nine successors in the manner of a single flame successively igniting a series of torches. The death of Guru Gobind Singh without surviving heirs created a serious crisis, for ever since the time of the fourth Guru, Rām Dās, the office had been hereditary within his family of Sodhī Khatrīs. An attempt was made to continue the pattern of personal authority (a disciple named Banda was widely acknowledged as leader until his execution in 1716), but disputes within the community and its dispersion during the period of persecution which followed Bandā's death eventually produced a different pattern of leadership.

During this period and the subsequent years of the Afghan invasions there emerged twelve separate guerrilla bands (the *misls*). In order to preserve a measure of cohesion the leaders of the *misls* assembled on specified occasions to discuss issues of common interest. Together they constituted the Sikh community and it was as a community (*panth*) that they deliberated. Well back in the period of the personal Gurus there had developed, in response to the increasing growth and dispersion of the community, the doctrine that the Guru's bodily presence was not actually essential. Wherever a group of the faithful gathered to sing the songs of the Guru, there the Guru was himself mystically present. The doctrine was now extended to cover the periodic meetings of the *misl* leaders. Assemblies were always held in the presence of a copy of the sacred scripture and decisions reached by these assemblies were acclaimed as the will of the Guru (*gurmattā*).

A further development in the doctrine of the Guru came during the early nineteenth century when Mahārajā Ranjīt Singh, having established his dominance over his fellow *misaldārs*, suppressed these confederate assemblies. The doctrine of the *Guru Panth* then lapsed into desuetude and in its place the theory of the *Guru Granth* assumed virtually exclusive authority. The presence of the Guru in the scriptures had long been acknowledged. All that was required was a shift in emphasis.

To this day the *Guru Granth Sahib* occupies the central position in all expressions of the Sikh faith. Decisions are commonly made by using it as an oracle, continuous readings are held in order to confer blessing or avert disaster, and the presence of a copy is mandatory for all important ceremonies. The scripture which is used in this manner is Guru Arjan's collection, the *Adi Granth*. It should be distinguished from the so-called *Dasam Granth*, a separate collection compiled during the early eighteenth century which derives from the period of Guru Gobind Singh. Although the *Dasam Granth* also possesses canonical status it is in practice little used. The bulk of the collection consists of a retelling of legends from Hindu mythology.

Another institution which deserves special notice is the Sikh temple, or gurdwārā (*guraduārā*, literally 'the Guru's door'). Following earlier precedents the disciples of Nānak in any particular locality would regularly gather in a room set aside for their communal hymn-singing (*kīrtan*). This room (or separate building) was called a *dharamsālā*. As the community's interests expanded beyond the narrowly devotional into areas of much wider concern the function of the *dharamsālā* expanded accordingly. In the process its name changed to *guaraduārā*. The gurdwārās still remain the centre and focus of the community's activities, partly because their substantial endowments provide a considerable annual income. Contemporary Sikh political activity (expressed through the Akāli party) depends to a marked degree upon control of the wealthier of these institutions. The most famous of all gurdwārās, and still the primary centre of Sikh political power, is the celebrated Golden Temple of Amritsar.

Out of these five centuries of history there has emerged the modern Sikh community, a community which occupies in the life of India today a position of prominence considerably in excess of its actual numerical strength. Sikhs today are renowned for their participation in progressive farming, the armed forces, sport and the transport industry. In all four areas the prominence belongs principally to Jat Sikhs, the caste group which still constitutes more than half of the total strength of the community. Of the other groups which have significant representations within the community, the Khatrīs and Arorās, both mercantile castes, are more particularly distinguished for their work in manufacturing industries, commerce and the professions. Other substantial constituents are a group of artisan castes, jointly known as Rāmgarhīā Sikhs; and converts to Sikhism from the scheduled castes (Mazhabī and Rāmdāsīā Sikhs).

Although a measure of caste consciousness certainly persists within the community, all can join the Khālsā brotherhood and observe the common discipline. Here, however, a final qualification is required. Although Khālsā organisations normally insist that only the Khālsā Sikh is a true Sikh, there are others who lay claim to the title without observing the formal discipline. These are the so-called *sahaj-dhārī* Sikhs, noted for their adherence to the devotional patterns taught by Guru Nānak and his successors. In a sense they can be regarded as the descendants of the early movement, largely unaffected by the changes which took place during the seventeenth and eighteenth centuries. Their number is impossible to determine and without the external insignia of the orthodox Khālsā Sikh they constitute a much less stable group. There can be no doubt that the Khālsā provides the community with its stability and that its success in this respect has largely derived from its insistence upon external symbols. For this reason one can readily understand the apprehension with which orthodox Sikhs of today regard any inclination to abandon the traditional code of discipline.

---

1 'It is altogether a distinct and original faith based on the teachings of Guru Nanak in the form of Ten Gurus, and now through Guru Granth Sahib and the Khalsa Panth.' Gobind Singh Mansukhani, *The Quintessence of Sikkhism*, Amritsar 1958, p. 1.

2 The original edition of *The Legacy of India* gives expression to both the second and the third definitions. Dr Radhakrishnan lists Jainism, Buddhism and Sikhism as 'creations of the Indian mind [which] represent reform movements from within the fold of Hinduism put forth to meet the special demands of the various stages of the Hindu faith' (op. cit., p. 259). In the following chapter Abdul Qadir, in direct contradiction, cites Sikhism in support of his claim that 'Islam has had a more direct influence in bringing into existence monotheistic systems of faith in India' (ibid., p. 291).

3 This aspect is briefly covered below in the discussion of eighteenth-century developments. For a more detailed discussion of this period and its results see W. H. McLeod, *The Evolution of the Sikh Community*, Oxford, forthcoming.

4 'There is neither Hindu nor Muslim.' See W. H. McLeod, *Guru Nānak and the Sikh Religion*, Oxford 1968, pp. 38 and 161.

5 McLeod, op. cit., pp. 151–8. Ch. Vaudeville, *Au cabaret de l'amour: paroles de Kabir*, Paris, 1959, pp. 7–9.

6 Ahmad Shāh Abdāli of Afghanistan invaded north India nine times between 1747 and 1769.

Source: A. L. Basham (ed.) *Cultural History of India* (OUP, 1975), pp. 294–302.

6.4 THE CODE OF SIKH CONDUCT AND CONVENTIONS: FROM *SIKH RAHIT MARYADA*

Sikh Rahit Maryada is a manual of Sikh conduct that was published by the Shiromani Gurdwara Parbandhak Committee in 1950. This developed from an earlier publication in 1915 by the Shiromani Gurdwara Parbandhak Committee, which in turn had attempted to codify codes of Sikh conduct laid down since the creation of the Khālsā.

Chapter I

The definition of Sikh

Article I

Any human being who faithfully believes in

 (i) One Immortal Being,
 (ii) Ten Gurus, from Guru Nanak Dev to Guru Gobind Singh,
 (iii) The Guru Granth Sahib,
 (iv) The utterances and teaching of the ten Gurus and
 (v) The baptism bequeathed by the tenth Guru, and who does not owe allegiance to any other religion,

is a Sikh.

Chapter II

Sikh living

Article II

A Sikh's life has two aspects: individual or personal and corporate or Panthic.

Chapter III

A Sikh's personal life

Article III

A Sikh's personal life should comprehend –

(i) meditation on Nam (Divine Substance)[1] and the scriptures,
(ii) leading life according to the Gurus' teachings and
(iii) altruistic voluntary service.

Meditating on Nam (Divine Substance) and scriptures

Article IV

(1) A Sikh should wake up in the ambrosial hours (three hours before the dawn), take bath and, concentrating his/her thoughts on One Immortal Being, repeat the name Waheguru (Wondrous Destroyer of darkness).

(2) He/she should recite the following scriptural compositions every day:

(a) the Japu, the Jaapu and the Ten Sawayyas [. . .] in the morning.
(b) Sodar Rehras.[2] [. . .]
(c) the Sohila – to be recited at night before going to bed.

The morning and evening recitations should be concluded with the Ardas (formal supplication litany).

(3) (a) The text of the Ardas:[3]

One Absolute Manifest; victory belongeth to the Wondrous Destroyer of darkness. May the might of the All-powerful help!

Ode to his might by the tenth lord.

Having first thought of the Almighty's prowess, let us think of Guru Nanak. Then of Guru Angad, Amardas and Ramdas – may they be our rescuers! Remember, then, Arjan, Harigobind and Harirai. Meditate then on revered Hari Krishan on seeing whom all suffering vanishes. Think then of Tegh Bahadar, remembrance of whom brings all nine treasures. He comes to rescue everywhere. Then of the tenth lord, revered Guru Gobind Singh, who comes to rescue everywhere. The embodiment of the light of all ten sovereign lordships, the Guru Granth – think of the view and reading of it and say, 'Waheguru (Wondrous Destroyer of darkness)'.

Meditating on the achievement of the dear and truthful ones, including the five beloved ones, the four sons of the tenth Guru, forty liberated ones, steadfast ones, constant repeaters of the Divine Name, those given to assiduous devotion, those who repeated the Nam, shared their fare with others, ran free kitchen, wielded the sword and overlooked faults and shortcomings, say 'Waheguru', O Khalsa.

Meditating on the achievement of the male and female members of the Khalsa who laid down their lives in the cause of dharma (religion and righteousness), got their bodies dismembered bit by bit, got their skulls sawn off, got mounted on spiked wheels, got their bodies sawn, made sacrifices in the service of the shrines (gurduwaras), did not betray their faith, sustained their adherence to the Sikh faith with sacred unshorn hair up till their last breath, say, 'Wondrous Destroyer of darkness', O Khalsa.

Thinking of the five thrones (seats of religious authority) and all gurdwaras, say, 'Wondrous Destroyer of darkness', O Khalsa.

Now it is the prayer of the whole Khalsa. May the conscience of the whole Khalsa be informed by Waheguru, Waheguru, Waheguru and, in consequence of such remembrance, may total well-being obtain. Wherever there are communities of the Khalsa, may there be Divine protection and grace, the ascendance of the supply of needs and of the holy sword, protection of the tradition of grace, victory of the Panth, the succour of the holy sword, ascendance of the Khalsa. Say, O Khalsa, 'Wondrous Destroyer of darkness'.

Unto the Sikhs the gift of the Sikh faith, the gift of the untrimmed hair, the gift of the discipline of their faith, the gift of sense of discrimination, the gift of trust, the gift of confidence, above all, the gift of meditation on the Divine and bath in the Amritsar (holy tank at Amritsar). May hymns-singing missionary parties, the flags, the hostels, abide from age to age. May righteousness reign supreme. Say, 'Wondrous Destroyer of darkness'.

May the Khalsa be imbued with humility and high wisdom! May Waheguru guard its understanding!

O Immortal Being, eternal helper of Thy Panth, benevolent Lord, bestow on the Khalsa the beneficence of unobstructed visit to and free management of Nankana Sahib and other shrines and places of the Guru from which the Panth has been separated.

O Thou, the honour of the humble, the strength of the weak, aid unto those who have none to rely on, True Father, Wondrous Destroyer of darkness, we humbly render to you . . .[4] Pardon any impermissible accretions, omissions, errors, mistakes. Fulfil the purposes of all.

Grant us the association of those dear ones, on meeting whom one is reminded of Your Name. O Nanak, may the Nam (Holy) be ever in ascendance! In Thy will may the good of all prevail!

(b) On the conclusion of the Ardas, the entire congregation participating in the Ardas should respectfully genuflect before the revered Guru Granth, then stand up and call out, 'The Khalsa is of the Wondrous Destroyer of darkness: victory also is His.' The Congregation should, thereafter, raise the loud spirited chant of Sat Sri Akal (True is the Timeless Being).

(c) While the Ardas is being performed, all men and women in the congregation should stand with hands folded. The person in attendance of the Guru Granth should keep waving the whisk standing.

(d) The person who performs the Ardas should stand facing the Guru Granth with hands folded. If the Guru Granth is not there, the performing of the Ardas facing any direction is acceptable.

(e) When any special Ardas for and on behalf of one or more persons is offered, it is not necessary for persons in the congregation other than that person or those persons to stand up.

Chapter X

Living in consonance with Guru's tenets

Article XVI

A Sikh's living, earning livelihood, thinking and conduct should accord with the Guru's tenets. The Guru's tenets are:

(a) Worship should be rendered only to the One Timeless Being and to no god or goddess.

(b) Regarding the ten Gurus, the Guru Granth and the ten Gurus' word alone as saviours and holy objects of veneration.

(c) Regarding ten Gurus as the effulgence of one light and one single entity.

(d) Not believing in caste or descent, untouchability, magic, spells, incantation, omens, auspicious times, days and occasions, influence of stars, horoscopic dispositions, shradh (ritual serving of food to priests for the salvation of ancestors on appointed days as per the lunar calendar), ancestor worship, khiah (ritual serving of food to priests – Brahmins – on the lunar anniversaries of the death of an ancestor),[5] pind (offering of funeral barley cakes to the deceased's relatives), patal (ritual donating of food in the belief that that would satisfy the hunger of a departed soul), diva (the ceremony of keeping an oil lamp lit for 360 days after the death, in the belief that that lights the path of the deceased), ritual funeral acts, hom (lighting of ritual fire and pouring intermittently clarified butter, food-grains etc. into it for propitiating gods for the fulfilment of a purpose), jag (religious ceremony involving presentation of oblations), tarpan (libation), sikha-sut (keeping a tuft of hair on the head and wearing thread), bhadan (shaving of head on the death of a parent), fasting on new or full moon or other days, wearing of frontal marks on the forehead, wearing of thread, wearing of a necklace of the pieces of tulsi[6] stalk, veneration of any graves, of monuments erected to honour the memory of a deceased person or of cremation sites, idolatory and such like superstitious observances.[7]

Not owning up or regarding as hallowed any place other than the Guru's place – such, for instance, as sacred spots or places of pilgrimage of other faiths.

Not believing in or according any authority to Muslim seers, Brahmins' holiness, soothsayers, clairvoyants, oracles, promise of an offering on the fulfilment of a wish, offering of sweet loaves or rice pudding at graves on fulfilment of wishes, the Vedas, the Shastras, the Gayatri (Hindu scriptural prayer unto the sun), the Gita, the Quran, the Bible, etc. However, the study of the books of other faiths for general self-education is admissible.

(e) The Khalsa should maintain its distinctiveness among the professors of different religions of the world, but should not hurt the sentiments of any person professing another religion.

(f) A Sikh should pray to God before launching off any task.

(g) Learning Gurmukhi (Punjabi in Gurmukhi script) is essential for a Sikh. He should pursue other studies also.

(h) It is a Sikh's duty to get his children educated in Sikhism.

(i) A Sikh should, in no way, harbour any antipathy to the hair of the head with which his child is born. He should not tamper with the hair with which the child is born. He should add the suffix 'Singh' to the name of his son. A Sikh should keep the hair of his sons and daughters intact.

(j) A Sikh must not take hemp (cannabis), opium, liquor, tobacco, in short, any intoxicant. His only routine intake should be food.

(k) Piercing of nose or ears for wearing ornaments is forbidden for Sikh men and women.

(l) A Sikh should not kill his daughter; nor should he maintain any relationship with a killer of daughter.

(m) The true Sikh of the Guru shall make an honest living by lawful work.

(n) A Sikh shall regard a poor person's mouth as the Guru's cash offerings box.

(o) A Sikh shall not steal, form dubious associations or engage in gambling.

(p) He who regards another man's daughter as his own daughter, regards another man's wife as his mother, has coition with his own wife alone, he alone is a truly disciplined Sikh of the Guru.

A Sikh woman shall likewise keep within the confines of conjugal rectitude.

(q) A Sikh shall observe the Sikh rules of conduct and conventions from his birth right up to the end of his life.

(r) A Sikh, when he meets another Sikh, should greet him with 'Waheguru ji ka Khalsa, Waheguru ji ki Fateh'.[8] This is ordained for Sikh men and women both.

(s) It is not proper for a Sikh woman to wear veil or keep her face hidden by veil or cover.

(t) For a Sikh, there is no restriction or requirement as to dress except that he must wear Kachhehra[9] and turban. A Sikh woman may or may not tie turban.

1 Is translated as God's attributed self.
2 The Rehras is the evening prayer.
3 Literally supplication or prayer. In reality, it is a litany comprehending very briefly the whole gamut of Sikh history and enumerating all that Sikhism holds sacred. Portions of it are invocations and prayer for the grant of strength and virtue. It concludes with: O Nanak, may the Nam (Holy) be ever in ascendance; in Thy will, may the good of all prevail!
This is a model of the Ardas. It may be adapted to different occasions and for different purposes. However, the initial composition and the concluding phrases must not be altered. Mention here the name of the scriptural composition that has been recited or, in appropriate terms, the object for which the congregation has been held.
4 Two words, shradh and khiah, occurring in this clause connote what appears to be the same thing – the ritual serving of food to the priests (Brahmins). The difference between the connotations of the two words is implicit in the dates on which the ritual is performed. The ritual of serving food on the lunar date corresponding to the date of death during the period of the year designated shradhs is known as sharadh.
6 A plant with medicinal properties.
7 Most, though not all, rituals and ritual or religious observances listed in this clause are Hindu rituals and observances. The reason is that the old rituals and practices continued to be observed by large numbers of Sikhs even after their conversion from their old to the new faith and a large bulk of the Sikh novices were Hindu converts. Another reason for this phenomenon was the strangle-hold of the Brahmin priest on Hindus' secular and religious life which the Brahmin priest managed to maintain even on those leaving the Hindu religious fold, by his astute mental dexterity and rare capacity for compromise. That the Sikh novitiates included a sizeable number of Muslims is shown by inclusion in this clause of the taboos as to the sanctity of graves, shirni, etc.
8 Rendered into English: The Khalsa is Waheguru's, victory too is His!
9 A drawer type garment fastened by a fitted string round the waist, very often worn as underwear.

Source: 'Sikh Rehat Maryada (The Code of Sikh Conduct and Conventions)' in *Sikh Reht Maryada – The Code of Sikh Conduct and Conventions* (Amritsar: Dharam Parchar Committee (Shiromani Gurdwara Parbandhak Committee), 1994), chs 1, 2, 3, 10.

—— ●◆● ——

KHALISTAN AND SIKH IDENTITY

———— • ◆ • ————

6.5 'WE ARE NOT HINDUS'

KAHN SINGH NABHA

Kahn Singh Nabha (1861–1938) was a Sikh scholar and administrator and a member of the reformist Singh Sabha movement. His studies of Sikhism blend deep personal commitment and the critical reasoning of a historian.

Dear Member of the Khalsa: You may be surprised when you read what I have written. You will ask why there should be any need of such a work as *We Are Not Hindus* when it is perfectly obvious that the Khalsa is indeed distinct from Hindu society. Or you may want to know why, if such a work is to be written, there should not be books which show that we are not Muslims or Christians or Buddhists. In answering these questions let me acknowledge that such a work is certainly not needed by those who already believe implicitly in the Gurus, who live in accordance with their teachings, and possess a sound understanding of the principles of the Khalsa tradition. This book has not been written for their benefit. It has been produced for the benefit of those brethren to whom the following historical parable applies. The tale, briefly, is as follows.

Guru Gobind Singh once covered a donkey with a lionskin and set it loose in the wasteland. Men as well as cattle thought it was a lion and were so frightened of it that none dared approach it. Released from the misery of carrying burdens and free to graze fields to its heart's content the donkey grew plump and strong. It spent its days happily roaming the area around Anandpur. One day, however, it was attracted by the braying of a mare from its old stable. The donkey cantered to the house of the potter who owned it and stood outside the stable. There it was recognised by the potter, who removed the lion skin, replaced its pannier-bags, and once again began whipping it to make it work.

The Guru used this parable to teach his Sikhs an important lesson. 'My dear sons,' he said, 'I have not involved you in a mere pantomime, as in the case of this donkey.

I have freed you, wholly and completely, from the bondage of caste. You have become my sons and Sahib Kaur has become your mother. Do not follow the foolish example of the donkey and return to your old caste allegiance. If forgetting my words and abandoning the sacred faith of the Khalsa you return to your various castes your fate will be that of the donkey. Your courage will desert you and you will have lived your lives in vain.'

Many of our brethren are in fact neglecting this aspect of the Guru's teaching. Although they regard themselves as Sikhs of the Khalsa they accept the Hindu tradition. They imagine that it is actually harmful to observe the teachings of Gurbani by acknowledging that the Sikh religion is both distinct from the Hindu religion and superior to it. The reason for this is that they have neither read their own scriptures with care nor studied the historical past. Instead they have spent their time browsing through erroneous material and listening to the deceitful words of the self-seeking. The tragedy is that these brethren are falling away from the Khalsa. They forget the benefits which the Almighty One has bestowed on them, exalting the lowly, raising paupers to be kings, turning jackals into lions and sparrows into hawks. Seduced by those who oppose the Gurus' teachings they are ensnared by deceit and thereby forfeit the chance of deliverance which this human existence confers.

This book is restricted to the difference between Hindu tradition and the Khalsa because our brethren are already aware that they do not belong to other religions. This much they know, yet they mistakenly regard the Khalsa as a Hindu sect. I am confident that my erring brethren will return to their own tradition when they read this book. Realising that they are indeed the children of Guru Nanak and of all ten Gurus they will stand forth as members of the Khalsa, firmly convinced that *we are not Hindus*.

> The bulk of *Ham Hindu Nahin* consists largely of
> proof-texts drawn from the Sikh scriptures and presented as evidence
> that Khalsa faith and conduct differ from Hindu tradition to such an
> extent that the Khalsa must be regarded as a separate religious system,
> distinct and autonomous in its own right. The proof-texts are grouped
> under such headings as religious texts, caste, avatars, gods and
> goddesses, idol worship, etc. Having thus pressed its vigorous
> claims to a separate Sikh identity the book concludes on an
> eirenic note.

Our country will flourish when people of all religions are loyal to their own traditions yet willing to accept other Indians as members of the same family, when they recognise that harming one means harming the nation, and when religious differences are no longer an occasion for discord. Let us practise our religion in the harmonious spirit of Guru Nanak, for thus we shall ensure that mutual envy and hatred do not spread.

Beloved brothers in the Panth of Guru Nanak, I am fully persuaded that having read the discussion recorded above you will recognise your separate identity as the Sikh community and that you will know beyond all doubt that *we are not*

Hindus. At the same time you will grow in affection for all your fellow countrymen, recognising all who inhabit this country of India as one with yourself.

Source: Kahn Singh Nabha, 'Ham Hindu Nahin', in W. H. McLeod (ed. and trans.) *Textual Sources for the Study of Sikhism* (Manchester: Manchester University Press, 1984), pp. 134–6.

6.6 CHARACTERISTICS OF SIKH FUNDAMENTALISM

T. N. MADAN

[To conclude,] I will first try to highlight and elaborate some of the major points that have emerged from the foregoing discussion in the hope that they will be of comparative interest. I will then close with a few observations about the future of Sikh fundamentalism.

Fundamentalism in the broad sense of insistence on certain basic beliefs and practices is perhaps an essential component of all religious traditions. What is specific to a particular fundamentalist movement is, I think, more significant for understanding it than what it shares with others. Fundamentalism as a forceful affirmation of religious faith and cultural identity, combined with a militant pursuit of secular interests, is associated in the Sikh cultural tradition with the tenth guru. Sikh fundamentalism is not therefore a recent phenomenon. However, its expressions, shaped by changing historical circumstances, have been varied. The situation in the wake of the decline of Ranjit Singh's kingdom and the rise of Hindu fundamentalism in the late nineteenth century was quite different from that faced by Guru Gobind Singh two hundred years earlier. The current manifestations of Sikh fundamentalism have several characteristics in common with the earlier ones, but they also have distinctive features. In what follows I concentrate on Sikh fundamentalism today.

Sikh fundamentalism is a reactive phenomenon, a defense mechanism. Its apparent confidence hides many doubts, and its aggressiveness is a cover for fear and anxiety, fear of the threatening 'Other', seen as people and processes: nonconformists, secularists, and Hindus; heresy, modernization, cultural disintegration, and political domination. Of course not all Sikhs experience these fears and anxieties about cultural identity, but the fundamentalists (in their own eyes, true Sikhs) would want everybody to. I would stress that any attempt to explain religious fundamentalism in terms of states of mind alone amounts to reductionism and is therefore just as fallacious as economic determinism. Complex phenomena, needless to say, have multiple causes.

While mono-causal explanations of fundamentalism must be rejected, the claim of fundamentalists to be in possession of the Truth should be noted if we are to understand what motivates them and how they mobilize and hold their following. This does not mean that we recognize their claim as valid. In relation to their followers, however, fundamentalists do not allow the legitimacy of dissent and multiple opinions or individual judgments: a single judgment representing the collective will must prevail. This is considered axiomatic. It follows that Sikhs must have political power in order to enforce conformity. In the words of Khushwant Singh, 'in the Sikh state the Sikhs would not only be free of Hindus and Hindu influences, but the Sikh youth would also be persuaded (if necessary, compelled) to continue observing the forms and symbols of the faith'.[1] This implies that if Sikhs are not rulers, they must be rebels; but when they establish the 'just order' and become rulers, they cannot be rebels against themselves. In short, fundamentalism is totalitarian.

As a response to circumstances that are believed to be adverse, Sikh fundamentalism is marked not so much by deep theological concerns or intellectual vigor as by religious fervor and political passion. Modern scholars generally serve it; they do not lead or guide it. Thus, scholastic efforts have been made to argue that although the Sikh scripture contains many words and phrases (such as *śabad, śunya, śiva, śakti*) which are also found in the Hindu and Buddhist religious traditions, they do not mean in Sikhism what they mean in the other religions. Similarly, the roots of Sikhism in the sant tradition of socioreligious reform are played down, but this is not easy, for the Granth Sahib itself bears witness to them. The first guru certainly made his choices regarding theological, cosmological, social, and other matters, but he made them out of the traditions with which he was most familiar, Hinduism and Islam, in that order. According to Grewal,[2] 'it was a rich and lively religious atmosphere. And it was this atmosphere that Guru Nanak breathed.' But such scholarly disputations are of only limited interest to the fundamentalists or their lay followers, who emphasize action. It may be noted here that, with some exceptions, scriptural exegesis has not been a major concern of Sikh intellectuals. Inside the gurdwārās scripture is read, chanted, and venerated (very much as idols are in a Hindu temple); there are no discourses on it.

Understandably, therefore, it is not so much to the canon or scripture that Sikh fundamentalists turn for authority as to the tradition about what particular gurus or martyrs did. Sikh fundamentalism is orthoprax rather than orthodox. The emphasis is upon action and the expected fruits of action, and these fruits are this-worldly – economic and political. Piety or conformity to codes of behavior is seen as valuable in instrumental terms. For the orthodox, who do not think of belief and practice in dualistic terms, piety is its own reward. If action is motivated by the desired fruits, it is propelled by its situational logic. In today's situation, it is the tradition of violent action, characterized as righteous, and retribution for any attack on Sikh honor, that are emphasized. Joyce Pettigrew[3] has shown how deeply rooted these values are, though not in scripture but in the cultural tradition of the Jats, who account for the great majority of the Sikh community. The assassination of Mrs Indira Gandhi, prime minister at the time of Operation Blue Star, by her own Sikh bodyguards, and of General Vaidya, then the chief of the Indian army, are notable acts of revenge which the fundamentalists consider honorable, for they consider these two persons responsible for the attack on the Golden Temple complex. The same is true of the assassination of the Sikh (Akali) leader Sant Harchand Singh Longowal, within weeks of his having entered into an accord with prime minister Rajiv Gandhi in July 1985, which the pro-Bhindranwale Sikhs considered a betrayal of the cause of the community. Betrayal by anybody is bad, but by a leader it is particularly grievous.

Sikh fundamentalism depends upon charismatic leaders who are seen in the image of the sixth and tenth gurus as saint-soldiers (*sant-sipāhī*). Such a leader must be willing not only to kill but also to die for the cause. Thus Bhindranwale said, using the words of Guru Gobind: 'when the struggle reaches the decisive phase may I die fighting in its midst.' And he did, achieving for himself the halo of a martyr among his followers. There has been official confirmation that Bhindranwale's men inside the Akal Takht, many of whom were apparently hardly virtuous persons, fought with uncommon bravery to the last man. They also inflicted heavy casualties on the troops. How important the role of a charismatic leader is has been borne out by the relative ease with which the Punjab armed police were able to flush out in May 1988 (Operation Black Thunder) the terrorists who had reoccupied the Golden Temple complex in 1986. But as Bhindranwale's case so well illustrates, charisma needs material and institutional resources for its magic to work. He had the support of the institutional apparatus of the All India Sikh Students Federation; besides, well-to-do Sikhs in India and abroad (UK, USA, Canada) provided him and his supporters with money to buy arms and for other activities.

The strategy of the fundamentalist leader, as is well borne out by Bhindranwale's speeches and actions, is characterized by a selective appropriation of the tradition in a manner which is simultaneously revivalist and futurist. The notion of a Sikh state perhaps took shape in the tenth guru's time, or soon after, but the hope has not been realized. Guru Gobind's avenger, Banda Bahadur, conquered territory but hardly established a state. Maharaja Ranjit Singh's kingdom (1799–1839) was multi-religious. Fundamentalism today nourishes the hope of a Sikh state and points to destiny: the Khalsa will rule! Fundamentalism is explicitly soteriological.

The revivalist-futurist vision is not, however, unproblematic. On the one hand, the Sikh religious tradition is presented as a perennial philosophy; on the other, sensitivity to contextual variation is stressed. While the Sikh way of life is said to be unaffected by space-time (*des-kāl*) differences, Sikhs try to establish a territorial state of the true (baptized or Khalsa) Sikhs (Khalistan). As Pettigrew has pointed out, 'Temporal power was vested in the Panth, but precisely what this meant was difficult to ascertain, since Panth was the religious community of all Sikhs and not the localized community.'[4] Similarly, Gopal Singh asks: 'if the Sikh must combine [religion and politics], what about others who must live in their realm?'[5] In other words, the fundamentalist strategy for political autonomy depends more upon emotive appeal than rational argument or – a much harder task – willingness and capacity to confront contradictions within the Sikh tradition.

---

1 Khushwant Singh, *The Sikhs* (London: Allen and Unwin, 1953), pp. 84ff.
2 J. S. Grewal, *Guru Nanak in History* (Chandigarh: Punjab University, 1979), p. 140.
3 Joyce Pettigrew, *Robber Noblemen: A Study of the Political System of the Sikh Jats* (London: Routledge and Kegan Paul, 1987).
4 Joyce Pettigrew, 'In search of a New Kingdom of Lahore', *Pacific Affairs*, 60 no. 1 (1987), pp. 6ff.
5 Gopal Singh, *History of the Sikh People* (New Delhi: Macmillan, 1978).

Source: T. N. Madan, 'The double-edged sword: fundamentalism and the Sikh religious tradition' in M. E. Marty and R. S. Appleby (eds) *Fundamentalisms Observed* (Chicago: University of Chicago Press, 1991), pp. 617–19.

6.7 WHAT IS AND WHAT IS NOT ANTI-SIKH

KHUSHWANT SINGH

Khushwant Singh is a prominent Sikh author, journalist
and historian. He is the author of a standard history of the Sikh religion
and an outspoken commentator on Indian communal affairs. In this
reading, Khushwant Singh is addressing militant Sikhs who have placed
him and others on a death-list for 'anti-Sikh' activities.

According to *The Statesman* of 22nd May, 1989, criminals who murdered Dr Ravinder Ravi, writer and professor, in Patiala had four other names on their hit list. [. . .] I am apparently on the top of this mini hit list. According to leaders of the All India Sikh Students Federation, the Khalistan Commando Force and Khalistan Liberation Force, our heads are to roll because of our 'anti-Sikh writings'.

I think it is time these killers were told in plain language what is and what is not anti-Sikh. At the risk of being accused of indulging in self-praise, I will start with myself. [. . .] I, more than any other person, am called upon by foreign radio and television networks for comments on events in the Punjab, particularly regarding the Sikhs. I have never made myself out to be a man of religion but zealously retain my Sikh identity and am emotionally involved in the Sikhs' fortunes. I condemned Bhindranwale[1] because I regarded him as anti-Sikh; I condemned Operation Bluestar because I regarded it as anti-Sikh and anti-nation. I condemn terrorism because killing innocent people is condemned by our gurus as a sin. I make no distinction between Hindu and Sikh victims of violence: my heart goes out to the widows and children who have been deprived of their bread-earners and I do the little I can for them. I know our gurus would approve of that. I oppose Khalistan because I know it will spell disaster for the Sikh community as well as the country. There is nothing anti-Sikh about any of this.

The three other writers on the assassins' hit list are doing more than me in spreading the message of goodwill between the two sister communities. They do so at enormous risks to their lives because they too feel that this is what the gurus would have liked them to do and because they feel it is the best thing to do for the community and country.

And now let me tell our would-be assassins what is anti-Sikh. Killing an old *Jathedar*[2] of the Akal Takht was anti-Sikh. Killing Sant Longowal[3] was anti-Sikh. Killing Master Tara Singh's daughter, Bibi Rajinder Kaur, was anti-Sikh. Hanging innocent Hindus was anti-Sikh. I could extend the list of their anti-Sikh activities to several pages. Those who committed these crimes disgraced their gurus and the religion they profess.

In spite of the massive security that surrounds me wherever I go, they came very close to getting me. [. . .]

I am not a brave man but being slain by a terrorist does not disturb my night's sleep. [A reporter] came to get answers to a questionnaire drafted by her editor. The last question was, 'How would you like to die?' I answered quite candidly and without bravado, 'I would like to be shot by a Khalistani terrorist.' At my age (77), a quick end would be preferable to wasting away with some old-age disease in a hospital. It would also give me the halo of martyrdom and the feeling that I had given my life to preserve the integrity of my motherland. Terrorist threats do not deter me, and many others like me, from writing what we are writing and doing what we are doing. If they succeed in getting us, I am sure many others will rise to continue this *Dharma Yudh* [righteous war] against these evil men.'

---

1 Jarnail Singh Bhindranwale was the leader of the Sikh militants who occupied the Golden Temple and provoked 'Operation Bluestar' – the assault on the temple by the Indian army.
2 *Jathedar* of the Akal Takht: the Akal Takht of the Golden Temple is the supreme seat of authority in Sikh religious affairs. It is managed by the *Jathedar* ('leader').
3 Sant Harchand Longowal was a leader of the Akali Dal, a Sikh politico-religious party.

Source: Khushwant Singh, *My Bleeding Punjab* (New Delhi: UBS Publishers Distributors Ltd, 1992), pp. 161–4.

6.8 SIKHISM AND POLITICS
BHAI SAHIB SIRDAR KAPUR SINGH

Let the Sikhs make no mistake about it that unless they wake up and delve deep into their own souls to rediscover the direction which the Guru gave them, they are facing the mortal danger of being pushed out of the main stream of History and of eventual extinction. This 'national integration', this talk of 'secularism' in which politics is supposed to be freed and disassociated from religion, originate from those who have now usurped the political strings of the destiny of India. They have brazen-facedly adopted [. . .] tactics to push the decent element out of the political life.[. . .]

They have managed to maintain a fraudulent facade of democracy, reduced politics to a filthy game which nobody wishing to keep his hands clean can play and have turned public life into an arena infested by hoodlums, hooligans and other undesirable elements. Their self-interest is their only concern.[. . .]

These people can be no guides, for us, the Sikhs, and the only True Guide for us is the Guru who can help us here and redeem us hereafter. Bishop Berkeley is right in saying that, 'he who hath not meditated upon God, the human mind and the *summum bonum* may make a thriving earthworm but a sorry statesman'.

This calamity to India and to our nation must be staved off. This can be done, in theory, by a good, efficient and honest government manned by competent persons of unquestionable character in whom the people can repose their confidence. It is in this context that the Sikhs have to consider as to what their duty towards themselves, towards the Guru, towards the country and the nation is. Not by following the string leads of these politicians can the Sikhs do any good to themselves or to the country. Not by giving up political activity and aspirations to political power can they discharge the duty which the Guru and History have placed on their shoulders.[. . .] This danger of 'march upon Hindustan' has been there since the dawn of history and [during] the [last] two centuries [. . .] this danger has assumed the form of a double threat, of military invasion as well as the more disastrous ideological invasion such as can destroy the very soul of India. This makes the duty of the Sikhs much more complex and onerous. Their duty, therefore, is firstly to carve out and establish for themselves a congenial habitat and *milieu* wherein the guiding impulses and postulates of the Sikh society freely operate and fructify. Their second task is to so organize and equip themselves as to play the vital role of being a cultural and political bridge between the Aryan India and the Semitic western Asia. India is, by nature and historical circumstances, now destined to become a great nation and a great power on the material and cultural planes, both. Unless the Sikhs play their part properly and well they shall be guilty of treason towards India and the Indian people, towards History and towards mankind. Above all they shall have betrayed the task entrusted to them by the Sikh Gurus, that of creating a just, forward-looking, [egalitarian] and plural society wherein the spiritual values of mutual toler-ance, cooperation and understanding can prosper and thus to play a vital role such as truly behoves and befits them.

The demand for Sikh Homeland arises out of this context and it certainly is not something conceived by this individual politician or that and harped on by those who are supposed not to understand either the tenets of Sikh religion or the spirit of Sikh ethos.

In the present age, when all political power has devolved upon the people, to try to renounce it would be the greatest act of folly on the part of the Sikhs in their collectivity. Those who would aspire to and legitimately acquire this political power at the decision-making levels shall become the elect and the chosen people and those who renounce or edge away from it shall become the defeated and the vanquished ones. *Vae Victis* is a Roman piece of wisdom which means, 'woe to the vanquished'. Do some of our Sikh intellectuals wish the Sikhs to have the fate of the vanquished and do these intellectuals know what this fate is, and has been throughout the ages? The vanquished are the dust under the feet of the conqueror and the dirt on his shoes. The vanquished are the hewers of wood and the drawers of water. Is the Khalsa of Guru Gobind Singh, the revered Khalsa of the Eternal God [. . .] to be reduced to this condition? Have these Sikhs read as to what happened to the women, children, treasures of art and culture of the Russians subjected to German invasion during the last World War? Have they read the accounts and *Diaries* now published by some women who were caught up in Berlin when Russians occu-pied it in 1945? Do they know what happened to the Sikh women, the Sikh sacred heirlooms, when the Punjab was invaded by the soldiery of U.P. in 1845? Every virgin and every woman on the road leading to Lahore was raped and degraded by this mercenary Uttar Pradesh soldiery, [. . .] and it was to avenge this, mainly, that the Sikhs joined hands with the British during the Mutiny of 1857. In the Indo-Pakistan conflict of 1965, it is now known that but for the obduracy of a certain Sikh General it had almost been decided to abandon the entire Punjab west of Ambala to the invading Pakistani tanks. Just a week or ten days of occupation of the Sikh Homeland by the soldiers of Marshal Ayub and not a single Sikh virgin or a single Sikh rupee or a single Sikh sacred spot would have retained its purity or dignity. And the Sikh world, its generals, barristers and psychoanalysts notwithstanding, would have been enveloped by darkness and decay for fifty years at least, if not forever. Guru Nanak has warned that, 'when the foci of holiness, the spots of sanctity and the areas of pride of a people are violated, desecrated and degraded, then the people sink down into despairing gloom and state of abject surrender' [. . .] Will the Sikhs not wake up and prepare themselves for such an eventuality which may befall them one fine morning when they wake up from under their greasy quilts after a long evening booze? No amount of fine exegesis of the Sikh scripture made by our intellectuals will come to the rescue of the Sikhs when such a fate overtakes them. No amount of joined supplicatory hands or muttering the name of God will save them from total degradation and humiliation. But if they wake up in time, turn their faces towards the Guru, and salvage their political personality in a constitutionally established Sikh Homeland within the Union of India there is every prospect of such a fate to the Sikhs and shame to India being averted.

Source: Bhai Sahib Sirdar Kapur Singh, *Sikhism and Politics* (Amritsar: Dharam Parchar Committee (Shiromani Gurdwara Parbandhak Committee), 1995), pp. 21–5.

6.9 THE STATUS AND POSITION OF THE GOLDEN TEMPLE
KAPUR SINGH

This position and this status of the Golden Temple is unique in the religious or political centres of world history.

It is the Mecca of the Sikhs, because it is the religious centre of the Sikhs, but it is vastly more.

It is the St Peter's at Rome, for it is the capital of Sikh theocracy, but it is very much more and also something less and different. Sikhism has no ordained priestly class and, therefore, there can be no theocratic political state of the Sikhs in which the priests rule in the name of an invisible God. They have no corpus of civil law of divine origin and sanction and they, therefore, must have a state based on secular non-theocratic laws. It is more, because it remains the real capital of ultimate Sikh allegiance, whatever the political set-up for the time being.

It is the Varanasi or Banaras of Sikhism, because it is the holiest of the holies of the faith, but it is not precisely that because the true Sikh doctrine does not approve of any tradition or belief which seeks to tie up theophany with geography.

It is the Jerusalem of Sikhism because it is the historical centre of the epiphany of Sikhism but it is not precisely that because Sikhism, as a religion, is not history-grounded, that is, its validity is not tied up with or dependent upon any historical event.

It is not precisely the political capital of the Sikhs, because political capital presupposes a state under the control of the Sikhs, and when the Sikhs do have such a state, it is not imperative that its administrative centre must be at Amritsar, and even when it is, the Golden Temple and its precincts shall still retain their peculiar independent character apart from this administrative centre. When the Sikhs do not have a sovereign state of their own, the Golden Temple, with its surrounding complex, continuously retains its theo-political status, which may be suppressed by political power, compromised by individuals or questioned by politicians, but which remains and never can be extinguished, for it is, *sui generis* [unique; autonomous] and inalienable, and imprescriptible.

It is owing to this unique status, grounded in certain peculiar doctrines of Sikhism, that many misunderstandings continuously arise concerning the use of the Golden Temple with its surrounding complex, for 'political purposes', for allowing ingress into it and housing of those whom the political state may deem as 'offenders', and for pursuing 'extra religious activities' from inside its precincts. The Sikhs, themselves, have never viewed any of these activities, started or controlled from inside the precincts of the Golden Temple, as either improper, or repugnant to the Sikh doctrine, or contrary to the Sikh historical tradition. The reasons for this Sikh attitude are three, in the main, not singly, but collectively:

One reason is that this geographical site itself is charged with theopathic influences such as no other known and still accepted site on earth, including the old site of the Solomon's Temple, revered by three great religions of the world, Judaism, Christianity and Islam, can claim to be.

Source: Kapur Singh, *The Golden Temple: Its Theo-Political Status* (Amritsar: Dharam Parchar Committee (Shiromani Gurdwara Parbandhak Committee), 1995), pp. 7–8.

— ●◆● —

A SIKH WOMAN OF
THE NINETIES

—◆◆◆—

6.10 SIKHISM, LOVE, AMRIT

When I drank Amrit and breathed 'Waheguru Ji Ka Khalsa, Waheguru Ji Ki Fateh! (the Khalsa of Purity is inseparable from Waheguru and the Lord's Everlasting Grace prevails)', Amrit pulsed into my heart and into the same body that had been battered by love and cruelty. My head and ears tingled with adorning flowers, kisses and freedom as I knelt humbly, for once in all my life, vulnerable in soul, and sat before my Love.

My Kes, hair, flowed in steely strength like Samson's before him and tingled in holy reverence. Never would I be able to deny that I was a Sikh and that I did not know or love Waheguru. I would help others in the fight against cruelty, and never could I become someone else to suit myself as Peter (New Testament) betrayed the world. Never would I be able to denounce that I loved the Ten Masters and that I loved the Guru Granth Sahib as my only Master and Guru that lived with me in this world. Never would I be able to deny Waheguru was my true friend in life.

My Kirpan clung beside me as a force in life. Saint Soldier. I wouldn't be a coward for others, nor for myself. My conscience would be as steely and strong as the force within my Kirpan, for Waheguru is the strength of us all.

My Kacchara would allow me to be freed from a world obsessed with feminine sexuality. It wouldn't curb my sexuality but free me from the syndrome created by the media, by the world. Are we as women sexy enough, are we beautiful enough? Surely there is more that we can burden our bodies with, make us more awkward more, more. . . . I would no longer be either a Madonna-like creature or a Whore-like woman, but be as morally free and equal in love as men.

My Kanga held my Kes, in spiritual braids, and cleansed my hair and feelings. I hadn't become perfect. My love grew each time I combed and brushed through my spirit. My emotions rejuvenated.

My Kara embraced my hand and wrist. Waheguru would not let go of me, even if I tried to wriggle free from Him. When you're angry you want to wriggle free from those who hold you near to love. I don't know if it's claustrophobia or fear of intimacy, perhaps you've never felt this, in which case you can miss this bit.

My Kara, my ring of love, held on to me. Waheguru holds on to us even when we're angry and upset. Waheguru held my hand sympathetically. Her/his arm around me as I sat feeling pretty pathetic. Waheguru's eternity and power could never allow me to waste my life away as the eternity of torturous lives before in some cruel Karma (to have to be born again after so many births and deaths). Oh I can hear you, who have not really come to terms with the philosophy of reincarnation, think, 'Oh to come back and to have a good time'. To come back! For us to be born again and again in some uncontrollable cycle, to have no control over life, to live through the pain of life and death as animals, as anything or anyone, any person, as part of the food chain, is to have wasted our one chance as humans to connect to Waheguru. It is to be hell in every sense of the word. Because you see your conscience goes with you, as you relive and redie thousands of times and your heart becomes so weary (Guru Granth Sahib). Like Ryder Haggard's 'She' burning, alone, all those you love die and then you have to love again. Not an enticing prospect. But that's what would happen if we lived like animals in this life, eating, drinking, procrastinating and not nurturing our conscience, our connection to Waheguru. Well if we decided to stay ignorant of our Creator then, well, our buried soul after the grave of this life is really lost. I suppose choice is not something we use well, nor the body of a human.

'Waheguru you are my father and my Mother in the motion we know as life' (Guru Arjan Dev Ji, Fifth Master). I wasn't frightened of the future of this love affair. For Waheguru is merciful and the Lord would allow me to grow on this path to love. As with all love it would be an eternally poignant, volatile love affair. But a love affair that would soothe my heart an eternity when everything else crumbled away.

'Much too fragile to grip tightly anything I love. I have been waiting all my life to be loved. Love is a gift which the kind ones give me, not because I deserve it, but because such love as I need cannot last long . . . Noble passion is a virtue if it sustains someone like me for a few flying moments. I am a small thing with the soul of a flower, not of a man with its awful dead body moral responsibilities' . . . Though years have passed and my hair has grown grey, I still fall in love with many things. I definitely have come to the conclusion that the love of men and women is always a volatile affair, it is an inspiration which comes in flashes and leaves us half dead to ourselves. Every fresh visit of this angel, though rare and far between, makes us unselfish. Nothing else . . . This volatile unselfishness and that fascinating evanescent feeling for beauty is to me all the essence of religion and love'. ('A Volatile Affair', *On Paths of Life*, Puran Singh, 1927).

When life snatched from me those I love, Waheguru still held on to me. When I sat all alone in the darkness, crying angrily, well where are You? It's strange you know, people always talk of God and Light. When I'm sheltering myself in some lonely but relatively safe darkness; sitting in a deep, dark cave of gloom, don't say 'Oh look on the bright side' and don't tell me that God is Light. I say relatively safe because, well life's got to be pretty bizarre and shaky for you to feel safe only in darkness. I guess your fears and thoughts are veiled safely. It does not help telling someone crying in a cave that God is Light because if any of you have been stuck in a pothole, light is not one of the most obvious things that you see. So you see I felt all alone.

For if God is just Light and I'm down a metaphorical pothole in life, then where does that leave me? Not somewhere nice I can tell you. When I prayed and thought of all this life and light it still did not help, because let's face it an ugly dark pothole or 'manhole' is ugly and dark, period. So Light and Waheguru seemed very, very distant.

But not long ago I meditated whilst stuck in my metaphorical pothole. It took a lot of effort but I thought I'd give it a go. I'd tried everything else from ... well I'd tried lots of things. My personal ritual, call it 'new ageish' if you wish, call it a love of candles, is to light candles. Those unfortunate enough to know me used to be inundated with such burning materials. I haven't a clue what they did with their candles or candleholders. My personal ritual was to burn small candles, you know the ones you get six in a box, in front of a metal Khanda (spiritual symbol of Sikhs) in the hazy start of a day, Amritvela. In the gloomy winter mornings I love burning candles and incense sticks as much as I can, for surely a lightbulb doesn't have the same charm! But this time instead of burning the candles in front of the Khanda, I burned them behind the Khanda. I thought nothing of it.

Now you may think me simple. If you do you can skip this bit, well perhaps you have skipped most of this anyway, in which case I can ignore you. But aren't the most wondrous things in life simple? Shouldn't our devotion to Waheguru be simple, not stupid, but simple? Yes, an intelligent yet simple love. Well something simple struck me. The Khanda was no longer its bright metallic colour. When the candles burned behind it, the Khanda was blazingly dark.

I was amazed. I'd always thought, as I festered in my emotional pothole, that if the Khanda was Light and Waheguru was light, it was light years away from me. Now I could see that God and Waheguru was not just Lightness but Pitch Darkness too. I wasn't alone, I had the Dark, Dark strength of God around me. God is everywhere.

Source: 'Sikhism, love, Amrit' in *Finding Our Way and Sharing Our Stories: Women of the Nineties Reflect on their Traditions*, compiled by C. Capey (Ipswich: Suffolk College Publishing, 1995), pp. 110–12.

—— •♦• ——

INDEX

——— •◆• ———